ROBERT WOOD
JOHNSON

ROBERT WOOD JOHNSON

THE GENTLEMAN REBEL

Lawrence G. Foster

LILLIAN PRESS

Manufactured in the United States

First Edition

Library of Congress Catalog Card Number 99-95297

ISBN 0-9662882-0-3

Jacket and Book Design: Omega Clay

LILLIAN PRESS

P.O. Box 107

State College, PA 16804

For ELLEN MILLER FOSTER

Contents

CONTENTS

CONTENTS

POSTLUDE

UMDNJ — Robert Wood Johnson
Medical School

Robert Wood Johnson
University Hospital
667

Nothing happens unless first a dream.
— Carl Sandburg

Preface

Robert Wood Johnson died in 1968, and for the last ten years of his life I assisted him from time to time with various civic, political, and philanthropic projects. A restless spirit and an incurable idealist, he was an intriguing individual. Still, he was pragmatic in his ways, and his thinking thrust him far ahead of his times.

Johnson's life was like a mosaic, a collection of many and varied parts that, when pieced together, form a larger and more meaningful whole. Close scrutiny reveals imperfections, but the man's flaws add to his humanness. He worked hard at being different from others, and his spirited wit and love of adventure enhance the enjoyment of tracing his footsteps through life. This biography, the only book ever written about this extraordinary man, portrays his character, the sum of his accomplishments, and the importance of his legacy, so that others may judge his merits.

I will not forget our first meeting. The year was 1957, and I had recently left as night editor of the *Newark News*, then New Jersey's largest newspaper, to join Johnson & Johnson to help form its first public relations department. The company was still relatively small, with annual sales under $300 million. Shortly before noon that day, a call came from the office of George Smith, the company president, summoning me to meet him promptly in the office of "The General," as he was known. (I later learned that such calls were treated with the same degree of concern as fire alarms.) Unfortunately, however, I was not in the office, having taken an early lunch hour to rummage through a local auto junkyard in search of a part for my aging car.

When I returned to the office quite a while later, I was told to report immediately to the General's office. I arrived there about the same time as a very agitated George Smith, and for the first time took the long walk from the entrance to Johnson's office to his circular desk in the corner of the room. Smith introduced me with a brand of gallows humor I had last heard from a very annoyed city editor.

"General, this is Larry Foster. When he was with the newspaper, he took a half-hour for lunch. Now it seems he takes an hour and a half."

Johnson rose, shook my hand, and without a hint of a smile, said, "Well, young man, I'm glad to see that you are growing in your job."

I knew right then that I would like him.

As I came to know this remarkable person — the range of his accomplishments and the adventures that made up his life — the idea of writing this biography was born. The prospects of writing the book helped feed the journalistic fire that still burned within me. Quietly, I started what ultimately became a vast amount of research on his life's work. In later years, after he died, I interviewed scores of people who knew him, including many members of his family. Along the way, I concluded that in order to maintain independent thought, the book about his life would have to wait until I retired from the company so that my objectivity would not be compromised.

Over the years several authors had approached Johnson about writing his life story, but he always brushed them aside, saying, "I'm not old enough yet." Late in 1967 I wrote him in Florida and asked if we could sit down and, in the interest of recording the company's history, talk about his recollections. That appealed to him.

He wrote back that at present he wasn't feeling well and planned to enter a New York hospital for treatment, but that later we would get together. He died in the hospital, and I was asked to write the eulogy delivered at his funeral. Later I wrote a company-sponsored book on the history of Johnson & Johnson, titled *A Company That Cares*.

When Johnson was sixteen years old, his father died suddenly. A year later he finished prep school, and over the objections of his family he decided to forgo college and go to work at Johnson & Johnson with the dream of someday taking his father's place. From an early age he learned from his father the philosophy behind managing the family business. For that reason, this story begins with the *first* Robert Wood Johnson, at the time of the Civil War, and with his pioneering exploits in the early days of medicine. That period was filled with fascinating characters who were relevant for not only the father's life story but also the son's.

After a sometimes errant youth, Johnson settled down. Within fifteen years he worked his way up to become company president, and under his leadership Johnson & Johnson experienced phenomenal growth. Spurred by the success of Johnson's baby products — which became synonymous with motherhood — Johnson & Johnson became one of the world's most admired companies. Under his leadership, the company grew dramatically — from $11 million to $700 million in sales. But it wasn't sales and marketing success that brought Johnson wide acclaim as one of the twentieth century's most visionary business leaders. As early as the 1930s, he proclaimed that business had a moral purpose, indeed a moral imperative, to serve society and the public interest. Most of his fellow industrialists scoffed at this concept, but Johnson responded by writing a corporate "Credo" that would become the best-known and most widely emulated statement of the responsibility that business has to serve the public interest. He set a standard that much of American business followed.

Most of all, Johnson was a man of ideas and ideals, which he pursued with the zeal of a crusader. He had a vast range of interests — business, health care, politics, government, the military, mass transportation, architecture, writing, aviation, yachting, and philanthropy — and he relentlessly searched for new and better ways to do things. Always a student of better management techniques, he saw that the nation's hospitals were not being run effectively, so he helped form the first school of hospital management. He wandered through hospitals all over the world seeking new ways to improve patient care. His formula for better care was simple. He put the patient first, with this pledge: "We have always been, are now, and always will be dedicated to the patient first."

Years before others, he built some of America's most attractive industrial plants, placing them in suburban settings on acres of handsomely landscaped land. It was right after the Depression, and his "Factories Can Be Beautiful" concept set a standard for industry, brought him national recognition, and helped to dispel the impression that industrial architecture had to be ugly. He constructed the nation's first complete textile mill town, with homes, schools, and churches for his workers and their families. He was an innovator who always had a larger purpose. "We build not only structures in which men and women of the future will work, but also the patterns of society in which they will work," he said. "We are building not only frameworks of stone and steel, but frameworks of ideas and ideals."

Two generations before others took up the cry, he was advocating a larger role for women in politics and championing environmental concerns. He had a passion for cleanliness in the workplace — in part because his company made sterile surgical products. He had the corners of manufacturing areas, including the stairwells, painted white so dust and dirt could be easily detected. Once, he shut a plant down for an entire week because of careless housekeeping and told workers and management to get busy cleaning it up. He was a character, and not always a lovable one. But his employees revered and respected him.

He never forgot his early years as a young factory worker, and the old-timers from the mill were the only ones who still called him by his first name. He spoke and wrote about his conviction that the term "common man" was disrespectful. Every individual, he insisted, was entitled to be judged on his or her own merits. "A man's character," he said, "should not be gauged by what he earns." He was once described as being "splendidly Baronial," but few of that ilk ever had a more common touch.

He enjoyed his wealth and the pleasures it brought him. But the creation of wealth, he felt, must have a greater goal than merely acquiring money. Long after his death, his sense of personal responsibility toward society is expressed imperishably in the disposition of his immense fortune—more than $1 billion—which he left to The Robert Wood Johnson Foundation to improve health care in America. The Foundation's remarkable work is described in the Postlude of this book.

He loved a good battle, and engaged in many, including one memorable period in wartime Washington when President Franklin D. Roosevelt appointed him to a high government post. He served as a one-star general for all of sixty days before losing out in a confrontation with the Pentagon brass. On his retreat from the capital, he snidely remarked to columnist Walter Winchell that Washington was "a mecca for mediocrity," one of the scores of quotable comments that endeared him to journalists. Wry humor was his constant companion. His politics swung wildly from conservative to liberal, depending on the issue, and made him unpredictable. He was the only one in the history of New Jersey's turbulent politics to be offered the nomination for U.S. Senate by both the Republican and Democratic parties in the same election year.

Fiercely patriotic, he had a profound sense of duty and spoke openly of love of country. Once, when he felt that democracy was being threatened by communism, he declared: "It is our responsibility to do something every day of our lives, however inconsequential, to support the American Constitutional principles." His

[xvii]

allegiance to his country glowed in his widely acclaimed book *Or Forfeit Freedom*. He left his mark in other ways too. In mid-century, when employee relations in the nation were at a low ebb, he rallied a group of national leaders and took the lead in writing a document titled "Human Relations in Modern Business," an action plan for bringing religious values to the workplace to restore harmony. Many companies and labor unions used the guidelines to settle disputes, and the concept gained wide acceptance. The *Harvard Business Review* described it as "a Magna Carta for management and worker."

Johnson was a study in contrasts. He could be fiery and combative or the essence of gentility. But despite all his strengths, his power, and his wealth, he had his share of human frailties, which brought him disappointment, despair, and loneliness. His bitter wrangling with his son was a low point in his life, and the relationship was only partially salvaged by a deathbed reconciliation. Still, during his final days his indomitable spirit and urge to achieve saw him sketching a design for a more comfortable hospital bed. He kept notes on his declining condition until he could no longer hold the pencil.

From beginning to end, Robert Wood Johnson pursued his dreams with unbridled energy and passion. As a colleague of his once remarked, "Unlike the Man of La Mancha, he would not accept the concept that the dream was impossible."

My goal in the following pages, as well as my hope for the reader, is to capture the essence of this remarkable man's life—and do it fairly and objectively and as dispassionately as possible. I make no apologies for being intrigued by the man. The reader will be too. Years ago, when I embarked on this book, a wise friend in publishing advised me to "tell it like a story."

Now it is time to let the story begin.

Lawrence Gilmore Foster
State College, Pennsylvania
May 1999

PART ONE

The Path of the Pioneers
1845–1915

1

THE FIRST RWJ

THE road leading out of Carbondale to the northwest crosses a viaduct and climbs along a ridge to open fields and a picturesque countryside. As the road rises so do the spirits, for the traveler leaves behind the stark somberness of the Pennsylvania coal-mining town and exchanges it for more welcoming terrain, lush and verdant.

It was along this route, some one hundred miles north of Philadelphia, that Sylvester Johnson and his young bride came in 1828 and settled on the shores of nearby Crystal Lake. Sylvester was from a family of early colonists who first settled in New England and then slowly pushed westward in search of the promises of the New World. He traced his lineage to John Johnson, who had left Hull, England, and reached the Massachusetts Bay Colony in 1638, eighteen years after the Pilgrims arrived at Plymouth Rock. In time, Sylvester's forebears moved to Rhode Island and then to Connecticut, where his father, Stephen, a carpenter, married Experience Wheeler in 1798. The daughter of one of the founders of the seafaring town of Stonington, Connecticut, she was described as "a lovely character, so kind to everyone . . . of good height, rather slender, very industrious at spinning and weaving."

The first child born of the marriage of Stephen and Experience was Sylvester, who arrived in 1800 and grew to be a sturdy young man with a flaming-red beard and a short temper. For several years he labored in an iron foundry in which he had a business interest, but eventually that proved unrewarding. And since his father's carpentry trade was no more promising, the family decided in 1827 to move on in search of a new homestead. Hitching a pair of oxen to a two-wheeled cart piled high with their belongings, they began their slow journey west. After ferrying across the Hudson River, they decided to spend the winter in Newburgh, New York. From there, Sylvester scouted the area and then pushed into Pennsylvania, looking for the most desirable place for the family to settle.

Pennsylvania's rich farmlands and abundant natural resources appealed to New England colonists, who had been discouraged by the paltry yields of hardscrabble farming in rock-strewn fields. Centuries earlier, glacial action had scrubbed much of the land clean of fertile soil, leaving behind gravel, sand, and boulders. It was therefore not surprising that many bone-weary farmers and their families, after assessing the meager harvests enticed from the stubborn New England soil, pulled stakes and moved on. Some were lured to the lush and fertile Genesee County of upstate New York, once the Indians had been driven away. Others pushed on to Pennsylvania, which had come to be known as the "Peaceable Kingdom." There William Penn and his struggling band of persecuted Quakers had forged a new brand of colonial freedom that proclaimed liberty for all. Penn called it his "Holy Experiment."

It was Penn's good fortune and foresight to have established his followers near the uncommonly fertile Piedmont Plain, which stretched inland from the Delaware River for nearly one hundred miles until its abrupt meeting with the Appalachian Range. Nature had been kind to the area, for the Plain was well beyond the ravages of glacial thievery that had robbed the land in New England. Its rich farmlands produced an abundance of food that more than satisfied the needs of the settlers, and in doing so even helped make Penn's new political concepts more digestible. Offering a breeding ground for tolerance, land that rewarded effort, and safe harbors for trading ships, Pennsylvania soon became a giant beacon that lured pioneer families pressing westward.

During the winter that he was based at Newburgh, and on one of his sojourns in search of a homesite, Sylvester acquired a wife, Louisa Wood of Goshen, New York. Said to be "dainty but durable," Louisa came from a family that was familiar with the hardships of frontier life. She was nineteen when she and Sylvester met and married. Her father, James, was a miller and grain farmer descended from Pilgrims who had come to the New World from Yorkshire, England, in 1630. The Wood family produced soldiers who fought with distinction on Revolutionary War battlefields, and later in the fierce battle at Minisink on the bloody heights above Goshen in 1777. Badly outnumbered by the marauding Indian warrior Brant, the town militia fought valiantly until their ammunition ran out. They were annihilated, but their bravery did not go totally unrewarded, for the settlement was saved and the Indians never attacked Goshen again. The memory of that courageous stand fueled fireside stories around Goshen for countless winters.

Though Indian hostility had subsided, Sylvester and Louisa faced the rigors of pioneer survival as they crossed into Pennsylvania and made their way to Carbondale, in the heart of the anthracite coal region. What Carbondale lacked in beauty it gained in the raw vitality that came from its growing strength as a mining and railroad town. Sylvester found a job as a butcher, but that held little appeal for him. His parents, Stephen and Experience, had pushed on to the settlement at Clifford, just to the north in Susquehanna County. It was an area its prideful residents described as being "poetically beautiful." Deep down inside, Sylvester Johnson, foundryman turned butcher, had the instincts of a poet. Surely he was a dreamer. When he visited the Susquehanna countryside, he became infatuated by it, especially picturesque Crystal Lake. He was determined to live there.

On April 9, 1828, Sylvester paid $755 for 151 acres of wooded land along the northeastern shore of Crystal Lake. Then he and his father cleared some of the land, and with the help of neighbors built a farmhouse on Onion Hill overlooking the lake. From the porch of the house, Sylvester had a clear view of the water, but the scenery so enthralled him that it clouded his judgment about the reality of working the land around the lake. The kindlier soil of the Susquehanna Valley was more to the west, and the rich fertile plain more to the south. The soil in the vicinity of the lake was marginal at best, a prelude to the nearby rugged terrain that the Indians called the "Endless Mountains." In time, Sylvester cleared more of the land and began raising cattle to supplement his meager income from the disappointing crops.

Sylvester took a variety of odd jobs in order to stay at Crystal Lake. He repaired fence rails along the Milford-Oswego toll road, which passed by the lake on the same trail that the Lenni Lenape Indians had blazed from the Jersey highlands north to Buffalo. Then for a while he sold hardware. Whenever he put a few extra dollars together, he added to his landholdings on the lake. He also came to be known as somewhat of a local character, mostly for his stubbornness and flashes of temper. Once an itinerant preacher riding along the toll road where Sylvester was repairing fence rails stopped and asked him what he was doing to save his soul. The reply was a carefully aimed spit of tobacco juice.

Louisa busied herself raising a family, eleven children in all. The first, a girl, died at birth early in 1829. Then came four daughters and a son, the first being born later in 1829. Between 1844 and 1856, Louisa gave birth to five more sons, fairly bulging the walls of the farmhouse on Onion Hill. There were many times when the Johnsons had to struggle to provide the basics for their large brood, let alone an occasional comfort. Nonetheless, it was a happy family, and Louisa was a bulwark of strength. She had retained the durability she was known for in her youth, but some of her daintiness eventually slipped away. She was as consistent as Sylvester was unpredictable.

The family's modest and sometimes frugal existence was richly

[6]

enhanced by Crystal Lake's storybook setting. It was the perfect stage for acting out childhood dramas. Groves of trees along the shoreline provided an ideal backdrop for conflicts with imaginary Indians. The lake was crammed with feisty pickerel and elusive bass. Swimming was only a stone's throw from the house. In the summertime a growing number of vacationers were lured to the lake, which shook off its lethargy and came alive. There was laughter, and children's voices mixed with sounds from frogs and birds that challenged serenity but never conquered it. A small steamboat poked its way around the five miles of shoreline, moving people from place to place and making frequent stops at Peter Coil's lakefront tavern for some refreshment and revelry. The summer passed all too quickly.

As fall approached, Crystal Lake began retreating to its winter solitude once again. The crowds drifted away, and the autumn foliage made its brief but colorful entrance and exit. The first sign of real winter was when snow flurries began to obscure the twin peaks of Elk Mountain in the distance, and the lake acquired a thin glaze. In the next stage the lake became frozen and snow encrusted, and remained that way for months. There were fewer winter pastimes, and the Johnson children arranged themselves in front of the fireplace and spent long hours with their schoolbooks.

Louisa's eighth child was Robert, born on February 15, 1845. They gave him the middle name Wood. He was a serious boy right from the beginning, and in time he was studious as well. When the other children were frolicking, Robert would often escape with a book and be as joyfully entertained. For several years he was enrolled in the nearby country school, and then, encouraged by his progress, his parents allowed him to go to school in Carbondale, where Louisa's sister lived. He did well in the public school there, and when he was thirteen and continued to show promise, they rewarded him with an opportunity to learn more.

The missionary zeal of the period had prompted the Oneida Methodist Conference in 1844 to build a coeducational boarding school, one of the first in the nation, at Kingston, Pennsylvania, just west of Wilkes-Barre. They called it Wyoming Seminary, and they selected a twenty-six-year-old, high-spirited circuit preacher by the name of Reuben Nelson as headmaster. Described as a man "admirably suited to pioneering," Reverend Nelson was also an excellent teacher. Hearing about this, the Johnsons decided to enroll Robert. When the next term began, the boy was put aboard the stagecoach for Kingston, some forty-five miles from Crystal Lake.

As the stagecoach rumbled along the toll road to Scranton and on into Wilkes-Barre, with its cluster of white frame houses and a church steeple rising in the center, Robert had ample time to ponder his fate. The stage disappeared into the covered bridge that carried travelers over the lazy Susquehanna River, and upon emerging moved into the tranquil Wyoming Valley. With its panorama of harvested fields, an abundance of orchards, and a scattering of farmhouses and barns, the valley was peaceful and perhaps a bit deceiving, for not more than a mile into this Eden awaited the fiery Reverend Nelson, with his burning desire to teach.

The red-haired headmaster had his own brand of drive and intensity. When he was a boy of fifteen, he had lost his right arm when it was caught in a cotton machine in Hargrave's Mill in Morris, New York, where Reuben was working to save for his education. Compassionate friends of the family decided to sponsor the boy's education because he had such a thirst for learning. In time he joined the ministry as a circuit rider, and he preached with such gusto that he frequently lost his voice. Then he was recruited to be the headmaster at Wyoming Seminary, and, though somewhat subdued vocally, he took on the assignment with a resolution that reached its own crescendo. The school's objectives were clearly stated: "We want an education that will provide a harmonious development of the physical, mental and moral power . . . that will make our graduates philanthropists, patriots and Christians."

In search of these goals, Reverend Nelson established disciplinary rules that had a certain flexibility: "The discipline of the institution combines mildness with firmness, avoiding harshness and un-warranted severity, yet inculcating strict order, prompt obedience, correct deportment and industry." But in practice he leaned more toward firmness, and his punishments were carefully recorded in the school's grade and demerit book, often with jolting finality. "Expelled! And ears boxed" was the way one student's fate was de-scribed. Still, he was known more as a teacher than a taskmaster. He had a soft spot for youngsters whose parents had trouble pay-ing the tuition, and he would trade coal, brooms, or even work to keep his students enrolled.

The instruction at Wyoming Seminary leaned heavily in favor of the classical subjects, and the enrollment was small enough to allow individual attention. While the quality of education was su-perior, the living accommodations at the school were spartan. The dormitory was minimally furnished, with bare wide-board floors, a washstand, a pitcher and bowl, and a woodstove that made a pre-tense of heating the room on bitter cold nights. There were long hours of nighttime study by the light of tallow candles or camphine light, which students were required to provide for their own use.

Life at the school was not all austere, for there were always a mis-chievous few to liven things up. The favorite prank was liberating a bull calf from a nearby farm and tying it to the bell clapper in the tower so that every time the calf kicked, the bell echoed through the sleepy valley. The daily study routine was occasionally broken by visiting lecturers who wended their way to the valley, lured by the persuasive headmaster. When journalist Horace Greeley came he told them: "The curse of our times is inordinate self-seeking. . . . Work so that you may be more unselfish." That pleased Reverend Nelson, for the admonition might have been his own.

Robert remained at Wyoming for three years. His departure was hastened by the dark clouds that had begun to form over the nation and would soon lead to civil war. The issue of slavery had badly split the young republic, and tensions continued to mount in all areas of the nation. In the 1860 election the Republican Party, primarily northern and antislavery, nominated a little-known politician from Illinois, Abraham Lincoln. Lincoln's opposition to slavery was unacceptable to the southern states, which for years had threatened secession. The election of Lincoln was the last straw. On December 20, 1860, South Carolina seceded from the Union, to the horror of the nation. Many people shared Lincoln's sentiments that "a house divided against itself cannot stand." Other states followed in rapid succession, and Jefferson Davis was elected president of the newly formed Confederate States of America. There were anxious, tension-filled weeks of waiting and hoping that war could be averted.

Early on the morning of February 22, 1861, on his way to Washington for his inauguration, Lincoln came to Pennsylvania to raise a flag with thirty-four stars over Independence Hall in Philadelphia. "I am filled with deep emotion," he said, "at finding myself standing here, in this place, where were collected together the wisdom, the patriotism, the devotion to principle, from which sprang the institutions under which we live." Word had reached Lincoln of a plot to murder him as he passed through Baltimore, and he was strongly urged to alter his travel schedule and not go to Philadelphia. Lincoln refused, saying that the impending crisis with the South made it imperative to maintain the goodwill of the Commonwealth of Pennsylvania.

Six weeks later, in the predawn hours of April 12, white-haired Edward Ruffin, Virginia agriculturist and publicist, pulled a gun lanyard, and the first shot of the Civil War exploded over Fort Sumter at the harbor entrance in Charleston, South Carolina. Three days later Lincoln called for 75,000 volunteers, and the Pennsylvania legislature unanimously pledged its resources "in men and money." It was not long before the echo of the call to duty filtered into the Wyoming Valley. Bands played and soldiers marched, and the tempo soon reached out and touched the small school in Kingston.

Boys barely in their teens began responding to the call for

"Ninety-Day Men," and Reverend Nelson was torn between patriotism, which he spoke about eloquently, and his desire to keep his young charges off the battlefields. In a very short time, two of Robert's older brothers entered military service; Charles became a second lieutenant in the Pennsylvania Volunteers, and William was a private in the Union Army. The thought of giving a third son, a boy of sixteen, to the bloody conflict totally dismayed Sylvester and Louisa, so they arranged to send Robert to Poughkeepsie, New York, to begin an apprenticeship in an apothecary owned by Louisa's cousin, James G. Wood. It turned out to be a fortuitous step.

Poughkeepsie was a thriving manufacturing center in 1861 when Robert Johnson arrived there to begin his apprenticeship. The town, located on the Hudson River sixty miles above New York City, was a popular stopover for tradesmen and travelers, and its cobblestone Main Street rumbled with activity from dawn until late at night. Crowds pouring out of the steamship docks as though from a spigot surged up Main Street to the hotels, cafés, and trading establishments.

Three- and four-story wood buildings were crammed along Main Street, standing side by side, cornice to cornice, giving the impression of leaning on one another. Displays of merchandise along the sidewalks spurred sales but slowed the movement of people, which was already impeded by the long rows of hitching posts that lined both sides of the street. There was the constant clack of wagon wheels against cobblestones, and amid all the noise and flurry was the matronly Poughkeepsie Hotel, reposing somewhat aloof behind a balustrade around its first-floor piazza, with the breathing room a grande dame required.

It was an eye-opening scene for a young boy fresh from the farmlands of Pennsylvania and the quietude of the Wyoming Valley. James Wood's store, doing business under the name Wood & Tittamer, was located at 288 Main Street, and Mr. Wood ran it with a certain flair. In addition to drugs and medicines, he sold chemicals, paints, perfumes, and window glass. An advertisement in the 1864 Poughkeepsie City Directory gave a clue to his competitive spirit:

> The proprietor is confident he can present greater inducements than ever to purchasers. They will find a larger stock of first quality articles, lower prices and more accommodating terms than can be found else-where, and invites all to call and see for themselves.

Robert boarded with the Wood family at their home at 66 Market Street. He was fortunate, for in James Wood he had another good teacher, and a kindly man as well. His early days at the store were spent pushing a broom and doing odd jobs, but soon he graduated to more important duties, and eventually he was initiated by Mr. Wood into the art of making medicinal plasters. This part of his learning not only changed the course of his life but also put him in contact with one of humankind's persistent and often frustrating attempts to aid the healing process.

From the dawn of civilization, people had sought new methods of treating injuries and ailments. One early technique was the application of the juices and gums of roots, herbs, plants, and trees, as well as animal substances, to the skin. These juices were believed to contain healing medicaments that could then be absorbed through the skin. Experimentation continued through all cultures. The Chinese tried opium and elephant fat, the Egyptians tried slime from the Nile, the Hindus tried arsenic and astringent herbs, and the Greeks tried poppy juice and mustard. At the same time, newer methods were developed to keep the medications in closer contact with the skin for prolonged periods, and led to the evolution of plasters containing healants. The Pueblo Indians, descendants of the Aztecs, made plasters spread on animal skins, leaves, and flexible bark. The early colonists learned these techniques from the various American Indian tribes and added improvements of their own. Primitive as it was, the concept proved to be sound. Many of the wonder drugs developed in later years came from plants that were first used for medicinal purposes in a primitive society. The methods of introducing healants into the body were varied, and none gained more sustained support than the skin plaster.

Robert's early efforts at making plasters, like those of everyone who toiled at the art, were back-breaking and frustrating. He labored in the workroom at the drugstore with an iron heated over a spirit lamp, trying to mold crude rubber into a pliable mass that could be shaped in the form of a medicated plaster. In later years he looked back on those early experiences: "Probably no other branch of the pharmaceutical art has been the occasion of so much toil, anxiety and failure and discouragement before any measure of success was met." And then, reflecting on the frustrations and drudgery, he added: "Expressive expletives could not be restrained."

Toward the end of 1864 Robert completed his apprenticeship, and with the help of Mr. Wood he got a job as an order clerk with the wholesale drug firm of James Scott Aspinwall in New York City. He was nineteen when he traded Main Street in Poughkeepsie for the surging unrest of New York City in the third year of the Civil War. Aspinwall, a descendant of a well-known New York family, had entered the wholesale drug business in 1830 in partnership with William L. Rushton, under the name of Rushton & Aspinwall, and later carried on the business alone. The firm, when Robert joined it, was located at 86 William Street in lower Manhattan.

As he began a new phase of his life in New York City, young Robert the boy began the process of becoming young Johnson the man. The transformation of New York from a robust young city to an increasingly complex metropolis had been accelerated by the steady tide of immigrants being deposited on its doorstep from Europe. The city's population had nearly tripled in the two decades before Johnson's arrival and was now a teeming 800,000.

The long and slender island of Manhattan formed the boundaries of the city at the time, the other four boroughs being added later. The immigrants during that period were predominantly Irish and German, seeking escape from oppression or poverty at home. When they arrived in lower Manhattan most remained clustered between the Battery and Twenty-third Street, some by choice and others because they had no other place to go. Jobs were scarce, many were untrained, and language was a problem. While some had chosen to make the perilous journey to the New World, others had the decision made for them. Steerage passage from Europe could be had for as little as the equivalent of twenty American dollars, and in impoverished areas of Europe it was not uncommon to pay the passage just to relieve the burden at home.

As the congestion in lower Manhattan grew, living conditions deteriorated. Politics were corrupt. Health conditions were alarmingly poor. Crime was rampant in the darkened streets and alleys, and the eerie glow from gas street lamps often seemed more ominous than comforting. The unpaved streets were caked with mud and strewn with garbage, and the streets that were paved were soon in disrepair. Little or no planning resulted in inadequate and disorganized housing, some of it makeshift shanties. There was such a constant crush of people and horse-drawn vehicles that just getting across lower Broadway was a challenge. And still, in the face of all of this adversity, lower New York and its humble inhabitants generated a vitality that fed their survival.

Uptown, life was kinder and more comfortable. Just a few miles north of Battery Park, the clutter suddenly emerged into open spaces, groves of trees, and gently undulating hills. Farmhouses and cattle pens dotted the landscape. At Fifth Avenue and Forty-second Street, the Croton Reservoir dominated the area, with its high walls and terrace on top for promenading. From there one could see the hundreds of ship masts that ringed the lower tip of Manhattan. Fashionable brownstones and ostentatious mansions were spread across midtown and formed a ring around Central Park. The good life was very good indeed, and family position and social standing were important to success and acceptance.

The impact of the Civil War added to New York's tumult. Before the war began, there was an element in the city sympathetic to the Southern cause because of business ties. The fall of Fort Sumter galvanized Northern loyalties, and New York became a strong supporter of the war effort. Soldiers thronged the streets, and flags were displayed in almost every window, giving the city a strangely festive air for such somber days. Walls of buildings were plastered with enlistment placards, shops sold engravings of recent battles, and some even displayed the bloodstained uniforms of soldiers.

Then, on April 9, 1865, the city joined in the celebration of the surrender that day of General Robert E. Lee to General Ulysses S. Grant at Appomattox in Virginia, ending the war that had claimed 620,000 lives. Five days later, on Good Friday, President Lincoln appealed to the nation for an attitude of forgiveness so the Reconstruction could begin. That night he was shot by John Wilkes Booth and died hours later. On April 24, tens of thousands of bereaved New Yorkers, wearing black arm bands purchased from street vendors, passed Lincoln's casket on view in City Hall — a few blocks from where Johnson worked. When the mourning period was over, New Yorkers quickly resumed their frenetic pace, led by those obsessed by business, money, and success. Each morning hundreds of horse-drawn omnibuses brought thousands into the downtown area of Broadway and Wall Street to begin another business day and to draw a step closer, or one removed, from their dreams and aspirations.

Johnson remained with Aspinwall's firm for nearly four years, and then in 1868 set himself up as a broker and importer of drugs and chemicals. He conducted the business from an office — actually a desk — at 36 Platt Street in the downtown business district, later moving to a factory loft at 30 Platt Street. It was there that he first met George J. Seabury, who had also started as a drug broker after his plans to become a physician were thwarted by the war.

Seabury, just a few months older than Johnson, was born in New York on November 10, 1844. His family was financially comfortable and well established socially, having "been represented in

America prior to the Revolution." When the war began, Seabury had just begun his medical studies. He served with the Twelfth New York Volunteer Regiment and was wounded at Gaines's Mill and Malvern Hill during the Peninsular Campaign in 1862. After the war he continued his studies in Europe at the Universities of Göttingen and Heidelberg, but not toward a medical degree. Seabury said: "While in Germany, I became interested in the discoveries of Joseph Lister relating to antiseptics and the applications of the germ theory."

Returning to this country, Seabury later recalled how he got started: "The war had knocked me out of my medical and pharmaceutical studies and I had to begin over, so I resolved on going into the drug business in some form, and the form I selected was that of a manufacturing pharmacist — to work up new things, and old things that were badly done, and create, you might say, a new branch of pharmacol chemistry."

While Johnson was still at 36 Platt Street, he and Seabury became acquainted and later began discussing opportunities that awaited them in the medical field. Then, in 1873, they decided to go into business together as equal partners under the name Seabury & Johnson. Seabury became president, and Johnson was corporate secretary and sales manager. They rented three floors at 30 Platt Street, the same building where Johnson was then working, and began making spread plasters and selling various other medical products.

Their business began at a time when medicine was still in its primitive stages and scientific knowledge was woefully limited and highly experimental. With sardonic humor, the distinguished physician Oliver Wendell Holmes in 1860 described the sobering realities of nineteenth-century medicine: "I firmly believe that if the whole *materia medica*, as now used, could be sunk to the bottom of the sea, it would be all the better for mankind — and all the worse for fishes." Although Holmes was referring specifically to medical literature, the same inadequacies existed in medical education. For the most part, the average physician had a high school or lower level of education and a medical degree obtained by attending the same four- or five-month course of medical lectures for two consecutive years, with no written examination to pass. The education of the "better physician" consisted of a bachelor's degree and an M.D. from a reputable school and one to three years of study abroad. Germany was the center of scientific and medical development at the time, and thousands of Americans studied medicine there.

In search of relief from a host of ailments, and often out of desperation, patients would grasp at any promise or product, even those dispensed by an array of pseudo-medical charlatans who offered an endless assortment of concoctions, most of them worthless. Actually, many were city versions of the "miracle" remedies being peddled from the back of buckboard wagons all over rural America by enterprising con artists. These homemade brews, often laced with alcohol, offered the buyer little or no medicinal help other than the temporary psychological (and alcoholic) lift of having done something to ease the pain or discomfort.

This was not the case with the therapeutic value of medicated plasters, which continued to gain the respect of the medical profession as the art of making them improved. Johnson later reflected on how he had managed to unravel some of the early mysteries of making better plasters: "We became imbued with the idea of making pharmacopoeial plasters in rubber combinations, and not knowing the secrets of patent plasters and of grinding rubber, we commenced upon the benzine process. With a barrel of benzine, a mixing pot, and a brush, we worked upon this method for two years only to find, after great loss, that many of the medicaments required by the pharmacopoeia were not compatible with rubber dissolved in a solvent. Then commenced the struggle to combine rubber with the gums and drugs without a solvent."

Johnson's early efforts at making plasters were both laborious and frustrating, and his associates recalled seeing him "clothed in jumpers, bare armed and struggling day after day with white wall brush and pail of mush . . . spreading benzine plasters." But in time his perseverance produced results, and the newer plasters made it to the marketplace. As the business grew slowly but steadily, the factory loft on Platt Street became cramped. Teeming lower New York was already overcrowded, so Johnson and Seabury moved to a small factory across the East River in South Brooklyn. Johnson continued living in Manhattan, where he was caught up in the pulsating life of the city.

2

LIGHT FROM LISTER

WHILE living in lower Manhattan, Johnson had become close friends with a young newspaperman, Edward ("Ned") P. Mitchell, protégé of Charles Dana and later to succeed him as editor of the *New York Sun*. Dana had made the *Sun* one of the nation's greatest newspapers and became one of America's most distinguished journalists. Mitchell, a reporter for the *Lewiston Journal* in Maine, submitted several freelance articles to Dana, and they caught his eye. In 1875 Dana wrote Mitchell and offered him a job as a reporter on the *Sun* staff. He immediately accepted and, at age twenty-three, went to New York. Not long after, Mitchell and Johnson met.

They were part of what Mitchell described as "a semi-Bohemian sodality," and later, in his book *Memoirs of an Editor: Fifty Years of American Journalism*, Mitchell recalled some of their experiences in flamboyant New York. "About the time of the centennial of national independence there flourished in the neighborhood of the Madison Square Garden a semi-Bohemian sodality which considered itself a partly worthy successor of the famous crowd at Pfaff's," he wrote.

The "Pfaff's" to which Mitchell referred was a cellar restaurant on the west side of Broadway, a few doors north of Bleeker Street. Run by Charlie Pfaff, it was headquarters for a group of young rebels who scandalized polite New York society from the late 1850s until the Civil War. They called themselves "the Bohemians," and when they gathered for frequent and noisy discourse in the cellar alcove of Pfaff's that stretched beneath the Broadway sidewalk, they were often accompanied by their idol and poet laureate, Walt Whitman.

The successor group that Mitchell and Johnson belonged to was more subdued, but interesting nonetheless. It included several writers, a musician, a cartoonist, and, as Mitchell described Johnson, "a young importer of drugs, who spent laborious days and nights in perfecting a ready-made mustard plaster." While Johnson's career pursuits were more mundane than those of his more artistic friends, the group found him just as stimulating, though largely self-educated. He had long ago fine-tuned his interest in reading, and now he had the chance to bandy ideas about with this group of young intellectuals. Pfaff's was the perfect place for an eclectic education, which Johnson absorbed with spongelike efficiency. It completed his transformation into a bright and urbane New Yorker.

Newcomers to the group came and departed, but Mitchell and Johnson continued their friendship. Mitchell brought to the relationship wide-ranging interests and a sense of humor, while Johnson, lacking the same flair for humor, was more intense. Mitchell liked to play off Johnson's solemnity, for it drew attention to his own humor and made it more successful. He also knew the value of good narrative and could orchestrate his recollections into a story that had symphonic qualities.

Mitchell would regale Johnson with a wide selection of stories, and one of his favorites was of the time he visited President Lincoln at the White House. Mitchell had an uncle, Dr. Henry M. Pierce, who at the time of the Civil War developed an intense interest in improving methods used for caring for the wounded on the field of battle. Dr. Pierce lived next to Mitchell's family on Fifth Avenue, between Forty-first and Forty-second Streets, and was president of the Rutgers Female Institute. But he devoted much of his time and energies to developing a system and equipment that he believed would provide better medical care for the war wounded. His plan required precision of movement by stretcher-bearers and careful coordination of all equipment despite the distractions of battle. Dr. Pierce was determined to have his system accepted.

One day Dr. Pierce took Mitchell to the Academy of Music in New York for a demonstration of his latest ambulance and stretcher technique. With the great Opera House filled to capacity, the stage was turned into a combat scene replete with the rattle of musketry, the boom of heavy artillery, and clouds of simulated battle smoke that drifted to the recesses of the cavernous theater. The stage, Mitchell said, was strewn with "dead" and "wounded" in blue and gray. Then Dr. Pierce swung into action aboard his new horse-drawn ambulance, with its gleaming coats of varnish, closely followed by his highly trained stretcher-bearers. In a matter of minutes they systematically removed the "wounded" to the imaginary field hospital somewhere in the theater's wings. That was it. The demonstration was over. Everyone in the packed Opera House got up and went home, puzzled by what they had seen.

Dr. Pierce was dismayed by the lack of response to his latest plan, but after the second and far more costly Battle of Bull Run, President Lincoln invited him to the White House to explain his system and methods. Dr. Pierce asked his young nephew to accompany him, and their excitement mounted on the train ride to Washington. They arrived at the White House early in the morning and an attendant promptly ushered them into a room where Lincoln was having breakfast. Walking in unannounced, they encountered a surprised Lincoln just as he was lifting a heaping forkful of baked beans. Mitchell summed it up this way: "Whenever I think of the greatest American, it is first as an extremely tall man with a sad, surprised countenance, seated at breakfast, with beans halfway between starting point and destination."

·

[21]

The decade of the 1880s brought no dramatic change in the patient's chances for survival, even in the better established hospitals of the nation. As uncertain as treatment by the physician was, and because the medicines of the period provided only limited help, the surgeon's task was quite complex and all too often fatal to the patient. Surgery was still considered nothing short of a dreadful gamble. As Sir James Simpson, a noted Edinburgh physician, described it, "The man laid on the operating table in one of our surgical hospitals is exposed to more chances of death than was the English soldier on the fields of Waterloo."

Ever so slowly, man's innate desire to heal himself started to prevail, and medical progress began to be made in the hospital instead of in the library. As one medical journal noted: "The physician who had been an artisan in ancient Greece, a priest in the Middle Ages, and a doctor since the Renaissance, now became a hospital physician." The progress of hospital care in the United States was well behind that of Europe, where the healing arts were at least a generation advanced. The original concept of hospitals in colonial America was to provide a place for medical care of the indigent and others who could not be properly cared for at home. Most early hospitals were independent institutions, known as voluntary hospitals and managed by trustees or governors, much the same as orphanages. They were staffed by physicians and surgeons who donated their services in return for access to interesting cases for teaching and research. But home was where infants were born, the sick were cared for, and most people died, if it was a natural death.

Once physicians began using hospitals for private patients, the public began to realize that many illnesses could be treated more effectively in hospitals than at home. But successful surgery, which logically could be performed better in a hospital environment, still eluded the medical profession—principally because sterilization had not yet been discovered. The typical surgeon of the time was described as a man "who operated in a Prince Albert coat, well-buttoned at the front, and stiff with the dried blood of many a previous operation . . . and assistants with well waxed ligatures adorning their buttonholes. It was quite the custom to follow the mode of the housewife by putting the thread in the mouth before inserting it in the eye of the needle." The mortality rate for surgical patients was shockingly high, and no one was sure why.

As the nineteenth century wore on, the science of bacteriology gained a stronger hold and began its telling and dramatic role in patient survival. The credit for that breakthrough belonged to Joseph P. Lister, the English surgeon who founded modern antiseptic surgery when he proved Louis Pasteur's theory that bacteria cause infection. Until that time, virtually all of medicine was oblivious to the relationship between bacteria, infection, and death following surgery. Born in England in 1827, at Upton in Essex, Lister was the son of Joseph Jackson Lister, a devout Quaker and a distinguished microscopist. He studied medicine at University College in London and later went to Edinburgh, where he worked under the noted surgeon James Syme. He married Syme's daughter, Agnes, in 1856, and four years later accepted a professorship in surgery at Glasgow, where he first became intrigued with the mysteries of wound infection.

In the early part of 1865, while conducting his continuing search of the medical literature, Lister came across a paper by the French chemist Louis Pasteur that summarized his experiments in lactic and alcoholic fermentations. Lister immediately realized its relevance for surgery and for his own unproven theories: Pasteur had drawn the first clear analogy between fermentation and putrefaction of wounds. Lister sensed that invisible microorganisms in the air were responsible for infecting the wound site and resulting in decomposition, and that wounds or surgical incisions had to be protected from the "invisible assassins."

In the beginning Lister experimented with his "antiseptic bandages" in the kitchen of his home on Charlotte Square in Edinburgh, with his wife as his helper. An associate of Lister's later recalled seeing those early and tedious labors: "With the aid of

Agnes, a wash tub and a clothes wringer, Lister began the great system of antiseptic pads, bandages, cottons, gauzes and dressings which later played such a large part in wound healing." Surgical dressings of that era were made of cotton in loose wads or bunches, or of lint, jute, oakum, or a preparation of resin and wax. Virtually any available material that could absorb or stem the flow of blood from the wound or incision was considered useable; that it should be germ-free had occurred only to Lister and a few disciples.

Lister had to decide what to use for an antiseptic to prevent contamination. He chose carbolic acid, or phenol, a coal-tar derivative commonly known as creosote. It was first used to preserve railway ties and ship timbers, and to reduce the odors of decomposition in sewage. There had been earlier studies of various medically therapeutic uses of carbolic acid, but on August 12, 1865, Lister used it in an operation that became a landmark in modern surgery. He put his theory of antisepsis to its first real test when he sprayed an operating room with carbolic acid, disinfecting the air around the operating table, the surgical instruments, and the patient's skin as well.

The operation itself, for a compound fracture, was minor. What was vital was the application of antiseptic dressings, and the total technique Lister applied to the wound site. The operation took place at the Glasgow Royal Infirmary, where James Greenlees, eleven years old, was taken after suffering a compound fracture of his left leg when he was run over by the wheel of a cart. (In compound fractures, the bone pierces the skin and leaves an open wound — a type of injury that usually required amputation, which more often than not was fatal.) Lister set the fracture and carefully put undiluted carbolic acid on the open wound, then applied a dressing of lint soaked with the same fluid. The apparatus and the procedure were cumbersome, but the wound healed.

Ten other compound fractures were similarly treated, with only one death, and in that case there were severe complications. The absence of infection amazed Lister's associates, but they did not immediately embrace his theory of antiseptic surgery or his techniques in the operating room. He pleaded with his fellow physicians: "You must see with your mind's eye the living germs which infect the wound from the air, see them as clearly as you see flies with your body's eyes."

Like many great pioneers, Lister was a prophet without honor in his homeland. "Humbuggery," "bug catching," and "pickling wounds in carbolic acid" were among the sneering descriptions physicians in Europe applied to Lister's practices. The more criticism he received, however, the more persistent he became. He soon began spraying the operating amphitheater with a heavy mist of carbolic acid pumped out steadily from atomizer-like machines. This caused surgical attendants and patients alike to gag, prompting his critics to remark that if the "invisible germs" don't kill the patient, the pungent odor of the carbolic acid certainly would.

At the time, Lister was preaching antiseptic surgery and striving for sterility. The difference between the two is important — antiseptic being clean, while sterile is the total absence of microorganisms. He believed that wound sites demanded total sterility for ultimate safety and that until sterility was achieved, survival was more a matter of luck. While Lister's technique greatly enhanced patients' chances for survival, the odds would get progressively better as they moved closer to the sterile state in wound and surgical care.

A second problem with open wounds and surgery was how to close them. Over the centuries, surgical pioneers made many attempts to develop ligating and suturing procedures. "Suture," meaning "to sew," described the strand of material used to bring tissue together, while "ligature" was the strand physicians used to tie off blood vessels. Through the ages, beginning with the ancient Greeks and Egyptians, various suture materials were used, including plant fibers and animal tissues. The Greek physician Galen tried hemp and silk cord. The Arabian Rhazes, in A.D. 900, described stitching wounds with thread made of sheep intestines, and he was close to what eventually evolved. In later years, thin strands of iron and silver were tried, but these triggered problems when embedded in the body. The alternative to suturing, which was still in use by physicians in Colonial America, was the ghastly practice of cauterizing wounds by applying searing heat to arteries to stem the flow of blood. Some considered this excruciatingly painful procedure better than bleeding to death, but others found that arguable. Often the shock of the red-hot iron pressed into flesh caused death.

While the surgeons who used ligatures were correct in the approach, they were as yet unaware of infection, so nonsterile materials used to close wounds frequently caused secondary hemorrhage, often bringing about the same result — death. Lister sensed the need for total asepsis at the wound site, including sterile ligatures. He ligated all bleeding vessels with antiseptically treated catgut, made from sheep intestines. The catgut suture evolved from the musical string. In ancient Greece, harp strings were made from the twisted intestines of sheep and other animals. The name "catgut" is said to derive from *Kitgut*, an old German word for "fiddle."

Though most of the American medical profession was still skeptical of Lister's radical theories on sterilization, a hard core of interest persisted in keeping his name in the forefront of discussions on surgical procedures. In 1876 the nation prepared for its biggest celebration, the 100th anniversary of the birth of the Republic, to be held in Philadelphia. As part of the Centennial Exhibition, the International Medical Congress decided to convene a meeting and to invite Lister to do a presentation on antiseptic surgery. With some misgivings about how his lecture would be received, Lister and his wife boarded the Cunard sailing ship *Sythia* for the long journey to the United States, excited about their first trip to America.

As it turned out, when Lister spoke to the Medical Congress that day, Robert Johnson was in the audience. He had read about Lister, and had become intrigued by the possibility of developing a sterile surgical dressing to combat infection. Johnson listened intently as Lister explained his theory to a mostly skeptical assembly of the nation's elite physicians. The longer Lister spoke, the more encouraged Johnson became.

The Centennial celebration was the talk of the nation in 1876. It would last six months and attract eight million visitors. The main theme was patriotic pride, and the timing was just right for a nation struggling to define itself, only eleven years after being torn nearly asunder by a bitter civil war. The 450 acres of the Centennial Exhibition grounds were full of marvels. Machinery Hall held thirteen acres of innovations, all powered by the Corliss Steam Engine. When activated, the huge machines carded cotton, combed wool, printed newspapers, sewed cloth, sawed logs, pumped water, and more, foreshadowing the burst of industrialization that the steam engine would soon make possible. In other halls there were new marvels: an electric lamp, a gas-heated flat-iron, the new type-writing machine, and one invention that attracted little attention, Alexander Graham Bell's telephone. In all, there were hundreds of buildings, including agricultural and horticultural exhibits, an art gallery (although most of the paintings and sculptures were from abroad), hotels, restaurants, coffeehouses, saloons, and the world's largest soda fountain.

Opening day was May 10, and hundreds of thousands descended on Philadelphia from every part of the nation. Three days before, every hotel and roominghouse for miles around was bursting with clergymen, doctors, lawyers, merchants, bankers, farmers, gamblers, and thieves. The city, now in a state of nervous excitement, was festooned with acres of bunting and the flags of every country. More than 1,000 press passes were issued for opening day, making it the best-covered event in the nation's history. At 9:00 A.M. when the Centennial officially opened, President Ulysses S. Grant was the guest of honor, flanked by Generals Sherman, Sheridan, and Hancock, resplendent in their full-dress uniforms. Bands played the "Centennial March," composed for the occasion by Richard Wagner. There were hundreds of dignitaries, from J. Pierpont Morgan to Dom Pedro, emperor of Brazil. As a form of national expression, seeking to underscore the sense of confidence, excitement, and progress that was taking hold of the nation, the Centennial was off to an impressive start.

In an international exhibit hall, Seabury & Johnson was showing its new line of plasters, for which it won a prize. Also exhibiting was the German firm of Paul Hartmann of Heidenheim, which showed a line of surgical dressings developed in support of Lister's methods of antiseptic surgery. The dressings were impregnated with carbolic acid and were an advanced form of the homemade dressings that Lister and Agnes had first experimented with in the kitchen of their home. Johnson took careful note of the bandages the German firm had developed in support of Lister's techniques, and then scheduled himself to attend the surgeon's long-awaited lecture.

Some 480 physicians came to hear Lister's two-and-a-half-hour talk at the Medical Congress, which was followed by a lengthy discussion. The articulate and diplomatic English surgeon opened with a tribute to the medical advances that had been made in the United States. "American surgeons are renowned throughout the world for their inventive genius, and boldness and skill in execution," Lister told them. "It is to America that we owe anesthesia, the greatest boon ever conferred upon suffering humanity by human means." He then went on to explain his system of antiseptic surgery in great detail, and actually demonstrated the atomizer machine, spraying clouds of carbolic acid into the air of the large auditorium and filling it with the pungent odor of tar. The ensuing discussion developed into a heated debate between believers and nonbelievers, prompting the correspondent for the *Boston Medical and Surgical Journal* to write: "These gentlemen used no button to their foils. Thrusts were given in earnest." While the huge audience of physicians remained divided at the end of Lister's presentation, it was clear that he had won some converts.

At the ceremonial banquet closing the International Medical Congress, Lister was seated to the right of President Grant, an honor that made the surgeon's evangelistic journey to America seem worthwhile. Then he and Agnes took a train trip across the country to get a close view of the still-untamed western frontier. Just weeks before, on June 25, the Sioux Indians, led by Crazy Horse and Sitting Bull, had annihilated General George A. Custer and his troops at the Battle of Little Big Horn in the Montana Territory. Ironically, some of Custer's army officers were not with him in the battle because they had gone to Philadelphia to attend the Centennial celebration that Lister had just left.

On his return to the East Coast, Lister gave lectures in Boston and New York, but the medical press continued to be noncommittal about his teachings. On October 12 the Listers sailed on the *Bothnia*, with the eminent surgeon still wondering if he would live to see the American medical profession embrace his teachings on sterility. Once back in Edinburgh, Lister and Agnes both immersed themselves in a new series of experiments to improve catgut ligature.

•

Although Johnson continued to think about the complex problem of developing a commercially produced sterile surgical dressing, he was forced to devote his time and resources to products that the medical profession had already accepted. This meant improving the technique for making plasters with an India-rubber base and eventually producing all the plasters in the United States Pharmacopoeia, the official list of national standards established for the production of drugs and certain medical products. When completed, these accomplishments were considered the most progressive steps in the craft for centuries and hailed as the start of a new era in the manufacture and use of medicinal plasters. Soon, Seabury & Johnson began developing business opportunities in Europe. In 1878 Johnson traveled to England, Germany, and France to generate export business and to visit a long list of European apothecaries in search of new product ideas. His journalist friend Ned Mitchell accompanied him on the trip. They sailed from New

York on the German Lloyd liner *Donau*, and Mitchell humorously recalled in his book some of Johnson's foibles.

"When we were jointly admiring some architectural marvel or sentimentalizing at some historic site, Johnson would suddenly pull his tall silk hat more firmly upon his brow and dart away to enter the shop of a neighboring chemist or *apotheker* or *pharmacien* and talk for an hour about dry mustard plasters and elastic bandages for the wounded. I came to love him much, and to hate his hat. He insisted on wearing it on all occasions, formal or informal; alike by Shakespeare's tomb at Stratford-on-Avon, on the battlefield at Waterloo, in the presence of the Eleven Thousand Virgins at Cologne, on a pedestrian tour along the Rhine, on the topmost wall of Heidelberg Castle, at the Righi Summit when the sun was rising.

"Finally at Lucerne, in front of the Lion, I dared my friend into the pledge that when we reached the Devil's Bridge on our walk through the upper reaches of the St. Gottard Pass we would sacrifice to Satan by simultaneously hurling our head-coverings, his beaver and my chapeau melon, into the abyss below. He consented reluctantly. We prepared for the ceremony by buying and pocketing each a cheap glossy black cambric cap of the peasant type.

"When the Devil's Bridge was beneath our soles some days later, his hesitation was painfully apparent. There was once a famous battle at that desolate, diabolical spot, but I doubt if the conflict was fiercer than that between Johnson's pride of possession and sense of honor. Not till I had shamed him by redeeming first my share of the vow did the cherished and detested stovepipe descend to the divvle, to be caught by the foaming Reuss torrent and whirled to the Rhine and out into the North Sea unless intercepted."

They wore their cambric caps faithfully until they reached Paris early one Sunday morning, whereupon Johnson hastened before breakfast to a hat shop on the Rue Vivienne and purchased the nearest duplicate to a stovepipe hat. Much to Mitchell's chagrin, he wore it throughout the remainder of the trip.

When Johnson returned to the United States his head was filled with ideas for new products, but George Seabury was not always receptive to change. He tended to be more conservative, while Johnson had difficulty restraining his enthusiasm and his entrepreneurial spirit. This led to frequent wrangling, and it was only a matter of time before it would get more serious. The relationship took on an added strain when both men decided to bring members of their family into the business.

The scenario that unfolded was carefully recorded by Johnson in the minutes of the business meetings they held as part of their trusteeship arrangement. He wrote in a large ledger in neat free-flowing penmanship that was almost artistic, and had a tranquil quality that contrasted sharply with the atmosphere of the meetings. In 1876, Seabury proposed bringing his younger brother, Robert, into the company. "Well, I suppose it is fair for *me* to take in a brother too," Johnson replied.

So that same year, Edward Mead Johnson, then twenty-four, was invited to join Seabury & Johnson. Born on May 13, 1852, on the family farm at Crystal Lake in Pennsylvania, Mead, as he was called, was Louisa Johnson's tenth child. Educated in local schools, he taught for a year at the local country school before enrolling in a law curriculum at the University of Michigan. After completing the one-year course in 1876 and trying one case, the results of which remain vague, he accepted his brother's offer to come to New York. He began as a "traveler," as salesmen were then known. Later, he did the company's advertising.

In 1878, Johnson suggested bringing his youngest brother, James, into the company. Seabury, in a letter, recalled his reaction: "When I came to look over the *dramatis personae* of the Johnson family I found he had six brothers (actually five), and I said 'Good gracious, don't bring in the whole six. You have got to draw the line on introducing any more male Johnsons, because on general principles I am opposed to nepotism in business.'" As it turned out, James would help solve many of the vexing mechanical problems of plaster-making.

From his early youth, James Wood Johnson, Louisa's eleventh and last child, had demonstrated an interest in mechanical things. He was born at Crystal Lake on March 17, 1856, and after attending school at Pittston, Pennsylvania, he transferred to Wyoming Seminary and came under the influence of its feisty headmaster, Reverend Reuben Nelson. He then became an apprentice surveyor with the Pennsylvania Coal Company, before heeding Robert's call to join Seabury & Johnson. At age twenty-two, James too started as a "traveler," to learn something about the business. He then went to work developing plaster-making machinery at the plant in South Brooklyn, and before long became assistant superintendent of manufacturing.

About this time Seabury took a prolonged trip to Europe to learn, firsthand, new developments in medical products and to initiate legal action against a British firm that had pirated his company's formulas and processes. Some of the products had been imported to the United States and were becoming a competitive factor. During Seabury's absence, Johnson had more freedom in the business, and that gave him an opportunity to test some of his ideas. "The difficulties in manufacture," he explained later, "were that we could make plasters that would stick but wouldn't keep, and we could make ones that would keep but wouldn't stick." The problem intrigued James, and the wheels in his mind began turning.

On the premises of a dental rubber goods supply house two blocks from the South Brooklyn factory, a small experimental laboratory was set up for testing the revolutionary India-rubber base for their plasters. First a machine was designed to wash and crush the crude rubber, then another to grind and plasticize it and roll it into long sheets one-sixteenth of an inch thick. Next the sheets were coated with various medicinal formulas, and a backing cloth and protective cotton fabric were added. The yard-wide plasters were then rolled on spools in 120-yard lengths.

The secret to the success of the entire process was getting the rubber base to just the right consistency to accept the various types of medicinal formulas used. The test plasters varied in strength and composition, but after tedious effort and many failures, James, the quiet one, achieved what was described as a "mechanical triumph" in the way he orchestrated the manufacture of various plasters. When Seabury returned from Europe, he was dismayed by how much had been spent on the experimental laboratory, but begrudgingly complimented the Johnson brothers on the progress they had made.

In his meanderings through surgical wards in Europe, the always inquisitive Seabury had learned how surgeons there were using absorbent cotton as "packing" during operations and in postoperative care. On his return the young firm decided to try making a similar cotton product, and the results showed promise. They arranged with Lancaster Mills in Pennsylvania to card, comb, and bleach cotton to new specifications. The product was lumpy and hard, and attempts to "sterilize" it with steam produced frustrating results. As a compromise, the cotton was soaked in a borate antiseptic solution, packed in crude paper boxes, and offered to American physicians. It was far from perfect, but it was a step forward.

In 1879 Seabury & Johnson put out a catalog listing various new products they had developed, including thirty pages of medicated plasters for treating a wide range of ailments from simple injuries to serious disease. There was also "Lister's Antiseptic Gauze," the first in a line of products to carry the great surgeon's name. There is no indication that Lister was consulted on the use of his name, or compensated for it, but in these days before trademark laws it was common practice for companies to just "borrow" a well-known name and put it on a package.

As a strong advocate of Lister's theories, Johnson wanted to expand the sterile surgical dressing product line, but Seabury was reluctant. His hesitancy was partially supported by a report of the

American Surgical Association, some six years after Lister's lecture in Philadelphia, that "Anti-Listerians were in the majority." It was not yet apparent, at least not to the majority of surgeons in the United States, that Lister's pioneering work in antiseptics would soon revolutionize nineteenth-century medicine.

3

THE BIRTH OF
JOHNSON & JOHNSON

Now thirty-five years old, Robert Wood Johnson seemed to be totally immersed in his business life, to the exclusion of any meaningful social relationships. Women found him engaging and at times charming, but he offered no encouragement to them beyond the pleasantries that the occasion demanded. He was, as they said, intensely wedded to his business.

By 1880 Seabury & Johnson had outgrown its manufacturing plant in South Brooklyn, and after a careful search a larger plant was leased in East Orange, New Jersey, and all production was moved there. James, still working wonders with his new machinery, became superintendent at the new manufacturing site, while the sales and advertising functions remained at the office in downtown Manhattan. Robert spent most of his time in New York, making periodic trips to New Jersey to inspect new production techniques.

On one of his trips to New Jersey, Johnson met the young and attractive Ellen Cutler, whose background is shrouded in mystery. After a short courtship they were married in the spring of 1880 and made their home in Elizabeth, New Jersey. They remained together for four years and had a daughter, Roberta. Then, as quietly as Ellen Cutler entered Johnson's life she exited it, and to the best of anyone's knowledge Johnson never spoke of her afterward. Following the divorce he was given custody of the child, who went to live with his brother James and his wife.

Despite the acrimony and discord that continued between Seabury and Johnson, the business flourished, and sales reached $381,765 by 1882. The third trustee in the company was mild-mannered George C. Hallett, whose title was Treasurer. In reality he was the bookkeeper. Every week or so the two owners would call a meeting of the trustees, and Hallett would reluctantly set aside his green eyeshade and ledgers and become the referee in the seemingly endless duel of words between the two owners. His was the thankless task of casting the deciding vote when Seabury and Johnson were at odds, which was often. No matter how he voted, one of the two owners would be unhappy, as reflected in the minutes that Johnson kept of the meetings.

In one exchange, Johnson questioned the merits of a business trip to Europe that Seabury's brother Robert was planning, and later during the same meeting Seabury demanded a monthly report on the work Johnson's brother James did at the factory. Seabury suggested that certain prices be lowered. Johnson objected. When recording such exchanges, Johnson often added his own comments, such as "Subject to usual discord!" And when Seabury got his copy of the minutes, he would add his own comments. It was a partnership in name but not in spirit.

At the trustee meeting of April 29, 1884, the disagreements took on a more ominous tone. Seabury wanted it on the record that, at the previous meeting, Johnson had offered his stock to the corporation at a price ten times the net profits of the previous year, and that he too wanted to offer his stock at the same price. Johnson replied that he wasn't interested. Seabury, he said, could sell his stock to whomever he wanted at any price he could get. Then he noted in the minutes: "If Mr. Seabury would name a price that he would give for my stock or take for his, then I would either buy or sell." Both partners kept their stock.

Talk of breaking up the partnership was unsettling to Mead

Johnson, who had earlier expressed his concern, and that spring he announced he was leaving the firm. Mead and his brother James had become interested in the infant business-machines industry, but this unsuccessful venture later would cost both of them their entire savings. With a partner, George Washington Newton Yost, they had formed what they called the American Writing Machine Company to produce a machine called the "Caligraph." It featured a nonsmudging ribbon with an India-rubber base and was supposed to be superior to the typewriter marketed in 1874 by E. Remington & Sons, the gunsmiths. But Yost became embroiled in a heated legal battle over patent infringements, and the Caligraph was doomed. Yost was credited with helping to bring the Remington machine notoriety and financial success, while the Johnsons had nothing to show for their involvement.

As 1884 drew to a close, the rift between Seabury and Johnson widened. On November 11 Johnson called a special trustee meeting to discuss reports that Seabury planned to resign and "engage in a business of the same nature." Seabury read into the minutes a letter denying that he had any such intentions "at present." Johnson called attention to losses of $20,000 in sales and asked Seabury and Hallett if they knew the cause. Seabury said he thought it was due to the "universal depression." Johnson attributed the loss to several causes, including "the unpopularity of one of the trustees." Seabury was affronted. Later he took the minutes book and added his own comments in the margin, initialing each of them "A lie, GJS." "A deliberate lie, GJS."

Still bristling, Seabury refused to attend the January 1885 annual stockholder meeting (there were only two stockholders) or any other trustee meetings held in the early months of the year. On July 10 Seabury called a special trustee meeting, which Johnson attended but Hallett did not. Seabury moved that Hallett's resignation be accepted. Johnson disagreed. Then Seabury objected to the way Johnson was recording the proceedings in the minutes book and demanded that he be allowed to keep the minutes himself, "to be responsible for their faithful reproduction." Seabury made a motion to declare a 6 percent dividend. The vote: Seabury, yes; Johnson, no. Seabury then moved to adjourn the meeting. The vote: Seabury, yes; Johnson, no.

Eight days later, on July 18, Johnson resigned from the company and sold his half interest in the business to Seabury for $250,000, taken mostly in promissory notes. At the same time, he entered into a covenant in which he agreed not to engage in a similar business for a period of ten years. His brother James resigned as superintendent of manufacturing the same day. That ended the stormy partnership between George Seabury and Robert Johnson, but the acrimony would continue in a prolonged legal battle that continued between the two for years.

Later that summer, Johnson rented a small office at 23 Cedar Street in lower Manhattan and at the age of forty pondered his future with some skepticism. For twenty-five years he had worked relentlessly to learn the medical products business, but all that time and toil now seemed wasted. In the breakup with Seabury he had agreed to stay out of the medical field for ten years.

James had different problems. While there were no constraints on his remaining in the medical field, his savings had been drained by the unsuccessful attempt to compete with the Remington company in the burgeoning typewriter business. Several years earlier, he had married Martha Law of Pittston, Pennsylvania, and their first child, Louise, was just a year old. Without a salary or savings, the young family faced a bleak future.

James kept in contact with Mead, for the two brothers had always been close. When the Caligraph venture folded, Mead too was broke, but being single eased his burden. He tried the coal business for a short time, but that was not to his liking. Whenever James and Mead were together, they spoke about possibly returning to the medical field. It was appealing to both of them, but they lacked the capital. Then in December 1885 they decided to give it a try on a small scale. As Christmas approached they began making plans to find a factory.

Early in January 1886 James was riding westbound on a Pennsylvania Railroad train in New Jersey. As it slowed crossing the Raritan River to stop at the New Brunswick station, thirty miles from New York City, he spotted a "To Let" sign on a four-story red-brick building amid a cluster of factories, right next to the Rutgers College campus and hugging the shore of the river. He got off the train and inspected the vacant space — the top floor of an abandoned wallpaper factory. Enthusiastic about the possibilities, James reported his find to Mead, and the brothers decided to rent it. Busily they began making preparations. James concentrated on what he knew best, getting machinery installed, and on hiring the first workers and familiarizing himself with the city. Mead went about establishing a small sales office in New York at 32 Cedar Street, across the street from Robert's office. To get the business started, the two brothers managed to borrow $1,000.

While spotting the vacant factory from the window of the railroad train had been serendipitous, New Brunswick was an excellent place to start a new business. The city enjoyed a prime location on the eastern seaboard — midway between New York and Philadelphia — and the Raritan River provided easy access to the sea. That is what attracted a band of early Dutch settlers to the area in 1730, when it was known as Indian's Ferry. When a charter was granted, the town was named in honor of the House of Brunswick, which had just succeeded to the throne of England. During the Revolutionary War, Alexander Hamilton took command of Seminary Hill above the Raritan and held off British troops while General George Washington retreated down the road to Trenton. The armies of Cornwallis and Howe entered the town in December 1776 and occupied it until June 1777, while Hessian soldiers camped nearby on what was to become the campus of Rutgers University.

Rutgers, which traces its heritage to colonial days, contributed significantly to the town's reputation as well as to its stability. Chartered as Queen's College in 1766 by the authority of King George III, it opened in New Brunswick in 1771. In 1825 the General Synod of Queen's College changed the name to Rutgers College after Colonel Henry Rutgers of New York gave a bond for $5,000 to the institution. The stipulation was that the interest be paid annually to the college. Rutgers became the land-grant college of New Jersey in 1864 and remained a stabilizing and positive influence on life in the town.

The first railroad linking New York and Philadelphia, completed in 1839, fortuitously passed through New Brunswick. It reduced travel time between the two cities to about ninety minutes, when by stagecoach it had been three uncomfortable days. Completing the railroad to New York was an awesome task that required the spanning of three navigable rivers—the Raritan, the Passaic, and the Hackensack—a quagmire of meadowlands, and the stubborn, flinty rocks of Bergen County's bluffs.

The Delaware & Raritan Canal had its northern terminus at New Brunswick, and after the canal opened in 1834 the city became one of the busiest inland ports in America. In just four years, workers had burrowed their way across New Jersey's slender middle to link Bordentown on the Delaware with New Brunswick on the Raritan. The engineering feat reduced the shipping distance by water between Philadelphia and New York to ninety-three miles. Legal wrangling would have killed the entire project had it not been for the persuasiveness of Daniel Webster and others.

A tidal river, the Raritan had for years stimulated an increase in commercial water traffic between New Brunswick and New York. The ocean tides enabled craft of modest draft to wend their way up the river to the city docks. Then the steamers arrived—one of them owned by Commodore Cornelius Vanderbilt, who ran it from Perth Amboy to New Brunswick, where he operated the Hotel Bellona. The steamer *New Brunswick* left at 6:30 every morning and offered "meals at all hours" and "good accommodations for cattle." The trip to New York City took a little more than four hours, down the serpentine-like river and up the Arthur Kill and the Kill Van Kull, past Staten Island and on to New York Harbor. The trip in 1886 was especially exciting, for workers were frantically putting the finishing touches on the Statue of Liberty in preparation for the gala dedication in the fall.

A network of bumpy, dusty roads converged on the city, bringing waves of travelers, tradesmen, and stagecoach passengers and keeping the hotel business flourishing. Fifty-four saloons kept six temperance societies on constant alert. The popular Opera House, a favorite stage for trying out shows bound for New York, filled the gallery at ten cents a seat. In the muddy streets, track was being laid for the city's first "horse railroad," and some citizens complained about spending $40,000 a year to educate 2,057 students in the public schools. Politics in the Sixth Ward, where the Irish were ensconced under Patrick Hagerty, was raucous. The treasurer of a local bank embezzled $80,000 and put on such a convincing demonstration of insanity during a church service that he was sent to the Trenton State Lunatic Asylum, leaving depositors to mourn their losses and search for the money. The ever-present college students provided youthful zest.

Despite its often robust personality, New Brunswick also had a genteel side. There was a solid base of hardworking, God-fearing citizens, most of them holding steady jobs in the numerous small and diversified industries that had sprung up—among them a hosiery mill, a fruit jar company, three rubber companies making footwear, and a needle maker.

The latest arrivals were the Johnson brothers, settling into their nearly obscure fourth-floor loft adjacent to the Rutgers campus. When word reached George Seabury that James and Mead were preparing to enter the medical business again, he immediately became suspicious that Robert was also involved in the venture, which would be a clear violation of the terms of their agreement. While there was no evidence of that, Seabury's concern prompted Robert to write the following letter to James and Mead:

My dear brothers —
Since talking with you about your prospects and after knowing your intentions, I fear you may feel inclined to think that I may be led to directly or indirectly assist you. I write this to say that under no circumstances can I be induced to take any part in any business that may conflict with the business of Seabury & Johnson.

I would be glad to join in any other business to a reasonable extent that in my judgment offered a fair return for my money.

I must again draw your attention to the fact that Seabury & Johnson are an old established house, have unlimited capital and credit and can at any moment sew up your small means. I strongly advise you to think the matter over very carefully before you engage in a contest with Seabury.

In order to fairly compete with them, you should have at least five times the capital you now have.

I will now add that if you determine to engage in the plaster business from this time on, I shall refuse to aid or assist you and will not even talk with you on the subject.

I wish you to accept this as final and whatever you may do of this kind you must act on your own judgment and stand on your own.

I wish you to show this to Mr. Cox so that he may not be misled.

Yours truly,
R. W. Johnson

The "Mr. Cox" referred to was Rowland Cox, a New York attorney whom James and Mead had consulted about starting a company.

Robert's letter apparently satisfied Seabury, and on March 3 the *New Brunswick Daily Times* carried a brief announcement under the headline "A New Factory":

Messrs. Johnson and Co., of New York, wholesale druggists and drug manufacturers, have made arrangements with Mr. James Parsons by which they hire of him the old Janeway and Carpenter factory on Neilson Street, near the railroad bridge. They will soon begin work with from 50 to 100 hands at the manufacture of standard articles of drugs. Mr. Johnson, the head of the firm, was in this city Tuesday afternoon making the arrangements for the opening of the manufactory. He has engaged Mr. Robert Adrain as counsel to complete all arrangements.

The following day the city's two other newspapers, the *Daily Fredonian* and the *Daily News*, carried similar articles, but all three accounts were far too optimistic regarding the new company's size. When James began operations in the coming weeks, there were actually only fourteen employees, all recruited from Seabury & Johnson in East Orange.

On March 25 James made out a check marked "No. 1" from Johnson & Johnson to pay $7.92 to John Ware, the local railroad freightmaster. The new business was officially under way. The first products produced were medicinal plasters made on machines designed and hastily built by James during the previous months. They were similar to the machines he had built for Seabury & Johnson, and there was no problem in duplicating them because he had applied for patents in his name. James was careful to hire skilled operators, which, he believed, were essential to making good plasters, and in a short time the new company was producing twenty-one different kinds. Soon the product line included lint and cotton for dressings, and corn and bunion plasters for aching feet. By July, Mead eagerly wrote to a customer: "We are ready to make all of the goods you may require." It was an inaccurate but understandable boast.

Despite Mead's enthusiasm, the business did not get off to an impressive start. The competition was intense, not only from legitimate competitors but also from a host of unscrupulous operators who grasped at every opportunity to foist imitation products and sure-fire "cures" on a gullible and unsuspecting public that simply wanted to ease aches and pains and feel better.

The late nineteenth century was the heyday of patent medicines — so called because only the names could be protected. The ingredients often were a mystery. Some contained as much as forty-proof alcohol, others contained opium, cocaine, or morphine. Addiction was not uncommon, and most of the extravagant claims for the "cures" were rank lies, although there was little denying that people often felt better after taking them. Women, including staunch supporters of the Women's Christian Temperance Union, were among the best customers for "tonic" patent medicines. Though WCTU members were avowed teetotalers, some took the forty-proof "tonics" regularly.

James confined himself to running the factory, where he was far more relaxed devising complicated machinery than dealing with complicated people. The more extroverted Mead continued his prolific output of letters to potential customers from the New York office, but the orders were only trickling in. The brothers were having great difficulty getting the business moving, and the future did not seem bright. The competition was also beginning to bear down on George Seabury. A year had passed since the split, and the business — if not Seabury — missed Robert Johnson.

The legal covenant with Johnson required Seabury to make periodic payments to his former partner, and by mid-summer of 1886 he had missed several. Confronting him, Johnson suggested that their arrangement be abrogated. Seabury was reluctant, but, lacking the money for the payments, he had little choice. The resulting agreement was that in return for cancellation of $120,000 in promissory notes, Johnson would be free to reenter the medical business.

On September 23 Johnson published an open letter to the drug trade in which he explained that, for "a mutually satisfactory consideration," he no longer had a covenant with George Seabury and would be joining his brothers and "taking charge of the business." Then the letter made a bold bid for Seabury's customers:

> I now beg to state that I have joined the firm of Johnson & Johnson who are engaged in manufacturing a full line of preparations similar

to those made and sold by Seabury & Johnson. As all those interested with me have had a long experience in the manufacture and sale of these preparations, it is needless to say that they understand the art of manufacturing India Rubber Plasters and are producing goods in every respect equal to those made by other manufacturers.

I trust old friends and patrons of Seabury & Johnson will be good enough to carefully examine the products of the new house and if in appearance and quality they are found satisfactory, that they will give them a reasonable share of their favors. I think no one will deny that legitimate competition should be encouraged.

Johnson lost no time closing his office and joining Mead at 32 Cedar Street. His arrival sent a jolt of energy and optimism into the struggling young company, and he brought with him badly needed capital. On October 23 Mead was brimming with enthusiasm when he wrote J. J. Edmundson, the "traveler" responsible for New York and Pennsylvania.

It may take a little longer than we anticipated but we are bound to get to the top in the end. You can see by this time that something more is required than the efforts of a good No. 1 salesman to create a boom. That something we are nearly ready to give the public in large doses. R. W. Johnson has at last completed arrangements with Seabury whereby for a consideration he is scot free from all contracts with Seabury. He has a desk in our office and will lead our forces. There will be no lack of funds after a little.

If logic alone had prevailed, the new company would have been renamed—Johnson & Johnson & Johnson—to reflect the new partnership of the three brothers. But good judgment suggested that a better marketing approach would be to leave it at Johnson & Johnson, and this would soon prove prophetic.

Robert Johnson entered the fray fired up. On November 19 he wrote to another traveler: "We have concluded to stick the knife right into the bowels of the plaster business. . . . We shall send you a new price list . . . and you will be surprised at the cuts." Two days later he wrote a dealer: "We have concluded to try and do all of our business through the jobbers and have just made some heavy discounts, as you can observe, to induce the various jobbing houses to take our goods in hand and push them. . . . We guarantee the quality of the goods in every way to be equal to Seabury & Johnson or better."

Modesty was not one of Johnson's strengths. He did not hesitate to say that his brothers had gotten off to what he described as "a feeble start" without him, but he was now ready to change that. This new surge of spirit was quickly transmitted to the small band of factory workers in New Brunswick, most of whom had known him from his visits to East Orange. They were well aware of his reputation for getting the job done and how determined he could be. As he established contact with larger numbers of customers, the orders began pouring in and the production lines moved faster. Both the motivator and the money had indeed arrived.

Down at the docks the steamships *New Brunswick* and *Lucy P. Miller* began making daily runs to New York laden with increasing amounts of cargo stamped "Johnson & Johnson." That fall, as they plied the waters to New York Harbor, their passengers and crews were caught up in the excitement that had been mounting for months as the time approached for dedicating the Statue of Liberty. New York, and all the nation, had watched with fascination as the majestic monument was slowly assembled to its full height on star-shaped Bedloe's Island. The gift from France, designed by sculptor Auguste Bartholdi and engineered by Gustave Eiffel, had already been assembled and tested in Paris, after which it was dismantled, packed in 214 crates, and shipped to New York on the French ship *Isère*. The reassembly took more than a year, but the long-awaited dedication day, October 28, finally arrived. Although it was a rainy and dismal day, the crowds that gathered for the celebration made it festive.

President Grover Cleveland and a host of American and French notables reviewed a sparkling parade in Manhattan that moved downtown to the Battery to cheers and band music. Then the President and New York Governor David B. Hill boarded the Navy vessel USS *Despatch* and led a flotilla of three hundred tugboats, yachts, and steamers to Bedloe's Island for the unveiling. More than a million people on boats and ashore peered through the rain and mist as Bartholdi, on a platform inside the statue's head, pulled the cords and undraped the French flag covering its seductive face. "You are the greatest man in America today," President Cleveland declared, and the harbor erupted in a din of boat whistles, band music, warship guns, and cheers, welcoming the lady to her new home.

The emotional uplift of the dedication celebration was but a symbol of the rising spirit and vitality sweeping the United States during the late nineteenth century. The resurgence was evident in many other ways. The young nation, spurred by the arrival of hordes of new immigrants, was now growing dramatically. New social, political, and economic concepts were being tested. And it was a period of contradictions. The nation was in the process of being transformed from a largely rural and agrarian society to an urban, industrial one, from a relatively homogeneous population to a melting pot, from an isolationist posture to the beginnings of a world power. The Indian wars were winding down and the push westward continued, followed closely by the building of new railroads. The surge of immigration now included an influx of people from southern and eastern Europe, bringing a babble of strange languages and customs. Discontent was evident in the factory, in the polling place, and on the farm, all for different reasons. Unions and strikes became a factor for the first time. Women advanced the suffrage movement in search of voting rights. And industrialization meant that the farmer was no longer the backbone of America.

Despite these upheavals of tradition, most people clung to a belief in the rags-to-riches dream. The Horatio Alger example had been popularized by the likes of Andrew Carnegie and John Jacob Astor. Carnegie, after all, had been a bobbin boy in a Pittsburgh textile mill earning $4.80 a month. Astor arrived in America with

$5.00 in his pocket, and when he died in 1848 was the richest man in the country. Their stories were told again and again, kindling hope among the poor, the less rich, and particularly the ambitious.

The climate was ideal for starting a new business. The morale of the country had been damaged by an agonizing and draining civil war and was now rebounding. The pioneer mentality of frugality and doing without had given way to a more adventuresome spirit and a desire to live in greater comfort. This change in national attitude coincided with an explosion of new products designed to meet the needs and whims of a population eager to buy them. At the top of the list were products that promoted better health. People were anxious to feel better, and the health of the population was truly in need of improvement, due to a good deal of ignorance and some neglect. But the quiet revolution taking place in medicine was beginning to manifest itself in ways not even dreamed of a short time earlier.

Although medicinal plasters were the basis of the early business, Johnson soon turned his attention to developing a line of surgical dressings in accordance with Lister's teachings. Ten years had passed since he had heard the British surgeon speak in Philadelphia during the Centennial celebration, and the message still echoed clearly. Ever so slowly, American physicians were beginning to accept Lister's theories on germs, and Johnson was convinced that someday all of medicine would be converted to these beliefs. He was now devoting greater effort than ever before to developing a line of antiseptic dressings.

In early 1887 the young company published its first catalog and price list under the name "Johnson & Johnson Operative Chemists," by which it was then known. The thirty-two-page booklet contained a wide array of products, dominated by medicinal plasters. The two most popular plasters were made from the lowly mustard seed and the belladonna plant. Mustard plasters generated heat and acted as a counter-irritant to relieve injured or diseased areas of the body. Most physicians agreed that the majority of diseases involved inflammation, and a leading medical journal noted: "No matter what remedies we may use, we cannot afford to treat disease without the aid of mustard plasters." Belladonna came from the root extract of a plant traced to ancient Greece, and when combined with boric acid caused the fatty tissues of the skin to hasten absorption of the belladonna into the body. Belladonna acted as an anti-spasmodic, and increasingly extravagant claims were made for its curative powers.

Almost overshadowed in the catalog by the popular plasters was a line of dressings for wounds. Some were made from tarred jute, a fibrous East Indian plant also used to make sacks; and oakum, a hemp widely used in construction work to caulk seams. Almost in desperation, these materials were being adapted for wound care. But it was Johnson & Johnson's new line of antiseptic dressings that would have a lasting impact on medical care. The carbolated dressings were prepared "according to Lister's formula" and the Linton Moist Dressings were made from cotton gauze, packed in hermetically sealed jars and impregnated with a solution of iodoform, commonly referred to as "the skunk of surgery." The smell was overpowering, but the iodoform routed germs.

As correct as Lister had been about the need for a germ-free environment, even he had failed to grasp that the materials from which surgical dressings were then made were not satisfactory. Nor had he seen the importance of absorbency in surgical dressings. From the beginning the Johnsons saw the value of absorbency and believed that cotton was the correct material to use. They found better ways to clean, bleach, and comb cotton to produce soft, white absorbent dressings, but the process involved forty separate steps. Making the cotton and gauze antiseptic, and later sterile, was yet another challenge. It was common practice to wash and reuse surgical dressings, thus increasing the risk of contamination. So Robert Johnson developed an ingenious disposable sponge, or dressing, made of layers of absorbent cotton, and coconut and manila fibers, with a small capsule containing an antiseptic hidden in the center. Just before using it, the physician broke the capsule, thereby releasing the antiseptic and saturating the dressing. The design made it highly unlikely that the dressing would be washed and reused.

The mystery of infection would not be solved until sterile suture material was developed. But sutures and ligatures were more complex than dressings because they were frequently sewn inside the body and had to be absorbed without incident. The catgut from sheep intestines worked best, but the highest quality of that material was reserved for use in musical instruments. To compound the problem, care had to be taken that the methods used to make the sutures sterile did not break down their natural properties, rendering them weak and brittle. After much experimenting, the sutures were first immersed in a corrosive solution, soaked for ten days in oil of juniper berries, and then packaged in vials containing a 20 percent alcohol solution. The result brought a grateful response from physicians. "I have used common sewing thread many times in lieu of anything better," one doctor wrote, "and oh dear how I as well as the patient counted the days when they must be removed."

When the company was incorporated with capital stock of $100,000 on October 28, 1887, Robert Johnson held 40 percent of it, while his brothers Mead and James each had 30 percent. Robert was elected president (although James held the position for five weeks while a legal issue with George Seabury was cleared up) and Mead became secretary. James was general manager of manufacturing. In a little more than a year, the work force had grown to 125 men and women, and the factory had expanded to 35,000 square feet. Most of the employees came from New Brunswick. The Johnson brothers had purchased a secondhand factory whistle, and its piercing blasts were a daily reminder that the company was alive and well.

Turning to advertising to spur sales, Johnson retained the services of J. Walter Thompson, a young advertising genius whom he had met several years earlier. The two became good friends, saw each other socially, and often traded investment advice. Thompson had begun his career as a bookkeeper with a small agency, Carlton & Smith, and in 1878 purchased the agency for $500. He handled the Johnson account himself, and it could be frustrating. Johnson approved every ad and measured its performance according to his own yardstick. He had an instinct for what would sell, but at times he would meddle, much to the consternation of Thompson and his agency staff. The "Dear Walter" letters were often blunt: "I return the sketch and hardly see how you can make an advertisement out of it. It needs to have a very black background in order to throw out the white letters." That particular ad perished, but the friendship flourished, no doubt because Thompson wisely followed his cardinal rule: "Never get on stage in front of your client. No advertising can stand even the suspicion that you, not he, could have been responsible for his success."

4

KILMER'S GENIUS

EARLY in 1887 Johnson began spending more time in New Brunswick running the business and less in the New York office. At the factory, workers dealt with him guardedly, and with some awe and a little fear. They saw him as dogmatic, which he was, and having a quick temper, which he did. But few questioned his leadership, and he had the knack of being able to rally his workers, even the fainthearted, to bolder challenges. "The worse thing that can happen to a man is to lose his courage," he would tell them time and again, until he had made believers out of the doubters.

Most of the time he used persuasive tactics to get the upper hand, but when that strategy failed he would drive home his point until he had the dominant position, which he then protected tenaciously. Johnson did not like the lesser role, and refused to accept it. One way or another, he gained control of the situation. For him, it seemed to be the only role. He immersed himself in every facet of the business, even opening the company's mail every morning — a ritual he followed throughout his business life. The mail was brought in sacks to a room where he and several managers sorted and opened it, paying closest attention to orders and complaints. With his excellent memory, Johnson could quote current sales figures "up to Saturday night," as he put it.

Socially, Johnson did little mingling in the city, though, not married at age forty-one, he was considered a very eligible escort. He was friendly with many local merchants and businessmen, and the sumptuous luncheons he had at the Kline Hotel helped to round out his already portly build. On his frequent noontime strolls to the downtown business district, a distance he covered in long, assertive strides, he chatted with storekeepers about business matters but had no time for chitchat.

It was common for Johnson to visit pharmacies, and the day early in 1887 that he stopped in at the Opera House Pharmacy at the corner of Albany and Spring Streets was to have special significance. It was then that he met Dr. Fred B. Kilmer, an astute and engaging proprietor who was on his way to becoming a giant in pharmacy. Many years later, Kilmer was described by *Time* magazine as "the most revered pharmaceutical chemist in the country" and by *American Druggist* as "one of the most fascinating individuals American pharmacy has given to the world."

Kilmer was in the early stages of his career, and it was clear that he was not only a talented pharmacist but also an individual with rare personal qualities. Johnson liked him immediately. They struck up a friendship that was to strongly influence events in their lives and have an impact on the delivery of health care in the nation and the world for the next twenty-five years. Six years younger than Johnson, Kilmer was born in 1851 in Chapinville, Connecticut, the son of a lay preacher of the Methodist Episcopal Church and a descendant of the Palatine emigrants who settled in Livingston Manor, New York, in the early eighteenth century. He too attended Wyoming Seminary in Pennsylvania, and after graduating from the New York College of Pharmacy he did his apprenticeship in pharmacies in Binghamton, New York; Plymouth, Pennsylvania; and Morristown, New Jersey, before settling in New Brunswick in 1879.

In appearance and demeanor, mild-mannered Fred "Doc" Kilmer gave no hint of the determined spirit that churned within him. He looked somewhat frail, with a thin, elongated face accentuated by a mustache and a goatee that tapered to a point. He had a perpetual melancholy look about him, and that was the impression he left with those who had neither the time nor the opportunity to know him better. But behind that facade was an arresting personality and a ready wit.

Unlike its proprietor, the Opera House Pharmacy was dominating. Its regal appearance was highlighted by tall wood columns flanking the entrance and flaring upward to an elaborate carved frieze. The result was a graceful arch in both directions that met two larger, rectangular wood columns at the outer boundaries of the storefront. A huge sign, "Drug Store," stretched over the entire width of the sidewalk and was supported by a pole at the curb. Hanging from that was a large "Soda Water" sign announcing that Kilmer was a dispenser of the new fad—fizzled water. In the center of both windows were two hanging lamps. Kilmer frequently changed the window displays, which were mostly educational and included framed paintings or photographs, adding to the overall professional appearance he wanted the pharmacy to have.

Another frequent visitor to Kilmer's pharmacy was Thomas Alva Edison, the prolific inventor whose experimental laboratories were located in Menlo Park, five miles from New Brunswick. The two became good friends, and on his frequent visits to the pharmacy Edison talked with Kilmer about various drug compounds and their uses. He would venture behind the prescription counter to watch Kilmer perform percolation, distillation, emulsification, and other pharmaceutical functions, and then follow him down to the cellar to watch soda water being made from marble dust and sulfurous acid. Edison became intrigued by a window display Kilmer had assembled with a map showing where certain medicinal drugs came from, along with specimens of the plants from which they were derived.

Once described as appearing young but acting old and anxious, Edison had an unmanageable mop of slightly graying hair, and his clothes were usually rumpled. "He had the look of a mechanic and the manner of a careless schoolboy," one journalist wrote. On evenings when Mrs. Edison insisted that her husband accompany her to the opera in New Brunswick, they would stop first at Kilmer's pharmacy so she could, Kilmer recalled, "help to spruce up the unconventional inventor and remove traces of his hurriedly prepared toilet." Edison would sit patiently in the back room of the pharmacy while his wife made him presentable for the performance. He acted like a child being dragged to a concert, going reluctantly and leaving little doubt that his thoughts were back in his laboratory.

At the Menlo Park laboratories, with the help of many assistants, Edison developed a veritable assembly line for turning out inventions. The most productive inventor of his time, he had the first laboratory devoted entirely to the research and development of practical inventions by teams of skilled people. At one point he was generating forty new patents a year, earning him the sobriquet "Wizard of Menlo Park." It was there he improved the automatic telegraph and Alexander Graham Bell's telephone, and worked on his most notable invention, a practical filament for the electric light bulb.

Some of the carbon, charcoal, and other materials that Edison used in the experiments on the incandescent lamp had been purchased from his friend Fred Kilmer at the Opera House Pharmacy. Kilmer's basement was a storehouse of assorted materials that other pharmacists had access to. Kilmer recalled broadening Edison's interest in numerous drugs and chemicals used in his experiments: "At my suggestion he purchased a U.S. Dispensatory in order to become acquainted with the nature of certain drugs and chemicals." The friendship between Kilmer and Edison was rooted in new ideas, and it flourished for years.

The same could be said for the even closer friendship that was developing between Kilmer and Robert Johnson. Even in their early meetings the chemistry between the two was special—each had a probing mind and a yearning to explore the frontiers of medicine and health. Yet their personalities were quite dissimilar. Johnson was openly forceful; Kilmer was inwardly forceful. Their common meeting ground, one on which they seemed to meld together perfectly, was the vast area of the health sciences, still in its infancy.

Kilmer had a special interest in advancing the professionalism of pharmacy, and in 1886, at age thirty-five, he served as president of the New Jersey Pharmaceutical Association. He had also become quite knowledgeable about the cultivation of plants for medicinal purposes, a subject that Johnson too was very familiar with. When Kilmer first arrived in New Brunswick he was appalled at the prevailing public health conditions, though they were typical of those that plagued hundreds of towns and cities across the nation. Commenting later on the deplorable state of community health that he had encountered, Kilmer said: "No attention was given to public health matters. Epidemics of measles, diphtheria, typhoid fever, smallpox and the like swept through the city uncontrolled. Malaria was rife. Babies died by the hundreds. Privy vaults adorned every yard. There were public wells in the streets. House sewage was emptied into the gutters. Garbage was dumped on vacant lots. The water was muddy, dark in color, and bad in taste. Things were in rather a bad mess."

The filth Kilmer saw revulsed him. He went to the mayor and urged the formation of a committee that included several local physicians. The committee later became the city's first Board of Health. Looking back, Kilmer said: "We laid the foundations for the prevention of disease with quarantines, vaccinations for smallpox, distribution of diphtheria antitoxin, food inspections, and a general clean-up of the city."

These early experiences generated in Kilmer a lifelong interest in public health. As an influential member of the American Public Health Association, he helped bring similar reforms in the water and milk supply, disease control, and sanitary sewage systems to many other American cities where conditions were deplorable.

During his frequent visits to the Opera House Pharmacy, Johnson would talk about the need to develop a broad educational program for physicians in support of Listerism, a subject on which Kilmer was both knowledgeable and sympathetic. The two men spoke about the need to awaken the medical profession to these beliefs, but then they began to devise a plan. Kilmer would start corresponding with a group of well-known surgeons who were believed to be advocates of Listerism, and their experiences with the sterilization method would be compiled into a manual and distributed widely to physicians and hospitals. Meanwhile, Johnson and his associates would work on improving the surgical dressings that would be required in the operating room in support of Lister's concepts.

By early 1888 Kilmer had completed his correspondence and was busily putting together the long-awaited manual. One of Kilmer's many talents was the ability to write on scientific subjects clearly and with style, which was evident when *Modern Methods of Antiseptic Wound Treatment* was published early that year. Subtitled "A Compilation of Recent Notes and Suggestions from Eminent Surgeons," it was essentially a "how to" manual for physicians who performed surgery. It included explicit drawings of complicated surgical procedures and gave a convincing argument for Listerism: "Antisepsis and asepsis have assumed important places in surgical procedures. The principles which underlie this cannot be successfully controverted." In another section, the foundation for Lister's philosophy was emphasized: "Antiseptics must be used both in aseptic and antiseptic wound treatment. Cleanliness cannot be attained, much less maintained, without the aid of cleansing agents, or antiseptics — angels of cleanliness. Perfect asepsis, unaided, is a myth. Perfect aseptic wound treatment, by the use of antiseptics, is an established fact."

The articles by physicians included "The Organization of an Operation" by Dr. W. W. Keen, Professor of the Principles of Surgery at Jefferson Medical College; and an article on "Sutures, Ligatures, and Knots" by Dr. John Blair Deaver, Associate Professor of Medicine at the University of Pennsylvania. Deaver, a founder of the American College of Surgeons, was chosen to operate on more members of his profession than any other surgeon. There were photos of Lister, the noted Professor Robert Koch of Berlin, and others—all described as "some of the World's Greatest Surgeons." The later pages of the manual showed the surgical products available from the company. Johnson's entrepreneurial touch had been cleverly combined with Kilmer's scientific educational approach.

The manual met with immediate acceptance and was soon being hailed by the medical profession as the most authoritative discussion of antiseptic wound treatment ever published. It was the most important stimulus that Listerism had received in the United States to date. Before long the manual was the "practicing handbook" for all who believed in Lister's teachings, and a persuasive argument for those who were not sure.

The demand for copies was overwhelming, and by March 1888 the company had distributed 85,000 manuals. In time, four and a half million would be in circulation around the world. To Dr. Samuel David Gross, a contributor to the manual and the originator of various surgical methods, including wiring together the ends of bones in a fracture, Johnson wrote: "We are glad to be able to inform you that the antiseptic brochures have been of marked benefit to our business." That was an understatement. The stimulating effect the manual had on the business was extraordinary. Even so, it was hailed in its own right as a major contribution to the advancement of antiseptic surgery during a critical period of learning.

The educational process had begun, and although the gap separating primitive and modern surgery was still wide, the new manual was helping to bridge it. The timing was perfect, and the fact that Johnson also had a line of products that fitted neatly with this enlightened approach made the effort that much more rewarding. Kilmer later reflected on the role Johnson & Johnson played: "In its very inception, while the consensus of surgical opinion was decidedly against the innovations of antiseptic and aseptic surgery, the company boldly stepped in with new forms of surgical dressings and won out. They led the way."

Recognizing Kilmer's many skills, Johnson wisely asked him to join the company as Director of Scientific Affairs. Because of his dedication to pharmacy, Kilmer pondered the decision for some time. After a while he recognized the opportunity to play a larger role and to have an influence on the direction of medical science, and so he accepted. In October 1889 he sold the Opera House Pharmacy to an employee and joined Johnson's firm, beginning a relationship that was to extend over the next forty-five years. When Kilmer arrived at the company's laboratory, he found a meager assortment of test tubes, a handful of beakers, and a Bunsen burner. Undaunted, he set about making improvements and was given broad latitude.

Soon Kilmer was providing much of the technical expertise needed to mass-produce sterile cotton and gauze dressings. In 1891 his bacteriological laboratory repeated with great care the classic experiments conducted earlier in Germany by Robert Koch, demonstrating the efficacy of hot air and steam in killing microorganisms. From these experiments, Kilmer developed a procedure for verifying the industrial process by using reference organism spores of *Bacillus anthracis*, an organism also favored by Koch. Kilmer inoculated a portion of the dressing material, and the contaminated dressing was then placed in the center of the other dressings in the sterilizer load. If the steam killed the test organisms, the remaining dressings were presumed sterile also.

When word reached Lister about the new methods of manufacturing and sterilizing surgical dressings, he wrote asking Kilmer for details, and on December 28, 1891, Kilmer sent him a lengthy response outlining every step of the process. The inquiry from Lister generated pride throughout the company. Kilmer later summarized the dramatic sequence that began with Pasteur and Lister and in which he and the Johnsons had played a part:

Just prior to the manufacturing days of Johnson & Johnson, a number of important events occurred in the history of mankind. Pasteur had overthrown the doctrine of spontaneous generation. A few microbes of disease had been caught and convicted. Out of the researches into wine and beer, the science of bacteriology had its birth. Then came Lister with an attempt to clean the Aegean stables of wound infection, gangrene, and pus, with rivers of carbolic acid. Lister's methods were based upon the principles established by Pasteur. He attributed the mischief in wound repair to "living atmospheric particles," aseptic germs which he attempted to drown in carbolic acid. Lister's first methods were crude but they were founded upon science and upon art. He was the first to see the light and show others the way out of darkness. From Lister's great conception was born modern surgery. It is acknowledged that the introduction of Johnson & Johnson dressings marked the real beginning of antiseptic surgery in this country; in fact, it placed reliable antiseptic dressings within the reach of every practitioner. This the Johnsons did at a time when many of the profession were still in doubt about accepting the doctrine and theory of antisepsis.

Next for the Johnsons, and for the nation, came an entirely new aspect of medical care: first-aid products. The unlikely inspiration for the development of first-aid treatment was the national railroad system then under construction from coast to coast. Down through the years, in accidents and battlefields everywhere, the instinct for survival prompted some type of first-aid treatment — though often it was more harmful than beneficial and overlooked what Kilmer defined as the goal of first-aid: "to prevent an extension of an injury rather than its treatment."

One day, aboard a Denver & Rio Railway train as it snaked its way through the Rockies, Johnson struck up a conversation with the railroad's chief surgeon, who lamented the growing number of railway accidents. America had begun a new era in travel when the Union Pacific and Central Pacific Railroads met at Promentory Point in Utah, back on May 10, 1869, dramatically completing the conquest of the continent by rail. The linkup gave the nation 52,000 miles of trackage, which would soon double as feeder lines, made it possible to ship Longhorn cattle from remote Texas prairies, farm products from the fields of the Midwest, and manufactured goods from factories in the East. As railway construction pushed into new frontiers, the accident toll mounted, and physicians were seldom nearby to help.

Johnson listened intently, and early in 1888 he began soliciting the views of numerous railway surgeons to see what their needs might be. Then he came up with a first-aid kit to meet those needs. The "Railway Station & Factory Supply Case," containing an array of antiseptic dressings and surgical supplies, was introduced in 1890. It was recommended that the kit be placed with station agents at railroad stations across the nation so they would have it handy when needed. According to the promotional literature, the kit contained "supplies sufficient not only for minor injuries, but also enough for a number of serious accidents." The grisly instructions in the kit included first-aid advice on "fingers or toes torn off" and "hands and feet crushed or torn off." Thoughtfully, advice on treating fainting was also provided. And instructions offered this additional warning: "If the accident is serious send for a surgeon at once. While waiting keep cool."

The influence of the railroads touched every American, even to changing the clock on the wall. Once trains were running from coast to coast, something had to be done about coordinating schedules, so the railroads solved the timetable problem in 1883 by dividing the country into four time zones — Eastern, Central, Mountain, and Pacific — each zone based on the mean sun time on certain meridians near Philadelphia, Memphis, Denver, and Fresno. Though less than ecstatic about the change, the nation adjusted its affairs to railroad time — banks opened and closed, and people got married and were born and died by railroad time. A cry went up that people preferred to run their lives on "God's time — not Vanderbilt's," but the railroads prevailed.

After adjusting to the time change, Americans came to depend on the railroads — even embrace them — not just for transportation but for news and communication as well. Elaborate and luxurious union stations and terminals were built in large cities to augment what already was a small-town American tradition — the local railroad depot. Neatly maintained and painted red, brown, or green, the local rail station was usually located at the end of Main Street and became a crossroads of life in the community. Because most depots housed a telegraph office and mail and express service, they were the main communications link with the outside world.

Johnson believed that every rail depot in America should have a Johnson & Johnson first-aid kit, and he was determined to see that happen. Until this point in time, no effort had been made to establish correct first-aid techniques because little was known about emergency care. Kilmer began studying the subject, talking with physicians who had handled emergencies, and doing extensive research. Some techniques had never been analyzed, while others were highly controversial. Hanging like a dark cloud over many early attempts at first-aid was the ever-present danger that volunteers would maim or kill victims by applying the wrong treatment. But Kilmer patiently sorted out the various conflicts in a series of bulletins and laid out a clear course of action for various injuries that was calculated to help the injured survive.

These early bulletins on emergency care were of such help in giving early treatment to victims that Kilmer later compiled the nation's first comprehensive manual on first-aid. The manual was widely distributed by Johnson & Johnson, along with a list of first-aid products the company offered. In the manual, Kilmer defined "first-aid" as "a bridge between the accident and medical and surgical assistance, over which the patient may be carried safely and securely from the scene of the accident or sudden illness to the doctor or hospital." Kilmer's guidance was credited with saving many lives and reducing the pain of countless victims. Johnson, seeing the trend, soon developed first-aid kits for farm, factory, home, and office, and later many others.

Though he managed all facets of the business, Johnson concentrated on marketing strategies, new packaging, strengthening the sales organization, and the quality of products being produced. Kilmer later observed: "He was firm in the belief that high-quality and handsome packages were valuable factors in obtaining trade and holding the good will of his patrons." Johnson's doting on quality, combined with his constant pursuit of perfection, made him a nag on the subject until things were being done to his satisfaction.

For his increasing sales force, Johnson concentrated on hiring "travelers" who were trained as physicians. Some had not completed their medical studies, and others needed the $100 a month he paid them. They traveled by rail, stage, and horseback and averaged $125 a month in expenses, which Johnson watched like a hawk, spurring them on with frequent, terse notes. "It will be necessary for you to get in some 'hard licks' in order to make your work pay," he wrote one traveler. He was coy when it came to sharing information with competitors: "Sales for March will be ten to fifteen percent higher," Johnson wrote one traveler, "but this I do not care to mention outside, but prefer to state that we are barely holding our own in sales."

In 1890 a doctor wrote Kilmer that one of his patients had complained of skin irritation from using medicated plasters. Kilmer thoughtfully sent him a small container of Italian talc, which he recommended the patient use to soothe the skin. After some discussion at the factory, it was decided to include a small container of talc with certain plasters. That was the genesis of the baby powder business, and the beginning of an American institution that was to spread worldwide — the powdering of infants' bottoms with Johnson's Baby Powder.

By now all of America, and most of the world, had been introduced to the products bearing the familiar red cross. What had once seemed to be unrelated events now assumed new importance when viewed in retrospect: Robert asking his brothers to join him; their correct perception that Lister's teachings could be translated into an important new business; Robert's fortuitous meeting with Fred Kilmer, and the successful blending of their talents; and, not to be overlooked, excellent timing and luck.

5

RWJ'S "DOMESTIC SHRINE"

EYEBROWS were raised and tongues wagged in New Brunswick when the portly, forty-seven-year-old Robert Wood Johnson married the slender and disarmingly attractive Evangeline Armstrong from Holley, in Upstate New York, after a brief courtship. Evangeline was twenty years younger, and most would have guessed that the age difference was greater. It was, indeed, an unlikely match, and it quickly put a crimp in any plans the city's hopeful widows had for catching the elusive, wealthy industrialist who had become their fair prey.

They were married in a quiet ceremony at Maryville, Tennessee, on June 27, 1892, and after a honeymoon in the south returned to New Brunswick and moved into a somewhat forbidding mansion — Gray Terrace — that Johnson had purchased for his young bride for $75,000. There was no larger house in all of New Brunswick and environs, or a prouder husband. Evangeline, with her angelic face and hint of shyness, seemed to quicken Johnson's already sprightly step. And she came from good stock, as they said.

Her father, Edwin Armstrong, had started out as a schoolteacher and principal in Rochester, New York, before turning to medicine. His wife, the former Martha Gifford, was a schoolteacher and an accomplished musician. Completing his medical studies, Dr. Armstrong moved his young family to a large house on the public square in the picturesque town of Holley, and for the next four decades practiced general medicine, surgery, and the emerging specialty of diagnostics. The couple had five daughters, who proudly traced their ancestry to William Brewster, the chosen leader and elder of the Plymouth Pilgrims.

Gray Terrace was an opulent and awkward-looking example of Victorian architecture. It squatted pompously behind a stone wall topped by decorative wrought iron, and was three ungainly stories high. At one end a tower rose above the rest of the structure, adding nothing to its overall appearance. An architectural critic was unflattering: "The Johnson residence used practically every motif of every style in the Romantic era, and combined them illogically and obtrusively. Masses of sculptured ornamental detail were used on the façade with much light iron work, giving the home the wedding cake effect so popular in the 'gilded age.' Irregularity of design and a mansard roof were the dominating architectural features, but so heavy were the ornamental details that they detracted from the appearance of the building as a whole."

It was quite apparent from Gray Terrace's long line of curbstone critics that few in New Brunswick liked the way the house looked, except its owner, or dared express disapproval of Gray Terrace in Johnson's presence. He loved every nook and cranny of it, and the spacious grounds around it, and the horse barn and the greenhouses where he doted over the orchids that he proudly grew there. Johnson was not given to small talk, so it is doubtful that he engaged in conversation about the mystery that had hung over Gray Terrace ever since it was built by Robert N. Woodworth, a wealthy carpet maker, in 1873.

Shortly after the mansion was completed there was a bank robbery in North Jersey, and the gold that was stolen was never recovered. That's when a rumor started that the cache of gold from the theft was hidden in the recesses of the mansion's walls, which were so wide that a thin person could squeeze between them. Twenty years later the story persisted. But even if he had wanted to, Johnson could not have squeezed between the walls of Gray Terrace to investigate, not even if the walls were twice the width. (Years later, when the mansion became the Kappa Sigma fraternity house, hordes of pledges were sent wedging themselves between the walls of the great house in search of the elusive gold, which of course was never found.)

As might be expected, the young bride Evangeline became the focus of attention in New Brunswick, and the object of idle gossip and constant curiosity. The more puritanical in the city had concluded that Johnson's marriage to a woman young enough to be his daughter was not proper, though no one told him so directly. An acquaintance of the couple summed it up this way: "New Brunswick society never accepted her, and Evangeline could not care less." And neither could Johnson, who had a special disdain for purely social occasions. Shortly after the couple moved into Gray Terrace they were joined by Roberta, Johnson's eight-year-old daughter by his first marriage. This required some adjustment on everyone's part, especially Evangeline, whose family was about to grow rapidly.

Just a little over nine months after her marriage, on April 4, 1893, Evangeline gave birth to Robert Wood Johnson the Second, in an upstairs bedroom at Gray Terrace. Now Evangeline had two children to care for, a burden made considerably lighter by the presence of a household staff of five that Johnson had retained to keep the mansion functioning like clockwork.

The estate was located at the corner of College Avenue and Hamilton Street, just across the street from the center of the Rutgers University campus and a block away from Johnson's factories. Every day at precisely one o'clock he would walk home from the office to take his main meal of the day and "check on things." Once there, he slowed his tempo and the household staff quickened theirs. Evangeline would join him for a sumptuous meal prepared by an accomplished chef, and then Johnson retired to his library for a rest before returning to the office. There he would enjoy a Cuban cigar, puff by contemplative puff.

After resting, his daily mid-day ritual took him on an inspection tour of house and grounds to personally check on the work being done that day by his household staff and the groundskeepers. He was a stickler for detail, and perpetually convinced that his way of doing things was best. He gave orders politely and crisply, and his praise for work well done was always abbreviated. Still, he had his stout defenders, because he was a generous man. A woman friend of the family wrote: "He is the most appreciative man I ever met. If I wanted a favor, I would prepare with my own hands some dainty. It need not cost much, but must show evidence of being well made, and of being prepared for his especial comfort or pleasure. This I would carry to his home, and his hearty gratitude would open the door to any reasonable request."

About household matters, as well as business, Johnson was often difficult to please, and sometimes impossible. He once complained to a cabinetmaker that the animal claws carved on the legs of a table were not sufficiently "realistic." Another time he wrote a harried shoemaker about a pair of $12.30 handmade shoes that he was sending back to be altered, and offered this advice for a better fit: "Transfer the width that is on the right side of the shoe to the left side. If you could cut off the point on the right side of the shoe and put it on the left side, making the sole and the upper one-quarter inch wider at that point, it would work perfectly satisfactorily."

Johnson's penchant for a business-like approach impressed the city fathers, who held him in high regard. He was once offered the nomination for mayor and asked if his policy would be for the good of the Republican Party, and if he would be amenable to cooperating with those in power. Johnson outlined what his strategy would be if he became mayor, saying that he would discharge all "useless" officials, cut the appropriations of many of the departments in half, refund the debt at a lower rate of interest, cancel all unfair contracts, buy supplies and hire labor in the best market he could find, improve the streets and public works, and lower the taxes. The politicians were dismayed and the offer was hastily withdrawn.

At the office, Johnson was consumed by every intricate detail of the business. His colleagues marveled at just how much detail he could absorb, and his associate Fred Kilmer once wrote about it: "Let anyone call into question how much of any given article is consumed in any given country or time; how much any particular salesman has sold in a month or year or series of years; what the stock on hand is, or was at any given time; how much has been made or can be shipped, or the statistics of trade and economics for various countries, and Mr. Johnson has the salient facts."

Kilmer, who was sometimes carried away in his nonscientific prose, once wrote this description of Johnson: "He is a tall, stout man, carefully dressed, with brown skin, black hair and big, sparkling, black eyes. If you see him you will always remember a peculiar roll of the head which accompanies his laughter and his arguments. It is performed by dropping the chin, and ascribing there a small circle, of which the spine is the center. It is a family roll. He has it and all of his brothers have it. It is done automatically and subconsciously, and it looks all right—for a Johnson.

"If you get into an argument with him, he will soon utter some dogmatic statement with a determined air and branch off into something else, as if he had settled the subject. While he is undecided he is willing to listen, but when his course is once settled, I would not care for the job of turning him in another direction. A competitor once said of him: 'He wants everything his own way.'"

Johnson's enthusiasm became a rallying point for everyone in the company. As Kilmer noted, "He injects his enthusiasm, his grit and his faith into everyone else, and when 'R.W.' says 'It's a go!' we push forward with all of our strength." But his colleagues were always wary of Johnson's quick temper, and they guarded against provoking him. Kilmer once mentioned Johnson's "hasty temper" in an article he had written about him, and when "R.W." read the draft he promptly tore that page out and discarded it. He was quick with his contempt for those with too much money who spent it frivolously—the idle rich. "If a man has money, inherited or acquired, he should keep it in motion," Johnson said. "Hire men, buy machinery and keep the wheels moving and everybody busy," was what he preached.

His wealth was growing steadily, and it was not all coming from Johnson & Johnson. He had a sizable portfolio of stocks and commodities that he traded frequently, with advice from his New York broker and social friend Archdale Clare. He blended his knowledge of the stock market with a gambler's flair, and he would often "take a flyer at it," to use his words. He made profitable investments in a cattle ranch in Colorado and from a venture in mineral water from springs in Bethesda, Maryland. When someone tried to get him to invest $50,000 in a substitute for yeast, he took the product home and tested it in his own kitchen. The bread was not white enough to suit him, so he backed out.

Johnson also made a number of sound investments in property, one of them sentimentally inspired. For years he had been making frequent trips back to the family homestead at Crystal Lake in Pennsylvania, an area he loved for its tranquility, and in 1889 he bought at auction the mortgage of the old family farm on Onion Hill overlooking the lake. That same year he had Tiffany & Robertson, builders in Carbondale, erect a resort hotel, which was called Fern Hall. Managed by his brother Sylvester and his wife, Fern Hall was so successful that in 1894 they built an addition that gave them a total of forty-seven sleepingrooms. On the same property, they also built twenty-two cottages and sold them to "city people." Old Sylvester Johnson, the father, had indeed been right about Crystal Lake's potential as a resort, but he never lived to see his dream come true. He died in 1883, still clinging to his visions of Crystal Lake as it might have been, and eventually was.

Like other wealthy people of his day, Johnson's vacations sometimes stretched into weeks and months. He owned an island in southern waters where he would shoot in winter, and belonged to a fishing club in Labrador that held exclusive rights to a long stretch of river. He and Evangeline, Roberta, and baby Robert took family vacations on a lake in Maine where they owned a comfortable lodge, but the place that suited "R.W." best was his home at Gray Terrace, which his colleagues referred to as Johnson's "domestic shrine."

But the real focal point of his life was Johnson & Johnson, and anything or anyone who threatened the company's success had to face an aroused "R.W." In 1895 he took on an unlikely foe, the national nurse heroine, Clara Barton, in a dispute over the Red Cross trademark, which had become a valuable company asset.

After her heroic acts of mercy on the Civil War battlefield, Clara Barton had formed the American Red Cross. It was patterned after the Permanent International Committee for Relief to Wounded Combatants, formed in 1863 by Henry Dunant, a Swiss businessman. Dunant, who had witnessed the Battle of Solferino in Italy in 1859 and was shocked by the suffering of unattended soldiers who had fallen in battle, decided to take action. The organization he founded later became the International Committee of the Red Cross, using the Greek red cross as its symbol.

When Barton formed the American counterpart, she became increasingly distressed over growing commercial use of the Red Cross symbol, which had been purloined by a host of products, including Red Cross Cigars, Red Cross Brandy, Red Cross Whiskey, Red Cross Playing Cards, Red Cross Washing Machines, Red Cross Stoves, Red Cross Churns, Red Cross Soap, and Red Cross Dog Collars. In 1895 Barton prevailed on the U.S. House of Representatives to introduce a bill allowing the American National Red Cross Society exclusive use of the Red Cross symbol, with power to license its use. The bill passed the Senate, but President Grover Cleveland refused to sign it into law.

Johnson naturally opposed passage of the bill, contending that he had established the right to use the mark in his business since its founding. After a number of meetings a compromise was reached, and on January 29, 1895, he and Barton signed an agreement that allowed Johnson & Johnson use of the Red Cross symbol for the payment of one dollar. It said in part: "It is agreed that the said Johnson & Johnson are now and for a long time past have been entitled at common law and otherwise to the exclusive use of the symbol of the red cross as a trade-mark." A decade later President Theodore Roosevelt signed legislation further protecting the right of the American Red Cross to use the mark and at the same time strengthening Johnson's claim to it.

Clara Barton later had several meetings with Kilmer at Glen Echo, her home in Washington, D.C., and recorded the meetings in her diary. On the first visit, August 17, 1897, Kilmer announced the company's plan to publish a journal for physicians that would carry the Red Cross name. "We had a lengthy conversation and decided to hold another meeting," Barton wrote. Kilmer returned on August 25, and the discussions continued for so long that he wound up spending the night at Glen Echo. Barton wrote: "We are glad he came and also that Johnson & Johnson have the decency as well as the courtesy to submit the journal proposition to us and not tear ahead and publish anyway." When he returned again on October 26, Kilmer had been carefully briefed by lawyers as to the company's rights. This annoyed Barton ("We are stupid about law"), but they reached an agreement for the company to publish *Red Cross Notes*.

Legal support for use of the Red Cross trademark, which the agreement with Clara Barton ensured, came at a time when product imitation was blatant. Some packages used slight variations of red crosses that were strikingly similar. Frustrated, Johnson took a bold step and had special stationery printed in color with some of his better-known products shown alongside pictures of the imitations. He sent these to every physician in the country with a letter that said in part: "Red Cross Aseptic Ligatures in the new sealed envelopes had scarcely been placed upon the market when several imitations appeared as illustrated. While imitation is a flattering acknowledgment of the superiority of the original, we fear that where the end sought is of a commercial nature the requirements of surgery are apt to be omitted. The cost for the original will be no greater than the other kinds."

.

Mead and Kilmer had been corresponding regularly with the originators of a new product introduced in Atlanta in 1886, called Coca-Cola. A pharmacist, John Styth Pemberton, had experimented with a syrup derived from the coca plant and cola nuts by mixing batches in a three-legged brass pot in his backyard. He took a jug of the syrup down the street to Jacobs' Pharmacy, combined it with carbonated water, and sold it for five cents a drink. But after several years of sluggish sales, he sold the business in 1893 to Asa G. Candler, a wholesale and retail druggist in Atlanta. Candler formed the Coca-Cola Company and began broad-scale advertising of the "exhilarating" and "invigorating" drink with tonic properties, which was touted as being good for "Headaches and Tired Feeling—Relieves Mental and Physical Exhaustion."

The Coca-Cola people were primarily interested in producing a refreshing soft drink, but it was the "tonic" potential of the extract from the cola nuts that intrigued the Johnsons. Kilmer called the nonaddictive stimulant an "excitant of intellect and imagination." In 1894 the Johnsons introduced the first of their "kola" preparations, which were recommended to help stop nausea, regulate the pulse, increase stamina and endurance, suppress the appetite, allay thirst, abolish fatigue, promote digestion, and "sustain tonic." If those claims did not satisfy prospective users, taking a "kola" product held out two additional hopes: It sobered drunks, and was suspected of being an aphrodisiac.

Wary of being classified with the notorious dispensers of certain "patent" medicines, the Johnsons decided to restrict the sale of their kola products to the company's regular drug outlets. For good measure, they also had the new products approved by the

American Medical Association. The best known and most popular was Vino Kolafra, or "wine of kola," a concoction that contained liberal quantities of inexpensive sherry wine along with the extract from the cola nuts. Sales of Vino Kolafra were disappointing, and the product was dropped when factory workers began sampling the sherry in ever larger quantities.

Mead and Kilmer were giving far more serious attention to further experiments with the papaya fruit of the pawpaw tree, which grew wild in Central America. This fruit was the basic ingredient of the papoid products first researched in Germany. The action of the milky papaya fluid on food in the stomach was similar to that of human gastric juices, and it was seen as the perfect cure for dyspepsia, or indigestion, then called America's "national disease." By 1897 Mead had nurtured his interest in the ferments from papaya juice well beyond that of his brothers. The time he was spending on the project was also becoming an issue. After assessing the future of his own career, as well as his interest in this area of medicine, Mead decided to strike out on his own. He sold his stock in the company to Robert, and the settlement included Mead's taking over the American Ferment Company in Jersey City, which had been bought to expand development of papain products. American Ferment was producing Cartoid, a product that helped infants digest cow's milk. Mead was especially interested in infant nutrition, which until that time had received scant attention from the medical profession.

Mead moved his office to Jersey City and added several pharmaceuticals to the product line, and in 1905 changed the firm's name to Mead Johnson & Company. One day a Mead Johnson representative met Dr. Jerome S. Leopold, one of the nation's few pediatric specialists, who was in charge of the milk station of the New York City Milk Committee. On a trip to Germany, Dr. Leopold had learned that maltose-dextrin was superior to other sugars for milk mixtures and provided just the right carbohydrate addition to cow's milk. When Mead heard about this he related it to the problem many infants had tolerating cow's milk. He succeeded in converting potato starch to dextrin and maltose to diastatic action, and when it was tested on sickly infants at the New York Post-Graduate Hospital the babies quickly gained weight. Soon he had an infant-formula product on the market. The product was promoted exclusively through the medical profession and the drug trade, using no consumer advertising. The packaging carried no dosage directions — that information was to come from the physician. With this approach, Mead established himself as a part of the "ethical" pharmaceutical business. (In 1915 he moved the company to Evansville, Indiana, where he had acquired an old cotton mill on eleven acres for $50,000. He and his sons proceeded to build Mead Johnson into a highly successful business, its growth strongly nourished by sales of infant formula.)

With Mead's departure, renewed emphasis was placed on further development of the more traditional products, which Johnson and Kilmer knew best. The company's early, primitive research laboratories had grown substantially in size and expertise, and by 1896 were installed in a new building in nearby Highland Park. Kilmer proudly proclaimed:

> The scientific department of Johnson and Johnson as amplified, strengthened and extended is probably unique. Employed is a staff of skilled workers in chemistry, bacteriology, pharmacology, and allied sciences. They are equipped with all the appliances and apparatus that modern science affords. Eminent specialists in surgery, medicine and hygiene have augmented the work of the laboratory by clinical experiments and by practical application.
>
> Through this source new preparations and improvements on old ones have been tested before recommendation to the medical profession. Workers in labs keep in touch with every stage of progress in the science of medicine, surgery and sanitation. Standards have been raised, and it is confidently expected that the great excellence attained will be upheld.

Kilmer's scholarly contributions to medical literature were significant. He produced two especially important scientific monographs. In 1894 he brought order out of chaos by painstakingly compiling "Belladonna Illustrated," an erudite study of the controversial drug's history, action, and uses in medicine, hailed as the most complete and scholarly treatise ever presented on the drug. He consulted every recognized authority on belladonna and skillfully edited their contributions into a factual volume for "students, teachers, and practitioners of pharmacy and medicine." The volume was published by the company, and the effort spurred belladonna plaster sales to $2 million a year.

Perhaps the most significant paper of Kilmer's career was issued in 1897 and titled "Asepsis Secundum Artem" ("Following the Art of Asepsis"). It was hailed as the "outstanding monograph of the year" and considered a classic on the subject of sterility in wound care and the most scientific monograph ever written on asepsis. Achieving sterility was now becoming an art with the company, and the new knowledge led to construction of "the world's largest sterilizer," capable of holding six truckloads of surgical dressings at one time.

Kilmer's seemingly effortless prose was once described as "running the gamut from pure science to ironic whimsy." He wrote papers on the cultivation of medicinal plants, pharmacopoeial analysis, sanitation, pharmaceutical professionalism and education, practical pharmacy, and the history of pharmacy. His rewards were the contributions he was making to medical progress, but as a writer he served the company as faithfully as he served science.

In 1897 he began producing the monthly publication *Red Cross Notes*, which reported on medicine in numerous ways, from recent developments in surgery to articles by leading physicians on new procedures. Articles in the digest-size *Notes* over time had a profound impact on emerging medical attitudes and techniques. Kilmer was not so much a creator of these attitudes as a conduit to them, and his selection and editing of materials helped set the direction. *Red Cross Notes* carried the latest bulletins on the most threatening contagious diseases—diphtheria, smallpox, typhoid, influenza, whooping cough, and tuberculosis. *Notes* soon became a forum for physicians, to share their hopes, concerns, and experiences in advancing patient care. "It is a matter of pride that we retain the humble attitude of the sincere student," Kilmer wrote, "and we therefore earnestly solicit correspondence." Letters from physicians arrived in endless waves. The usually placid Dr. Kilmer became aroused when a leading drug journal referred to asepsis as "a fad practiced by cranks." Kilmer shot back: "The pharmacist who holds such a conception should abandon his calling or open his understanding."

Kilmer unobtrusively blended chatty notes about products into his coverage of medical subjects in such a way that it did not seem like advertising. The company's advertising man, J. Walter Thompson, became sensitive to the success that *Red Cross Notes* was having as an advertising medium, for distribution was now reaching 50,000 physicians and 20,000 druggists, and in 1899 a Spanish-language edition, *La Cruz Roja*, was going to countries in South America. Johnson sent Thompson another of his "Dear Walter" letters, which read: "I enclose a copy of the last *Red Cross Notes* printed in our factory, including the cover, now in color. This is the kind of work that we find pays."

The publication was also used to record the company's involvement in three of the most dramatic events in the nation at the turn of the century: a war, a devastating flood, and the shooting of a president. Congress declared war on Spain on April 25, 1898, a conflict ignited by a mysterious explosion aboard the USS *Maine* in Havana Harbor on February 15. The blast killed 260 Americans and severely damaged the nation's "honor." The battleship was in Havana because Cuba had become rebellious toward its mother country, Spain, a dispute constantly agitated in America by unscrupulous "yellow journalism." To boost circulation for his *New York Journal*, William Randolph Hearst had dispatched artist Frederick Remington and writer Richard Harding Davis to Cuba, with the boast "You furnish the pictures, I'll furnish the war." President

William McKinley, still carrying painful memories of his own participation in the Civil War, valiantly attempted a diplomatic solution following the sinking of the *Maine*, then reluctantly put the decision in the hands of Congress.

To the beat of John Philip Sousa's "Stars and Stripes Forever," the nation rallied behind the war effort. At Johnson & Johnson 300,000 packets of a newly developed compressed surgical dressing were produced and delivered to the Army and the Navy in record time. When 18,000 American troops landed on Cuba near the Spanish fort, they also carried a new type of cloth stretcher that had been hastily designed by the company and rapidly made. Workers subscribed $100,000 to the War Loan drive, and when the ambulance ship USS *Solace* sailed for Cuba, it carried a huge quantity of medical supplies contributed by the company. When it appeared that the war might be prolonged, Fred Kilmer, speaking as patriot as well as salesman, pledged: "Millions of pounds of cotton, millions of yards of gauze, miles upon miles of bandages, plasters enough to encircle the earth. They are yours, Uncle Sam, if you need them, and they are made 'Secundum Artem Asepsis.'"

Fortunately, the pent-up spirit of a nation unified for its first major conflict since the Civil War did not run its full course. The war was short and ended officially with the signing of the Treaty of Paris on December 10, 1898. Soldiers and sailors came home to the tune of "When Johnny Comes Marching Home," but not before Teddy Roosevelt and his horseless band of Rough Riders had charged up San Juan Hill in Puerto Rico. Short as it was, the war had long-range implications. Spain surrendered Cuba to the rebels and ceded Puerto Rico and Guam to the United States, which also arranged to annex the Philippines for a $2 million payment to the Spaniards. In less than a year, America had been propelled from strong isolationism to global involvement, which had even President McKinley perplexed. "In a few short months," he said, "we have become a world power. . . . It is vastly different from the conditions I found when I was inaugurated."

On September 8, 1900, a devastating storm struck Galveston, Texas, destroying nearly a third of the city and wreaking havoc for miles around. The storm-tossed Gulf of Mexico, propelled by sustained winds exceeding one hundred miles an hour, ripped through the city in fifteen-foot waves that demolished homes and businesses. The death toll reached 6,000 in the city alone, and damage estimates were astronomical. Emergency medical teams, including eighty-year-old Clara Barton, worked feverishly to aid the victims. They were initially hampered by a shortage of medical supplies, which were promptly sent as a donation from Johnson & Johnson.

Over time, emergency teams were trained to cut the dreadful toll of such disasters through better first-aid techniques. For some years, Kilmer had been researching various new first-aid methods and issuing bulletins on his findings. In 1901 he prepared the first book ever written on the subject: *Johnson's First Aid Manual*. It dealt with the simplest, most effective methods for laypeople to treat the injured in an emergency, keeping in mind Kilmer's theory that the fate of the injured person depended on the actions of the person into whose hands he first fell. The various techniques for treating and bandaging were clearly illustrated, and Kilmer emphasized: "Extensiveness has in all cases been sacrificed to simplicity." The manual was an immediate success and was adopted for use in first-aid training programs nationwide.

At about 4:30 P.M. on September 5, 1901, while greeting people at the Pan-American Exposition in Buffalo, New York, the popular President William McKinley was shot twice by a young anarchist who had concealed a gun in his bandaged right hand. Aides led the stunned President to a chair, and minutes later an ambulance took him to the Exposition's medical facility. He was in shock, but conscious. When McKinley was examined, one bullet fell out of his clothing; it had apparently been deflected by a button. The other had cut a path through the stomach and was lost in the muscles of the back.

Attending physicians decided to operate immediately to determine the extent of the damage and to probe and cleanse the wound to prevent gangrene. However, doctors were unable to locate the bullet, even though, ironically, the new x-ray machines that could have located it were on display at the Exposition. In the failing afternoon light, doctors focused the sun's rays on the surgeon's work with a mirror. The incision was closed without drainage, and antiseptic bandages were applied. Still under sedation, McKinley was taken to his home, where his wife Ida waited.

McKinley recovered consciousness with no apparent complications. He spoke, moved, and smiled at his physicians, giving hope that his hearty constitution would see him through. On September 7, McKinley's secretary, George Cortelyou, issued a medical bulletin stating that no serious symptoms had developed in the fifty-nine-year-old President. Soon afterward, though, the President began running a fever, and other worrisome symptoms began to appear. By Friday, September 13, it was clear that a general infection from gangrene had set in along the bullet's track. Late in the afternoon, McKinley rallied from his comatose state, but he died the following morning.

It was later learned that Johnson & Johnson dressings and adhesives had been used on McKinley throughout his ordeal. In the next issue of *Red Cross Notes*, Kilmer gave a detailed clinical explanation of the President's case, including anatomical diagrams. The autopsy had exonerated the medical team and stated: "Death was unavoidable by any medical or surgical treatment" due to the course the bullet had traveled and the damage it had inflicted. Nonetheless, Kilmer felt that a wider knowledge of the medical treatment McKinley received would put future treatment of wounds of the abdomen on a "firmer basis." In presenting excerpts from the official records, Kilmer added philosophically: "Though nations come and go, republics flourish or wither, rulers pass away, the healing art moves on, and the surgeons will turn from the keen disappointment as to the outcome of this illustrious case to a study of the scientific aspects."

The practice of providing Johnson & Johnson products in emergencies was to become a tradition. Five years later, when the San Francisco earthquake struck, Red Cross Johnson & Johnson products were rushed to treat victims of a disaster in which the company itself was a victim. On April 18, 1906, at 5:20 A.M., an earthquake registering 8.3 on the Richter scale shook downtown San Francisco, leveling large portions of the city. By 10 o'clock, fire had destroyed what was left of the warehouse and offices of Waldron & Dietrich at 144 Second Street, the Johnson & Johnson agents for the Pacific Coast. The office staff there appealed to New Brunswick for emergency medical supplies, and within hours rail cars filled with Johnson & Johnson products were speeding to San Francisco from various company warehouses in the west. The products arrived in time to treat many of the thousands who were injured. The fires continued for three days, and scores of buildings were dynamited in an attempt to halt the inferno. The earthquake and fires claimed 452 lives and caused more than $350 million in damages. It took weeks for the rubble to cool, and then the rebuilding began.

6

YOUNG ROBERT

BEFORE Evangeline Johnson had been married five years she had given birth to three children. Following Robert, John Seward was born on July 14, 1895, and Evangeline Brewster, on April 18, 1897. Her stepdaughter, Roberta, brought her young brood to four, and there were times when Evangeline was harried and felt the strain, especially when the children were ill. Johnson wrote to a friend during one crisis: "My wife is not able to tend them."

Whatever Evangeline's burden, it was far less than it might have been had she been obliged to care for the children and the cavernous Gray Terrace without the assistance of her large household staff. Shortly after Robert was born they engaged a governess, Mary Donohue, whose stubborn Irish manner made her nearly impregnable — or so it seemed to the children. Repeatedly, Miss Donohue served as the children's Court of Last Resort, where the verdict was always the same: "No." It was not until several years later that the daughter, Evangeline Brewster — known as "Love" to the family and "Love" Brewster to her father — finally fathomed Miss Donohue's ironclad resistance.

"I wondered at the time," Evangeline explained, "when I would ask my mother if I could do something and she would say: 'Ask your governess.' And I thought, isn't that funny, why does she do that? And finally I said to my governess, 'Why does my mother say "ask your governess" when it's something she doesn't want me to do?' And my governess smiled — she was a wonderful woman — and she said: 'Your mother said when she engaged me, I wish never to say "no" to my children, so when there is something I don't want them to do I will say "Ask your governess." ' " That is how the children learned why Miss Donohue was the Court of Last Resort in the Johnson home and why her answers were always the same. Despite this imposed handicap, Miss Donohue was loved, respected, and at times feared.

Though immersed in his business, Johnson set time aside to be an attentive father, but he was not prone to dabbling in childhood frivolities with his young ones. His age often dictated his actions.

"My father was forty-eight when my brother Bob was born," recalled Evangeline, "and that was middle age in those days. My most vivid memory is that when he got home from the factory we children were sent down to the library to have a little talk with father. And father always had something he wanted us to learn from him. One day we went down and he said, 'I have a mirror for each of you.' It was a small mirror that would fit in your pocket, and he said, 'I want you each to take a mirror and hold it in front of your face, and then I'm going to say something that will make you very angry, or I want you to imagine that you are very angry. And then I want you to look at yourself in the mirror and see how perfectly absurd your face looks when you're in a bad temper, and this will make you laugh and you'll get over the temper.' That was a wonderful way to teach children things."

There were three separate libraries at Gray Terrace, and most of the books were on philosophy and religion. The family belonged to the Episcopal church, but Johnson rarely attended, though he spent countless hours reading his books on religion. When Sunday morning came, Evangeline said he always resisted attending services: "He used to say to my mother, 'You take the children to church if you want, my dear. This is my church — meaning his home.' He would sit and enjoy the flowers in the greenhouse while the family went to church." Evangeline continued: "My father was very interested in Catholicism as a philosophy, not as a practice. He always said, 'The Catholic Church from the inside out is inspired philosophy. The Catholic Church from the outside in is geared to more limited mentality.'

"He said that when a man falls down in the street and is wounded the Catholics take him to the hospital and give him emergency treatment, and only much later do they ask what religion he is. The Episcopalians, before they even take him into the hospital, ask what religion he is. He said that's no time to behave like that. So he would send me, along with my governess, to the Catholic hospital and I would walk around between the beds and give people flowers."

The flowers were grown by Johnson in several greenhouses at the rear of Gray Terrace, and he watched over them attentively, with the help of his full-time gardener. "He would send people all over the world to bring back rare orchids," Evangeline said. "I remember the first time I was ever permitted to stay up until ten o'clock was to see a night-blooming orchid, where the flowers grow out of the roots."

From Robert's earliest years he spent a great deal of time with his father, who in many ways tried to hasten the boy through childhood. It was obvious that he could barely wait for Robert to grow up. Evangeline recalled that before Robert was five he was accompanying his father to business meetings and going on hunting and fishing trips with Johnson's friends and their sons, all of them much older. At age six he was fitted for a tuxedo with short trousers so he could attend social functions with the adults. "Bob had very little free childhood, as father always treated him like an adult. He was very anxious to have Bob grow up," Evangeline said.

Being thrust at such an early age into an adult world, and substituting business meetings and hunting trips for wagons and sand piles, influenced young Robert's childhood and no doubt contributed to his being "a very serious child." But he seemed to adjust well, and being the firstborn no doubt contributed to his serious demeanor. "Bob was always told: You must set your brother and your sister a good example. Remember, you're the oldest." Robert remembered, and he played the role of the "good boy," though often with a demonstration of stubbornness.

John Seward, on the other hand, was a far more docile child, and, his sister recalled, frequently ill in his early childhood. "My brother, Seward, though two years older than I, was a frail child who seemed to be always recovering from one illness or another, and invariably smelled of cocoa butter, with which he was rubbed in an attempt to 'Put a little fat on him.' He had blonde curly hair which fell to his shoulders, and he looked like an angel. He behaved like one, too, which made my older brother, Bob, and me seem like devils in contrast. Mother used to say Seward looked so much like an angel that she often stood beside his crib at night to make sure that he was still breathing. When Seward was sick, they would isolate him in a room on the third floor and hang a sheet across the door wringing wet with Camphenol (made by my father's company), and that was supposed to stop the germs from getting out. I loved him very deeply, and would crawl under the hanging sheet. If Camphenol kept the germs in, it did not keep me out. I would hide under Seward's bed whenever the nurse appeared."

Evangeline, or "Love" to her family, was quite different from her two brothers. As it turned out, she was an incubating maverick, though that did not become clear for some years. But even at a young age, she was daring and unpredictable. The Johnson children had a pony named "Dandy," who lived in the horse barns at the rear of Gray Terrace. The pony would be hitched to a handsome black cart so the children could go for gentle rides around the estate or through the city streets. Recalled Evangeline: " 'Dandy' was mostly Robert's property, and the driving authority was principally his. I remember Miss Donohue made us get out of the cart and walk up hills as she thought it was too heavy a load for the pony." One day Evangeline took the pony and cart to an Irish festival being held in the city. One of her friends remembered "Love" at the whip: "She turned the pony cart into a jaunting cart and we all had rides. I remember hanging on around all the curves, but she was standing up and shouting to the poor pony 'Go, Go!' Evangeline was wild."

Johnson too sensed that his daughter was different. A painter had been retained to do a portrait of the three children without Johnson's knowledge, and when Johnson saw it he was disappointed in the rendition of Evangeline. In a letter to the painter he gave a hint of Evangeline's early ability to be seen in different ways, a trait that remained with her throughout her entire life, to the consternation of some and the pleasure of others. Johnson wrote:

"Had I known that the picture was to be painted I might have suggested a very difficult style. Love Brewster is rather an unusual type, having a unique character, of striking appearance, with as much expression as an adult. In many ways an ideal subject. To my mind she should have been framed in sunshine, flowers and fairy surroundings. I am therefore sorry this portrait is not an exact reproduction of this saucy, strange face, with all its shortcomings, all of its perfections, vivacity, life and animation. I grant that an artist is entitled to some leeway, can paint character, life or form into an average face, but I should deny his right to change the striking characteristics by attempting some foreign ideality."

Though Evangeline qualified early as a "tomboy," she also was an opportunist. "Being a girl had definite advantages," she recalled again. " 'Give the toy to your sister, dear. Remember, she is a little lady,' 'Always think of your sister first and be gentle with her. She is a little lady,' et cetera and ad nauseum! This 'lady' business was, of course, the racket of my childhood. How my brothers ever got to like women enough to each marry several times is a triumph of the sex instinct."

The same childhood friend who saw Evangeline as "wild" remembered Robert as being "such a physical boy" and John Seward as being "such a sweet boy." Young friends enjoyed coming to the

[86]

big house to play because their visits often became exciting and daring expeditions as the children raced through the labyrinth of upstairs rooms and over porches and balconies, where the climbing was superior to any other house they knew. "I remember all of the porches and cupolas of that wonderful house. We used to play hide and seek, in and out, over the roof, always to the distress of Miss Donohue, who usually was one step behind us."

It was a happy family. The children got along well, with a minimum of conflict and only occasional violence ("When the boys were very young they used to play Indian and decapitate my dolls," Evangeline recalled with a note of belligerence in her voice.) Johnson was much better than his wife at resolving differences. He was firm and tactful, the elder statesman who found merit in the art of compromise where his children were concerned. At home amid his books, his flowers, and his children he was serene and the picture of contentment. He constantly reminded the children of how blessed they were, and how the family's affluence gave them special privileges that other children in the city did not enjoy. Because of the family's prominence, the Johnsons were often the subject of social items in the local newspaper, the *Daily Home News*. This never failed to agitate Johnson, who regularly telephoned the editor to register his protest over what he considered an invasion of family privacy.

When springtime arrived the children began counting the days to their escape to Bellevue Farm, the Johnsons' summer retreat less than a mile away in Highland Park. Perched on a bluff overlooking the Raritan River, Bellevue was as relaxed as Gray Terrace was formal. The land had originally been purchased from the Indians in 1675 by Dr. Henry Greenland, who later sold it to William Wright, the coachmaker from London. The farmhouse had been built in the mid-1700s during the ownership of Abraham Van Horn. It was both distinctive and gracious, with deeply beveled paneling, exposed beaded girts and two-panel doors, and cornices from the original house. Bellevue generated a warmth that somehow managed to escape the big house on College Avenue, and the family always seemed more relaxed there.

Sloping gently back from the bluff on which the house stood were acres of fruit trees, where the children spent happy hours climbing and frolicking. A herd of dairy cattle lazily roamed the adjoining pastures and kept the family larder filled. The farmhands who worked the land lived in a small house near the horse and carriage barns, and ten greenhouses filled with exotic flowers and plants required the attention of a dozen gardeners. The gardeners also tended the experiments Johnson was conducting with the belladonna plant in search of improved strains. Studies in Europe had concluded that the climate in New Jersey would support the cultivation of belladonna. In recent years the supply from the continent had dwindled and the quality had become inferior. Since he was buying 100,000 pounds of belladonna a year, Johnson decided to learn to grow it himself at Bellevue.

Johnson supervised the management of Bellevue with the same crisp efficiency that he used in running his company and the household staff of Gray Terrace. When the orchards yielded a surplus of fruit, he negotiated a favorable price and sold it to the wholesale produce merchants on Greenwich Street in New York. When the farmhands got behind in their work, he took charge: "Everything is going well at the farm except the farmers—they seem to be a little slow. I have just issued peremptory orders to have every weed out of the garden by Sunday night," he wrote one friend. And with a little persuasion he had convinced the New Brunswick postmaster to extend mail delivery to the farm: "Inasmuch as we are the largest purchaser of stamps in the office, I trust my request will be given careful consideration." It was.

The summers at Bellevue were long and lazy and pleasant. Robert learned to ride the horses, and well. His brother Seward was a tinkerer, and his skill amazed his sister: "He was always calm, and had such a scientific turn of mind that he could always fix a broken toy, make wonderful things out of paper, time and again. 'Let's try this,' he would say after a long, quiet look, and to my complete amazement the problem was solved." But Evangeline reserved her special admiration for her older brother. "Being four years older than I was, Bob often seemed a hero to me. I considered him almost with awe."

When Johnson strolled to the edge of the Bellevue property, on the hill overlooking the Raritan, he had a commanding view of his industrial kingdom just across the river in New Brunswick. What he saw added greatly to his feeling of contentment and sense of achievement. The ever-expanding array of red-brick buildings were rapidly churning out a mounting number of medical products eagerly awaited by a multitude of satisfied customers. Just beyond the factory complex was Gray Terrace, which represented other accomplishments — a stately home, a beautiful wife, and lovely children. He was a happy, contented, yet driven man.

Later he built a fishing camp at Moosehead Lake in Maine, and this became another vacation retreat for him and the family. It was one his daughter particularly liked. "My father picked the location by going around the lake in a boat and choosing the spot where the sunset was most beautiful," she recalled. "He built the camp there, and since there was no road into Greenville, the nearest town, we had a boat, which he christened the *Evangeline* after my mother. We took it from the camp into Greenville, about a half an hour ride, and we did our shopping there." There were also family vacation trips to the seashore at Cape May in New Jersey, and to Delta, Colorado, where Johnson had an interest in a cattle ranch. He also acquired an island in waters off the coast of the Carolinas, where he and his cronies would go duck-shooting in the winter.

Johnson loved to fish and would travel hundreds, sometimes thousands, of miles to have a chance for the right catch. It was an era when vacations were savored over long, leisurely periods, not gulped in short bursts. He had enjoyed fishing since his days as a child at Crystal Lake, pitting himself against the wily bass with a makeshift rod and worms for bait. Now he and his fishing companions, Williams, Pike, Hodges, and Chapman (always referred to by their last names), had exclusive fishing rights to a section of the Natashquan River that flowed from Labrador down to the Gulf of St. Lawrence in Quebec, and each summer they would arrange a trip to the remote fishing camp, where the salmon fishing was superb.

Months in advance, they made arrangements for the trip, with as much precision as if they were planning an arctic expedition. They reserved the French Indian guides at $1.25 a day plus expenses and had fishing rods custom-made by William Mills & Sons, in New York, at $40 each. They ordered the "grub," found a native chef to cook it, and hired a waiter to serve it. Then they began the trip by taking the train to Montreal and the night boat to Quebec, where they would spend the night at the Château Frontenac. Then came another boat trip down the St. Lawrence to Natashquan on the Gulf, and, finally, up the river to the desolate camp.

Johnson was always cautious on the trip, "as I am very clumsy and have great trouble getting in and out of a boat," he once wrote a friend. The vacation often lasted three weeks, and sometimes his brother James accompanied the group. "I will fish with J.W.," he informed his friends in advance—James was always "J.W." to him. Before the trip, the group always made arrangements with Fraser & Viger & Company in Montreal to ship via the steamer *St. Olaf* an ample supply of spirits to ward off the chill and help wile away the long evenings. There was never a complaint about the Bonny Briar Scotch, the Pomerey Sec, the Tom Gin, or the Italian vermouth, but Johnson once found two quarts of olives to be "of no account whatever" and told Messrs. Fraser and Viger of his dissatisfaction with the olives in a tersely worded letter.

For Johnson, it would have taken more than bad olives to spoil the salmon-fishing trip to the Natashquan. "You will feel it is the first time you have ever been fishing," he wrote to a friend who was

going for the first time. Another letter was exultant about the results: "The high water in the river prevented our fishing many of
the pools where we ordinarily get salmon, still there were plenty.
I think I caught 75 or 80 and could, of course, have gotten many
more by hard work."

Robert was still too young to accompany his father on the long
jaunt to Labrador, and besides, the trip would have conflicted with
his classes at Rutgers Preparatory School, on College Avenue in
New Brunswick, a block from his home. He had been enrolled in
the primary grades there in 1898, at the age of five. Rutgers Prep
traced its origins to the charter granted Rutgers College in 1766,
and the school still reflected the objectives of the early English
and Dutch settlers to provide an educational breeding ground for
secular and religious leadership. The school provided a sound education in basic subjects, with liberal exposure to the classics. Attendance was required at chapel, and a rigid discipline was enforced,
all for a $9 tuition a quarter. The school motto, "Serva res est verum
gaudium," promised "Hard work is true joy," and among the small
but gallant band of scholars there was little doubt about the hard
work part of it.

Robert advanced through three primary and four intermediate
grades before moving to the First Form of the prep school in 1907,
where he encountered Collar & Daniel's *Beginner's Latin Book*,
Milne's *Arithmetic*, Maxwell's *School Grammar*, Montgomery's *History of the United States*, and, as with most schoolchildren, the
ubiquitous *Ivanhoe*. He showed a tendency to learn quickly and
was popular with his classmates, though sometimes "difficult" — a
trait he no doubt inherited from his father.

The boy — if indeed he had ever been a boy in spirit — was always
a serious young man, with a personality that prompted a variety
of conflicting opinions and judgments about him — and most were
at least partly true. As it turned out, his complexities accompanied
him throughout his entire life, and he nurtured them and enjoyed

them as one would a family pet. Being different from others, and infinitely more complicated, became quite natural and more comfortable for him, and he learned to enjoy it to the fullest.

At times he even reveled in his uniqueness. There were early signs of this. A grocery store he would stop at on his way home from school was presided over by three sisters more inclined to agree than disagree, but they always had difficulty agreeing on Robert — even in their later, reflecting years. They remembered him quite differently but vividly, from those daily visits after school and his inspections of the long, glass candy case that lined one side of the store.

"He was an arrogant young man," one sister recalled with absolute certainty.

"He was a very nice boy," the second sister insisted.

The third sister couldn't quite decide which was more true, but she was firm about the fact that the boy could be exasperating. She used to stand behind the candy case waiting for him to make up his mind as he made a complete and time-consuming inspection of the assortment of sweets. It was a daily ritual.

Finally, in a somber tone that bordered on the demanding, he would ask: "What can I get the most of for a penny?" She could never figure out why he didn't ask that in the first place. Later in life he would practice capriciousness as though it were his personal discovery, and the candy-case encounters were probably his early training ground.

Opinions about his personality and conduct came from a variety of sources. Some were undoubtedly hasty conclusions prompted by his being the son of the richest man in the city, others were more honestly earned. His childhood was, in fact, quite normal, in the context of affluence. He got along well with his classmates and with workers at the factory, whom he got to know at a young age. His childhood friends included his cousins, Louise and Helen Johnson, whom he and Seward would visit at the home of their Uncle James and Aunt Martha at 17 Union Street, just off College Avenue and not far from their own home.

Far less formal than their home, the big Victorian house was a small museum of artifacts that James had brought home from his many adventures—to the Klondike in search of gold; to Mexico, where he had an interest in gold mines; and the countless hunting and fishing expeditions. The fishing rods and guns and trophies seemed to be part of the decor and prompted tales of intrigue for young ears. James always obliged.

The only concession to formality in the house was the rare mural wallpaper depicting "The War of Independence" that covered the walls of the dining room. Thomas Wilson had created the block-print mural in 1874–75 using 1,674 wooden blocks, and it was one of only eleven in existence. The scene had first been printed by Jean Zuber at Rixheim in France from a design by Zipelius and Ehrman and called "La Guerre de l'Independence Americaine," although neither artist had ever visited America. They took "Scene America" and put in figures of Washington, Lafayette, and others. Some years later, Jacqueline Kennedy had one of the existing copies of the mural installed in the White House.

·

The Kilmers—Annie, Fred, and Joyce—also lived on Union Street, in a home more like a library than a house. There were books everywhere. It was a happy home, despite the sadness that had already plagued their lives, and would still in the years to come. Annie Kilburn and Fred Kilmer had been married on Christmas Day in 1871 at Sunbury, Pennsylvania, and two years later had their first child, Anda Frederick. Ellen Annie, born in 1875, died eleven months later, and Charles Willoughby, born in 1880, died at the age of three months. Their lives were brightened, however, by the birth in 1886 of Alfred Joyce, whom they named after the rector of their Episcopal church, the Rev. Elisha Joyce, a friend and spiritual support to many of the neighborhood families, including the

Johnsons. A happy and creative child, Joyce showed an early talent for writing—like his father and his mother, who wrote poetry and composed music.

But in 1899 tragedy struck again, when Anda committed suicide. The Kilmers were distraught but not bitter. Annie was as spunky and tenacious as Fred was calm and resolved. Their resilience amazed neighbors and friends and elicited admiration and respect. Joyce became the center of their family life.

He attended Rutgers Prep at the same time Robert Johnson did, though they were nearly seven years apart and so did not become school friends. Joyce was an odd sort, remembered for wearing outlandish combinations of bicycle breeches and stockings and for leaning toward the unusual rather than the traditional. He often found himself on the fringes of the schoolboy groups, and occasionally the butt of unkind jokes. The Kilmers doled out love to him in large measure, and his mother, especially, constantly encouraged his writing. Joyce went on to Rutgers University for two years, and there he met more compatible friends as well as the stately, spreading oak that was later to inspire his famous poem "Trees." After two years, he transferred to Columbia University, where he received his degree in English in 1908, and then taught Latin for a year at Morristown High School in New Jersey.

About the time that Joyce was taking up his studies at Columbia, Fred Kilmer was devoting time to the passage of the national Pure Food and Drugs Act, which marked the birth of consumerism in America. It was the nation's first attempt at curbing mounting abuses in the mass production of foods, drugs, medicines, and liquor. Kilmer referred to it as a "righteous law" and assessed it as "the most important and far reaching example of Federal legislation placed upon our statute books since the period of the Civil War."

Up until the law was enacted, the public had no protection, but was nonetheless eager to buy the new processed foods and medicinal products that came streaming to the market. Factory production brought increasing abuses, as the nation moved farther away from the home as the exclusive supplier of food, clothing, and home medicinal remedies. For every mass-producer of goods that subscribed to careful controls, there was an unscrupulous manufacturer ready to cut corners and, even worse, endanger health. While horror stories of sickness and death from contaminated food and drugs abounded throughout the nation, they had not come into focus sharply enough to ignite action by the authorities. It remained for author Upton Sinclair to light that fuse in 1906 with publication of his muckraker novel *The Jungle*. The book graphically described the exploitation of immigrant labor employed in the stockyards, and the nauseating methods of killing animals and preparing the meat for consumption.

Sinclair, who was an enthusiastic supporter of socialism and other causes, wanted his novel to generate sympathy for the workers, and it did. But it also generated a greater national concern for the plight of the consumer. Another author, Samuel Hopkins Adams, directed attention to the need for food and drug controls in his book *The Great American Fraud* and in a series of articles he wrote for *Collier's* magazine exposing quack patent medicines.

When a commission appointed to investigate the methods of food preparation verified the most shocking revelations in the two books, President Theodore Roosevelt and Congress were prodded into action. Roosevelt appointed Harvey W. Wiley, a strong proponent of the reforms, to administer the Pure Food and Drugs Act once it was in workable form. This called for an evaluation of the right controls, and Kilmer's expert advice was promptly sought because he was a recognized authority in the field of public health. The magnitude of the national problem the Act attempted to correct was evident in its title: "An Act for preventing the manufacture, sale or transportation of adulterated or misbranded or poisonous or deleterious foods, drugs, medicines, and liquors, and for regulating traffic therein, and for other purposes." It was passed by Congress on June 30, 1906, along with the Meat Inspection Act. Both took effect on January 1, 1907.

Though the Pure Food and Drugs Act provided only weak penalties for violators, its impact on the nation was profound. It succeeded in screening from the marketplace countless foods and drug preparations that did not pass tests in special government laboratories set up for the purpose. Many inferior products that did slip through were later removed from the market by a band of food inspectors who fanned across the nation. This touched off widespread concern about whether certain substances in foods and drugs were harmful to public health, and stimulated debates that raged on.

Beyond the immediate impact of the Act was the long-range effect of stimulating local and state legislation dealing with the chlorination of water, the inspection of milk, new methods of controlling flies and mosquitoes, the eradication of such diseases as diphtheria and tuberculosis, and the practice of giving physical examinations to schoolchildren. In many respects it was a projection to the national level of many of Kilmer's earlier community health improvements in New Brunswick and later in New Jersey. In time, this new concern with the nation's health, in terms of the foods eaten and drugs taken, had a positive influence on longevity, as did the latest advances in medicine. The average life span of Americans began to rise dramatically.

Both Johnson and Kilmer regarded the new law as a boon to their business and an obstacle to unscrupulous competitors. Every product produced by the company turned out to be in full conformity, and no changes in production methods were necessary. That was exactly what the two men had been advocating and implementing for years. Kilmer claimed the law would bring about "a marvelous revolution in the statements made by the proprietors of 'patent' or proprietary remedies and 'quack' medicines." The company was assigned "No. 117 — Guaranteed Under the Food and Drugs Act," which gave assurance, signed by Johnson himself, that these products were not adulterated or misbranded and conformed to the new law. Kilmer then made available to the Department of Agriculture, which was responsible for analyzing products, all the testing procedures and techniques he had developed in his laboratory.

It was more than a gesture, for Kilmer believed his laboratories could serve a larger purpose, which he had only recently described in these terms: "The department is not conducted in any narrow, commercial spirit, but is constantly engaged in purely scientific inquiry, and not kept going for the purpose of paying dividends or solely for the benefit of Johnson & Johnson, but with a view to aiding the progress of the art of healing." This, perhaps better than any other statement Kilmer ever made, explained his motivation and his reasons for leaving pharmacy.

.

While this national reform was taking place, Johnson was instituting a pioneer effort of his own, the formation of a company Welfare Work Department in 1906. This revolutionary step was taken at a time when much of the country was crying out against the abuses of workers, unsafe conditions in the factories, and the constant threat of occupational diseases. Johnson charged the staff of the Welfare Department with ensuring that company employees were well fed, properly housed, and generally content, and he made certain they succeeded.

Workers were given advice on health matters, referred to physicians, and in many cases had their medical bills paid. Legal advice was provided, and counseling on marriage and family problems. The only subject the Welfare Department was not permitted to advise on was religion. Classes were conducted in hygiene, gymnastics, millinery, embroidery, and English — the latter because many workers were Hungarian immigrants. A mutual benefit organization was formed to provide financial support during illnesses. Hospital and retiring rooms were set up for those taken sick on the job, and later became the company Medical Department.

When night shifts became necessary, a company kitchen presided over by a French chef served a variety of hot meals at midnight. With Johnson's encouragement, women employees formed the Laurel Club in 1907 for their social and educational enjoyment. They had a basketball team, a Glee Club, and a lending library, and the monthly dues of twenty-five cents helped support the club's charity work at St. Peter's Orphanage. Johnson soon became one of the first to provide pensions and insurance coverage for some of his employees. Later he bought up three blocks of houses in New Brunswick and rented thirty-two fully equipped homes to his key factory workers at reasonable rates; the company even paid for maintaining them.

The new program was scarcely in place and functioning when the nation was beset by the Panic of 1907, bringing unemployment and hardship to many. Johnson's company managed to weather the storm, and even continue a plant expansion, with some belt-tightening measures in the form of shorter hours and lower paychecks. The causes of the panic reflected some serious flaws in the American economic structure, including an inefficient credit system and too much "water" in the capital structures of the railroads and the new trusts. High profits, contrasting with the low wages of workers, resulted in low buying power, and this led to considerable speculation about mismanagement during the boom years from 1898 to 1907. When thirteen New York banks failed, followed closely by the collapse of several railroads, the panic was under way.

On the night of October 2, 1908, more than 2,500 of Johnson's workers gathered to celebrate the dedication of the new addition to the Red Cross Cotton Mill, which brought the complex to forty buildings and half a million square feet of manufacturing space. It was a festive evening, and the music and laughter helped everyone put aside the sad economic refrain of the previous year.

"Above all, we hope that the future will bring back the prosperity that has been missing for the past year," Johnson told them. He then added his praise: "You have put forth your best effort loyally and jointly . . . observing all the rules relating to modern wound dressings. When the products reach the surgeon he has absolute confidence in them. . . . We have been educators, teaching the world how to treat wounds according to modern methods and how to save life." He continued: "This factory is now undoubtedly the largest in the world, . . . and in the very near future we may be able to provide still further for the welfare and comfort of every employee."

A newspaper story on the celebration reported that "brain" workers mixed easily with those who toiled with their hands, and that all were "aglow with good humor and fraught with a feeling of fraternity." There was more fraternity that night than normal, for while Johnson had a cordial rapport with his workers the relationship was not a warm one. They were wary of him. Periodically, he would declare war on "the careless and the clockwatchers," telling them he wanted reforms or resignations. There were few resignations.

Johnson's constant vigilance manifested itself in other ways too. He viewed competing companies with suspicion and alarm. One new Chicago firm, Bauer & Black, worried him because it had been formed by a former Johnson sales manager, S. H. Black. Not convinced that the stories he was hearing about the success of that new venture were true, Johnson wrote his representative in Chicago: "I wish you would learn if Bauer & Black are as busy as they claim to be, even if you have to hire someone to watch their factory at night."

A far more serious threat was posed by the J. Ellwood Lee Company of Conshohocken, Pennsylvania, which produced a complete line of sutures and ligatures and medicinal plasters. Lee, a clever entrepreneur, had become a major factor in the trade. His firm had grown to five hundred employees, he had the only catheter factory in the nation, and he was a notorious price-cutter, which greatly disturbed Johnson. In frustration Johnson wrote Lee: "If you follow the start you have made, in a short time you will be giving away goods and paying people to take them. When you get tired of this fun, come down to Cape May, take a bath and cool off." Cape May was known for its therapeutic health baths.

In 1905 Johnson made a deal to acquire Lee's company for Johnson & Johnson stock. It was his first major acquisition, and the arrangements were interesting. Both companies listed the other's products in their catalogs and continued their independent ways. On May 2, 1905, Lee and two of his associates, Charles Heber Clark and Frank R. Jones, became members of the Johnson & Johnson Board of Directors. Fred Kilmer went on the Board at the same time, a well-deserved reward for his invaluable contributions to the success of the business.

Clark was a writer who was acclaimed as "one of the best humorists of the day." The son of an Episcopal clergyman from Berlin, Maryland, who was an abolitionist and a Northern sympathizer, he boasted that he was "brought up on sweet potatoes and among negroes." After serving two years in the Union army, in 1865 he became a reporter, an editorial writer, and a book reviewer for the *Philadelphia Inquirer*. Later he was music and drama critic for the *Philadelphia Evening Bulletin* and editorial writer for the *North American*. He wrote under the pen name Max Adeler, and his first book, *Out of the Hurly Burly*, became an immediate bestseller in 1874, when humor was the most popular form of writing in America. It was a collection of humorous sketches of life in a suburban town, and for thirty years the horseplay and labored extravagance of the book found an appreciative audience in the United States and in England. His second book, *Millburg*, was also a success. Tall and gaunt, Clark had the preternaturally sober face popularly attributed to humorists. He tried in vain to live down his reputation as a humorist by writing six serious novels and two collections of short stores, but none received the acclaim of his humor.

His connection with Lee was an interesting story, as Clark later explained: "The Calvary Episcopal Church at Conshohocken, in 1876, owned nothing but a little rough outbuilding, not handsome and not comfortable," Clark wrote. "I began to teach a class of boys in Sunday School a few weeks after moving to town. In the first class were two boys, sons of a laborer in the rolling mill. Their names were J. Ellwood Lee and Conrad B. Lee.

"When Ellwood left school, he came to me, as the boys often did, to have me help him find a situation where he might earn his bread. . . . Being upon the [Philadelphia] *Bulletin*, I inserted in that paper an advertisement in behalf of Ellwood. I received an answer from a maker of surgical instruments on Eleventh Street, Philadelphia. He wanted a boy and he took Ellwood. That was the event to which I owe my financial independence in my old age [and his seat on the Board of Directors of Johnson & Johnson from 1905 to 1915].

"Ellwood stayed there for several years and learned the business thoroughly. Not only this, but he developed some ability as an inventor, preparing devices not known to the surgeons. His employer was a dull fellow, not able to perceive that he had a treasure in this young man. . . . And so, after a while Ellwood left him and, having married, he began to make some small articles, chiefly his own inventions, in the garret of his little home. Before long he put up in his backyard a tiny wooden factory, to which his tasks were removed. In a year or two he built beside it a small stone mill.

"The townsfolk began to take note of him. Here was a man who, evidently, would 'get along.' In 1887 he dug the foundations for a third and much larger mill. Then he came to me (regarding me as his benefactor because of the small service I had done for him) and proposed that I should go into business with him. He showed to me that it would be worth while for me to do so. The change, however, was not regarded by me as advisable, but I turned in and helped him to form a company known as the J. Ellwood Lee Company. The stockholders included the two Lees, I, and my dear wife Clara Lukens. I and my wife owned one-fifth of the business, and I was made president.

"I made a handsome profit. It has been a large return for the small bit of kindness done by me nearly thirty years ago to a poor boy. I have reaped richly where I sowed without a thought of rec-ompense, and I believe in my heart that this is God's way of ful-filling his promise, that the good action shall not fail of its reward. This repays me ten thousand fold for all the help that I have been able to give to young fellows who came to me for help."

In conjunction with the merger of the two firms, Kilmer pre-pared a booklet titled "Handbook of Ligatures," which soon gained wide acceptance in hospitals and among surgeons. Clark was the unlikely collaborator in the writing of it. In the booklet the authors proudly proclaimed "These firms control the entire process," and indeed they did. Lee had developed improved manufacturing tech-niques, and after long effort Johnson had succeeded in producing the first truly sterile suture. It was a milestone in the history of surgery.

Five years after joining Johnson, Lee turned his attention to a new pursuit, producing tires for the infant auto industry. That also put Johnson in the tire business, but he quickly became dis-enchanted, and Henry Ford played a role. Lee had marketed a brand of tire he called "Jelco," a name derived from his initials. When Ford learned this he expressed dismay at having his autos riding around on tires bearing a name that suggested "jelly," so Lee promptly changed the name of the tire to "Lee of Conshohocken." Eventually all connections between Johnson's company and the Lee Tire & Rubber Company were severed, though the Lee company continued marketing tires for many years.

·

As for Johnson, he remained focused. The ever-resourceful Kilmer started a new publication, the *Red Cross Messenger*, in 1908, aim-ing it directly at druggists and pharmacists to help them "sell more goods and make better profits." By now the drugstore had become an institution, with the familiar red and green show globes in the window serving as beacons for everyone in search of medicines or sundries. There were tens of thousands of drugstores across the nation, all of them remarkably similar, with perfume and cigar counters, huge glass and wood display cases, and walls of gleaming mahogany with dozens of small drawers that held secrets only the proprietor knew. At the rear of the store the pharmacist communed with his mortar and pestle and compounds in isolation behind a discreet glass partition. Then came the invasion of the soda fountain, with its marble-and-onyx top, its swirly wireback chairs, and whirring ice cream mixer. Diehard druggists resisted creating a social center in their domain and a breeding ground for young romances, while the more enterprising reveled in the opportunity to lure new customers and hear the jingle of sales on the cash register.

The *Messenger* was an immediate success, with some 50,000 copies going to drugstores around the world, and the monthly issues had something for everyone behind the drugstore counter. Kilmer built up the role of the pharmacist with such declarations as "He is an educator and ranks with the clergyman, the teacher and the physician," or inspirational tidbits like "Grover Cleveland was a druggist." Through the *Messenger*, a Clerks' Club with the motto "Keep to the Front" was formed and there was always advice on selling and on building the drugstore career. Kilmer began devoting columns to the Women's Organization of the National Association of Retail Druggists, formed to promote a closer association among druggists' families, but also a strong proponent of suffragette causes. Under the heading "Leaders in the Woman's Movement," the *Messenger* included letters and articles on objectionable advertising that took advantage of women, and on opportunities for women as clerks and pharmacists.

Fred Kilmer had always been a good salesman, so sprinkled throughout the publication was a subtle reminder that the Johnson products were the best and the pharmacist and his clerks would do well to recommend them. Not surprisingly, it worked.

7

THE DEATH OF
THE LEADER

YOUNG Robert Johnson's life was about to be turned upside down. The sudden death of his beloved father would
change the course of events for him in ways that he could
not have imagined. He was sixteen when tragedy struck.

He had just returned to Rutgers Prep in the fall of 1909 after an
unhappy semester at the Lawrenceville School in Princeton. That
had been his parents' idea, and it was a mistake. The boy developed
an immediate dislike for his new surroundings, and to the annoyance of the faculty and the chagrin of his parents he ran away from
Lawrenceville several times. He would then go to the Trenton railroad station and wait to be picked up by his father or one of the
household staff. Finally, he was allowed to enroll again at Rutgers
Prep, where he was required to repeat his junior year.

Once back at school in New Brunswick, he settled down to his
studies and took an immediate liking to being a private in the
Company B Drill Team. From that point on, the military would become one of his life-long interests. At the school, military drill was
required of all boys enrolled in the scientific course, and a school
bulletin recommended it highly for all others, claiming: "There is
no better training in habits of attention, obedience, regularity and
neatness, and an upright and manly bodily carriage." He took the
discipline of the drill team very seriously and started exercising

strenuously until he developed a ramrod posture, which he would keep throughout his life.

No matter how engrossed he became in school activities, Robert found time to make regular visits to his father's factories and offices, a short distance from his home. There he showed an intense curiosity about the workings of the family business, the products made there, and the workers who produced them. By now he had become friendly with many of the office staff, and they listened patiently to his questions and willingly took the time to respond because he was such a polite young man. And also because he was "R.W.'s" son.

"R.W." had always enjoyed robust health, and he dismissed minor illnesses the same way he did minor annoyances — with dispatch. There were times, though, when the strain of business showed. "I have so many strings on my bow that I can hardly manage the bow at all," he once remarked in an uncharacteristic moment of uncertainty. The first hint of Johnson's onsetting illness came on the morning of January 31, 1910, when he left the office early, complaining of not feeling well. That was rare for him. Before leaving he told the office staff that he had "a touch of the grippe." His diagnosis was far off the mark.

The following day was the company's annual stockholder meeting, and Johnson was not well enough to attend — a clear indication of how sick he was. For him to miss an important business meeting was a rarity. The family physician, Dr. Frank W. Donohue, made several visits to Gray Terrace before gravely announcing that Johnson had Bright's disease, a very serious condition (named for the London physician who first diagnosed it) that affected kidney function. To confirm his diagnosis, Dr. Donohue called for help from one of the most distinguished physicians of his day, Dr. Edward Gamaliel Janeway of New York, who was also a friend of Johnson's. Janeway, a graduate of Rutgers and the College of Physicians and Surgeons at Columbia University in New York, had served as president of the American Association of Physicians and was a well-known diagnostician and pathologist. He was among the noted doctors summoned to Buffalo to try to save President McKinley's life after he was struck down by an assassin's bullets.

Dr. Janeway rushed to New Brunswick, the city of his birth, to the bedside of his friend Robert Johnson, but he could offer little hope. He confirmed the earlier diagnosis and said that the damage to Johnson's kidneys had already taken its toll. Even in the hands of a physician so competent that his skills "dominated his colleagues," the tools for fighting Bright's disease were totally inadequate. The futility of such critical situations lay in the fact that virtually the entire armamentarium of drugs available to physicians was carried in their leather valises.

The two physicians tried to make Johnson as comfortable as possible, and then turned their attention to consoling the family. Janeway soon returned to New York, because he himself was in failing health. A growing despair pressed down on Gray Terrace. Those who passed in and out of the big house moved quickly on their anxious missions, as though their own burst of energy could somehow be transmitted to the rapidly declining Johnson. The children had been herded off to a corner of the house with Miss Donohue, away from the increasing pessimism. Evangeline remained at her husband's bedside, trying to comfort him. On Saturday, the sixth day of his illness, Johnson slipped into unconsciousness.

Before daybreak on Monday, February 7, the doctors summoned the entire family to Johnson's bedside. Roberta had arrived only minutes before with her new husband, Carter Nicholas, after a long and tense train ride from Tallahassee, Florida, where they were honeymooning. James arrived in haste from his shooting box in North Carolina, where he had been enjoying a respite from the bitter winter weather. Newspaper accounts later said Johnson succumbed at exactly 6:38 A.M., and while the precise time made little difference, the accuracy would have pleased him. Evangeline and the children could not believe he was gone. Among Johnson's 2,500 employees, there was a pervading sense of doom and foreboding, and many were convinced that the company could not enjoy continued success without his leadership.

It was the city's largest funeral. Early in the morning of Wednesday, February 9, some 1,200 of Johnson's employees gathered at the plant, and at ten o'clock began walking the long block that goes through the campus of Rutgers University to Gray Terrace. They moved slowly up Hamilton Street in double file, and when the first of them reached the house, the line still extended all the way back to the factory entrance. All morning long they moved through the gates of the big house and into the drawing room, where the body reposed, then through the conservatory and out a side entrance. More than 1,500 people passed the casket that morning, including delegations from most of the business, civic, religious, and charitable organizations in New Brunswick.

Hundreds of floral pieces were crowded into the downstairs rooms. A huge stand of carnations and violets in the form of a closed book from Johnson's Board of Directors was placed at the head of the casket. The orphans of St. Mary's Home sent a modest bouquet. A standing easel of orchids and lilies of the valley came from the factory workers, and the salesmen sent white and pink roses in the form of a broken column. The London office sent a wreath of lilies, and the Montreal office sent palm leaves and white roses. Close to the casket was a small wreath of carnations from the household staff bearing the message "From his loving help." The most impressive floral arrangement barely made the funeral on time — an immense blanket of 2,000 pink roses, sent by the family and prepared by Thorley of New York. It was placed on the casket minutes before the services began. Thorley was fortunate that Johnson was not present when it arrived so late, or later when the staggering bill came. His frugality might also have rebelled at the casket chosen for him. The gleaming mahogany box lined with lead was an exact duplicate of the one in which President McKinley had been buried.

At three o'clock that afternoon the service began. It was simple and brief, with the Rev. Elisha Joyce of the Christ Episcopal Church, presiding. This was followed by a benediction offered by the Rt. Rev. Monsignor John J. O'Grady, pastor of St. Peter's Roman Catholic Church. Monsignor O'Grady's presence gave rise to speculation that Johnson had converted to Catholicism on his deathbed, but there is no evidence that he had — and because he was divorced, it is unlikely.

The funeral cortege included thirty carriages to carry the mourners to Elmwood Cemetery, a mile away, followed by a seemingly endless procession of other assorted vehicles and people walking. The flowers were so profuse they had to be loaded on a large truck, which had been commandeered for the burial procession and hurriedly draped in black. Along the route to the cemetery, hundreds of New Brunswick residents lined the streets to witness the departure of the city's leading citizen, some joining in the procession as it passed.

At the cemetery, Funeral Director W. J. McDede maneuvered the crowd close to the bier for a short committal prayer by Reverend Joyce. Snow and bitter cold had left the earth frozen and impenetrable, so the burial had to be delayed for several days until the ground thawed. Meanwhile, the casket was placed in a temporary vault, and when a group of Johnson's young male employees learned of this, they decided to post a twenty-four-hour guard at the door of the vault. Women employees prepared hot food and sent it at frequent intervals to nourish the grave-watchers. It never was clear what dangers they feared, but no one could deny that it was a touching gesture of loyalty. The *Daily Home News* summed it all up in its headline:

LAST OF EARTH
FOR R. W. JOHNSON

An editorial writer added:

Death laid its heavy hand on Robert Wood Johnson, robbing New Brunswick of its brainiest and most successfully aggressive man of affairs. . . . Few men have left this vale of tears for the great beyond with a life record so fine in private virtues and so rich and enduring in public usefulness."

The tribute from his longtime friend and close associate Fred Kilmer was the most eloquent of all:

Among his last official acts was the consideration of plans for the care of his employees in time of sickness and providing a pension for those long in his service.

The glory is his of having been in at the beginning of an era which snatched life from death.

When once convinced that an article which he could manufacture would save life and prevent suffering, he caused it to be manufactured and placed before the [medical] profession irrespective of any consideration of profit.

The results of his life work must be sought for in the thousands of hospitals, operating rooms, and at the bedside of millions of ill and injured patients everywhere upon the globe.

Probably more than any one man, he is entitled to credit for making the discoveries of Lister popular and for putting into practical application the great advances made from that time to this, in the technique of surgery.

Ten days later, on February 18, the Board of Directors named James as the company's new president. The choice was not an obvious one, for the company had developed a group of strong managers, and many doubted James's ability to lead as his brother had. Sensing this, mild-mannered Uncle Jimmy was quick to communicate with his employees:

I presume you have thought it possible that on account of the death of my brother changes might be made either in the policy of the business, or the methods of carrying out same. I take this occasion to tell you that there will be no change.

The business will be conducted with energy and vigor. My policy was my brother's policy. My brother's policy is my policy. . . . I feel qualified to carry forward the great work accomplished under my brother's supervision.

It was a valiant effort, and some felt inclined to give James the benefit of the doubt. Others were skeptical. They were two entirely different personalities. Still, it was really a moot point. James held the stock. James was the new president, for better or worse. Time would tell.

In the weeks after Johnson's death there was considerable speculation about the size of the fortune he had amassed and how it would be divided. Of particular interest were his majority holdings in the company. On February 23 his Will was probated, and the following day this account appeared in the *New York American*:

ROBERT W. JOHNSON'S WILL IS PROBATED
LEFT $2,000,000

The will of Robert Wood Johnson, probated in New Brunswick, New Jersey, shows an estate of over $2,000,000. The bulk of his estate is left to his widow, Mrs. Evangeline Armstrong Johnson. She gets all the household goods, horses and carriages at Gray Terrace, the New Brunswick home of the Johnsons, $40,000 in cash or securities, $20,000 from his life insurance, and the income during her life of $20,000 par value of the preferred stock of Johnson & Johnson. The Moosehead Lake, Maine, summer home is to be maintained out of the trust estate, and an income is provided for the maintenance of her three children, Robert W., John Seward, and Evangeline Johnson.

Mrs. Roberta Johnson Nicholas, a daughter, who recently received $150,000, gets one-fourth of the estate. The Bellevue Farm in Highland Park is left to the two sons.

But that account did not tell the full story. It failed to point out that the bulk of the estate, in the form of stock in the company, was left in trust for his children by his second marriage and was to be divided when the youngest reached twenty-five. This set the stage for a quiet struggle, beginning a decade later, for control of the company. When that took place, young Robert demonstrated his father's gift for taking charge.

•

Johnson's untimely death had a traumatic impact on his family. Without him, Gray Terrace ceased being a happy home. His wife, Evangeline, seemed lost without his presence. Her mother had died just two months earlier, and before she recovered from that loss she was beset by her husband's illness and death. The children shared her despair — especially Robert, who was closest to his father. To the surprise and dismay of friends and family, Evangeline decided to leave New Brunswick shortly after the funeral, though the departure was not quite as hasty as her daughter, Evangeline, remembered:

"The minute father died, my mother took an apartment in New York, and she took my brother Seward and me with her. She put him in the Browning School and she put me in Miss Spence's School, which was right across the street. Bob at that time sort of moved over, if you want to call it that, and stayed with my sister Roberta and her husband at their home in New Brunswick."

Robert's adjustment to his father's death was slow and difficult. He was turning seventeen. "Father died at the wrong time for Bob's development," Evangeline said. "He was just going into adolescence, . . . and what he did was to take the management of his life entirely into his own hands."

When he returned to Rutgers Prep after the funeral to complete his Third Form, or junior year, his classmates did their best to lighten his sorrow. He continued to be active in various school programs, and in mid-March was appointed manager of the basketball team, a responsibility he undertook diligently. Never a loquacious boy, he was perhaps more restrained than usual. He was lonely and he missed his mother, brother, younger sister, and especially his father.

That summer he asked if he could take a job at the factory and was encouraged to do so by his uncle. He got along well with the workers, many of whom were Hungarian immigrants. It was a sad summer, though, for the joys of previous summers spent at Belle-vue Farm were still vivid in his memory. But he enjoyed working, and he did a conscientious job all summer. During this period he first began thinking about returning to the company after gradua-tion instead of going to college.

In September 1910 he returned to Rutgers Prep for his senior year and was elected captain of the Company B Drill Team. Being the youngest member of his class and not as physically developed as the others, he found this to be a challenge. The drill team required a demonstration of authority and mastery of numerous compli-cated formations. He enjoyed that, and found the snappy military uniforms, with their wide-brim campaign hats, appealing.

As he approached his eighteenth birthday, Robert began to grow taller, closing the gap between himself and the other boys in his class, some of whom were now close to twenty. He increased his exercise regimen and kept trim. Later in life, slimness became such a fetish that he monitored his weight in terms of ounces and frac-tions of ounces. He combed his hair straight back, accenting the sharp features of his face. It was not quite the face of a young man, but one better suited to a much older person. Even his gray-blue eyes showed only an occasional youthful twinkle. His sister Evangeline was right. Childhood had eluded him.

In June he graduated, and the school magazine, *The Argo*, pub-lished its annual spoof of the senior class. They said of Bob John-son: "As others see him — Bluffer; Fad or fancy — Drill; Ambition — To be it; Destiny — To be — nit."

His family and friends assumed that he would enroll in college that fall, as most of his classmates were planning to do, but that summer he announced he would join the company instead. His mother promptly opposed that decision. While her influence over him had waned since his father's death and her move to New York, she persisted, and she gained the support of his Uncle James, who also thought that he should go to college and join the family business later. The impasse continued all summer, while Robert worked at a variety of jobs in the factory.

By September they reached a compromise. Robert enrolled at Rutgers Prep for several postgraduate courses and continued working part-time. Soon he began spending more and more time on the job, and less and less time at classes, as the school's attendance records attested. Then he began pressing various plant foremen to give him a full-time job. This was met with polite but firm refusals, because none of them wanted to go against the wishes of the family. The word had gone out that although part-time work was all right for Robert, no one was to take him on full-time. Finally he persuaded Walter Metts, foreman of the powerhouse that contained a pair of 2,000-horsepower turbines for generating electricity, to give him his first full-time job. Metts recalled how that came about: "No one would hire him full-time, but I finally relented. He worked with me for a while, then began to learn the production side of the business by spending as much time as necessary to get to know how each department operated. Then he would move on to the next one. He was a good worker, but he started in the powerhouse at the lowest job there."

Moving from job to job in the factory, Robert developed an easy rapport with the workers, a trait he retained throughout his life. He was at ease with them, and they with him. They called him Bob, or Bobby, and adopted him as one of their own, especially the ebullient Hungarians, many of whom came to America and to New Brunswick because a job opportunity awaited them at Johnson & Johnson. Others were recruited by the company on the docks in New York when the refugee ships arrived.

New Brunswick had become a center of Hungarian life in the United States. Spurred by their defeat in the War of Independence in 1848–49 by the Austrian Hapsburg forces, aided by the intervention of Czarist Russia, Hungarian immigrants began arriving in large numbers about 1850. Then in 1851 Louis Kossuth, Hungary's exiled governor and hero of the fight for independence, made a triumphant visit to America. In seven months he gave more than three hundred public addresses and spoke before the joint Houses of Congress. Dressed in sable and with headgear adorned with a plume—the symbol of honor and prowess—Kossuth was memorable. In flawless English he talked about Hungary's desire to be free, and made such an impression that William Cullen Bryant called him "the Washington, the Franklin of Hungary." With Kossuth's visit paving the way for a tide of immigrants, New Jersey and New Brunswick became havens for Hungarians at the end of the century. Once this link was established, they came to the city in droves, and in time more than one-third of the city's population could trace their origins to Hungary. New Brunswick became known as the "most Hungarian city in the United States."

Most of these new immigrants were young, and they came from the provinces of Zemplén and Veszprém at first, and then from the industrial centers around Borsod. Many had agrarian backgrounds, and some were craftsmen, but for a chance to come to the United States they were willing to take any employment they could get, and often at modest wages. The Johnsons liked the Hungarians. They were hardworking and honest, and, above all, fiercely loyal. Before long, the company came to be known as the "Hungarian University," for Hungarians made up two-thirds of the entire work force.

Robert later warmly recalled his early years in the factory when the Hungarians taught him their skills and became his friends: "Starting with the first day I went to work, and continuing throughout my business life, I have had many close friends among the Hungarian people in New Brunswick." They would invite him to their homes, to church celebrations, to weddings and christenings; feed him Gulyas, chicken paprika, and Dobos cakes; ply him with wines from Badacsony or Tokaj; and regale him with tales about old Budapest—all to the strains of gypsy music. He recalled the time he attended a wedding at John Susko's home and the next day he and Skinny Hardy went to work in the Mill Rooms with such hangovers that "we slept under the machines in the afternoon and Johnson Kenyon [the foreman] didn't catch us — thank God, and the muslin cover." Robert, in turn, made the Hungarians feel that he was one of them.

The Hungarians would tell him stories about themselves, like the time a disgruntled employee named Peter Uregas threatened to dynamite the plant unless his extortion demands were met. The threatening letter was written in Hungarian and demanded $22,000 — the money was to be put under a cross in a cemetery. But Uregas forgot to put a stamp on the letter. He waited in vain — with his unstamped letter still at the post office, undelivered and unread. He wrote a second letter, now demanding $33,000. Hundreds of workers stayed away from the factory, fearing that it would be blown up. Pinkerton Agency detectives were brought in from New York, but Uregas saved them the trouble. After writing a third extortion letter, he went to the Keasbey post office and handed it to the postmaster — who had him arrested.

Peter Uregas was an exception, for most of the Hungarians were model citizens who rarely violated the law. Their homes were impeccably clean and orderly and their tidy front yards were filled with garden flowers. At times, more than half the Hungarian employees were women, wife and husband often working side by side. The women were good workers and rode herd on the performance of male workers, and in so doing built up a strong esprit de corps. Comfortable restrooms were built for them, and special consideration was given if there were family problems, especially sick children. The Hungarian women, in their crisp white uniforms, kept their departments in the cotton and plaster mills as spotless as their kitchens at home.

·

In 1911 the company celebrated its twenty-fifth anniversary with the claim that it was producing 90 percent of the cotton, gauze, and bandages in use throughout the world. Now it had its own steamships, led by the *Robert W. Johnson*, leaving the city docks every day with cargoes of finished goods for the transportation terminals of New York, and returning at night with fresh supplies of raw materials. The fame of its products spread, and photos showed Red Cross products being carried by a camel in India, in the basket of a hot-air balloon in Germany, and by dogsled in the Arctic. Johnson & Johnson advertising was distinctive. One classic ad showed a girl and boy sitting on a log facing the ocean. The boy held an umbrella over the two of them, but high enough so that his arm was seen encircling her waist. The caption read:

FEELS GOOD ON THE BACK
RED CROSS KIDNEY PLASTERS

Professional advertising centered around the theme of a uniformed nurse with a red cross on her left shoulder and with various Red Cross brand products in her hand. The red cross symbol was even used on the mammoth lighted sign atop the factory buildings, visible for miles. Some 20 feet high and 102 feet across, the sign had the Johnson & Johnson name in white lights flanked by two huge flashing crosses in red. The monster sign all but blinded riders of the Pennsylvania Railroad as they passed on the elevated tracks, but it got their attention.

•

Robert did not lead a sheltered life during his prep school years. Along with some of his friends, he explored various city establishments, one of which he remembered particularly vividly in later years: "Fortunately a few of us boys learned of a restaurant known as Bustanoboys, which in no time came to be known as 'Busty's B.' I was introduced to this wonderful hideaway by Mother's chauffeur, who was related to one of the waiters. Through this very special connection, I met an exceptionally talented educator — a bleached-blonde hostess, who later drank up my allowance in bourbon whisky as fast as my allowance became due. This magnificent creature took the square waltz apart and made it really maneuverable. Hence I learned teaching and fact were not related."

During the summer of 1912, when Johnson was eighteen, he had begun to hang out with a new group of friends, who spent much of their time in the local taverns. Most of his boyhood friends had gone off to college. Robert started drinking more than he should have.

Some years later, impressed by his range of knowledge, a reporter asked him where he had received his education. "In Petey Tennyson's saloon," he replied with a wide grin of satisfaction, knowing he had set the trap and caught his victim.

Tennyson's was located on Easton Avenue, a few blocks from Rutgers University. It had the reputation of being an educational center of sorts, although uncredited and occasionally discredited. Upstairs over the bar was a social center known as the Excelsior Club, which attracted a loyal but odd assortment of "members" that included legitimate campus intellectuals, some pretenders to the literati throne, street-smart types from downtown, and drifters who added a wandering viewpoint to the spirited debates. Johnson nested among this group and began hatching his period of rebellion.

After work and on weekends he spent a great deal of time at the Excelsior Club — and below, in the precincts of Tennyson's. Being from the wealthiest family in the city gave him a special distinction and appeal, and he soon collected a host of new friends and became "one of the boys" — and even a folk hero among some of them. A prodigious reader, he was always well attuned to current events. The college intellectuals in the crowd rattled on about theory, while he invariably chose the more pragmatic stand. The debates raged on, with much rhetoric and few definable conclusions. More often than not he had the support of the working crowd, because he usually sided with them in the arguments.

"He had great rapport with the young men who weren't the socially elite," a contemporary recalled. "They weren't bums, but often they were the Roman Catholics. The Catholics weren't accepted by the Wasps in those days. But Johnson leaned towards them as individuals, and he liked them. And they liked him. He didn't know how to be a snob. He had no patience with snobs."

"Yes, Bob Johnson was a Bolshevik!" said another.

"He was a rouster," an elderly physician in the city remembered. "He had plenty of pepper in his pants. . . . He had a reputation. . . . He was a hell-raiser, and New Brunswick was a small community."

Downstairs, at the "lower school" of Tennyson's institution, the ebullient proprietor was perhaps the smartest of them all. The cash register never stopped jingling. Short and rotund, Petey Tennyson wrapped a white apron around his ample middle and paced the length of the highly polished mahogany bar, generating business. His "texts" were every handbill and notice he could lay his hands on, and whether they promoted causes or services didn't concern him. They all stimulated discussion and thirst among his patrons. And just to make sure they could be read, Tennyson kept a drawer full of assorted reading glasses that had been left at the bar and doled them out, as needed, along with the handbills. The Excelsior Club upstairs was the recognized forum at Tennyson's for the weightier issues of the day, but downstairs Petey kept the conversation and the liquor flowing. Prohibition had little impact on his business. "When Prohibition was repealed, all Petey had to do was open up the front door instead of the back door," a relative recalled.

The young Johnson's behavior and the reputation he was acquiring came to be of increasing concern to the staid management of the company, and especially to his uncle. It had been going on now for nearly two years, and he was approaching his twenty-first birthday. Then came a dramatic event, a turning point. Robert arrived at the company offices one day in a drunken stupor and prostrated himself on the floor outside the door of the room where the Board of Directors was meeting. He lay there until the meeting ended, and one by one the directors had to step over him to get out of the room. He told the story many times in later years—not in a bragging manner, but more to illustrate how erratic his behavior had become during that period.

The incident angered his uncle, and there was a confrontation over it. "Uncle Jimmy told him that if he didn't stop fooling around he would sell the business," Walter Metts, his first boss, recalled. "He stopped that kind of behavior almost overnight and became a very serious-minded young man," he added. James knew that the threat of selling the business was his most persuasive argument, for the company had become to Robert what it had been to his father—the focal point of his life.

The improvement was instant and dramatic, and as a result, on April 15, 1914, eleven days after his twenty-first birthday, he was elected to the Board of Directors to replace J. Ellwood Lee, who had died. In this role he had no direct responsibility for the management of the company, as that was vested in a Board of Control. But the election was in recognition of the fact that he would become a major stockholder in four years, when he reached the age of twenty-five, in accordance with the terms of his father's will. While his behavior improved, he found other ways to be a maverick.

The city of New Brunswick was on the brink of another of its many transitions—this one political. Over the years there had been numerous unsuccessful attempts to have a commission government replace the alderman form. It became an issue again in the elections of 1911 and 1913—and it was defeated each time, but by increasingly smaller margins. The effort to change the form of government had been led by one of James Johnson's executives, Charles McCormick, described as "the doughty leader." Dismayed at the defeat, and because he believed the company was being unduly criticized, James issued an order urging six of his management people to resign from various city boards on which they were serving. They did, and when asked why he had taken the action, James told a reporter: "We have tried to assist in the general betterment of the town, and have received nothing but kicks for our pains." Finally, on March 2, 1915, the electorate, by a majority of 818 votes, approved the commission form after a strong campaign by the Board of Trade. This set up an election for commissioners on April 6, and immediately the field became crowded with candidates for the five seats on the commission.

In the interest of trying to stabilize political unrest in the city, Dr. Austin Scott, the incumbent mayor and president of Rutgers University, decided to run again. Scott had the support of the old-line politicians, the Board of Trade, and various members of Johnson & Johnson's top management, so the Good Government League faction he represented seemed to have a clear path to victory.

Just before the filing deadline, Robert and some of his friends were discussing the impending election at Farrington's Tavern on Burnet Street and wondering whom they would support. In the middle of the conversation Eddie Farrington, son of the tavern owner, came to the table carrying a tray of fresh beers. Johnson looked up and said, "Why not run Eddie?" Everyone laughed. It was a story he always enjoyed repeating.

Young Farrington laughed too, but also expressed interest. At twenty-nine he had only a grammar school education, but he came from an area of the city populated by a strong Irish vote and had thought of perhaps running for public office some day. Beginning that night, the young group began putting together a fusion ticket of Republicans and Democrats, and in the ensuing weeks they worked feverishly on the campaign for Farrington and his runningmates on the People's League ticket.

For weeks the city of 27,000 rocked with political campaigning. The race had fifty-seven candidates, including tavern owner Petey Tennyson. Noisy rallies and street parades echoed through the city day and night. Eddie Farrington was humble and direct in his appeal to voters, promising "to establish intimate relations with the people of the city; to become familiar with their needs and desires, and to seek their aid and advice." His views on public office were also refreshing: "A commissioner's door should never be closed to the public. I do not believe the city wants to elect men who will sit in the sanctuary of a private room, working out public problems as he in his own wisdom thinks best."

By Election Day, April 6, the city was in a frenzy. The first returns did not reach the city clerk's office until almost midnight, and then the complicated counting procedure began, with some seventy-six sets of figures having to be tabulated for each of the fifty-seven candidates. It was nearly daybreak before the results were official — and when they were, Eddie Farrington had polled the most votes, 2,745, and New Brunswick had a new mayor.

There was dismay among the losers, especially the Good Government League candidates, who declared they had been "liberally decorated with the double cross." Far less upset was the philosophical Petey Tennyson, who had polled 444 votes. For Petey, who had conducted his campaign from his usual position behind the highly polished mahogany bar, his defeat required little adjustment. He just set up another round for the boys.

Eddie Farrington became New Brunswick's forty-third mayor and, to the surprise of many, one of the outstanding officials in the city's history. Early in his administration he led efforts to improve the water supply, pave the streets, and close the taverns at a decent hour on Saturday nights so the Sabbath would not be violated. Most of all, the door of his office was open to everyone — just as he had promised during the campaign.

Farrington and Bob Johnson became good friends, but three years later, the young mayor, then thirty-two years old, died following surgery for gallstones. Deeply moved by his death, Johnson said at the time of the funeral: "I have lost an intimate friend. . . . Mutual interest in civic questions and in the many charitable campaigns incident to the war had thrown us together a great deal, and I had the opportunity of knowing him as man to man. I am glad to say he was a lovable character, a man of principle, a man of sympathy, a man who understands his fellow man — a man among men."

Several years after the mayor's death, Johnson named one of the company's steamships the *Edward F. Farrington*. And fifty years later, when they removed the personal effects from Johnson's office following his own death, there was a framed photo of a smiling Eddie Farrington. It had been on the bookshelf all that time.

PART TWO

The New Generation
1916–1941

8

MENDING HIS
WAYS

MATURING Bob Johnson had put behind him the carefree, sometimes errant days of frequenting Petey Tennyson's tavern and was now playing a more urbane role among the young social set in New Brunswick, where again he stood out. His good looks, his wealth, and his family position set him apart from many of the others, and he made no effort to blur these distinctions.

"During that period Bobby bought fast cars and turned them over to the company's mechanical department and told the boys to speed them up," Walter Metts remembered. "Then he'd go out and wreck them. It's a wonder he didn't kill himself."

"He became quite a playboy, and there were people in the city who still thought he wouldn't amount to much," another old-timer said. Seward was attending Yale, and when he was home on vacation the two brothers, both of them handsome, would team up and charm the young ladies of their social circle. "Rounders, we called them," the elderly gentleman added. "When they weren't racing around in cars they were in speeding boats on the river."

Robert was now living with his Uncle Jimmy and his family in the big house on Union Street, and the elderly Johnson viewed his nephew's youthful escapades with quiet tolerance. The earlier rebellious period and excessive drinking was now over, and young ladies were entering the scene. One of Robert's closest friends was Miles Ross, son of a wealthy and socially prominent family. Mr. Ross was the city's largest coal dealer, and the Ross family had a spacious home on Livingston Avenue, where Robert was spending more and more time. Miles was one reason why Johnson went there so often, but so was Miles's pretty young sister, Elizabeth.

At the factory, though, Johnson was all business. He was always punctual and he worked hard and was learning fast. Still, he had his critics — he always would. His father had chosen and trained a group of serious-minded managers known more for their business acumen than their sentimentality. They were not about to jeopardize their own careers, or the business itself, by hastening the development of the young Johnson, who to many of them was still an unknown factor. Yet they had to deal with the reality of his substantial stock holdings in the company. Some of the managers viewed him with guarded optimism, others with guarded pessimism.

It was in 1915, at the age of twenty-two, that Robert was promoted to his first important position of responsibility, as head of one of the departments in the factory. The workers applauded his promotion, for they considered him one of them. At this time too, Robert began developing a close relationship with Fred Kilmer, who would become a father figure for him. He visited Kilmer frequently in his laboratory, always addressing him as "Doctor Kilmer." Robert saw little of his mother after she moved to New York following his father's death and then began taking extensive trips to Europe. (In 1915, she met and married John W. Dennis, a wealthy Englishman who had made a fortune growing potatoes.)

The kindly Kilmer was a wise man who was always generous with his time and advice. He welcomed Robert's visits, and the rapport they had developed. Kilmer's own son and last surviving child, Joyce, was now married and living in New York successfully pursuing his writing career. For a time Joyce worked as a reviewer for the *New York Times Review of Books* as his other writing was steadily gaining popularity, and he had stature as a lecturer. He was very much the idealist and deeply religious, having earlier converted to Catholicism along with his wife, Aline.

It was now five years after the senior Johnson's death, and the company's continued prosperity under James's leadership silenced some of his critics, who claimed he was not the leader his brother had been. The unconvinced insisted that the company was reaping the rewards of good management that "R.W." had put in place and was moving ahead under its own momentum. There was some truth to both arguments, but it was difficult to deny the healthy sales and profits figures.

James and Robert had a good, if somewhat guarded, relationship. Once he was convinced that Robert had mended his ways, James encouraged the young man's progress in the company, but still clung to his "wait and see" attitude.

A telegram from San Francisco on June 16, 1915, set off a noisy celebration at the factory: "Johnson & Johnson have been awarded a gold medal by the Panama-Pacific International Exposition for the display of their products. This is the highest honor and the only gold medal awarded to any exhibitor of medicinal or surgical dressings or dental specialties." Months had been spent building an authentic ten-foot scale model of the factory complex, down to the last windowpane. It was then carefully crated and shipped to San Francisco's Palace of Fine Arts, where the model was displayed along with samples of all the products the company produced. International exhibitions had become quite influential in developing new foreign sales opportunities, so the medal was an accomplishment worthy of the celebration it touched off back home.

But soon hopes for expanded international growth were replaced by concerns about involvement in the volatile war in Europe. There was increasing talk about moving away from America's policy of isolation and about the need to position the United States as a world power, using the nation's growing military strength if necessary. Involvement in a war of any magnitude would have serious implications for a company that was now the world's largest producer of many of the medical supplies that would be required. The apprehension that began to grip the nation was palpable.

Within months, tension over world peace would mount and be injected into the most spirited public gatherings. It was that way on the night of May 29, 1916, when the city's political and business leaders gathered at the Hotel Klein to officially open the first coast-to-coast transcontinental telephone lines between New Brunswick and San Francisco. Before the banter began on 3,500 miles of telephone lines the Bell System had laboriously strung across the country, there was an address on "Preparedness" by George Haven Putnam, organizer of the Security League in New York. "We should not sit back in timid neutrality when there is work to be done in the world," he warned. "If we are going to do our part in the fight of democracy against aristocracy, we have got to begin. . . . The responsibility now falls on the men of this generation." The all-male audience listened intently.

Then the somber mood changed. Guests picked up individual receivers at each place and put them to their ears. The historic moment was at hand. First came the roll call of wire chiefs — Pittsburgh, Chicago, Omaha, Denver, Salt Lake City, Winnemucca (with hasty explanation that it was 155 miles from Reno), and finally San Francisco, where it was 6:14 P.M. The connection was complete, and for the next sixty minutes greetings were exchanged — from grave pronouncements meant to sound historic, to frivolous banalities. James Johnson's comments were political, and intended to be funny. He said that as a delegate to the forthcoming Republican National Convention in Chicago he might be the only person voting against Teddy Roosevelt for the nomination.

Robert accompanied his uncle to the dinner, making his first public appearance representing the company. He too had been chosen as one of the greeters, and he chatted briefly on the open line with the company's San Francisco agent, H. D. Dietrich. Then, from the transmitter placed on Seal Rocks, the roar of the Pacific Ocean was sent along the wires eastward. Eric Goodwin sang "On the Banks of the Old Raritan." San Francisco responded with a Victrola playing "Little Grey Home in the West." With glasses raised, and in a cloud of cigar smoke, they closed with New Brunswick's lusty song of farewell:

> Good Night, Frisco!
> Farewell, Frisco!
> So long, Frisco!
> We're going to leave you now.
> We'll annex you by and by.
> Do not sigh! Don't you cry!
> We'll annex you by and by.
> Although we leave you now.

By 1916 the war in Europe had been under way for two years, and the demand by the Allied armies for surgical dressings produced by Johnson & Johnson was staggering. No company in Europe had anywhere near the same capacity for production, and in the United States the output was at a level significantly higher than all other competitors combined. Added to the war demand was the growing acceptance of the same products in American hospitals. Extra shifts were added, but the orders continued to pile up.

A search was made for a new source for textiles, and on June 1, 1916, Chicopee Manufacturing Company of Chicopee Falls, Massachusetts, was acquired for $1 million in cash. Chicopee had been founded in 1823 and was a consequence of the War of 1812, when it was realized that the nation had to move away from a primarily agrarian economy. The move toward industrialization began in the cotton mills of New England. Now, the entire output of Chicopee's spinning and weaving operations was being shipped to New Brunswick for finishing as surgical dressings and other medical supplies for the European war effort.

The announcement of Robert's engagement that summer to Elizabeth Dixon Ross surprised many who thought he wasn't quite ready to settle down, and comforted those who felt that marriage was just what he needed. Those who knew him best believed that he himself was not sure. But the wedding, described as one of the most glittering social events in the city's history, took place the evening of October 18, 1916, in the library of Elizabeth's spacious home. Her father, Millard Fillmore Ross, had spared no expense to make the merger between his family and the Johnsons a memorable event. The Ross family was widely known in politics. Elizabeth's grandfather, Miles Ross, was a prominent Democratic leader who served eight years in the U.S. Congress.

The huge house had been turned into a garden setting, with canvas enclosing the broad porches, and flowers and potted palms creating the proper atmosphere. Hundreds of American Beauty and Sunburst roses, and enormous white, yellow, and pink chrysanthemums, banked the walls, and woven into the flowers and greenery were hundreds of tiny twinkling golden lights. At one end of the library, an altar and chancel had been erected, banked by a screen of pale lavender orchids. At precisely eight o'clock, to the strains of Lohengrin, the wedding procession entered the library led by four young ribbon-bearers and four bridal attendants, and a similar number for the groom. Seward was his brother's best man, and their mother, Evangeline, was there from England with her new husband. The noted French caterer Monsieur Louis Monquin created a sumptuous supper, and guests danced long into the night to the music of Van Bear's Orchestra from New York. It was very late when the couple bid farewells and left on a wedding trip to Canada and the West.

·

For some time, Americans had viewed German aggression in Europe and the success of its U-boat attacks with a sense of detachment and unreality, many still clinging to President Woodrow Wilson's promises of neutrality. That attitude took a shocking turn on May 7, 1915, at the news of the sinking of the British liner *Lusitania* off the coast of Ireland. Almost 1,200 people lost their lives, many of them vacationing Americans. To some, a global war appeared to be imminent, but in November 1916 President Wilson was re-elected on the strength of his slogan "He Kept Us Out of War." The headlines of this campaign rhetoric were soon replaced by the appalling toll of new conquests by the U-boats and a new threat emerging in Mexico. There, Wilson had dispatched some 12,000 troops under General John J. "Black Jack" Pershing in an attempt to restore order and tame the elusive and notorious Mexican bandit "Pancho" Villa. That campaign ended in frustration, and the troops returned home. Pershing, with his bullhorn voice, volunteered to lead the American Expeditionary Force overseas after Congress finally declared war against Germany on April 2, 1917.

The declaration of war touched off a frenzy of patriotism throughout the nation. Overnight, enlistment posters appeared everywhere, the most familiar showing the tall man in red-white-and-blue attire pointing a convincing finger and declaring "Uncle Sam Wants YOU." Enlistment centers were jammed with new recruits, many of them boys barely in their teens. To band music and tears they marched off to training camps and then to battlefields far away. Pershing was already in France when the citizens of San Francisco raised $4,070 for the Red Cross on June 22 and presented him, in absentia, with the gold-plated "Johnson's First Aid Cabinet No. 1" for relief of the first "Sammies" to be injured in the war. The gift of a first-aid kit was to have an ironic twist, for when the war ended a year and a half later the wounded numbered nearly 500,000.

The sensitivities of Joyce Kilmer had been severely jolted by the loss of innocent lives in the sinking of the *Lusitania*, and ever since that tragedy his poems had emphasized the nobility of war and the warrior's calling, so long as the cause was holy. It therefore did not surprise his friends when two weeks after the United States entered the war he enlisted in the Army. At first the Army could not understand why the celebrity author wanted to become an ordinary foot soldier rather than a correspondent, which his status as a writer warranted. Kilmer replied that he was "a poet trying to be a soldier," a transition he was to make with bitter finality.

He went overseas with the 165th Infantry Regiment, the famous "Fighting 69th," a rambunctious group of Irish Americans. With them Kilmer found a new depth to the meaning of comradeship, and with some skepticism they accepted this newcomer of Irish heritage, of which he happened to be quite proud. That alone qualified him for their initial affection, and it was returned in his own unique way—by writing about them. His thoughts came mostly in letters, as opposed to the writing assignments he had disdained, but were no less meaningful. Of his comrades, he wrote home: "Say a prayer for them all, they're brave men and good, and splendid company. Danger shared together and hardships mutually borne develops in us a sort of friendship I never knew in civilian life, a friendship clean of jealousy and gossip and envy and suspicion— a fine, hearty, roaring, mirthful sort of thing, like an open fire of whole pine trees in a giant's castle."

Back in New York, Joyce's editors were puzzled that his poems and articles were coming only in a trickle. Kilmer wrote that he hadn't come to France to report on the war—"If I had, I'd have come over as a correspondent instead of a soldier." But in the mud trenches on the Western Front, he was moved to write what his fellow doughboys came to regard as his greatest work, "Rouge Bouquet." Ironically, it would soon be read at his own battlefield grave by Father Francis P. Duffy, chaplain of the 165th Infantry Regiment and later historian of the "Fighting 69th" with his "Father Duffy's Story."

Father Duffy and Joyce became good friends, and the priest sensed the impending fate: "Joyce was one of those soldiers who had a romantic love of death in battle," he wrote, "and it could not have missed him in time." The time came in the waning days of July 1918 along the banks of the Ourcq River. The adjutant and aide to Major "Wild Bill" Donovan had been killed in action, and

Kilmer, now a sergeant in the intelligence section, volunteered to replace him. He greatly admired Donovan's bold leadership, and on the morning of July 30 he accompanied Donovan on a scouting mission. Kilmer took up his observation of the German position at the north edge of the woods along the river, and Donovan moved ahead for a closer look. When the major returned, he found Kilmer shot through the head by a single German bullet.

News of Joyce's death moved swiftly through the regiment, and those who were in the vicinity of a little copse known as the Wood of the Burned Bridge, a stone's throw from the purling Ourcq and a short distance from the tranquil village of Seringes, gathered for his burial. Sergeant Alexander Woolcott, who had left his drama critic duties at the *New York Times* for assignment with the 165th, sent back an account:

> They all knew his verse ["Rouge Bouquet"]. I found any number of men who had only to fish around in their tattered blouses to bring out the copy of a poem he wrote in memory of some of their number who were killed by a shell in March. You see that there is a refrain that calls for bugle notes, and I am told that at the funeral services, where the lines were first read, the desperately sad notes of "Taps" sounded faintly from a distant grave when the refrain invoked them. The lines were read by Joyce's own beloved Father Duffy, and those who were there told me the tears streamed down the face of every boy in the regiment.

The opening lines of "Rouge Bouquet" are:

> In a wood they call the Rouge Bouquet
> There is a new-made grave today,
> Built by never a spade or pick
> Yet covered with earth ten metres thick.
> There lie many fighting men,
> Dead in their youthful prime,
> Never to laugh nor love again
> Nor taste the Summertime.

[133]

Some of the tears might well have been saved for Fred and Annie Kilmer, who had now lost their fourth and last child. Friends found it difficult just facing them to express their sorrow over Joyce's death. As they grieved for Joyce the son, an admiring nation grieved for the thirty-one-year-old poet, who had just begun to dispense the treasures of his talent. As they had done before, Fred and Annie buried themselves in their work. Annie took Joyce's death especially hard, for they had been very close. Fred tried to ease her sorrow by saying that she was the one who had inspired Joyce to write: "Joyce and his mother enjoyed a very close companionship throughout his life, . . . and he acknowledged his indebtedness to his mother for many of his writings." While it was no doubt true, it also was gallant of him to give her the credit.

Annie then decided to devote the rest of her life to perpetuating Joyce's memory, and friends remembered her attending countless meetings where she had been invited to speak about him. She set several of his poems to music and published a book of his previously unpublished poems and letters, which she called "Memories of My Son, Sergeant Joyce Kilmer." The War Department later named an army base near New Brunswick "Camp Kilmer," and streets, schools, parks, and bridges all across the nation would bear Joyce's name to keep his memory alive.

·

The Johnson & Johnson bandage-making machines worked day and night to keep up with the demand, now from all the Allied Forces as well as military and civilian hospitals at home, and some abroad. The factories ran seven days and hired hundreds of additional women who volunteered to take jobs to help out in the crisis. When author Janet Steward visited the production lines, she wrote "[The war] has forced this always busy factory to make machinery that can turn out in a given time one hundred times as much as the machinery in use before America went to war." While that estimate was high, production had reached mind-boggling figures.

Gauze and adhesive plaster was counted in terms of "thousands of miles," and bandages in the "hundreds of millions." The entire product line was revised to accommodate wartime needs.

In France, an American surgeon had discovered a new burn dressing developed at the Hospital St. Nicholas at Issy-les-Moulineaux, but the formula was a secret. He brought back a sample, and Fred Kilmer and his aides soon developed an improved version, which they called Redintol. The preparation was paraffin and resins with different melting points, and they produced it in brown bars resembling cakes of maple sugar. When applied to the wound site and covered with an air-excluding shell, the healing was remarkable. Later the laboratory staff turned its attention to the sad task of developing dressings to be used in "the reconstruction of American soldiers" who had been maimed in the Great War.

Even in normal times Kilmer was a prodigious worker who could be found in his laboratories long into the night. But during the war, and especially following Joyce's death, he pushed himself mercilessly. "It's this way," he explained. "If there are one million men under arms at the front, that means that hospital supplies for twice that number must be ready." Modern warfare had posed extraordinary challenges to even the most gifted surgeons, and the treatment of the war wounded was of compelling interest to Kilmer. The noted French surgeon Dr. Alexis Carrel, appalled at the high rate of amputations due to infection, began to develop a new antiseptic system, which would later involve Kilmer and his associates.

Carrel decided that deep wounds, such as those inflicted by exploding shells, required constant irrigation with a sterilizing solution. Working at his laboratory at Campiegne, he began devising the apparatus and asked Henry D. Dakin, an English chemist, to develop the right solution. The resulting Carrel-Dakin method consisted of a series of rubber tubes that carried a solution of sodium hypochlorite into the wound. The tubes were wrapped in toweling to hold and diffuse the solution, and every two hours a pinch-valve released more solution from a container hanging above the bed. The complex solution called for ordinary bleaching lime, which was unstable and often risky.

Kilmer set about developing chloris-soda ampules, which were dropped in water to produce the precise mixture recommended, and quickly made them available to surgeons trying Carrel's very successful technique. In his special "War Surgery" issue of *Red Cross Notes*, Kilmer examined all aspects of the complicated operation for physicians and explained them in detail.

With the onset of the war, Robert's responsibilities were greatly increased. The company soon became the major supplier of medical products for all of the Allied Forces, and there was constant pressure from the War Department to keep increasing production. These responsibilities kept him out of military service, and on April 12, 1918, he became General Superintendent in charge of manufacturing when the man who held that position was suddenly taken ill. In a letter announcing the promotion, James urged management and workers to "obey and respect" young Johnson in his new role. There was another reason why he gained new respect. A few days earlier he had turned twenty-five and now owned the large block of company stock left to him by his father.

To keep the production lines rolling at high speed, workers were spurred on by slogans and appeals for greater patriotism. Atop the factory, the huge electric sign bearing the company name was changed to read "Loyalty to America" in letters five feet high. Just below it, a large flag in blinking lights gave the appearance of waving and could be seen for miles.

During the late summer and early fall of 1918, work at the factory was directed toward the production of gauze masks to be worn by people in public to help stem the spread of the devastating flu epidemic raging in the nation. Untold thousands of civilians and more than 24,000 troops in military camps were felled by the scourge, compared with the 34,000 killed in battle. The epidemic, apparently started by a sailor who fell ill on August 28 aboard a transport docked in Boston Harbor, spread rapidly down the coast, killing 15,000 in Massachusetts alone. There was a severe shortage of medical supplies and personnel, many of whom were serving overseas. At the peak of the epidemic, New Brunswick reported 6,700 cases, or one-third of the city's inhabitants.

Gauze masks were one of only two effective methods of controlling the spread of the disease, the other being vaccination. Some cities, like San Francisco, made wearing masks compulsory while in public, and it was a strange sight seeing pedestrians moving quietly through the city with their faces covered with the white epidemic masks. But it was effective. "With everyone wearing masks in San Francisco," one physician reported, "the number of influenza cases was reduced from 2,300 to 300 cases a day."

The effects of the flu epidemic were still being felt when the New York metropolitan area was jolted by a devastating explosion that claimed fifty lives at the T. A. Gillespie shell-loading depot. Located on Raritan Bay at Morgan Station, a mile and a half south of South Amboy, the facility was the largest in the nation. It extended half a mile along the waterfront and three miles inland. In one section the government produced the shells, and in another the Gillespie Company loaded them on ships and land conveyances. At 7:40 P.M. on October 4, 1918, 7,000 pounds of TNT exploded with a deafening roar. The resulting fire touched off thirteen more explosions at intervals of one to five minutes, and the blasts were felt all the way to Long Island. Windows within a ten-mile radius were shattered, and hundreds of buildings were damaged. The nearby towns of South Amboy and Perth Amboy were in ruins and placed under martial law.

Within minutes of the explosion the call went out for doctors and nurses who would be willing to enter the sprawling munitions depot to aid the hundreds of workers who lay injured and surrounded by thousands of unexploded shells. Robert's sister,

Evangeline, had graduated from Miss Spence's School, learned first-aid, and become a lieutenant in the Red Cross Ambulance Corps in New York. She volunteered for the dangerous assignment.

"They couldn't force anyone to go, but they needed help, and at that age I thought it was exciting—so I went," Evangeline related years later. She remained at the explosion site for three days, driving the ambulance through the rubble and unexploded shells without incident. Looking back on the experience, and typical of Evangeline's humor, she remarked: "It seemed like I spent more time with that doctor than with some of my husbands [she had three]." She later received a government commendation for her heroics at the explosion site.

At age twenty-one, Evangeline was a free spirit. ("I would have become a debutante in New York, but the war came and saved me.") Tall and athletic, forceful and assertive in manner, she was more handsome and striking than she was pretty. Her presence never had to be announced. She was bright, she was humorous, and her friends never had to wonder what she was thinking—she told them.

Once, during her rebellious youth, she shook up Palm Beach the day she dropped leaflets from a plane, protesting the ban on the newer, more modern swimsuits. "I was crazy about swimming, and in those days you had to wear a bathing suit that was like a dress, with a skirt and a sailor-top sort of thing. I thought it was silly to put on a whole suit of clothes to go into the ocean. So I decided to protest. I wrote a flier and had them printed. I had learned how to fly a small seaplane based on Lake Worth, so I flew over the beach near the Breakers Hotel in this open-cockpit plane and threw out hundreds of fliers. They were very annoyed."

Evangeline's first marriage, some years later, was to the highly dramatic and brilliant conductor of the Philadelphia Orchestra, Leopold Stokowski, by whom she had two daughters, Lyuba and Sadja. "When I told my brother Bob that I was marrying an orchestral conductor," Evangeline said, "he was horrified. 'A conductor?'

he exclaimed, and I said, 'It's not a street car conductor, dear, it's an orchestral conductor.' And he said, 'Oh.'"

·

The Armistice for the Great War was signed on November 11, 1918, and people turned their attention to returning to a more normal life. It had been a costly and difficult conflict that drove deep into the nation's emotions and resources. The War Department awarded Johnson & Johnson a special commendation for its outstanding performance during the war. Hoover expressed his appreciation for the company's support of the food conservation campaign, and the Russian Minister of War presented James Johnson with a silver-and-gold cigar box with an etching of the Kremlin on the lid. James had bought into the Neverslip Horse Shoe Company in New Brunswick, and the largest order it had ever filled was from the Russian army for its cavalry.

Ever since his father's death, Robert had assumed a paternal role toward his younger brother. The two had always been close, but now he felt an added responsibility to try to steer his brother into the family business. Seward was in the Navy commanding a submarine chaser in the Mediterranean Sea when he received this letter from his brother:

Dear Sew,

As we have just completed our war drive and things are slowing down, it gives me an opportunity to write you a letter that I have been considering for sometime on a subject which is of the utmost importance to both of us.

It is quite evident, considering the entire situation, that demobilization will be quicker than hoped for before the cessation of hostilities, and whether your particular unit of the fighting force will be early or late, will of course, be a matter of detail. The Navy will undoubtedly remain large. In fact, it has been brought to my attention quite convincingly that the Navy program has been increased rather than cut down.

I am assuming, of course, that you are not going to remain in the

Navy. You would be surprised at the number of people who have spoken of this matter to me, and they stated that they wondered whether or not you would stay in, as there seemed to be some feeling that you might. I never entertained this thought, and therefore, my plans for the future as far as you are concerned are based entirely on your getting back in the harness within a reasonable time.

The success of our family largely depends on the activities of you and myself, and in these activities we must be brothers and partners. I mean by this, perhaps owing to the fact I have been at work for quite a number of years, and as this has brought me a fairly intimate knowledge of the business, that my position will, therefore, seem dominating. This should not be the case. It is only that I was a little older than you, and I neglected my school studies and college education to go to work, and had you been in my position, doing the things I did and run the race so far with me, I am mighty sure we would be neck and neck.

To put my thoughts in a few words, they are these: It is my greatest wish that you will come back to this business and take up the work here that will be detail in its scope at first, but with the idea of absorbing a general knowledge of this business, and finally settling into, what I consider a certain branch of it, making that work your part of the future success of Johnson & Johnson.

While I am not a prophet, it appears to me that the coming years will tax the executive ability of a business organization more than ever. There will be more energetic competition, not only in this country, but internationally, and a period of re-organization that must be handled most diplomatically, particularly on the part of those in industry.

This is placing the matter before you in rather a concrete form, but I know you must be giving the future some thought at this time.

Giving a little thought to the pleasure of living, I can say that I never really enjoyed myself until I went to work, and while I have certainly had my share of good times, and more so, I consider these good times made possible by the fact that I had a responsibility placed upon me, and a real job to do during the working hours.

In speaking about all these things, I am positive that I am voicing the sentiments of all the officers of Johnson & Johnson, who are the best friends you and I have, and each one of them is looking forward to the day when you will come here and take up the work.

I want to be complete and to have you know that my plan is to push responsibility upon you just as fast as you can absorb it, and a little faster.

These statements may be a little premature, but they are things that I have been thinking about for a long while, and I suppose you have, so that we might as well say them.

Your action during the war period has certainly shown what one brother was made of. My minor services were small in comparison.

We have just completed a successful War Work Drive here which I went the limit with personally, because I do feel with the war over, I want to do one thing right.

So, Old Top, with all this before you, pilot your gasoline launch home.

With a mighty optimistic outlook on the future and the fact that you have done your Country a service, these will put you in A-1 shape to get after the real job.

Elizabeth and I have your room at the farm all in shape, and as long as you are willing to put up with our company, we want you to make this headquarters.

Good luck to you and congratulations.

Sincerely,
Bob

In the spring of 1919, when his service in the Navy was complete, Seward followed his brother's advice and returned to the company, where he assumed duties in the purchasing and planning departments. The competition that one might have expected to develop between them in the family-owned business never materialized. Seward was content to allow his older brother to assume the reins, and Robert did not resist. Their personalities were well suited to that arrangement. Robert was as naturally assertive as Seward was restrained, and in the coming years they developed an unusually close relationship that ruled out head-to-head competition. It was a relationship rooted in mutual admiration, demonstrated in many ways, and best expressed by a longtime friend of both: "Seward spent all of his life trying to be more like Bob, and Bob spent all of his life trying to be more like Seward."

Several months later, tragedy struck when their mother died of injuries sustained in a fall on a street in London. Evangeline and her husband, John Dennis, had just moved into a new country home at Noxton, in Lincolnshire, and had made plans to sail to the United States aboard the *Mauretania*. Arriving in London to begin the trip, Evangeline fell, breaking her hip on a curbstone. She was taken to a London hospital and two weeks later, on September 9, died of a blood clot at the age of fifty-four. At the time, young Evangeline was in Germany with members of Bernard Baruch's family, tracing how noted works of art had fared during the war. She was at her mother's bedside when she died, and attended her funeral at Noxton, where she was buried.

The Times.

DAILY AND WEEKLY.

OFFICE: - - 189 BURNET STREET.

WEEKLY: Invariably in advance, $1.50 a year
Clubs of ten or over, $1.25 each, with a copy for the
getter-up of the club. The rate to subscribers residing outside the county is $1.70 per annum.

DAILY: Ten cents a week when served by carrier,
or $5 a year in advance when sent by mail.

Communications of whatever nature must be addressed to

A. E. GORDON.

NEW BRUNSWICK, N. J.:

WEDNESDAY, MARCH 3, 1886

A New Factory.

Messrs. Johnson & Co., of New York,
wholesale druggists and drug manufacturers, have made arrangements with Mr.
James Parsons by which they hire of him
the old Janeway and Carpenter factory on
Neilson street, near the railroad bridge.
They will soon begin work with from 50
to 100 hands at the manufacture of standard articles of drugs. Mr. Johnson, the
head of the firm, was in this city Tuesday afternoon making the arrangements
for the opening of the manufactory. He
has engaged Mr. Robert Adrain as counsel
to complete all arrangements.

The Johnson brothers,
Robert, James, Mead

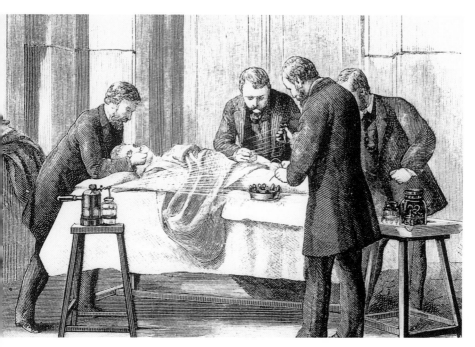

Surgeons use Lister's carbolic spray to kill "invisible germs"

Sir Joseph Lister

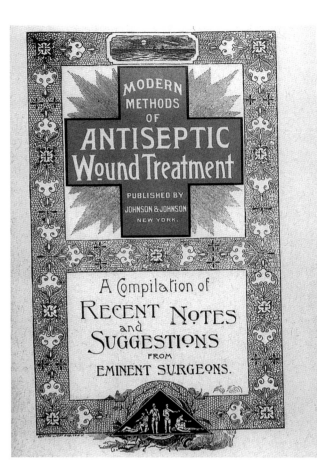

The "how to" manual for surgeons

Fred B. Kilmer

Robert and his mother

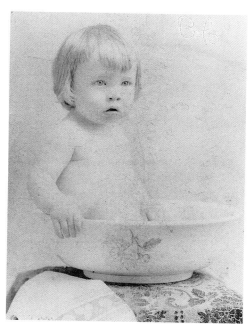

DAILY HOME NEWS
New Brunswick, N. J.
MONDAY, FEBRUARY 7, 1910.

DEATH CALLS A CAPTAIN OF INDUSTRY

Robert W. Johnson, President of the World Famous Johnson & Johnson Company, Succumbs at the Age of 65—Left Business Last Monday Ill—Bright's Disease Brought the End.

Robert Wood Johnson died at 6.40 this morning at his residence, College avenue and Hamilton street, surrounded by all his family and near relatives. He had been unconscious for some time before and passed away peace-

9

THE YOUNG MAYOR

WHEN Robert and Elizabeth returned from their honeymoon to Bermuda they moved into Bellevue, the Johnson farm estate overlooking the Raritan River in Highland Park. In the months before the wedding the gracious farmhouse had been extensively renovated, with frills and feminine touches added here and there, but not without some cost to the charm of the old house. The couple began to entertain often, since many of Elizabeth's girlhood friends were curious to see them in their married state, and to visit the house for the first time. Marrying the handsome and wealthy Robert Wood Johnson was considered a coup. Elizabeth was anxious to show their friends how she had transformed the old farm into a love nest.

The demands to increase wartime production consumed most of Johnson's time, and he put in long hours at the factory. But after moving to Highland Park he began showing an interest in local government and the problems confronting the tiny community of 5,000. Many of the streets were not yet paved, and, as one resident put it, "after a rain there was so much mud in the streets that the milk wagons couldn't get through." Johnson's interest in politics had been heightened by Eddie Farrington's victory in the 1915 City Commission election, and the euphoria of that triumph continued. Johnson was a registered Republican, and his political leanings, like those of his father, were by his own admission "conservative liberal." He made no attempt to resolve the contradiction that label suggested to many.

In early 1918, when a Republican member of the Highland Park Borough Council moved to another town, a vacancy was created, and Johnson was asked if he would fill it. He accepted, and on February 5 was appointed to the unexpired term. He was twenty-four years old. The experience generated an interest in public service and politics that was to last throughout his lifetime. He performed well and soon gained the respect of his older peers and the townspeople as well. When the election of 1919 came around, he decided to run for the council seat he would be vacating. It was a lackluster election, and he conducted a modest and low-key campaign. The Republican Committee, speaking on his behalf, said in its advertising: "Whenever he starts anything he sticks to the finish and sees that the thing goes 'Over the Top.'" A majority of the voters agreed when they went to the polls on November 5. Johnson received 412 votes and placed highest on the ticket. To reward his performance, the borough council decided to make him mayor at the reorganization meeting in January 1920.

New Year's Day 1920 marked the beginning of a new and frenzied decade in America that was aptly labeled the "Roaring Twenties." It began with a bold departure from social custom and convention, symbolized by the heady flamboyance of the flapper era, and it ended with the devastating Great Depression. Between these two extremes—the exhilarating surge upward at the beginning of the 1920s and the sickening plunge downward at the end, when the nation became gripped in the depression—was a decade crammed with highs and lows. To further complicate the 1920s, the nation on January 17, 1920, reluctantly ushered in Prohibition, which banned (until 1933) the production and sale of all alcoholic beverages.

Early that New Year's morning, Johnson made his way down the winding road from Bellevue carrying his inaugural speech carefully written in neat and flowing penmanship on two sheets of paper. It was in many respects a day of quiet triumph for someone whose antics in earlier years had so many heads shaking in despair. His reform had impressed even the doomsayers who had so carefully tracked his earlier escapades and predicted dire results. But it is more likely that his thoughts that morning turned not to his critics but to his father—How proud he would have been!—and perhaps to his good friend and, in some respects, his political inspiration, Eddie Farrington, who had been put to rest just a few weeks earlier.

When Johnson arrived at the borough offices tucked away on the upper floor of a two-story white frame house on North Second Avenue next to the firehouse, he was greeted by his fellow councilmen and a small contingent of townspeople. He carefully read the brief address. "Paving is our first consideration this year," he said. "Allow me to submit recommendations, which at this time seem to be the subject most worthy of your attention." He went on to name the streets to be paved, the equipment to be used, and the instructions the work crews would receive. In closing he said, "There is nothing on the horizon that should interfere with a successful administration during the coming year." The mayorship, not yet an hour old, was now an "administration." He took quite readily to the business of being mayor.

His performance as mayor, at the age of twenty-six, was commendable. The streets were paved, the water system was improved, and the cost of local government was reduced. And once the story of his collecting garbage in his tuxedo made the rounds, his corps of supporters among the townspeople grew rapidly.

There were numerous versions of what actually happened, but he told it best: "One night while I was mayor I was having a formal dinner party with about twenty guests. We were all at the table eating when I was called to the telephone. It was a woman who berated me as being a terrible mayor because her garbage hadn't been collected. So, still in my dinner clothes, I got in the station wagon and drove to her house and asked if she was the woman who had called about the garbage. She said she was, so I asked where I'd find it. She pointed it out to me, so I picked up the can, put it in the station wagon and drove it to the dump and dumped it. Then I went back to hosting my dinner party."

Years later, reflecting on the incident, Johnson admitted that the sudden surge of civic duty that night was stimulated by the second, or perhaps the third, very dry martini he was drinking when the woman called.

Even without such antics, he often drew people into his web on their first encounter. In the summer of 1920, Ed Olly, a recent college graduate working as a civil engineer, first saw him in a park in New Brunswick. Fifty years later, after having forsaken engineering for journalism and jobs on the *New York Evening World* and the *New York Daily News*, Olly wrote about that first meeting in his column in the *New Brunswick Home News*:

> He was on a horse. . . . I was bending over my planetable, taking a sight through the alidade at one of my rodmen, when this fellow comes along the road bordering the golf course. He stopped his horse and asked me what I was doing. I looked up. It is nearly half a century ago but I can still see him clearly. He was the most unbelievably handsome man I ever saw. He was sitting on a brown horse and he wore a blue polo shirt, and his face was ruddy and he had a shock of pure golden hair. He looked like a Viking come down to Earth in one of those Time Tunnel things you see on TV nowadays.
>
> "Who was that?" I asked one of the boys.
>
> "That's Bobby Johnson," he said.
>
> "And that's what he always was in those days—Bobby Johnson. When I saw him on the horse he was twenty-seven years old, but he was already a legend around New Brunswick."

The perception of Johnson being more mature and infinitely more responsible than he was in his teenage years was now accepted, but it was much more difficult not to be seen as a rich young scion, and he did little to discourage that. That reputation eventually spread far beyond New Brunswick, but at the time it was a localized but widely held belief that the Johnson boys could afford any frivolity they chose. And they chose many. The penchant for fast cars, tuned to peak performance by company mechanics, gave way to fast boats when Seward returned from the Navy. They owned a variety of small craft, each faster than the previous one. And often, like children's toys, they didn't last long.

The fate of one was recalled by a Staten Island resident: "Around 1920, give or take a few years, a very high speed boat travelled quite frequently up and down Raritan Bay. People in Tottenville referred to it as the 'Johnson boat.' The boat had been built on the Great Lakes. When Johnson placed his order he was fourth in line, with the promise of having to wait some time. For a payment of $4,000 to the one whose boat was currently being built, he was able to take it over. On the first day out, going hell bent for election, the boat hit a submerged obstacle and tore a good sized hole in the bottom. Nase Manley [who was aboard] said his most vivid recollection, after recovering from the shock, was Seward carefully studying the chart and exclaiming that there was no obstacle there."

Elizabeth did not take well to her husband's racing around in fast cars and boats. A homebody, she preferred a more sedate life. Ever since their marriage, Robert and Elizabeth had been consulting physicians in Philadelphia and New York about their inability to have children. Then, early in 1920, Elizabeth learned she was pregnant and, fearing she would lose the baby, stayed very close to home until the birth of Robert Wood Johnson III on September 9, 1920.

·

Some subtle changes that would soon become more abundantly clear were taking place in the business. The most important of these was Johnson's expressed intention to gain control of the company's common stock. Some of it had passed from the family's control with the acquisition of the J. Ellwood Lee Company in 1905, a transaction that brought to New Brunswick the services of Frank R. Jones, who now held the key position of General Manager at Johnson & Johnson. On January 26, 1920, Jones wrote to the company's attorney, Archibald Cox:

My dear Cox. The fact of the matter is, the Junior member of our organization, that is the son of your good friend R.W., is anxious to eventually control all of the common stock of the company, and I encouraged him with the hope I could make an exchange of my common for his preferred. But I fear nothing can be done in that direction until the obnoxious income taxes are removed, and from the manner in which we are spending funds in this country, I do not think, even if one would live as long as Methuselah, they would be able to see the day when these taxes are no longer in order.

In the background another situation was developing—the uncertain health of James Johnson. Then sixty-four, James had never been in robust health, and now there was some suspicion that he might be suffering from a form of leukemia. No firm diagnosis was made, but James began spending more and more time away from the office on fishing and hunting trips. When not engaged in those activities, he was content with a good cigar and a mint julep. Returning from one of his long absences, he wrote Cox on December 17, 1920.

My dear Cox:
This is simply to notify you that I am sitting at my desk in the office of Johnson & Johnson, not to do any work because I never did, but I have been away so long I did not want my friends to forget me.

Sincerely,
James W. Johnson

While his responsibilities dwindled, James's reputation for kindness did not. One day an enterprising youth talked his way past both the factory guard and the secretaries. He was a young apprentice engineer from Germany, then working at the Mack Truck Company in Plainfield, New Jersey, who had developed a toy airplane made of balsa wood. He called it the "Jiffy Plane," and his plan was to sell it on weekends at Coney Island to finance his passage back to Germany, to begin his formal engineering education. But his entrepreneurial efforts were stymied by his inability to find

[148]

a supplier of boxes to hold the twenty-five-cent Jiffy Plane. Then the engineers at Mack, perhaps as a joke, advised him to go see James Johnson, whose company produced its own boxes for many of its products.

Once in James's office, the youth demonstrated the Jiffy Plane by flying it around the spacious room. James told him that tooling up for a box for the Jiffy Plane was just not possible, but he did offer to try to convince one of his outside suppliers to take on the job. After a telephone call a supplier agreed to meet with the boy. The supplier then set up the machinery to cut, print, and assemble the cartons — ten gross of them — for a total cost of just three dollars. James, of course, had subsidized the Jiffy Plane project. The youth, Carl K. Hammon, later returned to the United States and became a successful consulting engineer. "I have never forgotten what I learned about the meaning of America from James Wood Johnson," he wrote many years later.

The absence of James from the business at this time was not nearly as important as it would have been a few years earlier, since the entire business was undergoing a major transition. The early discoveries of antiseptic — and later sterile — surgical dressings and sutures had already been improved to the limits of technology, and the machines for producing them, and the apparatus for sterilization, were operating at peak performance. New growth in the business would have to come from other sources, and the logical choice was to bring new consumer products to the market. Once again the timing was right, for the consumer public had been neglected in order to meet the nation's wartime priorities. A new toothpaste was introduced, in a strange-looking collapsible metal tube that had to be properly squeezed for the best results. Baby cream was added as a companion product to the already enormously popular Johnson's Baby Powder. Then these two new products were combined, along with several other products, into a single gift box for new babies.

The "accidental" introduction of baby powder, an outgrowth of including a small amount of talc with medicinal plasters to soothe irritated skin, was followed in 1921 by more serendipity—the creation of the Band-Aid Brand Adhesive Bandage. The first one was devised in the kitchen of a cotton mill employee, Earle E. Dickson, whose young bride, Josephine, kept cutting herself while preparing meals in the kitchen of their Highland Park home. Patiently, Dickson kept bandaging her fingers, but this happened so often he decided to make a ready-to-use bandage she could apply herself. On a large strip of surgical tape he placed small pieces of gauze at intervals, then covered the adhesive with crinoline for protection. From then on, whenever Josephine cut her finger, which was often, she simply snipped off a piece of the tape-and-gauze pad and applied it as a ready-made bandage.

When Dickson told a co-worker about his "invention" he was encouraged to inform his superintendent. "The boys in the front office loved the concept," Dickson recalled. On November 9, 1920, the first product was made by hand: a single adhesive strip measuring two and a half inches wide and eighteen inches long. The user had to cut it into small strips, just as Josephine Dickson did. Each retail package contained one strip, and sales that first year were an unimpressive $3,000. Next, machines to mass-produce the adhesive bandages were designed, but sales remained low for eight long years, prompting the company's advertising agency, Young & Rubicam, to conclude that adhesive bandages would never become a popular product. Following a failed test market, the agency, on May 31, 1928, wrote the company:

> Attached is a report covering the results of the Band-Aid Bandage test campaigns. From this it is clearly apparent that neither sampling nor advertising alone, nor even a combination of sampling, advertising and window display, is sufficient to create a popular demand for Band-Aid Bandages in sufficient quantity to justify the cost of the effort.

Rejecting the advice of the agency, Johnson & Johnson persisted in its marketing efforts, and the Band-Aid Bandage later became one of the world's most popular consumer products. And Earl

Dickson became a vice president, all because his young bride was clumsy in the kitchen.

The key to increased sales of consumer products remained the corner drugstore, which was now facing two new threats to business. One was the new mobility Americans were enjoying with their first automobiles, which allowed them to range far beyond the corner drugstore for their shopping. The other was the identity crisis confronting pharmacists because of the wide array of sundries being sold in their stores, from school supplies to hairpins to ice cream cones. They welcomed the new business, but they were concerned about this new challenge to their professionalism. Sensing an opportunity, the company created the slogan "Your Druggist Is More Than a Merchant" and made it the central theme of its national advertising. Someone even suggested putting it in lights on the mammoth sign on top of the factory—and it was. Thousands of railroad passengers also became familiar with the slogan.

To the delight of druggists, the popularity of the slogan grew with each new advertisement that used it. Soon it was appearing in thirty-five magazines, until one eminent pharmaceutical journal refused to accept it because, it claimed, the slogan presented an incomplete thought and too many people were supplying the ending "He is a bootlegger." Not wishing to encourage that conclusion, the marketing department quickly revised the slogan to read: "Your druggist is more than a merchant. Try the drug store first."

That did it. Pharmacy associations all over the nation adopted it as an official slogan. In England it became "Your Chemist Is More Than a Merchant," and Canadians translated it into French. A pharmacy leader proclaimed, "Such cooperation is entitled to the full support of the druggists of the country," and sales of Johnson & Johnson products in drugstores soared.

·

Robert Johnson had set his sights on gaining control of the common shares of the company long before he made those intentions known. He also believed that Johnson & Johnson's destiny would be in his hands as its president, and he was confident of this long before others in the company considered him ready for that position. He had made that determination at the time of his father's death, vowing that someday he would succeed him. Some in the company who had been so worried that Robert would never be successful were now beginning to worry that he would. They saw him as a threat to their own security, and representing a new generation of managers who had both ability and charisma.

As the consumer business continued to grow, Johnson began devoting more of his time and energy to sales and marketing, which he considered his area of strength. Along with this new growth came a concern that the company might lose some of the closeness it had always enjoyed with its employees. Johnson often used the terms "family of companies" and "family of employees," and he believed this spirit was responsible for much of the company's success. To keep employees "in touch," as he put it, he asked Fred Kilmer to start an internal publication that would bring employees closer together. Referring to it as "a sort of intimate family bulletin," he urged Kilmer: "Please do not let this idea get away."

Rapid growth brought another, even more pressing problem. In the aftermath of the war, production continued in high gear as supplies of hospital and consumer products were replenished. But as this tapered off, Johnson and his colleagues began to speculate on where future growth would come from. He later wrote to his uncle, Mead Johnson, "Sometime about 1921, I determined that America was being forced to a policy of isolation and that our export business was about to be destroyed." The answer, he contended, was to begin building an international business based on manufacturing in foreign countries.

At the time, there were strong arguments for isolation. Many Americans believed that the country had been drawn into the war needlessly and had paid bitterly. The nation had suffered staggering casualties, and all across America the memorials to the war dead being erected were painful reminders of the cost of becoming involved on foreign soil. A policy of isolation was seen as the only answer—let America take care of America, and let the foreigners take care of the foreigners. Political issues aside, the risks of expanding a business overseas were many, and the rewards were uncertain. The lines were soon drawn, Johnson noted later. He was in favor of establishing manufacturing facilities in international locations, and he was "virtually alone."

In support of his belief that overseas manufacturing should be established, Johnson proposed to the Board of Control, of which he was not yet a member, that he and Seward embark on a worldwide fact-finding trip to confirm the feasibility of the plan. This touched off a heated debate within management that continued for more than a year. Some favored expanding the network of agents and distributors already in place. A few clung to the belief that any international expansion would be inimical to the company's best interests. One or two supported Johnson's position, but not very vocally.

Toward the end of 1921, while the Board was still debating the merits of the worldwide trip, the two brothers decided to cruise the Bahamas for five weeks in two chartered boats—no business, this was to be a lark. They spent hours studying nautical charts of the West Indies and arranged to charter the *Zodiac*, a lumbering Great Lakes express cruiser with a 1,000-horsepower engine, and the *Tramp*, a Cape Cod catboat, for fishing and to haul the supplies. The planning rivaled that for a military invasion, with hundreds of five-gallon tins of gasoline delivered by an oil company to various remote anchorages throughout the islands. In early February they left the snowy north and took a train to Miami, where they were met at the Flamingo Hotel by the eight-man crew; two captains, sailors, stewards, and a Bahamian pilot who knew the waters.

Both brothers had a passion for the sea. Robert, especially, reveled in the adventure and romanticism of the journey and compared it with the stories about the South Seas that he read so avidly. "Who does not have the ambition to visit these islands as master of his own ship?" he later wrote. Where there was no adventure they created it. At Gun Cay they encountered the friendly "booze fleet" lying at anchor waiting for the "rum runners" from Florida to buy their cargo of English gin (at $14 a case) and authentic Scotch whiskey (at $28 a case). For the next five weeks, their days were spent lazily sailing and fishing, strolling native beaches, exploring the islands. At Nassau, they joined in the nighttime revelry at the Colonial Hotel, where two young, handsome, wealthy males were always welcome.

At the hotel dock, Seward arranged an elaborate launching of a shallow draft craft he had purchased by mail and hauled along on the trip. He named it "Puddle Duck." With much pomp, and quantities of champagne that cost more than the boat itself, he staged a noisy christening. The dozens of natives lining the dock for the launching roared with laughter as Seward swung a bottle of champagne for the christening and broke the bow of the boat.

Robert kept a diary of the trip, a casual recording of events ranging from treacherous seas to his brother Seward's persistent calm and casual disregard of anything remotely disruptive. He was in constant awe of that quality in Seward. In time, however, his brother's tranquillity took a toll: "While this life is restful," Robert wrote, "I am beginning to wish for the burning road of industry again."

The trip ended in Miami on March 17, after a harrowing sail from Bimini across a storm-tossed Gulf Stream. Still dressed in their sea togs, and wearing overcoats and derby hats, the brothers dashed to the train station for the trip back north, having satisfied for the first time their spirit of adventure. But as the wheels of the train clicked away the miles, they began talking about future trips, and someday building their own ship, "a ship that will safely take us anywhere we may wish to go," Robert wrote later. The daydreams were soon put aside, and it was back to work, and home to Elizabeth, who was patiently caring for baby Robert at Bellevue.

Now the company's Second Vice President, Robert was moving up the ranks. His stock holdings gave him a seat on the Board of

Directors, and the next big move up would be to the Board of Control, the domain of the small group of senior executives who made the day-to-day decisions. From the earliest days, his father had emphasized strong management—it was the rock on which Johnson & Johnson was built. One of the most competent managers, Frank Jones, took a liking to young Johnson, saw his potential, and became his mentor. Jones was a good teacher.

In the spring of 1922 Johnson decided not to seek reelection as mayor of Highland Park, citing increasing business responsibilities. His future role in politics would be as "king-maker," as newspaperman Frank Deiner put it some years later. As it turned out, Deiner didn't get to cover the election that year because he had become a "celebrity journalist." He had identified the bodies in the infamous Halls-Mills murder, which also thrust New Brunswick into the headlines and brought to the city such journalistic luminaries as Damon Runyon and Irwin S. Cobb.

That fall, Johnson again presented to the Board of Control his plan for a fact-finding trip to explore global markets. He later wrote: "Our company needed first-hand information about the chances of doing business in a vast and powerful family of nations spread all over the world. In addition to the British Empire, we need facts on other nations, such as France, China and Japan." The board was not receptive at first, and James Johnson resisted on the grounds that the present export business would be threatened. Finally, after much discussion, Jones and the other board members gave their approval for the trip. Young Johnson's foresight in recognizing the potential of global expansion would become a milestone in Johnson & Johnson's future growth.

"We spent a full year in preparation for the trip," Johnson later wrote, "in reading and talking to experts, and in securing letters of introduction that really would open the minds of the people we had to see. If we were going to consult a bank in India, for example, we wanted an introduction from the head of the Bank of England. If we were to call on an important public health official, our letter had to come from someone high up in the Rockefeller Foundation. Getting those letters took time, but they also spelled success for our investigation."

Laden with trunks filled with the fruits of their research, the Johnson brothers sailed from New York on October 1, 1923, aboard the SS *Olympic* on the first leg of a seven-month world journey. The ship was barely out of port when it encountered heavy seas and gale-force winds. Elizabeth and three-year-old Robert Jr. accompanied the Johnson brothers as far as London and Paris, and en route home their ship encountered more fierce storms on the North Atlantic. It was not a pleasant trip for her and the child.

Johnson had laid out three objectives for the trip: (1) to determine Johnson & Johnson's best course of action in international business over the next five years; (2) to determine whether establishing manufacturing facilities overseas was a viable option; (3) to learn more about the supply of cotton in foreign markets, since this was a major component of many of the company's surgical and first-aid products. The arduous trip took the two brothers to sixteen areas of the world, including London, Paris, Bombay, Sydney, Peking, Borneo, and Ceylon. They followed a rigorous routine of official meetings and informal talks, visited scores of pharmacies and hospitals, and step by step pieced together an evaluation of the business potential in the worldwide marketplace. The carefully planned letters of introduction paved the way for meetings with high-level officials who had direct knowledge about the purchase and distribution of medical products, about their particular government's approach to health care, and about hospital care. The brothers also probed to learn more about health education, which had always been one of the company's great strengths in building the business.

The initial meetings in London, with businessmen, bankers, and government officials, went well. Johnson was particularly interested in determining governments' attitudes toward providing health care for citizens. He also visited the first of many hospitals along the way—to gather facts for the business, but also to satisfy his intense personal interest in advancing patient care. But the meeting with Messrs. Selby and Butterfield, the company's London agents, did not go well, especially when Johnson brought up the subject of opening a manufacturing plant there and hiring a sales force. He was hardly out of the office when Selby and Butterfield, feeling threatened, cabled Frank Jones in New Brunswick to ask for "a guarantee of future employment." When Jones sought Johnson's advice on what to do, he replied that the business the English gentlemen were generating for the company "won't pay for your motor car tires." "I am astounded at their attitude," he cabled. Then, calming down, he urged Jones to give Selby and Butterfield a vote of confidence.

Johnson had arranged to send periodic reports back to Jones as the trip progressed, and then to present a final report to the Board of Control on his return. During the seven-month trip, he wrote Jones thirty-six letters, some of them very detailed. As always, he treated Jones with deference, addressing him as "My dear Mr. Jones." Seward undoubtedly contributed to the reports, but he sent Jones only one letter of his own during the entire trip, and that was devoted to regrets over the death of President Woodrow Wilson, and a prediction that the League of Nations would collapse. Jones wrote Robert twelve letters, discussing events happening at the company, and keeping him informed on sales and profits.

From London the brothers went to Lille in northern France to look at the textile industry there. En route back to Paris they stopped at Brussels. From Paris, Robert wrote: "I am not like some of the United States Senators who go to two Paris cafés and return to make a statement about the economic and political situation of France. I am considering our own business and nothing else, and am not at all disappointed. Some day there will be a great business to be done in France, and if we could establish ours inexpensively now or at some time in the future, it would be worthy of consideration."

They continued their journey overland to Marseilles and then by ship to Cairo. There they examined Egyptian cotton production, concluded that it would be too expensive for use in their products, and decided to look for lower-priced cotton in India or China. Johnson reported back to Jones that he saw a market in Egypt for absorbent cotton, a process not yet introduced there, and for medicated plasters if an advertising campaign could be launched in Arabic. Warehousing imported products in Egypt, he wrote, would make it possible to serve Sudan, the Holy Land, and Turkey, but he dismissed any thought of manufacturing in Egypt. While in Egypt they visited pharmacies and gathered information on general health and sanitation conditions. Johnson discovered, to his dismay, that retail business in Egypt was not, as he put it, "on a very high moral plane." Moreover, he believed that the local sales agent for the company, an Irishman, had "absorbed a bit more of the local color than we think is necessary."

Boarding the SS *Fan Peterszoon Coen*, they went through the Suez Canal for the trip across the Red Sea to Ceylon. "This ship is very comfortable, the food good, and the people terrible," Johnson wrote. "We have about ten books to read on India and Ceylon." Arriving at the British Crown Colony of Colombo, he toured the native bazaars and found that the company was getting a fair share of the business. The other opportunities he considered meager. "A traveller on a motorcycle will cover the entire trade in three weeks," he reported to Jones.

On December 4 Johnson wrote from Bombay: "The Surgeon General was not a bit cordial. . . . He seemed to view our travels with considerable suspicion." His overall impression of India was not much better: "The Indians seem to be more anxious to debate, build new capitals and to discuss politics than to get down to the work of educating their young people and improving sanitary conditions, which are deplorable and beyond description." Still, he saw the possibility of doing an expanding business in India. "We can develop this business with our own people," he wrote. They spent Christmas in Calcutta, and Robert reported from there: "We find that honesty is a very rare thing among the natives and that work is just as rare among the whites."

After visiting Darjeeling, the two moved on to Surabaja, Java, in the Netherlands East Indies, the smallest of the four islands in the Dutch archipelago. "Our plan has stood the test of criticism from London to here," Johnson wrote, "and that phase of the situation I now conclude is right. From now on it is simply a question of whether enough business can be developed to warrant its adoption." From Java they boarded the SS *Montoro* and sailed for Australia, and Johnson wrote from Sydney: "What we have done is very simple. We started from New York with an idea; we wished to know two things. Is the idea practicable and is it worthwhile. After nearly six months of study en route and nearly a year of study before leaving, I am now convinced that the method is all right that we have in mind. I am not yet convinced that it is worthwhile."

Aboard the SS *Albans* they sailed to British North Borneo, then on to Manilla, where they had tea with the archbishop and drank rum in the Army and Navy Club. "If we can sell any natives it should be the Filipinos," noted Robert. They then moved on to Hong Kong, where they arranged to give some of the Johnson & Johnson products on display to charity because they were dusty. They sailed up the Pearl River to Canton on a boat with barricades and machine guns to defend against bandits, then to Peking, noting: "Our plaster business in China is worth careful attention." After boarding the SS *Empress of Australia* for the long journey across the Pacific, the two brothers arrived at Seattle on May 9 — the end of their seven-month journey.

Returning to New Jersey late in May, Robert immediately began pushing to form a British company, recommending that a factory there be leased rather than built. "It would do until we learn how to run a plant in England, and prove that we can win customers there," he said. "Leasing would let us get going at once, and it also would save the firm money if our experiment fails." With some apprehension the board approved the plan and an executive was dispatched to London to search for a suitable factory to lease. The decision to begin international manufacturing, a result of Johnson's findings on his trip, and his constant urgings when he returned, planted the seeds of what became the world's largest health-care business.

By late summer the company was ready to sign a lease for a new British factory, once the Messrs. Selby and Butterfield could agree on a location. It was decided at the start that the two Englishmen would participate in the new venture, but every time a factory location pleased Selby, Butterfield would object, and when a location pleased Butterfield, Selby would object. Johnson went to England to try to get them to agree. "We soon found that the problem had little to do with either good or bad factories," he recalled later. "The trouble was that Mr. Butterfield lived about 30 miles south of London, while Mr. Selby lived 25 miles north. A plant north of the city would be inconvenient for Butterfield, while one south of it would be inconvenient for Selby. A location east or west of London was inconvenient for both."

The argument dragged on for three more weeks, at which time Johnson threatened to make the decision himself. Finally Selby and Butterfield agreed on a factory located at Slough in Buckinghamshire, twenty miles west of London. Machinery was crated in New Brunswick and shipped to Slough, and Johnson stayed on to help get the factory in operation. To the English workers, he was just another hand. "If I wanted a wrench, I first had to learn to call it an spanner. Then I blundered around until some workman told me to 'hop down the street and buy one from an ironmonger.' "

The factory was located in a bucolic setting along with a cluster of other plants on what was known as the Old Trading Estate. A British journalist from the *Slough Observer* wrote about his first visit: "There is a stretch of bright green lawns, at the end of which a golden lettered board announced the name of Johnson & Johnson, and crossing the lawns you come to the red wall of the factory building. The entrance is through a quaint porch, such as might lead into the abode of some alchemist of olden times, and upon the porch is a red peculiar cross, the symbol of the firm's cabalistic, and for all the world suggestive of the arts and lore of the Rosicrucian back in the Dark Ages. . . . Not an unsuitable first impression. Greater wonders are done here every hour of the day than all those alchemists performed in a hundred years. The firm is associated with two other companies, one in America and one in Canada, both bearing similar names, but it is an all-British firm using only Empire materials for its manufactures, and employing only British labour."

The reporter got just the impression that Johnson wanted to create, that it was an all-British firm. It was the beginning of a philosophy that was carried out at many of the company's international ventures through the years: Be as local as you can be.

10

"FACTORIES CAN BE BEAUTIFUL"

T H E view from the bluff on which Bellevue Farm perched overlooking the Raritan River was peaceful and comforting. Usually there was sublime stillness. In the fall of 1924, first occasionally and then with increasing audacity, the stillness was broken by the desperate whine of engines straining to keep a collection of flimsy airplanes aloft.

The source of this fascination for residents of the area was the new Hadley Field, recently carved out of the farm of John R. Hadley Sr. in nearby South Plainfield. The U.S. Post Office Department had prevailed on Hadley to relinquish part of his farm to accommodate the airplanes of the Air Mail Service introduced to the nation six years before. With understandable trepidation, Farmer Hadley agreed, and the airstrip became the new eastern terminus of the Air Mail Service, replacing a less-safe field on foggy Long Island. The new runway had only one drawback — a dip near the center that often sent unsuspecting pilots airborne again soon after touchdown.

Hadley soon began luring a collection of private pilots and their primitive aircraft, and together they filled the skies with noise and feats of daring. One of the most intrepid pilots was Kenneth Russell Unger, slightly plumpish and easygoing on the ground but a fearless daredevil aloft. Unger and his other pioneer friends soon were attracting hordes of onlookers and admirers, who would line the cornfields to watch in awe as the flying machines were coaxed to the heavens. One day Robert Johnson, who had gone to Hadley Field to watch Ken Unger perform, was himself attracted. Johnson asked Unger to teach him to fly, and what began as a student and mentor relationship became a friendship.

There wasn't much that Unger couldn't do behind the control stick of an airplane. His first venture into the skies took place in 1908, at the age of ten. His parents had taken him to Paris, and there he managed to talk a hot-air balloonist into giving him a free ride. When the balloon returned to the ground, his enthusiasm for flying was still soaring. Nine years later he was back in France as a fighter pilot with the Royal Canadian Air Force and earning the Distinguished Flying Cross for downing nine German planes and a kite balloon. "I ended up in command of Fighter Squadron 210 in France," he said. "It was what we called the RFC, the 'Refugees from Conscription.' "

Unger had joined the Royal Air Force in Canada when he learned they would teach him to fly, but two days before he was scheduled to get his commission as a second lieutenant, the U.S. Navy ordered him to report to Brooklyn for active duty as an apprentice seaman. "It was an embarrassing situation," Unger recalled, "but my father straightened it out with the recruiting officer and I received an honorable discharge from the Navy and a check for $6.26 — they called it retainer pay." Soon he was on his way to France, with a total of fifty-six hours of flying instruction. There he performed heroic feats in his Sopwith Camel.

Returning home after the war, Unger joined a group of war aces who were barnstorming in California. Later he became the "baby" of the new transcontinental Air Mail Service. Once, on the air mail route from Salt Lake City to Reno, he made a successful emergency deadstick landing in a treacherous mountain pass in Nevada.

Walking away unhurt, he decided to ride for help on a horse graz-ing nearby. "I figured I'd take a ride, but I must have forgotten to fasten my seatbelt. The next thing I knew I was going through the pony's version of a snap roll and Immelmann Turn. Not too long after, I was on the ground with a broken ankle." The next day he was back flying the route to Salt Lake City with his ankle strapped to the controls.

When Unger came east to Hadley Field, he formed Unger's Fly-ing Service, gave flying lessons, and on Sundays thrilled crowds as a daredevil with an aerobatic team, "The Three Black Crows." Later he teamed up with stunt pilot John Perri, who performed wing-walking acts and had more than three hundred parachute jumps to his credit. Hadley was to become a cradle of early commercial avia-tion, and on the night of July 1, 1925, a throng of 15,000 watched as Pilot Dean C. Smith took off carrying eighty-seven pounds of mail on the initial leg of the first coast-to-coast night air mail service. His DeHavilland biplane, named "The Fastest Dollar" (and with a dollar bill taped alongside the open cockpit), was forced down twelve miles short of Cleveland. Smith and the mail both survived.

Johnson became one of Unger's most eager students and soon gained the respect of the master for his skills in the air. "He handled a plane very well and was very keen in the air," Unger recalled. "He and I got along awfully well together, and we had a lot of fun." Some years later Unger would go to work for Johnson as chief pilot for Johnson & Johnson.

Unger recalled those early flights with Johnson: "Soon we were taking my open-cockpit plane on business trips. When we'd go cross-country he'd watch the clock and at the end of an hour he'd say, 'All right, toot toot!' That would be the signal for him to take over the controls for the next hour. Then he would turn it back to me an hour later. He loved to fly, and we always kept a special flying suit for him, with a nice helmet and goggles, and we had ear-phones so we could talk back and forth. We got ourselves a Curtiss

Robin and then a Wright. Those old planes you could sense with the seat of your pants, and they would talk to you and you could put them down on a dime. Then the new airplanes came along with all that garbage hanging on them, spoilers and brakes and all that stuff. They can get you in trouble."

As much as flying intrigued Johnson, the lure of the sea still had a strong hold on him. Ever since their odyssey to the Bahamas, he and Seward had talked about building the sailing ship of their dreams, and in 1924 they commissioned William H. Hand Jr. to design a two-masted 140-foot sailing schooner, which was built at the Hodgdon Brothers Shipyard at East Boothbay, Maine. Christening it the "Zodiac," after the ship they had chartered for the trip to the Bahamas, they began planning their first adventure—a six-week cruise along the coast of Labrador. They would be exploring for timberland and mineral deposits, they explained, and a Yale University mineralogist, Duane Stoneleigh, was invited to accompany them. But mostly the trip would be a pleasure jaunt devoted to sailing, fishing, and hunting.

As their departure drew closer, the two brothers added a more adventuresome twist by announcing that they planned to follow the route of the Nutting Expedition, which had mysteriously vanished a year before in an open boat off the coast of Labrador. An eager press added far more intrigue to the trip than was justified, and newspaper headlines announced the departure of the *Zodiac* from Humberhead, Newfoundland, on July 4, 1925.

There was a theory that the Nutting expedition had been shipwrecked and its survivors were stranded somewhere along the desolate Labrador coast. The Johnsons had promised to make a close inspection of the promontories along the coast where a shipwrecked Nutting party might have placed distress signals. This duplicated a similar search a year before by the U.S. Navy cruiser *Trenton* shortly after the expedition was reported missing. Now the press raised everyone's hopes again, and the suspense built up

[165]

during the six weeks the *Zodiac* was away and out of touch. When the party returned on August 20, the news was disappointing. The *Detroit Free Press* ran the story on page one:

NEW NUTTING
SEARCH FAILS

R.W. and J.S. Johnson returned today from an unsuccessful 4,000 mile search in northern waters for a trace of the lost Nutting Expedition which left Iceland in August 1924. Sailing from Nova Scotia in the yacht *Zodiac* they penetrated Hamilton Inlet to Labrador, interviewing natives at points along the coast without obtaining trace of the missing men. They said they believed the expedition struck an iceberg. The Nutting Expedition left Reykjavik, Iceland, in 1924 in a 40-foot sloop *Leif Erickson* for Baddeck, Nova Scotia, following the trail of the Vikings. William Washburn Nutting, commodore of the Cruising Club of America, was in command with Arthur S. Hilderbrand, a writer, John Towdahl, a marine painter, and a Norwegian skipper as members of the crew.

What began as a pleasure trip that Johnson had called the fulfillment of a boyhood dream was now being described by the nation's press as a failed search. Typical of the headlines across the country was the one in the *New York American*:

JOHNSON BACK WITH
NO WORD OF NUTTING

Undaunted, Johnson faced the reporters and seemed to enjoy it, as always. "We definitely established the fact that William Washington Nutting did not land on the coast of Labrador," he told them. Then he added somewhat sheepishly, "We made the trip for pleasure and not a dull moment was registered, as we all found enjoyment in the invigorating air and in our trips over the rock formations along the coast." When pressed for details he said that the "invigorating air" was filled with mosquitoes, black flies, deer flies, and moose flies that swarmed over their food and penetrated

[166]

every type of protection they could devise. Then he added that the Labrador mosquitoes were far more menacing than the infamous ones in New Jersey and had made the trip "distinctly miserable."

The rest of the party, including the Norwegian captain and the crew of eight Gloucester fishermen, felt much the same. When asked what he thought of Labrador, the Norwegian replied laconically: "Given a choice of thirteen cents and all of Labrador, I would take the thirteen cents."

A brighter note on the trip was a visit to the Grenfell Mission. Dr. William T. Grenfell, who had spent twenty-three years of his life running missions to serve the deep-sea fishermen of Labrador and northern Newfoundland, had a surprise visit from the Johnson brothers. Carrying with them a supply of medical products, cotton, gauze, sutures, mustard plasters, and even Lister's Dental Floss, Robert and Seward exchanged pleasantries with the doughty English physician, inquired about his work, and then, as mysteriously as they had appeared, left to continue their odyssey. Near Cape Mugford they encountered Indian tribes as they came into the Hudson Bay trading posts to exchange furs. When they returned they told intriguing stories of their adventures.

In a period when the calendar rather than the clock was more important for measuring most business and leisure activities, six weeks spent sailing to Labrador was not considered an abuse of time. But Johnson's long absences from home did not please Elizabeth, and added to the strain that, friends felt, was on their marriage from the start. Elizabeth still preferred to stay at home, tending to young Robert, who was then going on five years old. But those closest to the couple saw trouble brewing. The sojourns to the Bahamas and Labrador, and the extended business trip around the world, did nothing to smooth the troubled waters of the marriage.

The business, on the other hand, did not appear to suffer during Johnson's long absences. The proliferation of new products continued, and the new thrust into international markets held great promise as the manufacturing operation in England began to take shape. The outlook was reported glowingly by Kilmer in the *Red Cross Messenger*: "With the reputation for quality already established abroad, and with a factory as efficient as the one at home, worldwide familiarity with Johnson & Johnson products will be given an added impetus." Then, almost as an aside to his audience of drugstore owners, Kilmer added: "Products that are unquestionably accepted throughout the world add prestige to any drug store."

By then Fred Kilmer had gained what amounted to folk-hero status among the druggists of the nation for his steadfast promotion of the slogan "Your Druggist Is More Than a Merchant. Try the Drug Store First." With uncharacteristic immodesty he asked his *Messenger* readers: "Is it any wonder that the slogan has become a part of the language of the people?" After conducting his own "research," he concluded that the slogan had been used in company advertising more than "one billion times" since its introduction four years earlier. In fact, in his penchant for preciseness he put the number at exactly 1,010,006,496 times, though he did not explain how he arrived at that total, or vouch for its accuracy.

Kilmer now was busy unveiling another promotion he had helped concoct: the first annual National Pharmacy Week. As champion of this latest effort to boost the professionalism of pharmacy, Kilmer admonished drugstore owners that this was not an occasion for commercialism or special sales. "There are other weeks for that," he advised. "Now is the time to demonstrate that art, science and business are blended in pharmacy." He urged pharmacists to erect displays at the front of the store showing their apparatus for distillation, grinding, pressing, evaporation, and other processes used in their behind-the-counter permutations. For good measure, Kilmer commandeered the gigantic electric sign atop the factory and had "National Pharmacy Week" emblazoned in lights for all to see.

Kilmer's taciturn and usually undemonstrative manner was an intriguing contrast to his adroitness at promotion. Among his many talents, he was a born salesman and a promoter. He had an exquisite sense of timing, and was deft at turning just the right phrases to spark a response. He was also a serious writer, and his flair for words had an underpinning of knowledge of many subjects. When he took pen in hand — or began to peck away on his typewriter — the results could be fascinating, like the time he looked back, and then ahead at things to come.

It was in 1926, when the company marked its fortieth anniversary, that Kilmer used the occasion to look back over the four decades of medical and scientific progress that he and his generation had experienced. Seventy-five at the time, he was working daily just as hard as ever. (Kilmer, it was said, never did retire; he just died.) He wrote a paper titled "Land Marks 1886–1926," in which he traced the highlights of the company's development, along with advances in medicine and surgery, discoveries in biology and chemistry, and important inventions that had occurred during that period. Kilmer also looked ahead and speculated on what he termed "things to come." This is what he saw:

Light, heat, power derived from radiant energy from the Sun and the center of the Earth.

Ectogenesis.

Destructive wars — extinction of civilization.

Exhaustion of world's supply of coal, oil, wood, paper.

Decline of earth's food supply to exhaustion and revivification, leading to overproduction.

Interplanetary communication.

Disintegration of the atom; destruction of the world; end of this universe, with the creation of a new heaven and new earth.

Given his usual optimistic outlook, some of Kilmer's predictions were grim, but this was the scientist talking, not the kindly old gentleman.

While Kilmer was focusing on pharmacy and science, Johnson was nurturing new ideas about advances in industry and management. One area that concerned him greatly was that, in the eyes of many, run-down, poorly maintained factories had come to symbolize American industry. Nowhere was this more apparent than in the begrimed textile mills of New England and the South, where working conditions were appalling. In 1926 Johnson decided the company would build the nation's first modern, single-story textile mill on a large tract of land on the outskirts of Gainesville, Georgia. Adjacent to the mill, they would build two hundred modern homes for the mill employees, a grade school, a medical facility, and several churches. Nothing like it had ever been built before, and, when completed, it would revolutionize the construction of textile mills.

Work on the project began immediately. The land site included the watershed of the Chattahoochee River, to ensure a pure water supply for the spinning and weaving operations. The cotton gauze produced at the mill would be sent to New Brunswick to be made into sterile surgical dressings. Built into the sprawling, one-story mill was both technical excellence and an aesthetic beauty that was new to the textile industry. One visiting writer declared: "The plant in Georgia is as nearly perfect as a modern cotton mill could be." Even before its completion it was a showplace that attracted factory and mill designers from all over the world.

In Chicopee Village, as it came to be known, thirty-one variations of modern brick homes were built with three and four bedrooms and laid out on gracefully curved, attractively landscaped streets. Power lines were placed underground, and the homes were among the first in northeastern Georgia to have indoor plumbing, electricity, and hot water. The new mill and the adjoining village changed the lives of those fortunate enough to work and live there.

One woman employee described her experience some years later in a letter to the company. "There was no child labor law then so as we got big enough, not old enough, we went to work. Spinners were paid 10 cents a day and doffer's wages were 35 cents. We worked eleven hours a day. Then in 1927 we heard of the new mill at Chicopee, and moved there with our four children and my mother. We had a modern five-room brick house with all of the modern conveniences, and went to work in a modern mill where all was light and clean. A new life was opened for us."

To celebrate the opening of the new mill, local businessmen hosted a barbecue for employees and hundreds of area residents. Later, they sent Robert Johnson a gift of a silver bowl and pitcher, and his reply, printed in the *Gainesville News* on October 5, 1927, was as much a reminder to his own management as it was a thank-you. He said: "May we conduct ourselves that we shall continue to merit the good will and confidence of the citizens of Hall County." In the industry, the new mill and village were seen as the greatest advance ever taken to upgrade the status of the southern textile employee.

A visiting Englishman familiar with the contrasting conditions of the textile trade at Lancashire was impressed when he visited Chicopee. As the Cresent Limited slowed for the stop at Gaines-ville, the train conductor began extolling the virtues of the mill and village. Later the Englishman wrote: "The coloured population, in their gay clothing, seemed happy and free and not at all underpri-vileged." At the mill he was greeted by a thirty-two-piece employee band that "nearly took the roof off." But that night the incessant croaking of thousands of frogs kept him awake — reminding him of the one flaw in the plan for a perfect mill. Johnson believed that by not allowing animals on the property he could ensure a purer water supply. But the Englishman explained: "His obsession with the purity of the water made him overlook the social effects of ban-ning livestock, pets and chickens. The whole area was overrun with frogs and other amphibia which thrived because of a lack of natu-ral predators." After several sleepless nights the visitor departed, impressed by the mill but overwhelmed by the frogs. "I had no idea they could make such noise," he wrote.

In the years ahead Johnson carried out his "Factories Can Be Beautiful" philosophy by building more than one hundred attrac-tive and efficient plants and office buildings. Others would do the same, but in 1926 he was in the forefront of the concept of modernism that was just beginning to creep into the American consciousness. Not surprisingly, the trend was rebuffed by much of industry, where factories were expected to be "sweatshops" and "salt mines" and where ugly facades hid cluttered, dirty, and unsafe interiors.

From the outset Johnson made it clear that he was not motivated simply by the movement toward modernism. To him, building attractive factories made eminently sound business sense. Attractive factories and pleasant working conditions generated greater efficiency and pride among workers. Well-maintained buildings promoted community acceptance of the company and reflected the integrity of the company and its products. For a company dedicated to purity and sterility in its line of medical products, Johnson believed it made even greater sense. Later he identified what he saw as a still loftier goal: "We build not only structures in which men and women of the future will work, but also the pattern of society in which they will work. We are building frameworks of ideas and ideals."

On February 1, 1927, at the age of thirty-three, Robert Johnson was elected to the Board of Control, a key position in the company's hierarchy. His climb from factory hand sixteen years earlier had, for him, been a noble journey. He was no longer the "junior member" of the company. It was the beginning of a new era. Almost immediately he began involving himself in the company's strategic decisions and speaking out on them with authority. And while in some respects he was still the student, he was also the emerging teacher.

Looking to the future of the business, he told them: "We are passing through a time when the management who made this business is letting go of the reins, and the new management is beginning to operate." And, in a not so veiled warning to those who might oppose him, he added: "The stockholders of this business, realizing the necessity for bringing in young men, are also quite ready to sustain the expense of as much of the former organization as is willing to cooperate and help in the progress of Johnson & Johnson."

Neither Johnson nor his management was aware of it at the time, but by cautioning against overproduction he was identifying one of the root causes of the Great Depression that would soon grip the nation. His policy of conserving capital in 1927 had a profound effect on the company's ability to survive the coming economic collapse.

11

CHARMED BY MAGGI

IN the winter of 1928, Robert and Elizabeth reached an impasse in their marriage and began a two-year trial separation. To their friends it came as no great surprise. Those who saw it Elizabeth's way said that Johnson was married more to his business than to her and that he was far too fond of night life in Manhattan, sailing adventures, and other exotic interests to be a good husband and father. Those who saw the problems Johnson's way looked on Elizabeth as a homebody who made little effort to share his interests and who had trouble keeping pace with him, both socially and intellectually. He had, they said, "outgrown" her.

Making the separation an unusually long two years was Elizabeth's idea, though she promised she would give him a divorce whenever he met someone "he wished to be with." He moved out of Bellevue, leaving Elizabeth behind with young Robert, who was then going on eight. Johnson then began spending more time traveling, especially to England. He had grown fond of England and was spending more time there than the business either required or justified. On April 6 he sailed aboard the SS *Olympic* for a six-week stay in England, and soon after his arrival he rented a four-story townhouse in the Mayfair section of London, at 18 Charles Street, just off Curzon Street.

Later that spring he went to Paris for a short visit. There, a friend invited him to dinner and arranged for a blind date with Maggi Shea, a beautiful, vivacious model and aspiring dancer and photographer. Readers of the *Norwich (Connecticut) Bulletin* had earlier learned about the new and exciting life of the former hometown girl.

FORMER NORWICH GIRL IN
AMERICAN BEAUTY FOUR

Four of New York's prettiest girls have been chosen by Jean Patou, fashion creator of Paris, to be his American models and have sailed for France where they will be under contract for a year. One of the four to whom this honor has come is a former Norwich girl, Margaret Shea, daughter of Joseph Shea and Margaret Hinchey Shea, former residents of Hickory Street, but residing in New York City for a number of years past.

Miss Shea sailed last Saturday from New York on the *Acquitania*. She has been on the stage for the last three or four years and has last been appearing in the musical comedy Good News. This is the third time she has been picked for one of Patou's models, but on the two previous occasions she yielded to her mother's wish that she should remain in New York. When she was again chosen this year in the competition conducted by one of Patou's representatives in New York, her mother gave her consent for her to go abroad and Miss Shea eagerly grasped the opportunity.

That day in May, when Johnson walked into the Paris home of Maggi Shea's friend, Maggi immediately recognized him as the "handsome and sophisticated Bob Johnson" she had met casually and admired at various soirées in New York. "I recognized him, but I doubt that he had remembered me. The most he had ever said to me was 'Hello, how do you do.'" She added: "I was bug-eyed. I thought he was the most divine man I had ever seen." And she intrigued him. "I was a flapper," she said. "I was a product of the Twenties."

Maggi was twenty-five, petite, and blonde, and breathtakingly beautiful — the perfect enhancement for a visit to Paris in the spring. Johnson stayed a week, they saw each other every day, and when he returned to London he had more on his mind than business. He was also thinking of Maggi Shea.

Later in May he returned to the United States aboard the *Olympic* and when the ship docked in New York reporters asked him about the future of industry in Britain. He told the *New York Times*: "The British Empire will experience within the next twenty years the greatest industrial renaissance of modern history." But his predictions of a growing British influence in world trade proved to be excessively optimistic. The coming collapse of the U.S. economy, triggered by the stock market crash of 1929, would quickly spread overseas.

That summer Johnson went to Kansas City as an alternate delegate-at-large to the Republican National Convention that nominated Herbert Hoover. Later he offered strong support for Hoover's candidacy: "A people who have been enjoying a prosperity unparalleled in the history of the whole world are not going to gamble with the future by making a drastic change in their national policies. This country may be likened to a gigantic business concern. To keep it prosperous its affairs must be directed by the best trained and the best experienced executive available. I believe that Herbert Hoover possesses one of the best executive minds that the country has produced in many years, and that the country will not fail to avail itself of his services." Johnson's optimism was understandable in view of Hoover's own campaign rhetoric: "We in America today are nearer to the final triumph over poverty than ever before in the history of our land," he told the people. He did not know that the ship of state was sailing steadily toward the submerged economic crisis of 1929.

Once back from the Republican convention, Johnson's thoughts again began drifting to the alluring Maggi Shea, who was still on her modeling assignment in Paris. Then came the perfect opportunity to rejoin her in Europe. Johnson was invited to enter the

Zodiac in a widely publicized sailing race across the ocean to compete for the King Alfonso of Spain Cup. The invitation read, in part:

> At the King's request, the race will start in time for the boats to arrive in Santander during the time that the King and Queen are occupying their Summer palace in that port, so that they will be able to entertain the participating yachtsmen. Visiting Spain in this way, as guests of the Royal Family and Spanish yachtsmen, is something never to be forgotten.

The appeal of a challenging ocean race, and the chance to see Maggi again, was more incentive than Johnson needed. He hastily replied:

"You may rest assured that the *Zodiac* will be handled in such a way as to get her there first if possible."

In Gloucester, Massachusetts, the Norwegian Captain Norman Ross began preparing the *Zodiac* for the big race. The ship had been modified since the trip to Labrador. Her brief topmasts had been replaced by longer and heavier sticks taken from the *Henry Ford*, which finished second to the *Columbia* in the International Fishing Schooner Race of 1926. Captain Ross had been sailing master on the *Columbia*. Originally the *Zodiac* had carried only a jib, jumbo, foresail, and mainsail, but now she carried a large or small balloon, fore topsail, main topsail, and large and small staysail, and when all were set there was an impressive 2,200 yards of sail.

The *Zodiac* had successfully competed in races between New York and the Bahamas, but the 3,055-mile run from Sandy Hook on the New Jersey coast to Santander, Spain, would be a grueling test for ships and crews. The lumbering, 100-ton *Zodiac*'s best hopes were for severe weather, for in light winds she would be no match for the faster, trimmer yachts. Johnson made that clear to reporters: "We want to prove that a Gloucester-built boat, schooner rigged and handled by a fisherman crew, can beat the conventional type of yacht if it blows at all. It will be a fine test of seamanship and it ought to be great fun."

To race against the "flanneled yachtsmen," Captain Ross went to Nova Scotia and Newfoundland to pick his crew of eight pipe-smoking, churchgoing Down East fishermen. "Not a man in the fo'c'sle is an American," he bragged. With brand-new sails and trimmed to "the Queen's taste," the *Zodiac* sailed from Gloucester, with a noisy farewell befitting a departing hero, and on to a berth at the New York Yacht Club, where the boat was greeted quietly, with some disdain and a few sneers.

The New York press generated pre-race drama as the starting date drew closer. Sentiment built for the *Zodiac*, Captain Ross, and the Down Easters. The *New York Telegram* reported dramatically: "With them will sail the owners of the boat, young millionaires who wish to risk their lives to prove that a Down East crew can out-sail any group of men alive. Robert Johnson is a licensed aviator, but in a day when other men are crossing the Atlantic in planes, he prefers this oldest of all means. His *Zodiac* is as trim a bit of boat as ever eyes were laid upon. She cost more than $75,000.00. Down below she is finished in immaculate white and mahogany. Her brass shines jewel-like. Her hardwood floors would make many a Park Avenue home envious."

Finally, the big day—Saturday, July 7—arrived. The waters around Atlantic Highlands were crowded with spectator craft, dominated by the black-hulled yacht *Corsair* owned by J. P. Morgan, who was aboard with his party. The steamship *Edward Farrington*, somewhat of an ugly duckling alongside the sleek racing craft, had come up from New Brunswick with more than a hundred raucous, beer-drinking well-wishers. Captain Ross stepped gingerly from a dory to the deck of the *Zodiac* and took his place beside Robert and Seward Johnson for the raising of the colors. The Stars and Stripes was run to the top of the mast, and then, "for no good reason that anyone seemed able to furnish," it was followed by an Elks Lodge flag. Then the *Zodiac* weighed anchor and began maneuvering for a fast start (her engines sealed and her prop lashed to the deck to conform to race rules). The other contenders, the *Atlantic*, the *Elena*, the *Azara*, and the *Guinevere*, did the same.

"If it is to be a race let it be a real one," Johnson said bravely. The only thing missing was the wind. When someone suggested towing the *Zodiac* to the starting line, he balked. "We are not going to bother about any tugs to get us to the starting point," he replied. "We are going to sail out and we will sail until we reach the coast of Spain. The only thing we need to finish first is just a little luck."

Suddenly, what little wind there was vanished, and the deadly calm was disturbed only by the howling revelry aboard the spectator boats. The embarrassed crews, with sails barely slatting, waved farewell over and over as their craft bobbed up and down, going nowhere. This lasted two and a half hours. J. P. Morgan grew impatient and suggested to the race committee that the boats be towed to the starting line. Then at 2:30 in the afternoon there was a puff of wind, enough to nudge the *Zodiac* across the starting line. Its crew of sixteen and afterwatch of five crowded the deck and waved a final farewell. Most of the *Elena*'s crew had jumped ship the night before, but the hastily recruited replacements got her across the starting line first, aided by a sliding extension on the bowsprit that enabled the ballooner to catch what little air there was. There were three women aboard, prompting the *New York Sunday Times* to comment stuffily that the *Elena*'s new recruits "formed, in truth, a motley crew."

Ambrose Lightship was barely astern when the *Zodiac* encountered the first of many problems that plagued her crew for the next three weeks. As they reached South Shoal Lightship, a stiff wind suddenly came out of nowhere and broke the spinnaker boom, tearing the balloon. Then, three days later and 440 miles from New York, they were becalmed. Johnson radioed wryly: "We are teaching the crew to swim around the vessel."

Again the weather changed. On July 23 the *Zodiac* was hit by heavy gales that swept away her wireless antenna, ending any further radio communication. Anxiety for her safety mounted at home until an oceanliner reported spotting her in rough seas. The headlines then changed from apprehension to hope. Finally, on July 28 at 10:30 A.M., the weary crew sighted Santander and the *Zodiac* became the fourth boat to cross the finish line.

The race had been won by *Elena* and her "motley crew," which crossed the finish line four days earlier. As each of the other yachts arrived, King Alfonso and his entourage aboard the Royal Yacht hosted another welcoming party. Patiently, the party-weary King waited for *Zodiac*. When it finally arrived it was escorted to the dock by the Royal Yacht amid the din of ship's whistles and band music. Then the revelry began at nearby Magdalena Palace, where, it was reported, the Princesses Beatrice and Christina "danced with nearly all the yachtsmen." The celebration continued at bullfights and parties until exhaustion conquered everyone five days later. Asked later to comment on the race, Johnson said: "You probably have had the experience of a ride in a barrel of love [at the amusement park] and know the shaking up you get during those few minutes. Well, for twenty-one days we were given just such a tossing."

When the sailing buffs examined the results and the ships' logs, they decided that if the *Zodiac* had not lost two days by avoiding the Gulf Stream it would have won handily. This did not please the *Zodiac*'s navigator, Naval Commander Vincent Clark, who was touted as a "specialist in air currents and wind predictions." Clark's most recent exploits, however, had not been on the capricious Atlantic, but aloft aboard the dirigible *Los Angeles*. The race over, Clark returned to the skies and let the "flanneled yachtsmen" debate the strategy during the long winter ahead.

•

Johnson left for Paris, where Maggi was waiting. "I was there to greet him and we had a lovely week," she remembered. That was the week they fell in love, but their relationship remained innocent, Maggi was quick to point out. "I was a stuffy square, a country girl," she said. When the idyllic week ended, Johnson went back to London and then returned to the United States in the early fall. Maggi left Paris and returned home about the same time, worried about what her mother would say when she learned that her daughter, who had had a strict Catholic upbringing, had fallen in love with a married man.

Soon after returning, Johnson met with Elizabeth. They had agreed to a two-year separation, but when he told her about his love for Maggi she agreed that they would begin divorce proceedings. It was a very painful decision for Elizabeth, for she had always held out the hope that they would get back together. And it was especially hard on young Robert, who was then nine but had not yet seen very much of his father. The boy was puzzled and hurt. Elizabeth was embarrassed and hurt.

Johnson started looking for a new home, which he and Maggi would share once they were married. He decided not to live in New Brunswick, and he found the Princeton area appealing. There was a grand old house there called "Morven," which was one of the nation's most historic homes. The Georgian-style mansion, with its warm yellow-brick exterior, was located on five acres in the center of Princeton. It had been built in 1755 by Richard Stockton, a signer of the Declaration of Independence, on a 5,000-acre tract of land that his grandfather had purchased from William Penn in 1701. During the Revolutionary War the British occupied and pillaged the mansion, but once it was restored it again became a center of hospitality for the rich and famous. Monticello, Stratford, and other famous American manor houses could not claim more illustrious visitors than did Morven. It had been host to eight Presidents, including George Washington and James Madison, and others such as Aaron Burr, Alexander Hamilton, Daniel Webster, and Light-Horse Harry Lee enjoyed the warmth of Morven's hospitality and debated momentous issues around the glow of its fireplaces. It was under Morven's roof that plans were made to bring the College of New Jersey, later to become Princeton University, to the quaint village and locate it just up the road.

Johnson arranged to lease the grand house from members of the Stockton family. The mansion had been neglected for years, and his promise to restore it to its former elegance encouraged the Stocktons to entrust Morven to him. That was a good decision. As one Morven historian noted: "If the new occupants of the place were alien in blood, they were far from being so in spirit." With sympathetic understanding for preserving Morven's glorious past, Johnson began pouring untold amounts of money into major repairs to the home and its gardens in an effort to bring back the proud grandeur of Morven's past. Maggi was invited a few times to Princeton to spend a weekend in the house — always, she said, with a chaperone accompanying her.

The renovation of Morven continued, and Johnson began establishing a new circle of friends in Princeton, a town strongly influenced by its academic types, new and old money, and a distinctive tone of civility. It had few of New Brunswick's persistent ailments. And while Princeton was now his adopted home, it was New Brunswick that commanded Johnson's loyalty and concern. He was always trying to find new ways to stimulate the city's economy, and his ally in these projects was often Elmer Beattie Boyd, a contentious, civic-minded editor whose family had acquired the *New Brunswick Home News* a half-century earlier and turned it into a successful and influential daily newspaper. While Johnson's father had tangled with the Boyds over petty matters, such as social items printed about his family, Johnson saved his wrath for major issues. Most of the time he and Elmer Boyd worked together trying to find ways to improve the city.

Never at a loss for a new idea, or a quote to the newspapers that raised eyebrows, Johnson announced that he was thinking of providing airplanes for all of his company salesmen, so they could save time and improve their performance. He said this just before taking off in his own plane for Washington, D.C., to attend the All-American Aircraft Display at Bolling Field. By the time he landed in Washington his new idea was in headlines. Piloting a plane enthralled Johnson, and he was convinced that the fledgling aircraft industry offered great potential for New Brunswick if a major airport could be built at nearby Miller Field. Boyd's paper liked the idea, commenting: "With the establishment of a municipal airport, factories engaged in the manufacturing of planes and accessories will eventually follow."

Johnson bought a New Standard biplane and flew it around the New Brunswick area, to the amazement and often the amusement of local residents. The old-timers shook their heads—first fast cars, then fast boats, and now fast planes. During the summer of 1929 Johnson announced that he planned to build a plane of unique design, which, as he put it, "will serve my purpose for pleasure and business." Johnson said he got the idea for the design after making a study of aircraft on his trips to England, France, and Germany. He recruited the services of John Miller, an early airmail pilot and now a designer of small planes, who ran the tiny Miller Aviation Corporation at Miller Field and he in turn got Harlan D. Fowler interested. Fowler had invented the Fowler variable area wing and was another pioneer in aviation.

Word of this radical new aircraft soon reached the Wright Aeronautical Corporation, which sent technicians to Miller Field to watch the progress. The amphibious biplane was designed to take off from both land and water and had a huge forty-four-foot wingspan. There were two 200-horsepower engines, but they were mounted in tandem, one behind the other, and housed in nacelles that enclosed both the engines and the propellers (looking somewhat like the jet engines of later years). It was a strange-looking craft, but Johnson said it was designed to fly on one engine should the other engine fail.

Anticipation built as the big day for ground testing arrived. A crowd of onlookers and reporters gathered at Miller Field, where Johnson announced solemnly: "The plane at the present is merely an experiment, a laboratory." He then told them that what he really had in mind was not just one plane but an entire industry. "If after sufficient tests it proves that it can carry out definite performances, we shall start the building of an industry," he declared.

The engines were started and the plane taxied up and down the field without incident and then returned to the hangar. The newspapers carried such glowing reports that one would think the plane had passed the most stringent tests, for already they were calling the design a "revelation in aviation." The press stories now attracted the attention of serious-minded aviation experts, who were saying that the plane could become the best amphibian aircraft ever produced in the United States. A week later Johnson and Miller had the plane hauled down to Keyport on Raritan Bay in sections and reassembled for its maiden flight off the water. A large crowd gathered on the shoreline for the test.

It was windy and the bay water was choppy. The plane bobbed up and down, as if impatient to get started. Miller climbed aboard, strapped on his helmet, and gunned the engines. The plane taxied down the bay, turned around, and, Miller said later, became airborne nine seconds after he hit the throttle. All eyes turned skyward as the plane gained altitude. The crowd cheered. For the next hour Miller circled the bay performing a series of tests. Then he brought the craft down for a smooth landing and a hero's welcome. "It handled beautifully," Miller said enthusiastically. "It answered the controls perfectly and is well balanced." Everyone went home impressed.

The following day, Miller again took the plane up from the bay at Keyport, and circled back, this time to New Brunswick Airport, for its first landing on a runway. The crowd of spectators had grown larger, in anticipation of witnessing a momentous event in aviation. The weather was good and Miller made a perfect landing. But the left wheel strut snapped, and the plane rolled two hundred feet down the runway, slipped over on its back, and skidded to a crunching halt. Miller climbed out unhurt. The plane was destroyed. That ended the experiment and dashed Johnson's hopes for a new aircraft that would bring a new industry and jobs to New Brunswick.

The memory of that failure soon faded as Johnson became intensely interested in the new autogyros. He was back at Hadley Field, and, under the watchful eye of pilot Ken Unger, began taking lessons to learn how to pilot the strange-looking craft. He soon became proficient, and a government flight inspector qualified him as the first nonprofessional pilot in the region to receive a license to fly the autogyro — it read Number One. Encouraged, he would later purchase a Pitcairn, a three-place autogyro, for $18,000.

•

When the SS *Europa* left New York Harbor early the morning of July 25, 1930, Johnson was on board and heading back to England, this time with his chauffeur and motorcar. The trip would be both business and pleasure, he said, with the first stop at Slough, to be followed by a tour of the continent. No mention was made of other plans, but that September he and Maggi Shea were married in a quiet ceremony in Paris. They spent their honeymoon in southern France at the resort of Capbreton on the Bay of Biscay. It was nearly a month before the newspapers carried the announcement.

When they returned to the United States in October, Maggi and Johnson moved into Morven, which was still being renovated. All of Morven's fifteen rooms were being redone, and Maggi became engrossed in the project. She was impressed by Princeton's historic surroundings — where the cause of America's Independence had been debated and embraced and where the first Continental Congress was convened in 1782. "It was exciting to move into an old, broken-down historic house and to restore it," she recalled. "It had the beauty of the architecture and all of the potential. We found the original plans for the house and gardens. I finally got around to cleaning the attic, and exorcised the ghost of Cornwallis. Of course, I don't believe in ghosts, but someone said, 'You hear them, don't you?' and I did. It turned out to be an animal in the attic."

Next Maggi turned the old slave house at the back of Morven into a photography studio. Her interest in photography had begun as a child, and she studied it briefly in New York, then pursued it again in Paris between modeling assignments and while she was writing a fashion column for *Paris Vogue*. She became quite good at it, particularly her photos of nature and animals.

In time the grand old house, with its mellow front of yellow brick, white shutters, and broad, white-columned portico, was restored to its former elegance. The gardens were replanted with great care, and the gnarled wisteria and elms gave it a regal charm all its own. After years of neglect, Morven was once again worthy of its heritage and was remindful of the romantic, third-century poem for which it had been named.

Living in Princeton required a high degree of social stamina. Johnson rode with the Stoney Brook Hunt, and even teas were part of that ritual. As for Maggi, the social strata of Princeton were somewhat heady for someone who described herself as a "country girl." She had a limited education, but what she had she used wisely. She also had a way of delivering words with a burst of energy that made them sound more forceful than they deserved to be. It was an impulsive mannerism that sometimes reached staccato proportions. She liked to talk.

Maggi was an attentive hostess too, and her infectious enthusiasm for whatever she was doing compensated for any shortcomings. It bubbled over. Being very personable, a beautiful woman, and a gracious hostess helped get their marriage off to a successful start. She was also an arbitrator, and around Robert Johnson being an arbitrator helped considerably.

The couple entertained a great deal at Morven, mostly with frequent small dinner parties whose main purpose was to explore the depths of some business or political issue. This soon developed into a ritual that Johnson followed for years. It stemmed from a certain self-consciousness he had about his lack of formal higher education, now that he had expanded his public presence and become more deeply involved in issues of national concern. Already a clear thinker and an articulate and persuasive spokesman, Johnson wanted to fill the gap in his education. He delved into many subjects and studied them exhaustively. Usually they were issues of current concern to him, often having to do with economics, government, or some phase of business. He relied on his old technique of gathering as many books and reports on the subject as he could find, and then immersing himself in the information until he had absorbed quite a bit, and usually much more than he needed to know. He read constantly and relied heavily on contact with experts in the field. Often these were academics, and his proximity to Rutgers University in the early days, and to Princeton now, made that easy for him.

Morven was as close to Princeton University as Johnson's office was to Rutgers in New Brunswick, and this gave him a ready source of authority on almost any subject. Beginning shortly after his marriage to Maggi, he began inviting these authorities for small dinner parties and intense conversation at Morven two or three times a week. For Johnson it was a fascinating and effective way to learn. The guests came both from Princeton's faculty and staff and from among the many highly successful business and professional people who lived in the Princeton area. When the ladies were included, they usually drifted off to another part of the house after dinner, and the conversation among the men wore on, often for hours, amid the haze of cigar smoke and sips of warm brandy.

Johnson planned the guest lists for these forums with the intensity of an eager student preparing for an examination. The conversation would have a focus, and those who could contribute the most to it were the first invited. But the plan and purpose of the dinners was never openly discussed by Johnson. It was as though he were setting up his own private curriculum, and actually he was doing just that. Later, when he became more deeply involved in New Jersey and national politics, the dinner parties changed their tone, and the guest lists included leading national and state political figures. The Johnson dinner parties at Morven ranked high on many social calendars and earned a reputation for never being boring.

·

When he was living in New Brunswick, Johnson had spent a great deal of time out of town, much of it related to the changes taking place in his personal life. England was an escape, and he went there often. Once back in Princeton with Maggi, however, he began to devote long hours to his work again. The Depression was now beginning to have more adverse affects. The cutback of work shifts at the factory drew criticism from the Hungarian union, but still no one was being let go. "In comparison with many other large plants, either completely shut down or working spasmodically, Johnson & Johnson is fortunate to be able to keep so many employees working," the press reported.

To help bolster sagging business, Johnson announced that he would visit sixteen cities in the Midwest and Southwest where there were major wholesale drug customers, and that to save time he would be traveling in the Pitcairn autogyro piloted by his friend John Miller. The sleek green-and-white autogyro drew crowds wherever it landed. It was shaped like a conventional, low-wing racing plane, with short stubby wings flared up at the tips. Pulled forward by a propeller, it got its lift from the four huge rotor blades that whirled above the two open cockpits. It was slow, but it could land virtually anywhere.

When it did land, reporters were invariably present, and Johnson was always ready for them. They rarely went away disappointed. One day at the Wichita Airport he declared that the office desk was now passé. "Modern business declares action," he proclaimed. "The day is past when you can run a business from behind a desk. So I choose the autogyro." Then he added a note of local interest drawn from his brief observation from the air: "The Missouri Valley seems to be better off than any other section of the country I have visited. I couldn't say things are booming in the Valley, but business is so much better off, comparatively, and it should be a matter of congratulation to you people who live here."

The *Wichita Beacon* reporter was impressed. He wrote: "A forceful, attractive personality, enhanced by an observant nature and a keen interest in his surrounds, make Mr. Johnson one of the most engaging business visitors Wichita has had of late." He also liked the autogyro, describing it as "the most modern means of transportation at the command of the civilized world." Johnson charmed reporters at the other stops of the trip, which included Fort Wayne, Chicago, St. Louis, Kansas City, Tulsa, Little Rock, Memphis, and Louisville.

•

The election of Herbert Hoover failed to produce the prosperity the candidate had envisioned while campaigning. His pledge of "a chicken in every pot" turned out to be an empty promise. Hoover was barely in the White House when the dark clouds of the Great Depression began gathering over the nation in 1929, though the causes of the impending economic collapse had been seeded much earlier.

At a mid-year meeting of the Board of Directors, Johnson had warned of the need to curtail expenditures and pull back on new projects that required significant investment. Since much of the nation had been deluding itself about the health of the economy, it was not surprising that few within the company shared his concern. Fred Kilmer was an exception. Periodically he would express apprehension about the business, but always somewhat apologetically because he was aware that, in the eyes of others, pharmacists and writers (and he considered himself both) were not supposed to know about business and economics. Kilmer credited his instincts for most of his reactions.

Johnson and Kilmer had much in common. Both, in a sense, were "Renaissance men" in that their interests were wide-ranging and their intelligence and energy allowed them to put their thoughts to practical use. Johnson recognized Kilmer as a kindred spirit and seemed to regard the older man as somewhat of a father figure. And because Kilmer was one of the few who agreed with Johnson on the business outlook, they once again found themselves allies. Johnson was appreciative, and on August 9 he told Kilmer so:

> Dear Dr. Kilmer:
> I very much appreciate your feeling about the semi-annual statement, and people are beginning to see it.
>   You are one of the few who have been able to give intelligent analysis to the whole thing and see into the future. I am afraid that most of our colleagues, both inside and outside the corporation, like a good many other fair weather friends, find it all rosy when business is good and collapse when business gets a little bad.
>
> R.W.J.

The stock market crash that precipitated the Depression occurred that fall, with the most rapid decline in late October. The *New York Times* on Friday, October 30, described the previous day as "the most disastrous trading day in the stock market's history." The market crash shook investors' confidence and created a deflationary spiral as difficult to halt as the inflationary one had been, carrying the nation to industrial and financial depths. From the carefree "Roaring Twenties" the nation rapidly slipped into the clutches of the Great Depression.

The psychological scars were lasting. When things did not get better, optimism and courage gave way to apathy, despair, bitterness, and fear for the future. Millions of people were forced to live on handouts or eat at soup kitchens. Bread lines were commonplace. Thousands took to the road, traveling across the country in the hope of finding work. In every city, rickety shacks made from old boards, corrugated tin, and flattened tin cans sprang up to house the drifters, and sometimes entire families. They called these "Hoovervilles," after the once popular President they now derided.

The year 1930 saw the dawn of a decade marked by somber

reality—a marked contrast to the unrestrained optimism of the 1920s. Unemployment soared, and even the best-managed companies began to cut back. Many poorly managed firms went out of business. When Johnson addressed the Board of Directors on January 6, he spoke bluntly: "The directors of this company must realize that we are in the middle of a revolution." Yet the adjustments he called for—shorter shifts, no Saturday work, and three-day weekends twice a month—were mild compared with the measures other companies were taking. As it turned out, no Johnson & Johnson employees lost their jobs during the Depression.

Much of Johnson's January 1930 report was encouraging, in spite of the dismal economic climate. He broadened the bonus system to include the sales department and urged that bonuses be based on incentives. "I know of nothing more important than this," he said. Johnson had been stewing about the contributions members of the Board of Directors, comprised of members of his management, were making, and he took this opportunity to tell them so:

"I am anxious that this Board begin to function in some way that will be of use to Johnson & Johnson, and we would welcome any recommendations toward that end. As a body for disseminating information it is already useful, but for an intelligent discussion of a major problem it does not disclose its value. The fault for this may rest with the stockholders, and if so recommendations will be in order."

The "stockholders" he was referring to, of course, were the members of his senior management.

On a lighter note, Johnson announced the beginning of a brand-new advertising approach, a series of musical programs to be broadcast live on radio. He took a special interest in the previews and made some choice comments on what he heard. About the musicians, he said: "A liberal application of apple whiskey would help the orchestra." About the announcer: "Let the announcer name a whole string of songs and then leave the building." And about the soprano: "I wish she would join a sewing circle." About one of the songs he said: "Rackety Coo was awful, just plain terrible." The musical series was soon replaced by dramatic programs.

On February 4, 1930, a month after his wake-up call to the Board of Directors, Johnson became Vice President and General Manager of the company, making his control complete. His ailing Uncle Jimmy, no longer active in the business, still held the title of President, but it was more honorary and in recognition of his earlier contributions than an indication of his influence on the business.

•

Although the day-to-day needs of managing the business to cope with the effects of the Depression kept him busy, Johnson continued his visionary approach to health care. Ways to provide better care for hospital patients had challenged his ingenuity since his first exposure to a hospital environment at Middlesex Hospital nearly fifteen years earlier. For him it was a problem that seemed to defy solution. He could not understand why hospitals were not run more like businesses and less like foundering institutions. Their lack of management appalled him. He had gained a broad understanding of how hospitals in various parts of the world functioned, and in 1931 he outlined what he called "corrective measures" for Middlesex, which for him was a "laboratory" for his hospital reforms. He summarized his suggestions in a report titled "Service to the Patient" and had it printed and distributed. Two of his proposals turned out to be years ahead of their time for general hospitals across the nation.

First, he proposed that the medical staff of the hospital be organized into service departments according to medical specialties— such as, surgery, obstetrics, radiology, gynecology, pediatrics, and pathology. While there was already some specialization at major teaching hospitals, it was years before the larger general hospitals were organized this way, and even longer for smaller hospitals. Middlesex did not reorganize that way until more than a decade after Johnson's report.

Next, he posed a delicate question: "Are we to permit the inno-cent public to go on indefinitely believing it can intelligently choose a medical man? Because some emotional and probably confused patient decided that a surgeon should treat him medically, or that a medical man should perform a surgical operation, must we [the hospital] approve such a choice? He continued his argument: "After all, there are very few people in position to choose their medical attendants intelligently. A well-conducted modern hospital is the one institution that can do this, and it behooves the hospitals to perform this service for their public. One might say, 'That is true, but is it popular?' We have come to think that legislators are in-fluenced only by votes, but we surely have not come to the point where our hospital boards are thinking in the same terms."

It was a sensitive area, because for years Americans clung to the belief, as many still do, that the right of "free choice" of a medical practitioner was somehow sacred.

12

LIKE FATHER,
LIKE SON

THE once placid and even-tempered James Johnson was seventy-five and getting more feisty with each advancing year. Still clinging to the title of President of Johnson & Johnson, he was rarely seen in New Brunswick, but many in the company remembered, with admiration, the contributions he had made. What bothered James most was having to make way for his nephew, Robert, and the next generation of management. To him, it was like repelling an enemy invasion. In February 1932 James wrote his brother, Mead, from his country estate, The Locust, at Bernardsville, New Jersey: "The thing that gets my goat every once in a while, is the disrespect, if you like, or the inconsiderable estimate of ourselves on the part of the young ones."

Along with his thirty-two-year-old Scottish bride, who was also his nurse, James boarded the SS *President Hoover* for six weeks of sun in Cuba. The marriage had taken place the previous spring, six years after the death of his first wife. When James returned in April, still in ailing health, there was a letter from the company informing him that he was now officially retired, with no title and a $2,500 annual pension, the maximum benefit paid to retired senior executives. Incensed, he wrote to the Board of Directors on April 18 complaining about his small pension and the treatment he was getting after forty-five years of service. He again criticized the performance of "the youthful generation" and demanded to see the company's financial statement and a list of salaries.

In terms of company growth under the "young ones," James had a point. When he took over as president in 1910, sales were $3,873,000, and they rose to $15,172,000 by 1920, when he began to taper off his duties as president. The next dozen years of recovery from the war and the Great Depression saw very limited growth, so James had the numbers on his side.

Two days later Robert replied, giving James the financial information and list of salaries. He also reminded him that he was the one that had approved giving James a salary and bonuses totaling $835,000 during his years of reduced activity. "The crushing disappointment to me is that your letter disclosed that I have failed to gain your confidence," he wrote.

Still bristling, James submitted his resignation as "president, director and pensioner" on May 28, and the Board accepted it "with profound regrets," praised him for his contributions to the business, and wished him "health, prosperity and happiness." Two weeks later he and his wife went to Scotland, where his health seemed to improve, but on the return trip in late August he was taken ill and died at sea aboard the SS *Majestic*. Robert was in the West, but the kindly Dr. Kilmer and some of the other old-timers were there when James was placed in the family mausoleum next to his brother Robert. Early reports estimated James's estate at more than $4 million, but when his will was probated the amount was $1,354,007. His wife received $400,000 and the remainder was left to his daughters.

Robert waited a discreet amount of time, and then with little fanfare became President and General Manager of Johnson & Johnson on October 15, 1932, twenty-two years after the death of his father. He had achieved his goal. It had been a long journey to the presidency, but those many years of learning the business and demonstrating his leadership had finally brought its rewards. Almost everyone in the company felt he had earned the top job, but he always had his share of quiet detractors.

During their frequent vacations, Johnson and Maggi spent time at Ghost Ranch in Albiquiu, New Mexico, where he had been going since childhood, when his father had a financial interest in the Piedra Lumbre Cattle Company that operated the ranch. Maggi photographed the beautiful landscapes and spent time with friends, including artist Georgia O'Keeffe, who lived nearby. Maggi had never spent time in the Southwest, but she quickly adapted to it. "I learned to ride and rope cattle, and for my pictures we would go north to Colorado. I would photograph mountain sheep, goats, and cattle, and Bob would fish the mountain streams."

In August that year they joined Laurance S. Rockefeller and five others for a month-long packhorse trip in Jasper Park and the adjacent mountains of British Columbia. The trip was organized by a mutual friend, Arthur N. Pack of Princeton, president of the American Natural Association. Pack took several thousand feet of motion picture film of caribou, moose, bighorn sheep, and mountain goats, and later wrote: "Mr. Rockefeller proved an expert axman and cut all the firewood for the camp stove and the evening campfires, while Mr. Johnson kept the camp supplied with trout."

By the spring of 1932 much of the nation had become embittered over the degrading effects of the Depression and the failure of the Hoover administration to deliver on its promises. As the presidential election drew closer, many recalled the glowing rhetoric of the 1928 campaign, when Hoover told the voters: "We in America today are nearer to the final triumph over poverty than ever before in the history of our land." In truth, the nation was teetering on the brink of economic disaster.

Herbert Hoover had stubbornly clung to the belief that the best way to cure the nation's economic ills was to stimulate the growth of private industry and benefit from the "trickle down" effect. But his creation of the Reconstruction Finance Corporation, calling for loans to industry, never produced the intended stimulation of business, and he saw public works projects as "raids upon the public treasury," and the dole as debilitating to the American spirit. With no corrective action from government and with business activity stymied, the nation resembled a wounded dinosaur unable to struggle to its feet.

As the Republicans prepared to write the party platform for the upcoming presidential campaign, Johnson sent a telegram to former Ambassador Walter E. Edge, a member of the resolutions committee: "No intelligent person will support a political party which fails to demand real economies in federal, state, county and municipal governments," he said. "It is government that is on trial and unless corrective measures are taken we will have economic chaos. Give us a platform that a decent man can fight for and a leadership that is not guided by political expediency."

Prohibition was to become a major issue in the presidential campaign. The Republicans couldn't agree, so they adopted a compromise position that the *New York Herald Tribune* wryly referred to as a "wet-moist-dry plank." The Democrats, willing to admit that Prohibition had been a total failure, favored repealing the Eighteenth Amendment. Johnson's open support of the Democratic position further weakened his position for Hoover.

At their respective conventions that summer of 1932, the Republicans nominated Hoover for a second term, and the Democrats selected Franklin Delano Roosevelt, who had succeeded Alfred E. Smith as governor of New York. Roosevelt launched an energetic campaign that espoused vaguely liberal principles, while from its inception the Hoover campaign was mired in negativism ranging from outright voter hostility to increasing skepticism on the part of his strongest support, the nation's business interests.

Early in July, Johnson wrote U.S. Treasury Secretary Ogden F. Mills to express his displeasure with the platform the Republicans adopted. He said, in part: "I am, with millions of other Republicans, greatly disappointed in the Republican Platform. . . . We want a platform that is simple and concise — which will give responsible citizens something really constructive to work for. We must hold Mr. Hoover responsible for the Republican Platform, but that platform leaves an opening for Mr. Hoover to disregard the Convention and announce his own platform. I appreciate that it has been good politics to procrastinate and straddle for the past twenty-five years, but I should like to point out the course is no longer the one which will get votes."

Throughout the campaign, Johnson continued to criticize Hoover's economic policies, but he never threatened to bolt the Republican Party. A week before the election, he hosted a dinner in support of Hoover's reelection for some one hundred business and professional leaders, but even on this occasion his polite support of Hoover was mixed with strong criticism of his economic policy. "The problem before the country today is that of government," he told the gathering. "Business can take care of itself, but until the government adopts a sound economic policy there can be no sound business revival."

Franklin Roosevelt won in a landslide, sweeping the popular vote 23 million to 15 million. On January 25, 1933, six weeks before the March inauguration, Johnson wrote to Roosevelt outlining a four-point proposal for the nation's economic recovery:

My dear Mr. Roosevelt:
Some of us feel that it would be better if the present economic complexities could be reduced to a few simple generalities — not because everything can be said in a few simple terms — but because it is utterly impossible for the public at large to understand the situation unless some such attempt is made.

As a result of this effort the following program is offered:

1. It must be made clear to every citizen who has an understanding of addition and subtraction that we will have to live within our means, and this is also the case with the federal, state, county, city and township governments. It seems to be a fact that since 1914, and perhaps before, the world at large, and America in particular, has spent more

than its income until we have reached a point where our public and private credit has collapsed. We must face the truth or go back to barbarism. Therefore, all budgets should be balanced in fact.

2. Every legitimate effort should be made to increase prices of commodities. It ought to now be fairly clear that the payment of international debts in goods and in gold has a tremendous downward pressure on all commodity prices, and for this reason international debts should be drastically reduced. It would also seem clear that a modicum of inflation is indicated (I think the word "reflation" is better) so as to bring the dollar down to reasonable levels of value. Undoubtedly these two acts would at once result in increased commodity prices.

3. Wages should be increased and hours should be decreased. A federal law limiting hours of work to perhaps six or not more than eight seems worthy of careful thought, with the understanding, however, that such a law would be capable of easy and quick adjustment in the event of changed economic conditions, and perhaps a plan of practically universal wage increase should be attempted. I will be glad to enlarge on this, which plan, if properly handled, has a fair chance of success toward a universal nation-wide wage increase program.

4. It is well to remind the public at large that almost any government can make its citizens poor but no government to date has been able to make its citizens rich. The principle of taking from those who have and distributing these funds to those who have not is the expediency of economic suicide. Every major European country has tried it, and it has resulted in economic chaos and collapse. It must now be clear to the American people that under any sort of decent management the success of the few means the success of the many. Our present graduated surtax is nothing more than a tax on success. Industrial and commercial operations on a large scale are not profitable if viewed with a full realization of present taxes. It is obviously unfair to tax the many for the benefit of the few, and it would seem to be equally unfair to tax the few for the benefit of the many. Therefore, as a part and parcel of any plan of revival, the present graduated surtax must be adjusted downward to a very material degree.

Furthermore, the inheritance tax and death duties should either be eliminated or minimized. There is no greater incentive in life than working for the benefit of one's children, and it must be clear that the present inheritance tax and death duties, which will have the tendency to dissolve a business upon the death of the owner, are nothing more than a capital tax and are disastrous and unjust.

I am in a position to place before you a more detailed plan, which I think might be effective in bringing about a practically universal wage increase within sixty days.

Respectfully yours,
Robert W. Johnson

Johnson had released copies of his letter to the press, to various elected officials, to corporate leaders, and others. The Associated Press carried a summary of the proposals, and that led to headlines in newspapers all over the nation. Most of the articles focused on the call for higher wages and reduced working hours, since the national unemployment rate was then exceeding 25 percent. One editorial commented: "Many 'big men' have realized the necessity for higher wages, but Mr. Johnson is one of the few to come out publicly, not only in favor but in agitation for it."

The press sought an endorsement of Johnson's plan from national business leaders, but virtually all of them took the same position as New Jersey Governor A. Harry Moore and Pennsylvania Governor Gifford Pinchot, both of whom said they needed more time to study the plan. The major corporations, some of whom were struggling to meet their payrolls, were silent. Roosevelt's headquarters sent word that he would review the proposals after he took office.

The President-Elect, seeking some rest before the inauguration, accepted an invitation to spend eleven days aboard Vincent Astor's yacht, the *Nourmahal*, fishing and cruising in a warmer climate. When Roosevelt returned to Miami, he delivered a speech in Bay Front Park on the evening of Wednesday February 15 and had just settled into the rear seat of his open car when, at 9:35, a man fired five shots from a pistol. None of the bullets hit Roosevelt, but five people were seriously wounded, including Mayor Anton J.

Cermak of Chicago, who died three weeks later as a result of the wound in his chest. Police arrested the gunman, Giuseppe Zingara, a thirty-five-year-old brick mason, who told them: "I like Roosevelt personally, but I don't like presidents." The reason he didn't like presidents, he said, was because "rich men send their children to schools." It was three weeks before he took office, but that night Roosevelt was initiated into the perils of the presidency.

In his inaugural address Roosevelt declared: "This nation asks for action, and action now." The very next day he proclaimed a national bank holiday to save the country's financial institutions. On March 9, without a dissenting voice in the House, the new Congress passed the Emergency Banking Act, ending the run on banks by allowing sound banks to reopen under regulation and putting unsound banks under conservators. The bill eventually led to the Banking Act of 1933 and establishment of the Federal Deposit Insurance Corporation.

The Emergency Banking Act was the first of fifteen pieces of legislation enacted in the first three months — the famous "Hundred Days" — of the Roosevelt administration. It was the start of a strategy called the "New Deal" that was to revolutionize American society and introduce, for the first time, such sweeping federal reforms as unemployment compensation, food stamps, guarantee of bank deposits, supervision of the stock market, protection for collective bargaining, standards for wages and hours, support for farm prices, refinancing for farm and home mortgages, and Social Security.

The New Deal was based on improvisation and experimentation. One legislator described it as "an experiment in using unorthodox means to modify but to preserve the orthodox institutions of a free economy." Roosevelt's goal was both to get the country out of the Great Depression and to prevent future depressions. But by concentrating on making the economy relatively depression-proof, he also made it inflation-prone. Roosevelt persistently followed his own philosophy: "If it fails, admit it frankly and try another. But above all, try something." Actually, he was less prone to admitting failure than his words suggest.

.

For weeks Maggi planned a huge dinner party at Morven for Johnson's fortieth birthday, on April 4, 1933, but the party took on a somber tone, and some state officials had to cancel. Early that morning the dirigible *Akron*, pride of the U.S. Naval Air Forces, crashed at sea off the New Jersey coast. The accident claimed the lives of seventy-three naval officers, crewmen, and guests. The 785-foot silvery hulk (nine feet longer than Germany's *Graf Zeppelin*) had lifted off its moorings at Lakehurst Naval Air Station the night before on a routine training flight. Within a few hours it was caught in the center of a raging storm off the Jersey coast, the mighty airship struggling to outpace the wind but being tossed around helplessly like a toy balloon. Then, twenty-five miles off Barnegat, a tremendous downdraft drove the huge airship into the turbulent sea, and all but three aboard perished. The crash of America's "Queen of the Skies" was the beginning of the end of the brilliant era of dirigibles, which met its final fate with the crash of the *Hindenburg* four years later at Lakehurst.

Being forty didn't faze Johnson in the slightest; he had always seemed older than his years. He maintained an exhausting work schedule, but always found the time for his many leisure-time pursuits, which included riding his horses, swimming and tennis. He had moved into the company presidency with ease, and his management philosophy was now becoming an integral part of major policy decisions. He continued to push for greater decentralization of Johnson & Johnson operations, which gave smaller units the opportunity to function on their own. Johnson often recalled the incident that convinced him of the merits of decentralization.

An improved formula for making plaster products had been introduced, but some annoying problems had developed in the early production runs. Determined to find the cause, Johnson called a meeting of everyone who had any responsibility for producing the new adhesives, but when seventeen people filed into his office, he was dismayed. "I now know what the problem is," he told them. "Too many people are involved. The meeting is over." And so the meeting ended before it even began. Later he assigned one person to be responsible for finding and correcting the problem.

From then on, Johnson was convinced that the best way to run a business was to decentralize it, and that concept evolved into what came to be known as the "Johnson & Johnson Family of Companies." Over time, he became the foremost disciple of decentralized management—and both believing in it and preaching it, he also practiced it ardently. Once a product line was strong enough to support a separate management team, he spun it off and put a separate group in charge.

Another reason he believed in independent units was the human factor, which he later explained in an article in the *Saturday Evening Post*: "Workers need recognition and appreciation," he wrote. "They need to be esteemed in terms of the human equation as well as the production chart." Smaller operations, where more people could be recognized and rewarded, were the answer.

The same principles were applied to managing the rapidly expanding global business. First, new product lines were placed with agents. Then, when the business was able to sustain itself, new international affiliates were formed. Once an area of the world demonstrated sufficient growth potential, Johnson was ready to risk putting an affiliate company there, even during the Depression years—South Africa in 1930, Mexico and Australia in 1931, and Brazil and Argentina later in the 1930s.

The problems American business was facing showed no signs of abating, so in April 1933 Johnson again wrote to Roosevelt, this time urging him to convene a meeting of major industry leaders and allow them to help come up with a solution. At the heart of the problem, he told Roosevelt, was the nation's drastically reduced purchasing power, and a 10 percent wage increase would reverse that trend. This time he did not make the text of the letter public.

Five weeks later President Roosevelt announced a plan for uniting business and agricultural groups in a more cohesive effort. It was more detailed than what Johnson had in mind, but not dissimilar.

The Roosevelt plan called for companies to be grouped according to industry. When the Drug Industry Institute of America was formed in May, Johnson was elected a director of the Institute and joined the nine-member executive board. One of its first objectives, the Drug Industry Institute announced, was a wage increase, and two weeks later Johnson announced that Johnson & Johnson would give a 5 percent increase to all 1,600 employees. This further endeared him to his workers, but it enraged some of his fellow industrialists.

Johnson was not at all happy when he learned the details of the textile industry code under the National Industrial Recovery Act, for he found he was at odds not only with the government but with the other textile operators as well. In response to their proposed minimum weekly wage of $11 in northern mills and $10 in the South for a 40-hour week, he said it was inadequate to raise a family and recommended that the minimum be $15 a week in the North and $14 in the South. Even William Green, president of the American Federation of Labor, came in at $14 for the North and $13 for the South, slightly below Johnson, but he wanted a 30-hour workweek.

Because Johnson & Johnson was now the world's largest producer of surgical dressings, its stake in the textile industry was significant. While wages and hours were an issue, what really upset Johnson was the government's attempt to stipulate how many hours a week his textile machinery could operate. His mills at Chicopee Falls, Massachusetts, were older, but the textile complex he had built in Georgia was the most efficient anywhere. Limiting hours of operation, he said, would make it necessary to dismiss about five hundred of his workers. Irate, Johnson arranged to meet with Secretary of Labor Frances Perkins on June 30. The night before, he took off from Princeton Airport at five o'clock on the Bellanca, with Ken Unger as pilot, and two hours later they were in

Washington. He went right to the Mayflower Hotel to prepare for his confrontation with the crusty Perkins.

Frances Perkins had been Roosevelt's Industrial Commissioner when he was governor of New York, and when he became President he insisted she come to Washington. Perkins was above all an individualist. She was tenacious and at times disputatious, but both qualities suited her well. She soon became a familiar character in Washington, whisking around the city in her three-cornered hat. When asked if she felt handicapped in her position because she was a woman, Perkins replied: "Except in climbing trees, it never bothers me." She was also a favorite of Eleanor Roosevelt, who paid her the ultimate tribute: "If any woman in the world was equipped by experience and ability to be the first woman Cabinet member, Frances Perkins certainly was."

Johnson and Perkins met in her office, where Johnson had warm words for Roosevelt's Recovery Act, telling Perkins that it was the "opportunity of the century." But then he cautioned again about imposing restrictions on the use of textile machinery, saying it "would cost the consumer of textile goods an enormous penalty without any benefit to the working man." Later Johnson reported that Perkins was attentive to the argument he presented and that they got along well.

The same could not be said for his turbulent relationship with the new head of Roosevelt's National Recovery Administration (NRA). To implement the National Industrial Recovery Act, which was symbolized by a proud Blue Eagle, Roosevelt had picked a tough-minded fifty-one-year-old retired brigadier general, Hugh Samuel Johnson, to head the NRA. When tapped for the job, he was working in New York for Bernard M. Baruch, the wealthy stock-broker and political adviser. A graduate of West Point in 1903 and a classmate of Douglas MacArthur, Hugh Johnson spent his early years in Fort Scott, Kansas, when it was still Indian territory. Later that probably seemed tame to him, compared with running the NRA in its early years. For seventeen months, General Hugh Johnson was under relentless attack as he struggled to bring together disparate elements of business and industry to solve the nation's critical unemployment problem.

Earlier the same day that he met with Frances Perkins, Robert Johnson had presented his concepts before an NRA committee hearing. Newspapers reported that General Hugh Johnson and his aides were impressed with the industrialist's eloquent argument. A force and clarity in his voice made Robert Johnson a commanding speaker. Low-pitched—not deep-bass low, but low enough to be authoritative—his voice had a crisp quality, the kind you get when sound bounces off the walls of an empty room and you are surprised enough to repeat what you said. It was a natural gift that he used to his advantage. The words came out easily, but he was at his best when hammering a point home, as opposed to meandering through a labyrinth of ideas. "He is a fluent talker," one reporter wrote. "His choice of words is wide and his construction borders on the beautiful. His delivery is both smooth and energetic."

Robert Johnson's appearance at the hearing was the only amiable encounter between the two Johnsons. The fallout began over national employment issues, and later the attacks on each other became more personal. They escalated even further when General Hugh Johnson became a newspaper columnist after his government service and could peck away at his industrialist adversary from the columns of the daily newspaper.

·

Encouraged by the way his arguments for higher wages and lower hours were being received, Johnson set his sights on American Federation of Labor President William Green, and within two weeks he had Green as an ally. He and the labor leader met in Washington and posed for pictures, an impeccably dressed Johnson next to the shirt-sleeved Green. One newspaper called it a "strange spectacle," having the two on the same side. At the meeting, both men spoke in favor of a higher minimum wage and a shorter workweek, and against limiting the hours textile machinery could be operated. "Idle machinery means idle dollars, and idle dollars means idle men," Johnson declared. Green agreed. And the headlines followed.

By now Johnson's presence on the political scene was widely recognized. In early July, New Jersey Republican Senator Hamilton F. Kean recommended that he accept a position as adviser to Interior Secretary Harold C. Ickes, for the many federal public works programs then getting under way. In response Johnson said: "At this time I consider it more important to keep the heads of families in employment, which so far we have done successfully, than to take up other work."

Two weeks later, when Roosevelt issued his so-called "blanket code" for reducing work hours, Johnson telegraphed the President:

My dear Mr. President:
We enthusiastically agree to your blanket code of employers of labor, which we will put into effect August 1.

It was a moment of supreme triumph for Johnson. He had been pushing for a reduction in work hours for a long time.

In compliance with the code, Johnson's work force was reduced to a 35-hour week with no cut in pay. His quick adoption of the code touched off some grumbling among company executives, which he addressed in a memorandum defending his actions. The company, he stated, would henceforth concentrate on building volume growth rather than profits, adding: "For the present we are not interested in any more than the most moderate profits." He urged his executives to put greater emphasis on quality, productivity, and new products, and he promised that if they succeeded in this "the returns would be greater than ever." But his workers in Georgia did not fare as well. There, Johnson could not run his textile machines for three eight-hour shifts because the code set the limit at two eight-hour shifts.

On September 22 Johnson was back in Washington before the NRA official with a new plan. He proposed being allowed to run four six-hour shifts a day at his mills and promised he would pay his employees the same as they were now getting for eight hours. That way, he said, he could hire twice the number of people and help reduce the nation's unemployment, then at 13 million. Johnson was convinced that working six-hour shifts for the same pay would be efficient and enhance the "health and happiness" of employees. He didn't insist that the entire textile industry embrace the plan, but asked to be allowed to try it. "We are willing to prove it by practical tests," he said. "It will provide an interesting experiment," Johnson told General Hugh Johnson and the NRA officials. "Our reason for presenting the plan is the belief that the NRA is failing and that, through this failure, we will lose our only chance in this decade to prove that the theory of high wages and short hours will work. To my mind, a failure of the NRA principle would be a tragedy of major importance to the people of this country." The sharp criticism caused some of the NRA officials to bristle, particularly Hugh Johnson.

Returning from Washington after a weary week of meetings and no progress, Johnson, according to one newspaper report, "was disappointed but not discouraged." He had not given up. In addition to the shorter hours, he was openly suggesting a minimum hourly wage of 50 cents, as opposed to the 35-cent rate in effect. Workers across the country cheered that suggestion, while mill operators brooded in silence.

Many of Roosevelt's reforms and programs were aimed at enhancing the public welfare. The President went so far as to claim that the freedom of enterprise should be limited by consideration of public welfare. Johnson's philosophy of corporate responsibility also demonstrated an abiding concern for the public welfare. The principal difference was that Johnson wanted business and free enterprise to generate its own sense of public responsibility instead of being dictated to by government. He saw that jobs were the way to abolish welfare rolls. Unfortunately, however, the Depression climate was not conducive to changes by business, so many of

Johnson's suggested reforms fell on deaf ears in the business community, while Roosevelt's plans were gaining strong support from the public.

His most recent attempts to joust with Washington's politicians made him discouraged but still hopeful that he had some solutions to the nation's unemployment dilemma. Then there was good news. The new 35-hour work week he had been campaigning for soon resulted in 515 new employees at Johnson & Johnson, at a time when the bread lines in the nation were still long. In his jubilation he decided to run a series of company advertisements backing President Roosevelt and the National Recovery Administration, but shrewdly asking customers for the "sale." The ads carried a banner headline with Roosevelt's famous rallying cry to the nation—"Together We Cannot Fail." Under Roosevelt's picture, the message continued:

> Our leader points the way. America must follow. We cannot falter. Johnson & Johnson has been doing, and will continue to do, its part. We were among the first, if not the first, in our industry to sign the President's blanket employment agreement. Wages in our factories have been increased. Hours have been decreased. Already we have made a 10% increase in the number of our employees. We are observing the spirit as well as the letter of the agreement. Join with us in making the spirit of NRA a part of your daily life! Your cooperation is vital to its success. When you need merchandise such as we manufacture, you will be aiding the common cause of recovery if you specify Johnson & Johnson products. We say that proudly and unashamedly, for of such a mutuality of interests is the Spirit of NRA.

The ink on the ads was barely dry when the NRA reversed itself and proposed a new code calling for a 40-hour work week and a cut in the minimum wage to 32½ cents an hour. Johnson was flabbergasted—he would have to fire five hundred workers. So on November 24 he wrote his nemesis at the NRA, General Hugh Johnson, and detailed to him why the new rules would be bad for industry. Then his frustration showed, when he added: "I do not propose to waste any more useless discussions with the NRA."

The argument over wages and hours wore on, with much rhetoric and little relief for workers. Major manufacturers claimed they wanted changes, but they put the blame on the tens of thousands of small factory owners who were opposed to the NRA reforms. The earlier harmony that had prevailed between Johnson and AFL President William Green quickly disappeared when the union convened in Atlantic City that August. In his opening speech, Green castigated private industry for not putting the millions of idle back to work. Unless there was a resolution, he warned, "society may be compelled to take over the means of production." In response, Johnson sent a blistering telegram to Green, blaming him and his colleagues for the NRA's failure to accomplish its major objective. Labor leaders did not take a stand for higher wages and shorter hours, he told Green, because they feared that "a successful NRA might limit the future of labor unions." Many saw truth in the allegation, and the press reveled in the opportunity to carry on the debate.

The pressure on the NRA administrator intensified. General Hugh Johnson was getting it from all sides — from manufacturers opposed to the new codes for being too restrictive, and from a few, like Robert Johnson, who claimed the codes did not go far enough to offset the impact of the Depression. From yet another direction there was opposition from the vocal Secretary of Labor, Frances Perkins, and others in government who disagreed with the policies of the National Recovery Administration and the direction it was taking. Adding to Hugh Johnson's woes was a critical press that fanned the flames of the bickering every chance it got.

Finally, Hugh Johnson went to Roosevelt and suggested that he be allowed to resign as NRA administrator. He told Roosevelt that the multipronged attacks were having a murderous effect on the NRA and the entire recovery program. Besides, he confided, the strain was beginning to take its toll on him. While sympathetic and equally weary of the persistent attacks on the recovery plan, Roosevelt urged him to try to come up with a plan that would put the administrator of the NRA under the control of a board rather than one individual. But the general was insistent about leaving the post, and on October 1, 1934, he gathered the NRA staff together and made a poignant farewell speech that had many in the audience, including him, in tears.

In one of his parting interviews, Hugh Johnson told the press that he was opposed to a shorter workweek because it would increase the costs of goods by one-third. When Robert Johnson read that in the papers, he fumed, then sent the former administrator a caustic letter: "I never completely understood until this morning how great the distance between your viewpoint and the philosophy of a modern, enlightened industrialist" (Johnson was of course referring to himself). Then he fired another volley: "Your administration of NRA is one of the tragedies of the age and perhaps, due to poor execution of the principles behind that great institution, we have lost the opportunity of a century."

Having lost the Battle of Washington, Hugh Johnson went off to New York, where in another lapse of good judgment he became head of the infamous Works Progress Administration. He remained in that post for only a short but embattled period, which included a widely publicized fistfight with New York Parks Commissioner Robert Moses in the apartment of the general's former employer, Bernard Baruch. Then the general retreated to the more genteel role of newspaper columnist, where he waited in ambush for his old antagonist, Robert Johnson.

Back in New Brunswick, Robert Johnson pondered his next move in his struggle to be heard. For several years his proposals for shorter hours and higher wages had not gained acceptance, despite pleas to the National Recovery Administration, to labor, to business leaders, and even to the President himself. They got only token responses, but no action significant enough to deal with the nation's pressing unemployment problem. Voluntary compliance

[211]

now seemed totally unrealistic. There was only one other recourse, an appeal to Congress, which Johnson made in a written statement submitted through U.S. Senator A. Harry Moore of New Jersey on July 29, 1935. It was titled:

THE MOST IMPORTANT ISSUE FACING THE UNITED STATES OF AMERICA TODAY — THAT ISSUE IS UNEMPLOYMENT

The statement began:

> Let us not confuse ourselves with discussion of taxation, inflation, doles, the bonus or relief. These are effects, and not causes. The cause of our national distress today is the existence of approximately 10 million unemployed, men and women eager and willing to work, but for whom no profitable work can be found.
>
> We shall have no rest, peace, prosperity or happiness in this country until these men and women are back on jobs again, employed members of the consuming public, eager and able to buy the goods they make.
>
> We shall—on the contrary—until this one basic problem is solved —see only a continuation of the tragic disorder, waste and human misery of the past five years.

Johnson went on to urge Congress to take action to shorten the work day and raise wages to relieve the nation's present strife. He also called for the cooperation of his fellow industrialists, but stated that the issue of confiscatory taxes had to be addressed by the legislators. "It is futile to attempt to meet the problem with palliatives," he wrote, "for we can neither borrow ourselves out of debt, nor tax ourselves into prosperity."

"We are moving along a trend line," Johnson argued, "in which government, seeking to forestall the social unrest of unemployed citizens, must inevitably meet the problem by advancing into more and more projects ultimately competitive with private industry. It is a trend which inherently involves relief, doles and gigantic bureaucracies to administer them"

The Congress, Johnson wrote, had two courses to choose from—either live with the present chaotic unbalanced structure, with huge government grants for relief for many years to come, or adopt a new national wage and hour policy that would put people to work again and gain the enthusiastic support of industry. In his conclusion, he wrote: "Until unemployment is solved, taxation will feed its armies, to the benefit of neither the worker, the consumer, nor industry itself."

This time Johnson did not send copies to the press, so there was no burst of editorial support for his plan as there had been in the past. He waited, and waited, for a response from Congress. None was forthcoming, save for a few encouraging notes from congressmen whom he considered friends. From the others there was stony silence. He was dismayed. The silence could in part be attributed to politics at work. Roosevelt would be seeking reelection, and many in the Congress were not anxious to make it easier for him to win, even at the expense of easing the Depression crisis and extracting the country from the economic hole it was in. The timing was bad.

In November 1935, four months after the collapse of the NRA, Johnson came up with a new approach—actually the old plan with new players. He directed this new appeal to the U.S. Chamber of Commerce and the National Association of Manufacturers, the nation's two leading business organizations. He urged the two groups to present President Roosevelt with a plan whereby industry itself would be responsible for solving the national unemployment problem.

"Unless we do this," he warned, "we must be prepared to permanently support from 15 to 25 million people on relief at a cost that could reach $4 billion a year. The return of the unemployed to private payrolls is industry's own job, and I ask that we cease waiting for the government to do it and launch an immediately effective program, based on facing reality and accepting our responsibility as management. Private industry has not done an adequate job for the wage earners in the United States. American big business should give immediate consideration to the fixing of maximum working hours for all classes of labor, either by industrial cooperation or, if necessary, through constitutional amendment."

This time Johnson gave the newspapers copies of the letters the same day they were sent. The result was a brief flurry of news stories and editorials in support of the idea, but there was no response from the two national organizations. Not many businessmen were anxious to bail Roosevelt out of his dilemma. Nor were there many who, like Johnson, believed strongly that businessmen should bail the nation out. Some looked upon Johnson as a crusader. To others he was a maverick. And some wished he would just go away.

Witnessing the slow death of ideas he felt were vital to the nation was painful for Johnson. He had tried to penetrate the bureaucratic armor and failed. Little did he realize that this was only a rehearsal for the battles he would face when he became a brigadier general in the trenches in the nation's capital. The war, Johnson's as well as the nation's, was yet to come.

13

BOLD CONCEPTS

T HE kind, gentle, and very lonely Fred Kilmer died three days after Christmas in 1934, at the age of eighty-three. His beloved free spirit, Annie, had died on New Year's Day two years before, at the age of eighty. She had devoted the last fourteen years of her life to perpetuating the memory of their poet son, Joyce, through her writings and perky rhetoric. She never turned down an invitation to talk about her hero son or to dedicate a building or park named for him. The diminutive Annie, driven by bursts of energy and a cheerful demeanor, had become a sort of folk hero in her own right.

Annie was a gifted writer, conveying in her words warmth and kindness mixed with a lively sense of humor. She saw humor in everyday situations, as well as in what she called the "adventures" of life. But when she wrote about Joyce the humor quickly turned to sadness, as it did in the deeply moving poem "Memories of My Son, Sergeant Joyce Kilmer." In the years after his death she set six of Joyce's poems to music, which was another of her talents. They included his best-known poem, "Trees." The poem had also been put to music in 1922 by composer Oscar Rasbach, and it was his rendition, not Annie's, that became a favorite in the repertoire of popular singers across the land.

In her constant quest to keep the memories of Joyce alive, she received unfailing support from her ever-patient friend and spouse. No matter how obsessed she became, Fred always seemed to understand. In the dedication of one of her final writings, "Whimsical Whimsies," Annie paid a public tribute to her husband, and also expressed a poignant wish:

DEDICATION

To one whose counsel was always asked after I had accomplished something, the result of which I was a little dubious, and whose sympathy never failed me. Who, while he may not have always understood, at least fully appreciated me — who has always granted me every wish, and who, I trust, will grant my last, that of allowing me to go before him.

These scribblings are dedicated to:

My husband

Annie's wish was granted. Fred was now alone. Old age began to take its toll, not so much in how he looked or what he did, but in his lack of spirit. "My time and strength are well mortgaged," he remarked, and his friends, including Robert Johnson, privately nodded in agreement. Yet he continued to go to his laboratory almost every day, often at odd hours, burying himself in whatever work interested him. Though he still held the title of director of the laboratories, which was his for more than forty years, younger staff members had assumed his major duties. He spent many hours browsing through the company's historical museum, which he had organized to trace product development and trademarks.

Kilmer's daily visits to St. Peter's Hospital became a ritual in the last several years of his life. There he spent countless hours cultivating plants and herbs in the monastery garden he had created on the hospital grounds. It was supposedly the only one of its kind at a medical institution. From all over the world Kilmer had gathered exotic plants, many of which he used in the hospital's pharmacy to concoct medicines. His lifelong study of medicinal plants, combined with his knowledge of horticulture and chemistry, made him an expert on ginger, kola, pawpaw, belladonna, and other plants that had medical applications. The garden at St. Peter's enabled Kilmer to put one of his strongest beliefs into practice: "Closely allied with the practice of medicine is the preparation of medicine," he would say, and this also summed up his devotion to the profession of pharmacy.

At St. Peter's, Kilmer also became interested in the scientific training of nurses, just as he had taken an interest in the education of pharmacists in his earlier years. He used to engage the young student nurses in conversation, and they came to look forward to his visits, somewhat awed by his range of medical knowledge and bemused by his casual, sometimes unkempt appearance—something else Kilmer and his old friend Tom Edison had in common. He used to stop by the nurses' library, which had been given to the hospital in memory of Joyce, and often they learned more from him than from the books on the shelves. The first day his final illness prevented him from visiting the hospital, the nurses began mourning the loss of their friend and mentor.

Because Kilmer had outlived his contemporaries and all the members of his immediate family except his grandchildren, there were few mourners at the graveside at Elmwood Cemetery that crisp winter morning, compared with the number of lives he had touched. He was buried not far from his old friend, the first Robert Wood Johnson, with a headstone that reads:

> I have fought a good fight,
> I have finished my course,
> I have kept the faith.

Perhaps the epitaph did him justice, though Kilmer might have preferred the tribute in *American Druggist* magazine, "He was one of the most fascinating individuals American Pharmacy has given to the world," or *Time* magazine's description of Kilmer as "the most revered pharmaceutical chemist in the country."

The profession of pharmacy had lost its true champion, and the company was now without its strongest link to the past. Though the words of praise following his death were rich and eloquent, they too soon trailed off to a faint echo, as though planned that way by Kilmer himself. Johnson later named the company's historical museum after Kilmer, so future generations would remember him.

Robert Johnson's close relationship with the kindly Fred Kilmer after the death of his father had helped him through his period of uncertainty. Then, when Kilmer lost Joyce, his remaining child, Robert helped to fill the void. It would have been a more meaningful relationship for both if they had made their feelings known more than they did, but both were adept at disguising their feelings when it came to relationships, and that was unfortunate. Yet Kilmer spoke like a father, and Robert listened like a son.

•

In 1934, after several miscarriages, the last of which Maggi blamed on mountain-climbing in New Mexico, Robert and Maggi adopted an infant girl, Sheila. Johnson was charmed by the baby, and when he thought no one was watching he used to sneak into the nursery and talk to her for long periods, well before the child was old enough to communicate with him. Maggi, a doting mother, lavished the same attention on Sheila that she had received from her own close-knit Irish family.

Maggi rarely accompanied her husband on business trips, but when he returned she quickly brightened the room with her presence. Her beauty and youth enlivened their many social gatherings, and when they were alone her incessant chatter amused him and kept him from getting too wrapped up in himself. He could relax with her, and she provided support when he needed it. Maggi seemed good for him.

She could be mischievous too. That was part of her charm. Once Johnson was entertaining a group of male politicians at Morven, all of them strangers to Maggi. She and a young lady friend were biding their time upstairs waiting for the dinner to end. Suddenly, Maggi had a whimsical idea. She and her friend dressed up "as

French maids" and went down to the dining room to take after-dinner drink orders in their best French accents from the startled guests. Johnson went along with the gag without a word. Maggi remembered that he had little to say later that evening when the guests left.

Maggi and Sheila spent summers at Ghost Ranch, and Johnson would join them for as long as he could. In the winter they went to Nassau, where they decided to build a house on Hog Island. That gave Johnson the chance to get back to sailing, which he had sorely missed since disposing of the *Zodiac* after the race to Spain. The social pace in Nassau was almost as hectic as it was in Princeton. Their house guests on Hog Island included royalty and an assortment from the international set who flocked to Nassau in its golden days.

For all of his sophistication ("He was the most sophisticated man I ever met," said Maggi), Johnson did not know how to dance, or at least his efforts were awkward at best. He had developed a real aversion to dancing, and years later he explained why:

"As a young boy, I attended the Dodsworth Dancing School, a top-drawer institution. Little girls wore white dresses with huge sashes, long white stockings which invariably bulged with wrinkles at the knees, and white shoes—the invention of the very devil as they left an imprint each time a lad misstepped. The boys wore an even more impressive costume—a blue serge suit with an Eaton collar and silk bow-tie, black stockings, patent leather slippers that really had a shine, and, last but not least, spotless white gloves.

"So entering the ballroom, the young men bowed first to Mrs. Dodsworth, then to Mr. Dodsworth, and then to the assembled patrons and patronesses. . . . The boys retired to one section of the room and seated themselves in chairs arranged in rows. The girls sat across the room. The proper announcements were made. Completely out of step with the music, the students stiffly followed the instructor's 'left foot left, close; left foot front, close; right foot right, close; right foot back, close,' making a geometrically perfect box. . . . It was utterly impossible to perform with a partner, . . . there was only one place to put your foot and that was slap bang on your partner's little white shoe. This procedure was known as teaching. No doubt it had some merit, the outstanding one being that hundreds of otherwise happy children were convinced dancing was both unpleasant and abhorrent."

Maggi was a good dancer. One day in Nassau Robert told her he had decided to take dance lessons. Maggie was waiting when he returned home from his first lesson. He announced gleefully, "Maggie, there are all kinds of new dance steps!" "Really, Bob? Show me some," she replied. So they rolled up the rug, and from that day forth Johnson became a confirmed dancer, and later a superb dancer. "He would practice his technique for hours, dancing with a broom," Maggi recalled.

•

Early in January 1936, Johnson and Maggi went to Europe for a skiing vacation in Austria. He was a good skier, and the first five weeks were pleasant, but in early February he had a bad fall and broke his left ankle. When they arrived home on the liner *Europa* on March 17, he was walking with a cane and making light of the injury.

His serious thoughts on his arrival, however, were for the war clouds then gathering over Europe. "The French people are actually terrified at Chancellor Hitler's Rhineland coup," he told reporters. "As a matter of fact," he added, "every principal European country is anxiously eyeing France to see what steps she will decide to take against Germany. The situation is the gravest since the World War." Then he took the opportunity to underscore his hours-and-wages cure for the nation's economic ills, and reporters dutifully noted his views in their dispatches.

Midway into the 1930s, as threats of another world conflict started in Spain and began rumbling through Europe, there was a growing trend toward isolationism in the United States. It was not unlike the trend that preceded the world war two decades before, advocated by those who believed the nation would remain safer by not becoming involved. Johnson himself began to sound like a pacifist, and he took a more aggressive view on peace than the isolationists did. But he built his rationale for maintaining peace on an economic foundation, based on the principle that wars were caused by political mismanagement and the need to put idle people to work. It was not a new theory, but he gave it an interesting twist.

World Peaceways, an organization for disseminating information on peace and international affairs, had asked him to prepare a statement giving his views on the peace questions, and seeing this as another opportunity to present his solution to economic ills, Johnson agreed. He spent hours at Morven drafting the statement and developing an interesting tie-in between labor and industry and pacifism, which was later published in numerous newspapers. Johnson contended that the governments of the world were so badly managed that their leaders had to placate citizens with exploitation and war in order to get out of economic difficulty. "The key to this mystery of ever current war talk is to be found, in effect, in the existence of 20 million unemployed throughout the world," he wrote. "One reason nations fight wars for new territories is to solve an unemployment problem, even if it means employing men as fighters. Solve the problem of world unemployment and world peace and world prosperity will have a better chance. With more productive industry, jobs will become the weapons of peace."

•

When the National Recovery Administration was abolished by the Supreme Court in 1935, President Roosevelt was shocked because it cast doubt on all the other New Deal legislation he had managed to get passed during his first term. As a result of the Court's decision, more of his reforms were being challenged, and it was in the shadow of this growing crisis that Roosevelt ran for a second term. The Republican nominee was Governor Alfred A. Landon of Kansas.

Johnson decided to remain quiet on the sidelines during the presidential campaign, as had other liberal Republicans who believed that Roosevelt might, after all, be the best presidential candidate. It was not natural for him to be silent on any subject of interest to him. Supporters of Landon were somewhat miffed about Johnson's silence, while Democrats were encouraged by it. Shortly before Roosevelt was renominated at the Democratic National Convention in Philadelphia in June, Johnson gave all his employees a 5 percent bonus—one of several he awarded them during the Depression years. Immediately the pro-New Deal press interpreted the action as an expression of faith in Roosevelt. For once, however, Johnson did not take the bait. He let it pass without comment.

Johnson was a Republican, but he was also a patriot, and in that time of national strife he was more a patriot than a Republican. In his own way he was giving expression to the closing lines of Roosevelt's acceptance speech on June 27: "We are fighting to save a great and precious form of government for ourselves and the world." In that light, Johnson remained silent right through to November, which for him was a long time. Roosevelt needed no help getting reelected, polling nearly 28 million votes to less than 17 million for Landon. There was no hint of how Johnson voted, and no one, least of all Johnson, had any idea that one day he would be serving in the Roosevelt administration.

Unemployment remained a major challenge for the Roosevelt administration as it began a second term. With the National Recovery Administration now defunct, a new approach was taken with the appointment of Major General George L. Berry as Federal Industrial Coordinator. Berry called a meeting of the Council for Industrial Improvement, consisting of national business, industry, and labor leaders, for December 10 in Washington, D.C.

There, for the first time, Johnson announced yet another version of his wage and hour plan, proposing to classify all business and industry into one of three categories: 6-hour day, 30-hour week; a 7-hour day, 35-hour week; or an 8-hour day, 40-hour week. The idea was to allow "backward" industries time to adjust to fewer hours, while encouraging "progressive" companies to make the move to a

30-hour week right away. Simple as the change was, it cleverly took away the excuse that the full adjustment could not be made right away. Here was a plan for all, or so he thought.

The night before the meeting opened, Johnson hosted a dinner at the Mayflower Hotel for Berry, a score of leading industrialists, and a few congressional leaders, out of which came a glimmer of hope that something positive might happen. At the meeting the following day, one faction raised the question of "the constitutionality of work week legislation and the legality of maximum hour and minimum wage agreements in the face of antitrust laws," and Johnson recognized immediately that he was witnessing the slow strangulation of his plan. The next day, the press was enthusiastic ("The merit of the Johnson plan is that it is flexible enough for working out an arrangement satisfying to labor without disturbing industry"), but the majority of the council members offered no support. Discouraged, Johnson boarded the train and returned to New Brunswick.

.

It was more Johnson's philosophy of "corporate social responsibility" than his management style that set him apart from most of the industrialists of his era. In the mid-1930s, when virtually all of American industry was struggling for survival, Johnson came up with the bold concept that business had certain responsibilities toward society and that the more a company lived up to those responsibilities the better sales and profits would be.

The seeds of that belief came in a document he wrote and sent to every major industrialist in the nation in April 1935. He composed the first draft at Morven late into several nights, scribbling first the outline and then the text on his favorite lined yellow pads. He titled it "Try Reality." The focus was mainly his arguments on wages and hours, and his suggested solutions to the chaotic economic issues of the day.

Toward the end, however, he delved into what he called his "industrial philosophy" and went on to explain the larger reasons for the very existence of business, beyond merely the goal of making products and profits. These words to the nation's industrial leaders were Johnson's most profound and most prophetic:

> Out of the suffering of the past few years has been born a public knowledge and conviction that industry only has the right to succeed where it performs a real economic service and is a true social asset.
>
> Such permanent success is possible only through the application of an industrial philosophy of enlightened self interest. It is to the enlightened self interest of modern industry to realize that its service to its customers comes first, its service to its employees and management second, and its service to its stockholders last. It is to the enlightened self interest of industry to accept and fulfill its share of social responsibility.

Putting the responsibilities of business in those terms, and linking them to the belief that it was in the enlightened self-interest of business to serve customers, employees, and stockholders, in that order, was a new concept for much of American industry to embrace. In many companies the interests of the stockholder reigned supreme. But Johnson saw it differently. "I firmly believe," he later explained, "that if you put the customers, employees and communities [which he added later] first, and you carry out these responsibilities well, then the stockholders will be well served and the company will be successful."

Hoping that the message in "Try Reality" would elicit a groundswell of support from his fellow industrialists, Johnson waited, and waited, in vain. There was no meaningful response, not even at the urgings of the press, as in one editorial: "Mr. Johnson's challenge should not be ignored. He has placed the issue squarely before the nation's industrial leaders. If they continue to evade it in the interest of temporary profits, they can expect nothing but increased taxation and governmental interference with private enterprise."

The rejection by his fellow industrialists did not deter Johnson. Business, he believed, and people like him, were in the seat of power. He told an Associated Press reporter in Atlanta early in January: "America is in the hands of its captains of industry, including all kinds of employers." Nor did his setbacks keep him from being ranked with the nation's business leadership. That same month *Fortune* magazine carried an article and photos of him, oil magnate Jean Paul Getty, and Charles Edison, son of the inventor. And while it took decades to play out, Johnson's philosophy of corporate social responsibility, which he first defined in 1935, was tested and found to have substantial merit.

•

At the beginning of his second term in 1937, Roosevelt began formulating what came to be known as the "Second New Deal," a less radical approach to resolving the nation's domestic problems. That June a joint congressional committee began hearings on an administration wages-hours bill to revive the workable labor features of the NRA, and Johnson was invited to be the first person to appear before the committee. The bill called for giving a five-member board the authority to fix maximum hours and minimum wages within limits set by Congress. The Roosevelt administration was hoping that a 40-hour week would be written into the bill.

After the frustrating years of speaking out on the subject and not being heard, Johnson relished the opportunity and came to the hearing in Washington on June 3 at his articulate and persuasive best. Immediately, he caught the committee's attention by proposing a 30-hour workweek for what he labeled "modern industry," where labor represented less than 25 percent of total production costs; a 35-hour week for "semi-modern industry," where labor costs were between 25 and 50 percent; and a 40-hour week for "backward industry," with labor costs in excess of 50 percent. He also recommended a minimum wage of $16 a week. It was an old theme, but this time he was at the center of a new stage, and he knew it.

The committee had not been prepared for such a bold proposal from a businessman. The *New York Daily News* reported that the members registered "surprise," but "shock" might have been a better description, as the congressmen contemplated the reaction of supporters back home who were running "semi-modern" and "backward industries."

Johnson anticipated that. "My ideas are pretty unpopular," he told the committee. They were unpopular with his fellow businessmen, perhaps, but not with the members of the press at the hearing. Most of them liked his message as well as his performance. In a syndicated column, "In Washington," Raymond Clapper wrote:

[Johnson] looks well-fed and well trained, a golf club tan, a close-clipped "crew" haircut, a bright, easy way that bespeaks a successful, comfortable and prosperous existence, although questioning developed later that he had never attended college but had gone to work at 16 and, inheriting his father's business, built it into one of the best-known industries in the country. A practical man. Now we would get the real dope. Johnson told the committee:

"I am urging that this bill be approved in accordance with enlightened self-interest and that in passing this legislation you will be doing a great thing for business and a great thing for millions of American employees. Private management must assume new social responsibilities or forego the privileges of management and the satisfaction of creative enterprise."

Mr. Johnson has a six hour day in one of his textile mills and in some of his other establishments. He says with a laugh that some of his colleagues call him a philanthropist. He thinks it is good business.

Senator Black has a question: "Do you belong to the National Manufacturers Association or any other industrial committee of that kind?"

"Senator," the industrialist replies, "I have been unable to find a sympathetic group of colleagues in organized business and I've tried very hard."

Clapper ended the column by commenting, "Apparently the witness isn't a typical industrialist after all."

One writer in particular had an opposite view. Hugh Johnson, the retired Army general and former NRA administrator, was now a columnist for United Features Syndicate and saw an opportunity, at last, to fire a round at his longtime antagonist and critic. He didn't miss the mark.

"Mr. Johnson was just about the biggest pain in the neck that the NRA encountered under the cotton textile code," General Johnson wrote in his syndicated column. Having gotten that off his chest, he half agreed with Johnson's position, but saved a volley for his fellow journalists: "Before going off half cocked to applaud such seemingly enlightened views as Mr. Johnson's, it would be a swell idea to get the whole picture and his particular place in it."

All that summer the political process bounced the controversial bill back and forth like a rubber ball. Having been thrust in the center of the controversy, sometimes uncomfortably, Johnson was frequently sought out by reporters for comment. He had, in many respects, become a sometimes lonely business voice for the bill. In September, as it came closer to a vote in Congress, he issued a statement that reminded the public of the mounting costs of the Works Progress Administration in its efforts to put people to work. It said in part: "It is far more expensive to pay the taxes for WPA work and for doles than it is for business to increase its payrolls in accordance with a reasonable wages and hours bill."

The bill was passed by the Senate just before Congress adjourned in November. It had been favorably reported by the House Labor Committee, but a Rules Committee filibuster had blocked a vote on it and prevented it from being considered. The measure was scheduled for action in December by a special session of Congress.

Some of the bill's strongest supporters in Washington were fast losing hope, but Johnson was determined to stick it out to the bitter end. It was defeated in the House on December 18. Ironically, the very same day, Johnson was speaking on its behalf before the Chamber of Commerce in Gainesville, Georgia, lamenting that business had let the President down in his hour of need. Commenting favorably on Johnson's speech, the *Atlanta Journal* called him "one of the foremost industrialists in the country" and added: "So long as this spirit animates enough of our leaders, the goal remains in sight."

Someone suggested that copies of the editorial be sent to Washington, and Johnson did not object. So along with a cover note complimentary to Johnson, a local Democrat sent the editorial to James Roosevelt, then serving on his father's staff in the White House. Other copies went to the chairman of the Democratic National Committee, to Tommy "The Cork" Corcoran, the charismatic frontman in Franklin Roosevelt's brain trust (and a friend of Johnson's), and to James A. Farley, the Roosevelt loyalist and consummate politician then serving as Postmaster General. In terms of getting the President's attention, this was the equivalent of using the editorial and cover note to paper a room in the White House.

President Roosevelt's relationship with big business was under a constant strain right into the second term, even though the approach taken by the Second New Deal was more an oblique attack on the nation's problems, with more consideration given to prevailing sensitivities. In that respect, it was becoming more effective and more palatable to business. There were indications that business leaders were looking for reasons to cooperate more fully with Roosevelt.

At the end of April 1938 a series of events took place in Washington that had all the markings of a brilliant political plot that resulted in a coup for the President. Later Roosevelt said it was merely happenstance, perhaps fortuitous political happenstance. In his message to Congress on the recovery, and later in his radio fireside chat of April 14, the President asked for a rededication to teamwork between government and industry, for the common good.

Taking this cue, John W. Hanes, the newly appointed "Wall Street member" of the Securities and Exchange Commission, began calling some of the nation's top business leaders, urging them to join in a pledge of cooperation with the President in helping to bring about economic recovery. He got sixteen of the country's top businessmen to agree, including Johnson; Owen D. Young, Chairman of General Electric Corporation; and Winthrop W. Aldrich, Chairman of Chase National Bank. It was an illustrious group. Turner Catledge, writing in the *New York Times*, pointed out that these men represented "billions in industrial investment and employing power" and, through offices and directorships, some 130 major companies in the nation. The sixteen prepared and signed a pledge of cooperation with the President, which reached his desk just minutes before he was to begin a press conference. Roosevelt told the newsmen the document was "excellent."

That just happened to be the day before Roosevelt met with Henry Ford. The indomitable auto magnate, an outspoken opponent of the New Deal, had stayed away from Washington since the days of the Hoover administration, and this was to be his big return. The pledge from the business leaders made headlines nationwide and was the perfect prelude to Ford's visit. When reporters met the seventy-four-year-old Ford at Union Station and asked him what he expected from the meeting with the President, he replied gruffly: "I'm just a passenger."

True. Franklin Roosevelt was the driver, and the wheels were turning. A crowd of several hundred cheered Ford as he entered the White House for a meeting that produced no major news. But it didn't have to. Ford's visit, coming on the heels of the pledge of cooperation from the business leaders the day before, generated screaming headlines that many interpreted as a new truce between Roosevelt and all of business. It was more of a softening of opposition than a truce.

A few days later Johnson was called to Washington for a private meeting at the Mayflower Hotel with "an emissary of the White House" and Wisconsin Senator Robert M. La Follette Jr., an eloquent defender of the President's program. Present also was an unnamed "New Dealish publisher." Washington columnist Joseph Alsop, a cousin of Roosevelt, got wind of this and later filed a column calling the meeting "a significant one." He reported that

Johnson listened attentively but "was a little leery of buttering the White House" on the spending bill. The other subject on the agenda, Alsop wrote, was a new wages-hours bill. Johnson needed no briefing on that subject, since by this time his name had become nearly synonymous with it.

As the tug-of-war continued between Roosevelt and business, the infighting within Republican ranks at the national level was growing more intense. The previous December, Johnson had intensified the conflict when he called for the mass resignation of the Republican Party hierarchy. That was the same day the executive board of the National Republican Committee was meeting in St. Louis to select a committee to draft a declaration of principles for the party. In his statement, which made headlines across the nation, Johnson called for the "complete, permanent, political retirement" of National Republican Chairman John D. M. Hamilton, Governor Alf Landon, and Herbert Hoover.

"We must accept the fact," Johnson declared, "that the majority of American people are no longer willing to follow this leadership. The Republican Party must develop a vital new program which will find public acceptance. It must attract new leaders, new faces, with the young men and women of the country in an important majority position in high party councils if the two party system of government is to survive in this country."

Only the day before, a committee of "younger" Republicans had asserted themselves, recommending an infusion of new blood into the party and suggesting a steering committee that included Charles A. Lindbergh, Thomas E. Dewey, William Green of the American Federation of Labor, Henry Luce, and columnist Dorothy Parker. This echoed the plea of three New England governors for a housecleaning of Republican leadership.

Hamilton lashed back at Johnson's public challenge. "I have never run away from a fight, and I shall not now," he replied. One newspaper noted: "The chairman of the Republican National Committee has red hair, and some of the characteristics traditionally associated with that hirsute color scheme." Hamilton continued: "Mr. Johnson applauds the legislative tendencies of the New Deal. This is characteristic of certain Republicans who seem to think there is no place in the Republican ranks for those who actually oppose the New Deal and who apparently believe that the way to beat Mr. Roosevelt's methods is to surrender to them. I cannot agree."

Nowhere in the nation was Republican discontent more evident than in New Jersey. Jersey City's infamous mayor, Frank Hague, had engineered the election of Senator A. Harry Moore as Democratic governor, despite charges that the ballot boxes in Hudson County had been stuffed. These charges were not new, but Johnson was widely reported to have been the financial "angel" behind the defeated Republican candidate, Senator Lester H. Clee, who represented the new Clean Government Movement that Johnson had helped launch. It wasn't like Johnson to squander large amounts of money on a losing cause and take it lightly.

Johnson waited to go on the offensive with New Jersey Republicans at a huge rally in Camden County attended by more than 1,000 party faithful. Sharing the platform with the defeated Clee and Governor George D. Aiken of Vermont, Johnson addressed the gathering and launched a movement calling for a liberal wing of the Republican Party in New Jersey.

It was a stunning proposal. Johnson told his audience: "Nearly all well qualified Republicans running for important state office in recent years have been defeated by their own party. The Republican party in New Jersey has suffered from a rather strange collection of diseases. We have had more than our share of political liabilities." Reform at the national level, he said, must begin with reform at the state level, and the state Republican platform must reflect "the desires and appetites of the man in the street." He continued: "I believe that in New Jersey there are millions of people who will support a realistic liberal group whose objectives are better government at lower costs."

The challenge shook the traditionalists in the room. The *Phila-*

delphia Record reported: "[Johnson's] address was no less startling than his suggestion to rid the Republican Party of Alf Landon and Herbert Hoover." And one editorial called it "Enlightened Republicanism."

In many respects, Johnson sounded like a candidate. Some political pundits had him waiting in the wings to be asked to run for U.S. Senator, which he denied. He was often mentioned as a candidate for governor too, but he explained his reluctance to run for public office to a reporter in Dallas, Texas, who wrote: "He denied that he would make the race, . . . saying he preferred the role of private individual, with the private individual's right to fight for what he thinks is right, support whom he may please, and criticize without being accused of seeking political gain."

On June 16, Johnson stood before what should have been a hostile audience, the Eighth Annual Institute of Labor at Rutgers University. The assemblage included labor leaders and trade union delegates from the New York metropolitan area and the eastern states. At a time when organized labor was battling to get a toehold in American industry, when issues of the right to collective bargaining and strike-breaking were being settled with bloodied bats, it was not the most promising forum for an industrialist. Congress had finally passed a watered-down bill that was more of an embarrassment to Johnson than to the unions. Already the legal posturing over interpretation of the new 25-cents-an-hour and 44-hour-week limits had begun.

Yet Johnson was philosophical and hopeful. "It is not a good piece of legislation. It is a mighty weak start in a good direction," he told the labor union audience. Then he proceeded to blast labor for failing to support the provisions he had been advocating for years. Their fears that higher wages and shorter hours would make unions unnecessary, he said, were totally unfounded. He also had some advice: "You have not been able to sell the principle of organized labor to the underpaid worker in the past fifty years; you will raise the potential number of union members a thousandfold by establishing decent maximum hours and minimum wages." Later in the speech, he made what many considered a shrewd observation. "American businessmen," he said, "are probably the most efficient in the world, but I am afraid they are nevertheless political morons. I find we have as astute a group of politicians as we have anywhere, but I am afraid they are business morons. But there are more politicians who know something about business than there are businessmen who know something about politics."

The news wires hummed with that quote, which was covered as a story on its own. "The ovation at the end was without parallel," one reporter wrote.

Before business audiences Johnson's remarks were equally direct. He urged them to develop a strategy that would encourage well-managed labor unions, contending that the best way to control unions was to cooperate with them. He took comfort, he said, in the labor unions' support of free enterprise and their staunch opposition to communism. He told business audiences that it was their mistreatment of workers that brought on unionism in the first place, a charge that was not always well received.

More and more he began urging business to become politically active. "No man in business can be successful unless he has some knowledge of practical politics," he said repeatedly. Johnson later gave this concept practical application when he initiated courses in politics for his company's employees, the first program of its kind in the nation. In time, many business organizations began to make an effort to understand the political process better.

In the South, Johnson had become what the *Atlanta Georgian* described as the "stormy petrel" of the textile industry, with his persistent demands for a 40-cent-an-hour minimum wage. He was the scourge of southern textile manufacturers. "They stand convinced that he is a wild-eyed maverick in their midst," another paper said. But he used one reply to repeatedly quiet his opponents, and this gained him even more popular support. "Surely," he said time and again, "no industry will stand before the nation recommending a minimum wage of less than $16 a week for the head of an American family." There were no responses to that.

Johnson had spoken before many audiences in the past several years, most of them representing business, labor, and politics. On January 6, 1939, he went to Athens, Georgia, to address the student body at the University of Georgia, not far from where he had built the world's most modern textile mill. Some of his mill workers were the parents of students who gathered in the university chapel to hear him speak.

His thoughtful address was aimed directly at the subjects young people want to know about, or, more important, things students should hear. He had an uncanny ability to target his message to his audience and hit the mark. On that day he scored a bull's-eye. The migration of the textile industry from New England to the South was a thorny issue as well as a matter of Southern pride. The contention that lower wages in the South were justified because of worker inefficiency just wasn't true, Johnson told the students. He continued:

"We operate mills in this country, in Canada, and in foreign countries, and the efficiency at our Gainesville mills surpasses all others. Business in general follows markets and not low wage levels. If the South wants more industries, then let it increase the buying power of the consumer."

Other textile manufacturers had called Johnson a philanthropist for paying the highest wages in the industry. "I am not a philanthropist," he told the students. "I am in business to make a profit." But in doing so, he added, he saw a responsibility to consumers and employees that went far beyond the profit motive.

"If business leadership will assume their full social responsibility, I have no fear for the economic progress of our country," he told them. "It is the job of modern management to give the people they employ a full sense of security growing out of accomplishment and performance, as well as a declaration of purpose." Otherwise, he said, "no management is worthy of its position."

"Business has missed the greatest opportunity of the century," he continued. "Industrial leaders have largely ignored the negative public attitude toward management. Let business conduct itself in the community in which it operates so as to win the approval and the confidence of its neighbors. If this is done, we will not require any of the national business organizations which are said to speak for business. They have accomplished exactly nothing."

By their applause, the students gave him a high mark for the lesson in business management.

14

A PATTERN
OF GIVING

B y nature, Johnson was a very generous person. Some of his colleagues thought he might be too generous. "If you didn't watch him, he would give away the factory," one commented. Just before Christmas in 1936 he took 12,000 shares of his Johnson & Johnson stock (then a privately owned company) and formed the Johnson New Brunswick Foundation. This later became the Robert Wood Johnson Foundation, and with $1.2 billion from Johnson's estate it became the nation's largest philanthropy devoted to improving health care in America.

The Foundation's early focus was on the people of New Brunswick, many of whom were still feeling the effects of the Depression. Johnson had always felt an allegiance to the place where he was born and where the company had its origins, so when word got out that he had formed a foundation, the requests for assistance began pouring in. There was no pattern of giving. The help ranged from food and clothing for poor families, to fixing an orphan boy's teeth before he departed for Boy's Town in Nebraska, to a down payment on a house for a highly regarded black policeman with a wife and eight children. As long as the dividends from the stock held out, the needy were seldom turned away, and when they were depleted, Johnson dug into his own pocket to help.

A small group of local businessmen served on the Foundation's board, but Johnson ran it during the early years according to his own views on philanthropy. Because this was before the federal government began paying close attention to foundations, Johnson did as he saw fit. He was president and, perhaps more important, the person in charge of the petty-cash fund—which meant that anyone with a reasonably convincing story would be helped. "His hand was always in his pocket ready to help an individual or organization that needed it," a contemporary remembered. At one meeting a board member suggested that an attorney be consulted about a gift Johnson wanted to make. "Well," he said, "let's go ahead with it, and if we get in trouble, then we'll call in the legal talent."

He did, however, establish one ironclad rule, that the company was never to be mentioned in connection with a grant. Johnson saw the Foundation as his own, and he remained its only contributor. The one exception was a 130-acre tract of land on River Road in Highland Park that he and his brother Seward donated to the Foundation, then had deeded to Middlesex County to become Johnson Park. The Works Progress Administration put some four hundred men to work for a year to turn it into a recreation area.

His abiding interest in improving health care prompted Johnson to refocus the Foundation's various projects at the two New Brunswick hospitals, Middlesex and St. Peter's. Concerned about increasing the flow of physicians, Johnson had the Foundation provide no-interest loans to a large number of young men from New Brunswick who wanted to become doctors but could not afford a medical school education. They agreed to repay the loans when they established themselves in practice, but very few of them ever did, and this was always a great disappointment to him.

Johnson enjoyed his personal wealth to the fullest, but he was always concerned about flaunting it in the presence of his employees. He drove himself to work, albeit in a large sedan, a Cadillac or a Chrysler. In later years he owned a custom-made white Rolls Royce, which he used mainly to take Mrs. Johnson to New York for the evening. But the chauffeur was never permitted to bring the Rolls to the office entrance. Instead, Johnson would walk several blocks and meet the car at a pre-arranged place so his employees would not see him getting into the Rolls Royce. Everyone knew, of course, that he owned it.

His attachment to the business had become legendary. Women often commented that Johnson was "married to his company," though they never said that in his presence. He was quick to defend the company, and business in general. One night at a dinner party at Morven a woman guest asked him why his products cost so much. He thought a while, and asked: "Can any of you tell me the approximate cost of preparing this dinner?" They looked puzzled, so he challenged them to find out the true cost of preparing a dinner at their homes. Each time the same group got together, someone would offer new information. Johnson recalled how it turned out: "We had progressed in simple steps from a discussion of the menu to the contributive costs of the stove, light, heat, rent, and of course the food. After they learned the cost of a meal, they had less trouble understanding the cost of an industrial product."

He involved himself in every area of the company, but showed a preference for developing marketing and advertising strategy, and opportunities for expansion. The close relationship that had developed with druggists smoothed the way for the introduction of new products, even sensitive ones. Falling in that category was the new sanitary napkin developed for women, which had acquired the name Modess. Johnson's ultimate goal, which he later achieved, was to provide inexpensive sanitary protection pads to millions of women worldwide. He considered it undignified for women to have to resort to makeshift methods to meet these needs, and he was especially determined to bring sanitary protection products to women in underdeveloped countries.

Sales of Modess napkins grew so rapidly that Johnson decided to form a separate company, the Modess Corporation, later to become the Personal Products company. The new entity almost had a disastrous start. Sales offices had been rented at 500 Fifth Avenue, New York, and to gain the attention of the drugstore business a special two-for-one offer was widely advertised. Within days, even before the office furniture arrived, there were ten mail sacks bulging with orders. "We decided to sort the orders alphabetically," a Modess manager recalled, "so we got a bunch of empty cartons, and by midnight we finally completed the job." Returning the next morning, they were horrified to find that the janitor, thinking the cartons of orders were wastepaper, had thrown them out.

Johnson was particularly astute about judging executives and how they would fit into the business. In 1933 he met and was impressed by George F. Smith, a Chicago native who had never attended college but went into business after serving in the infantry in France in World War I. Smith enlisted as a private and rose to lieutenant. When Johnson met him, quite accidentally, he was managing a small chemical company. Johnson saw promise in Smith and brought him into the company as his assistant, and he later rose to become president of Johnson & Johnson, a position he held for seventeen years.

He was also right about the potential of Philip B. Hofmann, a gangling six-foot-five graduate of the University of Pennsylvania's Wharton School, Class of 1930. Hofmann's father owned a drugstore in their native Ottumwa, Iowa. When his son was about to graduate from Wharton, then an undergraduate curriculum, he wrote to Johnson, told him he admired his company, and said he would like to see Philip get started with a firm like Johnson & Johnson. Johnson wrote back and said to send the boy in. Hofmann was given a job as a shipping clerk, and Johnson made it a point to keep track of the young man's progress. Thirty-two years later, Hofmann succeeded Johnson as Chairman of the Board and Chief Executive Officer, but unfortunately his father did not live long enough to see how well his letter had paid off.

The rapid mechanization of industry brought with it a great deal of stress in the workplace, and this concerned Johnson, who spoke out on behalf of those who had become "a small cog in the huge production machine." In addition to machines that worked with robot-like precision, there was a flurry of new work-simplification programs and a rash of eager advocates of time and motion studies who brought their principles to industrial management with evangelistic fervor. Their methods took a heavy toll on some of the old-timers, and Johnson was one of those who resisted. In *Dun's Review* he wrote: "Having always enjoyed my work, I can imagine nothing more serious than facing a lifetime of workaday monotony. If industry hopes to win a fuller measure of good-will, ways must be found to break the monotony or to relieve it."

As the pressure continued to mount in industry, there was a re-birth of the term "slave driver." Ed Olly, who was now managing editor of the *New Brunswick Sunday Times*, mentioned one day to a Johnson & Johnson executive that the company was getting a bad name for driving its people too hard. "Slave drivers they call you people," Olly said. He later wrote about what happened next:

"A few days later I got a call that Bobby wanted to see me. So I met the 'Viking on a horse' in his penthouse office, and a man in a white coat served him (and Smith) and me as we talked over what to do about Johnson & Johnson being called 'slave drivers.' Bobby was aroused. 'Come on,' he said, and he took me on a whirling dervish tour of the factory. Up and down stairs, in and out of corridors we went, and everything was immaculate like a hospital. Everywhere we went he'd stop and talk to the people. 'Hello, May. Hello, Tom' he'd say, calling them by their first names."

The visit convinced Olly that the "slave driver" charge had no basis.

Johnson felt it was important to put that rumor to rest, because he prided himself on being an enlightened employer who looked out for the welfare of his people. And at the time, he was trying to convince high school graduates that modern industry offered them a rewarding and satisfying future. In a message to the schools in the area he said: "Gone is that era of thought that the only chance of a truly satisfying vocation lies in a profession. The professions need and will have a sufficient number to their ranks, but now in modern industry a wide range of satisfying livelihoods is opening up to our future citizens." Then he argued: "The chief role of education, and the future of the nation, lie in giving the individual a chance to work out a satisfying career. Modern industry wants to be part of this ideal, but it needs the continued help of education."

Part of his appeal to attract young people to industry was his personal campaign to eliminate the term "common laborer" from the vocabulary. He had been at this for several years and continued to pursue it in the years to come. "In modern industry there should be no 'laborers,'" he claimed. "Each position should be that of a technician, and these people should be classed with other skilled specialists. No industry has the right to exist that is not successfully striving to correct and eliminate all jobs that require what is known as 'common labor.'"

•

On May 17, 1938, Johnson announced to his Board of Directors, all of whom were members of management in the privately held company, that he was becoming the company's first Chairman of the Board. "I shall not work any less," he told them. "I am merely putting the New Brunswick plant under independent management, just as the other companies of the firm have been for the past ten years." He was now forty-five years old, and since he had taken over management of the company, annual sales had increased from $18 million to $33 million.

Whether he held the title of President or Chairman made little difference to the outside world. True, he was backed by a superb management team that ran the day-to-day operations, but Robert Johnson *was* Johnson & Johnson, and it would be that way for the twenty-five years he was Chairman.

Johnson's new role as Chairman of the company did not limit his range of involvement in the business. Shortly after becoming Chairman, he decided to make everyone in the company "employee salespeople," and he explained the role in a letter to every wage earner. He urged them all to engage in "friendly conversation" with store clerks about the benefits of carrying and selling the company's products. "I am not asking you to become a sales person, but merely to present our business in a favorable manner," he said. It worked. Employees, especially the factory workers, took great pride in the fact that Mr. Johnson, the Chairman, had asked them to become "company representatives."

During those years he was working long hours, and when the day was over he would drive to Princeton where he and Maggi would host one of their frequent dinner parties. The current subject of interest was politics in New Jersey, where tax reform had become a major issue. As he often did, Johnson brought dinner guests to Morven who could shed light on a particular topic. One of his frequent guests was a Princeton University professor, John Sly, and the two of them, along with other dinner guests, began examining ways to bring about tax reform in the state. Out of these discussions came a plan, largely Johnson's and Sly's, that became known as the "Princeton Local Government Surveys."

Essentially, the plan was a guide showing municipalities how to control costs and reduce taxes. Later, when New Jersey adopted a new state constitution, the "Princeton Surveys" played a key role. At the time it was first announced, however, New Jersey politicians lashed out in protest because they believed the plan would undermine their power. Former Governor Harold G. Hoffman, still a political power in the state, told the *Newark News*: "The Princeton Surveys is the product of a lot of academic gentlemen with their heads in the clouds and their feet on Bob Johnson's pocketbook." The governor underestimated its importance, because the plan was later adopted by municipalities all over the nation.

·

If historic houses can represent power, then Morven was a powerful place. Within its walls political schemes were hatched and the fates of both man and state debated and often determined. But upstairs at Morven it was a different world—one where a pretty little girl, Sheila, then five, would act out her storybook fantasies and wait patiently to spend whatever amount of time she could with her Prince Charming, her father. Sheila, like no other person, could bring out a side of Johnson that few others ever got to see. The memory of those wonderful years still brought a twinkle to her eye many years later:

"My Dad's presence in my life was very strong, and his coming and going in my little world on the second and third floors of Morven was constant. Indeed, my mornings often started with a visit with him as he dressed, me curled up on the huge polar bear rug in his room. Then we would have breakfast together. It was a time when he read his newspaper, supported by a silver holder, but it was also a time for many useful lessons, such as how to open a boiled egg and eat it out of the shell.

"Often there were more exotic items on the menu, such as finnan haddie. He introduced me to this dish the summer we visited Nova Scotia. I was still very young, but I was as 'hooked' as the poor fish, and so my Dad made up a poem for me:

> Finnan Haddie Sheila
> Went to the shore
> With her little basket
> For to catch some more.

"Most of the day I spent with my nanny, whom I loved. I remember the day my Mother called me down to the music room and introduced us: 'Sheila, this is your new nanny, Miss Caroline Hay.' That was in 1939, and we were together for five years. Miss Hay would have me bathed and ready for Father when he got home from the office, and the moment he was back he would come to see me. Then on evenings when they were not busy with their many friends, I would dine with them in that elegant dining room that seemed so large to me then but really wasn't.

"At a very young age, Father taught me about money, of which we had so much, when most of the country, indeed the world, had so little. When I was old enough to get a weekly allowance of twenty-five cents, he insisted that I give ten cents of it each week to the church collection. Much of the remainder was put aside, at his instruction, so that I could purchase Christmas presents for each person who worked at Morven and who did so much to make my life comfortable and secure.

"I remember how important security was for us in the days following the kidnapping of the Lindbergh child. I was never to go anywhere alone, not even to school. Miss Hay was given a bicycle so she could accompany me. Then at night once we had gone to our third-floor aerie, Miss Hay locked the door at the top of the stairs and was instructed not to open it for anyone other than my parents or a member of the household staff.

"As I look back, Robert Wood Johnson the businessman was not of great interest to my young mind. However, I remember having a discussion with my friend Mikie Erdman about the comparative importance of our fathers. His father was the mayor of Princeton at the time, and mine was the president of a company. The titles impressed us, but I cannot say that the different sizes of homes among our friends ever meant anything to me.

"On the other hand, my Dad the sportsman impressed me greatly. I loved to watch him exercise his two hunters, Vanity and Wild Oats, and later I tried to match his style when he gave me that black pony. But my most lasting memory was not of galloping around the ring but of falling off one day when the saddle slipped, ending upside down under a trotting animal, and not getting hurt. But it was his love of the sea that stays with me today and that has influenced my own life."

In 1935 Johnson had bought the 74-foot auxiliary sloop *Medora* from Trubee Davison, a New York banker and President of the Museum of Natural History. After sailing the *Medora* in Nassau and Florida waters, Johnson decided the boat was too tame for him — what he really wanted was another ocean racer. Then one day he spotted the sleek 54-foot yawl *Stormy Weather*, built by Sparkman & Stevens, and he developed an immediate attachment. He chartered *Stormy Weather* and entered her in the 1937 Miami-to-Nassau race, which she won handily. He then purchased the boat, and she went on to set the record for three consecutive wins in the Miami-Nassau race, in addition to taking the Lipton Cup as well as the Governor's Cup Race off Nassau, both in 1939. *Stormy Weather* won every race in which Johnson entered her.

Then he decided to build a faster boat, using the latest design and newer materials. "Design a boat that will be the last word in ocean racers," he instructed Sparkman & Stevens. The new yawl, 67 feet overall, was built at City Island in New York and had a beam of 13 feet, 7 inches. It was the first boat of its kind to have a duralumin mainmast and boom, although her mizzenmast and boom were wood. The sidelight boards were built into the rail to offer less wind resistance. She was launched just before Christmas in 1939, in time for the Miami-Nassau race in February. The yacht was christened *Good News*, the name of a Broadway musical that Maggi had worked in during her modeling days. Naturally everyone thought *Good News* would be unbeatable.

Maggi was appalled when Johnson announced that he was replacing *Stormy Weather*. She remembered her reaction. "You can't just get rid of that lady, Bob! She's been too good to you. She has won every race for you," Maggi said she told him. The new owners entered *Stormy Weather* in the 1940 Miami-Nassau race, but she was edged out by *Good News*. Maggi recalled that all the yachtsmen and their guests had gathered for the victory celebration in Nassau. During the party, word came that a new correction in the handicapped race placed *Stormy Weather* ahead of *Good News*, which was then placed third. "I was ecstatic," Maggi said. The new yawl made a comeback in March by setting a new record in the St. Petersburg to Havana race, and Johnson planned to race her in Europe, but by then the war was spreading rapidly across the continent.

Maggi was more of a good sport than a good sailor. In Nassau and at Newport, where they also vacationed, she and Sheila would sail with Johnson on day trips, but when he was competing they would remain on shore and cheer him on. Sheila recalled those wonderful days when she was allowed to go sailing, with her father at the helm: "There was one wild trip on Long Island Sound when we ran into a good storm. I was sent below for safety, and Mother was attached to a mast. It might have been safe below, but oh was I sick, but not Dad, never!"

Those carefree days would soon change as Americans watched with mounting concern as Hitler's armies marched across Europe. The nation was ill-prepared to engage in a world conflict, for in 1939 the U.S. Army had troops and officers numbering only 175,000, ranking it sixteenth in the world, right behind Romania. President Roosevelt offered a guarded warning that would have been difficult to back up: "Hitler should beware of an aroused democracy," he told the nation.

The arousal began in America's factories, where production was being ratcheted to record levels for all materials needed for defense and combat, including medical supplies. In a matter of months Johnson & Johnson was turning out a significantly larger output of wound-healing products, and Johnson involved himself in the planning of that effort.

Wherever there was an emergency, particularly one threatening the national interest, Robert Johnson became more energized than ever. The bell had to ring only once to bring out the patriot in him. He spoke openly about commitment and love of country, and without the slightest sense of embarrassment. These were troubling days for the country. The threat was there, palpable, and growing. But the enemy had not yet shown itself, which added to the anxiety and apprehension felt by everyone.

For the better part of two decades, Johnson had contributed generously to New Brunswick in countless ways. His loyalty to the city ran deep. There had been numerous attempts to honor him for his generosity, but he was always able to discourage them. It made him uneasy to be thanked publicly. Finally, the planning for a testimonial dinner at the Roger Smith Hotel on July 10, 1941, had progressed too far for him to stop it, though he tried. Henry G. Parker, the dinner chairman, commented on Johnson's reluctance to be honored in his opening remarks to the 150 business and civic leaders gathered for the tribute. Many had known him since boyhood. Parker referred to the fitting quotation from Lincoln that was included in the dinner program: "Let us have faith that right makes might; and in that faith let us to the end dare to do our duty as we understand it."

In his reply, Johnson spoke of the "emergency" confronting the nation. Just a few weeks earlier the Nazis had engaged the Russians, and the battlefields now stretched from the Arctic to the Black Sea. The world's dictators, Johnson pointed out, dealt with the destitution of the masses by forming armies, but democracies dealt with the problem by creating jobs. "What workers need most," he said, "is dignity and security." He described his own efforts to build modern plants and to bridge the gap between management and labor as "experiments to reestablish the personal equation which has been lost in American industry." In his work toward these goals, he said, he hoped to establish a pattern others would follow.

As a token of their esteem, they presented Johnson with Carl Sandburg's six volumes on Lincoln. He was touched.

Two weeks later, on July 26, the company threw one of its famous employee parties, attended by more than 5,000 people from all sectors of the work force. Harry James and his orchestra played, and the master of ceremonies was WOR's Jim Parsons, who sang his popular "I'm Nuts About the Good Ole Oo-S-A." The revelers drank one hundred barrels of beer and consumed three tons of food, and danced until the early morning hours. All evening long, Johnson had a steady succession of dance partners — the lively, robust Hungarian women from the factory, and the more timid ladies from the office staff. He charmed them all.

PART THREE

A Vision for America
1941–1950

15

THE BATTLE OF
WASHINGTON

EARLY on the morning of December 7, 1941, the Japanese attacked Pearl Harbor, inflicting shocking losses and throwing the nation into a frenzy. The next day, Congress approved a declaration of war on Japan, and three days later the United States was at war with Germany and Italy as well. Defense preparation suddenly became wartime reality, and citizens throughout the land—men, women, and children—sought to aid the cause in whatever ways they could. It was a time for mobilizing patriotism as well as arms.

On December 19, New Jersey Governor Charles Edison called Johnson to Trenton, explained the urgent need to establish a rationing program for civilians, and asked him to become New Jersey's rationing administrator. He accepted, on condition that he be allowed to resign if a more vital assignment in the war effort came later. The governor agreed.

The first priority in rationing was rubber tires and tubes, because 98 percent of the nation's supply for raw rubber came from the Pacific area, which was completely cut off. Johnson immediately began recruiting volunteer members for rationing boards from all of New Jersey's five hundred municipalities. Within a week it became unlawful for any dealer in the nation to sell car or truck tires or tubes without prior approval. On January 4 Johnson met with all the new members of rationing boards and explained that tires would be rationed at about 7 percent of normal purchases. The boards were to decide who would receive them, based on hastily drawn priorities. For some boards there wasn't much to do besides say "No." One community, Johnson said, would have a quota of "two-thirds of a tire for January."

In the following months, he handled the rationing job with crisp efficiency, a reflection of his ability to organize and keep things as simple as possible. Meanwhile, he made inquiries about entering Army service, and there was immediate interest — based on his business record and his demonstrated skills as an executive.

On April 21, 1942, Johnson submitted his resignation to Governor Edison, saying that he would be commissioned as an Army colonel on May 4. He was to report to the Army Ordnance Department in Washington, the group responsible for providing all military supplies, but first he made a hasty trip to Michigan to inspect the new plant of Midland Ordnance Foundation Inc., which Johnson & Johnson had set up as a nonprofit subsidiary to do war work, principally as a shell-loading depot.

When he returned from Michigan he began winding down his work at the company. By then, Johnson & Johnson and its domestic companies were frantically gearing up for what would be record-setting production of a wide array of medical and hospital products to be used by the American and Allied forces. Soon the company would be quadrupling its normal domestic output of medical supplies and converting some facilities to produce combat equipment.

Ever since he was in his prep school drill unit and in a junior cavalry troop, Johnson had been intrigued by the military. In World War I he was a captain in the Army reserves, and later he attended the Summer War College conducted by the military. He had no apprehensions when he arrived in Washington in early May to resume his "military career."

But he was totally unprepared for wartime Washington in the

spring of 1942. Later he explained: "I was assigned to a small desk in a small room with five other officers. My rank rated a stenographer. The ranks of my colleagues were such that each also rated a stenographer in a room that measured about twenty feet by twenty feet, with loops of telephone and light wires dangling in spiral festoons from the ceiling." The crowding of ten people in one small office was just the beginning of his Washington education.

Small businesses in America were hurting because most of the war contracts were going to large companies, which were capable of producing the vast quantities of goods needed for the war. However, some 165,000 businesses in the "small company" category were desperately in need of war contracts to ensure their survival, since most of them had been cut off from raw materials that were being diverted to the war effort. The government enlisted the services of Wall Street wizard Floyd Odlum and gave him an opportunity to deal with the problem, but he quit in disgust when he learned it was just an advisory role. Congress tried several times to come up with a solution before creating the Smaller War Plants Corporation, which had a $150 million budget for loans to help conversions to wartime production.

Three weeks after arriving in Washington, Johnson was summoned to the Shoreham Hotel to meet with Donald M. Nelson, chairman of the War Production Board, who told him President Roosevelt wanted him to take over the Smaller War Plants Corporation. "I hesitated, and finally declined," Johnson said later. "I felt committed to the Ordnance Department. I thought my experience was more appropriate to the procurement services than to the role of remedying what seemed to me, all things considered, a hopeless situation."

On June 25 a column in the *Washington Daily News* said: "President Roosevelt wants his good and liberal friend, Robert Johnson, head of a big pharmaceutical firm, named chief of the War Production Board's new Smaller War Plants Corporation. But certain WPB bigshots are trying to sabotage the appointment. And certain

Congressmen too. Mr. Johnson is a Big Business Man. They want a Little Business Man."

The inference was clear enough. The "big" and "little" had to do with whether he would be too independent for the bureaucrats to handle, not with the size of the business Johnson ran. Roosevelt wanted that kind of independence, but others saw Johnson as a loose cannon on deck.

That September, Johnson was transferred to New York City to become chief of the New York Ordnance District, where he had a staff of 2,800 and directed purchasing from some 7,000 manufacturers in the metropolitan area. Very little was being purchased from small businesses. On October 14, Johnson was summoned to Washington to appear before the Senate Committee on Problems of Small Business Enterprises. The fact that he was the first witness suggested that the committee had heard from the White House.

With his usual confidence, Johnson told the Senate committee he had the solution: "There is only one way that small business could be systematically built into the war effort, and that is to decentralize procurement services and establish regional offices in every major city, to act as liaison with local manufacturers, and to nurse them into the war effort."

The committee chairman responded, "You are willing to exercise your experience and skill in this direction, if you are permitted to do so?"

"Oh, yes," Johnson replied.

"That is fine," said the chairman.

Later Johnson wrote: "It was that statement that was to bring me again to Washington."

The next day, Lieutenant-General Brehon B. Somervell, chief of the Services of Supply, and Johnson's superior by several echelons, testified at the hearing. He stated flatly that hundreds of small industrial firms would have to close, "and you can put that down as a fact," because the Army could not fit them into its production schedule.

By the end of 1942, the Smaller War Plants Corporation had managed to place only 224 contracts totaling just over $9 million with small companies. With some 120,000 small companies on the verge of bankruptcy, the situation was critical.

Early in January 1943, Johnson was ordered to report to Washington for a new assignment. He went straight to the White House for an urgent meeting, where he was told that President Roosevelt wanted him to take over the Smaller War Plants Corporation. This time there was no refusing it. "I certainly did not want the job," Johnson recalled, "but I took it." On January 19 the White House announced Johnson's appointment as Vice Chairman of the War Production Board (WPB) and Chairman of the Smaller War Plants Corporation (SWPC).

Though most members of Congress were anxious to approve Johnson's appointment and send him into the fray carrying the banner for small business, there was some resounding vocal opposition. One of the shrillest outcries came from the Democratic Senator from Missouri, Harry S. Truman, who asked publicly how someone as closely identified with big business as Johnson was could possibly represent the interests of small business. Later Johnson revealed that he had visited Truman personally and offered to resign if the senator ever found any conflict between his industrial position and the new appointment. After the two men met, Truman withdrew his objections and the appointment was approved.

Johnson took over the SWPC on February 8, a job that Washington columnist Drew Pearson called "the most difficult, undesirable job in government." The *Chicago Tribune* described it as a "hot seat." From the beginning, Johnson displayed a certain bravado and arrogance about the assignment that won him both praise and condemnation. He already had a penchant for making bold comments to the press, which were quickly transmitted into bold headlines. His most recent daring and imprudent statement came when he told a reporter that he had given himself just six months to do the job—the job that most people in Washington considered impossible. "If I don't do it in that time, they'll get rid of me, and if I do it by that time they'll also get rid of me, because the job will be done." The United Press carried the story across the nation to the believers and the doubters, many of whom were in Washington, including some of Johnson's superiors in the Army.

The announcement of Johnson's appointment came directly from the White House instead of through regular channels. *Barron's* reported that this was done in order to give the "errant colonel" some needed clout with his Army superiors and the War Production Board. From the outset, Johnson missed no opportunity to annoy his Army superiors, to the delight of leaders in Congress, the press, and the droves of hopeful small businessmen waiting to be rescued. At one of his first press conferences, he was asked whether he was an Army officer or an executive of the War Production Board. He replied, "I am responsible only to Donald Nelson [Chairman of the WPB], and through him to Congress. I am not responsible to anyone else." That rankled the brass at the Pentagon.

"Rarely can an Army officer affront his superiors and get away with it," said *Barron's*, but Johnson got the SWPC job primarily because influential congressmen were burning to 'save' their business constituents and Johnson was the one official who had said, with table-pounding aggressiveness, that they could be saved."

Johnson began by seeking autonomy for the SWPC and outlined what he saw at stake. One of his most persuasive arguments came in a letter to New York's Governor Thomas E. Dewey, who was then grappling with a string of small-plant bankruptcies in his state. Johnson wrote: "If we are going to lose in this war the advantages of private enterprise and the enthusiasm that grows out of owner-management, we are going to lose one of the most important ingredients of production, besides losing the American way of life." Dewey made the letter public and it drew wide attention.

Nothing had worked so far, so it was up to WPC Chairman Nelson to take drastic action. He was acutely aware of the growing pressure from Congress and the White House on the War Production Board to take corrective action. Carter Brooke Jones of the *Washington Star* disclosed on March 23 that Nelson had quietly signed an order giving the SWPC complete authority over its own activities.

Now it was up to Johnson. Announcing that he had a plan, he said he would focus first on pulling together what he called "the greatest collection of buying-power ever generated in the United States to a given program." Then he would decentralize into regions and bring distressed companies face to face with those who had production orders, not only military procurement officers but also the big corporations and local and state government agencies that bought supplies. Then he would recruit experienced businessmen to volunteer their services as intermediaries until all the distressed companies were finally back to work. He was absolutely convinced the plan would work. "For good or evil," he declared dramatically, "I am proceeding with my plan."

His first tactical error was to promise too much and to make his promises public. The Associated Press reported on February 22, 1943: "Colonel Robert W. Johnson, new vice chairman of the War Production Board in charge of spreading work to the little fellows, says it is really going to be done this time, to the tune of $25 billion to $35 billion worth of business this year!" The story was carried all across the nation. In Wenatchee, Washington, the *Daily World* commented: "Colonel Johnson is the latest of a string of top-flight businessmen who have been assigned the job of getting work allocated to smaller plants. One by one his predecessors have fallen by the wayside." To those who knew the magnitude of the problem, it was inconceivable that 10 percent of the nation's $240 billion in war production commitments could be diverted to small business.

When Johnson returned to Washington after his New York assignment, he rented a lovely house at 86 Kalorama Circle, N.W., filled with rare antiques, crystal chandeliers, several fireplaces, and with a pleasant garden. Maggi and Sheila spent weekends in Washington, at first frequently, and then only occasionally. Johnson was spending more time traveling to the various district SWPC offices to implement his plan to decentralize authority, and finding less and less time to come home to Princeton on weekends. Maggi began to worry about the strain on their marriage of thirteen years. She sensed something was wrong, beyond Johnson's busy travel schedule, but she was not one to raise questions, for she did not like confrontations. Nor did Johnson ever approach the subject.

In Washington, he had moved the SWPC offices to the top floors of the Mayflower Hotel. At least this time, Johnson figured, there would not be ten people to a room, as there were on his first exposure to wartime Washington. He sent a secretary from the company to open his office, and she reported that it resembled a "pigeon loft." Actually, it was three rooms, a fireplace, and three baths. When Johnson arrived, he inspected work procedures in the office and called a staff meeting.

"I attempted a modest approach toward better working conditions," he recalled later. "Very gently I touched on the matter of courtesy to customers, I mentioned housekeeping, played up the advantages of a workable office, and suggested that every desk be relieved of extraneous materials by way of the wastebasket. I further suggested that nothing be left on desktops except materials in immediate use, that nothing be stacked on top of files, and that coats and hats be hung in their proper places. And then, as an afterthought, I concluded that nothing should be attached to the walls unless it was in a frame."

The staff members looked at one another in utter dismay. The clutter of paperwork and unanswered correspondence were like battle ribbons to Johnson's beleaguered staff. "In silence the meeting adjourned," Johnson said. "It plainly was not a success." Nor was the effort. To have removed a single poster from the wall meant war with the Civil Service Commission. It wasn't like the home office, he found.

That disastrous staff meeting came at the time of the toilet episode, another confrontation he lost in his early days on the job.

Being lodged in a hotel, as they were, there were far more toilets than the one-toilet-to-twenty-people ratio prescribed by the "regulations." A young man appeared in Johnson's office and announced that the excess toilets would have to be locked because there was no provision for cleaning them. Johnson was aghast, but that didn't change things. The padlocks appeared quickly and the 1-to-20 ratio was established. He bristled, but offered only token resistance.

In his grand plan, Johnson envisioned a field staff of 2,500 managed by governing boards at the twelve regional offices. The boards would be comprised of local businessmen serving without compensation, and Johnson would recruit them personally. He proposed taking the authority to subcontract away from the Washington-based military procurement agencies and putting it in the hands of his regional boards. He also wanted to give the boards authority to grant loans up to $25,000 to small businesses so they could convert to wartime production. Meanwhile, he began working on defining just when a small plant becomes "distressed" and eligible for special help.

Then he wrote to the Secretary of War, the Secretary of the Navy, the Chairman of the Maritime Commission, and the Director of Treasury Procurement, requesting detailed information on the terms and methods the big prime contractors used in awarding subcontracts. He attached a list of 252 large corporations that had the preponderance of war contracts and said he would like the information back by April 7, less than thirty days away. "We were seeking important information," Johnson said later. "Both the letter and the forms were carefully prepared."

The deadline came and passed and Johnson didn't get a single reply. And with each follow-up telephone call to procurement officers, he heard a new excuse for the delay.

"That's when he decided to tape-record his phone conversations," said Tom Deegan, a longtime friend from Princeton who was a public relations professional and working in Washington at the time. "He got so tired of hearing these guys change their stories that he decided to nail them by taping the phone calls. It didn't make him very popular, and they screamed to higher-ups."

The welter of correspondence was another problem. When Johnson got frustrated over the amount of correspondence it took to answer one question in government, he put all the letters on one issue on a scale, had a photo taken, and got it printed in the newspapers. This upset Harry Truman, among others.

Though the decision to focus on the regional boards was made for operational reasons, it became an enormous political advantage to the SWPC. Now when congressmen came crying for help for distressed plants in their districts, they were referred to the regional board run by their own constituents. By deflecting the problem away from Washington and back to the local level, Congress was off the hook. Johnson hadn't planned it that way, but it was, in the words of Ward Schultz of the *Detroit Times*, a "ten strike."

The White House had been carefully monitoring Johnson's progress at the SWPC and was aware of his handicap. As a colonel, he had little hope of pulling rank in a wartime Washington that had an abundance of military brass. Roosevelt decided to correct that, and on May 17, the White House announced that the president was naming Johnson a Brigadier General of Army Ordnance. Immediately, eyebrows were raised all over Washington, especially beneath the braided caps at the Pentagon. It was rare for an Army promotion to be announced by the White House. Roosevelt was sending out a clear but unspoken message about the standing of the man he had put in charge of the SWPC — that he was not to be taken lightly at the Pentagon and that he would have presidential backing.

An elated Johnson called Maggi and asked her to bring Sheila to Washington so she could be the one to affix the brigadier general star to his uniform at the promotion ceremony. Maggi declined to go, but sent eight-year-old Sheila on the train, along with a member of the household staff. Johnson was waiting at Union Station when the child arrived. When she got to her room at the Mayflower, Sheila wrote her mother: "Dearest Mommy, When I got off the train I saw Dad, and I ran to him and was glad to see him again. Then he told me that I was to pin on his star in front of a few people, and mind you those people are the office staff. I was never so happy in my life. At that minute I wished you were there. I am very proud of my Dad, and who wouldn't be proud of their Dad if he was to be made a Brig. General. Love, Sheila. P.S. I am sorry that my letter is not longer than this."

Many years later Sheila still remembered the thrill of that day. "At first I had great trouble attaching the star to his uniform. Minutes passed and then more minutes. Everyone was standing around and they offered to help, but I refused. Finally, my Dad sat in a chair and that made it easier for me. When I finished the audience applauded."

The promotion suited Johnson fine. General Robert Wood Johnson. It sounded much better than "Colonel." Little did he realize that he would be a general for exactly sixty-four days.

The military uniform was important to Johnson; it always had been, even during his prep school days. It was not clothing, but a costume worn by another personality within himself. He was a meticulous dresser—his clothes did not hang on him, they were sculptured. The tailoring was flawless, the standards having been set by the dedicated needle-wielders in the custom shops along Oxford Street in London many years earlier. And wherever he went, he pursued the same standards of sartorial perfection.

He had an Italian tailor custom-make his colonel's uniform, and he brought him back for the new fittings. They were tediously long, but for this purpose he had infinite patience. The results were impressive. He was slender, and he had a ramrod military posture. There was no better-fitting military wardrobe in Washington.

As brigadier general he began an exhaustive travel schedule to meet with his regional boards. Quietly, he had supplemented his staff by recruiting a number of senior-level business executives—

some from his own company—to contribute their time as "unofficial volunteers at $1 a year." When Civil Service Commission officials got wind of this, they insisted that the volunteers take proficiency tests, just like all recruits to government service. Johnson protested loudly, but to no avail. Next, he did battle with the Bureau of the Budget, and was again repelled. This time his bureaucratic adversary was a young man whom he later described as being "at least twenty years my junior, with, I think, a bright new degree in public administration."

At issue was whether the SWPC field force should have the 2,500 people that Johnson recommended, or the 1,000 the young bureaucrat said would be sufficient. Johnson tried holding his ground, but the young man told him it was useless. "He suggested that we avoid further controversy and that his opinion would prevail with the Bureau of the Budget; that whatever the Bureau of the Budget recommended, the President would accept; and that whatever the President would accept, the Congress would accept—and he wished us good day and departed." Johnson added: "It worked out precisely as the young man said it would. It was embarrassing to have my opinion summarily set aside in the presence of the directors and executives of the Corporation, but it was very simply done."

Being sidetracked by the Civil Service and worked over by the Budget Bureau was not as disconcerting to Johnson as the defeat of his budget request by Congress. The House voted 105 to 52 to cut the $18 million budget request to operate the Small War Plants Corporation to $12 million. Those genial congressmen he had encountered at the hearings were less understanding when it came time to vote.

Despite the frustrations, some positive things began to happen. Over a seven-week period that summer, the SWPC placed orders with small businesses for 2,625 prime contracts valued at $217 million. Among the companies were 1,285 that had not previously received war work. One problem with reporting on progress was the tediously slow system that was in place. Months elapsed before new gains were made public. It was a start, but it was only a fraction of the billions in contracts Johnson had so intemperately promised.

At the SWPC, Johnson's policy on public information endeared him to the press. Shortly after taking office he declared in a memorandum to his regional offices: "The SWPC is paid for by taxpayers, and its employees are at the service of the public. It will henceforth be the No. 1 rule of this organization to receive and talk to accredited representatives of the press. Since the outbreak of the war, the American press has commendably handled the matter of military security with self-imposed censorship which has been most intelligent. Hence, press representatives will be regarded as fellow American citizens, who are trying to serve their community by conveying to their readers the public information which is rightfully theirs." Then he wrote his district managers. "In the presence of press," he said, they were not "to pass the buck."

Johnson then began crossing swords with members of the War Production Board, where he was vice chairman. In a speech before the New York Advertising Club, he said that war production had been delayed some six months by the erection of new plants that were not needed. "We have made mistakes," he declared. "We built new plants, big ones and too many. We built facilities that existed across the street." The "we" meant "they," since Johnson had never participated in those decisions. In the eyes of his Washington critics he was becoming increasingly dangerous, yet his candor continued to win him new admirers.

By early summer 1943, the tide of battle in Europe was beginning to turn in favor of the Allies. The Nazis had lost in Africa, were losing the Battle of the Atlantic, and were suffering huge losses in Allied air strikes. In the United States there was cautious talk that the end of the war in Europe was in sight.

Planning the transition of industrial production from wartime to peacetime took on a greater importance. Johnson and others began to focus on releasing increased quantities of scarce but non-critical materials to small companies so they could begin their recovery. The concept gained immediate appeal, because for some companies it was their only hope of survival. But the more Johnson tried to negotiate the transition, the more he was rebuffed by the military brass. The tension grew.

16

ENTER EVIE,
EXIT MORVEN

WHEN he went to New York to head Army Ordnance in the fall of 1942, Johnson took an apartment at the exclusive Waldorf Astoria Towers, the hostelry that catered to potentates and presidents. He worked long hours, and when he first went to Manhattan he went home every weekend to be with Maggi. Then the trips back to Princeton became less frequent, but that wasn't due only to his work schedule.

His evenings in New York were often spent out on the town, and in his impeccably tailored colonel's uniform he cut a handsome figure. For years he had moved smoothly with New York's café society. Ever since his discovery in Nassau that he had a natural talent for dancing, he had become extremely fond of it. Once he had learned the latest steps from a succession of dance instructors, he became increasingly proficient and graceful. He was now a very good dancer. He knew it, and so did others. When he glided across the floor with a partner in his arms the couple often became the center of attention. More and more, his partner was not Maggi.

At the center of nightlife in New York at that time was dancing to the big bands in hotel ballrooms, or to musical ensembles in the smaller, more intimate supper clubs — El Morocco, The Stork Club, "21," Copacabana, La Martinique, and others in the same glittering orbit. The major hotels featured ballroom dancing, and most of them had floor shows starring a dance team that whirled through their intricate steps with eye-catching precision.

One of the best dance teams in New York was The Vernons, handsome Jim Bruff and his beautiful auburn-haired wife, Evelyne. Both were approaching forty, but she looked younger. Bruff, who had attended the Pennsylvania Military Academy, had a natural flair for the entertainment business. Earlier, when the celebrated movie star and dancer Irene Castle saw Jim and Evelyne Bruff dancing at the St. Regis Roof, she was very impressed — so much so that she encouraged them to take the name "The Vernons," after her late husband and dance partner Vernon Castle.

First in their native England, and then on to the ramparts of the world, Irene and Vernon Castle had captivated audiences with their elegant exhibition ballroom dancing, and the dances they created, like the "Castle Walk." They became world-famous, and reigned supreme until Vernon's tragic death while serving as a flight instructor during World War I. So with Irene Castle's encouragement and permission, Jim and Evelyne became "The Vernons." Under this new name they opened the new Persian Room at the Plaza Hotel, and soon all of New York was enchanted by them, and especially the dashing Colonel Robert Wood Johnson.

In addition to being a performer, Evelyne was a dance instructor, and Jim Bruff was co-owner of La Martinique, the smart supper club on Fifty-seventh Street. It was one of Johnson's favorite haunts, and it was there that he met the striking Evelyne and danced with her for the first time. They danced together beautifully. Johnson was captivated, and so was Evie (Eve-ie). When Johnson came to La Martinique they often shared a table.

Many of New York's eight or so daily newspapers had "gossip" columnists who would make the nightly rounds of the city's favorite bistros in search of titillating items for the next day's column. Some, like Walter Winchell, were syndicated and their "beat" extended far beyond the supper clubs. Many years later, Frank Farrell, one of the more popular columnists, recalled the night he first met Johnson at La Martinique.

"I came in with Walter Winchell," said Farrell, "and Evie called us over to the table where she and Bob Johnson were. We had a few drinks and swapped stories. Both Winchell and I knew Evie. In addition to her professional dancing she was also a dance instructor, and Bob Johnson became one of her students, and her husband was busy running Martinique. Maggi was back in Princeton. Bob and I became friends—a friendship that lasted more than twenty-five years. We did a lot together."

Johnson and Evie managed to stay out of the columns, and Farrell explained: "Winchell was a peculiar guy. If he didn't like you there was no way to persuade him to like you. If he did like you he would do anything for you, and if he respected you he would never, never tarnish your image. So that in all the time Bob Johnson and Evie were dancing partners, Winchell never referred to it. That was the kind of friendship he extended to Bob Johnson."

Johnson's courtly, old-world manner precluded his having a flaming romance with Evie behind her husband's back. On one occasion he invited both of them to join him for dinner at the River Club and said he'd like to get together again. But there was no doubt about his attraction to her, which began with the lessons on the dance floor.

As a gangly young girl in Cambridge, Massachusetts, Evelyne Paynter had loved to dance, but learning wasn't made easy: "My mother didn't think nice young girls should go to ballet." Finally she persuaded her parents that it was good exercise. "They decided it was all right, for the exercise. I never did anything very alarming in the ballet, and I think probably I could have, but my mother was against it, and my father." Her father was born in England and later became an American citizen. He made a comfortable living from his inventions, one of which was a type of medical needle used on cancer patients. They had a house on the beach, and the four children — three girls and a boy — were taught to make friends with books, many of them, at an early age.

As other women had, Evie found Bob Johnson intriguing, as well as a remarkably good dancer. When they were on the floor alone, and performing, it brought a slight hush to even the noisiest ballroom. They also talked well together. She had a quick mind, and although she never attended college she did go to drama school and was well versed in the theater and the arts. She had charm, poise, and a stunning appearance. All these attributes appealed to Johnson. The problem was that both were married, and Evie was a devout Catholic.

It wasn't long before the rumors about Johnson and Evie got back to Princeton and Maggi. She recalled the nasty rumors: "People would say to me, 'Maggi, where were you last weekend? We saw Bob dancing around New York with that red-headed girl,' " and Maggi said she would reply: "Oh, I know he was there. That's just his dancing teacher." But Maggi began brooding more over his absence, explaining: "I'm only happy when other people are happy."

Maggi did not confront him, preferring to believe that the problem was transient. Johnson, on the other hand, would become sullen and uncommunicative when something was bothering him. As a result, there was no resolution of what had now become a serious breach in their relationship.

"Finally," Maggi said, "he did come home one weekend in the late spring of 1943, and I said: 'Bob, I don't think you're very happy. I think you're under a strain. I don't like to see you under a strain. You have a very big job in Washington. You're not happy, and you've got to make a decision.' "

"Maggi, maybe you're right," he replied.

"He went to his room and I went to mine. I cried my eyes out all night long, but I knew I had done the right thing, for myself. I cannot live a lie."

Maggi continued: "The next day was Sunday. I drove him to

path. He had gone from civilian to colonel to general to civilian, all within a span of fourteen months, and from colonel to general to civilian in just sixty-four days.

Some two weeks later, Johnson and Evie were married in Salt Lake City, and word of the event sent the newspaper columnists scurrying for their typewriters. Syndicated writer Delos W. Lovelace wrote in the *Detroit News*: "Brigadier General Robert Wood Johnson hands his commission back to the War Department, interrupting his third honeymoon to pick a fight. (Urging that noncritical materials be released so small companies can resume business.) . . . He leaves the Army because he may seem to come in conflict with military needs, and if the General were in uniform that would look odd."

For someone who doted so on being well organized, Johnson's life had fallen into disarray. Between waging the battle of Washington and dealing with the changes in his personal life, he had worn himself to a frazzle, physically and emotionally. His march on Washington and the bureaucracy was now about over. It had been neither a supreme victory nor a crushing defeat. He had focused national attention on the plight of small businesses and diverted substantial war work their way, but he fell far short of the billions in war contracts he had promised in the early days as chairman of the SWPC. He never came close to that goal.

On September 16 the *Washington Star* speculated that he was about to resign as chairman of the Smaller War Plants Corporation: "Johnson recently went to the Cornell Medical Clinic for a check-up," the paper reported. "As a result of that his doctors advised that he would have to 'slow down.' He was in Washington today for a meeting of regional chiefs of SWPC and will return to the clinic for further tests." Eight days later, on September 24, Johnson called a press conference and announced he was stepping down as SWPC chairman because of poor health. "The corporation's work is now in hand," he said. That was only partially true, as subsequent press assessment would show. Johnson told reporters that the SWPC had become a "political football" but that the businessmen associated with its administration had "picked up the ball and made it into a job." And he had a kind word for Congress: "I thank God for Congress. I have a great respect for it every day. I think it is the greatest American institution in Washington."

Then he reviewed what he saw as his accomplishments. The position of small business, he said, was generally stronger than it had been for twenty-five years, despite idle facilities in many plants. There were fewer failures and bankruptcies than in any normal year. There were 8,000 to 10,000 small factories with some capacity remaining for war production, and between 4,000 and 6,000 of these were in a distressed condition. Their chief hope for survival, he told reporters, was in getting orders for civilian goods.

His parting words were picked up by Walter Winchell and newspapers all across the nation. "Washington," Johnson said, "is a magnet for mediocrity."

The comment stirred up even more debate about Johnson in Washington. There were sharply divergent views on why he had quit and how effective he had been while there. Johnson summed up his side of the debate in a letter to New Jersey Governor Edison: "The job was in hand, the organization was complete, the policies were established, and the house was in order. There was no widespread destitution in small business in America, and I had suffered a physical collapse, which for the first time in my life has put me out of circulation. These are the reasons; there are no others."

But *Business Week* magazine had a different view of why he left Washington: "Johnson's temerity in suggesting that as ordnance contracts are cut back the Army should release the materials for essential civilian uses so incensed Robert P. Patterson, Under Secretary of War, and Lt. Gen. Brehon B. Somervell, chief of the Army Service Forces, that they prevailed upon Donald Nelson as chairman of WPB to request Johnson's resignation. Just a few weeks previously Johnson had resigned his wartime commission as brigadier general to do battle for civilian industry without the restraint laid upon him by his uniform. And Johnson's parting shot when he quit SWPC was that more orderly administration of the home front would be one of the greatest contributions to the war effort. Pointing a finger at absenteeism, he said that when women have to stay home to do the family washing, a washing machine becomes as important as a bomber."

No one could argue that Johnson's health might have been sufficient reason for him to leave Washington when he did, but there was little support for his contention that small business was on the road to recovery, to the extent that he said it was. It would take the termination of the war, still nearly two years away, for small business to really begin its revitalization. So the suspicion lingered that Johnson had been ambushed by a group that didn't think mavericks made good Army generals on the battlefields of Washington.

Among the first letters he received expressing regret over his illness and resignation was one from President Roosevelt, written on September 28:

Dear Bob,
I am awfully sorry to have you leave. You have done grand work and I hope much that you will really take care of yourself and get well quickly. When you get about again, run in and see me.

Always sincerely,
FDR

One senior staff member of the SWPC wrote him:

Dear Mr. Johnson:
This place seems like a morgue since you left. Everyone would be most happy to have you return, health permitting.

These were not the sentiments at the Pentagon, where they were happy to be rid of him.

Several futile attempts to lure him back to government service were made, including creating a new post for him. But Johnson wasn't interested, and while his health had failed, his humor did not. "Government work is not good for my digestion," he said in a letter to a former colleague at the SWPC. "I cannot be happy with compromise, procrastination, delay, and confusion. Quite frankly, I would rather work in a ditch, and do a good job, than join the great debating team."

In addition to stomach troubles that plagued him throughout his lifetime, Johnson had an enlarged heart, which doctors traced to a bout with rheumatic fever in his youth. His emotion-charged Washington experience, coupled with the breakup with Maggi, tacked on a few more ailments. On October 14 he wrote the acting chairman of the SWPC: "Things are going very slowly with me, and I have learned that it is going to be two or three months before I will be in circulation again." Throughout that fall Johnson spent his time in Princeton, recuperating and drafting a book on his experiences in Washington.

.

Life in Princeton pleased Evie. It was easy to succumb to the town's combined charms of academics and affluence. But Morven was something else. The big old house looked and felt like it belonged to someone else, which it did—Johnson had leased it from the Stocktons.

Maggi Shea claimed she had exorcised the ghost of the British intruder Cornwallis from Morven, but Evie Johnson imagined another image there that might haunt her. Maggi. Johnson offered no resistance when Evie suggested they build a new house. For the past fourteen years he had paid the price of living with history. He later remarked that it had cost him dearly to negotiate the lease for Morven, and he then poured huge amounts into the restoration. The Stocktons had driven a hard bargain, including the demand that an elderly family matron be allowed to maintain her residence in the tiny wing on the northwest corner. She remained there for the next dozen years, a quiet interloper.

There was also the lack of privacy. One Fourth of July morning in the early 1940s Johnson looked out of the window and saw a score of elderly ladies in wide-brim hats strolling on the lawn and peeking in the windows. He went out, inquired cautiously, and learned they were from the Daughters of the American Revolution. By prior agreement many years earlier, they had received permission to visit Morven on the birthday of Independence. They had visited Morven every Fourth of July, had he been there to witness.

For years Johnson had ridden to the hounds with his red-jacketed friends of the Stoney Brook Hunt Club. They covered much of Princeton's open terrain, and one place always appealed to him: a broad expanse of gently sloping hillside one mile to the west of Morven just off Rosedale Road, some sixty acres in all. He and Evie decided to buy it. They engaged an associate of architect Frank Lloyd Wright and built a modern house in what was referred to as the "Florida style." During construction, they lived in one of several houses on the property, and when they moved in they named the estate "Longleat."

While Johnson left Morven with only a twinge of regret, his English butler, Clarke, was devastated by the departure. For him, the gracious old house and gardens were reminiscent of the civilized living Clarke had known in London. Leaving the Charles Street house that Johnson rented in Mayfair years earlier had been distressing to Clarke, but Morven turned out to be a pleasant surprise. Clarke knew he would not like a Florida-style house, and he didn't.

Longleat sat on the side of a hill, with an excellent view of the sprawling grounds. It was just one story, with an exterior of long, narrow fieldstones, a gently sloping roofline, and an enormous fireplace topped by nine pink-tile chimneypots. A huge living room on one side of the front of the house had expansive windows overlooking a sloping lawn and groves of trees. On one side of the entry foyer was a large master bedroom suite and study, and on the other side, the dining room, a massive kitchen, guest rooms, and servants' quarters. White marble curved steps flanked by a pair of white stone lions led to the front entrance, of varnished wood and glass.

Close to a mile of road stretched from one of Longleat's two gated entrances, up over the spine of the hill, past the house, and down to the large barns and several houses that were remnants of a previous estate that guarded the other gated entrance. By Princeton's historic standards, or, to be more precise, Princeton preference, the house was "out of place," but it is doubtful that anyone ever ventured that opinion to Johnson. Very unlikely. He played a large role in its design, which is perhaps why it was so, well, different. He claimed that he liked the house, but there were always doubts.

Evie Johnson was soft-spoken, intelligent, and an avid reader. The couple would spend hours together in the evening reading in the living room of Longleat. She adjusted quickly to having a large staff to care for the house and grounds, but lacked the skills needed to manage them successfully. At times there were tensions among the staff. Johnson set the tone and tempo of their social life, and Evie reveled in her new role as hostess of Longleat. She filled the house with an extensive collection of Dresden China, porcelains, and crystal pieces, which gave the house a distinctly feminine look. Johnson gave her broad latitude in these matters, which interested him little.

The most sensitive issue in their marriage was religion. She was a devout Catholic, he a part-time Episcopalian, at least in terms of church attendance. Despite their divorces, they would make vain attempts in the coming years to have the Catholic Church sanction the marriage, including an appeal to Rome, which the Vatican denied. In the early years of their marriage, Evie was hesitant about taking Communion when she went to Mass, and she constantly worried about her salvation.

Their relationship grew more platonic over time, and eventually Johnson had his own bedroom added to the house. It was near Evie's, and it gave him greater privacy and room for a desk and his books. This allowed Evie to expand her clothes closet, which was already huge. The arrangement worked for both of them.

17

THE CREDO

DURING his recuperation after leaving Washington, Johnson went to New Brunswick only once, on December 12, 1943, for a Board of Directors meeting. That day he announced that in 1944 Johnson & Johnson would become a publicly held company. All the members of the Board held senior management positions in the company, and they welcomed the news that they would soon become stockholders. Christmas came early that year. Johnson, of course, would continue to be the major stockholder. Years earlier he had added to his already significant holdings when he bought most of the stock owned by his sister, Evangeline.

Johnson emphasized to the Board that the company's management philosophy would not change under public ownership. He outlined the four areas of responsibility that the company would continue to follow:

The first concern should be to provide the consuming public with goods of the highest quality at the lowest possible prices.

Next in importance is the maintenance of full employment at a fair scale of wages.

Third, there should be adequate executive compensation to assure the corporation of the most efficient management available.

Fourth, we must have adequate return on the capital invested by the stockholders, with emphasis on the maintenance of an adequate cash position, enabling the corporation to take advantage of every opportunity for the profitable development and expansion of its business.

These were the same areas Johnson had introduced in 1935 and tried, unsuccessfully, to get other corporations to adopt. They would also become the core of the Johnson & Johnson "Credo," which he would write and introduce in the coming year.

·

The first week in April 1944, Johnson returned to the office after six months of recuperation. He reported that he was fully recovered and had never felt better, and he looked healthy and fit, his deep Florida tan contrasting nicely with the spring blizzard that blanketed New Brunswick that week. The first associates to greet him at the office that snowy day addressed him as "General," and he did nothing to discourage that. Nor did he for the next twenty-four years.

It soon became evident that the title "General" would have a far longer life span than his Army commission did. He would become "General" to all but his most intimate friends and close family—to them he remained "Bob." There were some exceptions: his old cronies from the early days and a few of the senior mill workers who had helped shepherd him through his errant youth. A few persisted in calling him "Bob," and when he strode through the mill an occasional daring "Bobby" could be heard, usually from one of the Hungarian old-timers.

Once, in later years, he mused about people addressing him as "General," contending that he had taken a neutral position. He said those who wanted to call him "General" could, and those who didn't need not. He made it sound a great deal more discretionary than it actually was. It is not surprising that almost everyone called him "General." Actually, "General" fit him quite well—a custom fit—and there was no question that he was again in command of the home forces.

Whenever he came back to the office after an absence, everyone was ready for his inevitable inspection. For weeks before, it was customary to apply paint and polish liberally to any area of the office or factory that might not pass his close scrutiny. His obsession with neatness and cleanliness was by now widely known, and feared. Nothing could arouse him quicker than even the slightest evidence of poor housekeeping. To him a smudge was tantamount to treason. He claimed that a medical products company should always glisten, especially one that claimed a state of sterility for many of its products. He was right and they knew it.

Another part of the ritual surrounding his homecomings was the fuss everyone made over him, and it was not contrived, for the place took on added vitality when he was there. They felt his presence and welcomed it, even though it meant being on the alert at all times.

One of the first things Johnson did when he returned after his recuperation was send a pleasant message to all the employees assuring them that he was back to stay. A fresh round of rumors had him running for public office, but he said he had no such intentions. "My responsibility will be exclusively to the company," he averred, "and to those who work with us."

As the demands of the war had increased, the business had accelerated to a frenetic pace, so it was not difficult for him to rationalize that he was needed. And even though the company was in the process of going public, he still saw it as "his" company—in terms of responsibility for its welfare.

The book he had been writing about his Washington episode had kept him busy and rekindled the constant desire he had to write. A few weeks before he returned to the office, he completed it, and then arranged to have the manuscript edited. He submitted the final version to the Princeton University Press, which published it several months later. The 150-page volume was titled *"But, General Johnson—" Episodes in a War Effort*, which mimicked the response he said he had often received: "But, General Johnson, it can't be done."

[279]

He was honest about the effort. In a cover note to business associates and friends who received copies, he called the book "something of a hodgepodge." But as readers discovered, it was more than that. In the preface, Johnson expressed his objective and hope for the book:

> . . . American small business is only a segment of the national environment, but it touches every phase of American life. To explore the public efforts to solve its problems in a war economy is to obtain an insight into modern government which, with understanding, may lead to progress, but which without understanding, will foster despair.

He then proceeded to describe, honestly and with a touch of humor, his Washington experiences in behalf of small business, drawing on newspaper reports and congressional testimony to support his views. He described how he had seen things working in the nation's capital:

> There are, broadly speaking, four types of public thinking in Washington, each occupying, at times, predominant positions.
>
> *First*, military thinking, which approaches all policies in terms of rigid regimentation, resolves all issues in terms of commands, and discourages personal independence, imagination, and initiative—this is essential to a combat division but fatal to an economic system.
>
> *Second*, public administrative thinking, which tends to adopt the government as its client, defends and strengthens its particular segment of service against all comers, and finds protection behind innumerable divisions of responsibility—this is essential to the maintenance of an administrative hierarchy but deadly to administrative efficiency.
>
> *Third*, legislative thinking, which sees most issues in terms of constituents, party, and personal hazards, vigorously and courageously seeks expression of public policy within this framework, and talks and listens to everyone—this is the keystone of popular government but the tombstone of administrative direction.
>
> *Fourth*, business thinking, which concentrates on quick and im-

mediate results, accepts policy as it would a blueprint, but insists on complete control of its own assembly lines—this is the magic of American industrial production but as disturbing to the public service as a hawk over a chicken yard.

One chapter was devoted to how news was gathered in Washington and disseminated nationally. Mostly it was a flattering assessment of the major newspaper writers, columnists, and radio commentators, with an occasional admonition that reporting should be more objective. For no apparent reason, he offered sometimes overly flattering evaluations:

Walter Lippmann, ". . . It will be brilliantly written."
Dorothy Thompson, ". . . Among the world's great women."
Danton Walker, ". . . One of the greatest news gatherers of the country."
Raymond Gram Swing, ". . . A perfectionist."

As a reminder of Fourth Estate responsibilities, he included in the chapter the entire text of the Code of Ethics (Canons of Journalism) of the American Society of Newspaper Editors, as well as the Code of Ethics of the Association of Radio News Analysts.

Also included in the chapter was a plea for greater voter participation at the polls and for involvement in government service as a way to preserve democracy. The spirit of patriotism ran deep in Johnson. He openly expressed love of country, flag, and democracy, and never missed an opportunity to reaffirm these beliefs. The roving nature of *"But, General Johnson"* gave him the latitude to challenge Americans to pay closer attention to their civic duties. He reminded them that they were allowing the national news media to "make up the mind of America on the great issues of the day" because they had failed to exercise their voting privileges:

American democracy has been down on one knee for a quarter of a century. It has been knocked there by Americans. The Americans who do not vote in the primary elections. The Americans who do not vote in general elections. The Americans who do not vote at all.

Our democracy is based on the principle that we shall have a government of amateurs, not professionals. It is built on the belief that an everyday citizen will run for office and be aggressively supported by everyday citizens—his friends and followers. The idea of leaving government to professionals is not American—and it is not safe.

The men coming back from our fighting fronts will be in no mood to be pushed around by bureaucrats and sub-bureaucrats. They will want, above everything, freedom of action. Freedom to work. Freedom to live their own lives. Freedom to succeed.

In the final chapter Johnson looked to the future, and it was here that the visionary businessman emerged, in an element he knew and understood well. "The time has come to look ahead," he wrote. "A reconversion period is upon us. It is no longer only a question of helping small business. It is even more than a 'transition' to a peace economy. *It is a matter of maintaining independent business as a permanent part of the industrial structure.*"

Johnson then presented for the first time his enlarged version of the corporate responsibility statement he had introduced in 1935 in the "Try Reality" document. Entitled "An Industrial Credo," it spelled out a company's responsibilities to customers, employees, management, and stockholders, in that order:

AN INDUSTRIAL CREDO

We believe that our *first* responsibility is to our Customers—

Our products must always be good, and

We must strive to make them better at lower costs.

Our orders must be promptly and accurately filled.

Our dealers must make a fair profit.

Our *second* responsibility is to those who work with us—the Men and Women in our Factories and Offices—

They must have a sense of security in their jobs.

Wages must be fair and adequate,

Management just,

Hours short, and

Working conditions clean and orderly.

Workers should have an organized system for suggestions and complaints.

Foremen and department heads must be qualified and fair-minded.

There must be opportunity for advancement — for those qualified — and

Each person must be considered an individual standing on his own dignity and merit.

Our *third* responsibility is to our Management —

Our executives must be persons of talent, education, experience, and ability.

They must be persons of common sense and full understanding.

Our *fourth* and last responsibility is to our Stockholders —

Business must make a sound profit.

Reserves must be created,

Research must be carried on,

Adventurous programs developed, and

Mistakes made and paid for.

Bad times must be provided for,

High taxes paid,

New machines purchased,

New factories built,

New products launched, and

New sales plans developed.

We must experiment with new ideas.

When these things have been done, the stockholder should receive a fair return.

We are determined, with the help of God's Grace, to fulfill these obligations to the best of our ability.

Shortly after the Credo appeared in the book, hundreds of copies were printed and distributed throughout the company, and framed copies began appearing on the walls of company offices all over the world. Beginning with the company's Board of Directors, Johnson declared that henceforth the principles set forth in the Credo would be the company's philosophy. Those who did not endorse it could look for employment elsewhere. The Credo became the heart of Johnson & Johnson's culture and guided its destiny from then on.

When critics quickly pointed out that it was not realistic to place the stockholders last, Johnson disagreed vehemently. "If we put the customer first and follow through on our other responsibilities, I assure you that the stockholders will be well served," he would say, and sometimes add, "And, don't forget, I am the largest stock-holder."

Johnson & Johnson did become a publicly held company in 1944, and for the next five decades the wisdom of Johnson's philosophy would become dramatically clear. The initial offering price of a share of stock was $37.50. An investor who purchased one hundred shares for $3,750 in 1944 and held the stock would see it grow, with stock splits, to 124,848 shares valued at about $12 million by 1999, not counting dividends.

Later, Johnson would be vexed by the New York Stock Exchange and Securities and Exchange Commission regulations on disclosure, especially with regard to the salaries of his executives, which were high. One time, to the delight of the financial writers, he threatened at a stockholder meeting to "de-list" from the NYSE, expressing regrets that he had ever taken the company public in the first place. He also had a dim view of the value of outside directors — there were none during his lifetime, and none of his executives served on outside boards. His contention was that it required full time and dedication to serve a company properly as a director, that it could not be done part-time. Moreover, he believed that the best management directors were those who owned substantial amounts of company stock. If their financial futures were at stake, he claimed, they would make better decisions. Selling company stock, unless for a very valid reason, was, in his view, treasonous.

Writing about corporate responsibility was not as important as taking action, Johnson believed. Of all the concepts embodied in his Credo, none became more visible to the general public than his "Factories Can Be Beautiful" concept. It had its origins with the first modern textile mill and 200-home village he built in Georgia in 1927. In the ensuing years, Johnson guided the construction of more than one hundred trend-setting plants and office buildings throughout the world. Many were unique and years ahead of their time.

In the late 1930s, Johnson had developed a formula for the results he wanted to achieve. Earlier, in 1934, he surprised everyone by calling in the widely heralded architectural firm of Shreve, Lamb & Harmon, which had recently completed work on the dramatic new 102-story Empire State Building in New York City. Having designed the world's tallest skyscraper, the architects were somewhat nonplussed to find that what Johnson had in mind was a one-story building. He wanted it to be expandable in all four directions and to utilize aluminum and plastic and other new building materials. Not satisfied with the initial design, he modified it with the help of his own construction staff.

When the pace of construction picked up in later years, the Johnson & Johnson plants became widely known for innovation. Virtually all the new factories were located on large tracts of land, often on hundreds of acres. Johnson believed that a company's manufacturing site could be as attractive as a college campus. Close attention was given to landscaping. That was a Johnson rule. He believed the new buildings should blend into the setting and be an asset to the community.

Johnson had a hand in the design and construction of every plant and made frequent visits to the construction sites to make sure the buildings were developing as he had anticipated. The changes he ordered drove the architects and builders to the brink of despair, but no one argued with the results. The facades of the buildings were all different — the most talked about was in marble — and all had clean lines and were superbly functional. Vast expanses of tinted glass made it possible for workers to look out and enjoy the pastoral setting. The plush lobbies and reception areas resembled movie sets, some with floor-to-ceiling windows, velvet drapes, and recessed lighting. And, to promote the feeling that it was their plant, employees were encouraged to use the lobby entrances.

Manufacturing areas were bright and airy and often air-conditioned. The walls were pastel-colored, as were the specially designed covers that shielded the moving parts of all production machinery. These covers kept oily bearings from soiling the white nurse-type uniforms that had been the traditional wear for women employees since the company's earliest days. There were strict rules regarding housekeeping, and heads would roll when they were violated.

When asked why he went to great expense to build plants of this quality, Johnson had a ready answer. In the long run, he said, they were less expensive. His employees took pride in their workplace, and morale was high — ensuring greater output and higher-quality products. What's more, the plants were an asset to the community. All of this might have been lost if the company had lower standards.

But the concepts and philosophy introduced in the Credo in *"But, General Johnson"* captured the most attention and comment. He had sent the book to an extensive list of industrial leaders, political figures, educators, and journalists, and it was reviewed in the *New York Times Book Review* and numerous other newspapers. All found some merit in what he had to say. The *Times* reviewer, Walter T. Beachboard, agreed with some of his recommendations but labeled him as "a true business liberal," which brought a prompt reply from Johnson. "Most of us feel that we can move toward better times if we can combine the merits of the Old Deal with the merits of the New Deal," he wrote. "It is unfortunate that our people are so tightly locked in camps. . . . I am for taking the good out of each and developing a postwar pattern that can be an improvement over the past."

By contrast, the reviewer for the *St. Louis Post-Dispatch*, Henry B. Kline, while agreeing with some of Johnson's views, saw him as a conservative who "somewhat resembles the enlightened conservatism of Eric Johnson and *Fortune* magazine."

That happened often. Many people had difficulty putting a label on Johnson because his philosophy embraced both conservative and liberal views, depending on how they were being applied. It was impossible to stamp him as one or the other. And while some saw this as contradictory, he did not. The confusion, he felt, rested not with him but with those whose vision was limited. He saw the wisdom of examining all sides of an issue.

18

THE RISE OF
THE WRITER

B y the middle of 1944, a growing confidence in ultimate victory both in Europe and in the Pacific began taking hold in America. Rome became the first European capital to be recaptured after Allied forces fought their way from Anzio Beach. Following the massive landing at Normandy, the invasion of Europe from the west was under way. And American forces were rapidly changing the course of the war in the Pacific. At home, Franklin D. Roosevelt won a historic fourth term as President, with Harry S. Truman as his running mate, by a heavy electoral vote but a much narrower popular majority over Governor Thomas E. Dewey of New York.

When the outcome of the war no longer seemed in doubt, Americans began to devote increasing attention and concern to the formidable problems that would accompany conversion to a peacetime economy. There were fears that the winding down of the spectacular surge of wartime production would result in a dramatic collapse of the economy. And those who had vivid memories of the painful Great Depression and its record unemployment and bread lines worried the most. The war had brought management and labor together to fight the common enemy and preserve liberty, but peacetime positioning would once again be dominated by divergent interests.

On the afternoon of April 12, 1945, at the Little White House at Warm Springs, Georgia, President Roosevelt died of a massive cerebral hemorrhage at age sixty-three. Three hours later Vice President Truman took the oath as the nation's thirty-second President. Three weeks later, Germany surrendered unconditionally, bringing the war in Europe to an end. Then, on August 14, the Japanese surrendered unconditionally. A week earlier the first atomic bomb, equal to 20,000 tons of TNT, had been dropped on Hiroshima, followed by another unleashed on Nagasaki two days later.

It had been nearly two years since Johnson's abrupt departure from Washington, and in the fall of 1945 he returned, in the familiar but still controversial role of an industrialist urging Congress to increase the national minimum wage. This time there was new tension surrounding that sensitive issue, but again Johnson volunteered to enter the fray. He had espoused the cause of higher wages so often and under such hostile circumstances that by now no one doubted the sincerity of his motives, though some questioned the wisdom of his actions.

But this time the wage issue had a new backdrop. During the war, strikes had been forbidden and national loyalty and pride kept the labor force producing at peak levels. But many months before the Japanese armistice, when the outcome of the war became a virtual certainty, labor unions began positioning themselves for their role in the reconversion to peace. The transition was not as smooth as had been anticipated, and with each new labor demand for wage increases came the threat of strikes and discord. The Labor Department and the War Labor Board tried hard to maintain stability, but it was like trying to contain a prairie fire driven by a brisk breeze.

The uneasy labor peace erupted into open hostility with the surrender of Japan, and the labor disputes reached crisis proportions when Ford Motor Company halted all production and laid off 50,000 workers, blaming "irresponsible labor groups" for strikes against its suppliers. The Automobile Workers Union demanded a 30 percent pay increase nationwide. But the auto industry was not the only one under siege. A CIO Electrical Workers Union began an enrollment drive among 12,000 striking white-collar workers at Westinghouse Electric. The American Federation of Labor's railway unions were demanding a 36-hour week with no pay cut, and at the United States Steel Corporation, President Benjamin Fairless said a union demand for a $2-a-day pay increase would result in a sharp rise in steel prices. Anticipating the postwar labor-management conflict, President Truman planned a parley between management and labor in what was billed as an effort to bring about "industrial peace."

The Congress too sensed the urgent need for action. In late September the Senate Committee on Labor and Education began hearings on an amendment to the Fair Labor Standards Act that would raise the minimum wage in the nation from 40 to 65 cents an hour. Almost immediately business formed a solid wall of opposition. The hearings continued into October, with only one bold industrialist coming forth to testify on behalf of the measure. He was Patrick W. McDonough, a California steel-mill owner who startled the committee by testifying that his company had made $1 million a year during the war and claiming that it was "too much."

Hope of hearing more from business in favor of a higher minimum wage was all but lost. Proponents of the bill had invited Johnson to testify, but still bearing some of the scars of his earlier battles, he took quite a while to make up his mind to return to Washington. At 10 o'clock on the morning of October 23, however, with shoulders squared and that familiar glint in his eye, he strode into Room 424B in the Senate Office Building to testify.

It was memorable, even by Washington congressional committee hearing standards. Johnson's opening remarks characterized the hearings as a discussion on "the plight of the underpaid," and then, having set the stage, he proceeded to jolt even the liberal-minded senators with his recommendation.

"I suggest," he said in a clear, forceful voice, "that the committee should take the position that the average American workman cannot keep body and soul together on less than $30 per week anywhere in the United States. On the basis of a 40-hour week, I, therefore, am compelled to recommend a 75 cents an hour wage throughout the nation."

Committee members looked at one another in dismay. The bill called for an increase from 40 to 65 cents an hours, and Johnson was proposing 75 cents an hour. The rebel industrialist had returned.

Johnson then took his argument to an even loftier plane: "What we are really doing is *creating a new code of business ethics* with the aid and guidance of our federal government. It would be hard to imagine a more important task, nor one that would make a greater contribution to the world." The senators listened intently. "It was the underpaid, the unemployed, and the destitute of Europe," Johnson continued, "that caused the political upheavals which led to this great war. . . . We have come to a time we can honestly say, at least in our country, that man does not have the right to employ his fellow man unless he can pay a subsistence wage."

It was a moving speech, and the hearing room stirred uneasily when he concluded. No one had ever defined the minimum-wage issue in quite those terms before.

The following day, beginning with headlines across the nation, Johnson's presentation received wide coverage, and it was generally highly favorable to his proposals. Editorial support followed, and magazine coverage was equally encouraging. A *Time* magazine article in the November 5 issue gave the story a man-bites-dog twist:

> When a businessman demands that labor get more pay for less work, that's news. Last week a big businessman made such news by telling Congress: the U.S. should boost the legal minimum wage from 40¢ an hour to a minimum of 75¢. At the same time, he recommended that Congress prepare legislation to establish a 40, a 36 and a 30-hour week. Commerce, industry, the trades and agriculture would be classified into three major divisions and three work weeks. But all would get the same weekly minimum wage, $30.

[291]

This suggestion came from dapper, poker-faced Robert Wood Johnson, 53, wartime brigadier general (in Ordnance and as boss of the Smaller War Plants Corp.) and board chairman of Johnson & Johnson (surgical supplies). To a Senate labor subcommittee, now considering a bill to raise the minimum to 65¢ an hour, Johnson said: "not high enough; the U.S. can now pay higher wages and sell at lower costs."

Bob Johnson's best argument was his own company. It now has the highest minimum wage in the industry. Average hourly earnings for day work, excluding overtime and premiums, are 76¢ for women and 85¢ for men, while piecework rates run higher. In his southern textile mills Johnson pays a minimum now of 65¢ — at least 10¢ higher than competitors. Anticipating critics who would not fail to point out that he does not practice what he preaches, Johnson said that he would be glad to pay more if competitors were forced to do the same.

The press continued to hail him as a hero of the working class, some members of Congress wrote letters of support, there was a flurry of encouraging mail from businessmen, and one company launched an advertising campaign on behalf of the plan. Chester Bowles, head of the Office of Price Administration, went before the same Senate committee to give his support to Johnson.

For a while there was hope that the Johnson plan might be embraced. Then critics of the proposal, led by major industrialists and the conservative factions in Congress, began their counter-arguments. Johnson had heard all the rebuttals before, but this time he hoped that with the end of the war, sentiments would change. Getting decent jobs for returning servicemen and women had been given top priority by many, and here was a chance to act on that promise. But no. All the arguments that had historically been raised against increasing the minimum wage were brought up again. Even Johnson's most convincing argument — It is much cheaper to increase wages and create more buying power than it is to pay for putting people on the welfare rolls — stirred no outpouring of support from business in general. More frustrating for Johnson were the large numbers of businessmen and legislators who remained stonily silent, preferring to avoid the delicate issue — the safer course. Labor, naturally, agreed with Johnson.

At one point the debate was cleverly shifted to Johnson's "motives." He vehemently denied having any hidden agenda, other than his long-standing desire for fairer treatment of workers and for a greater sense of responsibility on the part of management. "You may suspect that I have some hidden or obscure motive, or you may feel that there is some commercial aspect in this situation. Please accept my assurance that there is not," he wrote one critic. "I have an indirect interest, that might be described as commercial, in the sense that a successful America would make it better for all of us."

Months passed, and Congress was still considering various versions of a minimum-wage bill. The longer the discussions continued, the less hope Johnson had of triggering a dramatic rise in the pay scale. When he addressed an audience of seven hundred businessmen at the Spring Conference of the American Management Association on April 24, 1946, at the Hotel Pennsylvania in New York, he rebuked management for failing to deal fairly with the millions of employees who are "outside the zone" of union membership and influence.

"If the last ten years of depression and six years of war economy haven't taught American management this lesson, they're beyond the pale," he said. "I'm afraid that the job is going to be done by militant labor." He added: "It seems too bad."

At the conference, he also underscored the need for business to emphasize "human engineering" and not just technological advancement. This, he said, required devoting more attention to the people factor — not only employees but also the general public. "We stand convicted at the bar of public opinion," he told them, "and the verdict deals with crimes in the field of human engineering. We have a rather odd equation wherein the public believes in our products but chooses to give us a vote of 'no confidence.'" That could be changed, he told the managers, if business were to put the customer first.

Johnson's management philosophy had been receiving much wider attention during the previous two years because of the articles he was writing for major magazines, such as the *Saturday Evening Post*. Writing had always held a particular fascination for him. It was a way of expressing his ideas. The publication of *"But, General Johnson"* had brought a flurry of praise, some polite and some sincere, and it offered him further encouragement. The timing was right, for in the mid-1940s many of the leading magazines were eager to publish by-line articles by well-known businessmen who had something to say, especially if it was controversial. In this role, Johnson was a natural.

His approach to what some saw as the "writing phase" of his life was similar to the way he undertook any other new subject — he sought help from the experts. At the time, it was common practice for experienced journalists and authors to provide help, for a fee, to businessmen and others who were aspiring writers. Then too, the editorial desks of the major magazines offered critical advice and blunt evaluations of the writing efforts of well-known businessmen they were trying to encourage. Johnson soon developed a stable of tutors, some of whom surely did not realize what they were getting into.

With journalist friends, like Walter Troan of the *Chicago Tribune's* Washington bureau, Johnson cast himself in the role of student. He wrote Troan, who was helping him edit a manuscript: "Unfortunately I never write except as a direct result of convictions; therefore, I am usually in trouble. Perhaps there is another aspect of my writing that you may sense, though no one ever tells me about it. I may be too aggressive, controversial, or downright quarrelsome. I suppose it is only natural that some of the heat of my feelings gets into the manuscript."

Johnson believed magazine editors were wary of him because he had strong convictions, but he never quite realized that was actually why they found him appealing. When they would tone down a first draft, Johnson always reacted. "Magazines are afraid of most

Young Robert joins the company

Elizabeth Ross
and Robert marry

Bobby at five

Bellevue Farm

Robert and Seward
on world tour

Off to a business
meeting in Egypt

Pilot Evangeline
in Palm Beach

The *Zodiac*

Maggi

Sheila

Morven

In the garden at Morven

Aboard *Stormy Weather*

Flying to work

of my stuff," he wrote a reporter friend. "They seem to have the courage of a sickly gazelle."

One of Johnson's volunteer critics was Arthur Baum, the *Saturday Evening Post*'s expert on business writing and a taskmaster as an editor. Baum was to become a patient friend in disguise, but in his role as a critiquing editor he was merciless. When the *Post* turned down one of Johnson's early articles, Baum took the time to write an evaluation that covered four typed single-spaced pages. He wasn't gentle, but he was helpful. ". . . You are firing a bunch of rockets to attract my attention," Baum wrote. "Okay, but isn't it a bit choppy?" Then later, "Pretty late to be telling us what the article is about, isn't it? We have already read six pages!" Then Baum would intersperse some encouragement: "You have some wickedly pleasant needles along in here. Delightful." Painful as it was to hear, Johnson learned much from Baum, once writing him: "The Lord only knows how I got into this situation. But I have it. And I must get it off my chest."

Another of Johnson's journalistic helpers was Roger William Riis, a roving editor for *Reader's Digest*. Their association got off to a pleasant enough beginning, but that soon changed. Based on his Washington experience and his admiration for Congress, as opposed to the rest of the Washington bureaucracy, Johnson drafted an article titled "Thank God for Congress" and sent it to Riis for his review. The reply had sharp edges. "If this were Walter Lippmann," Riis wrote, "it would have plenty of justification. But you are not a professional student of Congress."

That critique did not sit well with Johnson. "Let's look at this thing squarely," he fired back. "First, the whole principle of our form of government is that the amateur should speak. Of course, that amateur should be reasonably well informed. You say it would be all right for Walter Lippmann, but that I am not a professional student of Congress. I wonder about this. Let's look at the background."

He then summarized for Riis his political experience, from his being elected Mayor of Highland Park, New Jersey, to his Washington service. "Congress," he told Riis, "is local government moved to Washington. . . . I hope you will find these arguments as convincing as I do."

Johnson prevailed, and when the article was finally complete it began making the round of editors' desks, but generated little interest.

The *Reader's Digest* was his greatest frustration. Try as he might, he could not get one of his articles published in it. The *Digest* had articles about him but not by him. He made a number of submissions, including articles published elsewhere that he felt were candidates for condensation. "That magazine is an enigma to me," he once said in despair. Even publisher DeWitt Wallace was involved in explaining to Johnson the types of articles the *Digest* was interested in. Johnson's assessment of publishers ranked them with editors. "I realize that only our Lord understands the mind of a publisher. Mere men could hardly be expected to fathom such intricacies," he wrote an editor.

Johnson's first triumph as a writer in a major magazine came in the July 15, 1944, issue of the *Saturday Evening Post*, then one of the nation's most prestigious general interest magazines. The article titled "What Business Needs" and carrying Johnson's by-line — Robert Wood Johnson — made a case for less government intervention in the affairs of business.

"We must free the dynamic capacity of independent business because it is the very fabric of our national life," Johnson wrote. "We must free it, if for no other reason than to maintain a strong civilian economy as a tax base. We can't destroy the most vital segment of industry [independent business], and then expect to raise taxes from it. Independent business is the most vital force in the United States."

The article went on to cite some of the adversities that small business — which Johnson said he now preferred to call "independent business" — was facing in Washington, but claimed that revitalization could be achieved if two conditions were met: "Access to venture capital through local bankers, and a tax structure which will permit the reappearance, the re-emergence, of individual initiative."

The response to the article was quite positive, and numerous reprints were circulated throughout the business community. Johnson the industrialist was pleased, but Johnson the writer was ecstatic—a by-line in the *Saturday Evening Post*! There was one negative, which he chose to overlook. To accompany the article, the *Post* selected a candid picture of Johnson taken at a Washington press conference. It showed him with droopy eyelids that gave the impression he had been up all night—a very unflattering photo. Nothing was said at the time, but later the *Post* editors would have their own patience tested by Johnson.

·

From the outset of his cradle days as a writer, Johnson turned to Evie for guidance and support. She had always been a prodigious reader, and she knew good writing when she saw it. Johnson was quick to give her credit for critiquing his early drafts, which he always worked on at home. "She must have read and corrected more than a million words of what I wrote, for style is one of her great interests," he commented in later years. In the early days of his new intensity, the words did not come easily, but the ideas were there. When they poured forth onto the yellow-lined pads, Evie often helped him put them in better order.

Though writing held great appeal for him, not being as skilled as he would like was a form of torture. He had always plunged into new subjects and learned them thoroughly with as many books and professors as he could muster. Writing was different, he learned. But being a realist helped. "I am a literary backwoodsman," he once confessed to an editor.

One of his helpers was Stuart Chase, a successful author whom Johnson admired and who doubled as an agent for freelance writers. "In plain language, I would like to develop a moderate position in the writing world," Johnson told Chase. "I shall never be more than adequate, if that, but there are certain things I want to say." Writing was an area that brought out Johnson's infrequent expressions of humility. He was very comfortable sharing his shortcomings with journalists and editors, something he would not normally do when it came to business. But as a writer, he gravitated to a lower echelon, and he accepted that.

Chase became interested in Johnson's views on business management and called him a "bold experimenter." For a while the two discussed collaborating on magazine articles—a suggestion that came from Johnson, who thought a dual signature like "Chase and Johnson" might work. The popular author gingerly sidestepped that, but he did submit an outline for an article about Johnson to the *Reader's Digest*, describing him as "a big industrialist with a fine, human philosophy who believes in shorter hours and who builds factories that look like art museums." DeWitt Wallace decided the story would have greater appeal if Johnson's textile mills returned to the six-hour day. Militating against that approach was the economist on the *Digest*'s staff, who felt that in the reconversion the nation would need longer hours to generate maximum production to avoid inflation. *Digest* editors could not agree, so the idea was scrapped.

The editors at the *Saturday Evening Post* admired Johnson's bold stance on vital business issues and often corresponded with him about writing other articles, even though he could be difficult. Once, his friend Associate Editor Baum wrote asking if he accepted "roving commissions." Fresh from a recent encounter with another editor, Johnson replied tartly: "No, I do not have roving commissions. If I were to wait for results from publishers, I would have to rove to keep warm." On another occasion, Baum told him he was "sermonizing" in his writing. Johnson bristled. But he kept coming back, and so did Baum and other editors at the *Post*.

One indication of the *Post*'s respect for him was an article that appeared in "Inside Information," a newsletter that went to *Post* staff members and a special mailing list. In the newsletter's December 29, 1945, issue, just a week before the *Post* was to publish a second Johnson by-lined article, there was a full-page feature on Johnson and his bold exploits as a businessman and writer titled "The General Poises Another Super Bomb." The first "atomic bomb," the article said, "whammed into the deeper dugouts of the sweatshop industrialists" when Johnson testified on the Senate labor bill and asked for an even higher minimum wage. The second "bomb," the feature promised, would be the upcoming by-lined article "Break It Up," urging industry to decentralize.

The newsletter went on to relate the highlights of Johnson's career and his skills as a flyer and yachtsman, and even described him as "an amateur writer with a professional punch." Accompanying the article was a photo of him at the helm of his ocean racer *Good News* plying through a choppy sea. The good story and a flattering photo almost made him forget the last one. It was the calm before the storm.

There was the usual tugging and pulling between the *Post* editors and Johnson during the writing of "Break It Up." The last encounter was over the title, which Johnson had dreamed up and was stoutly defending. When he submitted the final manuscript to Editor Ben Hibbs, he made a final pitch for it: "I realize that the *Post* is a very dignified affair," he wrote, "but even your great sponsor Benjamin Franklin had his light moments." The title remained as Johnson wanted it.

When "Break It Up" appeared, it gained wide acclaim among business people. In the article, Johnson wrote:

Industrially, we in America for a long time have had a psychosis for big business—for putting everything under one roof. But even P. T. Barnum's main tent got so big that he had to have side shows, and that was long ago. . . . We built huge plants on the theory that the total job should be done at one place. Later we learned that a good share of the work could be delegated elsewhere, and the end product improved as a result. . . . Our new theme might be, "Delete, delegate, decentralize and, if necessary, delouse the central staff."

The *Post* liked that last colorful language so well they ran it in a box at the top of the article right under the headline. The article continued:

All production problems boil down to two men—he who makes the product and he who uses it. Bring them together, and the conference is complete. I first heard of production planning in the early days of industrial engineering, when experts like Gilbreth, Gantt, Emerson and Taylor were blueprinting new concepts of how to make big enterprises efficient. It was immensely appealing. I cabled my brother, who then was in Spain studying old wines and young senoritas, and suggested that he come home to take charge of the new planning department. He cabled back, "Sure, what the hell is that?" The time came when I thought his questions mighty intelligent.

But with the article, the *Post* ran a photo of Johnson with his mouth agape, looking as though he was gasping for air. It was a candid photo taken at the same stressful press conferences in Washington that produced the earlier photo showing him with droopy eyelids. This time Johnson's vanity was too badly damaged to let it pass. He angrily wrote Arthur Baum:

"I wonder if there is something sadistic in the magazine business. Supposing I were to publish, say in *Collier's*, a picture of Mr. Ben Hibbs brushing his teeth, or a picture of your chief printer being informed that his house was burning down, or perhaps of the head of your photography department at the moment of being aggressively seasick? I would appreciate it if you would put it [the photo] in the bonfire."

Baum tried diplomacy in his reply. The photo, he wrote Johnson, "transmitted to the reader a sense of dynamism and vigor, whereas a possibly milder and better looking picture might only serve as a mask."

Johnson didn't buy any of that. He fumed for weeks. But while the incident did not deter him from writing for the *Post*, it might have spurred on his contentious dealings with *Post* editors, whom he had dubbed "the Benjamin Franklin boys."

Editor Hibbs sent Johnson $150 for writing the article, and, as all his writing fees, it was prized. In terms of the labor and time he put into writing it, the fee was surely less than the minimum hourly wage he was forever battling for. But for him, writing fees could not be measured in terms of mere dollars. They were triumphs that carried a value all their own.

Getting published in the *Saturday Evening Post* so early in his writing phase was somewhat deceptive, for the road ahead would be rockier—and, as ideas for new articles failed to ignite the enthusiasm of editors, there was a flurry of rejection slips. In fact, Johnson was told that certain editors suspected he wanted to get by-lined stories in national publications to expand his identity, because he was planning to run for public office. He repeatedly stated that he had no such intentions, but it really bothered him when some readers complained about businessmen writing articles. "If I were an Iowa school teacher," he wrote Stuart Chase, "the public would respect my statements on industry on faith. But being an industrialist I am suspected of having one rabbit up each sleeve and perhaps a white mouse or two in my hat."

Had he been a less forceful personality, he would have been only a classic nuisance to editors. But he engaged their interest and attention because of his bold ideas, his determination to make them known, and his letters of protest. An article by this now well-known maverick sold magazines at a time when it was editorially fashionable to have business, political, and social figures among the contributors. And Johnson was all three, so he was a bargain at $150 an article or less. His lowest fee was $30, and he never accepted fees for speaking engagements. When one college wanted to pay him for a talk he replied, "Forget the honorarium. I would like a good dinner and a glass of beer." But he never refused a fee for writing.

[301]

Not all his writing efforts were focused on major issues and aimed at national audiences. When the editor of *Army Ordnance* magazine, a civilian publication of the Army Ordnance Association, asked him to write an article, Johnson warned that, if he did, "bombs would detonate." Fearless, the editor gave him the go-ahead, and Johnson used the opportunity to vent his feelings about all the real and imagined indignities he had suffered while dealing with the Army's supply organization. "Buyers in Khaki" was a slashing diatribe that took potshots at the military establishment ("Give a small mind a uniform and a little authority and watch arrogance develop"), the Civil Service ("Let's avoid the Civil Service. If we really want to get properly 'loused up,' let's go down that road"), the Army brass (". . . the high-ranking girls [Army secretaries] who knew more than the generals, and as a matter of fact, brought them up from cadethood"), and even Washington itself ("Washington is the last place on God's earth to get a job done. The old town is a mecca for troublemakers, phonies, and sharpshooters").

Whenever he wrote an article he felt strongly about but couldn't get published, he resorted to printing it in pamphlet form. The distribution included business associates outside of the company, Johnson & Johnson employees, and others. To his credit, he always submitted his articles, the published ones as well as the nonpublished, to others for review before they were sent around the company.

One unpublished piece titled, "Three Steps to Moral Business," did not find favor with editors, but it was a thoughtful expression of Johnson's long-held belief that business and morals were intertwined. In it he wrote:

Three steps must be taken, it seems to me, if moral principles are to guide human relations in the world of business. The first step requires each employer to realize that he is bound by the laws of God to act justly toward his employees and to insure their welfare. It makes no difference whether he derives this obligation from encyclicals of the Pope, from statements by the Federal Council of Churches, or from the Law of Moses — the Torah — with its profound recognition of human rights and duties. The obligation exists, and unless it is accepted nothing else will count.

The second step is for businessmen to adopt an attitude of trusteeship. Today's employer is not the dictator of an economic empire. He is a trustee for investors and customers, for the people of his community, and especially for the men and women who make his business go. He must see that the rights of each group are protected and must make sure that all derive benefit from his policies.

Finally, businessmen must resolve to treat their employees as fellow human beings, not as mere animated machines. Wage earners are men and women; they have rights, dignity, ambition, pride, and they feel a deep need to stand well in the eyes of their associates. Until employers treat them accordingly, business will not act in accord with sound moral principles.

Johnson's continuing and often frustrating efforts to bring workers and business closer together inspired him to try working through the church, specifically the Catholic Church. Even though he was an Episcopalian, his marriage to Evie, a devout Catholic despite her divorce, brought him in contact with numerous people in the Catholic Church hierarchy. He often accompanied Evie to St. Patrick's Cathedral on Fifth Avenue in New York, not far from their apartment at the Pierre Hotel.

It wasn't long before he met the Archbishop, Francis J. Spellman, who lived in The Chancery, on Madison Avenue, behind St. Patrick's. In Spellman, Johnson found a ready listener to his unorthodox views on how business could improve employee relations. The demeanor of the gentle-speaking prelate was somewhat misleading. Spellman had become the most powerful member of the Catholic hierarchy in the United States, highly skilled at religious politicking, and a fierce defender of individual rights. He too was a friend of Franklin Roosevelt, who used to refer to him as "my favorite bishop." He also was Military Vicar to the Armed Forces, which gave him and Johnson additional common ground on which to base the friendship that developed.

Many of their early meetings, in the spring of 1945, were over luncheon at the Chancery Office at 477 Madison Avenue, where Spellman, with his network of friendships, hosted power brokers from all walks of life and all religious faiths. They came from government, society, business, industry, and banking, and his extraordinary diplomatic skills behind the scenes could be applied to almost any worthwhile cause with predictable and positive results.

Johnson felt he had a supreme cause: reduction of the growing tensions between wage earners and management, which he felt was essential if America was to prosper in the postwar period. The archbishop listened intently and sympathetically to Johnson's views on the controversial subject. How could he get his views to a broader audience? Johnson inquired. Himself a writer and poet of some note, Spellman suggested having a magazine article published in a national publication. That is not what Johnson had in mind, but he said he would begin to outline one.

After a few days, Johnson went back to the archbishop with a different idea. The subject of Christian ethics in business, he said, should be preached from every pulpit in Spellman's archdiocese, all 4,717 square miles of it, so that Catholic employers could hear and learn. Next, he and the archbishop should work together to construct a course for employers of all faiths that would outline the benefits of improved working and living relationships between wage earners, management, and owners. Spellman, ever the consummate prelate-politician, told Johnson he should talk to the Rev. John P. Monaghan, chaplain to the Association of Catholic Trade Unionists.

The very next day, Johnson was off to St. Margaret Mary Rectory on Staten Island, where Monaghan lived, for a lengthy talk. While very much aware of the problem, Father Monaghan said he didn't find Johnson's proposal very practical and didn't think it would work. Annoyed at that lack of enthusiasm, Johnson went home and fired off a biting reply: "I am disturbed by what could harshly be described as an element of defeatism. Of course there are difficulties, and it is only proper and right that we should be aware of these difficulties. It is possible that we may discover some reason or reasons why nothing should be done, but we cannot at this time decide that *nothing can be done.*"

Then he quoted from an encyclical of the late Pope Pius XI:

We approach the subject with confidence, and in the exercise of the rights which belong to us. For no practical solution of this question will ever be found without the assistance of Religion and the Church. It is we who are the chief guardian of religion, and the chief dispenser of what belongs to the Church, and we must not by silence neglect the duty which lies upon us. Doubtless this most serious question demands the attention and the efforts of others besides ourselves — of the rulers of states, of employers of labor, of the wealthy, and of the working population themselves for whom we plead. But we affirm without hesitation that all the striving of men will be vain if they leave out the church.

Clearly Johnson was greatly impressed by those words and by what he considered to be the mandate. "This is our constitution," he wrote the priest. "We have the springboard for action. How do you feel about it today?"

Father Monaghan wasn't any more impressed this time, and having a Protestant push him on the Pope's teaching didn't help any. Neither did Johnson's frequent reference to Archbishop Spellman's interest. Later he wrote the priest again: "Someone in your church has to decide that the job is worth trying and that the experiment should be made," Johnson said. "I will go as far as I can toward promoting such a program."

Meanwhile, Johnson had followed Spellman's suggestion and had written an article titled "Christian Engineering," but his attempts to place it with *Reader's Digest* and several other national magazines failed. He went back to the archbishop for help in getting it printed in a Catholic publication, but it was Father Monaghan who put Johnson in touch with the Rev. Benjamin Masse, S.J., associate editor of *America*, the national Catholic weekly. More determined than ever, Johnson began corresponding with the Jesuit editor—and learned, to his dismay, that getting along with archbishops was easier, for him, than getting along with that magazine editor.

The previous rejection notes were almost charitable compared with the critique he was about to receive from the Jesuit editor. In response to Johnson's request for a frank appraisal of his writing, Father Masse and a fellow Jesuit editor obliged by reviewing several of his articles and writing a two-page critique. It was like submitting saplings to a buzz saw. "A great many generalities but poorly organized and gets nowhere," they wrote. "You have a knack of crowding a lot of thought into a very pithy sentence, but these sentences need development if the ideas are to be palatable to the reader." Father Masse did hold out some hope though. "You have a gift for expression and you think deeply," he told Johnson. "You lack only technical proficiency, which can be acquired by practice and by study of some sound rhetoric text." Johnson took the criticism stoically.

His article "Christian Engineering" appeared in the July 21 issue of *America*. In it Johnson contended that the modernization of industry and the development of the science of industrial engineering—time and motion study, work simplification, rate-setting— had lost touch with the human factor. "There remains a blank sector in scientific management, and that is the job of Human Engineering," he wrote. "If the principles of Christianity are followed, employers will avoid pitfalls. We have been looking for lost formulas, and during all of that time the Sermon on the Mount has been directly under our eyes."

And once again Johnson quoted from the Catholic Church's

own teachings to justify his position, this time referring to Pope Leo XIII's encyclical "On the Condition of the Working Classes" (*Rerum Novarum*), first published in 1891:

> If Society is to be healed now, in no other way can it be healed save by a return to Christian life and Christian institutions. When a society is perishing, the wholesome advice to give to those who would restore it is to call it to the principles from which it sprang; for the purpose and perfection of an association is to aim at and to attain that for which it was formed; and its efforts should be put in motion and inspired by the end and object which originally gave it being. Hence to fall away from its primal constitution implies disease; to go back to it, recovery.

"This is a Magna Carta, a constitution for the employers of the world," Johnson declared solemnly.

On other occasions, Johnson had been accused of being "preachy," and the article tended to support that criticism. Yet no one could argue that industry had become more impersonal in its rush toward modernization. That was one cause of the sharp rise in unionism and the current labor unrest.

"We must recreate a state of mind," he wrote. "Somewhere along the course of modern business, that state of mind was lost." To restore it, Johnson said, emphasis must be placed on "Christian ethics," as in Pope Leo XIII's encyclical. He recommended that priests begin teaching these principles to employers. "From this," he said, "can be developed the Science of Christian Engineering." He added: "We must prove to the world that free society can employ its people in security and happiness, for without this we shall fail, and all that we have, including our freedom, will be lost. Our business policies from here on must be based on sound, ethical philosophy. . . . By the grace of God and the blood of our sons, we have been given another chance."

The blending of Christian ideals and business practices seemed quite logical to Johnson, and there was no better conduit for this action than the clergy. But the response to this concept was modest at best — flurries of support here and there, no sweeping storm of change.

He would keep trying. For him, no dream was impossible. In fact, his dreams often seemed to him to masquerade as demons dancing around in his mind in the form of new ideas looking for a home, a place to grow. He once explained to one of his tutor-friends, Aristede D'Angeli, also a friend of Evie and director of the Academy of Dramatic Arts in New York, what compelled him to push on with his constant efforts to bring about change: "I cannot sit by and fail to give expressions to certain convictions that I have, so I shall continue to butt my head against the wall until I find some medium of expression."

19

THE GENERAL'S WAY

WITH the end of World War II, the nation came down from the heights of frantic production and began to seek a more normal pace and economic design to encourage peacetime growth and prosperity. It was the beginning of a new era of modern industry, one that would require the resolution of social and technological challenges in the workplace.

When the first of a wave of "miracle" drugs captured the attention of the medical field, hopeful patients awaited results. Behind the scenes, numerous other less dramatic medical advances were contributing to patient care—among them the introduction of disposable products for use in hospitals. Many hospitals were still reusing surgical dressings after laundering and sterilization. The risk of contamination was high. After a decade of research, Johnson & Johnson, which had introduced sterile surgical dressings in 1886, came out with a new generation of disposable products for hospitals. For surgical patients, the danger of infection was always present, but the risks were now far fewer than when Lord Lister sprayed his operating room with carbolic acid to fend off what he termed "unseen assassins."

As medical science advanced, the management of hospitals became more complicated, and the fact that there was no formal training for hospital administrators puzzled Johnson. He had devoted many years to studying the role of hospital management and had often lamented the lack of training for that area. Then in 1943 he provided funding to establish the nation's first School of Hospital Administration, at Northwestern University. Working closely on the pioneer project with Dr. Malcolm T. MacEachern of the College of Surgeons, Johnson saw this new approach as the best way to bring sound business practices to hospital management.

Johnson was a hospital patient numerous times — for his heart problem and other ailments — and each time was a memorable experience for the medical staff that attended him. Once he was required to have four penicillin shots a day, and the nurses would always ask, "And where did we get the shot last time?" Annoyed, he sent out for an indelible pencil. Then, after each shot was administered, he drew a circle around the spot on his skin and noted the date and time. Soon his skin was covered with his notations. However, there were fewer questions about where he got his last shot. On another hospital stay, he decided that he would reorganize the nurses-training program, which he accomplished during the two weeks that he was a patient. He had learned a great deal about nursing through the years, and his ideas were helpful. Another time, he was a patient in the hospital at the University of Pennsylvania, and while there he pledged to build a new medical library for the teaching institution. It was a costly but gratifying stay.

·

The dramatic growth of the company after the war led to a significant increase in advertising. Johnson had an innate suspicion of advertising agencies and felt that copywriters were too impressed with what he termed "their personal phraseology" to pay attention to what he believed was the most basic ingredient of the ad: proper use of the company name. To combat this, he developed a formula that company ads were to follow, and then set out to see that it was adhered to. To get his point across, he had small display cards printed and sent to every marketing and advertising person in the company. In gold letters, the card gave his formula:

DRAMATICS · SIMPLICITY · CONTINUITY
BRAND NAME DOMINATES
BRIEF AND LEGIBLE COPY
CORPORATION SIGNATURE STRONG

Then he began to measure consumer and professional print advertising against his formula. (This was before the advent of television commercials.) His first targets were the various advertising agencies representing the company.

"Our record shows that the agency rarely comes forward with a basic idea worthy of a long-term campaign with DRAMATICS, SIMPLICITY, AND CONTINUITY," he wrote about one agency. "These creations must come from us. The agency can be of assistance and occasionally it can create," he continued. "Unfortunately, the agency too frequently confuses the management. The net of this is that we must create a format of advertising. The agency must collaborate, polish it, and above all, get out of the way so that they are not a liability instead of the asset that they should and can be."

Johnson also waged war against overstatement in company advertising. "Exaggeration is not good advertising," he insisted. "If you must be off the line, understate rather than overstate." On another occasion he proclaimed: "Should it be that all our firms, worldwide, are the only honest advertisers in the world . . . LET IT BE SO!"

Normally Johnson did not require that all advertising be approved by him, but he did read and evaluate it with great care. It might have been easier if he had prior approval, though, for when he found mistakes the entire campaign had to be abandoned. Repeated mistakes brought out his cutting criticism. Once he spotted an advertisement for a new Red Cross Improved Bandage that embodied all the mistakes he had urged the agency to avoid. His memo to the account executive was devastating:

When a mistake is made it is unfortunate. When we make the same mistake a second time it is serious. When we make the same mistake a third time we are guilty of incompetence, poor management and lack of competitive strength. When we make the same mistake fifteen or twenty times it is reprehensible.

You will note the attached advertisement. While the signature of Johnson & Johnson is improved it should be appreciably enlarged.

After long and contemplated consideration I conclude that you have generated a group deserving a new terminology. Henceforth such persons will be known as QUARTER-WITS.

Robert W. Johnson

An outburst like that was not typical. Usually he was more re-strained and constructive. He never criticized the agency directly, but always through his own executives. And he did praise advertis-ing he found appealing. Sometimes the praise was generous. But if a memo from him started off like "The Cotton Bud advertising is fairly good . . . ," trouble was sure to follow. "Fairly good" to John-son meant not as good as the words suggested. His instructions in that particular memo shot a gaping hole in the entire campaign. Suddenly "fairly good" was a disaster.

Johnson didn't rely solely on his own instincts and judgment. Once when he became upset over baby product advertising but couldn't put his finger on the problem, he arranged to bring in a panel of young mothers to discuss the effectiveness of the adver-tising (the forerunner of focus groups). He had the session tape-recorded so he could listen to their reactions later. Then he out-lined what he wanted done in a memo, adding: "I hope this has the consent of Young & Rubicam." It did.

Though Johnson's close attention to company advertising caused some grumbling, there was, over time, unmistakable improvement in all the company's advertising. It did become more dramatic and simpler. While there were jokes about the small white cards printed with his formula for good advertising, years later those cards were still on display in many offices. Most agreed that his for-mula worked. Johnson would not permit a competitor's product to be mentioned—let alone criticized—in his company's advertising. If a product couldn't be sold on its merits, then it shouldn't be advertised, he maintained.

As the business grew, so did Johnson & Johnson's reputation for being a skilled marketer of consumer products and an innovator of creative advertising. In the late 1940s an unusual marketing campaign added considerably to this reputation. The advertising of Modess brand sanitary napkins made by the Personal Products Company had been less than successful, and because of his concern about the product, Johnson often attended the advertising strategy meetings. One day he suggested that the next campaign be pegged to high fashion, a subject of interest to many women. He cautioned, however, that for the campaign to be successful the designer clothes, the models, the settings, and the photographers would all have to be far different from anything ever seen in magazine advertising.

Taking Johnson at his word, the product director and the agency account executives set out to do something radically different with a high-fashion theme. Many of the great couturiers — Valentina, Falkenstein, Hattie Carnegie, Balenciaga, Jacques Fath, Christian Dior — were engaged to design gowns to be used exclusively for the Modess ads. Famous fashion models, including Dorian Leigh and Susie Parker, were photographed by such notables as Ruzzie Green, Cecil Beaton, and Valentino Sarra. The exotic settings ranged from Park Avenue penthouses and European palaces, to Venetian canals, art museums of the world, and the snowcapped mountains of Switzerland.

The "Modess . . . *because*" campaign was an immediate success and was later chosen as one of the hundred all-time great advertisements. Sales of the product soared. But of all its clever aspects, the two simple words of the copy, "Modess . . . *because*" were the most ingenious. That too was actually Johnson's suggestion, according to a marketing executive present the day it was proposed. "When it came to the question of copy," he recalled, "we knew from past experience that women resisted reading about a sanitary napkin, no matter how well written. We were discussing this problem with General Johnson, and he said: 'Think in terms of as few words as possible, perhaps only ten words, maybe only five words, maybe only one word, just "Modess," maybe "Modess . . . *because*."'" The brilliance of the "Modess . . . *because*" copy was that it enabled each woman who read it to fill in her own reasons for wanting to buy the product.

The strikingly beautiful gowns designed especially for the advertising campaign made their debut in the major women's magazines of the day—and reappeared later when worn elegantly by Evie Johnson for social events.

By now many Johnson & Johnson consumer products had become institutions throughout America, and in many other parts of the world as well. Mothers by the millions dusted babies' bottoms with Johnson's Baby Powder and used copious amounts of its sister products—oil, lotion, and baby soap. Johnson's baby products had become synonymous with infant care, and the advertising slogan "Best for Baby—Best for You" lured countless adult users as well. The nostalgic scent of the baby powder was a pleasant reminder of the serene days of childhood, and the formula for the scent was so prized that for decades it was kept in a bank vault.

"First-aid" and the name "Johnson's" had become inseparable in the minds of consumers. Band-Aid adhesive bandages were being used by the billions, and the agency executive who had once predicted they wouldn't sell had retreated into merciful anonymity. Though hospital patients were less aware of the Johnson products used in their care, that was not true of the physicians and nurses who applied the surgical dressings or closed the wounds with Ethicon sutures. They constituted another army of loyal supporters of "The Most Trusted Name in Surgical Dressings."

Like his father, Johnson was relentless in his pursuit of quality and superior products. "We are dedicated to the unwavering determination to design, produce, package and deliver to the ultimate user the finest products in the world," he told his management. "Nothing less offers a reasonable chance of continued success."

In fact, the slightest hint of a drop in quality infuriated him. One senior executive made the mistake of writing Johnson: "There is no instance where our surgical dressings products are not *at least* as good as any competitor's, and in some cases we enjoy a quality advantage." Johnson scrawled in oversize letters on the memo: "NOT GOOD ENOUGH — RWJ" and sent it back.

The practice of stopping at drugstores and other retail outlets to check on his company's products, and the competition's, became an occupational disease with him, as with others in the company. No matter where he traveled, he always found time to "check the stores" and send the inevitable memo to the home office. The dreaded opening line, "Well, here we go again," would send shudders through the most stouthearted product director. One memo could trigger months of travail. "Instruct our sales force to remove these old, discolored, unsightly [dental floss] displays and replace them with fresh ones," he once wrote. "Then design a display that will retain its appearance." There was never any question about following his orders. It was a matter of job security.

Periodically he would order all division presidents and marketing directors to personally survey three stores each — a drugstore, a supermarket, and a discount house — to check on their own products and those of the competition. His favorite stop during the winter months was Kasden's Drug Store in Surfside, Florida. The clerks at Kasden's never realized that their casual comments sometimes altered the course of a carefully planned marketing campaign. When a memo began "Yesterday I spent a half hour at Kasden's . . ." it spelled trouble, and what followed might result in a year's work. His memos were brief, but the consequences were often catastrophic.

"Our packages must be designed to give maximum brand impact," he once wrote. "We should give new attention to line uniformity." That memo had far-reaching implications. The irony was that he was so often right. Another time he noted: "We are not selling baby powder. We are selling JOHNSON'S. Our baby powder container, while good, has the words Baby Powder larger and Johnson's smaller. This should be in reverse." The change was made, and the marketing people reluctantly conceded that it should have appeared that way all along. He placed great importance on brand-name recognition and demanded that the name "be instantly recognizable."

Johnson had deep respect for the competition, which he also conveyed in memos following his "store checks." "Mr. Charles Revson is a pretty good merchandiser. Please inspect his line display. . . . The Brillo package has impact, . . . the word Bromo for Bromo-Seltzer stands out. . . . Procter & Gamble and Colgate have learned their lessons well."

He got involved in some unusual episodes, which is not uncommon with corporate chairmen who are quick to volunteer. One of his newspaper friends was columnist Dorothy Kilgallen, who with her husband, Dick Kollmar, had a morning radio program, "Dorothy and Dick," on WOR in New York. In September 1949 Kilgallen mentioned on the air that she wished Bob Johnson made "Band-Aids" in colors to match her wardrobe. Johnson happened to be listening, and when he got to the office he asked marketing to make her some bandages in a variety of colors. After checking with Kilgallen, the colors included bottle green, mauve, and shocking pink.

The project was put in the hands of a young assistant product director, who soon got carried away. A whole series of experiments were run on various types of colored cloth before rayon was selected. Then each bandage was hand-cut, two hundred in all, fifty of each color. For ready identification, they were put in clear-plastic containers and delivered to Kilgallen, with a note of apology that the colored rayon prevented them from being sterilized. On the air the next day Kilgallen gushed over the accomplishment:

"I chose the shocking pink [first] because I thought it would go well with my finger nails," she told her listeners. She then vowed she would wear them everywhere. This stirred interest in the marketing department, and later colored Band-Aid adhesive bandages made their appearance.

Johnson had a habit of wandering around and visiting offices unannounced. Dropping in on young marketing executives, he would sit down in front of the desk and ask, "What's new with your brand?" It wasn't considered wise to be slow or deficient in the reply. The younger product directors used to compare notes about breaking out in a cold sweat when they saw The General stride into their office. On those visits, however, Johnson would demonstrate a genuine interest in their ideas about better marketing plans or advertising, and later they related the details of his visit with pride— if they fared well. He always remembered the workers who handled themselves well and had good answers. If he was impressed, it could mean a brighter future with the company. Surviving one of his unannounced visits was like coming out of battle unscathed. Doing well was like getting decorated.

One of his many passions was neatness in all forms, which was manifested in many ways. Those who worked with him knew he was a confirmed advocate of having a clean desk. Not just his own—he wanted everyone's desk to be clean. So, on his surprise "What's new?" visits he always cast a critical eye on the desktop. Marketing people especially were sometimes barely visible behind the mounds of paper on their desks, including the deluge of memos from Johnson. Numerous times they quoted him as saying: "A cluttered desk is a cluttered mind." In the cafeteria at lunch, or over a beer on the way home, they often talked about the perfect reply: "Yes, General, a cluttered desk is a cluttered mind, and what does an empty desktop suggest to you?" It was good for laughs, but no one ever said it to him.

His penchant for neatness and cleanliness extended to the manufacturing plants, but in this case it was based on his strong conviction that a company producing sterile surgical products had to be clean and properly maintained. "Maintenance is money in the bank," he contended. When it came to plant cleanliness, he was the strongest enforcer, and he did it in strange but effective ways. In the early days, when the factory buildings were old, he ordered all the corners of the factory floor and stairwells painted white so he could easily detect any accumulation of dirt.

He made frequent inspections, and his patience wore thin when he found violations. One day he spotted a dirty window over one of the stairwell landings and asked the foreman to have it cleaned. A few days later he came by and saw the window was still dirty. He said nothing, but he went downstairs, returned with a long piece of wood, methodically broke the panes out of the dirty window, handed the wood to the foreman, and said, "Perhaps now we will have a clean window."

Stories about the plant visits were abundant. One employee put the gist of them to verse, and that amused the General so much that he sent it to the company newspaper. It began:

> When bosses fly around the plant,
> With eyes all filled with fear,
> There is just one thing I'm sure of,
> General Johnson's mighty near.

Many of the visits were announced. On one the plant manager had a thirty-minute tip prior to his arrival, so he hastily had things spruced up by having several large rolls of paper hoisted to the roof of the building. When Johnson arrived he was furious. "What in the hell is all that junk on the roof?" he asked. He had come by helicopter that day.

The employees looked forward to visits because they usually led to improvements. A district sales manager told about the outcome of one visit. "In Chicago we were on the second floor of a building with a long hall running the entire length of the block. The General was standing at the east end of the hallway, near my office, and I was returning from the far side. As I walked noisily along the hall-way with my size 13EEE feet, he didn't bat an eye. We exchanged greetings and I continued to my office. It was the Depression days, but he gave the order to soundproof the floor and carpet it. A lot of people thanked me for making our work area more enjoyable."

When he built a showplace plant on U.S. Route 1 in New Jersey, Johnson became concerned because the expansive new reflecting pool—shaped like a boomerang—couldn't be seen from the high-way. The pool would have to be enlarged, he decided, so he called the plant engineer and told him to get forty wood stakes with pointed tips and painted green on the other end. Together, the next morning, they staked out the contours of an enlarged pool. Then, with the engineer at the wheel, they drove up and down the highway while Johnson raised and lowered himself in the passen-ger side to determine whether the new pool could be seen from the highway. It couldn't. He then inquired about the possibility of having Route 1 raised in front of the plant. The State of New Jersey wasn't interested.

Another time, he was driving past one of his New Jersey plants that had a large expanse of windows when he spied one misaligned venetian blind marring the perfect symmetry of the buildings. He stopped, marched into the plant, and had them straighten it. It wasn't just compulsive. He had a reason, which he expressed this way: "A disorderly plant is a symptom of confused management. I cannot look into a man's mind, but I can look into his plant."

Plant managers knew what they were up against. One described him as "a hound for neatness, a bearcat for cleanliness." Having the plant and grounds in perfect order was as important to Johnson as meeting production quotas, and they knew it.

·

The heady world of Washington politics, the amusing and frivo-lous café society crowd, even the stirring adventures on his boats and planes—they all held his interest. But there was never any doubt among those who knew Robert Johnson that he was happiest and most content when he was involved in day-to-day business decisions. He had made Johnson & Johnson the focus of his life, the source of his pride, his wellspring of satisfaction — and often at the expense of his personal relationships. Competing with that was a lost cause, and sometimes it took a painfully long time for those close to him to realize it.

20

VOICE OF A PATRIOT

POLITICS had a tantalizing appeal for Johnson ever since he became New Jersey's youngest mayor in 1920 at the age of twenty-seven. It was not a pursuit for the fainthearted, and the rules of gentlemanly conduct did not apply. In the first half of the century, New Jersey had become a breeding ground for political chicanery at its worst, and the challenge to bring about reform was a test of will and endurance. That was the kind of fight Johnson liked and, as with many of his encounters, he emerged bloodied but unbowed.

Writers who covered New Jersey politics referred to him as a "king-maker," and that made him a prime news source. It was at Johnson's home at Morven in Princeton in the 1930s that the plotting to overthrow political bossism in New Jersey, and the charting of a course toward reform, began. The principal villain was Mayor Frank Hague of Jersey City, the state's dominating Democratic Party leader. Between Johnson and Hague there developed a tense political jousting match that continued unabated for years, spurred on by some strange similarities in their personalities.

Hague was born of immigrant Irish parents in Jersey City's Second Ward, known as the Horseshoe District, in 1876. His father had fled Ireland to escape arrest for conspiring against the British. The Horseshoe area (named for its shape) was a flat expanse of teeming immigrant life that stretched west from the docks of the Hudson River directly across from New York City. There thousands of Irish, German, Italian, Polish, and Jewish immigrants disembarked, and many of them established homes in the Horseshoe and stayed for their entire lives. For the most part, they were honest, hardworking people struggling to keep their large families together. And despite their many origins, they managed to get along together in the brownstones and crowded tenements where they lived, in the boisterous saloons where the men drank, and in the quiet churches where the women prayed.

The Horseshoe was a blend of poverty and dignity and was the perfect spawning ground for the politically ambitious. Frank Hague had that ambition. What he lacked in formal education — he was expelled from the sixth grade as incorrigible and never returned — he made up for in shrewdness. In 1911 he was elected Jersey City's street and water commissioner, then became director of public safety, and then was elected mayor in 1917 on a reform ticket. Two years later he became New Jersey's Democratic Party leader.

Hague's "reform" methods were carefully calculated to ensure his political longevity. He collected a tribute from those who did business with Jersey City, and every city and Hudson County jobholder had to "contribute" 3 percent of their wages to the organization coffers. In the process he built a disciplined and fiercely loyal political machine. Hague rewarded his constituents for their support, primarily with steady employment, medical care, Christmas food baskets, personal condolences at times of family loss, summertime boat rides and picnics, and the knowledge that they had a "friend" in city hall. They also had the highest city tax rates in America.

When it was expedient, the political bosses of the two parties made deals, and it was against this kind of unholy alliance that Johnson lashed out in his speech in 1938, when he attacked the professional elements in both parties: "I am using the word 'professional' as an act of kindness instead of the more descriptive term 'political racketeer,'" he said. "There has been a combination between the Democrats and Republicans which has often worked to the detriment of the people of the state."

The opposition to machine politics in the state came in the form of the Clean Government movement that was spawned in the 1920s and gained momentum, and vital financial support, at the dinner meetings at Morven. Now the two forces were about to clash. Hague fired the first shot in 1939 when he publicly accused Johnson of being the "boss" of the Republican Clean Government Organization. Hague calling Johnson a political "boss" made headlines across the state and cleverly deflected the bipartisan dealings that Hague himself was being charged with.

Once on the attack, Hague cited Johnson's frequent visits to Washington "to confer with New Deal leaders in advancing the Democratic Party's national policies, and his conferences with Jim Farley, chairman of the Democratic National Committee." "If Bob Johnson is betraying the Republican Party, then I think the people of the state should know of it," Hague declared. The Democratic boss was not alone in trying to fathom Johnson's political preferences, which at various times had swung from archconservative to liberal. Johnson himself admitted the ambiguity, but insisted that frankness in politics was more important than consistency. One political analyst wrote: "He is an industrialist and a Republican but seldom talks like either."

Allied with Johnson in the Clean Government movement was a young, progressive-minded lawyer from Essex County, Arthur T. Vanderbilt, later to become Chief Justice of the New Jersey Supreme Court. Vanderbilt led a supposedly nonpartisan group that was vigorously opposed to corruption and machine politics yet liberal in its thinking. It was Vanderbilt's plan to wrest control in the northern counties, but Johnson insisted on attacking Hague and the other bosses on the flanks, and from the southern part of the state.

Political writers credited Johnson with the grooming and early selection of Alfred E. Driscoll, who became one of New Jersey's most distinguished governors and the one who wrecked the political machine that controlled the state. Driscoll, a young and scrupulously honest lawyer and Harvard Law School graduate, was first elected to the Haddonfield Borough Commission in Camden County, then to the New Jersey State Senate, and in 1941 became Senate Republican majority leader. He then served as State Alcoholic Beverage Commissioner, a sensitive post surrounded by temptation and scandal. Driscoll's reputation as a strict and impartial watchdog grew.

Under Vanderbilt's direction and with Johnson's strong support, the Clean Government movement began putting together one of the most powerful liberal Republican organizations in the nation. When it came time to do battle with Hague in 1945, the group that had become the Clean Government Republicans mustered strong support for Driscoll, and he was elected governor. Almost immediately Driscoll began work on a new state constitution, which was to be acclaimed nationwide as a model of government reform. The judiciary too was revamped, and Vanderbilt was selected as the new state chief justice.

Driscoll's drive and energy had enormous appeal for Johnson, and the two men remained close friends for many years. They worked together on improving transportation in the state, including the creation and construction of the New Jersey Turnpike. When progress wasn't fast enough, Johnson would unburden himself to Driscoll, occasionally forgetting that it was the governor he was criticizing. Once he realized that he had gone too far. He wrote Driscoll from Florida:

Dear Al:
On many nights since my recent letters I have been greatly disturbed. I have done you an injustice, and I am sorry. Being exhausted as I was is a poor excuse. The truth is that I sometimes forgot that government and politics cannot be as orderly as a closely knit industrial family.

You have done more than any governor has in my lifetime, and always for the good of the State. So, Al, let's go on pulling together. You can count on me for a little plain talk occasionally. Come on down and get a few days in the sun. Your room is ready.

Driscoll was gracious in his reply:

Dear Bob:

I was touched by your thoughtful letter the other day and I have found it difficult to answer. Your friendship has meant much to me. It has heartened me in times of adversity and strengthened me when the going appeared to be comparatively easy. Thank you very much. . . .

In other letters, Driscoll was equally generous in his praise of Johnson. "No one more than yourself deserves recognition for a very real contribution to the welfare of our society," the governor wrote. And in a later letter: "Our success in New Jersey is the measure of your wonderful contribution to good government in this State over a period of many years."

Having lost the governorship to Driscoll, the Democrats looked ahead to winning the U.S. Senate seat in 1948. Earlier the Republican leadership had quietly offered the nomination to Johnson behind closed doors, but he promptly and politely declined. Then Frank Hague sprang into action and publicly announced that in his capacity as state Democratic leader he was inviting Johnson to become that party's candidate for the Senate seat. Even the most blasé New Jersey politician was jolted by this move — which made Johnson the only person in the history of New Jersey politics to be offered the U.S. Senate nomination by the two parties in the same year.

With great flourish, Hague elaborated to the press on his choice: "I have great admiration for General Johnson," he said. "He is one of the outstanding industrialists of the country and one of the most distinguished citizens of New Jersey. He is a great liberal in his views and has distinguished himself in the service of his country.

From my observation of General Johnson's activities in New Jersey and my long friendship with him I feel that he will agree to present his candidacy to the people of the state for United States senator. I can predict without any hesitancy that he will be elected by an overwhelming majority."

Johnson was basking in the Florida sun aboard his yacht *Sirena* when the news broke. Enterprising reporters reached him on the ship-to-shore telephone and learned that he did not want to be the Democratic candidate or the Republican candidate. Hague then announced that he was heading for Florida to try to persuade Johnson to change his mind. It was a masterful political ploy that only someone of Hague's cunning could conceive, but Johnson wasn't buying it. He still bore the scars of his time in Washington and was not about to volunteer to run the gauntlet in the U.S. Senate.

.

Johnson managed to stir things up in other areas of politics. In the spring of 1947 he wrote an article for *Vogue* in which he sharply criticized women for failing to take advantage of their political rights and become more involved. During his research for the article, he wrote to the state secretaries of all forty-eight states requesting information on the number of female officeholders in each state. He also wrote to dozens of other organizations, including women's clubs and the U.S. Conference of Mayors, in an effort to determine why more women were not active in politics.

The article drew wide acclaim for its frankness—some said its bravery. Few men had dared to tackle the sensitive subject in a national magazine article, but Johnson forged ahead undaunted. He had broached the issue the year before when he spoke to the Garden Club of New Jersey: "It is often embarrassing at meetings and dinners of country and state officials to find only one woman in the room," he told them.

But that was mild compared with Johnson's *Vogue* piece, titled "Sugar, Spice and Everything Nice":

I recall a parade Mother took me to see as a little boy. It was a demonstration in favor of Votes for Women, with banners emblazoned with flaming swords and in blood-red letters, "Taxation without Representation Is Injustice?" I didn't know just what that meant, though Mother whispered something about the Boston Tea Party and Declaration of Independence. Just then Isadora Duncan marched by, leading a column of Amazons dressed in flowing Grecian robes. . . .

The ladies kept on marching and a lot of them made speeches from Stanley Steamers or Maxwell Fours. Then came 1920, and the Constitution was amended to say that the ladies might vote. Magazines all over the land broke out in a rash of articles on the New Age in Politics. In time "Ma" Ferguson was elected governor of Texas, and humorous cracks were made about the West "where men were men, but women were governors."

The joke wasn't very good. Many editors wrote pieces deploring the fact that women were getting political know-how without political ideals. Others urged that the ladies be given time—time in which to learn all the ropes, and to beat the old-line bosses at a new and better game.

Well, we have been waiting. Twenty-six years have passed since women got the franchise. During that time they have elected only one other governor, Mrs. Nellie Ross, of Wyoming. A handful of women, including a good actress and a well-known playwright, have been elected to the Senate and the House. Although we have had two women serving as Ministers in our Foreign Service, there are none at present. In the last Congress [the 79th], there were no women in the Senate and only nine in the House, while the present Congress shows an even poorer record with only seven in the House. All forty-eight governors are men. In twenty-five of our 1947 State Legislatures, the Democrats and Republicans have 16 women in the upper Houses and 180 in the lower, or a total of 196. This is 38 less than the 1946 total, which was an all-time high of 234. In cities over 30,000, there are no women serving as mayor or city manager—at least to my knowledge; but in some of the smaller villages and towns, there are women serving in those capacities.

The record is a poor one. Why? Are the ladies getting a run-around? Or are they natural washouts in the field of politics? They will campaign for beautiful roadsides, for health funds, for playgrounds, and worthy causes. In this department the distaff side cracks a whip, making whole communities sit up and be good. But politics are something else again. There women — or at least many women — are willing to follow the Old Guard, vote for its candidates, and scurry off to the bridge club. It was one thing to fight for the Disfranchised Woman-hood of America; it is another to buckle down to the grind of picking candidates, rounding up votes, and keeping a steady hand on the controls of the political machine right at home.

Women own a big share of the taxable property in the United States. They got some of it by sound business operations, they got some just by living longer than the average man. The whole net of modern politics touches women, and touches them every day.

What does all this add up to? That's for the ladies to say. They must admit, I think, that they have neither cleaned up politics, developed political leaders among their own sex, nor achieved a revolution. They aren't doing much in the places where politics start — in towns, counties, and states.

Leaders of a number of women's organizations believed that Johnson's scorching criticism would serve as a stimulant. Male reaction to the article was a stony silence, except for the editors of *Vogue*, who were delighted with the stir. Some of Johnson's critics accused him of grandstanding again and called him a male chauvinist at heart. But the facts didn't support those contentions. The majority of his work force was comprised of women, and he repeatedly took measures to improve their lives and give them opportunity to grow. On a number of occasions he even spoke out on women's rights. Once, when he was proposing an increase in the minimum wage, a businessman wrote him and asked if he *actually* intended the increase to be for *both* men and women. Johnson fired back a curt reply: "The answer is yes. It is for men and women. Does that clear up your question?"

When Wilma Soss, president of the Federation of Women Shareholders in American Business Inc., wrote a letter to the *New York Times* noting the economic potential of women, Johnson was quick to agree. "To strengthen your position," he wrote Soss, "you might go on to say that 70 million policy holders in the United States have as their beneficiaries women and children. . . . For years it has been known that the wealth of the United States is largely in the hands of women. . . . The sad part of the story is that women have not used their rights and have not been effective in defending them."

He added: "For the past fifteen years I have attempted to organize the women of New Jersey in support of the principle of good government, and I am sorry to inform you that the ladies have not responded. However, I do believe that women will respond to a direct appeal to their own financial welfare, and I further believe that a sufficient number could successfully change the atmosphere of government in the United States without regard to party. The Federation of Women Shareholders in American Business has a unique opportunity. . . . The time has come for women to accept the responsibility that goes with their ownership."

In Johnson's view, women were not alone in their failure to capitalize on their potential at the voting polls. He felt the same way about his own work force, but in this case he could address the matter. When the figures for the 1950 federal census were announced, Johnson was surprised to learn there were 28 million salaried and professional people in the United States, compared with only 20 million blue-collar workers. The white-collar work force had been growing and was directly related to industrial modernization.

As more modern machines were developed, there was a greater need for salaried technicians, engineers, and support staff, and as production increased with greater mechanization, there were more jobs for salesmen, clerks, and other white-collar workers. Johnson believed the change had come about so quietly that its political importance was scarcely realized, and certainly not by the white-collar workers themselves. "I am convinced," he said, "that 99 percent of these people believe themselves to be a part of an inconsequential political minority." Yet he considered them the most powerful force in the nation, and according to voting potential they were.

After mulling it over, he came up with the idea of forming "Sound Government Committees" in all his plants and offices. The purpose was to get white-collar employees interested in government, in the political process, and in issues directly affecting them, much as the unions were doing with factory workers. Johnson made it clear that he was not attempting to organize the unorganized or to promote any political causes — "It isn't appropriate that corporations should enter the arena of partisan politics," he said. Membership on the committees was to be voluntary, and meetings were held on company time. The limit was twelve members to each group, with no officers, no dues, no formalities. Executives above a certain level could not participate.

In anticipating reactions to his plan he thought some employees would wonder what difference even one person could make in a nation of 150 million people. He had a ready answer. "What have a few Socialists and Communists done to us?" he asked. Every American knew the answer to that question.

Once he put the program in motion, he stepped aside and waited to see what happened. Soon, dozens of Sound Government Committees had been formed, and although early discussions were disjointed, employees soon began to focus on issues that affected them. The agendas that evolved were formidable. The minutes of one group had a list of concerns that included "fair and just taxation, a sound dollar, integrity in government, support of fundamental constitutional rights, a vigorous two-party political system, and a resourceful and respected foreign policy."

In time, the talk became action. One group explained the economics of the current tax situation to seven hundred fellow employees at small gatherings. Another convinced a national business organization to create Sound Government Committees among its membership. Still another wrote a letter on fair taxation to the company's stockholders, and elected officials received a flood of mail and visits from constituents.

The news media quickly picked up on the idea, and countless articles were written about the Johnson plan for Sound Government Committees. Many echoed his belief that white-collar employees now represented a new force in American politics. An editorial in *Collier's* magazine, one of the most widely circulated publications in the nation, observed: "The white-collar workers are not only the country's most numerous, but also the most diversified in activities and interests. They certainly personify that famous character, the Average Citizen. As such, they are less likely to be special pleaders than the organizations of farmers, labor union members and business executives. We think a little less special pleading would be a mighty healthy thing for the country. And we're in favor of sensible moves like the Johnson & Johnson program."

The Sound Government idea did not become the national "crusade" Johnson envisioned when he proposed it, but it did make its mark as a new enlightened idea. It was impossible to determine how widely it had been replicated throughout industry, but employees in his own company kept the committees active for more than ten years. And they did it on their own initiative, because it gave them a better understanding of the political process and because they also saw results.

21

"OR FORFEIT FREEDOM"

LONG before the war came to an end the struggle for power in the peacetime economy had begun in workplaces all over America. Labor and management jockeyed to strengthen their positions. Now, rallied by the exhortations of labor leaders no longer bound by the wartime no-strike agreement, workers became increasingly strident. As their demands mounted, management strengthened its resolve to take a hard line in new contract negotiations. It certainly was not the peace the nation had hoped would come with the cease-fire, nor was it the tranquillity that returning servicemen and women expected as they came home to resume their lives as civilians.

Against this backdrop of national unrest and growing bitterness, Johnson began work on a book that he hoped would address the problems plaguing the nation and offer viable solutions. But the mounting hostility in the workplace was not the only thing that concerned Johnson. As the national debate became more heated and more shrill, there was increased discussion about the merits of communism and socialism — perhaps not seriously, but to Johnson the patriot it was cause for alarm. Furthermore, he rebelled at the thought of solving the nation's problems with increased government intervention. "So many of our people have lost their sense of freedom in the workplace that they turn to government as their only defense," he said at the time. "It is our duty to make what contributions we can to clear public thinking, and I simply cannot rest without continuing such efforts."

Out of this thinking, this concern, came the book *Or Forfeit Freedom: People Must Live and Work Together*, published by Doubleday & Company in 1947. It was the best writing he had ever done, and the *Saturday Review* called it "one of the most important books ever written by an American businessman." Writing the book gave Johnson the opportunity to bring together his philosophy on managing a business, his long-held concerns for the well-being of lower-echelon employees, and his commitment to the community, and to shape all these concepts into a solution to the troubles that business and industry were facing in the turbulent postwar era.

In the opening pages, in his usual blunt style, Johnson summed up his views on the decline of confidence in business:

Things have been going wrong with our economic system; they went very wrong in 1929 and again in 1937, and they took another tailspin during 1946. Because they did, and because a few business leaders both talked and practiced nonsense, private enterprise is in disgrace with one part of the public and on probation with the rest. . . . Yet the very ones who buy and boast [about products] no longer trust business to do its job well, at a reasonable profit, and with justice for everyone. . . .

This is shown by the number of people who suspect the motives of business, sneer at its claims to service, and favor punitive taxation. It also appears in such studies as the Fortune Survey. During 1946, for example, the Survey revealed an increase of more than forty per cent in the number of people who opposed business management in its disputes with labor. Though all income groups were represented, the shift was greatest among the middle class and poor, who form most of our population. Can we doubt, then, that business is still losing public confidence?

No industrialist had ever been that critical of the loss of public confidence by business, and no one could deny the truth of what Johnson said. The danger, he explained, is that more and more people are becoming convinced that in a democracy based on free enterprise, conflict between management and labor is inevitable, and this could lead to drastic controls and regulations that could take the nation in the direction of a form of socialism.

Johnson took eight months to write the book, though he later commented, "In some ways I have been thirty years writing this book." Its essence was the ethics of employment and the pressing need to elevate the relationship between American labor and management to a new level of understanding. Using many historical references, Johnson traced the evolution of industry from its earliest days and showed how the employer-employee relationship had changed over time. He then suggested ways in which the various differences could be resolved, in order to reduce conflict in the workplace, restore public confidence in business, and preserve the freedoms he linked to this whole process.

The book began with a warning that the nation's economic system had performed well during wartime but was now "staggering toward collapse." A reevaluation and recasting of the rules that govern the workplace were needed in order to restore the public's confidence in business. Johnson suggested that this begin by "throwing off our enslavement to the 'Laissez faire, laisser passer' [Hands off, let things alone] doctrine that became a code of business freedom that bordered on nihilism." That philosophy only justified exploitation and dignified greed, he wrote. At the turn of the century, the ethics of Christianity yielded to enlightened self-interest, and workers were delivered to "the callousness of employers and the greed of unrestrained competition." But now, Johnson continued, "big business" had developed monopolistic methods, and labor unions too often duplicated the "socially irresponsible performances of industry."

[334]

Whatever the errors of the past, Johnson wrote, they pale in comparison with the failures of modern business, which he described as an attempt to put "twentieth-century productivity into the straight jacket of eighteenth-century economic ideas." It was this failing, he said, that caused the increase in the minimum wages to be defeated, which would eventually lead to higher taxes and larger welfare costs. It would be smarter, he added, "to pay this bill at the source" and increase the workers' purchasing power.

Customers are voters — "Let us think in terms of 'voters for business,'" he said — but many of his fellow industrialists could not see it that way. "One of our greatest reconversion problems is to earn the respect of the public for the management of business. In doing this, it is vital to sell the customer the integrity of private management and to secure his support through votes as well as through purchases."

In the book, Johnson contended that the technology revolution that automated industry had created "faceless" men and women along the assembly line, shorn of dignity on the job and pride in their skills, and known only as badge numbers. The once proud worker had been reduced to a mechanical robot, and management had forgotten that emotional security is just as important as economic security in creating a healthy work environment. He called for a "new craftsmanship" that would provide workers with a meaningful explanation of their role in the production process and promote a greater sense of satisfaction. And the preferred setting for accomplishing this, he wrote, was a smaller, decentralized plant so that there could be greater personal contact between worker and management.

Throughout the book, Johnson kept his eye on the target: putting America back on the road to full production, full employment, full recognition of labor's rights, and full use of the technical mastery the nation had demonstrated during World War II. Failure to do these things would only encourage further government controls, he wrote, and nothing can be accomplished unless both labor and management redefine their responsibilities to the worker and to society.

Johnson reinforced the point by including in this book a slightly modified version of the "Industrial Credo" that appeared in *"But, General Johnson"* in 1944. This time he added a brief "preface" that gave a compelling rationale for the document and set the stage for his enumeration of a company's social responsibilities. Unfortunately, however, in later years the preface was rarely included with the Credo, as it was meant to be, even though many believed that what it said was vital to the whole concept. The modified Credo, with its preface and an additional paragraph at the end, read:

> We may be sure that both alarm and bitter anger will arise if huge corporations either abuse their power or fail to render the service required by society. The evidence on this point is clear. American institutions, both public and private, exist because the people want them, believe in them, or at least are willing to tolerate them. The day has passed when business was a private matter — if it ever really was. In a business society, every act of business has social consequences and may arouse public interest. Every time business hires, builds, sells, or buys, it is acting for the American people as well as for itself, and it must be prepared to accept full responsibility for its acts.
>
> We believe that the first responsibility of business is to its customers:
>
> Products must always be good, and manufacturers must strive to make them better at lower prices.
>
> Orders must be promptly and accurately filled.
>
> Dealers must make fair profits in order that they may give good service.
>
> The second responsibility of business is to those who work with it; to the men and women in factories, stores, and offices, as well as in service establishments and on farms:
>
> They must have a sense of security in their jobs.

Wages must be fair and adequate,

Management just,

Hours short, and

Working conditions clean and orderly.

Workers should have an organized system for suggestions and complaints.

Foremen and department heads must be competent and fair-minded.

There must be opportunity for those who are qualified to advance as workers and as people.

Each person must be considered an individual standing on his own dignity and merit.

The third responsibility of business is to its management:

Our executives must be persons of talent, education, experience, and ability.

They must be persons of common sense, endowed with full and trained understanding.

The fourth responsibility is to owners and stockholders:

Business must make a sound profit, since, in order for it to continue

Reserves must be created,

Research must be carried on,

Adventurous programs developed, and

Mistakes made and paid for.

Bad times also must be provided for;

High taxes paid,

New machines purchased,

New factories built,

New products launched, and

New sales plans developed.

At the end, Johnson added:

This fourth responsibility is the last — very much the last. Only if the other three have been met, or plainly can be met, is it worthwhile to consider the future of any business enterprise or ask what it should receive. Once basic responsibilities have been met, however, owners and stockholders should receive fair return on the money they have invested. Less than that fair return will discourage sound business and will therefore reduce, if it does not prevent, the success of private enterprise.

The strength of the Credo's message was in its simplicity, and in Johnson's conviction that it was not only a socially responsible approach but also a smart way to run a business. It had been ten years since he first introduced the concept of corporate social responsibility to fellow industrialists. Later he broadened the list of responsibilities to include the communities where employees worked and lived, and made other minor changes, but he never changed the basic concepts.

Johnson also alluded to how his views on corporate responsibility were influenced by Pope Leo XIII's "On the Condition of the Working Classes" (*Rerum Novarum*). The papal encyclical attacked the excesses of capitalism at the beginning of the transition from an agricultural-based society to an industrial-based society. It stated that individuals had the right to own private property, that material goods should meet the needs of everyone, and that the state should have limited powers.

Johnson wrote that his thinking had also been shaped by the Pope Pius XI encyclical "On the Reconstruction of the Social Order" (*Quadragesimo Anno*), which condemned the same abuses Pope Leo XIII had addressed forty years earlier. Pius XI's encyclical opposed the concentration of economic powers, favored collaboration between management and labor, and asserted that the place to meet social obligations was at the most local and least central levels.

Deep-seated personal convictions were also responsible for Johnson's path of thought. He viewed his inherited wealth as a further obligation to act responsibly, but strangely and rather ironically it was his lack of formal education that made him plunge into the subject so deeply and sent him in search of more information about the whole area of social justice. His propensity for diligently pursuing a single subject until he had gained what he felt was a respectable amount of knowledge about it had led him to the papal encyclicals—that and the fact that the Jesuits were linked to his writing efforts.

His philosophy, Johnson said, was rooted in two conclusions he had reached: that all human relations in the workplace should be based on a recognition of the primacy of moral and ethical behavior, and that because every act of business has social consequences that affect the public, business must accept full responsibility for its actions. His efforts to convey these beliefs to his colleagues in business and industry met with mixed reactions—and certainly no outpouring of support. Some accused him of sermonizing, while others saw the wisdom of his words but doubted the practicality of applying his philosophy in dealing with current problems that business was facing.

Johnson's book went on to advocate improved training and education programs, the development of a "new craftsmanship" that would be superior to that replaced by modern industrialization, a more realistic attitude in dealing with unions, and a stepped-up production program bold enough to provide a decent living for all. In his frankness, he was impartial in treading on the toes of both labor and management. One reviewer later commented: "Johnson wrote without fear of disapproval by his fellow industrialists or denunciation by labor leaders."

In many respects, the book was a compendium of Johnson's management philosophy, tuned to the trying times of a nation left badly scarred by a costly war. The message was, in effect, "Let's sit down and talk." It was sensitive to the needs of many, including returning war veterans who came back from hostile battlefields hoping to settle down to a decent-paying job only to find them-selves facing a belligerent and divided workplace. It was practical in its approach to solutions—"Five years of good management would do it," Johnson wrote. But it was also idealistic, and that was always Johnson's Achilles' heel.

By all measures, the book was Johnson's most distinguished con-tribution to change. It came out at a time when he was one of the few American industrialists or perhaps the only one bold enough to face the nation's labor-management unrest and offer solutions—even if they came from "Industry's Rebel," the pragmatic idealist.

The tone of the book was different from Johnson's previous writ-ing. It was composed in more measured terms and did not send out the shock waves of his earlier articles, which drew attention to his views. Yet, he was still direct and penetrating in his analysis. His more studied approach gave his words added weight and his con-clusions strength. To add to his own validity, he described himself in the book as "a businessman who had tried to fill certain public needs, apply certain useful innovations, and explore certain prom-ising fields in dealing with human beings."

Unlike some of his earlier, shotgun approaches to writing, when he scattered ideas all over the landscape, Johnson was more focused in this book. In a direct and forceful manner, he defined his man-agement philosophy and recommended solutions to the conflicts confronting labor and management. And he was not hampered by having too many editors, as had happened in the past.

This time he relied on the help of one editor, the talented Car-roll Lane Fenton of New Brunswick, who with his wife authored numerous books on science and geography for both adults and children. Fenton was quiet and patient and not given to the flat-tery Johnson had sometimes received—as well as barbs—from the magazine editors he had worked with. In addition to Fenton, the only other help Johnson got was from Father Masse at *America* magazine, who worked with Johnson on the section of the book dealing with the origins and evolution of the industrial movement.

Johnson preferred to work on one chapter at a time. With a large scrawl and using a heavy black pencil, he filled page after page of a lined legal-size pad, and then had his secretarial staff type it for Fenton to edit. Sometimes thoughts surfaced during the night, and, being a light sleeper, he would sit on the side of his bed and make notes on a smaller pad on his night table. The next day, the notes would be worked into the chapter he was working on. He was a creature of habit, particularly when it came to work. The writing was always done at home in Princeton or in Florida, during what he called his "off hours," but never in the office. One never did personal work in the office.

As the words evolved from the notepads to book form, they became Johnson's version of a philosophical road map that business could use to find its way back to the main thoroughfare of public and employee confidence, from which it had strayed so far. When the work was complete, he was proud of it, and so was Fenton. In expressing his thanks for having the opportunity to work on the book, Fenton wrote Johnson: "This was your book, General."

Throughout the 271 pages of *Or Forfeit Freedom*, Johnson did not make a single reference to his own company, even though Johnson & Johnson had served as a laboratory for his ideas and solutions since he first assumed a management role thirty years earlier. But in a touching gesture he dedicated the book to "Those men and women who have worked with me through the years" and added: "From them I have learned the lesson that business must and can do its work for the good of humanity."

Doubleday did an initial printing of 12,000 copies (later followed by a second printing of 8,000), and there was wide distribution to industrialists, members of Congress and the Truman administration, labor leaders, the press, political leaders, and educators. It sold in bookstores for $2.50. Almost immediately there was a flood of favorable reviews. One read: "This book should be required reading for every industrial leader, member of Congress and labor leader in the country. If enough ordinary citizens read it and heed what it says, they will be able to bring sufficient pressure to bear on recalcitrant labor and business leaders to reverse our present trend and head American industry on the right road."

Publications that reviewed the book ranged from the *New York Times Book Review* to the *Boilermakers Journal*, which offered high praise. The *Times* reviewer, Keith Hutchinson, liked the book but didn't believe business was in a mood to initiate Johnson's proposals. Johnson replied: "I hope you will not think I am idealistic when I say that management is, in fact, a 'state of mind.' If we can develop an understanding of the need for balanced service, I am confident that our American management can do a magnificent job."

Among the numerous radio programs Johnson appeared on was NBC's popular "Author Meets the Critic," hosted by John K. M. McCaffrey. One of the panelists was James B. Carey, secretary of the CIO and one of the nation's best-known labor leaders. There was little Carey did not like about *Or Forfeit Freedom*, so the sparks did not fly as anticipated. Carey later quipped: "When Bob Johnson wrote his book, he forfeited his freedom to be president of the National Association of Manufacturers."

In his opening remarks on "Author Meets the Critic," Johnson answered some of the criticism that the book had too basic an approach to a complicated problem. "Some reviewers have called *Or Forfeit Freedom* simplified economics, and some say it's labor relations with an economic twist," he said. "Neither statement tells what I set out to do. I believe America *means* business, and that business in its modern sense *means* America. The first and biggest job of American business is to make and distribute the things people need—enough to provide a decent living for every one of the 140 million people in these United States. The second job is to make it possible for American workers to live happy, useful, and dignified lives. Unless these things are done, business and workers too will be headed for dismal failure. American business is in deep trouble. It must begin to chart a clear course, and I have tried to set up some bearings for it in the book."

Over the CBS radio program "Of Men and Books," commentator Quincy Howe told listeners that Johnson had spelled out how the free enterprise system could be made to work. Not surprisingly, the liberal weekly *The Nation* applauded what it called Johnson's "sweet voice of reason." But it was dubious about broad acceptance of the changes Johnson was recommending, saying the book was "keenly intelligent in its analysis of the American economy, somewhat wishful in its recommendations, and probably obnoxious to the industrialists it is intended to reach." The weekly added that Johnson "may have presented an opportune time to change, for the longer it goes the harder it will be."

Monsignor Fulton J. Sheen, then at Catholic University in Washington, D.C., termed the book "forceful," and the Rev. Howard F. Smith of the First Congregational (Unitarian) Society Church applauded Johnson for his "insight into the psychological make-up of the average man." The dean of faculties at the University of Georgia said the book should be required reading in all college business courses. The owner of a textile plant in Pennsylvania telephoned Johnson to say that when he became embroiled in a labor dispute he called his workers in and they settled their differences using *Or Forfeit Freedom* as a guide. From Ketchikan, Alaska, came word that the book was used as the basis for discussions that settled a small dock strike.

While words of praise about the book—"courageous," "inspirational," "a stirring trumpet"—continued to come from many quarters, the one group Johnson had hoped to reach, had hoped to stir into action, was his fellow industrialists. Many of them wrote him polite notes about the book and its noble intentions, but when Johnson looked around to see if anyone was following his lead, he found he was alone. To realists, that came as no surprise, for as a writer for the *New York Herald Tribune* later commented, "Johnson set off a firecracker in top industry's face."

And perhaps for other reasons, small business was not inclined to join the crusade Johnson hoped to form. After reading the book, one small-business owner wrote poignantly to Johnson: "It is utterly impossible for me to do for my employees that which is in my heart and my mind but not in my pocketbook."

The book later received the Franklin D. Roosevelt Memorial Foundation Award from the American Political Science Association as the best book of the year in the field of government and human welfare. The citation read:

> For his approach to the perennial problem of improving labor-management relations; For the promise that his suggestions hold for a more equitable functioning of the private enterprise system; For his recognition of the dignity of the worker and his proposals to re-establish the employee's feeling of craftsmanship; and above all for his enthusiasm and firm conviction that this objective can be accomplished, this award is made.

While *Or Forfeit Freedom* did not become the sudden catalyst for change that Johnson hoped it would, a retrospective look at the later 1940s shows that business during that period underwent transformations that coincided with many of the concepts Johnson was proposing. One shining example was the new relationship that business and industry were developing with the communities where new plants were being built and employees were working as well as living. The bonding between community and business began in the late 1940s and continued to grow. That period also saw a deepening concern on the part of business for the emotional needs of employees in a highly automated work environment—another concept Johnson advanced in his book.

Perhaps most important of all, the message contained in Johnson's Credo influenced similar company statements of responsibility written over the next fifty years. Beginning in 1982, when Johnson & Johnson was confronted by the Tylenol poisonings, the Credo became a landmark document because the company used it as a guide in successfully managing that historic crisis.

22

ADDING THE
HUMAN TOUCH

I N many of his writings, Johnson came back to several basic
themes: human dignity; improving working conditions, from
worksite to compensation; blending moral obligations with
the pursuit of economic goals; holding business to higher standards of performance in areas where it had not previously ventured. Even before *Or Forfeit Freedom* was published, Johnson had
begun to seek ways to gain broader acceptance of these concepts,
and he concluded that he would need more support from others.
He wrote later: "It seemed to me that I was not qualified to do this
task alone. But who was qualified, and how could experts on ethics
[which he had decided would be the best place to start] put their
ideas into a form that made practical business sense?"

He began by asking a small group of clergymen and businessmen to meet with him in Princeton in the summer of 1946 to help
devise a moral code for business. As Johnson spoke to them, the
magnitude and complexity of the assignment became apparent to
the group, giving rise to doubts that they would be able to accomplish such a formidable task. Yet, Johnson told them, just such a
document was needed, not only to bring harmony to the American workplace but also to preserve confidence in the democratic
system. "They agreed," he said later, "that no problem [facing the

nation] is greater or more urgent than that of establishing sound, cooperative relations between workers and management."

At the meeting, Johnson called attention to the many complex relationships in the business environment and stressed that interdependence must be successfully achieved among many groups so that all can progress together. "The idea that business is impersonal is fiction," he said. If the workplace provided a more understanding environment there would be many fewer areas of disagreement.

One of the clergymen in attendance was Father Masse of *America* magazine, who later recalled how the initial meeting gradually took on a larger importance. "All of the participants were acutely aware of the present threat to our American way of life," he wrote. "It seemed to them that the cold war was not a power struggle in the ordinary sense of the term, but that a fundamental issue was at stake. They shared a conviction that a system based on a philosophy of atheistic materialism was challenging a system rooted ultimately in the Christian ethic, and the struggle would be finally resolved on ideological grounds."

The longer the discussion continued, the deeper it delved into philosophical issues and the more apparent it became that agreement on a document would be a lengthy and arduous task. Father Masse continued his recollections: "The discussants proceeded to the logical conclusion that the Western Powers would succeed in the cold war only to the extent that they returned to the principles whence their way of life derived, reinstated them in their original vigor, and applied them to their domestic and foreign policy. Just as the Imperialists in the Kremlin sought their inspiration from communistic ideas, so the Democratic West must find in its Christian beliefs the wisdom and power to check them."

"To those present at the initial meeting," Masse added, "it was obvious that if businessmen were to play their full role in the cold war, they would have to study how and to what extent Christian principles might be applied in the marketplace. There was no dearth of moral teaching on economic affairs. Over the past sixty years, all of the major religious groups had issued statements on the so-called social question. The problem was to apply these principles to the work-a-day world where the yardstick of profit and loss rules supreme — a delicate task which neither businessmen nor clergymen felt able to accomplish working in isolation. The latter knew the theory but not much about the practice; the former were familiar with practice but mostly ignorant of theory. Why not, then, pool their resources? Why not write in collaboration a sort of code of management conduct that would reflect religious inspiration and moral principles?"

That was precisely the mission Johnson had hoped the group would embark on, but as the discussion continued late into the afternoon, it became apparent that it would be a very long project. Was it too much of an undertaking? Would people be prepared to wait and see it through? Each participant was asked to comment, then Johnson suggested they take a vote. "Though aware of the difficulties, the group voted to get on with the job," Father Masse reported.

Looking back on the initial meeting, Johnson said: "They reached one unanimous conclusion, that the root of our problem is moral. The human equation is all important. We are dealing with men and women, with all of their hopes and fears, their loves and hates, and not merely with impersonal economic and political forces."

Johnson was skeptical about how the project would develop. "I expected one of two things," he said. "Either the group would develop a useful statement after a few meetings, or there would be polite expressions of interest and the project would die on the vine. Neither of these things happened. To my surprise, all of these experts agreed with my very cautious suggestion that the problem *was* one of ethics. They also went further and declared that giving employment policies a sound ethical basis was the most important issue facing America today. It was also a problem we were determined to solve, regardless of the time or personal sacrifices involved."

No one attending the meeting that day suspected that it would take three years and a score of meetings to complete their work. Shortly after the first meeting, the process of enlarging the group of collaborators began. From the ranks of business they added companies and representatives who had demonstrated a progressive approach to labor-management relations. The labor people who were asked to participate included the widely known and outspoken James B. Carey, Secretary-Treasurer of the Congress of Industrial Organizations (CIO). Boris Shishkin, the economist with the American Federation of Labor (AFL), was another labor representative.

Other Protestant, Jewish, and Catholic clergy were soon added to the group, and the Jesuits were well represented. One prominent Catholic priest was the Rev. John F. Cronin, S.S., an assistant director of the National Catholic Welfare Conference in Washington and a leader of its social-action programs. It was Father Cronin whom the collaborators called on to draft the final document. Several educators were added, including representatives from the Universities of Illinois and Wisconsin, and the Catholic colleges, St. Louis University, Rockhurst, Loyola, and Villanova. Rabbi Hirsh E. L. Freund, executive director of the Synagogue Council of America, was one of a number of Jewish leaders who joined the group. The Protestant representation included Dr. Cameron P. Hall, Executive Secretary of the Federal Council of Churches of Christ in America.

As new companies were added, representatives of General Foods Corporation, McCormick & Company Inc., Standard Oil of New Jersey, and Swift & Company joined the group. Two representatives from the Motion Picture Association of America were added, as was Thomas J. Ross of the New York public relations firm of Ivy Lee & T. J. Ross. The meetings were held in various cities every three or four months, including New York, Washington, and Baltimore, and sometimes lasted for two or three days.

[349]

"It was slow work at first," Father Masse recalled. "Definitions were hammered out, doubtful points cleared up, differences of opinion somehow reconciled. From time to time new members joined the group and made their contributions."

The people whom Johnson and the others recruited to work on the project were often recommended for their farsighted views on social and workplace issues. This included many of the clergymen, some of whom were seen as activists. Within the group were some very creative thinkers from a range of disciplines, and when they came together to address Johnson's challenge they developed a synergy. The discussions were lively, the debates were long and animated. Soon they were caught up in the subject, fascinated by its complexity and yet determined that something worthwhile come from their deliberations. Commenting on the work as it progressed, Johnson said: "This is not essentially a matter of compromise. It is rather a proposition wherein we take the good from the right wing, and the good from the left wing in its entirety, and combine this into a new and modern wing, which we hope will give us something to work by."

As the months passed, it became increasingly apparent that completing the document would take a long time. While some remained with the project for the entire three years, new people were occasionally added, and others withdrew because of a change in their jobs. In all, more than one hundred participated, some of whom were brought in on one or more meetings to discuss a particular subject. Women were conspicuously absent from the list of fifty-three who collaborated on the final document, but they did participate in the quarterly discussion groups, for women's issues in the workplace were frequently on the agenda.

The formidable task of recording what was said at the meetings fell to Father Cronin, and the time-consuming job of distributing new drafts and then dealing with the multitude of changes went to Robert J. Dixson, Johnson's associate and director of industrial relations at the Johnson & Johnson Chicopee company.

Johnson attended most of the meetings and frequently led the discussion. The two papal encyclicals were often points of reference, and Johnson told the story of how they first came to his attention. When he was chairman of the Smaller War Plants Corporation, a staff member had asked him to define the ethics of employment. He asked for time to think about it, and after much pencil-chewing and looking at a blank page he said he needed more time to study the subject. His research led him to Leo XIII's and Pius XI's encyclicals. Now, he said, he found himself leading a group that could, in effect, write an ecumenical version of the encyclicals that would apply to business in the mid-twentieth century.

Each time the group met, there were new ideas to be explored, evaluated, and debated. It became a test of endurance as well as intellect, and, perhaps most of all, a test of willingness to allow other viewpoints in the final document. Agreement on some points did not come easily, but gradually a consensus was forged. The final document was built around a set of principles and ethical values that, it was hoped, would bring about greater harmony between employer and employee. It had taken much longer than anticipated, but there was still a sense of urgency about making it public. Labor disputes were intensifying.

The group decided to call the final document "Human Relations in Modern Business: A Guide for Action Sponsored by American Business Leaders," and Prentice-Hall agreed to publish the fifty-two-page document as a book late in 1949. Meanwhile, Johnson, with consent of the group, wrote a major article about the document that appeared in the September 1949 issue of the *Harvard Business Review*. In it he gave the rationale for calling the group together and quoted liberally from the document itself.

The article generated widespread interest in the forthcoming book. Quoting from the document, Johnson wrote: "The world is looking to us for an example of what free men can achieve. We dare not fail. The destiny of generations to come is in our hands—we are making history. This is our challenge, and our opportunity." He also made it clear that it was a cooperative effort, and the names and affiliations of all who participated were listed. The *Harvard Business Review* commented: "The very fact that such a diverse group agreed upon a single document is, in itself, significant."

The document began with a Statement of Principles calling attention to the "complex relationship among the various levels of management and labor" and noting: "Men are social creatures, sensitive to considerations of pride, achievement, desire for esteem and affection, and similar non-economic drives. Likewise, men have a conscience and a sense of justice. They do not change their nature when they put on their business suits or working clothes."

These concepts, and the language, were alien to labor management discussions, and certainly to contract negotiations. The document continued along its philosophical course:

"The fundamentals of human nature may not be ignored in human relations. . . . There are [five] drives that profoundly influence conduct: man's sense of *dignity* . . . , the need for the *esteem of others* . . . , the basic *instinct for survival* . . . , the desire for *security* . . . , and *social instincts*, [the natural tendency] to associate with those who share their interests and to develop teamwork in pursuing common undertakings."

Moving from the human equation, it made the transition to religious and moral grounds: "Human relations . . . are subject to moral and religious laws that are reflected in the conscience of mankind and which have been confirmed by the experience of men in all ages. If we accept the brotherhood of man under God, important conclusions follow. Each man has an inner dignity, with basic rights and duties. Life has an over-all purpose. Men must judge their conduct, not merely in terms of personal gain or convenience, but also as right or wrong. Service to society, and to personal interest, become important. Teamwork and cooperation follow."

After giving a historical review of labor and management practices, and abuses, the document offered a perspective on the practical application of the new approaches it was advocating. It discussed basic needs of employees in the workplace environment, personnel policies, employee rights, labor unions and grievances, educational programs, and the need for better communications. Each was elevated to a level that encouraged greater awareness of human needs and a sensitivity to what was considered fair and moral. That was the theme that permeated the entire report, and broke new ground and set the stage for changing future discussions between labor and management.

Though the document made no reference to the encyclicals, and did not pretend to be an elaboration on them, the similarities were there. But there was no need to make that association, because *Human Relations in Modern Business* was a profound work in its own right. Nothing like it had ever been written for American business by such a diverse group. It was co-signed by six leading business leaders, in addition to Johnson. The other forty-six collaborators were also listed. The co-signers were all high-profile business leaders, and their names added weight to the document and helped to give it wider national recognition. Those who co-signed with Johnson were: John D. Biggers, President of Libbey-Owens-Ford Glass Company; Curtis E. Calder, Chairman of Electric Bond & Share Company; Erle Cocke, President of the Fulton National Bank of Atlanta; Frank M. Folsom, President of the Radio Corporation of America; Herman W. Steinkraus, President of Bridgeport Brass Company and President of the Chamber of Commerce of the United States; and Jack I. Straus, President of R. H. Macy & Company Inc., the New York department store, and a well-known civic leader in the city.

Prentice-Hall printed tens of thousands of the reports and sold them in bookstores and other outlets for $1.50. The committee sent thousands more to industry and labor, business associations, government officials both federal and state, religious leaders, educators, and the press all over the United States. A surge of positive reaction quickly followed publication. The *Harvard Business Review* called it "A Magna Carta for business." *Time* magazine described it as "The Capitalist Manifesto" (the *Communist Manifesto*, by Karl Marx, had been published a century earlier in Germany). The daily and weekly press, labor journals, and religious and education publications all joined in praise of the book. Writing in the *Rochester (N.Y.) Courier-Journal*, the director of the LeMoyne College School of Industrial Relations said: "It is the greatest statement of principles of industrial ethics to be issued under the names of leading businessmen of America. In contrast to the paternalistic 'pap' issued by clumsy propaganda machines of many industrial groups, it stands out as most nutritious food which will aid in bringing our economy to vigor and sanity."

Reports began filtering back from all over the nation that *Human Relations in Modern Business* was being used as intended—as a basis for discussion, a beginning point, a guide for giving the human factor greater visibility in discussions between labor and management than it had ever received before. One labor publication columnist wrote: "An increasing number of businessmen see labor not as an enemy, nor a rival for power, but as human beings. This is progress." The *Protestant World*, the national Protestant newspaper, offered another perspective: "The payment of these moral wages in human relations is a low enough price for a just industrial peace."

Johnson was greatly encouraged, but perhaps a little more cautious than others. "The first step will be hardest to take, since it means the achievement of new understanding," he said.

Father Cronin observed later that the most promising result of the project was that so many prominent corporate executives, all highly successful, "would subscribe to the view that God's law must prevail in the marketplace." The group was indeed able to accomplish what Johnson had been unable to do on his own. Hailing Johnson as a "man of action," Cronin wrote about the practical use the book would have in bringing about positive change.

Noting that although most of the business leaders who participated were not Catholics and yet had found inspiration in the social teachings of the Catholic Church, Cronin criticized Catholic business leaders for "knowing little about it, or not daring to speak out." He added: "Instead of the old idea that religion and business do not mix, we have very prominent industrialists declaring that only when they *do* mix can we have a healthy society." Another clergyman reviewer wrote: "For indeed a practical code for business has been devoutly hoped for and long forthcoming. The implementation of this tiny book in the policy of each individual firm is a task that should challenge every God-fearing business leader, every union policy maker, every school of industrial relations. . . . We must have not only a reform of morals today; we must have a reform of social conditions tomorrow. The codification of a set of business rules is a happy beginning. The practice of this code would be better still. But in order that this reform may be more stable, the structure itself of our capitalistic society must be more integrated."

Father Masse, reflecting on the project he had stayed with for the entire three years, wrote: "No one who participated thinks it is the last word on this very large subject. As it stands in its brief but pregnant 52 pages, it represents a compromise between those who wanted a short, succinct statement of unadorned moral principles, and those who advocated a full-scale book with everything spelled out. If it suffers from the defects of all such compromises, it is also capable of stimulating the interest of those who want to plunge more deeply into the subject, and of satisfying those who have little time and less inclination to read. The men themselves who participated in the project feel that the book will pay the largest dividends if it is used as a roundtable text by mixed groups of industrialists and clergymen."

The overall impact that *Human Relations in Modern Business* had on hastening change during the postwar period is difficult to gauge, because many other factors came into play at the same time. However, the overwhelming national response from various quarters—business, labor, religion, government, and the press—suggests that the principles the document espoused did gain a place on the American agenda in mid-century, for it was during this period that business and industry began to assume a role of greater responsibility. In the workplace the human relations factor became more important, and the rancor that had set in following the war did subside. It was also during this period that business and the community began developing a closer relationship.

The evolution of industrial America in the post-World War II era, from a focus on frenetic production to a pace that had to accommodate the needs of people rather than battlefields, produced no monumental heroes. But a small number of farsighted businessmen who had a sense of what was needed to move the nation forward had emerged. Robert Wood Johnson was one of those leaders, perhaps the most vocal one. Although it was not fully recognized at the time, in retrospect his concepts and philosophy coincided with changes that took place during the period he was advocating them.

Johnson's passionate belief that business organizations had a responsibility to their customers, employees, the community, and stockholders, in that order, began to be viewed as pragmatic rather than altruistic—which Johnson himself had maintained was the case since he first introduced the concept in 1935. Putting the customer first was sound business, not altruism, he said. But it was concern for the employees of the nation—and later the communities where employees worked and lived—that took center stage during a period of turbulence and uncertainty after World War II.

Johnson had been quick to grasp the significance of what was happening in this domestic conflict, and *Human Relations in Modern Business* brought a sense of hope and purpose to the deliberations. It was by all measurements a unique document, and a half-century later it still retains its ring of truth.

23

INNOVATOR AT WORK

THERE were recurring rumors in late September 1946 that President Harry S. Truman planned to appoint Johnson as the new Secretary of Commerce, to replace Henry A. Wallace, who had resigned at the President's request. Wallace had been Vice President during Franklin Roosevelt's third term, and Truman had replaced him on the ticket for Roosevelt's fourth term. Although Truman brought Wallace back as Secretary of Commerce, he was a strong-willed opponent of the "get tough" stand the administration had taken against Russia. The breach between the two men soon widened, and Wallace was out.

The *New York Herald-Tribune* gave credence to the rumor with a two-column front-page story quoting White House sources as saying that Johnson was the President's first choice for the Commerce post. Business had been clamoring for a businessman to head the department, and in Johnson the President had a highly visible businessman who had been accepted by both parties. Another candidate mentioned in the story was W. Averell Harriman, then Ambassador to England.

Reporters pressed Johnson for a response, and his reply was emphatic. He was not interested in returning to the bureaucratic wars in Washington, and while he would remain active and vital politically, he did not want to be Secretary of Commerce. Almost immediately Truman offered the position to Harriman, who accepted. Those who knew Johnson's proclivity for saying what was on his mind, and Truman's reputation for giving sharp responses, felt that the decorum at Cabinet meetings would have suffered badly had Johnson been given the appointment.

As the politics of the Cold War intensified late in 1946, there was increasing concern about the perils of atomic warfare, and rampant speculation about whether the United States, or any nation, could survive a concentrated attack with nuclear weapons. The horror of such a prospect numbed the mind, but military strategists began mapping plans that called for surviving an initial attack while still retaining the ability to strike back. Critical to this strategy would be protection of the nation's defense, and offense, industry. For some time now, Johnson had been pondering how industry might survive a nuclear attack. Late in 1946 he wrote a jolting article titled "Dig, Son, Dig," which touched off a storm of controversy that played out on front pages and radio programs all across the nation. One newspaper headline characterized the article as "a bombshell."

The article appeared the first week of January 1947 in *Army Ordnance*, the journal of the Army Ordnance Association. The goal of the association, comprising 50,000 executives and engineers of American industry, as well as officers of the armed services, was to enhance industrial preparedness for the nation's defense. With thirty-two local chapters spread all over the country, and well-attended national and sectional meetings, it was a powerful organization that carried weight throughout the military-defense establishment. Johnson was a frequent contributor to the journal.

Like many of Johnson's ideas, this one had a fuse ready to be lighted. In the article, Johnson called for industry and government to collaborate on a plan to protect industry from atomic attack and suggested underground plants as one possibility. The spark was provided by the catchy "Dig, Son, Dig" headline in the usually staid journal. When translated to newspaper headlines, Johnson's proposal for a defense plan quickly became a frantic plea to start digging. The *New York Times*, the *Herald-Tribune*, the *Washington Post*, and the *Baltimore Sun* ran the story on page one. Waves of editorial opinion followed, as the "Ban the Bomb" adherents, the doves, and the hawks entered the fray. Ministers felt compelled to speak out, one calling Johnson's suggestion "morally repugnant."

It was a moot point. From any angle, the article was not about to calm fears. "The atomic bomb is a reality," he wrote. "It may soon be possible to destroy the power of an industrialized nation in a few days, or even a few hours. If we have a third world war, that is what the enemy will attempt to do to us — destroy us in the first days of war. In the past two wars, our production lines were the fountainheads of victory. In a third war, an enemy could have no choice but to attempt to choke off the flow of these fountainheads at once. If the enemy should have its way, the Arsenal of Democracy would become the prime theater of war."

Johnson went on to recommend that this was a decision that neither the military nor the government should make independently. "This job calls for civilian leadership, not Civil Service — God forbid!" he wrote. "We in business are ready to develop a defense. . . . We are determined that this time the defense will not be fouled up by official red tape."

Then religious leaders expressed opposition to underground plants, saying that this approach would weaken their efforts to emphasize moral barriers to atomic warfare. Actually, the Army-Navy Munitions Board had already appointed an Underground Site Committee and authorized it to survey potential locations. Johnson's article mentioned the possibility of building plants in caves and caverns, and Richard R. Deupree, Chairman of the Munitions Board and CEO of Procter & Gamble, told the *New York Times* that Johnson's article prompted a flood of calls from cave and cavern owners who thought they had found a new market for their properties. (The *Times* speculated that stalactites and stalagmites would be a problem.)

The debate touched off by Johnson soon shifted to the need for underground shelters for civilians. In a letter to a physician friend, Johnson recalled that in wartime Washington "a White House deep shelter was built behind a board fence as one of the early steps of the war [but] the person of our President is no more [important] than yours or your patient's or mine."

Later, when he reread his article after publication, Johnson was dismayed to find that several of his more pointed jabs at the military had been deleted. One was: "The Army and the Navy will let the country down in this situation. Military officers do not have the mental stamina to meet this kind of problem." When he inquired about the editing, he was told that the "boys in the print" shop had to cut it to fit the space, to which Johnson replied: "By a rather strange process they eliminated the hottest lines in the story, aimed directly at the group with stars on the shoulders instead of in their eyes. . . . The next time ask the boys to delete some of the soothing phrases, and remind them that I wasn't born yesterday."

The threat of nuclear war would continue to be a constant concern that would hover over the nation for many years. Johnson's article stirred the debate about how to deal with the threat, and the press brought to light several previously undisclosed attempts to explore moving defenses underground — not just manufacturing, but military, government, and staff personnel as well. Several weeks after publication of his article, Johnson wrote to both Truman and Dwight D. Eisenhower, then Chief of Staff in the War Department. The letters were prompted by a new British report on the devastation of atomic bombing, and his question to both men was: "What can we do in the United States to strengthen our defense against this type of weapon?"

Truman chose to inject politics into his reply: "I wish everyone in the United States could have seen not only Hiroshima and Nagasaki but Berlin, London and a dozen other places that I can name. I think then we would never go isolationist again. Some of the Republicans seem headed in that direction and we must stop it if we can."

General Eisenhower's reply to Johnson, addressing him as "Mr. Johnson," not "General," noted that a jointly sponsored analysis by the British and Americans of bombing damage in Europe and Japan was expected to produce guidelines for building better defenses for the Allies. "I truly appreciate your patriotic interest in this subject," he added.

People often mentioned Johnson's deep sense of patriotism. He wrote and spoke about preserving freedom in America, and about allegiance to flag and country, with passion and visible emotion that could bring tears to his eyes. "The banner of freedom is as fresh and new today as it was when the rugged pioneers came to America," he wrote. "The crusading challenge of Valley Forge has been lost in the shuffle of foreign ideologies, but the truth is as real as it was to the soldiers under Washington. Our parents gave us the heritage of independence. Are we throwing it away? Freedom is still the brightest, shiniest, newest, most radical thought in the world."

Claiming that business held the key to tarnishing the appeal of communism, Johnson said: "The new purpose of business is to do everything so well that socialism and communism will cease to exist. It is no longer enough to produce a better product at a lower price. Business is our way of life and must accept the responsibility for all of the economic effects of our capitalistic system. . . . The handwriting is clear. American institutions, whatever their nature, exist through public sufferance. The new purpose of business is to serve the public, both with products and a code of ethics. We must perform all of the services that the public demands. If we do not, the voters will choose another system. . . . Once the public has made up its mind that our present system is inadequate, it will be too late to either repair it or defend it. . . . The new purpose of business is not only to do these things but to explain them to the people."

The best way to sell free enterprise, he contended, was to make it more appealing than any of the alternatives. He was greatly distressed in 1946 when he read a *Business Week* account of a speech by Howard Chase, then Public Relations Director of the General

Foods Corporation, before the Association of National Advertisers annual meeting in Atlantic City. Chase reported on the results of a recent poll showing that "the public today retains strong doubts regarding business leadership." Some of the causes of these doubts, Chase said, had to do with profits and prices. Various speakers at the conference recommended an advertising campaign to change the public's attitude.

Johnson doubted that advertising was the answer. He estimated that 25 million of the 60 million wage earners in the nation were employed in industry and commerce. "This is our sales force," he wrote Chase, "and we must first convince them that business is worthy of their support. When we have won their support then we can ask them to help us sell American business to the citizens of the United States. I am confident that wage earners are not properly informed, but when they are these men and women will do the job."

Around this time, Johnson had another new idea, one that would turn his 15,000 employees in thirty-five plants and offices all over the world into "salesmen for the company," as he put it. He believed that the rapid growth of the company had become its enemy, because its size made good communications difficult. Earlier, a sound system for announcements, and to relieve boredom in the workplace, had been installed in each of the decentralized plant and office locations, so Johnson decided he would do a series of in-plant broadcasts called "Robert Johnson Talks It Over." He described it as "an experiment in communications," and, as with most of his projects, it had to be done in a certain way.

He started out by drafting remarks for seven broadcasts that would explain the company's various operations, but the more he thought about it, the more he wanted to say, and the more broadcasts he added. Before he was finished there were forty-four broadcasts in all, and he insisted on participating in the writing of each one. When it came to communicating with his own employees, Johnson was masterful, but things had changed since the days when he could stand up and address most of his employees. This would be different, and everything had to be just right.

At the suggestion of Evie, he retained a tutor to help him develop a more chatty style — and not just any tutor, but Evie's friend, Aristede D'Angeli, who worked with him for many hours. Next, Johnson turned his attention to the recording sessions, which were done in a studio, on both tape and records, since not all plant and office locations had the same playback equipment. At one point Johnson insisted on getting the advice of a Hollywood recording studio that a friend had recommended. Finally, after many months of preparation, the broadcasts were ready to be aired.

In his opening remarks, Johnson said: "Years have passed since I knew everyone in our organization. There once was a time, however, when I did know — at least, I recognized — every man and woman who worked with Johnson & Johnson. Those men and women knew me, too, and we'd get together once in a while to talk about the company, its progress, and its problems. In those talks I learned how others felt, and they learned what was on my mind. Anyone might ask questions, and could get answers. We have grown too large for such discussions, . . . yet it is more important than ever that people know and understand what is going on in their company."

Once a week, one of the talks, lasting seven to ten minutes, was broadcast, but the timing was up to the local plant manager. It was always presented on company time, though, and frequently tied to small meetings, where employees and their managers could discuss issues of particular interest. To make the talks more personal, Johnson often referred to longtime employees by name, and to incidents from the past.

In the second talk, Johnson gave an overview of how the company was organized, beginning with the role of the Board of Directors (all members of management) and the shareholders, which then numbered 1,800. Then he went on to discuss the functions of the various departments, including research, manufacturing, product development, marketing, and advertising. He also explained how the decentralized family of companies, both domestic and overseas, fit into the overall corporate picture.

Speaking on the importance of keeping the workplace clean, Johnson related this story about a foreman who wasn't cooperating: "I ordered three white uniforms for every person in the department and told the foreman that every time a uniform became soiled from oily machinery or other messy housekeeping, the employee had to change to a fresh uniform." After a week of seeing employees constantly leave the work area to change their uniforms, the foreman came to him and told him that he had "discovered that the problem was poor housekeeping." "After that we had no more problems," Johnson said.

The talks enabled him to convey his business philosophy to employees in a personal way, and he wove this into the entire series. When he spoke about customers, he said: "If we fail they will fire us." And about the importance of being a good neighbor, he reminded them: "If we aren't a good neighbor, then find out what we are doing wrong and we'll change it."

Employees had a positive reaction to the series, and, as Johnson had hoped, saw the talks as a personal message from Johnson to each of them. He then decided to turn the broadcast into a 174-page paperback, *Robert Johnson Talks It Over*, which was published by the company and widely distributed. In 1949 the Freedoms Foundation awarded the book its Certificate of Merit. Johnson's "experiment in communications" was a success.

The broadcast series and the book led to several thousand meetings between employees and management at the company's thirty-five locations, and at the ensuing discussions many problems were resolved. Encouraged by this, Johnson decided to try adapting the series to a public-service radio series—first regional then national—that he would call "Business Is People."

But first he asked his senior management for a reaction to doing the series on commercial radio. "I want criticisms no matter how weak or how severe," he wrote. "After that I will decide whether the job [his synonym for the project] should be done this way, some other way, or abandoned." He received little encouragement, which was the best way to dampen his enthusiasm for an idea. Nonetheless, he went ahead and had a sample script written, with some help from him. It was done in radio-dramatization format, with several actors, and Johnson himself role-playing workplace situations that were to have both a lesson and a moral. The first rehearsal was a disaster, and Johnson was quick to recognize that. Then and there he abandoned the whole idea.

For someone who was constantly churning out new ideas, he had many more successes than failures. And then there were the good ideas that never got off the ground because they proved to be impractical. One such project was his idea for turning factories into places of learning, a concept he called "College While You Work." As always, he approached a new project with boundless enthusiasm and was miffed when others did not respond in a like manner. His plan was to offer college courses to production and office workers at the worksite, and mostly on company time.

"Workers cannot live happily or well in a world they do not understand," he wrote in his outline for the project, which he hoped would result in "a student body of 30 million." Using adult-education and plant-training courses as models, Johnson wanted to expand to include college-level courses in three areas: job-related courses like accounting and engineering; courses dealing with problems related to the family, labor relations, and international affairs; and cultural courses, which he described as ranging from "English to Egyptology." Some would extend beyond the work day into the evenings, but the "campus" would still be the company facility.

As someone who had not attended college, Johnson had a particular concern for others who hadn't, and here he thought he had a solution to a better education. "Why not do it at the place of work," he said, "and why not as a business expense? True, such a plan would call for additional overhead, but if it pays off in terms of lower costs then the scheme would not be an expense but a profit."

He added: "Were every business and every employer to undertake his own educational program in collaboration with their employees, and carried out in cooperation with unions, we would carry education throughout our working years. To think and think straight requires an ever-lasting flow of new facts. Unless we are prepared to expose our job holders to these new factors, how can we hope that they will understand the complexities of our age?"

It was a compelling argument, especially for employees. Least enthusiastic were the manufacturing people, who believed "College While You Work" would play havoc with their production schedules. For months Johnson tried to sell the idea to his fellow industrialists, who listened to his plan with polite indifference. He had paid several educators to work out a sample curriculum—and with that as a basis for an article, he tried to interest the *Saturday Evening Post*. They listened, but weren't buying. At his own company he could generate no enthusiasm whatsoever. No one thought it would work. Finally, the idea began to fade away. Johnson remained its only champion.

But for every Johnson idea that was abandoned, many more flourished. One that proved very successful was "A Day in Modern Industry," targeted at high school students about to graduate. In planning the project, Johnson remarked: "If industries would let the nation's youth be a part of industry for one day, millions of our citizens of tomorrow would have a new concept of the vital role that management plays in making possible our high standard of living." Months were spent planning the program and making a film to be used in schools and to encourage other companies to invite high school seniors to spend a day in industry, where they could "manage the company" for a day by assuming duties of key positions.

Not one to coddle young people, or anyone else, Johnson had some very direct words for the first of many high school groups that came to the company as part of the program. "American youth lacks the initiative of our pioneers," he told them, "and adults are to blame because you prefer personal security to pioneering. This is our attempt to show young men and women about to be on their own the roles that imagination and initiative have played in building American industry. Youth must be shown their responsibilities and sold on the American way of life. Our important duty of the day is to give you the facts and the truth."

That first day, three hundred students participated in the program, and a seventeen-year-old from St. Peter's High School sat at Johnson's desk and became "chairman of the board." The news media turned out in force, with fifteen national publications, wire services, and radio networks represented. In later years, with the help of continued press interest and promotion by Johnson's personnel department, "A Day in Modern Industry" was widely replicated by other companies.

.

Though strong-willed and highly opinionated, Johnson nonetheless tolerated discussion and debate on many business matters. He had an excellent management group, and he always claimed that he was wise enough to listen to them. In one area of the business, however, he was adamant, and that was in adhering strictly to the principles laid down in the Johnson & Johnson Credo. The Credo was law, and as long as he was running the company it would be followed to the letter. Anyone who didn't comply could look for another job. He made that point unmistakably clear.

Over time the Credo was modified slightly to reflect changing trends, but the basic philosophy never changed. Johnson used the 1948 Annual Report to Stockholders to introduce the Credo, which listed a new responsibility, "to the communities in which we work and live."

Sleepy small towns throughout America were being awakened by an influx of factories being built on the outlying roads, bringing with them new jobs, a revival of business for Main Street merchants, better schools, and an overall redefining of the sense of community. Johnson's new plants — he came to detest the term "factory" — were constructed in a dozen states in the postwar years, mostly in towns and smaller cities, and each had a different look. He insisted that their architectural design and detailed landscaping permit them to blend into the local setting, rather than be a jolting intrusion. Most were built on expansive tracts of land — often hundreds of acres.

Once the plants were up and running, Johnson urged his employees to become part of the community and to have the company assume a role of responsibility — which meant both financial support and service to the community. In explaining the philosophy of integrating companies into the community, Johnson said: "We build not only structures in which men and women will work, but also the patterns of society in which they will work. We are building not only frameworks of stone and steel, but frameworks of ideas and ideals."

The Credo passage that Johnson wrote to meet the new needs of the community read as follows:

> We must be a good citizen — support good works and charity.
> And bear our fair share of taxes.
> We must maintain in good order the property we are privileged to use.
> We must participate in promotion of civic improvement, health, education and good government
> And acquaint the community with our activities.

In introducing this new responsibility, Johnson reminded shareholders that the company had been following the Credo philosophy for ten years and would continue to do so. No one could argue with that, in light of the results he reported. In those ten years, sales rose from $30 million to $165 million, and earnings went from $2 million to $11 million.

Though an idealist in many respects, Johnson was also a pragmatic, hardheaded businessman, and he applied this sense of reality to the Credo. "This Credo is not perfect," he wrote. "We have changed it and expect to change it again. We also know that it is better than we are; being humanly frail we sometimes find it difficult to live up to its declarations. But we believe that it is both a set of goals and a guide which helps us to do better than we would without it."

Adding the community as a new obligation under the Credo coincided with the construction of numerous new plants by Johnson & Johnson following World War II. Johnson explained his rationale for this responsibility:

> Our approach to this field is not a matter of individual impulse. It is, rather, one aspect of the philosophy that underlies our whole business. Such success as we have enjoyed in community relations has been won by the people with whom I work, and for whom I speak. Let me summarize four premises that underlie our community relations.
>
> First, we believe that business has a real and continuing obligation to every community in which it operates. A few critics still deny this, insisting that business management should limit itself to the job of making money with which to pay dividends and wages while improving plant, equipment, and products. Some stockholders share this attitude, as we see when they take legal action to keep company funds from being used for civic betterment. But these holdovers from the past are decreasing in both numbers and influence. The great body—and the best brains—of American business are convinced that companies share the obligations as well as the rights of citizenship. The question is not whether we shall accept these obligations. It is how we shall meet them wisely and well.
>
> Second, we hold that the obligations which rest on business differ in no essential way from those of the private citizen. A corporation can do some things private citizens can't do; it can call upon experience which no one citizen has had. But both company and individual share the obligation to make their community a better place in which to live—better physically, culturally, morally, and politically.

Third, we find that good community relations are an outgrowth of realistic organization within the company. For us, this means decentralization, which both meets our corporate needs and allows each plant to become part of its community.

Fourth, although good community relationships demand company understanding and planning, they must be carried out by people who act according to their own opinions and beliefs. This is true in a political campaign or in building a hospital; in developing a water system or in adding a music room to the local library. We therefore expect our people to act as people and we must give them elbow room to do so. Corporate citizenship does not mean that any citizen should become a mere mouthpiece for his corporation.

Johnson also set the example for community involvement, and he had as his allies Elmer Boyd and his son, Hugh, the family publishers of the local daily, the *New Brunswick Home News*. All three men had a deep commitment to the sometimes beleaguered city of New Brunswick and came up with many improvement projects. Some of their ideas became realities, others took years to materialize, and some remained only dreams. One plan was for extensive, new low-cost housing, and another was for a more modern railroad station with a landscaped mall and more parking. Both projects became reality, but much later. These three men generated many ideas for the betterment of the city. The Boyds provided enthusiastic editorial support and could turn to Johnson for financial help or to lead a fundraising drive. They made a good team.

Along with his deep interest in the community, Johnson never forgot old friends who had helped him when he was young, untrained, and trying to learn the business. Nearly forty years earlier, when Johnson first came to the company after his father died, James McGarry, a superintendent in the mill, took him under his wing and patiently taught him the basics of manufacturing. The two became friends, and Johnson never forgot the kindness. McGarry was now dead, but his two daughters were nuns. Sister Mary was with the Society of Our Lady of the Cenacle, a semi-cloistered order that conducted religious retreats for laypeople, and Anne Marie was a Sister of Charity.

Overlooking the Raritan from a hilltop in Highland Park was the lovely Bellevue Farm, which had been the Johnson family summer residence and later Robert's home when he married Elizabeth Ross. The spacious, twenty-room farmhouse with wide, inviting porches and spacious grounds had a look of quiet solitude. Johnson thought it would be ideal for religious retreats, so in 1949 he decided to give the house and thirty acres to the Cenacle order. The only stipulation was that each year on March 6, the day McGarry died, a Mass be celebrated there in his memory.

Soon after, Sister Mary was transferred to Bellevue Farm and it became The Cenacle retreat house, which it still is fifty years later. "We made very few changes," Sister Mary recalled, "one being the outdoor pool, which we had to fill in with dirt. Nuns weren't supposed to have pools. The General would stop by regularly, and anything we needed all we had to do was ask. One hot day he said: 'Where are the fans?' We didn't have any, but a few days later we did. He replaced the carpeting and had the outside painted. We made larger sleeping rooms into smaller ones, more in keeping with our living style. He thought they were too small. He could not do enough for us."

Some years earlier Johnson had met Brigadier General Henry Dries of the Salvation Army, then assigned to New Brunswick. A slightly built, gentle man, Dries could become a relentless, persistent fundraiser for any project that benefited the Salvation Army. Johnson was a perfect target for that tenacity.

"I first sought his help to purchase the Hebrew Ladies' Aid Society building," Dries recalled. "We then housed transients there when they traveled between New York and Philadelphia. They were homeless, but we didn't call them that then. They were 'transients,' and often alcoholics. Mr. Johnson didn't like the term 'alcoholic,' and he referred to them as 'men with drinking problems.' Once he helped us buy the building—we were caring for sixteen transients a night — and he would ask me 'What are your needs?' I would tell him and the next day the beds, blankets, food, anything we needed, would arrive. He would say to me, 'I like your slogan — A man is down but never out.' Then when we opened Star Lake Camp for children, I told him what we needed and he supplied it."

"Some years later," Dries continued, "he did a wonderful thing for me and my wife, Viola, who was also in the Salvation Army. We hadn't had a furlough in all of those years, so General Johnson decided to send us on a vacation to the Miramar Hotel in Miami. He called in one of his executives who vacationed near the hotel and said: 'I want you to adopt Henry and his wife. Being in the Salvation Army, they don't know how to spend money on themselves, so I want you to teach them how.' We went on his yacht. It was wonderful, and everywhere we went this man introduced us as 'my children, Johnson and Johnson.'"

While some of Johnson's philanthropy received public recognition, most of it did not. His generosity to individuals was always carefully concealed. When a local reporter's wife was stricken with cancer, Johnson arranged and paid for an operaton at a major medical center in New York, and then sent the woman to Asbury Park to convalesce. When a New Jersey senator's young daughter needed an iron lung and other expensive equipment to survive her illness, he provided it. If he heard on the radio about a child in need of medical care, he often sent a check to the station to be forwarded to the family. His gifts frequently came with a personal touch. When a clergy friend was sent to a cold climate, he made out a shopping list of warm clothes to be purchased and sent to him, being specific about color, size, and quality. Details were important to him.

•

Community concerns were important, but the national and international problems continued to mount. The economy was struggling to regain its strength after the war, hampered by America's commitment of foreign aid to help rebuild war-torn nations. The darkening cloud of the threat of communism hovered over the nation, adding to the unrest. A small group of business leaders, Johnson among them, were willing to step into the public arena to debate solutions, but the vast majority remained on the sidelines, and most were silent.

Writing in the *New York Times Magazine* on October 5, 1947, Chester Bowles, whose latest high-level Washington assignment was as Economic Stabilization Director, identified the threat to free enterprise in an article titled "Challenge to the Business Man": "Karl Marx was convinced that capitalism was doomed to smash itself to bits in a period of recurring inflations and depressions. The leaders of the Soviet Government today are Marxists. Their policies since 1945 have been predicated on the assumption that Marx was right and that our American capitalistic system would eventually come apart at the seams. At the rate we are moving, it is wholly possible that within the next ten years Karl Marx' judgment will have been proved correct."

Bowles claimed that American business had been myopic. When V-J Day arrived, he wrote, those who knew economic history were aware that a dangerous inflationary period lay ahead, yet the monopolists clamored for lifting controls and returning the nation to the workings of a free market. This position, he pointed out, had the strong backing of the National Association of Manufacturers. As it turned out, Bowles said, the majority of business and the Association were wrong. Inflation continued to soar, endangering the entire economic system.

Some enlightened business leaders disagreed vigorously with the National Association of Manufacturers and its "fellow-travelers," Bowles wrote, and he named Johnson, Nelson Rockefeller, and Henry Ford as being among them. "But so far," Bowles said, "the majority of our businessmen seem reluctant to support these leaders." Unless there was an awakening by business and labor in general, and action taken to stabilize the economy, the Karl Marx threat might materialize, Bowles contended. "The future of our

[373]

present economic system rests largely in the hands of those who own and manage American industry."

Another national figure who was outspoken on major issues was Joseph P. Kennedy of Boston, patriarch of the Kennedy family. He and Johnson had been longtime friends, though they were not always in sync politically. Long before his sons John, Robert, and Edward entered politics, Joseph Kennedy was influencing the direction of national policy. In an article in the *New York Journal-American*, he took a stand against foreign aid, claiming that the top priority should be stimulating the domestic economy. It was a position that Johnson did not agree with, and he told Kennedy so.

In his reply, Kennedy praised Johnson for persistently speaking out on national issues: "Sometimes when I get a little frustrated at the results that I feel one can get crying in the wilderness, I remember fellows like Herbert Hoover and yourself who are always in there punching for the best interests of the country, and it gives us all a little more zip to continue." But on his position on foreign aid, Kennedy gave no ground: "Everybody hates us now and giving money isn't going to make them love us any more."

Being conciliatory on some national issues was far easier for Johnson than being soft on communism, where he drew the line. He erupted in opposition to any hint of sympathy for communist causes, and the patriot in him prompted him to lash out at any individual or group. No one was exempt, and late in 1948 his target became the clergy. An article in the *New York Times* had triggered his concern, and he followed with a letter to the Rev. Cameron Hall, a leader of the Federal Council of Churches in America. Johnson wrote:

> Dear Reverend Hall:
> I was Christened and confirmed an Episcopalian in Old Christ Church, New Brunswick, New Jersey. In later years a growing suspicion has developed in my mind to the effect that the church is responsible in part for the development of the ideas of totalitarian socialism and even communism.

[374]

A few weeks ago I met with 150 ministers and was shocked by some of their questions. Last week I met with another group of 35 or 40 members of the clergy and had the same experience. In the press recently I noticed that the Red Dean of England was visiting this continent, and from the press I am informed that the Bishop of York is a declared socialist. In *The New York Times* this morning I found the attached article with the headline "RED INFILTRATION FOUND IN RELIGION."

The Federal Council of Churches must be immediately aware of this problem. I ask you, how extensive is Red infiltration in religion? What does the Council of Churches offer as a solution? I would also be interested in your opinion as to what part the church played in England toward the development and sponsorship of the present Socialist government. These are issues that cannot be side-stepped. I want to be friendly and I am determined to cooperate because I feel that Christian ethics offer the only solution to our present-day problems, but I think in honesty I should tell you that for several years I have been informed that the Federal Council of Churches has a pink cloud floating over it.

For the record, it is best that you know that I am a political liberal and independent, but I am an enemy of socialism and communism, not only because one is totally atheistic and the other leads toward atheism but because I do not believe that the aims of social justice can be attained through either of these ideologies.

Sincerely,
Robert Wood Johnson

The *Times* article Johnson referred to was based on a report out of Washington in which the House Committee on Un-American Activities claimed that the Communist Party of the United States had made inroads into church organizations. The charges were contained in a pamphlet directed to the public and part of a series dealing with what the committee called "the Communist conspiracy." It read, in part: "The Communist Party of the United States assigns members to join churches and church organizations in order to take control where possible, and in any case to influence thought and action toward Communist ends. It forms 'front organizations' designed to attract 'fellow travelers' with religious interests."

The Federal Council of Churches was a formidable Protestant organization, representing twenty-five national denominations working together "on matters of common interest and concern." While its primary concern was spiritual, it also had on its agenda "working progressively for constructive measures of human welfare." The reply to Johnson's letter came three weeks later from the Rev. Samuel McCrea Cavert, General Secretary of the Council, who wrote: "If you have the impression that there is a 'pink cloud' over the Federal Council I believe that this is due to the propaganda which has been carried on by a little group of extreme sectarians of the most narrow point of view—the point of view which insists that churches have nothing to do with the daily working life of the world."

Cavert complimented Johnson on the philosophy put forth in his book *Or Forfeit Freedom* and said he was in "warm accord with it on most points." He also informed him that the Council was forming a new department called "The Church and Economic Life," which would bring together industrial management, labor, and agriculture to explore problems "from the standpoint of the fundamental Christian principles concerning human relations" in the workplace—precisely what Johnson had been advocating for years. Cavert added that the Rockefeller Foundation would be giving a $100,000 grant to the Council's new Church and Economic Life group, "for studies in the ethical aspects of corporate economic practice" and told Johnson: "Basing my judgment upon my reading of your book, I have no hesitation in saying that I believe this program of the Federal Council's to be one which moves in the general direction which you yourself have in mind. It is certainly poles away from any doctrinaire Communism or Socialism and is based solidly upon Christian ethical teachings." In closing, Cavert said that he and Hall wanted to meet with Johnson in New Brunswick "for the purpose of interpreting the spirit of our work and the direction in which we are moving." (The meeting was delayed because Johnson had an emergency appendectomy in late December and then went to Florida to recuperate.)

For Johnson, who felt he had spoken more often than he was heard, this news that a major organization would be pursuing ways to bring Christian values to address problems in the workplace was heartening. To him it meant that he was being heard, that his message was getting across. A Protestant though not a churchgoer, he was also sensitive to undercurrents of criticism about his close working relationship with Catholics, particularly the Jesuits. "It so happens," he said, "that a large part of my work has been in collaboration with Catholic officials. This is because the Catholic Church is giving more attention to the all-important question of management-worker relations than any other organized sector of society."

Concerned that this might be misinterpreted, however, he instructed his associate Robert Dixson: "Our work must take on a nonsectarian atmosphere at the earliest possible date." Dixson, himself a devout Catholic and the principal intermediary with the Jesuits, made certain that the "Human Relations in Modern Business" project had a solid ecumenical base. This satisfied Johnson, though he continued to dialogue with Catholic priests more frequently than Protestant or Jewish clergy.

Actually, Johnson had more Protestant support than he realized, though much of it came from individual clergy. One minister likened him to "St. John the Baptist, a voice crying in the wilderness but preparing the way for greater times." This amused Johnson.

24

PUTTING PEOPLE
FIRST

B Y the late 1940s Johnson had become one of the nation's
most articulate and forward-thinking business leaders.
His reputation was constantly being reinforced by a
steady string of feature stories about him in national magazines
and newspapers. He drew from a wellspring of new ideas, and his
interviews were sprinkled with the kind of colorful quotes that delighted journalists.

He had a knack for putting together just the right mix of words
to create a punchy, often shocking, and sometimes even amusing
phrase to enliven a story. "Every time I hear the term 'common
labor,' it hits me in the belly." Or, on decentralization: "Put a man
in charge, give him elbow room, and go fishing." Or, on where to
locate a factory: "Place the plant where it best belongs, and not in a
place just because the old man who founded the business was born
there."

This Week magazine, the nationally syndicated newspaper sup-
plement, referred to him in a headline as "America's Most Unorthodox Big Businessman" in the January 4, 1948 edition of the
Sunday *New York Herald-Tribune*. Journalist Jack H. Pollack was
quickly caught in the Johnson web: "A slender, dapper boyish 54,
Johnson is a complex personality. Though he laughs easily, relaxes
with his feet on the desk and barks orders like a typical tycoon, he

is essentially serious, sensitive and introverted. Author of the controversial book *Or Forfeit Freedom*, he is a constant headache to more conservative fellow industrialists."

Johnson always managed to work into the interview some of his favorite solutions. That day he addressed the welfare problem: "The eleven million people earning less than a subsistence living are a liability to society, which must meet the deficit to feed them and their families through charity and subsidies. Why not avoid this waste and pay the bill at its source with a living wage?"

Labor leaders applauded Johnson's social-mindedness, though they were wary of his "excessive paternalism." The president of the Textile Workers Union of America was quoted by Pollack as saying: "The cooperative spirit [of management] shows what can be done when an enlightened management is responsive to a program of responsible unionism." To that Johnson added: "If we don't get private enterprise going, we'll have some other system forced on us — and not by revolutionaries from Europe either. We can't treat labor nowadays like a mere commodity to be bought, sold, and scrapped like so much machinery." Johnson's critics, Pollack added, "argue that he makes grandstand plays to apple-polish the labor crowd." If so, no one did it better.

The writer exuded abundant praise over the design of Johnson's factories: "Every day, on much-traveled U.S. Route 1 between New York and Philadelphia, motorists blink their billboard weary eyes in disbelief. For rising out of these grimy smokestack surroundings is a white-marbled, green landscaped building which looks like a Hollywood version of the Twenty-First Century. No mirage. It is Robert Johnson's 'Factory of the Future.' . . . The employees have their own showers, modern cafeterias, lounges, where they play bridge and ping-pong—and a plant broadcasting system for dances and educational programs."

When Pollack asked him why the company had never hired a public relations professional, Johnson replied: "If there are any public relations problems I want them to reach my desk. I won't risk having my thirty years of work gummed up by an intermediary." Actually, Johnson had several senior executives who were skilled in government and community relations, and they helped him immeasurably though their titles were only "Assistant to the President." It would be another decade before Johnson would agree to form the company's first public relations department, and then a journalist would be hired to help get that accomplished.

Despite his sometimes cavalier approach to public relations, Johnson was a master at it, and in 1949 the Public Relations Society of America honored him as the nation's outstanding industrialist for his "application of sound public relations philosophy, in civic leadership and in service in the public interest. . . ." When Howard Chase of General Foods Corporation, who headed the awards committee, informed Johnson of the award, he urged him to be "challenging in his acceptance speech" at the Society's annual dinner at the Waldorf-Astoria Hotel in New York.

Johnson did not disappoint them. Addressing the four hundred guests at the dinner, Johnson said: "The issue of the day is Socialism versus a free society. Where did the notion grow that government can do for us what we will not do for ourselves?" And then, with Secretary of Commerce Charles Sawyer awaiting his turn to deliver the principal address, Johnson added: "Government—our government and all other governments—are inherently incompetent." He had been asked to give a challenging talk, and he obliged, perhaps too well.

Though Johnson's philosophy of decentralizing a company into smaller units for more efficient management and higher employee morale was now several decades old, the practice was not widely accepted by American business. Bigness and central power in an organization still appealed to many companies. Not until years later did the movement toward decentralization gain wider acceptance and momentum. A *Reader's Digest* article in 1949 detailed how Johnson's approach to decentralization worked in one of his textile mills in Cornelia, Georgia, where the business and the community were blended into one. "I've kept Robert Johnson out of this [story] because he keeps himself out," the author wrote, "but he is the moving spirit behind the whole idea of decentralization."

"The experience of Johnson & Johnson indicates," the article continued, "that the problem of labor unrest can be solved within the framework of modern technology. That the solution does not have to be imposed by government. That the solution can be found by management and labor working together. And that the key to it is that the worker takes satisfaction in his job and in his way of life. . . . The mill in Georgia is one man's contribution toward the solution of one of the most deep-seated of all labor problems — an attempt to make the factory worker feel that he counts and that management knows he counts."

In *Or Forfeit Freedom*, Johnson had expounded on how and why the policy works: "Whoever made the observation that a factory should be as long as a man's shadow understood the conditions making for industrial efficiency. A factory which one man can fully comprehend is just about the right size. It is adequately simple and understandable. It is managed by one executive and a small staff who can and usually do know their business. Facts are available; action is fast; decisions are made on the spot. There seldom are conferences, meetings, and confusion for overlapping authority. And, because the workers in the plant know each other and are known to management, results can be checked easily. Perhaps the most important factor of all is the absence of excuses. In the small plants there can be no passing the buck, because there is no place to pass it. There are no overlapping departments, no joint responsibilities, and no attempt to fit policies into a general pattern conceived by a group of well-meaning executives who sit in remote offices and have no direct contact with the processes of production."

Johnson practiced what he preached. Some years later, when Johnson announced he would be visiting the company's operations in Brazil, the general manager there told what happened: "In preparation for his visit I went to the files to check the correspondence from him, and I found just twelve letters and memos from him over a span of seven years, and several of those were Christmas greetings."

The business press referred to him as "the chief apostle of decentralization" and often quoted his particularly memorable line: "Delete, delegate, and decentralize, and, if necessary, delouse [the central staff]." Some argued that decentralization took many forms. It could be physical plant and production, or it could be the decentralization of management methods and controls. Johnson recognized that too, and explained it from his viewpoint:

> At its simplest, decentralization is the scheme of distributing plants in various places to take advantage of regional markets and supplies of raw materials, at the same time escaping problems presented by huge operations in crowded urban centers.
>
> This is *physical* decentralization, but it is only part of the story. *Full* decentralization involves a change in organization and in management. While plants are being distributed, top management must delegate authority to run them without a constant stream of home-office directives. For us, the entire organization may be compared to a large shipping company, with vessels of various types and sizes that carry different cargoes in different parts of the world. Management knows where each vessel is going, how long it should take to get there, and the probable profit from its voyage. But every vessel is a self-contained unit, with its own crew, its own officers, its own captain. He is in charge of operations. When problems arise, he and his officers solve them without instructions from a home office on the other side of the globe. This sort of decentralization is a thoroughly practical matter. Like many other companies, we adopted it in order to improve our operations, our products, and our profits. But every one of its practical advantages helps to build a foundation for our work as good citizens. Decentralization also increases effectiveness by cutting problems down to manageable size and allowing men who are on the ground to do what must be done to solve them.
>
> Finally—and most important—decentralization builds good rela-

tionships between management and workers. The top boss and his executives are no longer mere names and pictures in the company magazine.

Sometimes in his sermonizing style, but more often directly and forthrightly, Johnson addressed business organizations that had been anxious to hear him but were not always happy with what they heard. *Time* magazine commented after one appearance before the American Management Association: "[Johnson] tells businessmen what they don't like to hear . . . and once more made them squirm."

In October 1949 the national magazine *Coronet*, a *Reader's Digest* look-alike, ran a feature on Johnson that said he had waged a one-man campaign to bring a "new look" to factory design and a new philosophy to business management in America. Johnson confessed to the interviewer that he sometimes had trouble selling his new ideas to his own management, who sometimes were embarrassed by his constant crusading. When that happens, he said, "you simply have to try to educate the executives as well as the workers."

In a rare moment, exhibiting doubt about whether some of his concepts would ever be accepted, Johnson said a better time for new ideas would be coming—when the nation wasn't enjoying so much prosperity—for in a downturn people are more apt to listen to new ideas. But then he quickly reverted to the Johnson everyone knew: "I am not worried about the future of my company, but about the future of American industry."

Newsweek magazine called him the "Lone Wolf" of American business, saying that he "was born with a silver spoon in his mouth, but has replaced it with a gold one." The steady growth and success of Johnson's family of companies was compelling evidence that, despite his maverick tendencies, he knew how to build a business. The magazine noted the recent flurry of plant expansion, presided over by Johnson and "exemplifying Johnson's belief that factories can be beautiful as well as useful."

Of one of the new factories, *Modern Industry* magazine said:

It might be an H. G. Wells industrial futurama . . . , production workers in spotless blue and white uniforms . . . , foremen in surgeons' coats. Lustrous aluminum paint. Restful light-colored walls and dirt-free buff floors. Machinery completely enclosed to keep dirt out. Neatness, efficiency. To effect a workable compromise between his dream machines (with all parts enclosed), Johnson employed a sculptor who has made a hobby of streamlining industrial equipment. The sculptor is now busy designing panels to cover ready-made machinery. . . .

What kind of person is this highpowered, scrupulous industrial manager whose main difficulty is being thirty years ahead of his time? His management ideas are sound, they say, but sometimes get so far ahead of the main stream that carrying them out creates practical problems.

When *Cosmopolitan* magazine asked how young people could get ahead in business, Johnson advised: "If the boss doesn't think you're good, quit the job."

A group of young business executives searching for more youthful views on business management decided to form the Young Presidents Organization. They asked Johnson, then fifty-seven, to speak at their first dinner meeting. Despite the age difference, the group believed that Johnson represented a new generation of management-thinking. In a rousing talk, he urged them to go out and regain the confidence the public had lost in business twenty years earlier. "Business must get back the respect of the man on the street if it hopes to remove itself as a sitting duck for driveling politicians to shoot at," he told them.

•

Many awards and honors for his contributions to and interest in medicine came Johnson's way, but none moved him as much as becoming the first layman to be named an Honorary Fellow of the American College of Surgeons. In accepting the award at the College's annual convocation in Boston in the fall of 1950, Johnson was moved. "This fulfills the ambition of a lifetime. Now I am almost a doctor," he told the gathered surgeons. Frequently he referred to the award as "one of the highlights of my life." The same honor was later bestowed on him by the Royal College of Surgeons in England, when he was made a member of the Court of Patrons of that august group.

At times Johnson had reflected on career paths he might have taken, and becoming a physician was always high on his list. Over time he acquired a remarkable amount of knowledge on medical subjects, sometimes to the amazement of doctors who either treated him or were collaborating on a medical project. It was his usual practice to read everything he could find on a particular medical subject and to consult the experts in that field. In analyzing the state of his own health, he frequently got too many expert opinions.

He became deeply involved in the restructuring of Middlesex Hospital and for six years served as chairman of its executive committee. He encouraged company executives to volunteer their time too, and there was a steady succession of them among the hospital's volunteer leadership. Johnson always had a deep personal interest in how hospitals were managed, and as with business he felt it could always be done better. It was not unusual for him to visit the hospital several days a week, roaming the corridors with several "recruits" from Johnson & Johnson in tow — time and motion study experts, engineers, accountants, personnel specialists — any discipline that could contribute to improvement.

He soon expanded this project to include numerous other hospitals in the area, and he persuaded the area chapter of the Society for the Advancement of Management to send new volunteers. In time, his efforts gained national attention, and the *Reader's Digest* published an article about the reforms Johnson was helping to bring about in hospitals and the volunteer movement spreading across the nation, which they gave him credit for.

Some of Johnson's insights about problems in hospitals came while he was a patient. On one hospital stay he was appalled at the high noise level and called in a company sound expert to take readings. They were comparable to the noise in heavy traffic. The hospital then began an intensive noise-abatement program. Metal containers were replaced by plastic ones, rubber bumpers were put on supply carts, typewriters and telephone switchboards were put in soundproof areas, and patients' radios were toned down. It took a while, but Johnson had made the hospital quieter.

His interest in improving the way hospitals were run continued through the years. He made many efforts to improve patient care and bring professional management to these institutions. He wrote frequently for hospital publications, where he would make the case for better human relations practices for hospital employees. "While hospitals have special problems, many are similar to those faced by workers in business, and it is reasonable to think that they can be resolved by methods industry has found useful," he wrote. He deplored the "rigid caste system" that had developed in hospitals and said it should be abandoned in the interest of fairness, efficiency, and better patient care. Like the customer, the patient always came first.

Nursing was another area of patient care close to Johnson's heart. Well-trained nurses, he believed, should have a more important role and could be given greater responsibility for patient care. He did not hesitate to say that physicians were part of the problem because a subservient role had been carved out for nurses. Several programs to elevate the professional status of nurses were sponsored by Johnson, and as far away as Brazil he funded a nursing program, which was named for him. He also devised a program to bring nurses out of retirement to meet a current shortage.

Years later, his interest in nursing inspired the founding of the Johnson & Johnson Wharton School Fellows Program in Management for Nurse Executives at the University of Pennsylvania, the leading program of its kind in the nation. But the innovative nursing program at the Wharton School was only one of Johnson's many legacies. In recognition of his personal commitment to Middlesex Hospital and his generous financial gifts, the hospital

[386]

was later renamed the Robert Wood Johnson University Medical Center and became one of the premier hospitals in New Jersey. The medical school at Rutgers University became the Robert Wood Johnson Medical School. But the primary legacy was The Robert Wood Johnson Foundation in Princeton, New Jersey, the nation's largest philanthropy devoted to improving health care.

PART FOUR

The Man and His Mystique

1950–1968

25

READY, AIM, FIRE!

WHILE Johnson's highly acclaimed book *Or Forfeit Freedom*, and the praise he received for his leadership and collaboration on *Human Relations in Modern Business*, brought him wide recognition, he still struggled to gain the approval of hardened editors as a writer of magazine articles. It was a battle that he never really won. Editors admired him for his fresh ideas, but would admonish him for the way he expressed them. The jousting went on with every new article he submitted.

The exchanges were sharp but never acrimonious, and there was also humor, which for Johnson was often painful humor. When one editor suggested outright that he spend more time thinking before he started writing, he replied: "It is impractical for me to sit quietly under a tree and think these [articles] through before I go to work. Beyond that, I get my inspiration from working."

At *Harper's* magazine, which printed several of his articles and rejected many more, Johnson had a teacher in John Fischer, an editor with an equally direct style. "You asked me to be frank to the point of bluntness about your manuscript, which is enclosed," Fischer wrote. "Well, here goes. Some passages are both witty and pointed, and they set forth an argument which badly needs to be made [on being born rich]. Other passages, however, are at best pretty pedestrian." On occasion, Fischer could be generous in his comments. When he read *"But, General Johnson"* he said: "It was the best comment on government administrative problems I've ever read." In that case Fischer was more generous than the book actually deserved.

Johnson had titled the *Harper's* article on being born rich "Dough Boy." While most of his writing was on the philosophy of managing a business, on promoting harmony in the workplace, on the shortcomings of the military, and on the need — the desperate need, he felt — to preserve freedom, "Dough Boy" was different. It was a cathartic effort to defend inherited wealth and to point out the obligations that someone thrust into wealth had. The article included some poignant comments:

> If the individual considers wealth as a license he is soon poor.

> Money in the bank is a real source of embarrassment. One has a sense of guilt, and also a sense of fear. Of course, it is all right if it is other people's money, which apparently can be spent with impunity — but not so your own.

> "Playboy" and "richboy" are synonymous, but I wonder if it is true. I have known playboys at all levels. Most of them are very poor, but, I must admit, frequently attractive. There are rich playboys, but many more poor ones.

> Money makes it difficult to know people, and hence, hard to balance one's judgment.

> Naturally the rich are proud of the industries they build. They are proud of their sons, and want them to carry on where they leave off. Is that wrong?

> What's wrong with being rich, except the headaches that go with it? The wealth amassed by individuals soon passes into other hands, and in competitive society performs a greater service than if consumed by the government.

Harper's and several other major magazines passed "Dough Boy" off like a poor relative, and the article never did gain acceptance. Still, it contained thoughts that Johnson carried with him throughout his lifetime. He was the perfect candidate for the role of self-made man, but his substantial inheritance rewrote that scenario. Now he wanted to defend being rich, and nobody was listening.

•

Ever since leaving Washington, Johnson had become increasingly critical of the military. He saw the growing military establishment as a threat to the national economy, and most military officers as inept businessmen. "For some strange reason," he wrote a journalist friend, "these military fellows have the courage to walk standing up into a blazing machine gun, but they cringe from a public or even a private discussion of executive practice."

He was opposed to universal military training—"A conscripted man is not a Free Man," he said—and believed that a volunteer army was workable. The problem, he wrote his publisher friend John Knight, was that "the Army is so poorly managed that it does not attract enough men." These and other thoughts he set forth in an article titled "The Maginot Line of America," which *Harper's* received warmly and published in August 1948—just when the nation was debating the merits of legislation on universal military training. He built a reasoned case for training civilian specialists during peacetime to prepare for future wars, and a case for using modern management methods, as opposed to the whip of authority, for military personnel practices. But he also sowed some jolting suggestions that were vintage Johnson. In his usual aggressive style he wrote:

> If enforced military training is allowed to encourage and enlarge upon the malpractices of our present military system, it will weaken our defenses from the top down. It can easily become the Maginot Line of America.
>
> One way to improve human relationships would be to do away with

all of the brass and braid and officer insignia. In a modern age, all these things are a sad mistake. They date back to the day when the military men were looking for a way to awe the peasants. Today we are not dealing with peasants, but with well informed men and women. They must be treated accordingly. The Chairman of General Motors does not find it necessary to wear insignia. Neither does a vice president of the Chase National Bank. Their colleagues know them and that is enough.

I believe all commissioned officers should wear the same designation of rank, both as to tunic and insignia. Let it be something like a single star for everyone from the second lieutenants to the top generals and admirals. Non-commissioned officers could wear a somewhat different star in all ranks.

[He then went on to recommend] the elimination of West Point and Annapolis as they exist today. Despite their many conspicuous merits, these military academies are the fountainhead of the military caste system, which dominates the professional officers of both services. This system sets up insurmountable barriers between the enlisted men and an officer aristocracy and teaches blind obedience to the orders of the ruling class. . . . The evils and abuses of the system are many and well known. . . . West Point and Annapolis should be converted into postgraduate institutions, no longer Army and Navy but coordinated with the merged services.

The news wire services immediately shaped Johnson's suggestions into a short "bright" that appeared in hundreds if not thousands of newspapers and magazines across the nation. Most readers chuckled, the GIs roared, the military brass bristled — their longtime nemesis, the maverick businessman, had struck again. But even though some of his suggestions were outlandish, few people dismissed Johnson summarily. His ideas always had some substance, something of value. Behind his flair for shocking solutions were always problems that did need attention.

Some time after he proposed stripping the military of its brass, he wrote to the distinguished military editor of the *New York Times*, Hanson W. Baldwin, suggesting that they collaborate on an article enumerating the military's deficiencies. He added that he would be perfectly satisfied to have Baldwin, the leading journalist on military affairs, have "top billing" in the by-line. Turning him down most tactfully, Baldwin did not criticize Johnson's suggestion or deny the need for the series of articles. And he added: "I have read a number of your articles and they have always seemed to me to be very cogent and well expressed." However, pointing out that he did not work well as a collaborator, Baldwin told Johnson: "[I] was intrigued and much flattered by the suggestion . . . and should certainly be honored to have my name associated with yours." Baldwin proved himself a diplomat, and Johnson gracefully accepted his decision. They stayed in contact, but not as joint authors.

The military wasn't Johnson's only target. He had written an article in 1946 that few people knew about except the various magazine editors who had rejected it for publication. Titled "Or Else," it advocated expelling Russia from the United Nations in order "to isolate the sick patient from the rest of the world," as Johnson put it. His reasoning was that Russia had kept the rest of the world from making strides toward a lasting peace through such diverse methods as vetoes, walkouts, boycotts, and threats. Call Russia's bluff, he urged, and get on with a workable plan for world peace. It was a radical solution, and Johnson couldn't find anyone to publish it.

Five years later, in 1951, Ed Olly of the *New Brunswick Sunday Times*, learned about the article and got Johnson's permission to publish parts of it. Olly wrote: "As usual, [Johnson] was ahead of his times. He wrote the article when the 'Cold War' was just starting to warm up, when many people thought we could be friends with Joe Stalin. It is easy to say now 'Kick Russia out of the United Nations,' but it was not so easy in 1946." Former President Herbert Hoover made the same recommendation in 1950, Olly noted.

There was always a stack of unpublished articles that had made the rounds, unsuccessfully, and had been returned to Johnson, unclaimed for publication for one reason or another. Yet they all contained thoughts and challenges worthy of a better hearing. In one titled "Barricade," Johnson lamented the public apathy, the failure to vote on critical issues, and the submission to the will of politicians, and asked, "Where are the rebels? The rebels for right? Are we conforming to inertia?" All this, he said, adds up to the loss of hard-won freedom. In "Lawful Rebellion," which warned about the dangers of central authority and was also rejected, he wrote: "Bureaucratic commissars differ from the war lords only by the weapons they use."

Johnson's writing output gradually began to taper off in the early 1950s. There seemed to be no less zeal for changing things, just fewer words coming forth. One of his goals was to encourage what he called "amateur politicians" to run for office—they would be more honest and more effective than professional politicians, he believed. Dwight D. Eisenhower was cited as a good example of an amateur politician. In an article in the June 1953 issue of *Dun's Review*, Johnson wrote: "Last December [1952] we witnessed a political amateur win the highest office in the nation. Mr. Eisenhower's lack of knowledge of the political ropes was no roadblock in the minds of a great segment of the public who gave him the largest vote yet recorded in a Presidential election."

Though Johnson gave some editors pause for thought, many organizations constantly sought him out to speak at major events. He often accepted, noting: "I have a series of weaknesses, one of which is that I accept invitations to speak." There were few disappointments, for he was an excellent public speaker who had been well trained by experts. The problem was that no group was fully prepared for what he might say—which was part of his appeal.

When the Atlanta Chamber of Commerce was launching a long-range program to promote the region—called "Opportunity in America"—Johnson agreed to be the keynote speaker. Before a capacity audience he gave a stirring speech titled "Welfare Capitalism versus the Welfare State," in which he outlined the pitfalls of "complete government domination of our affairs." The speech got wide press coverage, and more than 83,000 reprints were distributed.

Welfare capitalism must prevail over the welfare state if freedom

is to survive, Johnson told the audience. "The errors of management and the errors of labor have led us to a semi-social state. . . .
Free management and free labor, under the guidance of Christian
principles, offer the best hope for the future. . . . I see the enlightened American worker as the defender of free men, free unions and
free business."

An address Johnson gave at a Labor Relations Forum at Catholic
University in Washington was also well covered by the press, and
university officials were inundated with requests for copies of the
talk. After reading one news account, noted New York advertising
executive Chester La Roche told Johnson in a letter that such views
would "speed up democracy" and recommended that the Advertising Council become a vehicle to accomplish that.

Occasionally something Johnson said had repercussions back
in New Brunswick at the company. For instance, at one talk in
Rochester he said: "For many years, business has been content to
select its management from the ranks of technical specialists. These
men are able lawyers, designers, engineers, sales leaders, experts
on materials or on production methods. Unfortunately, however,
few of them have received training in the art of dealing with their
fellow men, and especially with fellow men over whom they have
authority." When those remarks got back to the company, some
were chagrined, especially so-called "technical specialists" who
saw themselves as future senior executive material. At the time,
Johnson's speech material was coming from a new breed of human
relations and training experts who had gained a toehold in the
company and were preaching that line. Johnson later became more
sensitive, but the resentment of a few was lasting.

His speeches were confined to business subjects — he never spoke
on the military, though he did write about it. In his first presidential message to Congress after taking office in 1953, President
Dwight Eisenhower recommended a reorganization of the military
establishment to give it a greater concentration of power. Incensed
over the proposal, Johnson immediately took his objections to the

news media, even though he had supported Eisenhower in the election. He sent copies of his letter of protest to members of Congress, and to Nelson Rockefeller, whom Eisenhower had appointed chairman of a committee to recommend improvements in armed forces unification.

In the letter he said: "It is with reluctance that I exercise my rights as a free citizen to oppose one, but vital, segment of the President's program concerning reorganization of the military establishment. Our freedoms must be defended at home and abroad. The threat of undue military influence on our society grows with the size of our military budget. We should avoid, at all costs, too great a concentration of power. . . . The Congress and the President should, through resolution, proclaim that the civilian authorities of the military establishment shall at all times control and direct our policies and procedures. This declaration should be stated unequivocally and announced to the people of the United States and to the world."

Because he felt so strongly about this issue, Johnson agreed to state his argument before a congressional committee on June 18, pitting him against both Eisenhower and Rockefeller. The results on armed forces unification did not turn out the way Johnson had hoped, but Eisenhower later changed his own mind about what was best for the nation, though not until his moving farewell address at the end of his second term. At that time, the outgoing President spoke out against military dominance, much the same as Johnson had eight years earlier: "In the council of government," Eisenhower told the nation, "we must guard against the acquisition of unwarranted influence, whether sought or unsought, by the military-industrial complex. The potential for the disastrous rise of misplaced power exists and will persist. We must never let the weight of this combination endanger our liberties or democratic processes."

Johnson was never reluctant to profess his patriotism openly, and he was never embarrassed by it. But he was always appalled by voter apathy. In late October 1952, he had been touched by a

[398]

newspaper photo showing soldiers of the Army's Seventh Division struggling up Triangle Hill in Korea, burdened by machine guns and looking spent. Days of artillery fire had shorn the hilltop of its foliage; it was a desolate scene. He wrote his publisher friend, Elmer Boyd: "I know this is old stuff in the news, but we must find a way to carry this message to the people. It seems to me this picture does it."

Boyd agreed, obtained a copy of the photo from the Associated Press, and the next day ran it in his paper with excerpts from Johnson's letter, which said in part: "The attached picture tells many stories. Here is a horrible mess which we are asking our young men to clean up. It shows a terrain so disheveled by blast as to extinguish life. Something has happened to this United States when, on the one hand, soldiers suffer this way to defend our right to vote, and then 50 million persons, through downright disinterest, fail to exercise that privilege."

Johnson had a soft spot for war heroes, and he occasionally brought them into the company, with mixed results. Usually these were flamboyant and attractive individuals, with good family backgrounds, adept at the social graces, and not very good businessmen. One was William Pancoast Clyde Jr., son of Lord and Lady Clyde of the Clyde-Mallory Steamship Lines. Billy Clyde was a dashing Group Captain and fighter pilot in the Royal Air Force whose heroics in air battles over Dunkirk and Britain won him the Distinguished Flying Cross. The two met after the war, and Johnson was so impressed that he offered Clyde a job, though at the time neither knew exactly what he would do. As it turned out, he worked for years on international assignments as sort of troubleshooter and diplomat. Clyde was clearly one of the most engaging but unconventional employees Johnson had, and after several years they both decided he had no future in the company. He moved to Acapulco with his pockets full, which was Johnson's traditional way of terminating an unproductive but pleasant relationship.

Johnson had mentioned to his journalist friend Frank Farrell the possibility of coming to work for him, but Farrell resisted. He explained why: "I admired and respected [Johnson], and truly liked him, but it doesn't surprise me that people didn't get close to him. When I was a kid I trained polo ponies for General George Patton. I was one of Patton's favorite characters. But as I studied Patton, I swore to myself it's a good thing we're friends and I don't have to work for him, because I would go crazy. And I swore that I would never get into the Army because he might request me and I couldn't work for him. He tried to get me to go to West Point, and I'll tell you that's one of the reasons I volunteered for the Marine Corps [during World War II, Farrell was a captain in the Office of Strategic Services and served in the South Pacific], to stay away from Patton. My relationship with Bob Johnson is the same. As long as we were on a parallel as personalities where wealth didn't matter, fine. But the idea of working for Bob, no. I never gave it a moment's thought."

Farrell, a handsome, charismatic columnist for the *New York World-Telegraph and Sun*, covered nightlife in Manhattan and also wrote about more serious subjects. His engaging Irish manner, quick wit, and ready smile made him enormously popular with the ladies. Being single, he was a popular choice of the Hollywood studios to escort their rising young starlets around New York, making the rounds of Copacobana, the Stork Club, El Morocco, "21" and others in that glittering orbit—naturally becoming "items" in the next day's columns. Farrell escorted Elizabeth Taylor when she was a rising star, and later he was linked romantically to a string of starlets, including Rhonda Fleming and Maureen O'Hara. He loved New York and knew it well, later being largely responsible for bringing the aircraft carrier *Intrepid* to its Hudson River mooring to become a museum popular with tourists.

Johnson and Farrell forged a friendship that continued for twenty-five years. "I admired Bob Johnson so much," Farrell recalled. "I found him fascinating. To me he was a personal hero; I loved to be with him. He was a very handsome man with a very commanding personality. He had the heartiest laugh, and when he laughed the whole room would turn around, because it was a deep voice and a very honest laugh. He had the voice of a military commander in the field—though not in combat, because combat overturns the voice."

"We did a lot of sailing together on *Gerda*, his newest boat, when she was docked at City Island in New York," Farrell said. "We had a Danish captain, a mate and a cook, and Bob and I took turns at the helm and stood regular watches. One time he decided to stop by and see his old friend, Joe Kennedy, at Hyannis Port. Jack was there. Bobby was there. Most of the family was there. About five o'clock Joe, Bob, and I were in the library, and Joe said: 'Bob, what about your stock?' Bob replied: 'Joe, it should be selling at about half of what it's selling right now.' Two years later I ran into Joe Kennedy on Fifth Avenue and he said: 'Frank, you must be a millionaire now.' I said, 'No, still working for about $20,000 a year at the newspaper.' He said 'What did you do about Johnson & Johnson stock after I set Bob up for you that day?' I said 'Nothing. I took Bob at his word. The stock was high.' He said: 'You fool, the chairman of the board can't tip you on his stock. That was the surest statement I've ever heard to buy the stock, because I bought it and made $2 million.' I said, 'Joe, that's how millionaires are made and I guess I'm destined to be a poor man all my life.' He said: 'Frank, keep your ears open on these things.'"

"Another time," Farrell said, "we sailed up to Chatham and stopped to visit his brother, Seward. We came ashore and there was Seward, barefooted, with a long scraggly beard. My first impression was that he looked like St. Francis of Assisi. There were kids crawling all over him. His kids and other people's kids. The kids loved him and he would tell them stories, and he had fourteen Weimaraners running all over the place and barking. It was a very enjoyable afternoon. Seward insisted we stay overnight in the guest cottage, but he didn't tell us that one half of the cottage was for guests and the other half for the fourteen Weimaraners. The dogs knew we were there and they objected to it, barking and snarling all night. We got no sleep at all. We thought it was one of the great put-ons of all time because Seward had no reverence for Bob whatsoever. He thought Bob was the stuffiest SOB he'd ever met. Seward was a sailor and he loved kids, and Bob could do without kids. I think Bob was envious of Seward's easygoing life. He was a natural born beachcomber."

On occasions when Evie was not in town and Johnson was staying at their apartment at the Hotel Pierre, he would join Farrell on his rounds of the cabarets, once with Joan Crawford and several times with Ginger Rogers. "Ginger Rogers called me and Bob the best non-professional dancers in the world, and the papers picked it up," Farrell said. "Johnson was fascinated by Walter Winchell, who was probably one of the extraordinary characters of all time. If he joined Bob and Evie at their table, he would tell them stories for an hour. He loved to tell stories. Bob was never a playboy. He was far superior to those characters. He could belt a few, and then not drink for a week. Now and then he would have a moment of eccentricity."

"I would love to hear Bob and Fulton Sheen go at it," Farrell recalled. These meetings with the Catholic bishop were usually over lunch or dinner in one of Manhattan's better restaurants, he added, and Evie was often present. She had been a good friend of Fulton Sheen's since her marriage to Johnson, and she was a generous contributor to the missions that were close to the bishop's heart.

Fulton Sheen (Fulton was his mother's maiden name) had become the best-known Catholic orator in America because of his spellbinding sermons on his weekly network telecast, "Life Is Worth Living," which ran on NBC. He had riveting eyes and would appear on the set of a study wearing a cape and pectoral cross and in a deep, rich voice make a flawless, forceful presentation without benefit of notes or teleprompter. Set in prime time against Milton Berle and Frank Sinatra, the series was expected to die a quick death, but Fulton Sheen's appeal sent the ratings soaring. Earlier he had hosted "The Catholic Hour" on radio and spent sixteen years in mission work as national director of the Society for the Propagation of the Faith. But it was his television program that catapulted him into national prominence and gave him an entrée to business, society, and politics.

Getting into a discussion with Fulton Sheen on a serious issue was a mental and verbal challenge that intrigued Johnson. A brilliant scholar, the bishop had written more than a score of books, but he was skillful at putting people at ease. He used his humor to great advantage. When he received an Emmy for his television show, he quipped: "I feel it is time I pay tribute to my four writers, Matthew, Mark, Luke, and John." After returning to his television show following a summer-long absence, his opening line was "Long time, no Sheen."

Johnson had great respect for him and did not back off during their many friendly but intense encounters. Farrell recalled the lively discussions between Johnson and Fulton Sheen: "I would hold back and not even enter the conversation unless I thought there was a point they were missing."

The bishop too remembered: "We had many discussions. [Johnson's] favorite subject was business, and we were often on opposite sides. He was constantly emphasizing labor-management relationships, and along with that the independence of business from government bureaucracy. The position I took was that business should work toward profit-sharing—that is to say, the workers should be given some share of the profits. In those days there were many sit-down strikes, which had started in France. The argument I gave was that workers were willing to sit down on someone else's tools but not willing to sit down on their own. His position was never that of paternalism, of being good to them just to win their goodwill. His argument was that business required that they be given more than an adequate wage. He often told me that he raised wages above the comparable wage scale of other industries simply because he felt that it was good business. Hence, the response he received, he felt, was as good or better than that which would be received from profit-sharing. . . . I admired him so much."

Sheen also said Johnson fit the definition of a gentleman that John Henry Cardinal Newman gave in his book *The Idea of a University*: "It is almost a definition of a gentleman to say he is one who never inflicts pain." The bishop continued: "We in America are not always inclined to stress decorum and the qualities that go to make a man of refinement. But [Johnson] stood out among other men in that respect, and, as such, I will always remember him."

Farrell recalled that his association with Johnson and Fulton Sheen almost made him wealthy. "In all the years I knew Bob, I never accepted money or asked to borrow any, not even expenses for some of the things I did for him—except, that is, for the Fulton Sheen deal that fell through. Bob had this great admiration for Fulton Sheen, and one day he called me and said he had found a way to make me a rich man. I said, 'Go on.' He said, 'How do you think it would be if Johnson & Johnson sponsored Fulton Sheen's television programs?' I said that would be very interesting, because he can't find a sponsor easily—Kent cigarettes wanted to sponsor him badly, and Budweiser beer wanted to sponsor him, and Fulton told me: 'I can't be sponsored by even a minor vice.'

" 'But surgical supplies,' I told Bob, 'that's a matter of mercy.' 'Fine,' he said, 'you line up Fulton Sheen and we'll give you ten percent of everything we spend, his fee, air time, advertising, everything.' So I said, 'That's a lot of money,' and he said, 'That's what we're talking about, a lot of money.'

"So I called Fulton Sheen and he said nothing would please him better, but he was leaving NBC for Dumont Television and wanted me to hold the story for a month until the switch was made. Bob was delighted. A couple of weeks went by and I'm waiting. Then one night about four in the morning I bolted up in bed and said, 'Oh, no!' I waited until ten in the morning and called Bob. I said, 'By any chance do any of your companies manufacture contraceptive products?' He said, 'Ortho, the best there is.' He had dropped the bomb. No cigarettes. No beer. No contraceptives. No Fulton

Sheen. Four hundred thousand dollars a year went out the window."

Though Farrell and Johnson enjoyed the café-society life in New York, that was not the basis of their relationship. Both had an interest in politics, the military, and a broad spectrum of domestic and international issues. "Average people are not very good copy and not interesting to spend a lot of time with," said Farrell. "I could spend eight hours a day with Bob and look forward to the next day. In five minutes you'd be involved in the darnedest analytical conversation. He was the most forward-thinking man I'd ever known."

26

RELATIONSHIPS

ROBERT Wood Johnson was not an easy person to know, but Evie Johnson felt that she knew her husband as well as anyone. She was a realist, and she confronted his shortcomings more directly than he did. Reflecting on their twenty-five years of marriage, she described her husband in these terms: "He certainly wasn't a Saint Francis. He was more like a Saint Augustine"—who, she noted, found his way back from his errant ways.

"Bob had a great sense of authority and a presence," she said. "He was not what you would call *pretty* handsome, he was *arresting* handsome. You always knew when he came into a room, because he suddenly became the center of attention."

At their weekly dinner parties at Longleat in Princeton, and at Wycombe House, their spacious home on Indian Creek Island in Florida, Johnson would station himself at the door with Evie at his side, he dressed in flawlessly tailored dinner clothes, she in an elegant gown from a fashionable couturier. He offered the hearty welcome, she a soft-spoken one. At dinner, and encouraged by the dry martinis and the vintage wine, Johnson shaped and directed the conversation, while Evie listened more than she spoke.

Despite his striking good looks, Johnson was not a ladies' man. "He was awkward with women," Evie said, "and not at ease with many of them. Women did not see him as the type of husband they would want. He was too much wedded to his business. Women thought he was very formal. He had a great sense of humor, but was very subtle. He used it in a very adroit way, and he could cut you down with one look."

For Evie, there was no need to be jealous. In all the years of their marriage, no woman tried to steal her husband from her. Only when she spoke of his two previous wives was there a hint of disdain for his other relationships. "Elizabeth Ross was a homebody," she said abruptly, "and Maggi was the antithesis. She was a feather in a breeze." It was a subject Evie did not want to dwell on.

Hard as his business shell was, there was a sentimental side to Johnson. As Evie put it, "He could, on occasion, be very warm and sentimental, but you didn't see that very often. I remember one night at the Plaza Hotel when Peter Grace asked Bob if he could dance with me. It was a Viennese waltz, and when I came back to the table there were tears in Bob's eyes. But it may have been because Peter could do a Viennese waltz as well as he could."

"We had a very honest and friendly relationship," Evie explained. "He would say that most of the men he knew had outgrown their wives. That wasn't the case with us. He would ask what I thought about this and that—not that he ever paid attention. But I did try to help him with his writing and speaking.

"Bob was a very impressive speaker, even though you couldn't take apart his sentences grammatically. But he spoke with such authority that nobody ever paid any attention to the construction, and I thought that was wrong. I took him one time to the Academy of Dramatic Arts, to a man named D'Angeli, and he taught him how to speak more effectively. Bob was doing some radio work at the time and he got to be an even better speaker. He had a booming voice, yet he couldn't sing for peanuts. He couldn't carry a tune.

"Another time, I suggested he see our friend, John Gielgud, the actor, for some instruction. They were drawn to each other's strong personalities and would get involved in animated discussions. John would say, 'Stop dropping your voice at the end of a sentence.' And he did, and he got even better.

"Bob was fiercely competitive. He wanted to be the best at everything he did. He had a very inquisitive mind, and what he didn't know, he learned. He wasn't always right, and he knew it. And he could do something I could never do: When he was wrong he could handle it with some grace. He didn't mind being wrong, but I did.

"Bob was so competitive he would try to compete with his instructors, who naturally were more skilled than he. If he couldn't compete, he got discouraged. Once he tried taking golf lessons, and when he wasn't able to compete with his instructors he threw his golf clubs in the brook and walked off. He never played golf again.

"It was important to him to do everything just right, even when it came to his clothes. He was a meticulous dresser, always wore gray and navy, never brown. He couldn't stand having a crease in his shirt sleeves, so Elsa, my lady's maid, would take the sleeves of his shirts down and press them and then sew them back on. He made the cleaners stop stapling their tags on his clothes. For him, they pinned them on. And when he wore gloves, he always turned the tops down. I could never understand that, but he did.

"He was always dressed just right, flawless, except on his boats. Then he wore these floppy hats and tan slacks and looked like a member of the crew. That's what he wanted to look like. On a boat he was a different person.

"We both liked to read, and those evenings when we weren't entertaining or he didn't have business, we would settle in the living room and read. He was never into the classics or poetry, but if it was about business or politics he would devour it. He enjoyed reading mysteries a great deal. But he was very prudish, a bit of the Old School—no, very much the Old School type. If he came across a page that he thought was too lewd, he would just tear it out of the book. Just like that. One evening, we were reading and he became very upset over this particular book. I don't know what it was. He said to me, 'Are you dressed to go out?' I was puzzled, but I said yes. 'I'll get the car out,' he told me, and he did. We drove for several miles in silence. Then he stopped at a bridge that passed over a swift-flowing stream, got out, and threw the book into the water. Then he drove home in silence. He felt the book deserved that fate, and I didn't question him about it."

Books were more than just books for Johnson. They were his private education, his classroom, his university degree. He believed that people like him, without a formal education, needed to be motivated to learn more, so he decided to write a "self-help" book aimed not only at the working class but also at college graduates, to remind them that learning doesn't end with a college degree. In the outline for the book he set the stage:

> It is a young man's graduation day from the best engineering school. During the ceremony he heard a muffled boom. The next day the newspapers carried headlines that a river had blown up. Someone evolved the notion that by placing Product A on one bank, and Product B on the other bank, the oxygen in the water would be released so rapidly as to explode the river. This brought rains to the countryside. People saw great economic potential in the experiment.
>
> Our young graduate was educated up to the moment of the muffled boom. He is no longer a well informed engineer—and this will go on every day for the rest of his life. Only there will be no boom to alert him. This is just as true of the man on the street. Perhaps there was a time when one could get an education and stay educated for life, but no longer.

When Johnson presented the outline to the editors at Doubleday, which had published *Or Forfeit Freedom*, they liked the idea, but thought it would sell better if he included his own experience of rising to the top without a formal education. He objected to that approach though, so the project was abandoned. Later he went back to his ever patient contact at Doubleday, Clara Classen, with an outline for a novel he wanted to write. The plot revolved around a family that owned a business in a small town, but Johnson had concluded that a successful novel had to be, in his words, "red hot, like *Forever Amber*." Not wanting to be identified with what he called "racy" sequences, he suggested that Doubleday get the noted author Louis Bromfield to write it. Johnson would give Bromfield the plot and accept 10 percent of the profits from the novel. Doubleday politely declined.

Johnson wrapped his disappointments in a brooding silence. When his ideas did not work out, Evie would, very cautiously, console him. He abhorred sympathy in its purest form, and Evie became adept at saying just the right thing. They had an accommodating relationship. Neither liked to argue, so they never argued. When a disagreement began to be serious, Evie said, they would walk away from it, leaving the issue unresolved. They learned to accommodate many unresolved issues.

Yet theirs was a caring relationship. Evie had an abiding concern about her husband's health, which had never been robust. "He had many health problems," she said, "and after he was diagnosed as having endocarditis by Dr. Paul Dudley White, the noted heart doctor, I watched him like a hawk. But he didn't know I was watching. Dr. White had given me a book on endocarditis, in which I underlined several symptoms to watch out for and had the book covered in silk and put ribbons in it. Bob thought it was one of my own books. He would sit across from me reading, and I would look at him and watch for the symptoms."

Her concern moved him, and he usually responded the way he knew best — by buying her something expensive. Evie had several room-size closets filled with expensive clothes, and in 1956 the Fashion Academy named her the best-dressed woman in society, displacing the Duchess of Windsor. Evie's couturier clothes were complemented by her dazzling collection of jewelry. Her favorites were large and lavish necklaces of precious stones from all over the world. They became her trademark in café society, and she bought most of them in the Bulgari salon at the Hotel Pierre, where the Johnsons had their New York apartment.

To Evie's way of thinking, none of this was extravagance, but rather the role her husband expected her to play. And for those who knew and observed the couple, there was never any doubt that Evie reveled in the role of being Mrs. Robert Wood Johnson.

"Bob was quite generous and showered me with jewels and furs and flowers," said Evie. "Wherever I went, there were more flowers than there was room for. When I would tell him I had enough fur coats, he would say, 'But this one is different.' Where money was concerned, Bob had two sides. He was meticulous about having bills paid promptly, but he never knew what anything cost because all of the bills were turned over to his staff for payment.

"He was penny-wise and pound foolish. He would pay a million dollars for a boat and walk away and never see it again. Then he would complain and carry on about some insignificant charge, some small thing.

"He didn't feel that women should be left a lot of money, or else they would become targets. He believed they should be comfortable but not affluent. I never questioned his decisions, and I never read a single thing he asked me to sign because I felt that if he brought it to me it was all right to sign."

"And yet Bob did what I asked him to do. Largely. And I did the things he asked me to do, and I never questioned him."

Having been divorced, and being married to Johnson outside the Catholic Church, disturbed Evie deeply. She felt alienated from the church for some time, until she met a kindly priest, Father Martin D'Arcy, when he was at the Farm Street Church in London. He persuaded her to renew her regular attendance at Mass, and in later years she went to church daily. Once, on a trip to Rome, the Johnsons arranged to have an informal conference at the Vatican, but they received no encouragement about having their marriage sanctioned by the church.

Evie was careful not to push Johnson in any areas, but where religion was concerned she exercised added caution. "It was his choice to make," she said. "He worked hard to bring Christianity to the workplace, and he got deeply involved in that subject with representatives from many different churches. But what he did personally about religion was, I felt, up to him. Bob would often accompany me to Mass at St. Patrick's in New York, but most often I think he went there to hear Fulton Sheen preach. He enjoyed him very much."

Johnson had always contended that his interest in the Catholic Church was more intellectual than spiritual. After reading about an American-sponsored project for a study team to go to Rome to translate more of the early teachings of Christianity, Johnson became intrigued and wrote the scholar in charge of the study group to offer his services:

> For many years I have considered what might be called a businessman's sabbatical year. It was my hope that one day I should go to Rome with a small secretariat, and in collaboration with the Vatican authorities attempt certain social studies aimed to disclose patterns that might be published later. I appreciate that this is really a lifetime job, but I was going to take a stab at it if the appropriate time ever arrived. From the report in the *Times*, I gather that you are planning such a work, but that you have properly realized the magnitude of the task and arranged for the collaboration of a large number of experts. Perhaps you might find some use for my part-time services.

The scholar — perhaps through divine inspiration — declined the offer to have Johnson as a part-time assistant.

•

When it came to sharing her deepest thoughts with someone, Evie usually turned to her brother, Tom Paynter, with whom she was close. Several years younger than she, Tom had become a legendary figure in the book world. He was a senior buyer at Walden Book Company in Stamford, Connecticut, and had purportedly over a span of three decades bought more books than anyone else in the business. For Evie he was like both a father and a son to her, and a large framed picture of Tom in her living room was a constant reminder of the support she received from him.

Though she had learned to love books as a child, it was Tom who sent Evie a steady flow of the most current books, which she read and passed on to others. Johnson found his brother-in-law's knowledge of books fascinating and enjoyed spending time with him. Over the years, Johnson had developed the regular practice of sending books he found interesting — usually on the subjects of business, government, or politics — to a long list of executives at Johnson & Johnson. He purchased the books from Paynter's company, and the deliveries had to be prompt — Johnson saw to that.

Johnson himself had few close personal friends, but there was a strong bond between him and his brother Seward. It was never more evident than when they wrote memos to each other, usually on the traditional blue company memo paper, and signed the correspondence "Love, Bob" or "Love, Sew." Sometimes the memos were about projects that involved other executives in the company, and they would get a copy. Thus, over time, this open demonstration of affection between the two brothers became widely known — and admired.

Soft-spoken, and mild-mannered, Seward was different from his brother in many ways, beginning with appearance. He too had a slight build, and he was a few inches shorter than Robert. In his youth, Seward was strikingly handsome and much more adept at courting the ladies. He first had a mustache, then in later years he grew a beard and elaborate sideburns that arched down to the graying beard, giving him an old-man-by-the-sea appearance, which suited him well. While Robert was always impeccably dressed in custom-tailored suits, Seward preferred the rumpled look of someone who had just been attired by the camping department of Abercrombie & Fitch. Getting Seward into a tuxedo was a struggle, and even then he would often don a brown fedora as a final gesture of rebellion. He liked his life as a country gentleman.

Seward was deceptively bright. Despite his laid back, casual approach to life, he had an excellent grasp of engineering and the sciences, especially oceanography, and when he put his mind to things he excelled. But by choice he didn't do that very often. Long ago Seward had decided not to compete with his brother in the company, and colleagues of both men agreed it was the best test of Seward's good judgment. He clearly was not cut out to be a business executive, and competing against his compulsive brother would surely have led to clashes. Yet, Evie pointed out, "the General secretly admired Seward's relaxed ways."

Several common interests brought the brothers even closer: their passion for sailing and the sea, their desire to help New Jersey deal with its problems, and their concerns about how their mounting wealth should be used to accomplish their individual philanthropic goals—which, like their personalities, were different. Seward's Harbor Branch Foundation in Florida would focus on various aspects of oceanography, including the medical potential of marine life. Robert, from the outset, concentrated on improving health and health care through the resources of The Robert Wood Johnson Foundation, then a largely local philanthropy.

Earlier, with encouragement from his brother, Seward had tried a career with Johnson & Johnson. He had organized the company's purchasing and planning departments, after admitting that he had no idea what planning was all about. Then, in the challenging Depression years, he served as treasurer and held a tight rein on expenditures. It was during the World War II years that Seward demonstrated his greatest skills and technical knowledge when he directed the company's wartime operations that included producing parts for combat aircraft and for torpedoes, and the shell-loading plant in Illinois. In that job, Seward excelled.

After the war, Seward held the title of vice president, but his duties were limited and his lack of interest was apparent. In 1955 he announced that he was taking "semi-retirement" to spend more time with his oceanography research and cattle-breeding experiments at his farm estate in the rolling hills of New Jersey.

Seward's "semi-retirement" passed almost unnoticed by his brother, who long ago had perceived that Seward would never be a major factor in the family business. Colleagues who knew both men well considered that a blessing. Some said that's the way the General secretly preferred it, some believed that the relationship would otherwise have suffered badly. One noted: "Seward was the submissive one, and how fortunate it is that he did not have the spunk and bite and disposition of their sister Evangeline, or they might have been battling constantly. The General wanted to run things." And even though Robert was only two years older than Seward, the General played the role of father figure. Seward probably never saw it that way.

While clearly not in awe of his brother, Seward had an abiding respect for him and shared many of Robert's views about the inherent dangers of excessive government control and confiscatory taxation. They both railed against the onerous estate taxes, which they saw as a vulture feeding on their personal fortunes, and they established a series of trusts to minimize the tax impact when they died. Seward's politics leaned to the right, and by this time, in the late 1950s, Robert had become far more conservative in his views. Only occasionally now did he venture into the liberal camp (he preferred to call it "progressive") on certain issues.

Attendance at Board of Directors' meetings was given a low priority by Seward, much to his brother's annoyance. On one occasion he wrote that he would not be present at a board meeting because, "being a farmer, I don't like to change from overalls more than I can help." Coming from anyone else, that excuse would have made the General apoplectic, but by now he had a high tolerance for Seward's casualness about the business. He had lost that battle. Besides, an active and involved Seward would have presented other problems. There could only be one captain of the ship.

Yet he sought Seward's astute advice on many things—and did not always like what he heard in response. That was particularly true in politics, where Seward's approach was less emotional and more pragmatic. Once when Johnson had put together a list of requirements a candidate should meet, Seward, with obvious enjoyment, accused him of making "pious statements" and needled him for grouping communists, socialists, and liberals together. "Thinking people are confused and angered by this combination of words," Seward admonished. And when he used the phrase "a sincere conservative," Seward shot back: "There are all kinds of conservatives. A substantial block can't think. If you added 'thinking conservative' or 'intellectual conservative,' it would appeal to more people." Johnson made the change. Critiquing another portion of Johnson's creative effort, Seward asked: "Is it supposed to be funny or free verse? If I knew what it meant, I don't think I would like it." Seward had a license to be flippant and irreverent with his brother in ways that others did not dare to be.

Seward was much more consistent than his brother in many ways, if not in the desire to climb the corporate ladder. For one, he was content to sail the same vessel for years—his beloved 61-foot ketch, the *Ocean Pearl*—and he sailed her skillfully. Robert constantly changed boats. After he sold the *Good News* he acquired a 112-foot Mathis yacht, *Sirena*, a shallow draft houseboat that was almost an embarrassment for a blue-water sailor like him to own. Perhaps as a cover for his crime against the sailing fraternity, he referred to the *Sirena* as "Evie's boat," and when he bought it he remarked: "Apparently I am at a point where my ocean-racing days are over, and I have sunk to the houseboat level." The *Sirena* spent most of the time at the dock near their home in Florida and provided comfortable sleeping accommodations for an excess of house guests.

Johnson saw Seward frequently and corresponded with him regularly, but he saw his sister, Evangeline, only occasionally. Usually they had a good rapport, though Evangeline regretted selling her Johnson & Johnson stock to Robert. Many said she came out on the short end of the deal.

Both were hard-driving and relentless. Johnson once remarked that if Evangeline had been a man she would have been the one to run the company. It was an amusing compliment that Johnson probably did not believe—just like the time he said to her, "Babe [a nickname only he used for Evangeline and that she barely tolerated], if you had not been my sister, you are the one woman I would have married." Evangeline said she knew better.

Evangeline's marriage to Leopold Stokowski lasted twelve years, and began falling apart when Stokowski became involved with Greta Garbo, the actress. After divorcing Stokowski Evangeline married a Russian nobleman who had escaped the revolution, and she then became Princess Zalstem-Zalessky, a title that suited her regal airs. She continued her interest in the arts—the Metropolitan Museum of Art made her a Fellow in Perpetuity—and for years she and the Prince hosted some of Palm Beach's most memorable soirées.

•

Sheila, the child that Johnson and Maggi adopted, had grown up to be an intelligent, attractive, and very independent young lady. When she decided to transfer from Wells College in Aurora, New York, to Sarah Lawrence College in Bronxville, New York, Johnson was very upset. "My father thought Sarah Lawrence was very liberal, which it was not. I became liberal later, not while I was there," Sheila recalled. "But I do remember I was one of only seven Republicans that I knew about. When I was at Sarah Lawrence, I would visit him in Princeton, and we would spend Saturdays at the plant."

"My father was truly a little boy when we went to the office on those Saturdays," Sheila continued, "for he was playing hooky in reverse and showing up when he wasn't expected. Johnson & Johnson was his wife, his mistress, his child, his friend, his toy. It was his life, much more than the rest of us of flesh and blood. We all knew that, and either we decided to go through this as my brother Bobby did, and love it as much as he did, or we could avoid it. That's what I chose to do, because I did not feel close to the company in any way, shape, or form.

"Dad had qualities that could be both very kind and very tough. I saw little of the toughness. I was lucky. He didn't think girls had to see the tough side. I remember that when I was younger he would lean over and pat my hand and say, 'I'm proud of you,' and to get his approval I would have killed myself three times."

Through the years after the divorce, Johnson and Maggi exchanged friendly, chatty letters. Their affection for one another had clearly prevailed, Maggi's lighthearted manner had always amused him, and lifted his spirits. It still did. Maggi had remarried and was now Mrs. Edward A. Eily, but she and Johnson continued to discuss decisions involving Sheila, even to the wearing of a bikini. "I am against bikinis," he declared, and suggested that Sheila wear "a full-pleated skirt on the moderate side," adding: "I am a stylist at heart, but not in the Oleg Cassini class." Maggi was good at calming him down and reassuring him that Sheila would be just fine— which she was.

After studying in England for a year, Sheila decided to return to Sarah Lawrence for an extra year. Then she encountered some of Johnson's toughness, which she had escaped earlier. "He could not stomach the idea of paying any more money to Sarah Lawrence," said Sheila. "He thought that after twenty-one, children should be on their own. He took a stand and so did I. So I paid the final year of tuition out of my trust fund, and when I graduated I went to work in the admissions office at Sarah Lawrence. He worried so much that I would be a wealthy young lady, changing swains and unhappy and with too much money, that he erred on the other side. I always had a job and I never regretted it. I liked my jobs and was never happier than when I was working and productive. I don't like frivolity any more than he did. I'm uncomfortable with possessions, and I don't consider myself particularly heroic. That's just the way I am."

A friend of Sheila's overheard her discussing with Johnson the impending debutante season, and a New York social columnist printed the account of the conversation. "How much will it cost you for me to become a debutante?" Sheila asked her father. "About $50,000," Johnson replied. "I suggest that you give the $50,000 to charity because I don't want to be a debutante," said Sheila. And she wasn't.

•

Just as likeable and unpretentious as Sheila was Robert Wood Johnson Jr., who years earlier had decided to join the family business. As a youth, Bobby spent four summers in various jobs at Johnson & Johnson, following an apprenticeship pattern very similar to the one his father had charted for himself. Known as both "Bob" and "Bobby" to his friends and colleagues, the young Johnson graduated from the private Millbrook School and spent two years at Hamilton College before joining the company as an hourly worker in the plaster mill. There the second generation of Hungarians who had taken his father in tow to teach him that aspect of the business were delighted to have another Johnson protégé. It was difficult not to make comparisons between the two Johnsons, and few resisted the urge to do so. It was a burden Bobby would carry all of his years with Johnson & Johnson.

A year after the outbreak of World War II, Bobby enlisted in the Army. After taking specialized training at the University of Kentucky, he served four years in Europe with the First Armored Division, and then the Fourteenth, completing his tour of duty as a sergeant. He then headed back to New Brunswick to continue working under his father. The two had never had a close relationship. When Bobby was a child of eight, his father divorced his mother, Elizabeth, to marry Maggi Shea. Elizabeth and her son grew very close, and Bobby shared with her the pain of the divorce and the absence of his father. In later years he remarked ruefully that it was the family chauffeur who used to take him fishing and on other boyhood adventures, not his father.

When Bobby returned from military service, his career at the company began to accelerate. He held positions in manufacturing, engineering, and the personnel department before moving to merchandising and advertising—the aspect of the business that he liked best and where he began to demonstrate considerable talent. In 1947, at the age of twenty-seven and largely because he was Robert Wood Johnson Jr., he was elected to the Board of Directors. His next six years were spent at two of the company's affiliates—first in a management role at Ethicon, then in a series of positions at Personal Products, where he became vice president of merchandising and advertising. Personal Products happened to be an area of the company that Bobby's father watched most closely—particularly its advertising strategy, which he had helped create in earlier years.

Bobby and his father had one very strong common interest—their total commitment to Johnson & Johnson. The company was at the core of both their lives, but beyond that they were more different than they were alike. To begin with, Bobby preferred a lower profile. Instead of the headline-making political and public-service roles pursued and enjoyed by his father, Bobby could be found at the local Junior Sportsman's Show explaining a wildlife exhibit to youngsters, or serving as finance chairman of the First-Aid Squad in Highland Park, where his father had been mayor. He disdained the café society life in New York, which his father reveled in, and his preferred version of a "yacht" was a fishing boat, the *Wild Goose*, which he kept on Barnegat Bay in New Jersey.

Johnson & Johnson had become the center of Bobby Johnson's life, just as it was for his father, and this intense mutual interest seemed to ease the tension that had hovered over their relationship for years. After his marriage to Betty Wold, the attractive and personable daughter of a St. Paul, Minnesota, physician, Bobby began seeing more of his father away from the office. Johnson was quite fond of his new daughter-in-law—and delighted when she and

Bobby had the first of their five children, a boy, which they named Robert Wood Johnson IV. With the infant cradled in his arms and Bobby standing at his side, Johnson posed for a photograph under a portrait of his father, thus showing four generations of Robert Wood Johnsons in one picture.

It was a proud moment for the new grandfather. Beneath the surface, however, the hurt was still there for Bobby, and as one colleague remarked: "Bobby never forgave his father for leaving home and divorcing his mother, and that cloud always hung over their relationship."

As the young Johnson rose in the company ranks, there was a steady increase in the number of times he and his father took stubborn stands on opposite sides of a business decision. Then, in 1954, the opportunities for disagreement came more often. The General had decided to form an Executive Committee of the Board of Directors, which, with twenty-three members, had become increasingly unwieldy as a management group. The new Executive Committee had just seven members, including Bobby, who had just turned thirty-four. His father, of course, was chairman of the committee. The arena in which the two had been dueling on issues had suddenly become much smaller.

One of General Johnson's great skills, the ability to manage, also became one of his liabilities when he overmanaged. He perfected the practice of micro-management long before the term became popular. On large projects as well as in small, even petty areas, it could become an obsession. Some who knew him said he couldn't help himself, that he just did things that way. Others were less forgiving. Bobby's promotion to the Executive Committee required that he move his office to "The Penthouse," down the hall from his father's office. Just before the move, the General wrote Bobby suggesting that he make use of some office furniture that was available, adding, "I might remind you that in my office there are no drapes, and I think the classic appearance is very fine." But Bobby had always had modern furniture and artwork in his office, and without hesitation he chose that style for his new Executive Committee office.

The secretaries of executives in the Penthouse offices ate lunch in a small private dining area. In a memo, the General suggested to Bobby that because that dining area was getting crowded he should consider having his secretary eat in the general cafeteria, and the company would pay for it. Bobby replied that his secretary would eat with the others in the private dining area, and she did.

It soon became apparent to the General that Bobby was going to stand his ground on issues both large and small, but because both men had a distaste for open conflict, they managed to keep their differences from flaring into arguments, for the time being. Another factor contributing to the tensions that would build between father and son was the highly competitive environment at the senior executive level at Johnson & Johnson, where ambition ran strong and the rewards for success were great. Those competing to occupy the top rungs on the corporate ladder were not about to concede any advantage to Bobby just because he was the General's son. He would have to run the same race as the others who were hoping someday to succeed the General at the helm. And, in fact, good news about Bobby Johnson's progress was often slow to reach the General's ears.

27

Awe, Respect, and Fear

It was rare for the General to address a large audience of his managers, but on November 23, 1957, nearly five hundred of his executives gathered at the Far Hills Inn in New Jersey for the 70th Anniversary celebration of the founding of Johnson & Johnson. The event, titled "Looking into the Future," included an exhibit of company products from around the world, followed by a reception and then a dinner. Because of conflicts in travel schedules the event was not held in 1956 — the actual anniversary year.

The Far Hills Inn was the site of many Johnson & Johnson events, and the management of the restaurant was aware of the importance of having this special occasion go well. When he arrived in late afternoon and saw the size of the group that had gathered, the General promptly inspected the entire building to check on the number of fire exits. He decided there were too few exits to meet his standards, and he informed the Inn's management that no future company events would be held there until more fire exits were added. He was assured that new fire exits would be added soon, and they were.

At the exhibit focusing on the company's new products, Johnson moved from table to table, commenting with interest, until he had seen everything. During the reception, a large group gathered around him, for many of the younger managers had never seen or met this legendary figure who had led the company for so many years. Johnson chatted quietly, more subdued than usual. He seemed to be moved by the occasion and the size of the management group.

Nearly fifty years had passed since he had joined the company. During those five decades, he had helped to build Johnson & Johnson into one of the world's most successful and highly regarded companies. In many respects, he symbolized Johnson & Johnson, and no one recognized this more than his own people. As for Johnson, he saw the success of the company as his greatest achievement, and he had intense pride in his management. These were *his* people. He cared for them deeply — and they for him.

Following the dinner, he rose to make brief remarks. The crowded room fell silent. His voice was less forceful than usual, and filled with emotion. He spoke about the past, and optimistically about the future. Then he focused on the present.

"This room frightens me a little," he said, "for before me there are four hundred and seventy men — and their wives and children at home. This is a greater responsibility than I had ever realized. To each of you, and to your families, we owe a great sense of responsibility, and I can only pledge that we are dedicated to the success of this business, and it will continue to succeed if we adhere to the principles of our Credo —

> "First, the serving of our customers.
> Then to the people in the plant,
> And then to the management,
> And then to the community,
> And, finally and last, to the stockholders."

He then wished the assembled managers well, and stepped down from the podium. The sound of the standing ovation followed him as he left the room and departed.

In defining his hopes and aspirations for his management, Johnson had once again invoked the Credo as the yardstick by which he wanted them to measure their performance. A few observed that the document was idealistic, and Johnson agreed with them. But he was quick to remind them that written guidelines were better than no guidelines at all because they set goals for all to strive for. He acknowledged that there would be times when they fell short of the objectives. But he always came back to his original premise — that adhering to the Credo was also a sound way to manage a business, and over time would be reflected in its success.

Later in 1957 Johnson wrote a one-page document, which he titled "Our Management Philosophy." The opening line captured the essence of his message:

Our concept of modern management may be summarized in the expression *To Serve*.

The document read as follows:

OUR MANAGEMENT PHILOSOPHY

Our concept of modern management
may be summarized in the expression "to serve."
It is the duty of the leader
to be a servant to those responsible to him.
He accepts the problems of others
and the right of others to help and advise.
High position does not imply the wielding of authority
but rather to inspire others by effort
within the framework of the corporation policy.

We expect little of the organization chart
but much of policies and objectives.
Once these are understood and accepted
we expect management to reach its peak efficiency by
its own energy.

To lead in any human situation
means to give direction to human energy.
It means to be ahead of others in perception of the
goal,
which means reaching such goals in the face of new
problems.
It is the duty of management
to stimulate and develop the aptitudes of others.

To be responsible to others for their progress
is a far cry from the concept of authority with
autocratic control.
It is a question of giving subordinates
not only an understanding of policy
but of thinking independently.
It is a process of participating in other men's
initiatives, stimuli, ideas and incentives.

This concept of command helps to overcome intellectual
stagnation,
the great problem of large organizations,
thus increasing their fertility in the field of ideas.
The greatest responsibility of modern management
is to develop the human intellect
in order that it may express its talent.

When Johnson sent the management philosophy statement to his executive group, it was received with mixed feelings. Some said it was ambiguous, while others felt it impractical to apply. Still others expressed concerns that employees would interpret the statement too literally, thus creating problems for management. After the statement was distributed to a limited number of management people, Johnson sought their views and found little enthusiasm for it, so he decided not to send it to the entire management group. He was disappointed, and said that perhaps the statement was more of an expression of his own personal views. Even so, he adhered to his policy of letting the managers decide what was in the company's best interests. All except the Credo. To Johnson, that document was sacrosanct.

For Johnson, good business began with good management. To emphasize that point, he often resorted to words that summarized his thinking on the subject: "Management is cause," he would say, "all else effect." He also referred to himself as a "student of management," perhaps as a reminder that there was always more to learn. He saw his role as a builder of management teams, and he was inordinately proud of the glowing reputation Johnson & Johnson had earned for developing highly competent managements throughout its vast global network of companies. "My job is creating and managing managements," he declared.

"Trust" was a word Johnson used frequently when talking about his executive group, and he summed up his thoughts in this way: "I acknowledge that I have placed substantial trust in my management. I have done this deliberately for the reason that I am satisfied, after long and close association with these executives, that those who occupy these positions are qualified by character and experience to make the best decisions." Character was important to Johnson.

The intriguing aspect of his policy of decentralization was that it offered young and talented managers the opportunity to build what many viewed as "their own" business. Wherever they were located around the world, there was little interference from Johnson so long as the business was successful and growing. In 1957, the *Wall Street Journal* ran a series on the organizational philosophies and practices of American industry, and one lengthy article was devoted to Johnson's unique approach to the managerial art. He had one reservation about complete deputization of authority, Johnson noted in the article. When a business showed signs of illness, that's when he stepped in. "If a man is doing his job, you leave him alone, but if a business sickness or administrative illness sets in, it may be necessary to call the doctor," he told the Journal writer. "It's like in ordinary life—when the doctor says 'Go to bed' there's no argument."

Johnson's scheme of "associate companies," the *Journal* article pointed out, went far beyond mere divisionalization as applied by many companies. He said that before deciding on his formula for management he had studied the administration techniques used in the Roman army, in Lord Leverhulme's British enterprises, and in the great German chemical combine IG Farben. He concluded that instead of one chef with a very large soup, he would have many cooks and give each one a soup of his own. And to emphasize the need for individual authority, Johnson said he had read and reread Andrew Carnegie's biography. He vividly recalled one particular line: "There is no such thing as a degree of deputization; you either give someone authority or you don't."

At the time, Johnson & Johnson had thirty-two separate companies, twenty-four of them outside the United States. "The parent company prints no policy manuals," the *Journal* article reported. "It merely presents the operating heads with a Credo, which is contained on a single sheet of paper. If a new product or group of products becomes a sizeable entity in itself, it is cut loose into still another company, normally financed out of earnings."

In summing up his philosophy of decentralization, Johnson dealt with the all-important question of central authority: "Where power is an open question, both the central staff and the decentralized people grasp for it. Inasmuch as the central authority has more power to begin with, it soon ends up with everything and the rest become errand boys. This must be prevented in advance. Sometimes the price is high. It's a trying circumstance to stand aside and watch mistakes, but when you start to dilute the idea of local responsibility, the results are unsatisfactory."

Proof of the wisdom of Johnson's management philosophy, the *Journal* article continued, were the spectacular results achieved over many years. The price of the company stock had climbed steadily upward, and even though he was already the company's largest stockholder, Johnson bought additional shares on a regular basis. Purchasing and holding Johnson & Johnson stock was, he said, his way of showing confidence in the company. He flatly refused to discuss the price of shares, and when others welcomed stock splits he was ready with a warning: "Many, perhaps most of the stock splits, have motives that run counter to our desire. They are intended to increase the number of stockholders. They are intended to increase the market price of the stock, and frequently they give the impression that the corporation is rolling forward in success and profit. We had better earn this reputation the real way."

One family member who held a significant number of Johnson & Johnson shares wrote him that she had been urged to diversify, and asked for his advice. "You already have one of the most diversified stocks you can own," he wrote her. Another family member had received the same suggestion, to diversify, from a lawyer and a banker. Johnson responded: "Bankers and lawyers are usually wrong when it comes to investment advice, and bankers, especially, have never been good investors."

When the New York Stock Exchange issued an order requiring its member companies to solicit proxies from its shareholders and to reveal the salaries and stock holdings of its top executives, Johnson became incensed. It was at the time of the 1958 stockholder meeting, and he took that opportunity to blast the Exchange, declaring that he was seriously considering "de-listing" from the Big Board. The financial writers had a field day with Johnson's threat, and the *Newark News*, New Jersey's largest newspaper, took him to task in an editorial:

> General Johnson says he may accept delisting rather than comply with disclosure requirements. His reasons are comprehensive. Publications of such lists is a "disturbing factor" in a company, intrudes on "community relations," is bad for the company's competitive position, and, finally, "no executive likes to have his pockets turned inside out before

the public." He [Johnson] may not like it, but it is one of the penalties that goes with acceptance of the public's investment. . . . His stand must be causing acute distress in his public relations department. His stockholders can't be overjoyed either.

In reality, Johnson's public relations people were amused by the fuss he stirred up, and the stockholders were unwavering in their support of him. In time, the tempest passed. The General resorted to the advice he said he had received years earlier from his friend Bernard Baruch: "Pay no attention to the barking terriers." Still, he never forgave himself for agreeing to take Johnson & Johnson public in 1945, terming it a "basic error." His colleagues listened to this for years, mostly in silence, because no one agreed with him. The stock had served them well.

On numerous occasions Johnson had professed his tolerance for mistakes, and he was once quoted as saying "Mistakes are our most important product." Lofty and tolerant as this sounded, though, not many were anxious to test just *how* tolerant he was of mistakes. One of the bright stars of the marketing group was James E. Burke, who had come to the company from Procter & Gamble and was rapidly rising through the ranks. But shortly after Burke took charge of new consumer products, he made a costly error that led to his first face-to-face meeting with the General. Burke remembered it well:

"I had helped develop a new product that was a failure, and it cost the company a substantial amount of money. General Johnson sent for me, and I was convinced I was going to be fired. I was kind of excited about it because, I thought, well, you gave it your best shot and at least this company has the decency to have the Chairman of the Board fire you.

"I entered his office, and it was a long walk to his desk. He was dictating memos, which he did all the time on blue memo paper that we used to call the 'Blue Blizzard.' He looked up and said: 'Mr. Burke, I understand that you made a decision that has cost this company a great deal of money. Is that true?' 'Yes, sir,' I replied, and with that he stood up and shook my hand and said: 'Congratulations! Making decisions is what business is all about, and you don't make decisions without making mistakes. Don't ever make *that* mistake again, Mr. Burke, but please be sure you make other mistakes.'"

The outcome was fortunate for Jim Burke—and for Johnson & Johnson. Some twenty years later Burke would become Chairman of the Board and CEO and serve with great distinction. The General's tolerance paid off handsomely.

Johnson's associates knew that it was painful for the General to admit his own mistakes, and that he did so with some hesitation. Eric Marsh, a British manager, recalled how Johnson handled one situation. "I was visiting the States, and he invited me to his office for a chat. Out of the blue he asked: 'What do you think of the new Modess packaging?' Without thinking, I blurted out: 'It's the worst packaging I've ever seen on a product.' Then he said, 'Well, I'll have you know that I designed that package.' I was numb. The only thing I could think to say was, 'Well, General, when you make a mistake you sure make a good one.'"

"When I left his office that day," Marsh continued, "I went straight to the personnel office to check out what the severance pay was like. A little while later, he did a really fine thing. He wrote to the president of Personal Products saying that the Modess packaging was bad and that he was responsible for it and that it should be changed. He sent me a copy of the letter. There was no note attached. Nothing. And we never spoke about it again, but the packaging was changed."

·

The old-timers, especially, knew that Johnson was sly as a fox, even when they thought they were putting something over on him. Alcohol was never allowed in the executive dining room, except at the Christmas luncheon. Some overseas companies regularly served drinks at lunch, but when those managers visited New Brunswick they abided by the local rules—except the wily Bill Northam, an indomitable Australian who was a particular favorite of the General's.

Like Johnson, Northam was a sailor, and at the age of fifty-nine the bold Aussie would capture an Olympic Gold Medal in the five-and-a-half-meter yacht class, endearing him to his countrymen. Whenever Northam came to New Brunswick he was an odds-on favorite to join the General for lunch—not once but often. This meant an endless round of questions from Johnson, and, as Northam lamented: "Another foodless day, because you didn't get a chance to put a fork in your mouth, the questions came so fast about the business, and sailing." And, most regrettable, it meant no drink at lunch for Northam.

The enterprising Northam found a way, and he explained how: "I used to arrange with the steward, Valle, to have a snort of whiskey in the kitchen before I went into the dining room to join the General for lunch. One day Valle put it in my tomato juice, and when he served it the General said: 'Bill, your tomato juice is rather dark, isn't it? Is it all right?' 'Oh, yes, General,' I replied. 'The Worcestershire sauce changes the color, you know.' He looked at me, smiled, and said: 'You think you're putting one over on me, don't you?'"

On another occasion, the irrepressible Aussie talked Johnson out of sending him to take a special course at the Harvard Business School. The course, which lasted for many weeks, had a bad reputation at Johnson & Johnson because a number of the dozen or so executives who had been tapped to attend were no longer with the company, and not all left of their own volition. With amusement mixed with trepidation, some executives decided that being picked to go to Harvard was "the kiss of death," and there was much banter about it.

When Northam was called to Johnson's office that day, he said, he felt very apprehensive. "When I entered his office, I said: 'It's about going to Harvard, isn't it, General?' And he replied: 'Yes, Bill, it is.' So then I said, 'You know, General, in Australia I'm the only member of the Board of Directors who didn't attend college, and I guess it must be the same here with you.' He said it was. Then I said: 'You know, I'm the only bloke down there who thinks differently. They all think the same. Have you noticed that?' And he said: 'Bill, I have. You don't have to go to Harvard.' I rolled out of his office fast and right down and collected my bets, and some were betting 100 to 1 that I would have to go."

Some colleagues found it easier to relax in Johnson's company than others. Personality was a factor. Richard V. Mulligan was by nature a relaxed, affable Irishman—some said too relaxed. With little formal education, he had worked his way up in local politics and became mayor of New Brunswick during the Depression years. Mulligan had assisted Johnson on a Community Chest drive in the mid-1930s and made a favorable impression on him by being the first volunteer to get his report in. Mulligan related what happened next:

"He came to my office to thank me, and while there spotted a photo I had of my old friend Eddie Farrington, who had been mayor some years earlier. He asked if I could get him a copy of Eddie's picture. When he left, I called the City Clerk's office, and they had an extra copy. So I had a messenger take it to his office, and it arrived there before he got back. He called to thank me for being so prompt, and asked me if I would join him for lunch some day. Two weeks later I did, and he hired me on the spot. When I got to his office, I noticed that Eddie's photo was on the shelf behind his desk, and it remained there for the next thirty years."

Mulligan joined the company's personnel department, later handled labor relations, and went on to the Board of Directors, thus making the leap from precinct politics to the corporate hierarchy largely on his skills with people. When he arrived at the company, Johnson put Mulligan in charge of the company's "welfare department," created to help employees in need. Mulligan recalled:

"He told me to spend whatever I had to so long as the right people—the needy people—got it. It ranged from a ton of coal to a

[433]

bag of groceries to bailing a guy out of jail after he drank too much. And he told me he didn't want any thank-you letters. Another thing he did: he taught others to be generous. Every morning and night of my life, I say, 'God bless him.' "

Other facets of Johnson's personality drew more condemnation than praise. A newspaper writer once referred to him as being "egocentric," and some of his own people felt that at times he could be too demanding. There was no better evidence of that than in his constant nagging of plant managers over what Johnson termed "good housekeeping." Years earlier he had established himself as the nation's leading pioneer in the "Factories Can Be Beautiful" concept.

Once his new buildings were completed and in operation, he began his incessant — and some believed unreasonable — demands for superior maintenance of the buildings and grounds. And no plant manager felt the sting of his demands and the harshness of some of his "blue memos," more than those who were unfortunate enough to be running plants located between Johnson's home in Princeton and his office in New Brunswick. By varying the route he drove to work each day, Johnson could personally inspect some ten or more company facilities. He thoroughly enjoyed those daily inspections, while managers often found them painful.

By now, Johnson had perfected his formula for building handsome plants in bucolic settings, and when he completed a new addition to his so-called "family of companies" he doted over it like a proud parent. In the spring of 1957, the company opened the sprawling Eastern Surgical Dressing Plant on U.S. Route 1 in North Brunswick, on the well-traveled corridor between New York and Philadelphia. The cluster of connected buildings had more than one million square feet of manufacturing and shipping space, and with its gleaming red, white, and blue facade, large reflecting pool, and vast, carefully manicured lawns, it was soon touted as one of America's most handsome industrial centers.

The new complex was on the route that Johnson most often took between his home and the office, and this made personal inspections convenient for him, and distressing for the plant manager. The morning following one of his visits the inevitable "blue memo" would arrive with his suggestions — for "deep feeding" the birch trees, for making the elm trees look healthier, for ways to coax the ivy to grow higher up the walls, and how to remove rust stains from behind downspouts. He missed nothing, and his follow-up would be as certain as the sun rising.

In one memo he inquired: "You might ask the boys if they want to hire me as inspector." There was no need for that. He already held the job. On his visits, he expressed the desire to "roam about unattended," as he put it, adding that he did not want to "embarrass those who are with me should I decide to inspect remote areas." This usually meant back stairwells and the boiler room — places that the seasoned manager, or one who had been caught before, had carefully checked. But a cracked sidewalk, or cartons piled so high in the warehouse that the bottom one was crushed, tripped up even the veteran managers.

The North Brunswick plant site had hundreds of acres. Not satisfied that he could make a complete inspection in his car or by walking, Johnson decided one day to take a ride on the Pennsylvania Railroad, whose mainline tracks ran directly behind the new plant. That was when he decided that rail passengers should not have their view of his new plant spoiled by seeing the cars in the parking lots. The next day, the order came to landscape the parking lots with tall evergreens that would screen the cars from view. After he once rode the train to Trenton to see what other companies' plant sites looked like, he summed up his impression of some of them in two words: "industrial garbage."

Even the State of New Jersey was not spared from Johnson's wrath when he found that a tract of state-owned land that abutted one of his plant sites on U.S. Route 1 was poorly maintained and not up to his standards. He wrote to the highway commissioner, and when action was slow in coming Johnson declared that henceforth the company would take over the maintenance of the state property, which it did. "Sometimes it is harder to persuade people than to do the job oneself," Johnson said.

His Saturday morning inspections caused managers the most problems. He would drop in at a plant or office and roam around, checking out the entire place. Usually, he encountered a surprised employee who had come in to do some work dressed casually and never expecting to find the Chairman of the Board there. In a friendly and inquisitive manner, Johnson would ask a volley of questions about matters the employee often knew little about but nevertheless made a valiant attempt to answer. The replies to the questions, some accurate and some not, would be referred to in Johnson's follow-up memo to the manager on Monday morning, stating that he had been there, giving his impressions of what he saw, and usually offering suggestions. About the worst way a manager could begin his day on Monday was to be informed that the General had paid a surprise visit on Saturday. He knew, of course, that the inevitable memo would soon be there.

Some of the plant managers grumbled over his constant vigilance and the inspection visits, but they were all smiles when accepting accolades and awards for the appearance of their plants, or when they received letters from total strangers who passed by and were impressed. And those who remembered Johnson's purpose, as expressed three decades earlier, understood what he meant when he said: "We are building not only frameworks of stone and steel, but frameworks of ideas and ideals." Other American industrialists shared these goals, but Johnson was one who led the way.

As he approached his sixty-fifth birthday in April 1958, Johnson showed no indication of retiring. He was still going through the process of evaluating candidates who might succeed him, seeking from them their vision of the company's future. Growth that was too accelerated scared Johnson. "None of us likes to lose volume," he told his management, "but it may be more intelligent to lose some volume and search for opportunities with a greater growth factor over the next twenty-five years." He added: "We must be sure, however, that our ambition to grow does not exceed our capacity to manage."

In the late 1950s, the senior management decided that in order to keep pace with developments in health care it would be necessary for Johnson & Johnson to expand into pharmaceuticals. The General offered strong resistance. He had created within the company a corporate culture that came as close to being a reflection of one man's thinking as any American business, and the thought of diluting that culture by absorbing another company was abhorrent to him. Further, he had an admonition that had a chilling effect on any negotiations for an acquisition — "Never acquire a business when you can't fire the board of directors or the president."

．

Over the years, the company had ventured from its traditional product lines numerous times, most notably with Ortho, which had become a pioneer in products related to family planning and was managed by Philip B. Hofmann, who started in the company as a shipping clerk and was now a senior executive. In trying to persuade Johnson to acquire a pharmaceutical company, Hofmann and his associates pointed to the success that Dr. Philip Levine was having as director of the Ortho Research Foundation. He had brought considerable recognition to the company when he discovered the Rh blood factor. (Later, Levine's colleagues would develop a lifesaving vaccine that was a preventative for Rh hemolytic disease of the newborn.)

Finally Johnson relented and said he would go along with acquiring a pharmaceutical company if, in his words, it would be a "right fit." In 1959 the search ended with the acquisition of McNeil Laboratories Inc., which traced its beginnings to a family-owned drugstore in the mill district of Philadelphia in 1879. It later grew into a successful company that was run by Robert L. McNeil and his two sons, Henry and Robert. McNeil specialized in sedation and muscle-relaxant drugs, and later introduced Tylenol, first a prescription product and later an over-the-counter pain remedy that became hugely successful. Johnson liked the "fit," especially the company's heritage and family ownership.

Shortly after, the company learned of the brilliant pharmacological research of a young Belgian physician, Paul Janssen. Borrowing $1,000 from his physician father, Dr. Janssen had opened a small laboratory, with two assistants, in the town of Beerse, Belgium. Over the course of several years, he discovered two original compounds that became successful pharmaceutical products. From this emerged Janssen Pharmaceutica, still very small and highly skilled in research but lacking marketing prowess. That was Johnson & Johnson's strength, and Janssen Pharmaceutica became part of the family of companies. Paul Janssen went on to become one of the world's most prolific and highly acclaimed pharmacological researchers. Over time, he developed more than seventy compounds that became products, five of which were on the World Health Organization's list of "essential drugs."

For Johnson, the acquisition of McNeil was like bringing new relatives into the family. He dealt with that more easily than he did with parting with 622,000 shares of Johnson & Johnson stock, which was what the $31 million acquisition price amounted to. Parting with company stock was always painful for him. Over time, Johnson developed a degree of rapport with the McNeils, especially with Henry, the son, but for years he continued to grumble about the price that was paid for the company. Over the long term it became a good investment, but Johnson saw only the shares the company had to part with.

Janssen, the distinguished scientist, and Johnson, the maverick businessman, were both complex individuals, incurably inquisitive and frequently stubborn. "He liked people who spoke their minds," Dr. Janssen recalled. "I gathered that most people were afraid of him. I was not. On many occasions we had differences of opinion. There were lots of arguments. He wouldn't yield and I wouldn't yield."

The two remained friends and enjoyed each other's company, even when the discussions became heated. In the area of research, though, Dr. Janssen's patience was often tested. "The General had this idea of cottage research," Dr. Janssen recalled, and that was to hire all these bright people and then build a cottage for them in the middle of the woods somewhere and let them do whatever they wanted. Then they would come out years later with grandiose ideas. I pointed out to him that research was teamwork, certainly in the modern world."

"He was interested in so many things," Dr. Janssen added. "And he was a complicated man. I've never met anyone like him. He's not comparable to anyone I've ever met in my life."

While Johnson had strongly held views on many areas of business, he was wise enough to step aside for progress. His early resistance to building a pharmaceutical business soon changed as the Janssen team began registering success after success. In the years that followed, pharmaceuticals would become the fastest-growing segment of the business.

.

Johnson had his own method of determining how the business was progressing and where the problems were. He did this in the executive dining room of Kilmer House, and it became a daily ritual that was good for the free flow of information and bad for the digestion. Arriving in the dining room promptly, as always, Johnson would sit at his corner table, which had a commanding view of the doorway. Then, as his senior executives arrived for lunch, he would invite one, two, and sometimes three of them to join him at his table. The probing began immediately. "How is such-and-such product doing?" "Tell me about your marketing plans." "Do you have any production problems?" "I've seen your advertising—how can we improve it?" Question after question.

"I never made it more than halfway through the main course," said one executive who was the frequent target of Johnson's lunchtime interrogations.

Being asked by the General to join him for lunch was not as dreaded as it was made out to be in casual conversation. For those executives who had reasonable responses it could be an intriguing and rewarding experience, and many a career in the company got a boost if the General was impressed by what he heard. But when he wasn't satisfied, trouble followed.

The conversations almost always included a "suggestion" or two from Johnson that, like his "blue memos," could result in months of laborious effort. From the other tables in the executive dining room came furtive glances toward Johnson's corner table, and if glances could be interpreted they would have indicated both compassion and envy.

Johnson's unwritten contract with his management was unmistakably clear. He demanded of them loyalty to the company, personal integrity, and proven performance. In return, they received very generous compensation, which included substantial amounts of stock, some of it tied to long-term service. "We manage this business for the long term," he would remind them. He never fired anyone on a whim, only for what he considered just cause. And he always left that unpleasant task to others, but saw to it that the banished left with their pockets full.

There was a mystique about Johnson that generated in those close to him a sense of awe, respect, and affection. His colleagues worried about his health. As one put it: "Physically, he was a rather frail man. He smoked excessively, and when he started to cough you would think he was going to die right in front of you. But he'd catch himself and put the cigarette out. Why he never stopped smoking I'll never know. He was wiry but not strongly built, and he pushed himself about as hard as anybody could."

Between himself and his associates, Johnson had built a barrier that screened out relationships when they became too personal. Bob Dixson explained how this worked: "Friendships and associations were allowed to go just so far. People sensed this, and your conduct was governed by it. Those who were permitted a degree of familiarity with the General knew the boundaries, and confidences that were exchanged between friends were never expressed to him or by him. He didn't permit that. He would never ask you to comment about others in a personal way. If it was about business, yes, but never personal. There was nothing petty about the man. He had no close relationships with anyone, and some thought that included Evie. Basically, he was a very shy person, and some saw him as a very lonely man."

But for someone who did not allow close personal relationships, Johnson could be deeply paternalistic with his colleagues and constantly caring about their well-being, but always in a business-like way. When he went to Roosevelt Hospital in New York for a checkup, he would use the time there to arrange for a program of elaborate annual physical examinations for his executives. He monitored the luncheon menus carefully, insisting that high-calorie foods be avoided. He directed that only modest portions be served, and he was constantly concerned about those who were overweight. His son, Bobby, was inclined toward obesity, and this was a constant source of friction between the two of them. Bobby often had lunch downtown, where he could enjoy his martinis and a meal his father would not approve of.

Johnson's generosity and concern for others was expressed in many ways and with little fanfare. When he learned of employees who were in need, he "made arrangements," as he would say, to take care of the situation. "What better place for a part of our earnings than to give it to our people," he wrote once to the Board of Directors, adding: "Some have ample independent resources, others less so. We should plan our actions accordingly."

When a manager of one of his Texas plants suffered a serious illness and was sent to Arizona to recuperate, Johnson was concerned that the man would not have enough visitors. So he asked for a list of every salesman in the company who traveled to Phoenix, and then wrote a personal note to each of them, asking them to pay a visit to the ill man even if they had never met him. "Just talking about the business will cheer him up," Johnson wrote. Soon the manager had a steady stream of visitors, and they did cheer him.

If he didn't get the action he wanted in a particular situation, he would take action himself. In one case, when Canada passed a 19 percent increase in personal income taxes, Johnson telephoned the managers there and ordered a 20 percent salary increase for everyone on the payroll in Canada. "He did it without consulting us," a senior executive said, "because he knew we would have tried to talk him out of it."

The company's flight operations reported directly to Johnson, and he had strict rules governing the use of corporate aircraft. No expense was spared in purchasing the best equipment and servicing the aircraft, and stringent safety measures were always adhered to. The General was devastated when, on December 15, 1958, one of the company's planes, a Lockheed Lodestar, got caught in a blinding snowstorm and crashed in a desolate area of Rhode Island, killing all seven aboard—three crew and four company executives. The storm had come up suddenly, surprising weather forecasters. Ice quickly formed in the carburetors and manifolds of the engines, and the plane lost power and crashed. For months, Johnson mourned the loss of what he called "my business family" and vigorously defended the pilot's decision to fly on to his Boston destination instead of altering his course and trying to fly out of the storm.

28

DEAR MR. PRESIDENT

THE term "Cold War" became a familiar part of the American lexicon in the late 1950s. Throughout the nation there were growing fears about Russia's military and nuclear capabilities, and when the Soviets sent *Sputnik* into orbit on October 4, 1957, it was there for all to see, marvel at, and worry about. Circling the earth fifteen times a day and shining brightly in the clear night sky, *Sputnik* served as a wake-up call for many Americans.

In Washington, the Eisenhower administration was cautious about expressing concern that might trigger a wave of panic, but behind closed doors the level of anxiety was high. "The nation faces the possibility of direct, swift attack by weapons of unprecedented destructive power," the commander of the Veterans of Foreign Wars told a U.S. Senate Committee on Preparedness. Many families followed civil defense advice and began storing food and water in their basements, and some even purchased low-cost bomb shelters that a new breed of entrepreneur was advertising in newspapers. Industry too was stirred into action, as *Business Week* magazine noted: "With mounting concerns over the possibility of a nuclear attack, the time is evidently ripe for a new specialty in management consulting—planning to insure industrial survival in the event of atomic war."

Ever since sounding the alarm in his sobering article "Dig, Son, Dig," Johnson had been planning ways to protect his factories and employees in a nuclear attack. From a practical standpoint, everyone knew there was no protection from the destruction wrought by an atomic bomb, but to make no preparations made little sense and did nothing for morale. Johnson wrote his associates: "We feel a moral responsibility to do what we can for those who work for us while they are in their place of work." He also reminded them that Johnson & Johnson had supplied the military with critical medical products during every conflict since the Spanish-American War. That proud record, he said, must be continued, which meant protecting manufacturing as best they could.

Most companies assigned the civil defense responsibility to a special task force, but at Johnson & Johnson the General took charge. It was a project ideally suited to his penchant for detail. He sought the advice of civil defense experts who had worked for the government, and he attended numerous confidential briefings in Washington, some with his friend and adviser Donald J. Hittle, a retired Marine Corps general. When Johnson learned that all his factories in three states, New Jersey, Illinois, and California, were in the "prime target area," it gave a greater sense of urgency to his planning.

The senior management was much more concerned about making forecasts for the next quarter than they were about atomic bombs, but in one report Johnson wrote: "We continue to study all types of shelters, large-scale ones for plants and administrative buildings, as well as home shelters, management control centers, underground caves, surplus Pullman railroad cars, ships, distant locations to be reached by airplane, and secure areas in a valley with steep hills." After numerous inspection trips by helicopter, Johnson leased two hundred acres near Elk Mountain in northeastern Pennsylvania, where the terrain offered the type of protection that the experts recommended. The area, Johnson decided, could be used both as a corporate control center and as an evacuation site.

The General began thinking about building the nation's first underground manufacturing plant to produce medical supplies. It should be an Ethicon plant, he decided, because that company produced the surgical sutures essential in any emergency. Ethicon management reminded Johnson that climate control and the elimination of moisture were critical in the production of sutures, and that an underground plant would pose major technical problems. Johnson listened patiently but was not dissuaded. "We have a responsibility that overshadows all else, and that is the security of the country with respect to an essential surgical product," he responded. That ended the discussion, but it would be years before the problems were overcome and the underground plant was finally completed at San Angelo, Texas.

In looking at the overall civil defense planning, Johnson was concerned about how long his workers would be willing to remain in a company shelter in an emergency. "Employees who were in shelters would want to go to be with their families," he told his managers. "They would not be willing to stay in company shelters for long." So he decided to expand the project to include the testing of various designs of home shelters. Despite the seriousness of the project, it soon developed amusing aspects. First, he asked for volunteers. Actually, Johnson suggested "candidates"—that was his usual method of "recruiting" volunteers.

Construction of Johnson's underground test shelters in volunteers' backyards began with a power shovel and a bulldozer digging gaping holes in the lawn. Then a work crew spent weeks building the concrete, metal, and wood structure large enough to accommodate four people and food and water to last for several weeks. Fate, and a wonderful good nature, made Doris Little, a gentle, soft-spoken British lady who was a senior member of Johnson's secretarial corps—his "office family"—the first "volunteer." She lived next to the Ethicon plant in Somerville, in a home that once had a large, sweeping back lawn, until the invasion of the earth movers. But the doughty Mrs. Little soon turned "superintendent" and immersed herself in the details of construction so she could give daily progress reports to Johnson. In his reports to management, he referred to it as "Mrs. Little's Shelter," and that pleased her and drove her to become more knowledgeable about the technical aspects of building bomb shelters.

After the first heavy rainfall, Mrs. Little reported to Johnson that her shelter had become a quagmire. Then the heater that was added to reduce dampness made it difficult for her to breathe. And she had problems operating the long-range radio receiver and the Geiger counter. But through it all, the indomitable Mrs. Little persevered, and emerged somewhat of a heroine.

Another "volunteer" was Philip Hofmann, who had become Chairman of the Executive Committee and whose country estate had ample room for an all-metal shelter that protruded slightly above ground under a mound of dirt. When Hofmann tried to enter the shelter, he could barely wedge his six-foot-five-inch frame through the entrance.

Johnson would personally inspect the test sites, always with a new and sometimes involved idea for change. Meanwhile, the rolling lawns of his Princeton estate, Longleat, remained as impeccable as ever. He had wisely put his shelter in a corner of the cellar.

·

The early years of the Eisenhower administration were marked by the President's enormous popularity and the "I Like Ike" sentiment that swept him into office. His war hero and father image served to unify the nation, notably during the Korean War. But over time, some of his presidential decisions began to rankle the Republican hierarchy and blossom into open criticism.

A week before Eisenhower began his second term, Johnson, prone to pontificating, wrote the President and urged him to avoid "second term arrogance and willfulness."

Dear Mr. President:
Among the more malignant infections peculiar to Washington is that of "second term arrogance and willfulness." This usually affects White

House and State Department staff with particular virulence. We have lived through two epidemics in recent times, and I trust that we are not threatened with another.

This infection, like others, is as likely to affect one's political friends as it is one's political opponents. A strange aspect of this malady is that the patient is usually unaware of the affliction.

In modern times, the Congress has exhibited a fine sense of judgment and responsibility. More than that, Congress is immune to this disease. It may be wise for Congress to retain the power of decision in matters of great consequence.

Best wishes,

Sincerely yours,
Robert W. Johnson

In his reply, Eisenhower assured Johnson that his team at the White House would avoid those pitfalls. That did not turn out to be the case, however, for as the President's laxity and seeming indifference grew, so did the criticism. His shining image was then tarnished by his handling of the much publicized Sherman Adams incident. A former governor of Massachusetts and now Eisenhower's chief of staff, Adams was accused of interceding with government agencies on behalf of a New England textile manufacturer, and of accepting gifts from him, including the famous $69 vicuna coat. When Adams refused to accede to a clamor for him to resign, an impatient and critical press turned to Eisenhower for action. The President, who had always been portrayed by his supporters as the essence of political propriety, refused to fire Adams. Wrote one journalist: "The high priest of sanitary government has been caught defiling the altar." Adams eventually resigned, but Eisenhower's image had been seriously damaged.

In a letter to a business friend, Johnson laid out his complaints about Eisenhower: "Certainly, he is a fine, honest man, but in the very field which he professed to know more than anyone in the country, namely the military, he made some of his greatest mistakes—his opposition to the Polaris submarine, opposition to aircraft carriers, opposition to modernized ground forces, and a lack of foresight in space vehicles. And, he was one of the most important partners in establishing the island of Berlin, a problem that has plagued the world ever since."

Hoping to bring about change, Johnson drafted a letter containing these same criticisms of the Eisenhower administration and said he planned to send it to three hundred Republican leaders. But first he sent a copy to White House aide Henry Roemer McPhee and asked if he could discuss the letter's content with someone on the staff. McPhee replied that all members of the White House staff were very busy, so Johnson sent the letters to the Republican leaders. A few days later, he received a letter from McPhee inviting him to come to the White House "to meet with any particular member of the staff you would like to talk to. . . ." Johnson decided there was no longer any need for a meeting.

Though a prolific writer of letters and memos, Johnson did not consider himself a chronic complainer. That was true, but some felt that at times he could be too critical and dogmatic in his views. There was no disagreement, however, about Johnson's readiness, even eagerness, to do battle when he thought he was right.

The election of John F. Kennedy brought no joy to Johnson, who had offered modest financial and political support for Richard M. Nixon's candidacy. Following Kennedy's election, Johnson sent a warm note of congratulations to his old friend Joseph Kennedy, saying how proud he must be of his son. It would not be long, however, before Johnson was firing a shot across the bow of the Kennedy presidency.

Johnson's most recent foray into New Jersey politics had not gone well. For years Johnson had been working to revive New Jersey's Old Guard Republicans, who through age and by failing to keep up with the times had lost much of their influence. When U.S. Senator Clifford P. Case sought reelection, the Old Guard conservatives, citing Case's liberal tendencies, decided to oppose him. Johnson hosted a dinner for about fifty of the state's wealthy conservatives at the Far Hills Inn (which now had an abundance of fire exits). When Johnson's turn came to speak, his words had a familiar, historical ring: "We must pledge to each other our lives, our fortunes, and our sacred honor for the restoration of the conservative spirit to Republican politics in New Jersey."

This was far more than anyone present, including Johnson, was willing to do for the good of the party.

He then outlined to the group a plan that he said would become "a political structure at the precinct level, led by patriots who are unshakably committed to the principles of *natural rights*." The following day, the newspapers jumped on Johnson's political strategy and his reference to "natural rights." The headline of Roscoe Drummond's column in the *New York Herald Tribune* read "How To Wreck Republicans." Another reporter who was suspicious of the meaning of "natural rights" did some research and concluded that it could be traced to those Greek philosophers who taught that the only valid right was the right of the strong to rule.

Cast in this light, Johnson's comments did little to help the Old Guard cause. As it turned out, his campaign against Case suffered another blow when the New Jersey Conference for the Promotion of Better Government, an organization Johnson helped to found, backed the senator for reelection. Case was reelected by a wide margin.

Despite his failed efforts to resuscitate the Old Guard that year, Johnson was often sought out by political reporters. They felt he had insight into New Jersey politics, always had a new plan for improving the state, and was rarely without a quotable quote on politicians who stymied progress. Johnson had once commented: "Politicians are salesmen who have accomplished the impossible. Repeatedly they sell us a bill of goods or a scheme to solve our problems, and then they ask the Internal Revenue Service to send us a bill for twice what it is worth."

He could be just as hard on journalists. "Reporters," he said, "have developed plush habits. They sit at a typewriter or in a saloon and make a story from the news services and by scanning the boiler plate releases." That quote was not as popular with the press as the one that described politicians.

It was as an innovator and behind-the-scenes planner that Johnson contributed the most to progress in New Jersey, working with elected officials of both parties. After Alfred Driscoll, whom Johnson had "discovered" in the lower echelons of state politics and then helped get elected governor, Robert B. Meyner, a Democrat, became governor. Meyner served two terms and was succeeded by Richard J. Hughes, also a Democrat. When it came to projects that benefited New Jersey, Johnson had no compunction about working with Democrats, and in fact he became good friends with Meyner and Hughes, as well as neighbors of both of them, in Princeton. Johnson's former home, Morven, was now the governor's residence, and it was but a short distance from his estate, Longleat.

Hughes recalled the first time he met Johnson — many years before he was elected governor, and at the time that New Jersey was making critical decisions about the New Jersey Turnpike. "I was then the Democratic leader of Mercer County," Hughes said, "and the powers in the state were called to New Brunswick to finalize plans for the Turnpike. Some of those present were very skeptical and asked, 'When will New Jersey ever need a six-lane highway running through the state?' But that night Bob Johnson provided the fireworks and the enthusiasm that turned the doubters around, and we approved the plan for the larger Turnpike. And, of course, the skeptics were wrong and Johnson's vision was right. The Turnpike now has twelve lanes in many places."

When the Turnpike plan was finally approved and the project was under way, Johnson "volunteered" the services of George Smith, president of Johnson & Johnson, to serve as one of three Turnpike commissioners. With Johnson's support and guidance, Smith helped steer the Turnpike project through the long and difficult financing and construction stages.

While the public service of Smith and other executives of Johnson & Johnson was applauded by many, there were those in the company who thought Johnson carried his conviction too far. "Some felt that he did the business a disservice by elevating public service beyond its proper place," one of his executives once commented — privately, of course. That view was shared by other industrial leaders who criticized Johnson for asking too much from business, and particularly the extensive time commitments required of their senior management people. "A do-gooder," they grumbled.

During his two terms as governor, Meyner sought Johnson's help on various state projects. "We agreed on some things and fought on others," the governor recalled, "especially on civil defense. I was against the General and Nelson Rockefeller on that issue, and we argued and argued. But on other major New Jersey projects, like developing Spruce Run and Round Valley as major new sources of water supply, he gave me strong support and helped me overcome some opposition. I had a great respect for him."

Not long after taking office, Meyner began to acquire a reputation for unremitting frugality, a quality that Johnson admired in public officials. Hughes quipped: "I always told Bob Meyner that before he would spend a quarter he would look at both sides of it and weep." And Brendon Byrne, a subsequent New Jersey governor, remembered that when he took office he called Meyner and asked him whether he could recall what his salary was when he was governor. "I don't remember," Byrne quoted Meyner as saying, "but if you are interested in knowing, I will go home and count it."

Meyner was the first governor to live at Morven after it became the governor's residence. His wife, Helen, was a cousin of Adlai Stevenson, and she later served two terms in the U.S. Congress, where she built on her reputation for being outspoken and forthright. Once settled in Morven, the Meyners began entertaining there regularly (at taxpayer expense, of course), and their guest lists were studded with Democrat bigwigs — Harry Truman, Eleanor

Roosevelt, John F. Kennedy, Lyndon Johnson. Even Fidel Castro attended one party, which must have given Johnson a sleepless night at his home up the road.

The governor and Helen frequently went to Florida as houseguests of the Johnsons at Indian Creek. "Your room is ready," Johnson would write them, in words he used with many of his friends. "We went there often," Meyner recalled, "but one time something Helen said almost ended our friendship. Helen was seated next to the General, and during dinner she commented: 'General, in a democracy such as ours, don't you think it would be a good idea if everyone started from scratch?' The General saw this as a dig at those who had inherited money and he was furious. I expected to have our bags packed and to be sent on our way!"

Amused at the retelling of the story, Helen added: "I liked the General, but he didn't like women intellectually very much. I felt that he thought they should be in the bedroom and the kitchen — and maybe not the kitchen, because they didn't live that way. I found him hard to talk to about a world event or something that I would have liked to talk about."

Helen Meyner was not alone in that assessment. Though it was before the time that the term "male chauvinist" came into vogue, Johnson would have qualified as one. Periodically, he made attempts to add women executives to senior positions on his staff — more women than men were employed by Johnson & Johnson overall — but it was never a concerted effort on his part. It was still the era when male guests adjourned to the library for cigars, brandy, and discussion, and the ladies retreated elsewhere.

At dinner parties, especially his own, Johnson would dominate the discussion. "He was a great conversationalist, but he would monopolize the conversation," a close associate said, "and he was the empirical expert on everything. He enjoyed being the center of attention, and that put some people off. Not everyone liked him. But the people in the company, those who saw all sides of him, idolized him — well, most of them.

"Still, getting invited to one of his dinner parties was considered very special for people in the company, though the ladies fretted about competing with Evie's couturier gowns and lavish jewels. It was important to be there precisely at six, so at five-thirty the company people would be riding up and down Rosedale Road. By the time we went through the gate a few minutes before six we knew exactly who was coming. One time Governor Meyner and the president of Harvard were there. They were always interesting dinner parties."

When Meyner ran for his second term as governor, he was opposed by State Senator Malcolm S. Forbes, publisher of *Forbes* magazine and widely viewed as a maverick Republican candidate. Johnson offered only token support for Forbes, who was roundly defeated by the incumbent governor. After losing that election, Forbes faded from New Jersey politics, but he remained a popular figure in the state. Looking for an excuse for this latest Republican defeat, Johnson accused Forbes of contributing to the further downfall of the Republican Party in New Jersey, whereupon some political writers said that Johnson too had contributed to the party's downslide.

While Johnson could lend support to a Democratic candidate or cause, he was still firmly anchored as a conservative Republican. He once explained his politics this way: "In my early political days I fought for the wage-hour bill and certain carefully selected modern legislative actions. In recent years, I have been labeled a reactionary. This is wrong, but it is the luck of the draw."

He could criticize Republicans just as readily as Democrats. When one of his senior executives, Richard B. Sellars, was tapped to become treasurer of the National Republican Committee, Johnson gave his approval, but described the committee as "little more than a haunted house" and predicted that becoming treasurer would be a frustrating experience. Sellars survived nicely, and a decade later became Chairman and Chief Executive Officer of Johnson & Johnson.

When Johnson became depressed over the plight of the Republican Party in New Jersey, his old friend Congressman Robert W. Kean often lifted his spirits. Johnson admired Kean for his twenty years of service in Congress and for his steadying influence on the party. Webster B. Todd, the patient and persevering chairman of the Republican State Committee, had difficulty keeping Johnson in the fold of the party faithful.

Once Todd telephoned Johnson to try to pacify him over the selection of a candidate. Johnson, who taped and made transcripts of many of his phone calls, told Todd: "I'm finished. I have washed my hands of it [the party]. I have crossed the road, and if you see a fellow going up the road and you see his back, that will be me. So you can forget me." Todd replied: "You can say 'Forget you,' but I can't forget you." Johnson eventually came around, commending Todd for "the days, weeks, months, and years you give to better government." Congressman Kean's son, Thomas H. Kean, and the party chairman's daughter, Christine Todd Whitman, both became distinguished governors of New Jersey.

In 1961 Richard Hughes emerged as the Democratic candidate for governor but was not expected to win. A former judge and assistant U.S. attorney general, and an excellent campaigner, Hughes won by a slim margin. He and his large family moved into Morven and became friends of the Johnsons.

"I knew that the General had added an outdoor pool at Morven when he lived there," Hughes said later, "but then I discovered the pool had no shallow end to accommodate children. This didn't bother Betty or me because all our kids were 'water dogs.' Then we heard the story that the General had omitted the shallow end to discourage the patronage of young people who, he was convinced, found much delight in urinating in swimming pools."

Throughout the years Hughes was governor, he often called on Johnson for help. "One day at Morven," Hughes recalled, "I told him I was going to seek a $750 million bond issue, and he said he thought it would be too rich for the people's blood. Then I enumer-

Evie

General Robert
Wood Johnson

Longleat, photographed by Cecil Beaton on a weekend visit

Night life in
New York

Sailing on the
Queen Mary

Our Credo

WE BELIEVE THAT OUR FIRST RESPONSIBILITY IS TO THE DOCTORS, NURSES, HOSPITALS,
MOTHERS, AND ALL OTHERS WHO USE OUR PRODUCTS.
OUR PRODUCTS MUST ALWAYS BE OF THE HIGHEST QUALITY.
WE MUST CONSTANTLY STRIVE TO REDUCE THE COST OF THESE PRODUCTS.
OUR ORDERS MUST BE PROMPTLY AND ACCURATELY FILLED.
OUR DEALERS MUST MAKE A FAIR PROFIT.

*

OUR SECOND RESPONSIBILITY IS TO THOSE WHO WORK WITH US —
THE MEN AND WOMEN IN OUR PLANTS AND OFFICES.
THEY MUST HAVE A SENSE OF SECURITY IN THEIR JOBS.
WAGES MUST BE FAIR AND ADEQUATE,
MANAGEMENT JUST, HOURS REASONABLE, AND WORKING CONDITIONS CLEAN AND ORDERLY.
EMPLOYEES SHOULD HAVE AN ORGANIZED SYSTEM FOR SUGGESTIONS AND COMPLAINTS.
SUPERVISORS AND DEPARTMENT HEADS MUST BE QUALIFIED AND FAIR MINDED.
THERE MUST BE OPPORTUNITY FOR ADVANCEMENT — FOR THOSE QUALIFIED
AND EACH PERSON MUST BE CONSIDERED AN INDIVIDUAL
STANDING ON HIS OWN DIGNITY AND MERIT.

*

OUR THIRD RESPONSIBILITY IS TO OUR MANAGEMENT.
OUR EXECUTIVES MUST BE PERSONS OF TALENT, EDUCATION, EXPERIENCE AND ABILITY.
THEY MUST BE PERSONS OF COMMON SENSE AND FULL UNDERSTANDING.

*

OUR FOURTH RESPONSIBILITY IS TO THE COMMUNITIES IN WHICH WE LIVE.
WE MUST BE A GOOD CITIZEN — SUPPORT GOOD WORKS AND CHARITY,
AND BEAR OUR FAIR SHARE OF TAXES.
WE MUST MAINTAIN IN GOOD ORDER THE PROPERTY WE ARE PRIVILEGED TO USE.
WE MUST PARTICIPATE IN PROMOTION OF CIVIC IMPROVEMENT,
HEALTH, EDUCATION AND GOOD GOVERNMENT,
AND ACQUAINT THE COMMUNITY WITH OUR ACTIVITIES.

*

OUR FIFTH AND LAST RESPONSIBILITY IS TO OUR STOCKHOLDERS.
BUSINESS MUST MAKE A SOUND PROFIT.
RESERVES MUST BE CREATED, RESEARCH MUST BE CARRIED ON,
ADVENTUROUS PROGRAMS DEVELOPED, AND MISTAKES PAID FOR.
ADVERSE TIMES MUST BE PROVIDED FOR, ADEQUATE TAXES PAID, NEW MACHINES PURCHASED,
NEW PLANTS BUILT, NEW PRODUCTS LAUNCHED, AND NEW SALES PLANS DEVELOPED.
WE MUST EXPERIMENT WITH NEW IDEAS.
WHEN THESE THINGS HAVE BEEN DONE THE STOCKHOLDER SHOULD RECEIVE A FAIR RETURN.
WE ARE DETERMINED WITH THE HELP OF GOD'S GRACE,
TO FULFILL THESE OBLIGATIONS TO THE BEST OF OUR ABILITY.

* * *

Johnson & Johnson

Credo/1948

RWJ built scores of beautiful plants and modern workplaces

Four generations of Robert Wood Johnsons

Bobby

Sheila

Richard B. Sellars and RWJ

Evie and Bob in Miami

Sirena, known as "Evie's boat"

The rugged *Gerda*

ated item by item the desperate needs we faced in the state, and he said: 'If New Jersey needs it, let's go for it!' He and Guy Gabrielson, who had been treasurer of the Republican National Committee, endorsed the bond issue, and a newspaper headline read 'Big GOP Guns Boom Bond Issue.' But everybody else was against us. Labor left me, as did the Chamber of Commerce and all of business. The bond issue lost, and I was crushed because I had campaigned harder for it than I had for my own election. The morning after the bond issue vote, the General left on the front porch of Morven a bottle of very old brandy as a consolation prize, and a note that said: 'Keep on fighting!' It was a very nice gesture."

Hughes the politician was combative and tenacious, but the persona that made him so appealing was his warm, affable nature. The two had an easygoing relationship that softened some of Johnson's harder edges and brought his sense of humor to the surface. Once, when he was inviting himself to Morven to discuss a project, he wrote the governor: "If you have enough food in the house, why not invite me to breakfast some morning next week when you are not getting up at dawn. This will give us both time for a discussion. Furthermore, I do not talk much at breakfast."

.

New Jersey's paralyzing highway traffic problems, and the need to improve all forms of public transportation, remained at the top of Johnson's list of priority projects. He rarely had a short list, but one project that meant a great deal to him personally was the relocation of thousands of Hungarian refugees who fled to the United States following the revolt against Russia.

Johnson never forgot his allegiance to the Hungarian workers who had befriended him in his youth. Thousands of Hungarian refugees were given temporary shelter at nearby Camp Kilmer, which had been vacated by the Army. Johnson then played a leading role in helping some one thousand refugee families find homes in New Brunswick, and many of this group were given jobs at Johnson's company. Moved by the bravery of the Hungarian Freedom

Fighters, Johnson said: "Their love of freedom and their sacrifice should motivate every American to a greater sense of responsibility in the battle of the free world against communism." The American Hungarian Studies Foundation bestowed on Johnson its highest honor, the George Washington Award.

The Sound Government program that Johnson had created years earlier was now an unqualified success. Some 2,200 of his employees all over the country were engaging in forums on civic issues, and 80 held public office. "What this country needs are more *political amateurs* with the mind and the heart to enter government," he wrote in an unpublished article he titled "The Pendulum of Hope." In an earlier article, published by *Dun's Review* and titled "How to Light a Candle," Johnson urged fellow industrialists to encourage their employees to run for office. He had planted the seed for employee involvement in civic affairs and was watching it grow.

Many of Johnson's views on public improvements were ahead of their time and considered farfetched. He predicted, for example, that high-rise public housing would not work and that the buildings would eventually have to be demolished. But this came at a time when cities were just erecting some of the high-rise housing projects he said would be doomed to failure. He also recommended tearing down ghettos and starting all over—an idea he expressed in a letter to his publisher friend Hugh Boyd: "We should raze all the major Negro ghettos in the United States and give the people living there a fresh start in life with new housing." The cost, Johnson said, should be taken out of funds allocated for foreign aid.

From his office window, Johnson watched as the tidal waters of the Raritan River became more and more polluted with industrial waste from the scores of companies that had settled along its banks in a dozen towns upriver. With each change of tide, the thick, black sludge washed onto the banks of the pristine public parkland that he and Seward had provided years earlier. Here was a problem he could help eradicate, though it would take years of effort and vast amounts of public funds.

[456]

He assigned a chief aide, H. Mat Adams, to head the project and rally the support of the communities and industry in the Raritan Valley. Johnson attended countless meetings in support of the project, and after years of effort a giant trunk sewer system was built. Johnson kept watch from his office window, and as he saw the waters become cleaner, his memos to Adams became more encouraging — until, finally, he declared victory.

The growing problem of New Jersey's horrendous traffic jams and inadequate public transportation systems for commuting to New York was addressed by Johnson over several years. "The problem is colossal, and it will take a crusade to correct it," he declared. The "crusade" that he tried to inspire never materialized. Contributing to the traffic bottlenecks at the river crossings to Manhattan was the vast number of cars and trucks now traveling on the New Jersey Turnpike. Ironically, Johnson had pressed for the wider turnpike, which now became the problem — too many vehicles funneling into the bridge crossings and two river crossings, the Hudson and the Lincoln Tunnels. Constructing new tunnel crossings and bridges posed serious cost problems, as well as endless debates over the land in both states that would be required to accommodate approach roads.

When Johnson suggested that the approach to an expanded Hudson Tunnel could be built in Chinatown in New York, there was little interest in his idea. "Some feel that I represent a past era," he once remarked. "This is amusing to me, as my principal job is planning for the next twenty-five years. My sights are geared forward." Discouraged by the lack of progress on developing a plan for transportation needs in the decades ahead, Johnson decided to sponsor an exhibit and a conference to consider bold new approaches. For several months he orchestrated the exhibit, a panorama of sketches and models ranging from swift monorail trains to sleek commuter helicopters. The event, staged at Rutgers University, attracted many New York and New Jersey officials who were temporarily inspired by what they saw and heard. But their enthusiasm soon subsided, and the planning reverted to the less ambitious goals.

An underlying reason for wanting to improve the flow of people between New York and New Jersey was the frightful possibility of an atomic attack on Manhattan that would result in evacuation of the island. It took no study to determine that New York City could not be evacuated in a safe and orderly way. Those who scoffed at the possibility of an atomic threat revised their thinking as a result of the Cuban Missile Crisis — later described as "the week that shook the world."

In late October 1962, after American U-2 aircraft detected the presence of Soviet missile sites in Cuba, the tense standoff began. On October 22, in the most blunt speech of his presidency, John F. Kennedy revealed to the nation that the Soviet Union had broken its promise, lied to the United States, and started to build offensive missile and bomber bases in Cuba, only ninety miles off American shores. Kennedy announced an air and sea blockade to prevent the Soviets from landing offensive missiles in Cuba. Soviet Premier Nikita Khrushchev threatened to retaliate against the United States for the blockade. New intelligence reports said that construction work at the Cuban missile sites was speeding up. Tensions mounted as the world waited for the final showdown, which came when the Soviets backed down and Khrushchev ordered his ships to return and the launch sites to be dismantled.

Johnson laid the blame for the situation leading to the Cuban Missile Crisis at the doorstep of the State Department, which he believed was populated by ineffective bureaucrats. "We should suspend the Civil Service rules in the State Department for ten years, clean house there, and begin all over with new people," he said. Then he fired off a letter to President Kennedy, recommending that the President himself examine the level of State Department competence.

There was other unrest in the nation. The steel industry was struggling through the longest strike in its history, and Johnson took this opportunity to restate the "harmony in the workplace" message contained in "Human Relations in Modern Business," published a decade earlier. In an advertisement in the Jesuit magazine *America* Johnson stated: "If religion is what most Americans say they believe it to be, then religious principles should guide human relationships in business and industry. Such principles might well be the key to better labor-management relations." The ad then enumerated ways in which the document had been an influence: it had been a textbook for courses in human relations at twenty-eight colleges, more than 100,000 copies were now in circulation, and it had been translated into seven other languages.

While Johnson saw labor as a thorn in the side of industry, he often viewed government as the greater enemy of business. In the spring of 1962, at a meeting in the Oval Office, President Kennedy castigated business during a heated discussion with representatives of the United States Steel Corporation, which had just initiated a price increase for steel. Claiming that the move was against the public interest and dangerously inflationary, Kennedy said angrily: "My father always told me that all businessmen were sons-of-bitches, but I never believed it until now!"

The next morning, when Johnson read the account of the meeting in the *New York Times*, and the President's remark about businessmen, he was furious and marked the words with the heavy black pencil he always used for emphasis. At the time, Joseph Kennedy was convalescing at a New York hospital and receiving no visitors. The following week, and still fuming, Johnson wrote to Rose Kennedy saying he would like to visit her ailing husband—and assuring her, perhaps deceptively, that he had "nothing to talk about and no mission." Johnson's colleagues surmised that he was itching to confront Joseph Kennedy about his "S.O.B." remarks. A wise Rose Kennedy decided Johnson should not visit her husband in the hospital, which was probably good for Kennedy's recovery.

The turbulence of the 1960s—bringing student uprisings, civil disorder, and a loosening of moral behavior—was difficult for

Johnson and others in his generation to adjust to. Sheila summed it up best: "The 1960s were very hard on my father." Following one student outburst, Johnson wrote to Sheila: "As far as I can see, students throughout the world have become a source of uncontrolled bad manners." And whenever he suspected that Sheila herself might be developing what he termed "more liberal tendencies," he tugged hard on the parental reins.

To a colleague, Johnson wrote: "I am getting so allergic to the nonsense of our times that I sometimes wonder if I should have an opinion on anything." Then, quickly recovering from this aberrant thought, he added: "However, I shall continue to have opinions and express them." Whereupon he did: "I believe that our wonderful country has drifted into an acceptance of mediocrity. More than that, we have made a virtue of mediocrity."

It was one thing for Johnson to complain, but it was uncharacteristic for him to sound depressed, as he did in a letter to his nephew, Mead Johnson: "Certainly there is almost everything wrong as far as the world and our country are concerned, but in the meantime my solace is to work daily at the job. I have often thought what I would do if I did not have my work. Certainly it would be a difficult experience."

To Robert Wood Johnson, work continued to be a refuge and a constant companion. The work ethic was so important to him that he could not bring himself to recognize that in recent years he had gradually delegated some of his responsibilities without abdicating his role of ultimate authority. This reduced his work load and allowed him more time for his other interests, which often brought him both joy and despair. And sometimes his joy triggered someone else's despair.

29

MADISON AVENUE'S
NIGHTMARE

WHEN the train pulled into the railroad station in Boston in 1933 and a young Philip Hofmann lowered his lanky, six-foot-five-inch frame to the platform, his new boss, Harry Brandhorst, was there to greet the new junior salesman sent from New Brunswick for training. He remembers taking one look at Hofmann and exclaiming aloud, "Oh, my God!"

Hofmann wore a bulky beaver coat, gray spats on his well-shined shoes, a derby that made him appear even taller than he was, and pince-nez glasses perched on his nose. Clenched between his teeth was a large cigar, though not so large as to hide his broad, friendly, impish smile. When Brandhorst recovered from the initial shock, he took his exuberant young protégé in tow—and eventually turned him into a very good salesman. Hofmann's budding career as a young salesman with the company took him westward, and wherever he went he proved himself to be aggressive, strong-willed, and imaginative. When his salesman's bag of products included the hard-to-sell "Lister's Dog Soap," he decided to train his dog, Sandy, to help him by sitting up and barking at precisely the right moment during the sales pitch. When the act was down pat, Hofmann took the dog on his next tour of western states. "Tell the pharmacist how much you like Lister's Soap," Hofmann would say, and the dog would bark a response. "Tell the pharmacist how much we need this order." Sandy would bark again, usually closing the sale. Years later, Hofmann was still telling the story, adding mischievously, "After that trip with Sandy, those druggists had more Lister's Dog Soap than they could sell in ten years."

Some thirty years later, in the spring of 1961, Robert Wood Johnson personally chose the flamboyant and often irrepressible Philip Hofmann to succeed him as Chairman of the Executive Committee of the Board of Directors. The move came quietly and with little fanfare. The General continued as Chairman of the Board, and many believed that only death would pry him from the position. Johnson & Johnson and its Family of Companies now were the largest health-care enterprise in the world. Though Johnson had taken one hand off the company steering wheel, he would still keep his foot next to the brake pedal and the accelerator, ready to apply pressure when needed.

At the age of sixty-eight, Johnson moved comfortably into the role of patriarch, and that gave him even greater latitude to offer his philosophy and guidance as he saw fit. The fact that he no longer had part of his title meant little. He had become such a legendary figure within Johnson & Johnson that nothing more than his palpable presence was required. But even legends have critics. A small and cautious group, usually those who bore the brunt of his criticism, grumbled privately that the General now had more time to "meddle" in the areas of the business that interested him most. For the most part, however, his help was welcomed, and those who listened to him learned from his wealth of experience—though some of the lessons often came the hard way.

Being adamant was part of Johnson's nature—he was incapable of giving halfhearted opinions. And some of his most intransigent views were voiced on the ethics of advertising. When he thought that the rules he had set down were being stretched, he would fire off another blistering memo. "It has become the ingrained habit of the marketer and the copywriter to step over the edge of simple honesty," he once wrote. "Those persons are following the pattern of the day, but this is not the foundation of our success. Should it be that all of our firms worldwide are the only honest advertisers, then let it be so." He kept emphasizing his key points: "Exaggeration is not good advertising. If you must be off the line, understate rather than overstate. Under no circumstances are our competitors or their products to be referred to in a disparaging or critical manner, directly or indirectly. It is our policy to market and promote our products on the strength of their own superiority not on any weakness of the competition."

Of paramount importance to Johnson was the company's reputation, and he was constantly reminding his associates to keep strengthening it. "We are long on spending money for advertising and promotion to enhance our reputation," he wrote, "but let us be more careful about preserving our reputation." He kept saying that advertising had its limitations. "Industry is built on quality and service, and no amount of advertising, promotion, sales meetings, and similar effort will take the place of quality and service."

The advertising agencies—in particular Young & Rubicam, which for years had the major portion of the company's business—came under heavy fire from Johnson. After attending a three-hour presentation that he felt missed the purpose of the meeting, he exploded. He had asked for a review of what he termed "past mistakes," but instead got a presentation on new approaches. He kept his silence throughout the meeting, but when he returned to the office he dashed off a memo: "It was a repulsive experience. The wall charts were meaningless, and they indulged in a long recitation of complete drivel. The copy was third-rate, and the participants were a large gathering of flannel-headed human scenery." Agency people cringed when they knew he was going to be at a presentation.

Johnson's formula for successful advertising copy was very basic —too basic, his critics claimed—and he kept repeating it: "The copy should be simple. It should have continuity and repetition. The brand name should have major impact. The Johnson & Johnson signature should always be prominent." ("People may be bored hearing this," he admitted, "but we will ignore that phase of it.") His views on what he called the "new generation" were clear: "We are in a generation of advertising and marketing men who have been brought up through various schools and book learning. Through this education, many have lost the art of continuity or simplicity and the basic rules of advertising. They remind me of graduates of what might be termed the 'Julliard School of Musical Chairs.' I advise these men to get out of the way voluntarily. We are coming through, and some may be hurt."

"The General was not as autocratic as many thought," one long-time colleague said. "He honestly, forthrightly, and objectively sought advice, and he would accept advice and guidance and opinions if they were served up and handled in the proper fashion. But people never recognized this. They construed what he was saying as inflexible and a mandate, but it wasn't. If he suspected people were 'yessing' him too much, he would become annoyed."

If the General became interested in a particular product, it usually sent chills down the product director's spine. It meant that Johnson would be popping into the office unannounced, making suggestions, giving advice, and offering terse observations like "It's a good thing your competitor is such a poor advertiser." Worst of all, he would ask an interminable number of questions about market strategy. Anticipating the questions and having the answers ready became a challenge. If he was impressed by what he heard, he often conveyed that to management. Therefore, having the General interested in your product group was both a risk and an opportunity. But it was also nerve-racking.

Of all the products bearing the Johnson & Johnson signature, the one that interested him most was Johnson's Baby Powder. He felt that this product most clearly defined the company in the eyes of the consumer, and he hovered over the advertising, package design, and marketing strategy like a doting parent. For years he had helped to nurture the growth and success of the brand, and he was not about to let anyone tinker with the product without first doing battle with him. The entire marketing group was aware of this, and there were moments of silent prayer for the brand manager and the advertising agency in their encounters with the General over marketing strategy for Johnson's Baby Powder.

The product had an intriguing history, of which Johnson was a part. His old friend Fred Kilmer had presided over the "birth" of baby powder in 1892. In the early years, exhaustive research had been conducted to find just the right fragrance for the powder. After much experimentation, a complex and distinctive floral scent was selected, and it involved more than two hundred ingredients — natural oils, extracts, and aromatic compounds — from all over the world. The tantalizing fragrance was a mixture of floral, musk, and citrus notes with a sweet vanilla-like base. There were overtones of jasmine, lilac, and rose — all present, but in subtle ways. Once the aromatic triumph had been achieved it was never changed.

After generations of acceptance, some 60 percent of all babies born in America were being dusted with Johnson's Baby Powder. The scent became so familiar and so identified with "mother love" that in adults it conjured up fond memories of their childhood. Then came serious scientific research that identified the most important value of baby powder: the intense interaction it generated between mother and child through the sense of touch. The researchers found that the gentle caressing of an infant's body with the silky powder promoted a closeness between mother and child that had a lasting effect on both of them. The benefits of touch became even more important than the benefits of the powder itself.

Even though Johnson's Baby Powder represented only a fraction of the company's worldwide sales, Johnson believed that it deserved his special attention because it had attained a stature none of the other products had. He later agreed to modifications in the advertising and the packaging, but each change meant having another encounter with him. When the switch from tin to plastic containers was made, he even challenged the size of the new sprinkle holes. He would search for baby powder containers that were years old so he could be reassured that the fragrance was still there. (The curator of the Kilmer Museum later reported that a can of baby powder produced eighty years earlier still retained its fragrance.) The product had always generated a flood of laudatory letters from mothers, many claiming that the powder "made their baby smell like a baby should." Comments like that strengthened Johnson's resolve to remain the product's guardian.

He constantly stressed the importance of trademarks and at every opportunity would remind his people: "The trademark protection we are building around the world is the most important thing we have, next to our people. A patent lasts for seventeen years, a trademark lasts forever."

No one disagreed with that philosophy. But some of his other views stirred up disagreement among the younger marketing people—and when that happened Bobby Johnson always seemed to be leading the rebellion and in his father's line of fire. Yet Johnson respected his son's ability, once writing: "Bob Jr. is one of our outstanding modern merchandisers, knowledgeable in the latest tools and realistic in economics." He then added, "But Bob does not have a flair for copy, and those who do not have a flair for copy will find it very difficult to select a person having such a talent."

The General saw himself as a judge of what was good or bad advertising copy. Quick with his criticism, he was also ready with praise when he felt that a company advertisement had hit the mark. One time he wrote: "This is one of the best ads we have ever had!" And then added his usual note of caution: "Now, we will see if it sells baby powder."

Somewhat begrudgingly, he gave credit to the agency for the ads he liked. When he spotted advertising from other companies that he thought was good, he would call attention to that too. Two of his favorites were Revlon and Volkswagen. About Revlon he commented: "We think Charles Revson does the copy himself." And about Volkswagen he wrote: "The ad is a show-stopper, and in this unique case it is said that the agency did it."

•

In his new position, Johnson worked out a close working relationship with Philip Hofmann, urging him to make more decisions without the benefit of a committee. In a memo to Hofmann, he said: "There is merit in group decisions, and there is merit in individual leadership. It is increasingly clear to me that certain types of decisions are best made by the chief and not appropriate for a group." (He later noted, "There are no monuments to committees.") It was clear that Johnson believed the company now had two chiefs, with their respective areas of responsibility. The two men worked well together, and later Hofmann remarked: "I cannot recall the General ever countermanding a major decision that I made."

Johnson's method of examining the state of the company was to do a country-by-country rundown. He provided his input, and Hofmann did the necessary follow-up. He did the same with his other senior executives, and put on paper for them the qualities he believed were most important:

"We have developed what might be described as the 'J&J type.' He is a sound man of good character. He is a man who knows his job and has inherent good judgment. He is a person of reasonably good appearance, neat and orderly in the conduct of his affairs. He has a sense of humor, and is a solid type of person without peculiar, stylized habits or method of address. He is also a man of civic consciousness and responsibility. In my experience, men and women who do not approximate this description will fail to find a place in our industrial family."

One senior executive who fit Johnson's description precisely was Gustav O. Lienhard, the company's no-nonsense Chief Financial Officer. The General, who would introduce him as "the penurious Mr. Lienhard," said that he slept soundly knowing that Lienhard was in charge of the company coffers and eager to take on the spendthrifts at any time. In terms of their fiscal conservativeness, Johnson and Lienhard were blood brothers. It was Lienhard who endorsed Johnson's perpetual campaign to keep strengthening the company's cash position. And while Lienhard lacked Hofmann's salesmanship and flair, he was the perfect person to sit on the cash box.

In the financial area, the most egregious offense in Johnson's view was to tout the price of Johnson & Johnson stock. He would stamp out any attempt to fan further interest in the stock, which was already soaring. The General would confide privately that the stock was overpriced, yet systematically he kept buying more of it for his personal account.

Financial journalists grumbled about the company being "close-mouthed," and in the more than fifteen years that Johnson & Johnson had been a publicly held company, it had yet to hold its first group meeting for stock analysts. Instead, analysts were invited to have a one-on-one meeting with the laconic Lienhard, and when they were seated he would turn his desk clock around to face them and say pleasantly but firmly: "All right, you have thirty minutes to ask questions, but, understand, I'm not going to tell you much." That was the General's kind of financial officer, and during an era in which Johnson & Johnson and a select group of other companies were flying high and seemingly invincible, the approach worked.

In other areas of the business as well, Johnson insisted on the conservative approach. For years he would not allow the annual report to stockholders to contain information about the new products, preferring instead to limit the report to a straightforward financial statement with none of the adornments. "In honesty," he wrote, "if we are to mention new products, we should also list our failures and the old products that we have deleted from the line." While that was not easy to accept, it was difficult to argue against his philosophy.

If he found managers gloating about their successes, he drew them up short. "We have certain illusions of grandeur, and we had better get rid of them," he warned. When he believed that company presidents were losing contact with customers, he told them to "hit the bricks" and get out and meet them. Constantly stressing the importance of building the business for the long term, he would tell young managers not to be preoccupied with producing short-term results and to plan ahead. "Older men are said to look backward," he said, "and younger men forward, but I have found the opposite to be true."

Despite the aggressive style in which he managed people, Johnson also blended in a mixture of diplomacy and old-world charm. The exception to that was when he went on a tirade over what he saw as a serious transgression. Most meetings in his office were congenial. "The General had a knack for putting people at ease, even when they were apprehensive about meeting with him," said Foster B. Whitlock, a longtime colleague. "Number one, he liked people—he truly liked people. He was always searching for information, something new that he didn't know about. You could come into his office all worked up and tense, and he would quickly put you at ease and create an environment where you could be at your very best. He had a rare talent for getting the most out of people. You always did your best in his presence, because he encouraged it and made it possible."

The desk in Johnson's office was a light-wood, round table near the window at one end of the long room. Some maintained that the walk from the door to the desk seemed interminable, but Johnson quickly put most of his visitors at ease. On the table, which rarely had on it more than a single piece of paper for that particular meeting, Johnson had a large telephone console that enabled him to place direct calls to members of the Executive Committee. He did not like spending time on the phone any more than he liked meetings. In later years he installed a recording device on his phone so he could later review typed transcripts of the conversation. Sometimes the transcripts were circulated to others, which was good reason for executives to choose their words carefully.

"To understand the General, you had to accept the fact that he was a perfectionist," one colleague commented. "With him there was no room for error. He also had a tremendous ego, and whatever he did had to be number one—everything. He lived, acted, and behaved in a very controlled way. There are illustrations of his compulsiveness, his impatience, and lack of tolerance, but that was not a consistency of his. On the more important issues he was fair. Because he was so self-disciplined, he demanded that his people be self-disciplined. That was one of his great consistencies, and if you did not have self-discipline, you had a problem."

No one in the executive group came under closer scrutiny from the General than his son, Bobby, who had recently been elevated to the presidency of Johnson & Johnson. More than ever before, Bobby was now under his father's watchful eye in all that he did, business as well as personal. Bobby often had a problem with self-discipline, and the relationship between the two became, over time, more and more tense. Some claimed that the root cause of the problem was Johnson's misguided belief that he could mold his son to his own image, and that he became increasingly disappointed when he found that could not be done. "Bobby didn't fit the image," one of the General's associates commented. "He wanted him to be an alter ego, and he wasn't. We'd all like our sons to grow up in the image we have created for them, but it doesn't work that way. And Bobby rebelled against that."

From a physical standpoint, the molds did not begin to match. The General maintained a wiry physique, and actually measured his weight gains and losses in ounces on a special scale; Bobby was prone to gaining weight, sometimes alarmingly so. The General always dressed impeccably in the finest clothes from the best tailors on Saville Row in London; Bobby was far less interested in sartorial splendor.

"You could see that Bobby was falling short of his father's expectations," a colleague of the two said. "As father and son they were not close at all, except in their mutual love of the company. They tried to be close, but it didn't work. Some said the General didn't know how to be close. A hug here and there would have done wonders. And both of them were very stubborn, which didn't help."

Beyond all of this, basic changes taking place in the marketing areas of the business drove another wedge between father and son. Going into the 1960s, Johnson & Johnson was a relatively unsophisticated consumer products company that was sustaining its growth largely through favorable demographics, the quality of its products, and its strong reputation with the consumer. A paltry amount of market research was being done, and only feeble efforts were directed at developing new products.

The Bobby Johnson generation was attempting to bring about a sea change in marketing strategy at Johnson & Johnson, and he had brought into the company a group of young and highly skilled marketing people—including Jim Burke, from Procter & Gamble —who were blazing new trails and taking risks. This troubled the General, for the traditionalist in him was not always ready to take risks, and it created conflict both within himself and with his son. He would refer to the young marketing group as "Bobby's team" and to his son as being "hardheaded and competitive." Many believed that was an apt description of the General himself.

The kindly, mild-mannered, and now aging Norris Harding, the General's personal assistant, was one of those who did the most fretting about the storm he saw brewing between father and son. Harding's desk was just outside Johnson's office. He tended to the General's personal financial account and was the official gatekeeper. Harding had now been with the company some fifty years, most of them working for Johnson, and during that time he had come to know every bend and blind alley in the General's complex personality. Johnson, who often said they were as close as brothers, once said of Harding, "Every person he ever met was his friend."

The General had a habit of visiting offices unannounced, but he usually let Harding know where he was going. As soon as Johnson was out of earshot, Harding would call ahead and give the warning, always with the same terse message: "The General is coming." That meant "Get ready."

It was difficult to convince those who encountered the combative side of Johnson that under the surface he was a shy and gentle man. "That was a side of my father that few others were allowed to know," Sheila remarked. There is little doubt that Sheila saw more of the gentle side of Johnson than Bobby did.

Away from the pressures of business, Bobby and his father had a cordial if not close relationship. They did not spend a great deal of time together, but one leisure-time project they planned together was the conversion of a car into what they called the "Fordillac." A company mechanic who worked on the hybrid car explained: "In Florida the General liked to drive a smaller car, the size of a Ford, but he preferred the Cadillac engine. So he and Bobby (who had a winter home near Pompano Beach) decided to have a Cadillac engine put in a Ford, and they called it a 'Fordillac.' It was a tight squeeze, and we had to put the air-conditioning unit in the trunk. To everyone's amazement, everything worked. Bobby called it an expensive hot-rod."

The "Fordillac" was one of many autos modified for the General in the Johnson & Johnson machine shop over the years. The call announcing that he was buying a new car, which was every two years, began a project that sometimes lasted for months and taxed the abilities of the work crew. One of them explained:

"First, we had to remove all of the chrome — the General detested chrome on a car, and this was at a time when the automakers were just beginning to load them up with chrome. This meant taking off all the door handles, the trunk latch, the window trim — everything — and then painting them to blend into the car. The cars were all repainted a deep blue with a thin red stripe down the sides. It was called 'Johnson blue.'

[472]

"Then things got harder. On a visit to the Vatican, Pope Pius gave the General and Mrs. Johnson a large Saint Christopher Medal for their boat. (Christopher is the patron saint of travelers.) When he got home, the General decided to have a replica of the medal mounted on the front of his car right above the grille. So we had a bronze casting made, the size of a dinner plate, and over this we put a clear plastic coating for protection. We then built this into the grille of his Cadillac just below the hood emblem. Then we bought a second grille from Cadillac in case we damaged any parts. A local body shop helped us.

"Every few days he would come down to the shop to see how things were going, and of course to make suggestions. If we used the soldering iron too close to the plastic shield, it would melt it, so this was heart-and-ulcers time. For added safety, he wanted a brake signal light mounted in the rear window—this was long before other cars had these, so every time the car went through inspection the window light had to be removed so the car could pass. It was a feather in our cap to be picked to work on the General's cars, and when the job was finished we would each get a note of thanks from him, and the fellows looked for that. I worked on six cars—five Cadillacs and one Chrysler."

Each time he bought a new car he had another medal cast. One year he wrote to Evie: "You may be trying to find something to give me for Christmas. I would really like to have one of those medals, and you should have it properly *treated* by our friends on 50th Street." She knew that meant getting the medal "blessed" by a priest at the New York Archdiocese office.

Evie and Johnson had been married now some twenty years, and the seas had remained calm. Both of them saw to that, because they disliked confrontation and carefully avoided it. Evie had once remarked that being married to the General required a considerable amount of "accommodation," and by now she was well practiced at it. He, in turn, treated her in a friendly, respectful manner, but with no great display of affection. They had never been given to that.

[473]

Age had slowed both of them, and the days of being one of the dazzling couples of New York's Café Society were behind them. No longer were they stepping onto the dance floors of Manhattan's fashionable clubs in perfect step to the music. They settled now for an occasional quiet dinner in New York with old friends like Ed and Pegeen Fitzgerald, the WOR morning radio show hosts and their neighbors at The Pierre, and Cecil Beaton, the noted British photographer whose penetrating camera lens imprinted a certain "style" on his celebrity and fashion subjects. Evie was a great admirer of Beaton's keen sense of style and was influential in having him do some of the high-fashion photography for the widely heralded Modess advertising. An occasional weekend guest of the Johnsons at Longleat in Princeton, Beaton once took some memorable photographs of their home and the estate after a snowfall.

Johnson always seemed to establish an instant rapport with people who had new ideas. Another Princeton visitor was investment counselor John M. Templeton, who at the time was gravely concerned about the influence of communist propaganda. He wrote Johnson that a World War III would be "the struggle of free individualism versus Communist dictatorship for the minds of men." To offset the impact of Russian propaganda, Templeton wanted to create what he described as "a sort of Nobel Prize for Freedom and Individual Liberty." Using the prize as a catalyst, Templeton hoped to bring "fame and honor to those intellectuals who speak out for free individualism." He envisioned student interest, and the formation of "Freedom Clubs" on campuses across the nation. The two met several times to discuss the concept, but Johnson finally decided not to finance it.

Although Johnson had now moved to the perimeter of politics, he continued to generate ideas of his own, and in turn tried to sell them to others. One idea he had been mulling over for years was to make tuition for college and private secondary-school education deductible on personal income taxes. "This would enable people to get better educations, and it seems like an economically sound and socially and politically attractive thing to do," he wrote. "Millions of parents and many teachers may think well of such a scheme." They did, but the obstacle was Congress, and there was little support for his idea in Washington.

A longtime friend of Johnson and fellow conservative was Captain Eddie Rickenbacker, the leading United States air ace in World War I and now Chairman of the Board of Eastern Airlines. The two would exchange the public pronouncements they made in lashing out against communism, seeking each other's approval and support. Rickenbacker knew how to hit hard from the podium, and in one speech before the Miami Kiwanis Club identified the enemy as the "left-wingers, one worlders, do-gooders, Fair Dealers, socialists and communists, and left-sided individuals who call themselves Americans." Rickenbacker's alarm over the communist threat ("There is no cold war—there is a hot war") supported Johnson's contention that the nation should be better prepared to defend itself against attack.

Johnson also relied on Rickenbacker for guidance when he was planning to purchase a new company aircraft, this time a Lockheed Electra, which Johnson wanted to make into a "flying office." As he did on many subjects of interest to him, Johnson had acquired a depth of technical knowledge on various types of planes suitable for corporate use. Pilots often expressed amazement over how much he knew about commercial aircraft. When airborne on company planes, he would often go to the cockpit of the DC-3, the Convair, and later the Jetstars, sit in the jumpseat, and gab about the plane's performance and the joys of flying. His enjoyment of flying was one reason he never relinquished direct responsibility for the company's flight operations, though his interest in maintaining high safety standards was another.

He shared with Rickenbacker a deep sense of patriotism, but Johnson spoke about the rewards of being an American more than most people. He was not reluctant to proclaim his patriotism, and urged others to do the same. "Freedom is everybody's job," he said often. He once hired a new senior executive to work in the public sector and told him that part of the job was to go out and stimulate patriotism. Baffled, the man asked how he should do this. Johnson replied: "If we can get people together and promote freedom and Americanism, there will be greater acceptance of private enterprise and the American way of life." He urged the man to begin at the community level, in communities across the nation where Johnson & Johnson had built manufacturing plants and created harmonious work environments. At the grassroots level, he said, the message could be personalized and people would be more receptive to the benefits of the American way of life. One way to accomplish that, Johnson maintained, was to get people involved in community programs and public service, and the workplace would serve as a spawning ground for this activity.

He believed passionately that the well-being of America was irrevocably tied to how well business and industry performed, and how well it carried out its responsibilities to society. This was an area Johnson believed he could influence, and he approached the task with a sense of duty—and some believed a sense of destiny.

The rewards came in small doses. That year, 1962, Evie accompanied him to a ceremony at the Princeton Inn where the Garden Club of New Jersey, representing some two hundred chapters, presented him with a gold medal and referred to him as "a builder of an industrial empire who still retains an interest in community betterment and pays back to nature all he has had to disturb in the name of progress." That particular award, and the spirit in which it was given, pleased him greatly.

•

In late June of 1962 Johnson entered Roosevelt Hospital in New York for a checkup. There, his physician of many years, Dr. Scudder Winslow, diagnosed the problem as atrial fibrillation—an irregular heartbeat. He was treated with medication and remained in the hospital for ten days.

During his hospitalization, he eased the anxiety he felt over his health by concentrating on the ship he had been wanting to build for years and the long sea voyages he was still yearning to take. Thoughts of the sea brought out the dreamer in him, and he reveled in the thought of sailing to faraway places. He had always spoken of the sea with great affection as well as reverence, and he once wrote: "I love the sea and most of its moods. I fear its bad moods, but any sailor who does not is unsatisfactory to go to sea."

Planning for a new boat had always been one of his greatest joys, and this time he was determined to do it right. In recent years he had owned the *Sirena*, which was elegant but not very seaworthy, and later the rugged and lumbering *Gerda*, a 75-foot North Sea trawler that his journalist friend Frank Farrell described as having "a beam as broad as the actor Sydney Greenstreet." Then Johnson engaged the noted boat designer Olin Stephens, of the New York firm Sparkman & Stephens, to begin drawing up plans for a long-range motor vessel that could take him to distant ports. Originally, he was planning to build a boat about 175 feet long. "After discussing this with my old seagoing friends," he wrote, "I decided to dismiss this project. Friends today are not interested in joining me in extended ocean voyages. A ship of this kind can be lonely indeed for an owner navigating in distant ports alone." It was then that Johnson decided the boat should be smaller.

In planning the boat, he followed his familiar process of getting ideas and suggestions from many sources — from his brother, Seward, and even from George H. Morris, the commodore of the *Queen Elizabeth*, whom he knew from his numerous transatlantic crossings. As was always the case with Johnson in his search for perfection, there was too much information and it often became confusing to those working with him. Finally, Johnson decided that a vessel of 140 feet in length would be about right for him. Proving that he had great intuition, Stephens diplomatically suggested to Johnson that yacht designer Philip Rhodes might be better for this assignment. The General had worked with Rhodes in the past, and he took the suggestion, thereby relieving Stephens of the headaches that were to come. The responsibility for designing the "dream ship" now was in Rhodes's hands.

The General could be difficult, and in his determination to get his way he could wear people down. (In another situation he once confessed to being "annoyingly insistent," and there was no disagreement with that.) Now Philip Rhodes was bearing the brunt of the constant flood of changes the General was making during the frequent visits he made to the boat designer's office. Mrs. Little recalled some of the conversations between Johnson and Rhodes. "Mr. Rhodes would say: 'You know, Bob, I think we should do this.' And the General would say, 'No, let's try it this way.' That went on. He kept insisting on making changes and doing it his way."

As the work progressed, Rhodes found himself capitulating to Johnson even when he didn't fully agree with the changes. Johnson wrote a friend that he was "having fun" designing the ship. The harried Rhodes wasn't. Then Johnson solemnly declared that this would be a "working ship" and that he would call it *Freedom*. This seemed a contradiction to some, but not to the General. No matter, the name *Freedom* was soon to be changed too.

·

In the fall he was feeling much better, and he and Evie sailed to England, this time on the *Queen Mary*. They were invited to dine at the captain's table, and the General used this opportunity to talk about his new ship, and solicit ideas from the experienced mariner. In London they stayed at The Claridges, where they occupied their usual suite. Both of them always enjoyed London's civility, and they had many friends there. Invariably they would go to the old Farm Street Church of the Immaculate Conception in fashionable Mayfair. There, in a rustic, park setting, the Jesuits had built an unpretentious edifice that Johnson found very appealing. Evie was always pleased that he liked Farm Street Church so much and would accompany her there so willingly.

Johnson's sense of modesty was not always apparent, but it was there. It came forth when he had to stand before an audience to accept an award and listen uneasily to the accolades. He had made the trip to London to become the first American to be admitted to the Court of Patrons of the Royal College of Surgeons of England. In the formal setting of the College's paneled chamber, garbed in academic robes and surrounded by gilt-edged portraits of legendary Britishers, he listened to the words of praise for his generosity and his lifetime of leadership in providing improved medical care. He smiled shyly as the medallion was placed around his neck and as he posed for a photo that included Evie.

Shortly after returning home, he phoned Leonard Bailey, managing director of his Ethicon company in Edinburgh, Scotland. Bailey recalled the conversation well: "The General had read in the *Wall Street Journal* that the Hall Russell Shipyard in Aberdeen was going to sack many of its employees for lack of work. The yard was famous for building excellent small ships. He told me he had decided to have his boat built there to help save the jobs, and would I oversee the project from Edinburgh. I told him I knew nothing about shipbuilding but would do what I could. He said it would not be my responsibility if anything went wrong. Well, when the ship was built and it went on its maiden voyage, everything went wrong."

30

STEPPING ASIDE,
NOT DOWN

T EXANS like to do things in a large way, and in the spring of 1963 a huge crowd of 30,000 came to tour Robert Wood Johnson's latest factory creation — the new Ethicon facility at San Angelo. They could not see much until they went underground, because that's where the surgical suture production facility had been built.

The massive cement entrance protruding aboveground looked more like a giant mausoleum than a tribute to futuristic industrial design. The story in the *Dallas Morning News* read:

> From a highway on the outskirts of San Angelo, the Johnson & Johnson Ethicon division's plant looks somewhat like the great monument of Goliad to Col. James W. Fannin's unfortunate little army executed en masse after surrender by President Santa Anna's order during the Texas Revolution. From the road you can see only a huge amount of earth, with fountain-like front of creamy concrete and concrete wall around the top of the rise. The U.S. and Texas flags fly from the low roof of concrete and steel. It is all landscaped to blend in with the surroundings.
>
> Beneath the mound and eighteen feet underground is 90,000 square feet, and several million dollars worth of building, one of the world's unique manufactories and laboratories, the inspiration of a man who has had tremendous influence on industrial architecture for industrial needs, Robert Wood Johnson.

Only the colorful flags fluttering in the steady Texas breeze, and the graceful spout of water arching upward from the fountain in the center of the large reflection pool, kept the entrance from being a grim setting. At night, colored lights played off the water from the fountain, and the scene caught the eye of highway travelers. That was no accident. Johnson, who wanted his manufacturing plants to be admired, even when they were below ground, had dispatched an aide to the New York World's Fair to copy the design of the water fountains he had found so appealing.

A bit of subterfuge was taking place in San Angelo. Against Johnson's better judgment, the rationale for building the plant underground was being ascribed in the local press as a protection against devastating Texas windstorms and a way to control the climate for production of the delicate surgical sutures. But that was only partly true. Johnson wanted the plant underground so that in the event of a nuclear attack there would be an uninterrupted flow of critical medical supplies. And while the tide of public concern kept rising and falling, Johnson's level of concern stayed high.

"We have a responsibility that overshadows all else," he told his people, "and that is the security of the country with respect to an essential surgical product." When it came time to design the entrance, some of his people worried about its "fortress-like" appearance. Johnson resisted all attempts to disguise that, saying: "The appearance of this building is a radical departure and it should look like just what it is, an underground fortress. It should give the effect of great strength." When it was built it did resemble a fortress, but Johnson looked the other way and allowed them to say it was a measure to control climatic conditions for production.

Ironically, the federal government was building its first underground control center at Denton, Texas, at the same time. It would become the regional headquarters for the Office of Civil Defense and the Office of Emergency Planning, a part of the Executive Office of the President of the United States. When these groups in the White House learned that Johnson was building his own plant underground, they wrote him praising him for his "leadership" and for the example he was "providing to industry to improve its survival and rehabilitative capacity." Then, at their invitation, Johnson flew to Denton to inspect the new underground control center.

Back in New Brunswick, the finishing touches were being added to another building that was inspired by Johnson, this one a gracious Georgian Colonial design. It was located across the street from the main campus of Rutgers University and close to the historic Old Queens Building. When it came time to tear down the old red-brick mill and replace it, Johnson announced that the design of the new structure would "blend with its neighboring university buildings so as to accomplish a harmonious theme." It was a thoughtful and sensitive decision, because in many ways the Georgian Colonial architecture was more costly and less practical than a modern design. Johnson decided to take personal charge of the project, much to the distress of the architect and the builders. Their reward came later, when the building was acclaimed as one of the finest Johnson had ever built.

The four-story building, with its red-brick facing, Colonial wood trim, tall white entrance columns, and cupola with the traditional clock, blended perfectly with the campus architecture and was often mistaken for a university building. The sweeping entrance led to an elegant grand reception room, with authentic cornice work, parquet flooring, and a balcony overlooking the reception area. The walls were done in a soft Wedgwood blue, and on one wall was a life-size painting of Johnson by the artist Gerald Brockhurst. That was the Board of Directors' idea, not Johnson's. He had planned to hang a portrait of Lord Joseph Lister there, but the Board changed his mind. On the opposite wall there was a huge rendition of the Credo, done in metal.

Until that time, the complex of buildings that was Johnson & Johnson's headquarters, along the banks of the Raritan River, was a sprawling array of ancient structures, some dating back to the late nineteenth century. They were carefully maintained and upgraded, at considerable expense, in order to meet Johnson's demanding housekeeping standards. There were so many buildings, and additions, that they carried numbers for identification purposes. But assigning a mere number to the handsome new Georgian Colonial structure seemed most inappropriate. Given the academic environment that the building blended with, a member of Johnson's public relations staff suggested that the building be named Johnson Hall, which had an academic ring to it. The General liked the idea, but quickly wrote the Board of Directors that it was not his idea but that he "would agree to go along with the suggestion" if the Board approved. It became Johnson Hall, and the handsome structure was a fitting tribute to the man who had pioneered so tirelessly to improve industrial architecture.

The only ominous note in the otherwise uplifting spirit that the new building generated was the bomb shelter that had been constructed in its basement. It was large enough to accommodate some 450 people and was stocked with water and food and an array of survival equipment. But there was room for only about half the people employed at the headquarters site. That bothered Johnson greatly, and he ordered that other areas in the complex be selected as temporary havens in the event of a nuclear attack. This was serious business to him, not game-playing. Yet everyone knew that a shelter, regardless of its type, would offer little protection in the event of an atomic attack. When Johnson tested the interest his international managers had in building shelters, he found they were not "in the mood" to discuss shelters. They didn't share his concern.

Johnson wasn't a true eccentric, but as journalist Frank Farrell put it, "Now and then, the General had moments of eccentricity." Johnson consistently did strange things where personal safety was concerned — his own as well as that of the people close to him. Each new local or national incident of violent crime drove him to take some new safety precaution. Clear plastic shields were placed over the windows of the first and second floors of many office buildings in New Brunswick. From a bank construction project that went awry, he purchased bullet-proof glass and had it installed on the first floor of his Princeton home. He also bought police whistles and tear-gas pen guns for members of his household staff, though they were terrified of them.

Johnson admired the work of the New Jersey State Police. Beginning in the early 1960s, when riots became more prevalent and crime was increasing, Johnson began hiring retired state police officers to bolster the company's security. One of them, Captain Charlie Hanna, recalled the unusual security measures Johnson was taking:

"The General decided he wanted two of his secretaries, Doris Little and Olga Ferretti, to have added protection if they went out alone at night, so he bought them revolvers and got them licenses to carry them. He asked me to train them in how to use a handgun. Now, these were very gentle ladies, and they resisted, but the General insisted. That's what he wanted. The guns were .38 caliber snubnoses complete with ladies' shoulder handbags and built-in holsters. I took the two of them out to a firing range, and later on the tow path on the canal behind the office building. There was a sponge-rubber pellet that came out of this tear-gas bullet, and it went only about twenty-five feet. We'd go along the canal bank and practice. They weren't very enthusiastic, and they were not very good shots, but we reported back to the General that the training was complete, and that made him happy, even though they never once carried the guns."

Olga Ferretti held a graduate degree in nursing and kept a close check on Johnson's health, giving him his daily shots of penicillin for endocarditis, and other medications he required. Having excellent secretarial skills was a great asset as well. More important, she had the right demeanor for Johnson. She was poised and soft-spoken, well groomed, attractive, and intelligent. She had a low-key, restrained approach that was very lady-like. Johnson had great respect for her and treated her politely and in his usual courtly manner, always addressing her as "Miss Ferretti," in the same way he addressed his other personal staff members—always "Mrs. Little" and "Miss McBurney"—and the others who comprised his "office family." Only Norris Harding did he call by his first name.

For Olga Ferretti and Doris Little, working for Johnson required total commitment. Saturdays and Sundays were just like any other work day. Yet neither woman resented devoting years of their lives—Mrs. Little, fifteen years, and Miss Ferretti, ten—because they understood the unspoken terms of their jobs, and both were in awe of the man and the manner in which he involved them in everything he did. Mrs. Little worked with him most on his writing and other projects, while Miss Ferretti served as a combination nurse, secretary, and travel companion. Said Mrs. Little:

"He was demanding but unfailingly polite. He would call at seven o'clock on a Sunday morning and come over with a batch of cryptic notes that he had made when he woke up with an idea during the night.

"He never used a chauffeur unless he was going to New York. So he would drive to the office on the weekend and dictate, and I would take notes—sometimes I would drive. He would do the same with Olga.

"He was a man with so many ideas and so many concepts milling around in his head that they were like a chain around him when it came to breaking loose and enjoying some of the other things in life. He was a man obsessed by his work, and he was lonely. He had a real rapport with so few people. He had so much knowledge and such a diversity of interests that you got caught up in his work with him, and it made it all worthwhile. You felt you were helping him, and what you were doing was important."

For all of the work involved, being an assistant to Robert Johnson carried prestige, and it paid well. But it was also Johnson's personal appeal. Olga Ferretti remembered:

"My mother was of Italian extraction, and her English was not

perfect. When he came to my home to pick me up if we were working on a weekend, he would always get out of the car and come
in to say hello to my mother. He would go into the kitchen and
have a coffee and spend time talking with her. He was very kind
to her, and she was fascinated by him. He told my mother he liked
macaroni, so one Sunday we invited him to dinner, and he really
enjoyed it. We invited Mrs. Johnson too, but she didn't come. He
seemed to need family, and he always talked about how he missed
that. My mother would often say that he was a poor man. She used
an Italian expression — the poor rich man is what it amounts to.

"With all that he had, he couldn't seem to find happiness. Therefore, he had to keep working and pushing himself. But when you
heard him laugh — it was a real hearty laugh — it was such a great
feeling for anyone who knew that he was a lonely person to hear
him have this moment of laughter.

"He was always so thoughtful, and he did so many things for
us [Doris Little and others on his staff] aside from monetary consideration. There were many little things that he did which made
you feel honored to work for him. He never let you think that he
was such a great person. He was very humble. He had a sense of
humor, but not directed at himself. You had to let him laugh first."

Having survived her role of supervising the experimental bomb
shelter constructed in her backyard, Mrs. Little now faced another
daunting task. Johnson asked her to supervise the year-long construction of his new "working ship" at the shipyard in Aberdeen,
Scotland, and to plan and purchase the interior decor and furnishings. Said Mrs. Little:

"I knew nothing about boats, and I told the General that. I made
two trips to England, for furnishings for the boat, and then on
to Scotland, where I worked with John Wright at the Hall-Russell
Shipyard. I would bring the changes the General wanted made, and
he never made a single trip there, and didn't see the boat until a
few days before its maiden voyage."

Johnson still hovered over the business, but increasingly showed signs of wanting to back further away. For the first time ever, he decided not to attend the annual meeting of stockholders, placing the responsibility for conducting it squarely on Philip Hofmann. He had quietly requested that his photo not appear in that year's annual report. Increasingly aware of how old he was getting, when it came time to celebrate his seventieth birthday he wrote to Evie: "This year, will you be willing to dismiss my birthday. I would like to do this." Evie acceded to his wishes, as she always did, and there was no celebration.

He had considerably more trouble, though, suppressing his ideas on national and local issues that were of concern to him. One of his neighbors at Indian Creek Island in Florida was newspaper publisher John S. Knight. Johnson had written an article on why many nations remained "undeveloped" and sent the article to Knight for publication in his *Miami Herald*. The publisher replied: "Thank you for your latest controversial thought." The *Herald* carried Johnson's article on the editorial page. It read, in part:

> It is time to realistically evaluate the place of responsibility in giving consideration to the complexities of the modern world. No individual nation such as the United States, or the Western group of nations, has the surplus, competence, energy, and capital to pull a reluctant world forward unless the peoples of the undeveloped nations choose to devote their intelligence and energy to progress.
>
> This world observer can find but one logical reason for the progress of the West in contrast to the remainder. It is the relative competence of Western man and his acceptance of and devotion to the application of Judeo-Christian principles. Which came first is for you to decide.

Evie was certain that the article would provoke a reaction in the Miami community and told him to expect phone calls, at the very least. But nothing happened, and he was disappointed, commenting later to Knight: "I guess no one cares."

In New Jersey, Johnson had become increasingly disturbed about the way newspapers were carrying fewer articles on free enterprise and the role business was playing in preserving freedom. So he came up with the idea of purchasing a group of weekly newspapers throughout the state and pulled together a group that included his publisher friend in New Brunswick, Hugh Boyd, and Raymond Bateman, a state senator whose family had ties to publishing. For several months they researched and evaluated the new publishing venture before deciding it wasn't feasible.

His politics continued its swing to the right, and when the Senator Barry Goldwater bandwagon for the presidential nomination began to roll, Johnson was one of the first to jump aboard. "I don't want any equivocation on this," he wrote one associate. "I am a Goldwater Republican." He later wrote directly to the senator, declaring his enthusiastic support for him: "As each week passes, I am more impressed with your political philosophy and the continuing increase in your popularity." Very few others in the executive group agreed with the General's political views, which leaned to the right, yet he made no attempt to influence their thinking. They were free to support whomever they chose. (Goldwater won the Republican nomination in 1964 but was soundly defeated by Lyndon Johnson for the Presidency.)

Nearly two years had passed since Philip Hofmann succeeded Johnson as Chairman of the Executive Committee in the spring of 1961. Hofmann continued to demonstrate strong leadership, and Johnson seemed quite comfortable with his own reduced role in the company. No one anticipated the decision Johnson was about to make. Late in May 1963, Hofmann was attending a pharmaceutical industry meeting at the Greenbrier, a splendorous resort nestled on the eastern slopes of the Allegheny Mountains in White Sulphur Springs, West Virginia. As the conference was about to end, Hofmann received a call from Johnson, who said he wanted to come down to the Greenbrier to meet with him on a very important matter. The business he wanted to discuss, the General said, would take a few days, and he told Hofmann to reserve one of the resort's cottages, where they would have complete privacy.

Some years later, in a fortuitous encounter aboard the liner *Queen Elizabeth II* on a transatlantic crossing to England, Hofmann related to this author, in leisurely fashion, what took place at the meeting with Johnson at the Greenbrier:

"The General arrived the next morning, and I still had no idea of what was on his mind," Hofmann said. "He came right to the point and said he was going to make me Chairman of the Board and Chief Executive Officer of Johnson & Johnson. It came as a complete surprise. No one had been willing to believe that the General was going to step down, because the company was his whole life. Many thought he would never let go.

"Over the next three days, he led me through an intensive review of our worldwide operations, company by company. We covered several dozen of our major operations, and for each one we discussed the state of the business, past failures, and future opportunities. And we discussed the strengths and weaknesses of every member of senior management. He had given this very careful thought and planning, and it was extremely well organized. He didn't miss anything. He gave me his thinking on each company, and then he would ask me for mine. We didn't agree on all of the points, but we did on the basics.

"During those several days he was reviewing the results of his entire career. He was a great businessman—but a shy man, in many respects—and he had a mind that he couldn't shut off. It was always working. His number-one love was the business, but it wasn't a monetary thing. It was his desire to create a business that would bring better health, serve the welfare of the people, and at the same time make a profit.

"He didn't give me any specific instructions on what I should do as Chairman. He wanted to put the business in the hands of people he trusted, and he was smart enough to know that the most dangerous thing you can do is to write an exact blueprint for an unknown future. He told me he had made mistakes and if I wanted to see them just go to the Kilmer Museum and look at the products that never made it. He chased a lot of rainbows, but he also caught a lot of them. He devoted his life to Johnson & Johnson, and everything else came second.

"But he could be very tough and dogmatic," Hofmann continued. "He was generous to a fault, and he could do very kind things for people. I remember once during the war we were walking up the concourse of the 30th Street train station in Philadelphia, and he was in his brigadier general's uniform. Ahead of us was this little girl in a WAC uniform, and she was struggling with a heavy duffel bag. He came up to her and said, 'Come on, soldier, I'll give you a hand.' He swung the duffel on his shoulder and carried it to the taxi stand. She was all aflutter, having a general carry her duffel.

"He explained to me why he would not be attending any more stockholder meetings. He said someone would be bound to ask what he thought on a subject, and when that happened I would no longer be the Chairman. 'You might have the title,' he said, 'but you wouldn't be the Chairman.' On the second or third day, he asked me to go over the changes I would like to make in the company. I had given it some thought, so I had a list of things I wanted to do, including some extra stock to senior managers that came from me, not from him. He said, 'Fine. Go ahead.'

"By the time the meeting was over, he was very tired. He was sitting in a big chair and got up and crossed the room and shook my hand and said: 'Well, kid, the job is now yours.' And I replied: 'I'm not sure I'm saying this well, General, but you have put your life's work in my hands, and all I can tell you is that I'll do the best I can.'

"From that day forth he never once ordered me to do something his way, and never countermanded a decision I made. I respected him greatly for that, because I know how tough it was for him to let go. This was tested very soon. He came into my office a little later, very enthused about an idea he wanted the company to pursue. It did not appeal to me, and I told him so. He said to me: 'There are two ways to make a decision — one is logic and the other is intuition. If something tells you it's wrong, then forget it.' And we forgot his idea."

The General decided that he would remain on the Board of Directors (later he became chairman of the Finance Committee). Before leaving the Greenbrier, the two agreed on several other key management changes, which would be announced on June 7. Gustav Lienhard succeeded Hofmann as Chairman of the Executive Committee, and Bobby Johnson and Richard B. Sellars were named vice chairmen of the Executive Committee.

The changes came as a complete surprise to Bobby Johnson, who was informed about them on June 5 — and not by his father but at a meeting with Hofmann and Lienhard. The next day Bobby wrote his father:

Dear Dad,
Needless to say, I was shocked by my conversation with Phil and Gus last night. I hoped that I would never see the day during your lifetime when you resigned as Chairman of the Board of Directors. After reviewing in my mind overnight the changes in the executive structure of the business that you are planning, I have come to the following conclusion. I will not pretend to you that I agree with some of these changes, but I will pledge to you my continuing loyalty and devotion, and I will continue to bend every effort to make your plans, and this company, as successful in the future as they have been in the past.

Affectionately,
Bob

At forty-two, Bobby Johnson was just completing twenty-three years with the company. He was not a great fan of Hofmann, and Hofmann was not a great fan of his. At the time, it appeared that Bobby, who had risen through the ranks to become president of Johnson & Johnson, would someday follow in his father's footsteps and become Chairman of the company, and there was little doubt that this was Bobby's aspiration. But his father never spoke about that to Bobby. In his eyes, it was not a role that could be in- herited — it had to be earned. The well-being of the company took precedence over all else, even family relationships.

The Board of Directors that Hofmann headed was made up of twenty-three members of management with a collective total of 581 years of service with the company, or an average of twenty-five years each. They knew one another, and the company, well. They were there because they measured up to the standards of perfor- mance that Johnson had set for them, and because each one was personally committed to fulfilling the responsibilities contained in the Credo. For years the General had been preparing for the tran- sition, and now that it was here he was confident that it would go smoothly.

There were no farewell speeches from Johnson, and no messages to employees — no doubt a reflection of his belief that he would still be around tending to things, and in his own way. He did write a memo to the Executive Committee, which began: "It has been my painful duty to review the errors of my chairmanship." He then proceeded to list them, referring mostly to areas of the business that had been hurt by slow decision-making. "We intend to avoid such practice in the future," he said. "Management that is ponder- ous, slow-thinking, and slow-moving will not survive." It was as much a warning as a confession of his errors.

He was not amused when he tried to call a meeting and found that none of his senior executives was around. That prompted him to write: "Typical of my first week after having shed my important position, I find that everyone is in Europe." On another occasion, he wrote: "I will not be as active, and this will probably be a relief to you [Hofmann], and a good thing for everyone."

Some things did not change, nor could they as long as Johnson was around. A few days after stepping down, he was driving along the highway and came across a group of strikers in front of one of his plants. He stopped and asked if they would move their cars to

the rear so they wouldn't detract from the appearance of the building from the highway. He also told them that if it rained he would
see to it that management provided a place under cover for them
to picket, and that if they were still on strike when winter came he
would put up a tent for them. The strikers were delighted to meet
"the General," and they chatted with him amiably.

Among Johnson's concerns for the future was his failure to develop senior women executives. When Sears, Roebuck & Company
named its first woman director, Claire Giannini Hofmann, a fer-
vent supporter of equal opportunity for women in business, Johnson wrote to her seeking help in finding women executives. He was
specifically referring to the Personal Products Company, where he
said various women professionals had been hired, but none was yet
ready to move up to the Board of Directors level. He wrote: "I am
determined to develop a group of three to five women of sufficient
stature and experience, and we are appealing to you for advice,
guidance and assistance." Mrs. Hofmann replied that she could not
provide any names of specific candidates.

Johnson continued to carve out for himself an area of responsibility that he labeled "forward planning." For years, there had
been rampant speculation about what would happen to Johnson &
Johnson when he stepped down, but the change brought none of
the dire consequences many had predicted. Johnson did not need a
title to make his presence felt, or permission to explore those areas
of the business that interested him most. Now he looked forward
to the maiden voyage of his "working ship," where he could do his
planning in greater solitude—or so he thought.

That summer, he spent a week at a spa on the island of Ischia
in the Bay of Naples, hoping to rejuvenate himself in the Santa
Restitua thermal springs. Even though he was in Europe, he did not
go to Scotland to see his boat under construction. There, the always
persevering Mrs. Little was undergoing her on-the-job training in
ship construction and interior furnishings, and hoping all would
go well and to the General's complete satisfaction. At one point she

reported being "busier than a bird dog," but in her letter she also said she was looking forward to completing the assignment. "If anyone says 'ships' to me again I'll not be responsible," she wrote.

Johnson had decided that his new ship would, for tax purposes, be registered in Bermuda. But when he learned that several other boats had the name *Freedom* he changed it at the last minute to *Pilgrim*, ignoring the old sailors' caution that changing a ship's name, after it had once been decided, would bring bad luck.

His frustration over the name change turned to annoyance when he heard rumors that some company executives were grumbling about the company having to bear some of the cost for the boat. This was not true, and Johnson promptly fired off a stinging internal memo to his senior staff, which read:

> There will be no charge to the company concerning the ship I am building. This will be paid for and operated out of my personal account. I will use this ship for business conferences, but I do not contemplate charging any portion of such expenses to the company.
>
> You and all the rest of the stockholders can take a quick dip in the Raritan River.

31

THE HARROWING
VOYAGE

ABERDEEN, Scotland, November 5, 1963. Under the watchful eye of her new master, Captain Peter Hamilton, and the proud workers at the Hall-Russell Shipyard, the *Pilgrim* slid slowly down the ways, moving more briskly as she splashed into the water for the first time, on this her launching day. She was a pretty sight, and deserving of the cheers that went up.

The *Pilgrim*, created by the noted designer Philip Rhodes, had the classic lines of a motor yacht. She was 140 feet long and had a 26-foot beam, a high, rakish bow, and a gently curved canoe-type stern. On the upper deck, behind a spacious wheelhouse, was a large oval stack tapered slightly toward the stern, making her look like a serious ship, not just a large boat. The protected walk-around decks, the steel construction, and the powerful Caterpillar diesel engines added to the ship's credentials for seaworthiness and capability of cruising the world.

To the curious Scots who came by to admire the gleaming white ship that cost well over a million dollars, it must have been an outrageous example of American extravagance. But to the workers who helped build her, the *Pilgrim* had helped save their jobs. The shipyard had fallen on hard times until Johnson came to the rescue. The General had yet to lay eyes on his new "working ship," claiming later that he couldn't attend to his company duties and still come to Scotland to oversee the vessel's construction. That was fortunate for the shipyard, which had enough problems without having Johnson there to supervise.

The adventuresome Captain Hamilton was an intrepid mariner who had sailed solo across the Atlantic, and then wrote a book about his odyssey titled *The Restless Wind*. He lived nearby at Buchlyvie in Stirlingshire and came highly recommended by the shipyard management. For months he had been putting together his crew of eight: an engineer, an assistant engineer, a mate, two seamen, a cook, a steward, and a mess boy. Now he was ready to put both ship and crew through their paces during sea trials, and then return to the yard, where the bugs could be worked out before the *Pilgrim* headed for the open sea.

As one might expect of someone who had challenged an ocean and won, Captain Hamilton was not the retiring type. He called things as he saw them, and shortly after the launching he toured the *Pilgrim* from stem to stern and declared her "a hell of a mess" — an opinion he wisely kept from Johnson. Having been around boats for most of his forty-odd years, Hamilton was philosophical about the chaos that accompanies a ship's fitting out. Somehow the final equipment would be installed, the finishing touches would be added, and order would be restored.

Over the coming weeks the *Pilgrim* began to look more like a lady, and the first of several sea trials was under way. During that first trip, one of the propeller shafts driven by the Caterpillar diesel engines overheated. When the ship returned to the yard, that problem and others were corrected. On the second sea trial, the weather turned foul and water from a driving rain came through the foredeck into the cabins below. Johnson had insisted that the yard use a new type of caulking that had recently been developed in the United States. The yard manager, John Wright, argued that Hall-Russell had been building ships for four hundred years and preferred to use the traditional caulking. Besides, he told Johnson, applying the new material required special skills. Johnson insisted,

Wright gave in, and the new material was used—and the decks leaked.

When the vessel returned to Aberdeen, the leaks were corrected, and Captain Hamilton began to plan his first voyage. The ship would go to Portsmouth, England, where Johnson would board, and then cross the Atlantic to Trinidad by way of the Canary Islands. Johnson planned a series of voyages that would take him around the world, visiting Johnson & Johnson's far-flung plants and offices and giving credence to the *Pilgrim*'s status as a "working ship." The ship would be away for several months at a time, and at certain intervals Johnson would fly back to check on how his new management in New Jersey was running the company in his absence. That's what he planned to do.

In anticipation of being at sea for long stretches, and growing increasingly concerned about his health, Johnson decided to have a physician accompany him on the ship. He turned to Leonard Bailey at Ethicon in Edinburgh for help. Using his medical contacts, Bailey located a young Scottish physician, Dr. Hugh Murray, who was intrigued by the prospect of seeing the world before settling down in his career. When Bailey met Dr. Murray at an interview, he was impressed by the tall, good-looking chap with an easy manner and an unfulfilled sense of adventure. Grasping what he deemed a rare opportunity, Dr. Murray signed on as the ship's doctor.

Young Dr. Murray had another admirable quality. A devoted son, he wanted to share his travel adventures with his parents in Scotland. So he wrote a series of long, descriptive letters about his experiences. His observant eye and a desire to share his impressions of people and events made him a skilled chronicler. Years later, he generously provided copies of his absorbing "Dear Mum and Dad" letters to this author. Those letters provide the details of Johnson's trips when Murray was ship's doctor.

In mid-December, Hugh Murray left his home at Drem in North Berwick to spend a few days with Captain Hamilton and his wife and to learn more about the *Pilgrim* and the maiden voyage. Although he had never been to sea before, he displayed refreshing enthusiasm for learning the skills he would need for standing watch on the bridge—which would be one of his duties. In extending the invitation to visit the ship, Hamilton had written: "On board you will have a double cabin and attached bathroom, so I think you should be fairly comfortable. The designed speed is fifteen and a half knots, and we will probably cruise at twelve or thirteen knots."

It was a pleasant visit, and the captain clearly enjoyed the company of the bright, young physician who seemed so eager to learn the ways of the mariner. Murray was awed by the size and luxurious appointments of the *Pilgrim*, and before leaving Aberdeen he began making a list of medical supplies he wanted to have aboard. Captain Hamilton showed him the cartons of medical products that Johnson and Nurse Ferretti had sent from New Brunswick and remarked: "This is beginning to look more like a hospital ship than a yacht!" Dr. Murray went home for the Christmas holidays, to return to the ship in January.

Another series of annoying delays postponed the departure from Aberdeen until a gray and misty Monday, February 10, when the ship finally sailed for Portsmouth. En route, Captain Hamilton began tutoring Dr. Murray on the principles of navigation and general seamanship. He had an eager student. The captain was a strong believer in learning by doing. After showing the young doctor the basics of watch duty and steering the ship clear of harbor traffic, Hamilton promptly announced that he was going to his cabin for some rest. "Let me know if you get worried," he said as he departed. "I was already worried," Dr. Murray wrote.

Alone on the bridge, Dr. Murray took stock of the situation. "I was mildly surprised to find that each time a ship or buoy appeared, it was where the radar said it should be. And I soon learned that a ship doesn't have brakes like a motor car. Later, Peter asked if I would take another watch, as there was only the mate and himself to take duty on the bridge. He informed me that when General Johnson came aboard he would be taking *his* turn on watch. By the time I got back to the bridge that evening, we could see the lights of Newcastle in the distance, and a few small ships were moving on the Tyne.

"By the end of the watch, I was reasonably pleased that the ship was still on course, but the stabilizers had decided to stop stabilizing, and from then on they didn't work. The next day we were just north of the mouth of the Thames, and headed for the outer Goodwin Channel, off the coast of Kent. By now I was beginning to get the hang of it. That night the *Pilgrim* anchored just off the north coast of the Isle of Wight, with the lights of Portsmouth blinking in the distance."

Early the next morning, they sailed into Portsmouth Harbor, dipping the ensign to ships of the Royal Navy as they passed. Shortly after docking, several groups of visitors from Johnson's various companies in England came aboard to tour the ship. "Peter grew weary of this," wrote Dr. Murray. "Then we learned that it would be another week before General Johnson would arrive in Portsmouth. We then had to anchor the ship about fifty yards off the wharf and use the launch to get back and forth."

On February 18, the *Pilgrim* went to a fuel dock an hour away to take on fifteen tons of diesel fuel. As she eased alongside the jetty, a guard rail on deck made contact with a piling and the rail snapped with a resounding crack.

"Peter was understandably annoyed," Dr. Murray wrote. "Then, out of nowhere, a harried group of people arrived from the florists, and rushed on board to decorate the ship with various bouquets of flowers—azaleas, hyacinths, carnations of all shades, and lilies—all carefully arranged in expensive vases, some of them Wedgwood. They came from various Johnson & Johnson companies, all with a bon voyage message for the General. While we were still at the fuel dock, word came from Portsmouth that the General would be boarding when we returned. We left hurriedly, and when we got back to the wharf he was standing there, waiting for us."

It was the General's first look at the *Pilgrim*, and whatever he felt

[499]

he kept to himself. If he spotted the broken rail as Captain Hamilton eased the ship along the dock, he didn't let on. But when the gangway was in place, he noted that it was a poor fit (and said so later) and lacked the padding he thought it should have for safety. It was a tense moment for the young Dr. Murray, who for several months had been wondering what his new and vaunted employer would be like.

"I was rather interested to meet this mythical man, for my curiosity had been stimulated by meeting several of his managers and other employees during the past week. They all seemed to regard him as a kind of wonder man, who should be approached with a kind of fearful awe! In fact, he turned out to be a pretty normal-looking chap, and while there is no doubt that he has an excellent brain and is used to being treated with some respect, I found him quite pleasant and approachable. He came on board with his secretary, Miss Ferretti, who is coming with us on the trip. He had a quick look around the lounge, the salon and the bridge before retiring for a nap. He duly appeared again at suppertime, and the meal went off without too much strain.

"After supper we sat and talked, mainly about the yacht. The General told me he would be occupying the cabin next to mine, and that Miss Ferretti would be in the owner's quarters in the forward part of the ship. He then asked me if I found any faults with my cabin, and I told him no, that it was more than adequate.

"He began rattling off a list of alterations he wanted made—the cabin lights were not in the right place for reading, the mattresses were too wide, the clothes hooks in the cabins weren't in the right place, the waste-baskets were too small, and so on. Obviously his idea of what was adequate was different from mine, but I suppose if you pay that kind of money for a ship you are entitled to have things exactly as you like them.

"I had a quick talk with him about his health and the medications he was taking, and I finished up checking his pulse, apex rate, and blood pressure—none of which gave any rise to serious concern. On the whole he seems pretty fit, but there is no doubt that he seems pretty anxious about his health, though not, I think, to the extent of being hypochondriacal.

"He is a very well organized sort of chap, and before we went off to bed the following day's program was all carefully organized for each of us. I was detailed to accompany him to the Johnson & Johnson factory in Portsmouth to look around it."

On the way to the plant the next morning, Dr. Murray told the General that he would check his prothrombin when they got to the company medical department, and this he did, drawing five cc's of blood from the General, without incident. "Fortunately, I did it on the first attempt," Murray recalled, "because a group of attentive company managers were looking on and it was the ideal moment for a complete failure of my veno-puncturing technique as a circle of hand-wringing minions stood by."

The tour of the plant that followed, and seeing the General in action, intrigued Dr. Murray. "In a rapid and sketchy tour, Johnson picked up on numerous points requiring explanation or elaboration, and he really put his managers through the hoop. He knows the business inside and out—was familiar with the baby powder, elastoplast, plaster of Paris, and bandage production methods—and I should think he is a very difficult man to hoodwink. He eventually announced that he was very pleased with the factory, and everyone looked relieved. I could see why he is regarded with such awe by his employees."

Last-minute preparations were made for the sailing, and Johnson seemed quite pleased with his new ship. He expressed his satisfaction to designer Philip Rhodes in a cable:

DEAR PHIL

PILGRIM MAGNIFICENT　STOP　PLANNING DEPARTURE
THURSDAY　STOP　THANK YOU FOR EVERYTHING

BOB JOHNSON

In New Brunswick, Doris Little anxiously awaited word of how the General liked the way she had furnished the ship, and then the cable arrived:

PILGRIM EXCELLENT   STOP   FURNISHINGS PERFECT   STOP
THANK YOU FOR ALL YOU DID   STOP   BEST WISHES

JOHNSON

Mrs. Little breathed a sigh of relief and vowed to retire from nautical assignments.

•

Late on a beautiful sunny afternoon, February 20, the *Pilgrim* began her maiden voyage, heading first for the Azores. The harbor was calm and the wind was light as the handsome ship moved past the Isle of Wight and into the English Channel, with the coast of France on the port side and the Channel Islands dead ahead. When it got dark, Johnson, Miss Ferretti, and Dr. Murray went below for their first meal of the voyage, along with one of the crew. It was Johnson's shipboard custom always to invite one of the crew to join him for the evening meal. "The meal," Dr. Murray reported, "was not an unqualified success, as the yacht moved into open water and began to behave like a big dipper, with something of a lateral roll despite the stabilizers, which were now working.

"As we moved toward the sweet at the end of the meal, there was diminishing interest on my part. Then Miss Ferretti began turning somewhat green and asked to be excused. The General seemed just fine. I stuck it out, making rather distant conversation with him. He told me that he never gets seasick, but I excused myself rather hurriedly and went out and parted company with my dinner. I returned to the lounge for a while, but I continued to feel very squeamish. The General seemed to be enjoying himself."

As the *Pilgrim* moved into the Bay of Biscay, she continued to labor through the night in seas that grew rougher with each passing hour. At daybreak, Dr. Murray, after a restless night, looked out the porthole of his cabin and described the view as "alternately sky, then submarine." Getting about the ship had become increasingly difficult, and the rattle from things moving around in the cabinets and drawers was constant. Bravely the young doctor made a stab at eating some breakfast — and that was a mistake. "I pushed the food down, and it was completely wasted, as it came back up again." Miss Ferretti had absented herself from the meal. The General, feeling fine, enjoyed his breakfast, alone.

As the day wore on, the weather grew worse and the ship struggled hard to make headway. One huge wave sent the flowers and vases, believed to be secured, crashing to the deck of the lounge and the salon. Broken Wedgwood and splinters of expensive vases were scattered everywhere, and the General, who liked a tidy ship, helped clean up the glass and flowers. Dr. Murray was in his cabin — feeling, as he put it, "rather unhappy." He reported: "My only visitor was General Johnson, who dropped by now and then to borrow some more Johnsonplast tape so he could go around and tape the doors and cabinets shut. They were banging loudly, and that bothered him."

On the bridge, Captain Hamilton was struggling valiantly to keep the ship on course. He too was not feeling well. As the howling wind grew in intensity to force nine (winds in excess of 47 miles an hour), the *Pilgrim* would slowly climb to the crest of one huge wave after another, and then rush quickly down to the trough, sometimes taking water over the bow as she reached the bottom. Then she would begin the arduous climb all over again. Up and down, up and down, often shuddering as she went. Soon all the members of the crew were seasick — a few desperately so.

Of the twelve on board, only Johnson was feeling fit. He volunteered to take additional watches and turns at the wheel when others were too sick to go on the bridge. He had always said he was happiest when at sea. In Dr. Murray's words, "the General was as happy as he could be."

The fierce storm had reduced the ship's headway to just five knots. As water cascaded over the bow, the foredeck began to leak badly, and soon it was pouring into the crew's quarters below. The caulking that Johnson had insisted on using was separating from the deck planking. It became so bad that the crew had to be evacuated from its quarters and their mattresses moved to the dining salon and other parts of the ship that were still dry. The General helped organize the move.

"By this time," wrote Dr. Murray, "we were slowly moving down the coast of Portugal toward Cape St. Vincent, and hoping that things would improve, when we turned south along the coast of Spain. Unfortunately, this turned out to be prematurely optimistic. Later Sunday afternoon, the weather got even worse and the winds were now at gale force ten (more than 55 miles an hour), and coming directly at us. It was depressing to see how little progress we were making."

The deck below now had several inches of water sloshing around, along with broken crockery and tins of food that had fallen from the cabinets above. It was a mess. Each time the ship rolled, the water and debris moved across the deck. Johnson went to the galley numerous times to prepare pots of hot tea, which he brought to the crew members and to Miss Ferretti and Dr. Murray in their cabins. "He made the rounds with cups of tea, and I thought that was so nice of him to do that," Miss Ferretti said. "We were desperately ill and he was fine. He was trying to cheer us up."

In addition to his mal de mer, Dr. Murray was feeling guilty about not being able to help the patients he had aboard. "The junior engineer was so seasick that he went about looking like death for three days," Dr. Murray wrote. "He didn't speak to anyone for three days, but he continued to do his job down in the engine room, where one of the generators had gone down. Both engineers had to stay down there until it was fixed."

Captain Hamilton's prediction that the storm would be over in another twenty-four to forty-eight hours did not cheer Dr. Murray. "On Saturday afternoon I felt that I ought to get out of bed and try to help," the doctor reported. "I volunteered to take a watch and went to the bridge. The weather was no better. We passed a freighter that looked to be in even worse shape than we were. The ship signaled us to stay out of her way since the seas were so rough they couldn't control the steering. Then we discovered that the chocks holding our two launches on the top deck aft of the wheelhouse were loosening. Crew members had to go out and tie down the launches so we wouldn't lose them overboard. Then the gyro-compass failed and we had to resort to using the magnetic compass."

Meanwhile, Johnson was compiling a list of the ship's short-comings, which he later called "Pilgrim's Problems." It kept growing longer and longer: The water sloshing around the decks in the crew's quarters sent wisps of smoke out of the electrical connections in the corners. The portholes were leaking. A compass directly over the General's bunk, installed by the yard at Johnson's request so he could look up from his bed and see the ship's heading, had water coming through it, onto his pillow. He added the compass to the list.

In an understatement of classic proportions, Dr. Murray wrote: "By now, General Johnson was naturally a bit put out by the yacht and its constant breakdowns."

After five harrowing days, the weather started to ease on Wednesday afternoon, February 26, and the sun came out late in the day. The *Pilgrim* was two hundred miles north of the Canary Islands and now moving at eleven knots. Thursday was a marvelous day, even warmer, and the crew began the arduous task of cleaning the ship's exterior. The decks and all the outer surfaces and brass fittings were caked with salt, and the storm had lashed the ship so hard that some of the paint had chipped away. Remarkably, Dr. Murray noted, no one had been injured — except for the crew's pride as seafarers.

Early on an overcast Friday morning, the *Pilgrim* approached Las Palmas, whose high volcanic mountains rose sharply from the sea. To the others, it was a welcome sight, but as the ship eased into the harbor and went directly to the fueling dock, the water became murky with oil that had been discharged from ships in the harbor. The General was appalled, and when the Spanish customs officers came aboard he admonished them for their laxity, which they didn't accept very kindly. By now the oily water was lapping against the *Pilgrim*'s hull, adding to its scruffy look and Johnson's distress.

As soon as the refueling was completed, the *Pilgrim* moved to a cleaner area of the harbor and dropped anchor. Johnson could not wait to get ashore, and he went directly to the cable office and sent the same message to both Philip Rhodes and John Wright at the Hall-Russell Yard in Aberdeen:

PILGRIM FINE HULL   STOP   FINE MAIN ENGINES   STOP
OTHERWISE THIS SHIP IS A MESS   STOP   AM DEEPLY
DISAPPOINTED   STOP   SHE WILL RETURN ABERDEEN FROM
TRINIDAD   STOP   ALL SUBSEQUENT PLANS CANCELLED   STOP
SHE WILL BE MADE RIGHT OR SOLD   STOP   A TRULY BAD JOB
JOHNSON

That evening, he and Miss Ferretti and Dr. Murray went to the Hotel Santa Catalina for dinner. Before they got there, the doctor was given a good supply of pesetas to pay the bill, since the General disliked getting involved in paying bills. The young physician was delighted to do so, and wrote his parents: "It was quite an interesting experience to be able to hand out money à la millionaire, even if only for an evening." He continued: "The General was an extremely interesting dinner companion. When we got back to the ship we talked for another hour, and he retired at ten o'clock, as he always does."

At three o'clock on Monday afternoon, March 2, the *Pilgrim*, looking much snappier than she had in some time, weighed anchor and sailed from Las Palmas for Tenerife, sixty miles away. On the way out of the harbor, they passed two lavender-colored ocean liners — the *Windsor Castle* and the *Cape Town Castle* — whose odd color blended remarkably well against the deep blue sea. All was at peace on the *Pilgrim*—for the present, at least. The plan was to stop briefly at Tenerife to take on water, and then to move on to Palma, the westernmost of the Canary Islands, for a few days of swimming and pure leisure. The General liked to swim but not to be idle, so he planned to keep Miss Ferretti busy with dictation. It would take them twelve days to cross the Atlantic to Trinidad, the next port of call.

Dr. Murray related what happened at Tenerife: "All of the usual papers were signed on our arrival there, but the authorities informed the General that it would take until eleven o'clock the next morning before they could grant clearance for the ship to move on to Palma. This irked him considerably, and with some force he informed them that if this was an example of their efficiency, he was not going to remain on Spanish soil but would sail for the West Indies as soon as we got clearance."

The General could be very stubborn, and he often paid a price for it. His fit of pique cost him the leisurely days at Palma, and the Spanish authorities, perhaps in retribution for his outburst, didn't clear the ship to depart for Trinidad until noon the next day. When they finally left the harbor and sailed past the 12,000-foot ice-capped Pico de Teide volcano, it was quiet, as usual. It was Johnson who was erupting over Spanish bureaucracy. He calmed down as the *Pilgrim* headed across a tranquil North Atlantic, a school of porpoises playfully racing alongside the ship.

For someone with no nautical experience, other than surviving the horrendous gale they had been through, Dr. Murray caught on quickly. He had a keen eye for the ship's behavior. "The surface of the sea was like glass, but the yacht rolls quite a bit in this kind of sea," he noted. At certain speeds, the canoe-type stern seemed to dig in, riding lower in the water than it should have. Someone speculated that the ship might have been overpowered, but because the General had personally selected the engines, nothing more was said about it. As the days and nights grew warmer, the *Pilgrim*'s air-conditioning began to labor. "The cabins are beginning to get really hot now," Murray wrote in his understating manner, "and the ventilation isn't completely successful, so I began sleeping on a cot on the deck, where, except for the flying fish that came aboard and flopped around, it was very pleasant."

The yacht had picked up the northeast trade winds and, aided by a following sea, was moving along at eleven knots. Dr. Murray and the General, standing the same watch, spent hours engaged in easy conversation. Johnson did not rant about the *Pilgrim*'s problems — that was not his style. To him it was a personal matter, but the shortcomings were very much on his mind. He had trouble sleeping — he often did — and on this crossing he got up at odd times during the night and prowled the ship. Murray could hear him moving about.

At the halfway mark to Trinidad, Johnson suggested a celebration dinner. Captain Hamilton and a few crew members joined them, and Dr. Murray wore his kilt for the occasion. The General allowed himself one or two dry martinis. He had put on board a case of House of Lord's gin and a single bottle of vermouth — a ratio he adhered to on both land and sea. The chef prepared a special meal of lobster and chicken, with strawberries and ice cream for dessert. They all talked and laughed about their harrowing experience earlier in the voyage.

For nine days they did not see a single other ship, then a fishing trawler was spotted on the horizon, and then the first faint sounds of Barbados Radio put the *Pilgrim* back in touch with civilization. When the transmission improved, Johnson sent a message to his office in New Brunswick. His "working ship" was now in action, even if it was no longer his "dream ship."

The *Pilgrim* arrived at Port of Spain in Trinidad on Friday, March 13. By then the General had made up his mind to sell her. Shortly after they docked, a concerned Philip Rhodes arrived unannounced, from New York. The General was not happy to see him, but they engaged in gentlemanly conversation about the ship's failings, and Rhodes asked to see a copy of Johnson's list of the ship's shortcomings, "Pilgrim's Problems." Reluctantly, Johnson agreed.

He did not want to engage in a lengthy discussion about the ship, for he had already made up his mind to sell.

When Johnson stepped off the ship in Trinidad, he never boarded her again — and he never looked back.

Later he confided to Leonard Bailey: "The trouble with me was I had to interfere with the design of that ship. I should have left it to the designer. There were problems with it, and they were largely problems that were made rather than problems that were inherent." To another associate, he wrote: "Pilgrim did not turn out well. Yes, it was a real disappointment, but the book is closed. Such is the life of a sailor."

But a sailor without a ship is not a sailor, and he was already planning his new dream ship.

32

A NEW BEGINNING

I T was a very important occasion at the new home of The Robert Wood Johnson Foundation. The Board of Trustees was coming to dinner. When the meal was about half-cooked, the aging stove faltered—and then quit altogether. Frantically, the cook went to the home of a neighbor and finished preparing the dinner in her kitchen.

When the dozen guests arrived, the tiny dining room in the modest, two-story frame house at 142 Livingston Avenue in New Brunswick was very crowded, but no one seemed to mind. The rest of the house was almost barren of furniture, but one desk was sufficient to conduct the business of the Foundation, in this its first home. The year was 1963. The trustees exchanged warm words and fond recollections of their years of service in a philanthropic effort that doted on privacy and preferred anonymity when possible. That's the way Johnson believed philanthropy should be practiced, but on this special, family occasion he could not avoid the warm words of praise from his colleagues on the Foundation's Board.

The austere Klemmer Kalteissen, a judge of the Superior Court of New Jersey and president of the Foundation, rose to speak. Like Johnson, he was a native son of New Brunswick and intimately familiar with the city's needs. That's one reason why Johnson chose him to be president—that and his discretion. Judge Kalteissen briefly traced the history of the Foundation, saying it had been formed in 1936 and was known then as the Johnson New Brunswick Foundation. In 1952, he continued, it became The Robert Wood Johnson Foundation, but its resources were limited and the scope of its activity was largely local. Now it had assets of some $20 million, all in Johnson & Johnson stock contributed by Johnson, and its annual level of grant-making was about $225,000, which came from the stock dividends. Though tiny when measured against other foundations, it had grown large enough to need an office for its headquarters. At Johnson's insistence, that would be in a home setting rather than in a downtown office.

"This house," the judge said solemnly, "is dedicated to the alleviation of the suffering of mankind, and the training of men in the medical profession and women in the noble profession of nursing. We are here to assist our local hospitals in the care of the sick, the injured, the aged, and the suffering, and to help worthy organizations in the development of character in our youth, to help individuals and families in times of stress, accident, and need, and to help those confined to correctional institutions get a new start in life when they leave their respective places of confinement."

The judge continued: "We dedicate this building to the honor and glory of God and to the welfare of mankind, and to the benevolence, thoughtfulness, and devotion of General Johnson to the welfare of his fellow man. We are constantly reminded of the nobleness of his character, and of his constant reminder that we must improve the standard of service to the patient, and give aid to the sick."

When the Board decided to buy the house, for $33,000, Johnson called an old friend and company colleague, Frank Cosgrove, out of retirement to supervise the renovations. The two had known each other since boyhood and had spent so many years working together that Cosgrove needed no instruction in the General's likes and dislikes. The house had to blend into the neighborhood, not dominate it. The furnishings would be basic. With great care Johnson had selected a Williamsburg chandelier that hung in isolated splendor in the center of one room. After the experience of the failed stove and crowded dining room, Johnson decided that future Board dinners would be held elsewhere.

When the time came to name the building, Johnson decided that it would be called simply "Foundation House," and not "The Robert Wood Johnson Foundation." After checking out the professional offices along Livingston Avenue—mostly doctors and dentists—he concluded that their signs in front were much too large to be tasteful. So he ordered a small brass plaque—"Foundation House"—and had it placed near the entrance. It was so small that only those with keen eyesight could read it from the sidewalk.

Realizing that his foundation was destined to grow—though he hadn't the faintest idea how large it would eventually become—Johnson looked ahead and saw reason for concern, which he expressed in a letter to his brother:

> Seward:
> My Foundation has few rules and no bureaucratic procedures. I suppose some day some smart fellow will come along, or some trustee, who will want to formalize the whole show. God forbid! If you are around, vote against it. When Foundations fall into the hands of their paid secretariat, their trustees, in time, seem to abdicate their responsibilities.

Bobby Johnson had become a member of the Foundation Board. He and his father agreed on philanthropic goals more readily than they did on many business issues. Again looking ahead to what might happen after he was gone, the General wrote Bobby a poignant letter in which he expressed concern about ideological threats to the Foundation. It read:

> Dear Bob:
> The greatest issue before the United States and the world is the issue of free capitalism versus socialism. I have never felt that you grasped this. It seems to me that men of your age have been subjected to an era of temporizing with the fundamental concept of the United States.

I believe that everything we have was given to us by the framers of our Constitution. Only a return to this concept of a Christian Society under law can save the United States.

I am deeply concerned that the present or future trustees of The Robert Wood Johnson Foundation in some way may depart from this concept. Many foundations have done so, including several of the largest, such as the Fund for The Republic, the Ford Foundation and others. Foundation trustees have become involved in strange intellectual and esoteric objectives framed for them by academic men and women suffering from a confused state of ideology. It would certainly be no tribute to my memory if this were to happen to our Foundation. I look to you, among others, to be clear in your understanding of my convictions and, of course, I hope that you join me in these convictions with at least as great a determination as my own. Put this in your strongbox where you keep your private papers. Some day you may choose to reread it.

Johnson also wrote to Philip Hofmann, who had succeeded him as Chairman of the company, this time expressing his concerns about the future direction of the Foundation's grant-making activity. In this letter he said:

Many well-intentioned donors have set up a trust fund, which, like the Ford Foundation, proceeded in directions not intended by the original donors. I hope that my efforts will not be bent in that direction. My work is dedicated to hospitals, care of the aged and the injured, the afflicted and the sick.

Even his brother Seward, the person he was closest to, could not persuade Johnson to expand the activities of The Robert Wood Johnson Foundation into other areas, notably the support of educational projects outside the health field. Seward had a personal interest in these areas, but when he wrote his brother, Johnson remained adamant: "In my lifetime," he replied to Seward, "I have rarely been impressed by the education boys. There is no area of social responsibility more important than the care of the sick and the injured, and I think it best to confine my Foundation to the area of healing."

In everything he ever said or wrote about his philanthropic goals, Johnson never once deviated from his belief that care given to the patient was his principal interest. He once wrote: "Improved patient care is my greatest responsibility." He was distressed that others did not view this as he did. "There is a universal lack of understanding of patient care," he wrote. "Such is the sad commentary on what is purported to be the most forward-looking nation in the world."

One reason there was not better patient care, Johnson contended, was because scant attention had been paid to training a sufficient number of nurses and using them wisely in the hospital setting. Nurses, he said, were underutilized and often relegated to lesser roles in hospitals because physicians resisted giving them broader responsibilities. As a result of this phenomenon, and too few young women entering nursing training to begin with, a nationwide shortage of nurses began to develop. Johnson had the Foundation increase its funding of nurse training programs, and then came up with the idea of retraining retired nurses who had left the health-care field to raise families. Once the children were older, he said, the nurses could be persuaded to return to their profession. He was right. The program was successful, and many of them did return.

Increasing the flow of well-trained nurses had become one of Johnson's primary goals. At his urging, Johnson & Johnson's Board of Directors passed a resolution requiring every one of the company's affiliates, as well as the major plant locations, to provide financial support for nurses' training at local hospitals. And as usual, Johnson was impatient about getting it done. "We want to move rapidly," he wrote to the Board. "The shortage of nurses is upon us." Then he reminded the Board: "Resolutions are of no value until converted into action."

Six years had passed since the beginning of the medical education loan program, and not one loan had been repaid. Finally, a physician from Chicago who had received $2,800 in loans sent in a payment—a check for $100. He received a letter of thanks and was told he had the distinction of being the first to make a payment on a Foundation loan. Throughout the course of the loan program, few repayments were ever received, however, and this disappointed Johnson.

The patients who needed the most attention, Johnson said, were the elderly and those in frail health. He called them "the gentle folk." He believed that, in addition to the local hospitals—Middlesex and St. Peter's—and the Middlesex Rehabilitation Center, the nursing home was an important component of the health-care system. So he "adopted" the Francis E. Parker Memorial Home in New Brunswick and gave it generous gifts of Johnson & Johnson stock from his personal holdings, not from the Foundation. Over time, the Parker Home, with an endowment approaching $500 million, became the nation's most affluent care center of its kind.

The Parker Home reached this pinnacle of nursing home prominence quite by accident. Mrs. Parker had founded the home in 1905 with a modest gift in memory of her late husband, and in the belief that elderly patients could be cared for best in a homelike setting. After struggling along for some fifty years, the home got Johnson's attention because it matched his views of what a nursing home should be. He began channeling personal gifts of stock to the Parker Home, but he also spent long hours there helping the staff improve the facilities and patient care. He recruited Johnson & Johnson executives to serve on the Parker Home board, a practice that continued through the years. Like the local hospitals, the Parker Home became a "laboratory" where Johnson could test his approaches to patient care. He insisted that he wanted no special recognition for his efforts on behalf of the Parker Home, but years later they put a small brass plaque on the wall in his honor.

•

Over a period of years, Johnson had developed a close relationship with several physicians at the University of Pennsylvania Hospital. One who treated his medical problems was Dr. Francis Wood, an

[515]

erudite physician who loved literature almost as much as he loved medicine—and who became a good friend of Johnson. Another was Dr. Isador Ravdin, a noted surgeon and cancer specialist who taught generations of medical students at Penn. Ravdin was one of four surgeons who were roused in the middle of the night in 1956 to perform emergency surgery on President Dwight Eisenhower. Whenever Johnson and Ravdin were together they began their playful needling of each other. At one luncheon when Johnson was there to make a major gift, he kidded Dr. Ravdin about "having his hand in my pocket." Ravdin didn't deny it.

Because of the General's relationship with Penn, the Johnson & Johnson Board of Directors decided to give $1.5 million to the university's medical school for a building to be named for him. The six-story teaching, research, and library building would be called The Robert Wood Johnson Pavilion and was to be built along Hamilton Walk, on the main campus in Philadelphia. Johnson approved a brief list of mementos to be placed in the cornerstone—including one of his books and a copy of the Credo—and joined Penn President Dr. Gaylord Harnwell for the cornerstone-laying ceremony. It was a warm summer day, and the podium and chairs for several dozen faculty members and guests were set up on the lawn. Johnson listened to the introductory speeches and then went to the podium to give his response. Just then a group of coeds passed by, and he began his remarks by noting: "My, what a wonderful spot this is for girl-watching."

The need for new buildings did not interest Johnson nearly as much as the basic needs of people who were in distress. For a short time, that was the one area outside of health care that appealed to him, and he credited his son, Bobby, with first calling to his attention people who were desperately in need of help and had nowhere else to turn. To locate people in dire need, Johnson urged the Foundation trustees to join him in checking with clergy, the welfare departments, and the courts. "I am not interested in their guilt or innocence, only in their need for help," he told them.

At times the Foundation's resources were far less than the demand for them, and Johnson often used his own funds. When it was learned that one local hospital was getting more aid than the other, he made a personal contribution of $100,000 to the other hospital for a new laboratory. Still, it was not enough to meet the needs of all. "Apparently the bottom of the [cash] box is showing," he wrote to one group seeking help from the Foundation.

The cash box was much larger for Johnson's personal philanthropy, and the rules for distributing it were less formal. The requests came from the remote corners of the globe—the flying priest at the Arctic Circle; American nurses in Vietnam; the mission on the Island of Lepers; the Old Age Pension Club in Oxford, England; Sacred Heart nuns on the Island of Tonga. "It seems as though you are always willing to give another gift," one person wrote, and that was close to the truth. It was easy to trace the route that Johnson had taken in his travels by the letters that followed him back to New Brunswick asking for his help—which he had already given in small amounts on his trip.

As was his way, Johnson sometimes gave advice with the money. When a Salvation Army hospital in India proudly sent a photo of its small marching band—along with a request for money—Johnson noted in his reply that it was a good-looking group but that the marchers appeared to be out of step. And when sending a contribution to one children's school, he urged the teachers to be sure to give their charges a "sense of discipline, a sense of cleanliness, and a respect for God."

The compass of Johnson's giving from his personal funds pointed in all directions, and some of the salesmanship used on him was worthy of an award. Perhaps top honors went to Father Ed Moffet, the poetic priest who ran Blessed Andrew Kim Hospital on Paengnyong Island in the Yellow Sea in the Republic of Korea. Father Ed, as he called himself, wrote passionate appeals on an old erratic typewriter with bumpy letters, and yet the message came across as stirring and seamless prose.

[517]

"How long have I known your mercy," Father Ed wrote to Johnson. "In this crisis I lean on you again [the ambulance ship had been hit by a typhoon]. I beg it in the name of my sick and my poor here in the ocean." And another time: "Your personal, great gift of love for my little ones just arrived. With the agony of this hurt for my little ones breaking over me, I keep afloat by the power of your mercy—my stricken ones are safe with care and the cure of your love. My clumsy mind and full heart stall each time I try to thank you for the hope and the life your compassion has kept alive here on this lost isle in the ocean. In the love stories and epics and sages of all human history, no love has ever worked greater change, reaching out to save these little ones oceans and half a world away from Bayonne [Father Ed meant New Brunswick]. I can only whisper again what you must know by now. You belong to this isle—you own my heart."

The letters kept coming, and the checks kept going out.

Johnson was not always a pushover. Sometimes his tendency to give was tempered by practicality. One day he went into St. Peter's Church, near his office, for "a look around." The monsignor who was the pastor was the brother of Norris Harding, Johnson's personal assistant and gatekeeper. On the visit, he decided that the church needed, as he put it, some "touching up," so he arranged a Saturday morning meeting at the church with the monsignor and George Bahash, one of Johnson's maintenance managers.

Bahash recalled what happened next: "We went through the church, and the General and the monsignor kept adding to the list of things that should be done, and the list kept getting longer. When I reported back to him later that the work would cost $100,000, he was surprised. So he told me to cut it back to $60,000 and get it done."

After agreeing to pay for the interior painting of a Protestant church in New Brunswick, Johnson learned that the congregation also wanted to include gold-leafing of the church organ. Here he drew the line. "It seems to me that if the good church members want the organ gold-leafed, then they should pay for it," he wrote. Yet he would spend money to correct a problem that only he saw. On a visit to another church, he noticed dark blemishes in the grain of the walnut wood of an altar rail. He thought they detracted from the beauty of the setting, so he got permission to hire a wood-worker, and after considerable effort the blemishes were removed. Johnson went back to check the results and was satisfied.

"The General liked to see action in these projects," said Bahash. "If he couldn't see action, you were in trouble. Once I took a crew to his home in Princeton, where water was leaking into the basement. All day long we looked for the source of the leak and couldn't find it. Late in the afternoon, I got worried because he would be home soon. I had the men dig a big hole next to the foundation, for no good reason other than to show him we were taking action. It worked. When he came home he looked at the hole and was satisfied that we were making progress."

Some of the personal checks Johnson mailed out were accompanied by a touch of humor. He wrote to one friend, a nun, that he hadn't been feeling well and jokingly attributed his condition to having "fallen off a bar stool." Concerned, the sister wrote back that she was having Masses said for his recovery and urged him "to be more careful of bar stools."

Johnson did not need a special reason or event to prompt his generosity. Once he spontaneously sent his friend Francis Cardinal Spellman a check for $25,000 for the New York Foundling Home, saying he had "found the money in the bottom of the strongbox." And when he learned that a clergyman needed transportation, he bought him a new car. Once he gave a group of nuns in Boston a station wagon he himself owned, and had it delivered filled with Johnson & Johnson products. He always had a new concern. "I have been disturbed," he once wrote, "over the plight of women prisoners when they are released. A man finds it difficult enough, but a girl or woman much more difficult."

The most personal aspect of his generosity was extended to

members of his family, for whom Johnson at various times established trusts. (Seward did the same with members of his family, beginning in the early 1940s.) In the early 1960s, he formed substantial trusts for Bobby's children too, using gifts of Johnson & Johnson stock, as he had done earlier for Bobby himself. Bobby wrote his father: "Since words are never adequate, I can only hope that you understand just how much we appreciate your generosity."

But the warmth that accompanied Johnson's gifts of stock to Bobby and his family did not carry over to their business relationship, which was becoming increasingly strained. The General saw family and business as separate matters. Johnson often said, "The company is my life," and no one ever doubted that. It *was* his life. Fewer people understood, however, that Johnson & Johnson was also a large part of Bobby's life.

On the rare occasions when Bobby talked about it, he made it clear how he felt: "My whole life revolves around this company," wrote Bobby. "It began when I was three years old, and I cannot conceive of this changing." It is doubtful that the General ever understood how deeply his son felt about Johnson & Johnson. If he had understood it might have influenced his thoughts and actions in the stormy days ahead.

Late in the fall of 1964 the General became increasingly concerned about his son's health, and he summoned Bobby to his office. They had a lengthy, combative discussion that included the state of Bobby's health, his lifestyle (the General thought Bobby drank too much, which he vehemently denied), and his performance as president of the company. Bobby stoutly defended his performance and his business decisions. As was often the case when the two went head-to-head, there was more sound and fury than resolution.

When Bobby left his father's office he was highly agitated, but he had agreed to have a thorough physical examination. On November 22, Bobby entered Middlesex Hospital for three days of tests. When he came out of the hospital he reported to his colleagues that he had several health problems, including a peptic ulcer, high blood pressure, and his excessive weight. In mid-December, Bobby left for his division's annual sales meeting in Florida.

Though it seemed unthinkable at the time, Bobby Johnson would never return to the company.

33

THE PERFECTIONIST

ONE evening several weeks after his return from the disappointing maiden voyage of the *Pilgrim*, Johnson was seated next to an old friend, William J. Hughes, at a hospital board meeting in New Brunswick. Hughes and his two brothers ran a well-known company at 17 Battery Place in New York that chartered, bought, and sold marine vessels of all types. Johnson suddenly turned to Hughes and said, "Bill, you know a lot about ships. How would you like to work with me on my next boat?"

Hughes replied, "Sure, General, I'd be glad to."

Years later, and with a sigh of resignation, Bill Hughes looked back and remarked, "I never realized when the General asked me the question that evening, and I responded as I did, that it would change the course of my life for the next three years."

The Hughes Brothers company stationery prominently displays the slogan "Clearing House For Marine Difficulties." In their years in the marine business, the brothers had been tested many times, but they had never encountered the nature and number of problems that Johnson was capable of generating. Reflecting on this experience, Bill Hughes had a theory: "I truly believe that the General created problems so he could then go ahead and solve them."

The next morning, and with the sense of urgency imposed on the assignment by the General, Bill Hughes began his search. Earlier, Johnson had decided that this time he would not build a ship, but purchase one about 200 feet long that was seaworthy and capable of taking him anywhere in the world. Once he found a vessel that met his basic specifications, he would have it modified to meet his particular desires. As it turned out, the General's "modifications" would become Bill Hughes's "problems," but through it all Hughes remained cheerful and, above all, patient. "My mother taught me that patience is a virtue, and besides, I truly liked and admired the General. He fascinated me. But he was a perfectionist."

With a feeling of relief, Johnson put the matter in the hands of Hughes and turned his attention to business and the new role he had created for himself: Chairman of the Finance Committee of the Board of Directors. It was not a "committee," however, but one person — the General — who gave himself the assignment of riding herd on Johnson & Johnson's financial matters. It soon became clear that he would approach this role with his usual zeal.

One of the first things Johnson did was research and write several thoughtful memos on economic trends in the nation and the world and relate them to the company's business and spending patterns. He noted the generous expenditures for "market research, advertising, and promotion," and he criticized what he termed "penurious investments in research and experimental mechanical development." He began to influence higher investment in research, and this trend would continue into the future.

Johnson's wisdom had the greatest impact in the basics of the business, not in sophisticated financial strategy. It was his unwavering belief that management should concentrate on building the business for the long term, and not be lured by the temptation of short-term profits. He wrote to the Board: "We want enough profit to remain liquid. We want enough profit to progress, to make up for obsolescence and to develop our companies in a sound and reasonable way. We want enough profit to add each year to our safety fund of free and unencumbered cash. Beyond this we do not wish too much profit." He advocated channeling profits back into the business, and he had little or no concern for the amount paid out in stock dividends.

He could not tolerate having the company in debt, and he was delighted when a *Forbes* magazine article on the company's progress under Philip Hofmann's leadership commented that Johnson & Johnson "doesn't owe anybody a dime." That, and a Hofmann quote—"We try to be dynamic in research, manufacturing, and marketing and sales, and ultraconservative financially"—warmed Johnson's heart.

Hofmann was doing a credible job as Johnson's successor, which the *Forbes* article pointed out. Even more important to the General, though, was that the present management was preserving and building on the culture that he had spent so many years creating and nurturing within the company. That aspect of the business was paramount to Johnson, who made his intent clear: "I am leaving a business, not money, and it is of great importance to me to maintain the integrity and personality of the company."

In the role of patriarch, Johnson was exercising as much restraint as possible to keep from interfering with routine decisions. He tried to stay away from that area, and for the most part he did. But through his endless storm of memos—the "blue blizzard"—he would advise and counsel, cajole, nudge, push, and occasionally intimidate, until he got his point across. He was crafty in his variety of approaches, but so was Hofmann, who had developed a technique for dealing with the General. "At times he could be exceedingly dogmatic, and therefore difficult," said Hofmann. "When he took a stubborn position, I wouldn't oppose him on the spot. I'd let it rest a few days, then come back and say, 'Now, General, let's review that matter again.' And if I had a logical argument, he would always listen and often change his position. It was how you approached it."

Philip Hofmann had not been shy about taking the reins of the company. In fact, he was not shy about anything. When presiding at the annual stockholder meeting, he conducted the business portion with crisp efficiency, resorting to his usual practice of taking the shareholders on a rapid tour of the worldwide Family of Companies and commenting in greater detail on the larger ones. Because the General had decided to absent himself from these meetings, Hofmann had the podium to himself, and he reveled in the role. Then came a usually benign question-and-answer period, often shortened by the shareholder rush to the traditional bowls of iced extra-large jumbo shrimp—which later disappeared in an economy wave.

Occasionally Hofmann added a touch of humor to the meeting. Once when a news reporter asked him during the meeting if he wasn't worried about owning so much Johnson & Johnson stock and having all his eggs in one basket, Hofmann replied: "As long as I am sitting on the basket, I am not worried."

Johnson had once chided Hofmann about his lack of humility, an occasion that Hofmann recalled with amusement. "The General came to me and said: 'Phil, you have all this ability and drive and punch, but you don't have enough humility.' Now, he thought *he* was humble because he felt that's how he should be. But he wasn't humble. He and I had the same problem with humility, and people with certain characteristics often do. Humility didn't fit him any more than it did me."

"There was nothing humble about Bob," said Don Hittle, Johnson's friend and retired Marine Corps general. "He was a big man. He was an able man. He was a powerful man, and he knew it. He wasn't humble, but he had a sense of responsibility."

These opinions never reached Johnson's ears, so he continued to preach humility to his people. In particular, any boasting about the company's rapid growth bothered him. "We are a large family of small companies," he wrote. "We only reach large size when we put these all together. This may be good for our ego, but from a management standpoint we must think in terms of operating small and medium-size companies." Whenever he heard someone boast about the quality of management within the company, he reminded them: "It would be better manners if we stopped patting ourselves on our own backs." Despite his admonitions about boasting to outsiders, he had a glowing opinion of his management: "We have a fine management and we are proud of it."

In one letter to the Board of Directors, Johnson discussed the pitfalls of boasting about the company, but he was probably more concerned that it would drive up the price of the stock. Urging restraint, he said:

> At social gatherings, please do not brag about our companies. First of all, such conversation is considered bad manners. Further, there are people in the banking, brokerage, and competitive areas who would like to know more about the fabric of our enterprise. While there may be times when it is all right to brag, most of the time we would do better to follow a course of humility. We do not wish to make a mark on the speculative exchanges [his term for stock exchanges] of the country. We are essentially interested in making better products at lower cost. We are interested primarily in performing an important professional service to the public-at-large. Let this be the measure of our success. A degree of dignified advertising is appropriate. A larger degree of high-powered merchandising is appropriate to the trade. When we are interviewed by Wall Street analysts it would be best if we played down our optimism. If for no other reason, then consider the attitude of our government towards success. Governments throughout the world are not in favor of individual private success. Hence I think you should paint a very moderate position in terms of your public relations.

For the most part, Johnson kept an open mind and could be persuaded to revise some of his business decisions of the past, providing the new circumstances warranted it. Decisions could be amended, but he was adamant about holding to his philosophy. One area of decision-making that he considered sacrosanct had to do with matters dealing with the company's stock. "I have made many errors," he said, "but never with Johnson & Johnson stock."

He strongly resisted splitting the stock, even when it was selling at more than $100 a share and had one of the highest multiples (earnings per share) in the health-care industry in the mid-1960s. "Broadly speaking, the market will take care of itself. It is not our desire to run with the pack. Our value in the marketplace will be determined by our competence," he told his management. The argument that a high price per share kept the stock from having broader ownership carried no weight with him, because he preferred having fewer shareholders to begin with—except for his employees. He wanted as many employees as possible to own Johnson & Johnson stock. Not just as a reward, but as an incentive to do their jobs better.

The General could be tough on nonperformers. Once he wrote to directors in his companies around the world: "Now is the time to rid ourselves of all weak men and women in management. We have carried borderline cases for many years in the hope that we could improve them and out of a sense of charity. Today, anyone from Johnson & Johnson can find employment. Now is the time to separate them from our team." On the other hand, he was extraordinarily generous with those who performed well, and he constantly sought new ways to reward them. He wrote Philip Hofmann: "I think the executive salaries are too low. It is wise to remember that the people who developed this business should have an important equity interest in the company."

He urged his managers to be decisive, noting: "It is increasingly clear that only the 'Combat Executive' will survive the present era, one who has the state of mind to move towards aggressive and realistic administrative procedures." He resisted attempts to group people together in any way that removed their individuality, and he detested what he called the "Civil Service Philosophy." "Humans are not that way—grades, stratification, uniformity," he said. "These are degrading and don't promote human relations. The incentive for expression is diminished. It is not humanly possible to fit people into ten or twenty grades, and in the end it makes for mediocrity."

"He was a tough taskmaster," a longtime colleague said of Johnson. "He could be difficult and demanding, but he was fair. You could dig yourself into a hole, and that was all right, as long as you could climb out. But when he saw that you couldn't, that was it. The project or the person was finished. He would give you enough rope to hang yourself, and some did."

Despite constant change in the workplace brought on by rapid modernization of high-speed computerized equipment, Johnson held on to his basic belief that the secret to better performance was in workplace relationships: "When management masters the human side of the job, we'll get the orderly life we seek," he said

He continued his practice of avoiding meetings, particularly large ones. "Bad decisions are made at large meetings," he wrote. "It is better to have more competence and fewer people." He was critical of sales meetings, saying: "Many of our executives do not realize the sales meeting is a captive audience. Those listening cannot escape. It would be interesting to know how many of the audience would have bought a ticket to attend." And he could be sarcastic: "I am in favor of making mistakes and learning from them. As a matter of fact, I am quite impressed with the number of mistakes we make, but not so impressed that we learn anything."

He was clearly enjoying his new role as patriarch, philosopher, planner, and, in the view of some, royal second-guesser. He summed up for a friend how he saw his involvement in the business: "An important segment of my time is spent stopping some people from committing suicide. Another segment is spent identifying opportunities others do not grasp, but which offer progress, better service, and more profit, yet do not require great investment."

He carefully watched the performance and the management style of his senior management, observing how problems were handled. "When you face a complex situation," he said, "split the problem into its components and correct the components." And if someone got bogged down in too much detail he would say, "Sounds like Harvard thinking to me." Yet, as he was grappling with one difficult management problem, he noted: "There must be someone in the United States who can help us with this problem. Perhaps it is the Harvard Business School—God forbid!"

Johnson's presence in the company was as palpable as ever, even though he wasn't as visible as he used to be. In addition to the flood of memos, there was still the stream of books on business and national issues that he distributed to "enlighten" his people or drive home a point of view that he was sympathetic with. It was not unusual for him to purchase books in quantities of a hundred or more, depending on how far into the executive ranks he wanted to go. Some in the company, particularly younger managers, labeled this brainwashing.

Virtually everything he did, said, and wrote had a practical aspect. Yet he was quick to recognize the part that "luck" played. He wrote a friend, saying: "We have made our mistakes, we have had our failures, and by the grace of God and the competence of our team we have had our successes. As you know, there is luck in industry. When we succeed, we are likely to tell ourselves that it is the result of our intelligence and competence. When we fail, we are likely to blame it on bad luck. For your private information, there is some luck either way, and those of us who fail enough know it."

He also had his strong biases, and these he clung to tenaciously. "Never allow yourselves to set up a department of forward planning, for it will be an expense and a failure," he warned the Executive Committee. "Forward planning must begin at the highest level and carry through to the company presidents. It is part of our job, and it can't be done by a department of planning." He was also adamant about not giving the personnel department any responsibility for selecting and training future management, maintaining that "only a top-flight executive can evaluate an embryonic executive."

•

The General's prolific output of memos and letters kept three secretaries busy, and others on reserve nearby. By the time he had finished breakfast at home he had a long list of notes, some of which he made when he awoke during the night and wrote on the pad at his bedside table. One of his two senior aides, either Olga Ferretti or Doris Little, would drive to his home at Longleat in Princeton about nine o'clock in the morning. Johnson would then drive them to the office in New Brunswick (in the Cadillac with the huge Saint Christopher's medal mounted on the hood). Before the car got to the gate of the estate he would begin dictating memos and letters. If a plant inspection was on the day's agenda, he would stop there en route.

Once at his office, he continued working with his other secretaries, or the dictation machine, and by mid-afternoon he had churned out a staggering pile of correspondence. Leaving the office before the evening traffic rush, he often did more dictating on the ride home, or visited another of the dozen company plants between New Brunswick and Princeton. "His happiest moments were when he lived with his work," his colleague Gustav Lienhard observed.

The General's memos demanded attention, but they weren't always easy to deal with. Some of his ideas were farfetched and required more delicate handling. None of his memos died a natural death, because of his efficient system for reviving them from his bulging follow-up file. It wasn't possible, or prudent, to simply ignore a subject he had written about — it demanded either action or a plausible explanation. No subject was ever just forgotten.

For years he followed the practice of having stand-alone cards printed with a motto or message, most of which originated with him. The cards were usually four by six inches and nicely printed on heavy stock with red or gold beveled edging. He would have them distributed to some one hundred executives in the company, usually the same ones who received books from him. Among his favorites were:

MANAGEMENT IS CAUSE
ALL ELSE EFFECT

ANY FOOL CAN SPEND MONEY.
ONLY A COMPETENT MAN CAN
MAKE SOUND AND SECURE PROFITS

THIS IS NO TIME FOR AVOIDANCE
EVASION OR EXCUSES

WHY BE DIFFICULT
WHEN WITH A LITTLE EFFORT
YOU CAN BE IMPOSSIBLE

WE LEARN THE HARD WAY
THAT PROCRASTINATION DEVELOPS
A NEW COMPETITOR

All told, he distributed about two dozen different messages during his final years at the company. Some of the cards found a place on office shelves or side tables, and occasionally on desks (which went against his admonition that "a cluttered desk is a cluttered mind"). Others wound up in desk drawers or the scrap basket — but not right away. It was considered prudent to have one or two in evidence in case Johnson made one of his surprise office visits. Being added to his distribution list for the message cards and books became a status symbol for mid-range executives — a rite of passage.

Johnson now had more time to visit drugstores, especially local, independent druggists who helped build the company's business in the early years and were now threatened by the influx of large chain stores. He believed that the local druggists suffered from what he called "owner frustration." After returning from one of his drugstore patrols, where he had checked the product shelves and commiserated with the owner, he wrote a company colleague: "If you hired me to sell the local drugstore I would practice the art of friendly, personal selling to gain the owner's confidence and good will. We need to find the *pulse* of the independent druggist." He then offered suggestions on how to accomplish this.

On his visits to drugstores — a routine that he had now expanded to include supermarkets and what he called "discount houses"—he was also on the lookout for company products where the packaging had been damaged, discolored, or became dirty from handling. He called these "injured products" and said they were unacceptable for Johnson & Johnson because they reflected on the company's reputation with consumers. To make his point, he personally recruited a dozen or so secretaries and told them to go to various stores in the New Brunswick area and purchase all the "injured products" they could find. He then assembled the packages on a large table and invited the marketing groups in to view them. He told them to correct the problem immediately.

He routinely checked store shelves for what he termed "brand impact," which he said was the impression a product display left on consumers. He was always impressed by the displays of what he called "the soapers"—companies making soap products and toothpastes. "Brand impact" was as important as advertising, he explained, because "on any given day more people pass through the aisles of retail stores than read all the magazines in the country." When he didn't find the "brand impact" he wanted, he would fire off another memo: "I am weary of riding herd on those executives who stray from the path of brand impact."

On one of these forays to a supermarket, the General wheeled a shopping cart for the first time. When he returned to the office, he reported excitedly on the experience. One staff member recalled: "He was like a big kid, telling us how he maneuvered the cart up and down the aisles and how easy it made shopping. You would think shopping carts had just been invented."

People outside the company were always trying to get his ear to tell him about an idea they had for a new product for Johnson & Johnson to market. Even when there was room for skepticism, he faithfully reported back on the suggestions, as when his podiatrist had an idea for a new kind of toothpaste. "My local foot doctor is a man of ideas," he wrote, "but I am not keen on the toothpaste business." No matter how farfetched an idea was, he usually had it evaluated so he could report back to the originator—whom Johnson saw not as a bother but as a customer who should not be treated lightly. To his way of thinking, the customer always came first.

·

About the time of his seventy-first birthday, in April 1964, Johnson's associates began noticing a change in him. He had always been impatient, but now it was more noticeable. One colleague noted: "When he wanted something done, he wanted it done yesterday." Another said: "He was becoming quite a different person, perhaps attributable to his poor health and advancing age. He may have come to the inevitable realization that at some point you begin to lose your leadership. He was getting more and more irascible."

For the first time, Johnson began discussing the future of the company after his death, and the process for selecting a Chairman to succeed Hofmann someday. He also spoke about being tired and about how much he looked forward to returning to the sea on his next boat so he could sail it around the world to visit his companies. Tired or not, he would make it a "working ship."

In the months following his new assignment for the General, Bill Hughes presented Johnson with photos and details of dozens of ships that were for sale, hoping that one would appeal to him. But for one reason or another there was something wrong with each of the ships. It was not an easy assignment, but Hughes was patient—you had to be when working with the General.

Having grown up in New Brunswick, Hughes knew many of the same people and places that Johnson did. During Prohibition, a very young Bill Hughes used to deliver beer from Tennyson's Tavern at a penny a pail to imbibers in his neighborhood—and this was during the errant phase of Johnson's youth, when he was upstairs at Tennyson's drinking and talking politics. The two men laughed easily about the old days, and how angry Petey Tennyson would get when the pail had been coated with butter to reduce the amount of foam when he filled it with beer from the tap.

Hughes's frustrations were just beginning. Often when he got home in the evening there would be a packet of correspondence from Johnson, with new questions about a certain ship or changes in his earlier list of specifications. He was constantly changing his mind about what he wanted. Hughes tried, but he could not keep up with the flow of correspondence from Johnson and his corps of secretaries. His replies were terse as he pressed on with his search for Johnson's "Dream Ship."

At one point Vincent Astor's splendid yacht, the *Nourmahal*, became available. Johnson remembered seeing it in Nassau Harbor years earlier, when Franklin D. Roosevelt was a guest aboard it. But the *Nourmahal* was more than 300 feet long and had a crew of thirty. "I might have been interested at one time," Johnson wrote Hughes, "but she is larger than I want and would require too many men." It was also too expensive, for, as Hughes put it, Johnson was at heart a "horse trader" when it came to boats.

Hughes finally located a steel-hull ship in excellent condition in Baltimore. It had been built after World War II, as an Army mine planter known as an ACM 12, for active duty in the Harbor Defense Forces at the Panama Canal. It was called the *Weaver*, for Major General Erasmus Weaver, but was better known as "the ACM 12." When President Truman ordered the armed forces unified in 1949, the *Weaver* became a Navy ship. Later it was sold to the current owner in Baltimore and renamed the *Kipman*. She was 190 feet long, had a beam of 37 feet, was steam-powered, and the price—$85,000—was right. The vessel also had the full endorsement of Bill Hughes, and after careful consideration the General gave orders to buy it. The good ship *Kipman*, which had been leading a rather dull existence, was about to become adventurous under Johnson's ownership.

Among the specifications the General had given Hughes was that the ship had to be diesel-powered, which meant finding engines and installing them. Hughes quickly located a pair of General Motors diesels that were available from the *New York*, a vessel known as a trailership, and he purchased them for $65,000. Johnson would bear the expense of dismantling and moving them to a yard for the conversion. Hughes had scouted out a dozen shipyards before settling on the Avondale Shipyards in New Orleans, run by the tough-minded, no-nonsense Henry Zac Carter, who had boasted in a *New York Times* article, "We work hard." Mr. Carter had yet to encounter the General's interpretation of hard work.

After months of frustrating effort, Hughes was encouraged by the progress he was making. He had acquired a suitable vessel and located diesel engines and a shipyard to do the conversion. He had persuaded the Moran tugboat company to tow the *Kipman* to New Orleans. Just before the ship was to leave, Hughes got instructions from Johnson to change the name to *Ocean Star*, which he did. Evie Johnson, who was less fond of boats than she was of naming them, had suggested that name. But by the time the *Ocean Star*, under tow, reached the shipyard on the Mississippi, Johnson had decided he liked the name *Zodiac* better — after one of his earlier boats. Evie's choice of names had a short life.

The list of changes to be made to the *Zodiac* grew longer after the General went to New Orleans to inspect the ship. When Avondale presented an estimate of $985,000 for the work Johnson wanted done, he hit the ceiling and threatened to have the ship towed out of the yard into the Mississippi River. A calmer Bill Hughes said he would put the job out for bids, but after negotiating with Avondale they agreed on a price and the extensive conversion was begun. And relations with the yard improved after the General returned home.

The ship never got its hull wet under the name *Zodiac*, for before it came out of drydock at Avondale the name was again changed, to *Golden Crest* — a name that one of the General's secretaries spotted on a sign along a New Jersey highway. The name "Zodiac" had to be abandoned because it duplicated the name of another ship in the Bermuda registry. At long last the ACM 12 had resolved its identity problem, and the *Golden Crest* was prepared for its maiden voyage.

Meanwhile, the *Pilgrim* was back at the Hall-Russell yard in

Scotland getting the expensive "corrections" that Johnson wanted made to her. When asked why he wasn't selling the ship as it was, he replied that it was a matter of ethics. It should be made "right" before going to a new owner, he believed. By the time the *Pilgrim* was offered for sale, the General's attitude about it had changed. No longer was it "a floating disaster," as he had once called it. Now he was the seller, and his opinion of the *Pilgrim* was getting better and better. That was partly because of the salesman in him, and partly because the improvements to the ship had cost him $400,000.

"There are no cards that are not face up on the table with regards to the sale of the *Pilgrim*," Johnson wrote. As his attitude about the vessel changed, the real reason he decided to sell it surfaced. "Why does a man of my experience choose to dispose of her?" he asked theoretically. "The answer is I want a bigger ship."

The *Pilgrim* was not the ship of his dreams. An Englishman, spotting a bargain, went to Scotland and bought the boat for just over $300,000. (Thirty years later the *Pilgrim* would be resold in the United States for ten times more and become part of the Palm Beach scene as a still-handsome yacht.) But Johnson was philosophical when he approved the sale. "I have closed the book on *Pilgrim*," he said, "and I will not look back." And he never did.

34

CONFLICT WITH
BOBBY

ANY colleagues of both men believed that a tragic clash between Bobby Johnson and his father was inevitable. The signs were all there, and had been for years.

"One of the hardest things in the world is to be the son of an outstanding father," observed Dr. Joseph Kler, the kindly, wise, and aging physician who had treated members of the Johnson family for decades and knew both father and son well. "The General expected too much of Bobby. He wanted him to do more than he himself did. Young Bobby had the potential, but he never had the chance."

Certain things Bobby did annoyed his father, and he made no attempt to change. Bobby had brought into the company a small group of marketing people whom he considered friends as well as associates. His father labeled them "cronies." Senior executives traditionally lunched in the executive dining room, where the General held forth at his corner table, but most days Bobby and his "cronies" were at the Edgebrook Restaurant on the Route 1 traffic circle, enjoying a two-martini lunch.

The General, himself rail-thin, was obsessed with Bobby's weight problem and health in general. Whenever the subject came up, the conversations always became agitated. "The General was concerned for Bobby," a colleague said, "and with the profile he presented." Another added: "They clashed because they were quite the same personalities. And then there was Bobby's lifestyle, which the General objected to strenuously."

After receiving a copy of his son's medical report, following Bobby's medical tests at Middlesex Hospital, the General wrote Philip Hofmann on December 1: "He [Bobby] and I are greatly relieved to learn that there is no evidence of further, perhaps more serious, medical problems." Meanwhile, after attending the company's sales and marketing conference at Hollywood, Florida, Bobby went to his winter home near Pompano Beach, Florida, where he began an intense effort to restore his health. Just before Christmas he wrote to his father and the Chairman of the Executive Committee, recommending that James E. Burke be named acting general manager until he returned. That action was promptly taken. There was little communication between father and son during the ensuing weeks.

Starting with the new year, the General began a not-so-subtle effort to undermine his son's performance as president of the company. In a number of memos he used the phrase "if and when he returns to the company," giving rise to the suspicion that the General had already determined in his own mind that Bobby would not be coming back. When Bobby had not returned by February 15, he was informed in writing that he was placed on an indefinite leave of absence, at half pay, until his full recovery. He concurred with that arrangement in writing.

In the company, the impression was mounting that the division between father and son was growing even wider and went far beyond a temporary health problem that had to be corrected before Bobby could return. For executives with careers on the line — and perhaps sympathetic with father or son, or both of them — it was a delicate matter. Crossing the General could be perilous. Few were willing to serve as mediator, but Dick Mulligan, the gregarious Irishman who was head of personnel at the time, remembers trying. "Bobby would never give an inch," he said, "and his father was the same way. They were both of the same mold. I told Gus and Phil [Lienhard and Hofmann] that I could try to bring the two of them together, and I was told to stay out of that situation. And that's one of my regrets in life, that I didn't make a college try."

Another effort to bring father and son together was made by Jim Burke, now acting general manager and a good friend of Bobby's, though not one of the "cronies." Burke had a good rapport with the General too, and one day in mid-March he raised the delicate issue and pointed out the importance of maintaining the continuity of the Johnson family policy and leadership in the company. The family influence on the business could be lost forever if Bobby did not return to the company, he told Johnson. In being so outspoken, Burke, a person of exceptional integrity, was jeopardizing his own rise in the company, because he was the logical successor to the young Johnson. Still, he made the effort.

After thinking about what Burke had said, the General replied in writing: "Without question this [argument] has merit, and in its best form it has great merit. However, you have heard of the saying 'overalls to overalls' in three generations. This became something of an American tradition." He then went on to say, in a rambling way, that Burke's argument, good as it was, would not change the situation.

On April 10, upon learning of the rumors at the company, Bobby began a lengthy and impassioned letter to his father. In it he denied any responsibility for new product ventures that had gone awry and reportedly cost the company a lot of money. The losses were far less than some had mentioned, he said. He also contended that the advertising strategy devised for Johnson & Johnson, the parent company, was sound, accounting for the increase in sales figures. He denied that attempts to launch a tampon product had resulted in mismanagement, and pointed out that his father had approved many of the decisions to move ahead. He denied accusations of "cronyism," saying that being friendly with his executives was proper. He denied having a problem with alcohol. He described the accusations as being not criticism but "character assassination." "You would not accept this," he wrote his father, "nor can I." Bobby continued:

> Dad, I'm truly sorry that we seem to have gotten at cross purposes. Believe me, it was not through any desire on my part that it happened. I love and admire you tremendously. You have been and are one of the greatest businessmen that America has produced.
>
> Some of the things that I do in business undoubtedly annoy you greatly. Some of my methods and approaches are without question at variance with the traditional. But, I believe that the world and the marketplace are changing and that some new techniques not only work, but are important to success. The fundamentals haven't changed — honesty, decency, high quality, integrity, etc., but some of the procedures, I believe, have.
>
> I have made many mistakes. If I am not mistaken, our Credo, which you wrote, says: "We must make mistakes and pay for them." I believe that over the years I've paid for mine.
>
> Johnson & Johnson is almost my whole life. I have worked for the company for twenty-five years. From the time I was three years old I have had but one goal — our Company. I have brought my own boys up in the same atmosphere.
>
> My greatest desire now is to return to Johnson & Johnson. Nothing else is so important, but you will understand when I say that I cannot do this without honor, and that which accompanies honor: responsibility and authority. I feel that I have earned and deserve this, and I do not intend to lose my self-respect.
>
> Your son,
> Bob

Bobby Johnson did not complete the letter to his father until late in the day on April 11. Earlier that day, the Board of Directors abolished the position of President of Johnson & Johnson, the operating company, and created the position of President of Johnson & Johnson Worldwide, which went to Gustav Lienhard, Chairman of the Executive Committee. This action took away Bobby Johnson's title of president, made him general manager instead, and continued him as a member of the Executive Committee.

When Bobby received word of the changes, he added this postscript to his letter to his father:

I have just heard the results of the Annual Meeting. Considering the above, my removal as President would seem to preclude the possibility of my return. This to me, to say the least, is tragedy.

Bob

Though the official action had been taken, the General was moved by the warm personal words in Bobby's letter and on April 24 wrote in response:

Dear Bob:

I am deeply touched by your expression of love and affection. I assure you from my heart that this is reciprocated.

When you were a tiny infant and for several years thereafter I gave you a good part of my free time and greatly enjoyed seeing you grow into boyhood.

Then came a tragedy which you could not then have understood, and probably do not understand to this day. All that you can do is take my record on faith, agree that it has its unfortunate segments, but I did what I thought was best for all hands.

Affectionately,
Dad

Bobby's close friends urged him not to be precipitous about resigning from the company, hoping that he and his father could reconcile their differences. The relationship had always been haunted by one impediment: when the father was willing to speak, the son would not listen. When the son was willing to speak, the father would not listen.

On May 12 Bobby wrote his father:

Dear Dad,

The request for yet another medical examination is unacceptable to me. You are aware, because I have told you, that my health is now excellent. My ulcer is cured and my blood pressure normal. I weigh thirty pounds less than I did five months ago. In recent weeks, I have had doctors both in the north and in the south examine me. I have had three separate physical examinations in three different locations, including complete GI and stomach examinations, by top doctors in their field. My ulcer has healed, my heart is functioning normally, my blood pressure is normal. I have had enough radiation to choke a horse. I do not wish to have any more at the moment.

Taking the above, you may consider this letter to be my resignation from the Executive Committee and from whatever position I now hold on the Management Board of the parent company. I hope that you will allow me to continue as a member of the Board of Directors, but if you consider this impossible, so be it.

Your son,
Bob

Bobby's resignation at the age of forty-five was now official, and his lifelong dream of someday running Johnson & Johnson was shattered. So was the relationship with his father.

Some weeks later, Bobby received a cordial note from his father expressing the belief that business differences should in no way affect personal or family relationships and inviting Bobby to get together and "go for a swim." Bobby's reply was brief and to the point. There would be no swim. No meeting.

In another brief note to his father, Bobby summed up his feelings. "If you wish to concentrate on a person's weaknesses you can destroy them. It is better to concentrate on their strengths." Bobby felt that he had been destroyed. His father believed that the decision he had made was in the best interests of the company.

Within Johnson & Johnson there was no open debate about the merits of what had occurred, but there were opinions, ranging from feelings that Bobby had been unfairly treated to feelings that the decision was not only correct but fair. "I don't believe anybody shot Bobby down the chute," one senior executive commented. "His father was patient with him. I would have been less patient."

The estrangement between the General and Bobby, like their earlier relationship, had odd twists to it. They did not see each other, but over time they would exchange occasional brief notes, none of them warmly written. Bobby remained on the Board of Directors for the rest of 1965, but he was not reelected because his father recommended against it. That action severed Bobby's final link to the company.

•

During the months that the breakup was taking place, the General was having his own health problems, complaining of abdominal pain and shortness of breath. He went to Bermuda for a rest, and being away from New Brunswick and the conflict with his son seemed to improve his condition. "He was not a tense person, but he was intense," one of his physicians remarked. In Bermuda, he continued his "intense" involvement in the extensive conversion of the former mine-planter to a new dream ship at the Avondale Shipyards in New Orleans. Upon his return, he made the first of a series of trips to personally check on the progress of the work, and it was not long before the shipyard foremen were the ones who needed a rest in Bermuda.

At the shipyard, workers referred to the *Kipman* as a "survey ship," a new term Johnson had given the boat. "Working ship" didn't mean anything to anyone but him, and he forbade calling it a "yacht." Once in drydock, the ship was virtually stripped, and the rebuilding began. The steam power was replaced by diesels, and new generators were installed, as well as an exhaust system Johnson helped design because he had been unhappy with the high noise level on *Pilgrim*. From engine room to pilot house, the ship underwent major renovations: wood paneling in the lounge and staterooms, a new galley, new teak decking and mahogany rails, a new ventilation system, and a complete overhaul of the electrical system.

When Johnson saw the detailed lighting plan for the entire ship, he began recommending changes, from the crew's quarters to the light at the top of the ship's mast. He became involved in the location of each electrical outlet and the type of wiring used. "I have a deathly fear of fire," he explained to the foreman. With each change he ordered, the Avondale bill went higher. He rebelled against the cost of the washer and dryer that had been built to resist corrosion and the rigors of use at sea, and insisted on installing less-expensive models made by Sears & Roebuck. The foreman reluctantly gave in to Johnson's wishes, but he was vindicated many months later when the washer and dryer made for home use failed at sea.

Throughout the conversion process, Bill Hughes remained patient and philosophical. He had been in this role many times before with wealthy and often eccentric yacht owners, and he enjoyed the challenge offered by both the vessels and the personalities of their owners. As for the degree of challenge, he later admitted that Johnson and the *Golden Crest*—nee *Ocean Star* and *Zodiac*—took the prize.

According to the plan, the *Golden Crest* would use the run from New Orleans to the island of Barbados for sea trials. Once there, last-minute corrections would be made before the ship fueled and readied for the 6,000-mile passage to Cape Town, South Africa. When the vessel was ready to leave New Orleans, Johnson invited the local parish priest to bless it. Perhaps the pastor should also have offered a prayer for Bill Hughes, whose trials were far from over. The General then returned home to prepare for the first leg of his long-anticipated world journey.

As the day of his departure from New Brunswick drew closer, and he began to anticipate the invigorating gusts of sea air on the bridge of his new vessel, Johnson's spirits lifted. He was happiest and most content at sea. "The sea is the one remaining place without congestion, annoyance, noise, neon lights, inaccurate news reporting, political creatures and synthetic disturbance," he once wrote. "The sea and all of its moods is a charm to some men, who fear its bad moods but are challenged to survive and bring the ship and its people safely to port. Here one has almost the complete pattern of life."

The first problem he faced when he arrived in Barbados was finding a new captain for the ship. The captain he had hired was dismayed when he learned that Johnson planned to spend eight hours a day on the bridge in two four-hour watches. He liked it better when owners stayed off the bridge. Then there was the matter of the $300 stopwatch the captain ordered in Barbados and had delivered to the ship. Johnson did not like the captain's extravagance, and he told him so. The captain said a few choice words to Johnson, and stalked off the ship several days before it was scheduled to sail.

Johnson phoned Bill Hughes, the problem-solver, in New York and asked him to come to the rescue. Hughes made an urgent call to his friends at Moran, the tugboat company, and they miraculously came up with a captain who was willing to take over the ship on such short notice. To ensure that the new relationship between the General and his captain got off to a good start, Hughes flew to Barbados with Captain Dan Halpin in tow. That turned out to be a wise choice, and Hughes breathed a sigh of relief—another of the General's ship problems was solved.

There wasn't much about being master of a ship that experienced, and diplomatic, Halpin didn't know. He made it clear that there would be no co-captains on any ship of his but that an owner, even an opinionated one like Johnson, would be welcome on the bridge. Immediately, the two developed an easy rapport. The maiden voyage was delayed another two days waiting for a replacement part for the ship's automatic pilot to arrive. To Hughes's horror, it arrived damaged and could not be used. It was then that the General decided there had been enough delays and that the *Golden Crest* would sail the following day without a working automatic pilot. Hughes bid the ship, crew, and passengers farewell and flew back to New York for a well-earned rest.

With colors flying proudly, the gleaming white *Golden Crest* eased out of the harbor at Bridgetown, Barbados, late in the afternoon of September 1, 1965. It headed southeast for its first port of call, the remote island of St. Helena, some 3,700 miles away. The sky was blue, the seas were gentle, and the General was at the wheel on his first watch. He was happy.

Standing next to him on the bridge was the adventurous young Scottish physician, Hugh Murray, who had been the ship's doctor on the perilous maiden voyage of the *Pilgrim*. Undaunted by his first experience with treacherous seas, Dr. Murray took leave from his medical clinic in Regina, Saskatchewan, to accept the invitation to serve again as ship's doctor. Leaving the frigid tundra of the Canadian north and exchanging it for the embracing warmth of the South Atlantic was not a difficult decision for the young physician now interning as a mariner.

Murray and the General got along well, and the young man's enthusiasm for this new adventure seemed to further energize Johnson. He was also good company on the bridge, unfailingly curious about running the ship and the challenges of navigation, and always eager to learn. Worrying about his health, as he was prone to do, Johnson felt more comfortable having Dr. Murray aboard, especially on a sea journey as long as the twenty-two days it would take them to reach Cape Town. Conversations often focused on medical treatment and hospital care, and Murray was constantly amazed and impressed by how knowledgeable Johnson was on these subjects.

As he had faithfully done before, Dr. Murray recorded the highlights of the maiden voyage of the *Golden Crest* in a carefully kept log that he sent periodically to his parents in Scotland so they could share in his adventures. And the General kept notes on the ship's behavior and problems, so between the two of them little of consequence that happened went unrecorded. Captain Halpin had a crew of thirteen, including three hastily recruited Barbadians, to work in the engine room and the galley. Only two of the Scottish crew who had served the *Pilgrim* were signed on for the new ship, and it was perhaps just as well, for the General wanted those memories to fade.

The other passengers aboard were the General's nurse and secretary, Olga Ferretti, and Dr. Robert Page, the research director at Johnson's Ethicon company, and his wife, Barbara. Having someone to talk business with on the trip was important to the General. He also selected guests who would be good company, and he made his choice after carefully screening candidates when the trip was being planned. For company people, there were both advantages and disadvantages to being invited to join the General aboard his ship for a long trip. It could be career-enhancing, but in such close quarters, and for so long, there was little room for error. Yet, it was not an invitation that was easy to decline, and the couples who did accept no doubt experienced a strain on their marriage. The General was a gracious host, but not always easy to take in close confines.

Nearly two hundred feet long, the *Golden Crest* was a reasonably comfortable ship even in rough seas, and Johnson had supervised the decorating. (Doris Little had wisely retired from this duty after her draining experience with the *Pilgrim*.) The decor was warm and inviting, with a masculine touch. In the spacious lounge, the decks were covered with royal-blue nylon carpeting, the walls had fireproof walnut-color synthetic paneling, the furniture was heavy wicker. Two long couches on either side of the lounge had sky-blue damask cushions and faced long marble-top coffee tables. On side tables in the four corners were large wrought-iron lamps painted white and on marble bases. Six plush wicker chairs had oatmeal-colored cushions that matched the short curtains covering the expanse of porthole-type windows that looked out on the walkaround decks. In one corner, facing the lounge, was Johnson's office-type desk and a smaller desk and typewriter for Miss Ferretti. A narrow table against the wall was mounted on an old teakwood sea chest. The royal-blue carpeting was used in the dining salon, which had the same fireproof paneling and wall brackets for lighting. The large dining table seated ten.

There were three paneled and tastefully furnished guest staterooms. Johnson's stateroom was located on the main deck at the bottom of the outside stairway leading to the bridge. Lying on his bunk, he could look up at the compass mounted overhead and keep track of the ship's heading. He always had trouble sleeping, and he could detect the slightest change in the throb of the ship's engines. That gave him a good excuse to go to the bridge in the middle of the night to check on things. One time he caught the watch sleeping. It was the last time that happened.

The ship had been equipped with an expensive radiotelephone but had no Morse code telegraph. After several days the radiotelephone failed, cutting off all communications with the outside world. The radio went out when the General was on the bridge, and to everyone's surprise he was not overly upset. The *Golden Crest* would press on without radio contact and without an automatic pilot, he declared. Johnson's sense of adventure had triumphed over his annoyance. He saved that for his reaction to the first fire drill aboard the ship. In his view it was a disaster because the crew did not know how to manage it. He would correct that, he said, and promised that future fire drills would be better organized. They were, and organized with precision under his direction.

Eleven days into the journey, the General commented on the shaggy locks of some of the crew members, particularly young Billy, a deckhand who hadn't had a haircut in a long time. When the General suggested half-jokingly that he would give him a haircut, the boy foolishly agreed. A pair of scissors was located, and "General Johnson's Barber Shop" was set up on the deck. The barber went to work amid laughter from the passengers and taunts from the crew aimed at their helpless mate. "Even the General admitted it was not a thing of beauty," Dr. Murray reported, "and Billy looked forward to getting his hair tidied up when we reached shore." (After this failure as a barber, Johnson ordered an electric hairclipper for the boat.)

When he wasn't working or standing watch on the bridge, Johnson would attempt to organize some group exercises on the foredeck. With little success, he tried to get the others to do the same ballet exercises he had been doing for years to stay nimble. In the evenings, he had better luck gathering his guests in the lounge to play various board games, like Parcheesi, which he found amusing. Perhaps for lack of anything else to do, other than read, the game-playing became quite animated. The lounge had a large collection of books too, many of them mystery stories, Johnson's favorites. That was the limited evening entertainment offered on the *Golden Crest*—no films and, of course, no television, even in port. Johnson would retire promptly at 9:30.

The ship's cook was talented, and the quality of the food was exceptional. In keeping with the General's disciplined eating habits, the portions were not large, but guests could have more if they wanted. Johnson was adept at orchestrating the conversation during meals, though he was also inclined to dominate them. His range of knowledge and experiences was some justification for that, however, and he was seldom overbearing. He enjoyed humor. Guests had to stay alert, because he asked a lot of questions to draw others into the conversation. He solicited opinions but wasn't always pleased with the responses. Barbara Page, for example, had her firm opinions that often were not in accord with the General's, so sparks flew during some of the dinner conversations.

Party nights aboard the ship were Thursdays, when the General mixed the very dry martinis before dinner and allowed himself two liberal drinks, sometimes three. Usually he would not drink again until the following Thursday, but for other nights guests knew where the bar was. Thursday was Johnson's party, and he often invited some crew members to join the group. Captain Halpin had planned a special celebration when they crossed the Equator, but it was canceled when boisterous seas dampened everyone's party spirit. There were queasy stomachs—except for the General, who liked rough weather.

On the broad expanse of the South Atlantic, they saw no other ships for a week at a time. The tireless albatross that relentlessly followed the *Golden Crest* for days looking for handouts from the cook was the only sign of life, except for the flying fish that landed on the foredeck—and then in the frying pan for dinner. On the morning of the fifteenth day out of Barbados, St. Helena hove into view and the ship moved into Jamestown Bay and anchored close to the wharf. At the time, the island had no airfield, and it would sometimes be months before a ship stopped there. Every time the passengers and crew of the *Golden Crest* went ashore, they were welcomed by some of the island's five thousand lonesome inhabitants. Johnson, as was his custom, organized a dinner party at a local restaurant for members of the crew, with the ship's cook, Fred, as the guest of honor. The cook's labors were not made easier by the lack of air-conditioning in the galley, an egregious oversight when the ship was being converted at Avondale.

The island of St. Helena offered little in the way of sightseeing, its best-known landmark being the place where Napoleon lived during his exile and was buried after his death. Having covered that ground thoroughly, the passengers of the *Golden Crest* were anxious to set sail for South Africa, but first the ship had to replenish its rapidly dwindling water supply. The level in the fresh-water tanks had been dropping faster than it should have. The captain surmised that there was a leak somewhere in the ship's labyrinth of waterlines and ordered two thousand gallons of fresh water. The General, widely known for his compulsive cleanliness, blanched when a grubby-looking, dilapidated water barge pulled alongside to deliver the fresh water—to which he had Dr. Murray add far too much chlorine.

Just before weighing anchor, the ship took on mail pouches the captain had agreed to carry to Cape Town, because the next boat was not due at the island for two months. With the assignment came an official "mail flag" that the *Golden Crest* would fly en route to South Africa, some 1,700 nautical miles away. The ship was averaging a speed of eleven knots, and it would be about a week before it reached Cape Town. As much as he loved being at sea, the General loved his work even more, and he was growing uneasy with the less-demanding work schedule.

At mid-afternoon, a week later, the *Golden Crest* eased into the harbor at Cape Town, a city picturesquely situated beneath the 3,000-foot Table Top Mountain. A large delegation of Johnson & Johnson people — much larger than the General had expected — was on hand to greet him, along with a horde of reporters and photographers. Patiently, he posed for photos and replied politely to the usual barrage of questions about the ship's size, range, and cost (a question he always dodged). (Bill Hughes later said that before the General was finished tinkering with the ship and getting it the way he wanted, he had spent $1 million on it.)

During the interview, a reporter asked where Mrs. Johnson was. "Well, I'll tell you," the General replied, "it is not her cup of tea to accompany me on my excursions on my ship. I love being on the water, and she loves flying over it. She doesn't like the daring waters the way I do."

.

Among those on the wharf awaiting Johnson's arrival was nurse Dorothy O'Neal, on special assignment for the General. It was an unusual assignment that brought her to South Africa and other remote corners of the world. Throughout his fifty years in the medical field, Johnson had made many personal commitments to visionary projects that resulted in better health care. In the early days these included organizing hospital services according to medical specialties, helping develop the nation's first school to train hospital managers, and working to vastly improve nurses' training.

In recent years, Johnson had been focusing on a very basic but elusive goal — to provide a low-cost sanitary protection product to women in the undeveloped countries of the world for use during their menstrual cycles. His goal, he said, was to bring dignity and an affordable product to poorer women who were forced to improvise, even using such substitutes as fibrous plants in place of feminine-hygiene products they could not afford. An affordable and acceptable product would "be a great service to millions of women," he said. That was the challenge he took on, more as a personal project, separate from his successful Personal Products Company, which made an array of feminine-hygiene products.

Nurse O'Neal had spent five years as a missionary nurse in the Belgian Congo, where she was supervisor of a leprosarium. A native of Pennsylvania, she had a college degree in religious education and psychology, spoke several languages, and gave the impression of being a rugged individualist, which appealed to Johnson. So he personally hired her, and then planned her assignment: to go to undeveloped countries in South and Central America, Africa, and the Caribbean and learn from women there what type of feminine-hygiene product would be most acceptable to them. "We know that traditions and habits vary from country to country," he said.

"The day after he arrived in Cape Town," Nurse O'Neal related, "he told me he would show me how to conduct store checks to gather information for my assignment. It was winter there, and he wore a black raincoat and a black hat and looked like a preacher. When we went into the first pharmacy, he asked to speak to the manager, who happened to be a woman. 'My name is Johnson and we're doing a store check,' he said. 'Do you sell a lot of cotton wool?' 'Oh, yes,' the lady replied. 'What is it used for?' he asked. The lady's face turned red. Then he said 'Do you sell many of Dr. White's sanitary napkins, and could women be using the cotton wool for the same purpose?' The woman got even more flustered, and the General turned and left the store, leaving me and the manager alone. She said to me 'Everybody except that Baptist minister with you knows that women buy cotton wadding for that purpose—and it's none of his damn business.'"

Because the company had no manufacturing facilities in Cape

Town, Johnson spent his time meeting with the company's sales and marketing people and got involved in lengthy discussions about a price war between the larger retail outlets and the small pharmacies. And when he visited other pharmacies with Nurse O'Neal, he was more discreet in his questions than he had been the first time. He spent hours at the major hospitals talking about hospital administration and patient and medical care. He was always warmly received by hospital staffs, and he asked knowledgeable questions. After three weeks at sea, the burst of activity energized him.

His parting words when he left the office in New Brunswick some two months earlier had been: "The show must go on!" When he arrived in Cape Town, he cabled Hofmann: "The ship is able. I feel better than I have for some time. Basically I am as happy as a lark." A friend who received the same kind of cheerful message wrote back to Johnson: "It is difficult for me to tell you how genuinely happy I am that you are realizing such personal satisfaction and happiness from your new ship." The friend was not alone in that thought. The many people who cared about the General often wished he could find that kind of happiness more often.

The *Golden Crest* sailed from Cape Town in clear weather for the three-day trip to Port Elizabeth and other stops in South Africa. As the ship rounded the Cape of Good Hope, it encountered a perilous gale and heavy seas that it was taking on its starboard side, causing it to roll badly. "Everything started crashing about. Chairs tipped over, crockery shattered in the cupboards, and everything was a bit of a shambles — shades of the Bay of Biscay on the last trip!" reported Dr. Murray. "I was totally exhausted trying to battle my way around the ship, and it was impossible to stay in bed. After being pitched out several times, I finally managed to anchor myself by spread-eagling on the bed and gripping the sides. It was all right as long as I was awake, but as soon as I fell asleep I was pitched out again."

Many hours behind schedule, the ship arrived at Port Elizabeth. It was not until later that the passengers learned two ships had sunk in the treacherous equinoctial gales they had just been through. This bolstered Johnson's confidence in the seaworthiness of the *Golden Crest*, even though the ship's problems, including an erratic radar, kept mounting. But as Bill Hughes noted, the General enjoyed having problems to solve on his ships. It was early evening, and by the time the ship was tied to the wharf it had attracted a band of onlookers, and the press. Reluctantly, Johnson agreed to have the reporters and photographers aboard the next morning for an interview.

The interview attended by a group of reporters went well, but when a woman reporter from the *Evening Post* arrived late, Johnson told her the interview was over and left the ship. She busied herself interviewing crew members instead. The headline in the afternoon paper read "NOT ALL BEER AND SKITTLES ABOARD YACHT," and the story had to do with complaints from some crew members about "their disgust with conditions on board" and the General's rudeness to the reporter. When he saw the story Johnson was angered, mostly by the quotes from the crew members. His loyal physician friend, Dr. Murray, promptly wrote a letter to the editor extolling "conditions" on the *Golden Crest*. The letter was published the following day. Meanwhile, Johnson sent the unflattering newsclip back to Hofmann in New Brunswick with a note: "Word may have reached you of an unattractive article. It was an unfortunate interview between an aggressive woman reporter and certain members of my crew who will soon be leaving the ship."

Several days later the *Golden Crest* left Port Elizabeth for East London, where the company had major manufacturing facilities. Johnson was on the bridge. As the vessel moved slowly through the harbor and headed for the breakwater, engine power increased and the ship suddenly yawed dangerously to starboard and out of control. Those on the bridge were startled by the ship's action. "Fortunately, there was nothing in front of us to hit," Dr. Murray noted in his log. The ship's engineer speculated that the fluid in the flume tanks that controlled the ship's stabilizer system had suddenly shifted, causing the yaw. Johnson wasn't satisfied with that explanation. Now he had a new problem to solve, one that would soon involve Bill Hughes and eventually the French navy.

Without further mishap, the *Golden Crest* sailed into East London Harbor the following day. The General had sent word ahead that he was not to be met by either a reception committee or the press. They acceded to his wishes, but by the time the ship had docked a crowd of onlookers had gathered — private yachts were a rarity in East London. For the next several days, he inspected the manufacturing plants, spoke to the workers, met with managers, and spent hours visiting the local hospitals and pharmacies. He had let it be known that he did not want to be lavishly entertained — a quiet dinner with executives and their wives would be all right, but nothing elaborate.

Still, the General's visits overseas generated excitement, anticipation, and apprehension as well. They were like the visits of royalty. During his fifty years with the company, he had become a legend. His Credo hung on the wall in hundreds of offices and work areas. His framed photograph was in many of the reception areas. The General and his philosophy had permeated every corner of Johnson & Johnson. He had influenced the way management conducted the business, the way employees were treated, and how both managers and employees viewed community responsibility. He had become part of the local company's culture. He would spend a great deal of time touring production areas, stopping to chat with the workers, asking questions — and of course offering advice.

On many of the visits, local officials wanted the opportunity to greet Johnson. The mayor of East London had arranged to have him attend a noon reception at the city hall, but was told that it should not be an elaborate affair since Johnson was scheduled to attend a luncheon with a group of businessmen. When the General and his entourage arrived at the reception, they were dismayed to find that the mayor had set up an elaborate buffet. Johnson stayed only briefly, and left without eating. Also present was a reporter for the *Evening Post*, the newspaper he had tangled with in Port Elizabeth. The next day's headline read: "GENERAL JOHNSON WALKS OUT OF MAYOR'S RECEPTION."

A few days later he left East London, leaving the local management to make peace with the mayor. The *Golden Crest* sailed for Durban for a scheduled layup before going on the next leg of the world journey. From Durban, Johnson flew home, anxious to see how things were going in New Brunswick and to feel the pulse of the business once again.

The maintenance department at corporate headquarters in New Brunswick went on red alert well before the General returned from one of his lengthy trips. The lawn was carefully trimmed, tire marks were removed from the white curbing in the visitor parking area, the fingerprints were wiped from the glass doors of the river entrance — the one Johnson used.

It became a guessing-game — to catch what his eye would catch. And they always lost, and waited for his memo.

35

WHAT IS SUCCESS?

THE record was intact. It was impossible to anticipate what the General might find on his inspection rounds. His first memo on his return read:

Yes, I am back.

1. The garage roof leaks.

2. I understand the floor of the garage is to be improved.

3. The girls' sharp heels must not catch in the bricks in the new walk at the River Entrance, especially the lower step. Perhaps this should be changed to pink granite.

4. So as to give this emphasis, you can tell the boys they will have to wear high-heeled slippers and walk this daily if trouble develops.

Johnson had returned from the six weeks at sea energized and resumed his routine with new gusto. During his long absences, the trade and consumer magazines containing company advertising piled up, awaiting his return. He went through every one, judging how well the company's advertising measured up. At the office, he would ask to see advertising layouts, and his reaction could make a product director despondent. "The fingernail [of the woman shown in the ad] is definitely too pink," he once wrote. "This should either be natural or one of the platinum treatments. Slightly modify the lines and wrinkles of the thumb. Also consider slightly slenderizing the thumb on the right-hand side." Otherwise, the picture in the ad was fine.

Most of Johnson's involvement with advertising decisions ended with the suggestions he made, but when ethics or what he termed "poor taste and ill manners" were involved, he took a much firmer stand. In one case, he found the advertising of mouthwash products, including his own company's Micrin, offensive because of references to "bad breath," but each time he raised the issue he was told that was the only way to sell mouthwash. Finally, he had had enough. "This is hurting the image of Johnson & Johnson," he wrote, "and the Micrin business isn't worth that. We should instantly — repeat, instantly — find a more acceptable approach or else we'll cancel all Micrin commercials immediately." He got instant action, and the script was changed. Another time, he was annoyed when a television commercial for Procter & Gamble's mouthwash product, Scope, featured a character named "Mr. Johnson." That was probably done, he wrote, by "some smart aleck copywriter who is always on the edge of ethics."

Constantly railing against what he called "the silly comedy of the television commercials of the day," he would describe them as "stupid guff" and the product of Madison Avenue ad agencies that had wandered off the path. What consumers needed, he maintained, were "messages that conveyed a product's quality — and it doesn't have to be a tricky message." It was no secret that Johnson was no fan of television — and some of its story lines. When the company became the first sponsor of the television series "The Adventures of Robin Hood," he is said to have telephoned an advertising executive and asked: "What is this business about stealing from the rich and giving to the poor?"

While television remained unproven to him, he did enjoy radio, which he tuned in early every morning when he was home in Princeton. Long after television became the advertising medium of choice among consumer products companies, Johnson was still trying to convince his people to do more radio commercials. He could be annoyingly persistent, and he knew it. One memo began: "Now hear this! As MacArthur said, old 'chairmen' never die, they simply fade away. No doubt you will add that some fade away better than others!" He was much better at dispensing humor than being the recipient of it.

His most recent weeks at sea had changed his thinking about the importance of building the company's pharmaceutical business, and he was now enthusiastic about a new analgesic called "Tylenol" that had been developed at McNeil and was available by prescription only. The product had great promise, he believed. Looking ahead, too, he wanted the company to consider creating the position of "worldwide product director," so that one senior executive could oversee the marketing of the same product group in various companies. That concept became the pattern for product management — two decades later.

Johnson's brusque handling of business matters contrasted with his soft and tender treatment of employees who were down the line in rank. When he learned that an employee he had known for many years had become a grandmother for the first time but couldn't afford to go see the child in a distant city, he paid for her fare and insisted she travel first class for this important occasion. And when one worker happened to mention that his parents were celebrating their fiftieth wedding anniversary, Johnson went back to the office and wrote a congratulatory letter to the couple. He bought four new tires for the cars of every nurse who did "special duty" at area hospitals for company executives and their families, because he didn't want them to have a flat tire when they traveled at night. The tires should be the same make as he had just put on his own car, he stipulated. However, he did insist that the dealer give credit for all the nurses' tires that still had mileage left.

He was far more sentimental than he would have others believe, and incurably nostalgic. He liked going to the Kilmer Museum, which was tucked away in musty isolation in an ancient red-brick building, where samples of products since the company's founding were displayed in long lines of wood cabinets with glass doors. Portraits of his father and his two uncles, James and Mead, the company's co-founders, hung on the wall, and standing in the corner was a three-foot-high factory whistle that had summoned workers to their jobs in the early 1900s. The museum was a poignant reminder of the past, and he enjoyed being alone there with his thoughts. It had never been open to visitors, with the exception of occasional groups of employees — mostly those from overseas companies who knew nothing about the company's rich history. In a vast storeroom at the rear were scores of metal file cabinets containing trademark documents. Off to the side were several dozen additional spacious file cabinets containing Johnson's personal and business correspondence, family photos, and other memorabilia.

Much of his personal memorabilia had been at his office or home, until he decided to put it in a room in the Kilmer Museum that he personally would design and have constructed at the rear of the display area. He spent many hours planning what came to be referred to as "The General's Room." The entrance to the 20-by-25-foot room was done in handsome cherry wood. The double doors had small translucent glass panes and "Robert Wood Johnson" carved in the wood facade above the doorway. Against soft blue-gray walls were shelves holding framed photos, awards Johnson had received, his old ship's bell, and a prized needlepoint of his personal burgee, crafted by Sheila. Several academic robes he had worn when he was honored were in a display case in the center of the softly lighted room. The flagpoles stood in metal bases — one an American flag, the other his Army brigadier general's colors. He had spent a large amount of time planning the room and supervising its construction, and when it was complete it was locked and few people ever saw it. He had never intended it to display his accomplishments. To him, that room was more personal.

For years, Johnson had been making regular visits to the family mausoleum at the local Greenwood Cemetery, where his father was interred. Sometimes he went as often as every two or three weeks and fussed over the landscaping or the flowers in the large urns that flanked the entrance. Accompanied by Miss Ferretti on one visit, he said wistfully: "I wonder who will visit me when I am buried here." "I will," she replied. His mother was buried in a small church cemetery at Nockton in England. He visited there only occasionally, but he carefully monitored the care of the grave through the church sexton.

One of the unbroken links between Robert Johnson and his son was Bobby's wife, Betty. He truly liked and admired his daughter-in-law for her strong-willed ways and her unflagging loyalty to her husband. She had never been intimidated by the General, and she had wisely kept the lines of communication open while Bobby was no longer with the company. Betty believed, and emphasized to her father-in-law in a sternly worded letter, that Bobby had been victimized at the company. After he read the letter, the General put it first in one envelope and then in a second envelope, marked it "Confidential," and placed it in his safe-deposit box. No one else read it. He did not let the letter affect his relationship with Betty, for she was his principal contact with Bobby during a difficult period.

The Christmas holidays were sad that year, 1965, in terms of family togetherness, which for Johnson had never reached a level of great warmth. He was not imbued with the spirit of Christmas, but Evie was, and she tried to make up for his deficiency. He would lavish her with expensive gifts, usually jewelry, but she would be hard pressed to come up with a gift that would please him, and one he would use and enjoy. He was not easy to please with surprise gifts.

Communicating with children had always been an elusive skill for Johnson. He was perhaps at his best in Sheila's early years. A staff member once commented: "He just didn't know what to say to children." When his grandson Robert Wood Johnson IV was a young child away at summer camp, the General used to write him an occasional letter. "Woody" Johnson talked about them years later: "After the first few sentences, the letter would get into an explanation of how the business was doing. I had no idea what he was talking about, but I always enjoyed hearing from him."

Despite his awkwardness with children, he made a pretense of being relaxed around them. When one of his staff members had a baby and wrote to tell him the news, he replied: "First chance you get, bring the baby to the office. There is no reason why you shouldn't, and if the little creature wants to cry and make a fuss in the office that will be just fine. We will start a nursery on the directors' table." Though a well-intentioned invitation, the thought of a squealing baby having its diaper changed on the directors' table in Johnson's office was unthinkable.

After the holidays, Johnson began preparing to continue his world voyage on the *Golden Crest*. He planned the itinerary carefully and outlined it in a letter to his physician friend Dr. Francis Wood: "In early February we will board the ship at Durban, South Africa. Our first stop will be at the Island of Mauritius, and then we make the long voyage across the Indian Ocean to Western Australia. Then on to Sydney, and up to New Zealand."

To accompany him on this trip as a guest, and also to serve as ship's doctor, the General invited Dr. D. Stanley ("Pat") Pattison, director of medical research at his Personal Products Company. Dr. Pattison was gregarious, good-humored, and well read—and he loved the sea. He and Johnson had many animated discussions at company meetings, and he enjoyed the doctor's flair for interesting conversation. Before extending the invitation, though, Johnson checked with an executive who was friends with the Pattisons to determine whether the doctor and his wife, Joyce, got along well, since she too was to be invited. Before inviting any couple on a long voyage aboard the *Golden Crest*, Johnson always checked on their marital harmony. Once assured that the Pattisons were happily married, he extended the invitation and they accepted. They turned out to be an excellent choice.

Johnson and Miss Ferretti (by now a seasoned sailor) flew to Durban, where they were joined by the Pattisons. After inspecting the newly painted and polished *Golden Crest*, Johnson was pleased by all the improvements the conscientious Captain Halpin had made. He wrote to Seward: "This is now a fine, able vessel. We started off with approximately 150 problems and are now down to perhaps thirty, which may be par for the course." That was an optimistic appraisal, for Johnson would continue to find new problems, so he could have something to fix.

The ship stopped at Port Louis, Mauritius, for a few days so the General could "check the stores" and meet with the Johnson & Johnson agent there. But the amount of business the company did on Mauritius scarcely covered the fuel costs for moving the *Golden Crest* in and out of the harbor. Then the ship began its long journey across the Indian Ocean, encountering some "boisterous weather" for the first several days. Years later, Dr. Pattison recalled how he had enjoyed the voyage:

> The General was a rebel, and I am somewhat of a rebel myself, being of Irish heritage. And one rebel always has a sneaking respect for another, and I think that is why we got along so well. I got to know him much better during those many days at sea. He was a very astute gentleman, and his observation was phenomenal. He was a most remarkable man, and, to me, he fulfilled every verse of Rudyard Kipling's poem "If": "If you can walk with kings and not lose the common touch, . . . If you fill the unforgiving minute with sixty seconds' worth of distance run, . . . Yours is the Earth and everything that's in it."
>
> His health was better at sea and he was relaxed. I know he didn't sleep well, because when he came to breakfast he would have a stack of notes, and after we ate he would say, "Come now, Miss Ferretti, we have a lot of work to do," and he would go off and dictate from the notes. His mind was never filled. He never stopped thinking. He was an extraordinary person, but a very lonely man.
>
> He often spoke of his son, Bobby. He felt very badly about what had happened between them. On the other hand, he felt that he did the right thing. But it was a great thorn in his side. I remember on Easter we had a celebration, and the crew made a punch. The chief steward was Italian, and he gave a little speech and a toast—to our

brides and our loved ones, and our sons and our daughters. And the General walked out, and my wife followed him, and he was leaning over the rail on the starboard side and the tears were streaming down his cheeks. He was thinking of Bobby.

One evening at sea, Joyce Pattison, descending the stairway from the bridge, happened to glance at the porthole in the General's stateroom and saw him kneeling by his bed praying. Surprised, she mentioned it to Miss Ferretti, who replied: "Oh, yes, he does that often."

Since the breakup a year earlier, the General and Bobby had not seen or spoken to each other. In Menlo Park, New Jersey, Bobby had formed Johnson Industries Inc., and with only a few employees, he set out to develop a skin cream called "Vedra." It was a far cry from being president of Johnson & Johnson.

Reaching Australia, the *Golden Crest* stopped at Perth for a few days, then headed south for Adelaide. As ship's doctor, Dr. Pattison had few duties other than an occasional check of the General's blood pressure. As usual, Johnson ate in moderation and exercised every day. But he could not break his addiction to cigarettes, despite constant urging. He had a persistent cough, and for someone so conscious of good health practices, it was difficult to understand why he continued to smoke. He tired easily, but still managed to do his ballet exercises on the afterdeck, and even persuaded Dr. Pattison to try. "He showed me how to put my foot up on the rail," the doctor recalled. "I had trouble doing it, and the roll of the ship made it impossible for me. Thank God the weather got worse and I begged off."

Dr. Pattison, who knew far more about medicine than he did about ships, nonetheless had an interesting explanation of why the *Golden Crest* had a tendency to roll under certain conditions. "The boat was built to be a mine-seeder or mine-planter, not a mine-layer, and this type of design was for use in shallow waters or estuaries. The General had a big bow welded on it to weather the storm, but that didn't change the way the ship handled. He also discovered that both props turned inward instead of outward, which is normal, and this affected the steering at slow speeds. They conned him by saying 'This is the best thing you can have,' but he suspected the diesel engines were reversed when they were installed."

"The General knew a lot about boats," the doctor continued, "and so did his brother, Seward. He and Seward were very close. He showed me several memos from him and they were to 'Dear Bob' and signed 'Love, Sew.' I was brought up in the old country, where we didn't use such affectionate terms among brothers, so I was impressed. Seward was invited to join us on a later trip in the Caribbean, but he couldn't make it and the General was very disappointed. Seward never got to see the ship."

In Adelaide, the press was again clamoring to come aboard the ship and interview Johnson. He agreed, and a reporter asked him how he was enjoying his retirement. That was a mistake. The General bristled. "I am not retired," he declared. "I have no intention of giving up until I die. I'm not seventy-four as most people think. I'm only seventy-two, just going on seventy-three. Relax! Hell, no. I would not think of sitting back with my money and living a nice, senseless, easy, soft life. I have plans and work to do."

The wire services sent the story back to New Jersey, and his colleagues chuckled over something they already knew.

At a later interview in Australia, a reporter asked Johnson how many millions of dollars he had.

"Well," he said, "I've been at sea for some time and I haven't had a chance to check my bankbook."

"You don't seem to like to talk about money," the reporter observed.

"Yes, I know," said Johnson. "Everybody likes to convert what I do into money. I find it poor form. Anyone who is successful is unpopular."

Asked what success was, he replied: "Good gracious! What a question! Most decidedly, *I* have been successful." Then, obviously thinking twice about that reply, he added quickly: "I'll be damned if I can answer that. I don't know. I've always had new objectives."

•

When the ship reached Sydney, Johnson's friend and colleague Bill Northam, straight-talking Aussie sailor and Olympic gold medalist, was waiting on the dock. "I had arranged to have the *Golden Crest* tied up to the circular key, right in the center of things," Northam said. "He didn't like that, because he thought the ship attracted too much attention. But once that ship was in the harbor, everyone knew he was there. We had the American flag flying at the plant. Even the toll collector on the bridge asked me about him. I wanted to invite people aboard and have a party, but he wouldn't go for it. 'No parties,' he said. 'This is a working ship.'"

At the major ports of call, a packet of mail and reports on the progress of the business would be waiting for Johnson. One summary from Philip Hofmann had a note of apology for passing on some unsettling news about the business. The General fired back a reply:

"Please don't feel I would prefer to hear only good news. The truth is that I have lived all of my life on bad news, and I would feel lost without it." When one report suggested there had been some discussion at the office about the merits of decentralization, he wrote "RIDICULOUS" on the memo and returned it. That ended that.

Once ashore, the General began his rounds of visits and inspections. When he got to the Sydney office, he asked Northam to arrange a meeting with all the people on the marketing and advertising staffs. At that meeting, Northam said: "Johnson began by apologizing for talking to them about an old theme, then launched into his basic rules of advertising: Dramatics, Simplicity, and Continuity. He told them that was the most important thing he had learned about advertising in his fifty years in business. He went on for an hour, and they loved it, especially the younger people who had never heard him speak."

[566]

On his visits to international companies, he occasionally dropped in on a meeting unannounced and took a seat at the back of the room. Once when he did this and his presence was acknowledged, he told the group: "I'll have nothing to say at this meeting. Just go ahead." One manager recalled what happened next: "In no time, he was on his feet gesturing and making points, and soon he was completely involved in the discussion. He couldn't help himself."

At higher-level management meetings during his visits, the General would discuss many aspects of Johnson & Johnson's corporate philosophy. He seldom referred to the Credo, however, because it was hanging on the wall for all to see and, in his view, there was no compromise when it came to those responsibilities. Many of the discussions he engaged in had to do with land acquisition for future expansion and with designing office and manufacturing buildings — two areas in which he was especially skilled. He probably thought he was contributing to key business decisions more than he actually was, not realizing that his very presence was the most important contribution he could make.

The *Golden Crest* next sailed east to New Zealand, stopping at three ports there before going to Auckland. The ship would remain there for repairs and maintenance in preparation for the next leg of its journey. The company in New Zealand was vigorous and growing, and Johnson helped select an expansion site. Before leaving, he sent a message to the home office. "This has been a straight industrial voyage [translation: all work and no play]. We have laid out plans and policies for the next twenty to thirty years. We will succeed. We shall grow rapidly in South Africa, Australia and New Zealand [the areas he had recently visited]. . . . I shall return to Auckland in July and continue the voyage. We are on the march!" Feeling that he had made a contribution, he took a plane home, tired but happy.

•

Back at his desk, the General turned his attention to the growing shortage of nurses in the country, which had become a national problem. He wrote to Defense Secretary Robert McNamara, urging him to have the Armed Forces, the single largest user of nursing services, renew the nursing education program that had been abandoned after World War II. "The Armed Forces should be graduating 25,000 nurses a year for the next ten years," he told McNamara. "This can be done in the military hospitals and is vitally necessary." To support this plan, he sent a group to Washington to talk to Congressional leaders about it.

Another of his ideas for nursing—an intensive refresher course he had conceived and tested at Middlesex Hospital—had been adopted at twenty-four hospitals, and its rapid expansion to other hospitals encouraged him. And during his "improvement" visits to St. Peter's Hospital in New Brunswick, he was impressed by the young women in the nurses' training program and decided to put each on a monthly allowance of ten dollars for the three years they would be in the program. "I realize this isn't much," he wrote, "but it will give them a little spending money."

For years he had been sounding the alarm over New Jersey's strangling traffic problems, and when his friend Governor Richard Hughes decided to form a State Department of Transportation, he was elated. He stopped at Morven for breakfast, to thank the governor, but didn't succeed in convincing him to back a plan to put a new supersonic jetport on the site of McGuire Air Force Base in the Pinelands in central New Jersey. Hughes told Johnson he had political problems with that proposal. The General then started pushing for a New Jersey Jetport Authority, which Hughes also resisted. His persistent appeals to the governor to have the Port of New York Authority, as it was then named, reorganized to better represent the interests of New Jersey met with some success, but not until later.

·

The General became an outspoken critic of President Lyndon Johnson, who had soundly defeated Senator Barry Goldwater. The General had enthusiastically supported Goldwater. National defense was one of the issues the General faulted President Johnson on. By now the General was having a third test-model home air-raid shelter built in the backyards of two of his executives, who had "volunteered." He also ordered several dozen compressed-air horns, the type used on small boats, and distributed them to a group of women employees for use as a warning signal in an emergency. He told them to carry the horns in their pocketbooks but hadn't figured out how they would fit there.

Within a few months, he was ready to continue his world voyage, and in late July he flew to Regina, Saskatchewan, on the company plane to pick up Dr. Hugh Murray, who had again signed on as ship's doctor. At Vancouver they took commercial flights to Hawaii, and eventually to Auckland to pick up the *Golden Crest*. With Miss Ferretti as nurse and secretary, an eight-week voyage began with the enchanting islands of the South Pacific — including stops at Raoul, the Tonga Islands, Samoa, Tahiti, Moorea, Bora Bora, and the Marquesas.

There were no Johnson & Johnson plants on the remote islands, so the General had to be content with visiting tiny shops that carried the company's products, and small hospitals and clinics, often run by missionaries. Regardless of size, he dutifully called on them, and when he saw their meager medical supplies he usually promised to send them a shipment of Johnson & Johnson products.

On the tiny island of Vavau, in the Tongas — also known as "the Friendly Islands" — Johnson visited a church that had been destroyed by a hurricane and rebuilt by the natives. He was quite concerned that there were no pews or kneelers, and he couldn't get that scene out of his mind. When he got home, he wrote the Catholic bishop in Trenton, New Jersey, asking where he might find pews and kneelers. The bishop directed Johnson to a church in New Jersey that was being rebuilt, and there the General acquired several dozen church pews and kneelers. He had them crated, and after months of red tape they were shipped to Vavau on the deck of a large fishing vessel that left from San Diego. Eventually, the natives had pews and kneelers, and they used the wood from the large crates to build housing.

Captain Guiseppe Spano, of Genoa, Italy, was now in command of the *Golden Crest*, having been recommended for the job when Captain Dan Halpin went back to delivering oceangoing tugboats. Nattily attired in dress whites, Spano, an experienced mariner, cut a dashing figure on the bridge. He just wasn't Johnson's type. The General preferred "working" captains, who got down and scrubbed the decks with the crew. On shore, Johnson was unmatched for his sartorial splendor—in custom-made suits from Saville Row—but on board ship he dressed in khakis and a floppy, wide-brim hat. A captain who wore dress whites on a "working ship" was therefore suspect, in the General's eyes. Johnson's only concession to formality was a New York Yacht Club captain's jacket on which he had put Army brass buttons and which he wore to special shipboard dinners.

On the dock to greet them when they arrived at Papeete, Tahiti, was Nick Rutgers (grandson of James Johnson, the General's uncle and one of the company's co-founders) and his wife, Nancy, daughter of Norman Hall (co-author of *Mutiny on the Bounty*). The Rutgers home commanded a spectacular view of the harbor, and the couple shared their treasure of knowledge about the islands with their guests from the *Golden Crest*. Nick Rutgers had for years served as Johnson & Johnson's unofficial emissary in Tahiti, and for the General's visit he made sure the product displays in the Papeete shops were at their best. Spaulding Dunbar, one of Johnson's sailing mates from earlier years, and his wife, Doris, joined the ship and added more salt to the sea air with the tales they told as they proceeded across the Pacific. Johnson kept to his work schedule, filling Miss Ferretti's notebook with memos to send later and a flurry of new ideas for the business. He kept thinking about the reporter's question that had flustered him in Australia—"What is success?"—and began making notes for a suitable answer.

He wrote regularly—in the only way he knew, a business-like way—to the ever-patient Evie, who was alone in Princeton, taking an occasional trip to London to break the monotony. Her letters were warmer, as were Sheila's, and letters from both were waiting for him at the major ports of call. When Evie went to London, she was not fussed over in the same way as when she accompanied her husband on a trip. As one of her friends put it, "She was still Mrs. Robert Wood Johnson, and she would go to London, and stay at the Claridges, see the same people and do the same things, but it was never the same. The force of the General's presence was missing."

Two weeks later, the *Golden Crest* reached the Galapagos Islands off the coast of Ecuador, stopped there, and moved on to Panama City, then through the Panama Canal to the Caribbean. From there it went to Aruba and to the island of Curaçao in the Lesser Antilles, where the ship was laid up for maintenance and prepared for its next voyage.

The General flew back to New Brunswick, full of new ideas stimulated by the eight weeks at sea. "Here is an idea that is far out," he wrote a colleague after he returned to the office. "If we were able to take a plastic sheet, and through a fast process give it a pattern with thousands of open spaces, do you suppose we would have a cheap fly screen that campers could use?" The same memo contained an idea for making an open-mesh collagen burn dressing that could be absorbed by the body. His third idea, also in the same memo, was to develop a plastic covering that would protect insulation wrapped around pipes. He described these as "wild ideas," not realizing their future potential.

Finally, after much thought, Johnson formulated his personal answer to the reporter's question:

WHAT IS SUCCESS?

Success is being happy in one's work. Success is doing something with meaning and satisfaction. Success is working in a pleasant, inspiring, cheerful and stimulating environment. Success is working in fine facilities placed on attractive sites in structures of good design, well maintained.

Success is working with intelligent, dedicated, understanding and tolerant associates. Success is pride in the appearance and social attributes of those who surround you. Success is knowing we are well remunerated for our effort, encouraged for our achievements and sincerely advised on our deficiencies.

Success is knowing that the greater our contributions, the greater our reward, both monetary and otherwise. Success is being respected by our associates for our integrity, our honor and our total character.

In other words, success is having the ability to rise to greatness.

36

PEACE ON THE "GOLDEN CREST"

IN early January 1967, Johnson wrote his brother, Seward, his closest confidant: "I've been thinking a great deal of the future management and control of Johnson & Johnson. As a matter of fact, you know that this has been uppermost in my mind for a lifetime.

"At one point you and I owned in excess of eighty percent of the stock, I think at its highest point it was eighty-six percent. Since then, through good efforts and an attempt to do what we can for others, we have built trusts for children, trusts for charity, a trust for this, that and the other. In most of this we have tried to protect the continuity and competence of management but, nevertheless, we have engineered a very considerable dilution. Then came the great step after the war where we made the mistake of issuing stock and putting a portion of the company holdings on the open stock market.

"Now we must give great attention to an era that has developed, namely control and continuity. I hope you will think about this carefully and whenever the question arises do everything you can to give us the solidity of the closely held corporation we once had. I doubt that we can ever attain the majority at our highest point, but we should at all times be sure that we have as close to seventy percent of the stockholders with us as sooner or later there is going to be some kind of raid or organization engineered by those who, for one reason or another, dislike us.

"This sort of thing is as old as man himself. The beneficiary bites off the hand of his benefactor just as in Roman days Caesar said 'Et tu Brutus,' If you've forgotten your Latin, it's translated — 'And you, too, Brutus.'"

Johnson had already decided that the bulk of his own stock holdings would go to The Robert Wood Johnson Foundation, though he did no advance planning for the dramatic expansion of the Foundation following his death. An associate explained Johnson's thinking:

"The target he clearly defined for the Foundation was that it be used to improve health care in the United States. He had great faith and confidence in his executives, those that he had put on the Foundation board, and he relied on their judgment. He didn't dictate what was to be done, but he had confidence that it would be done right. In his mind he felt 'I cannot control this thing from the grave,' so he placed his confidence and trust in his colleagues to produce the results he would have wanted.

"He never said it in so many words, but I think he felt that the American people had made Johnson & Johnson what it is, so he was discharging his responsibility in turning his wealth back to the people that gave it to him. Now that's an idealistic thought, but I believe it was his thinking. He was a very generous man, but I believe that his generosity was also motivated by certain pragmatic thoughts. He felt that if a substantial part of his stock could remain in the Foundation, the future management of Johnson & Johnson would conform to the pattern of management that he and others believed in."

•

In the early months of 1967, there was some concerned speculation about Johnson's health. He was quiet about it himself, but others were worried. One colleague later commented: "Looking back, I

[574]

believe the General knew that his health was much worse than he led us to believe." At the time, the nation was embroiled in the war in Vietnam, and Johnson wrote to a friend: "I do my job each day the best way that I can, and close my mind to much else. This may be a cowardly view, but I ease my conscience as I have done my tour of duty in public, military and political life, and still stand ready for emergency and crisis service to the extent of my physical capacity." There was still a spark of his old energy there, and he was going on seventy-four.

As it turned out, Johnson had twelve months of life left.

If he sensed that he was failing, he made no attempt to slow his pace or confine his activity. If anything, an urgency crept into his schedule—the things he did and how he went about doing them. His first priority was to board the *Golden Crest* to continue his worldwide "inspection" of Johnson & Johnson companies. He took particular pride in the dramatic growth of the company overseas, because forty years earlier he had planted the seeds of the global business when he embarked on a world journey to explore new markets. In some respects, this was a retracing of that pioneering venture, and it probably added to his sense of accomplishment to see firsthand how the business had grown.

When the General arrived in Curaçao, where the *Golden Crest* was undergoing maintenance for the voyage to South America, he met his new captain, Arthur "Flash" Harris, a young and energetic master recruited with the help of the ever-patient Bill Hughes and his host of mariner friends. Remembering Johnson's reaction to the last captain's affinity for dress whites, Hughes this time chose a younger man with a buoyant spirit and a relaxed, informal manner. Johnson liked him immediately. But the real test came later when he spotted Captain Harris, dressed in khaki trousers and open-neck shirt, down on the deck helping a crew member scrub the teak. "Now there's a captain!" he exclaimed to Miss Ferretti with a burst of exuberance—and from that moment on, Captain "Flash" and the General were bonded as shipmates, despite the nickname.

For someone who had been a lifelong slave to perfection, Johnson found the *Golden Crest* a formidable challenge, but one he was clearly enjoying. By now, everything on the ship that was replaceable—or could be duplicated—had been replaced or duplicated. There were three radar systems and, as Johnson wrote, "enough radio on the bridge to confuse everybody." He added, "But, I figure some of it will work at times."

Earlier he had told Seward: "I am unalterably determined to bring this ship to perfect condition"—a pledge that Seward, knowing his brother, was sure would never be kept. Soon after leaving Curaçao, he reported again to Seward: "She is a strong, able, hard working deep sea ship. She is going well, but we still have a few major jobs ahead of us. We are running a happy ship and nearly all the men are competent." Certainly not perfection, but, for the General, pretty close. He signed off to Seward: "Take care of yourself, kid." The sea made boys of both of them.

After a stop at Puerto Cabello, Venezuela, and a visit to the plant in Caracas, Johnson began the long voyage to Brazil, where the company had major facilities, founded some thirty years earlier and nourished to substantial growth by an old friend and colleague Andrew Rohlfing. He had invited Rohlfing aboard for the trip to discuss the business in Brazil, and because the two men were quite comfortable with each other.

Rohlfing, an ardent boatman and an adroit engineer, was a handy person to have aboard. When the air-conditioning went sour just as they were crossing the Equator, Rohlfing fixed it. He recalled Johnson saying to him: "You're a guest aboard. You're not supposed to fix anything." "Yes, but I'm the guy who is sweating," Rohlfing said he replied. "On that trip we spent most of the time talking over old times. He was nostalgic," Rohlfing recalled.

But Johnson saw it differently: "We are working steadily on questions of better products for South America," He reported back to the office. Believing he was working hard made him feel better.

Johnson was greeted warmly when he arrived in São Paulo, Brazil, where the company was headquartered. They were fond of him, and some time later a Brazilian manager explained why:

"Brazilians are emotional, and they like people with personality and flair. We admire these traits, and on his visits here he always made a strong impression. We embraced the Credo he wrote because no one had ever conducted a business here under these kinds of guidelines. His philosophy of running a business and treating people the way he did was totally different. Spotless plants and manicured lawns were uncommon. He was referred to here as 'our beloved General Johnson.'"

In São Paulo, Johnson stayed at the Hotel Cadoro, and years later the manager there remembered his visit: "General Johnson was planning a dinner for the local managers and their wives, and when he came to me to choose the menu, he asked if I knew how to cut lettuce for the salad. I said I thought we did, we had been cutting it for years. He wasn't convinced, so an hour before dinner he came down to the kitchen and demonstrated to the chef and me just how he wanted the lettuce sliced. He cut it on a diagonal. I'll never forget it."

It was in Brazil that Johnson received word that his son, Bobby, had been taken seriously ill and was in a New Brunswick hospital. Dorothy O'Neal, the missionary nurse Johnson had hired for his low-cost sanitary-napkin project, was present that day and recalled his reaction. "We were at a meeting in the office of José Sanches when the telegram came," she explained. "The General read it, then said: 'My son is in the hospital and he's terribly ill. I have to make up my mind what I am going to do. I realize it's early in the meeting, but we are going to have to continue this tomorrow.' He wasn't able to take any more, and left the room. He was very much affected by the news of Bobby's illness." When he telephoned New Brunswick he learned that Bobby's condition had improved but that colon surgery was being considered.

The General remained in Brazil for another week and helped resolve the important question of moving more of the company's manufacturing to São José dos Campos, away from overcrowded São Paulo. After inspecting the production line, he decided that the baby powder was a shade off-color and had to be corrected, and that the package design should be improved. He and Rohlfing also worked out a new design for the Serena sanitary napkin that would reduce the cost of the product—which had always been his goal. Satisfied that his visit had been productive, Johnson departed for Santos, where the *Golden Crest* was docked, to begin the long trip back.

Before leaving Brazil, Johnson sent a blistering response to an internal memo discussing the color of the home-office memo stationery—just the sort of trifling matter that was certain to rouse the General's ire. (It should have been screened out of his mail pouch, because his agitated response was predictable.) He fired back: "Hell's breakfast! I already have sharp pains in the abdomen and the attached letter does not help. The million-dollar Law Department labors and brings forth a mouse. Now hear this! I shall use any color paper that comes to mind, including miscellaneous polka dots with Paris perfume. We will for the moment accept the judgment of the first-floor genius division and use the darker blue, but of all the trivia that ever came out of our Law Department this takes the cake. It makes me want to 'FROW UP'."

On the long voyage northward from Brazil, the General turned his attention to the company in the Philippines. He had invited an executive responsible for that area, Edward Walker, and his wife, Shirley, to join him on this portion of the trip. "He was a gracious and considerate host, always including you in the conversation, but he worked Olga Ferretti awfully hard, and I told him so," Shirley Walker said. Dr. Pattison was unable to make the Brazil part of the trip because he had contracted bronchial pneumonia. He would join the ship at Trinidad, thus leaving Nurse Ferretti in charge of Johnson's medical needs. "He relied on her a great deal, and I sense that he had an affection for her, a deep affection," Mrs. Walker said.

At every port, Johnson would find long, chatty letters from Evie.

His replies were usually a progress report on the business he was dealing with on the trip, and they always came with an apology for not being handwritten. (He would put them on an IBM dictation tape for relay to New Brunswick, where they were typed and sent to Princeton—and always signed "Love, Bob.") About his son, he wrote: "According to reports, Bobby's condition has improved and all looks better for him at this moment." In another letter, he spoke about shortening his journey. "It is time I returned," he said. He had never said that on any previous trip on the *Golden Crest*.

As the ship headed for Trinidad, and a meeting with the manager of the tiny Johnson & Johnson company there, the General made plans for his visit. Meanwhile, Alan Donawa, a Trinidad native, just recently named manager there, awaited his arrival with some trepidation. Friends in the company had warned him about the perils of the visit from Johnson. Donawa made sure there was no greeting party when the *Golden Crest* docked at the U.S. Navy wharf on March 26, but, as instructed by telex, he was at the ship at eight o'clock the next morning. The events that followed were etched in his memory, especially the horror of the sauntering cockroach during the General's inspection of the tiny production line.

"I had been alerted about the General's passion for cleanliness," Donawa recalled, "and I thought I had prepared well. The day before his arrival, I had the exterminator in. The girls' uniforms were sparkling white. We were standing next to the production line, and out of the corner of my eye I spot this cockroach casually walking across the top of a package and heading for the General's line of sight. I'm hoping to God he doesn't see this thing. I knew immediately that I should have had the exterminator in weeks earlier—all we did was stir them up. Very carefully, I made two attempts to flick the thing away. He turned to me and quietly said: 'Is this the sort of thing you get down here?' Then, when the inspection was over he said: 'Mr. Donawa, I don't think this is the place for you or the kind of place where we would like to manufacture. Tomorrow we will look for a new plant.'

[579]

"He ordered a car and driver and early the next morning we toured all around Port of Spain so he could get the feel of the place. After about three hours, he spotted a vacant building, and said: 'Mr. Donawa, I think this is an ideal location for our business.' It was a large building—very large—with ceilings about forty feet high. Very much larger than what we had. He said: 'I don't care if we have to pay dual rent. We will move here.' Here I am, new to the company, with no approval from my line management to move to a new plant, and now I will have two plants. I thought about it all the way back to my office on Sackville Street—yes, Sackville Street. I later signed a lease, and we moved, and it was a very nice location. I heard rumors of grumbling from New Brunswick, but no direct complaints."

About a week later, the *Golden Crest* left Trinidad for Martinique in the Windward Islands. The General had cabled Seward, asking him to join him for this portion of the trip. Alan Donawa remembered how disappointed he was when he received the telex from Seward: "He said, 'I wanted Seward to go with me on the ship, and I just received word that he can't make it. I am very disappointed.' And he stopped speaking for a while, and then continued: 'You know, Mr. Donawa, my brother Seward is the kindest man in the world.'"

En route to Martinique, Johnson read *The Brain Watchers* by Martin L. Gross, which Dr. Pattison brought with him when he boarded the ship at Port of Spain. It told of the methods employers used to scrutinize their employees, and the more he read the more he fumed. In his large scrawl, he wrote notes in the margins and across entire paragraphs, and he was so upset when he finished that he told his office in New Brunswick to send 150 copies of the book to senior management and personnel directors around the world. He also instructed that in each copy his marginal notes be written with a similar felt pen, and that a note be typed and inserted at the beginning of the book on a blank page. The note read:

How can we believe that our people will have confidence and admiration for a management subjecting them to this treatment? I suspect that such procedure, especially when applied through an outside agency, does irreparable damage to team morale.

It has come to my attention that recently we issued an extensive questionnaire to all hands which resulted in each of our people being given a number. This is a mistake. It may be comfortable for the computer but it isn't acceptable to men and women.

As a first step I advocate the total elimination of all outside services impinging on this problem. Good screening, good selection, reasonable interviews by members of our own industrial family are acceptable. We must be sure, however, that no unqualified person passes harmful judgment on any of us. Please design your procedure accordingly.

It was April 10, Johnson's seventy-fourth birthday, when the *Golden Crest* reached Kingston, Jamaica — its final destination. In the mail pouch was a cheerful greeting from Sheila: "Happy Birthday, Dad, wherever you are!" Sheila loved her father deeply, but he did not make it easy for people to love him. Said Sheila later: "Following the divorce of my parents, my relationship with my father changed, and there was a loss of intimacy due to my choices and attitudes. But I saw in him a gentle, shy, and caring person that most others were not allowed to know. Unfortunately, it was a person I was not able to reach as often as I would have liked in later years, but at least I know I was one of two who can call him 'Dad,' and his approval and love meant more to Bobby and me than either of us sometimes cared to admit."

After flying back to New Brunswick, the General resumed his work schedule. The time away had not dulled the barb of his humor. After consulting his follow-up list, he realized that he had not received a response to a much earlier suggestion and wrote the tardy associate: "When I graduated from Kindergarten in short pants I wrote you about this. I am now a grown man. What happened?" And he still could not refrain from involving himself in every facet of the business. When he learned that a physician who had treated him was entering the hospital, he wrote him: "As long as you are going there, why not do some practical product testing for us?" He then sent the doctor a supply of disposable pillow-cases and asked for a report on them—which he eventually got. In his role as chairman of the finance committee, his message—reduce costs wherever possible, and build up cash reserves—had not changed. When his recommendations met resistance, he offered this advice: "Twenty-five years from now, those in charge will be glad we acted in such a manner. If this seems painful to you now, I remind you that almost everything worthwhile is at times painful."

.

Johnson was now tiring earlier in the day, so he decided to see Dr. T. Scudder Winslow at Roosevelt Hospital in New York for a checkup. "The x-rays came about quite accidentally," Nurse Ferretti recalled. "He was in the waiting room, and one of the radiologists whom he had consulted earlier stopped to say hello. When the General described how he felt, and the pain he was getting in his shoulder blade, the radiologist suggested an x-ray." They discovered a small tumor on the lobe of his left lung. He took the news stoically.

"For good or bad," he wrote Seward, "Dr. Winslow and I have decided to dismiss surgery [dangerous because of his heart condition], and we will begin treatment at once with anti-tubercular medication. After three weeks, we will x-ray the lung again. This, of course, leaves open the question of the lesion being benign or carcinogenic. I am told it is in an inaccessible spot and cannot be biopsied."

For the next several weeks he kept a hectic schedule visiting six of the company's textile plants in the South, including Chicopee Village, near Gainesville, Georgia. It was there in 1926 that Johnson had built the world's most modern textile mill and a 200-home village for employees. A few years back the company had sold the village, and in a report Johnson wrote to the Board of Directors on his visit he lamented that decision, of which he had been a part. He had taken a nostalgic stroll through Chicopee Village and noted: "The sidewalks are going, the streets are breaking up and many of the house roofs need repair." It was a painful sight and condition for what had once been one of his proudest and most innovative accomplishments. "If we still had the Village it would be an aid to our employment position," he wrote. "The lesson here is that we must not sway to the changing winds of temporary economics."

When x-rays showed no improvement, it was decided that he should undergo treatment by lineal accelerator at the Ravdin Clinic at the University of Pennsylvania Hospital in Philadelphia. The radiation therapy would be given to him six days a week for a period of five weeks, and he began it in early June. His uppermost concern appeared to be the adjustments he would have to make in his work schedule, but he resolved that problem. Because he was an outpatient, he was able to take up residence at the nearby Barclay Hotel, go to the hospital for treatment in the morning, and return to the hotel to carry on his day's work, with the help of Miss Ferretti. "I shall proceed with my usual way of life, except to somewhat modify my schedule," he wrote Seward.

It was highly unlikely that the General could spend time at a hospital without attempting to make some changes. He kept his record intact in Philadelphia. "The first thing he did was revamp the nursing service at the hospital," a colleague said later. While this was an exaggeration, Johnson spent many hours each day conferring with the nurses and the hospital management. When he met a nurse supervisor from the Philippines who impressed him, he began exploring ways to bring more Philippine nurses to the hospital. "I am now working on a program for more nurses in the hope that I can help Pennsylvania University Hospital in that segment of their work," he wrote Seward.

It was also a certainty that drugstores in the area would become a target — in this case the C. Elbert Hoffman Pharmacy on Rittenhouse Square, near his hotel. "I have just completed a brief study of

the finest drug store I have ever seen in my life," he wrote exuber-
antly to a marketing executive in New Brunswick. This resulted in a
delegation coming to Philadelphia to see what Mr. Hoffman's pharmacy had that others didn't. Johnson visited the store frequently
and became friends with Elbert, who called him "Mr. Red Cross"
(a reference to the symbol on Johnson & Johnson packaging).

Johnson was in Philadelphia only a short time when he got a letter from Bobby: "Dear General, I have just now learned that you
are ill and I want you to know how sorry I am. I certainly hope
that the problem is remedied quickly and that you are soon back
on your feet. Good Luck. Your son, Bob."

It was still an armed truce between father and son. His sister, the
ever-philosophical Evangeline, now living at Cloud Walk Farm in
New Milford, Connecticut, wrote: "I have come to the conclusion
that the art of life is thinking beautiful thoughts as much of the
time as possible." The General was already philosophical about his
current illness and the tedious treatment it required: "It is the price
of staying alive and enjoying my work," he wrote one of the many
company workers who had sent words of encouragement. Johnson
responded to every note and card he received.

After five weeks of radiation treatments, Johnson was fatigued.
"I am only operating on a few cylinders," he admitted. But his
spirits were sent soaring on July 19. "The final x-rays this morning
disclose that the lesion is practically eliminated. All of the specialists are pleased. . . . I am one of the lucky ones," he wrote jubilantly.

He left that day for home, to finalize plans for the last leg of
the world journey that would complete his personal inspection
of Johnson & Johnson's major facilities, this time in Europe. The
Golden Crest had proceeded to Amsterdam and was awaiting his
arrival.

Evie Johnson, though gravely worried about her husband's illness, knew there was no way to deter him from continuing the trip.
He had persuaded her to go to London at the same time he was

leaving for Amsterdam. He made the usual arrangements for her at the Claridges in London, and for the Rolls Royce and her favorite driver to be at the airport to meet her. Johnson, accompanied by Nurse Ferretti, flew to Amsterdam on KLM Airlines, and from there he visited the company's Chicopee plant at Cuyk, Holland, and Janssen Pharmaceutica in Beerse, Belgium. A skeptic in the beginning, Johnson was now quite supportive of the pharmaceutical operations and the research accomplishments of Dr. Paul Janssen. Returning to Amsterdam, he wrote to Evie just before sailing: "The treatment [radiation] has left me somewhat weak, and I have some lower back pains that are troubling me." A recent letter from his former captain, Dan Halpin, expressed a sentiment that was on the minds of many: "Which ever way you go, General, may God go with you."

Johnson had carefully planned the itinerary so that he could visit a number of company facilities along the way and have several executives join him for short portions of the trip to discuss the future of their companies. From Amsterdam, the *Golden Crest* would sail down the English Channel to the Bay of Biscay and into the Atlantic, making stops at La Coruña, Spain; Lisbon, Portugal; Gibraltar; Cagliari on the island of Sardinia; and then Naples, Italy. Next the ship would continue back through the Mediterranean Sea, stopping again in Spain and Gibraltar before heading for the Madeira Islands and then across the Atlantic to the final destination, Port of Spain, Trinidad.

The journey would be a long one. Unknown to anyone but the captain, Johnson had a simple wood coffin placed in the hold of the ship and had designated certain passages from the Bible to be read should he die when the *Golden Crest* was far from port.

For the remainder of the trip, Johnson planned to concentrate on the new, smaller companies that were expanding rapidly and causing him some concern. "We are probably trying to move with too many products at this time, and trying to go too fast," he cautioned their managements. "This has proven time and again to be a mistake. It is the result of perfectly sound ambition, but lack of business judgment. Try to simplify your procedure and build a better management."

When the ship docked at Gibraltar, the General was confronted with a new problem—trying to get three of his crew out of jail. While riding in the ship's launch, they had entered Spanish waters by mistake and were arrested by Spanish authorities. The launch was confiscated, and they spent the night in jail before Johnson and the captain were able to negotiate their release. "This is one of the vicissitudes of foreign travel," he wrote Evie, but he had a few choice words about Generalissimo Francisco Franco, the Spanish dictator. "As for Franco," he wrote, "I wouldn't start a St. Bernard farm in Spain. The place is almost as bad as Cuba. We really had a devil of a time getting these men out of jail, and they were there over nothing."

The General was especially pleased with the new plant outside of Rome and its classic Roman architecture—which he had approved earlier. He described the architecture as "grand," but he decided the acoustics in the executive dining room were bad and suggested carpeting would help—a hard, wearable carpet." As he drove around the grounds, he dictated a memo suggesting places where seeding and new shrubbery were needed. Also unhappy with the appearance of a cement drainage ditch that passed under the entrance road to the administration building, he recommended that it be refaced. All in all, the Italian plant manager escaped virtually unscathed, compared with other new plant inspections. (Johnson once described a new plant in Scotland as "ghastly.")

The world journey was now almost completed, and in a span of just over two years Johnson had logged more than 35,000 miles on the *Golden Crest* and had managed to visit most Johnson & Johnson companies around the world. At times during this final part of the voyage he became bone weary, but he was still standing watch on the bridge. That was important to him. He complained little about his health, and for reasons he did not explain — perhaps it was a sense of fatalism — he had not arranged to have a physician aboard for this trip, as he had for the others. His spirits were high as the ship cleared Gibraltar and headed south, to pick up the trade winds and begin its long voyage across the South Atlantic. The longer trips gave him more time to think.

"This letter finds us two-thirds of the way across the southern Atlantic," he wrote Sheila, "and we are two days out of Trinidad. The sea is calm, with a very mild swell. The ship has worked well. She adheres to schedule and navigates straight as an arrow. We have a few minor things to correct, but they are truly minor and I find that she is, without question, the best ship in the world of her type. All hands are well this morning, and we have a happy and competent crew." It was the most glowing report he had ever given from the *Golden Crest*. To a friend in Bermuda, he wrote: "At long last I am really proud of this ship. I am sure that we have the best long-range private vessel in the world. It seems strange, but no other vessel is doing what we do. Even those with large yachts really don't take them to sea."

When the ship arrived in Trinidad, the General went to the new rented factory, which he had chosen, and found that the cleaning, painting, and moving of machinery was progressing nicely. "The new property is excellent," he reported to New Brunswick, "but the question is can we develop a profitable business here." The home office was wondering about that too, because rent was now being paid on two plants — thanks to the General's impulsiveness.

When Johnson decided that the *Golden Crest* would remain at the dock in Port of Spain until the next voyage, Alan Donawa, the local manager, received the news with mixed emotions. The very next morning, the General was back in Donawa's office with ideas for changes in the product line that he believed would boost local sales. "Then," Donawa recalled, "he asked about the local hospital.

[587]

When I told him about the problems they were having he said, 'I wish I had six months to devote to that hospital, and I could reduce their costs by forty percent — because I know the hospital business." Donawa then added, "Maybe he was trying to say something."

Arriving home in late September, the General began catching up on the political news. A few days later he wrote Nelson Rockefeller, then governor of New York: "This morning on the radio I learned of the Reagan-Rockefeller or Rockefeller-Reagan ticket. Either way, this scheme gives me great enthusiasm. I know you said that you will not take it, however, this country is in such a mess that you may have to make the sacrifice."

He wrote essentially the same letter to Ronald Reagan, then governor of California, saying he would support the ticket with either man heading it. The General had liked Reagan since he first entered politics and began lashing out against communism in televised speeches. Once he sent for a thousand copies of a Reagan speech, "A Time for Choosing," along with a message that said, in part: "I have rather vague plans of working for you. . . ." Reagan wrote back that he would be grateful for any help.

Shortly after his return — and after reflecting on what he had learned from his world tour — Johnson shared his observations with the Executive Committee in several memos. While he remained a strong proponent of decentralization, he said, he had found some flaws in that philosophy. "We have yet to learn how best to operate small companies. We are a large family of small industries, and we become large only when we put them all together. We must think in terms of managing small and medium-size companies. . . . We have a fine management, but we must constantly improve." Then in a company-by-company evaluation, he used his familiar metaphors: companies "in intensive care" or "in the repair shop." He was particularly concerned about countries that had erected political and economic barriers to growth of the business. "Should we diminish the business? Should we quietly fade away?"

In his franker moments, he confessed that he was happier when there were some problems. "It gives me some things to fix," he confided to Seward.

It was only a matter of time before the General resumed his inspection rounds of Johnson & Johnson companies in the New Brunswick area. "We are roaming outside your building," began one memo, followed by a critique of the exterior paint and the "scar" in the landscaping. He took the same trip twice on the Pennsylvania Railroad before concluding that a new warehouse was "cheap looking" and that the exterior had to be changed. So did the American flag in front of the building—it was too small.

Parking lots bothered him greatly. "Most people do not recognize that a parking lot should be a part of the architectural and landscaping design of a fine property," he wrote. "Unfortunately, car parking has become a very great liability to many otherwise fairly good industrial properties. Parking lots are also ruining the appearance of college campuses, hospitals and churches." Driving by a new elevated parking lot near the home office, he could see "the tops of motor cars" so he had a two-and-a-half-foot wall built to screen the cars from the street below. After an early snowfall, a sidewalk plow threw snow against the red brick of Johnson Hall, and it stuck to the side of the building, creating what he felt was an eyesore. "If they have forgotten how to use a shovel, ask someone from the retired list of pensioners and they'll tell you," he suggested.

In some respects, Johnson was conducting a reprise of his life's work that fall. He reminded his successor, Philip Hofmann, of the origins of the Credo: "We devoted much thought to the phraseology. Our attempt was to simplify a brief document that we believed could be understood, could be used as a declaration of our policy and principles straight down to the bench level in all of our facilities worldwide." He got the idea to translate the Credo into various languages and send it as a New Year's greeting card to every company employee worldwide, but when he learned how much it would cost he thought better of it. He decided instead to have a reunion of all the people who had worked with him in writing "Human Relations in Modern Business" some twenty years earlier, to see whether those principles could be revived. That idea was scrapped too, though, when he learned that many of the participants in that project were dead.

His medical problems had now grown more serious. The pains in his shoulder blades and around his lungs were recurring more frequently, and he had developed a persistent cough. On October 29 he returned to the University of Pennsylvania Hospital for five days. During that time, he was diagnosed as having a possible pulmonary embolus (a foreign body that occludes a blood vessel), and after he left the hospital he was required to have medication injected into his abdomen every six hours. For the next few weeks, he gave himself many of the injections. "This is the price of staying alive," he wrote. He dreaded that he might have cancer. As for surgery, he would not consider it.

Bobby's health problems had also persisted. Sheila visited Bobby frequently during his illnesses and continued to be attentive to her father as well. She was walking a fine line in the strained relationship between father and son.

In late November, Johnson began making plans for another voyage, which he said would depart on February 1 for Jamaica, Puerto Rico, Barbados, Venezuela, and Colombia. He wrote his newspaper friend, Frank Farrell, who agreed to go along, as did Philip "Flip" Cochran, a friend from his days in Washington twenty-five years earlier. All three had a lot to talk about from the old days. "I was looking forward to the trip," Farrell said, "but unaware of the severity of his illness. The General loved the sea more than anything else in life, and he had the courage of a pirate."

One of his physicians, Dr. Winslow, saw Johnson's courage in another way. Before leaving for the Christmas holidays in Florida, the General received this letter from the doctor:

Dear Bob:

A letter from me, I know, will surprise you. I just wanted to let you know how magnificently you have handled yourself in a most difficult medical situation during the last year. As a doctor, and a man, I have never seen the equal in courage. You will ever be a goal as a man to aim at. I am most proud of our friendship.

Sincerely,
Scudder

37

RECONCILIATION

I N the coming weeks, which would be the last of his life, Johnson's courage and tenacity would be tested as never before. Spells of tiredness and weakness were now recurring with greater frequency, and not being able to pinpoint the cause frustrated him. He was also feeling pain more often, but not in the same places, and this made self-diagnosis — a practice he often indulged in — more difficult. On his notepad, he kept track of the times pain came and went, but there was no pattern to it, and this baffled him.

Despite all the medical attention he was receiving from specialists in New York and Philadelphia, Johnson had never had a physician who kept close watch on his health on a regular basis. Realizing that this may have been a serious oversight on his part, in late November he wrote seeking the opinion of a professor at the Rutgers Medical School. The physician's reply was disconcerting: "I have long been impressed that the wives of physicians and wealthy persons are frequently the recipients of the poorest medical attention, often because corners are cut and responsibility becomes diluted." It was information that Johnson should have sought much earlier.

It took more than a perplexing medical condition to dampen his spirits when there were everyday problems to be solved. Over Thanksgiving weekend, the basement of the house in Princeton became flooded. Unable to find a plumber because of the holiday, Johnson took charge and, in his words, "laid out a scheme to correct the problem," which also included "reorganization of the household staff." Back in the office the following Monday, he wrote a friend that he had gone from the problem of a leaking pipe to the one dealing with "the world's dislocation of currency." "So you can see, it's going to be a nice, easy day," he added, with good spirit.

The joys of Christmas had always eluded Johnson. It was never a special day for him. Evie tried, with presents and frilly wrappings, but they were no substitute for the holiday spirit that was missing. For some reason Christmas made him uncomfortable, and his estrangement with Bobby added a note of gloom.

Johnson woke up in the early morning hours of Christmas in great discomfort. "Awakened with abdominal pain that roams around my midriff," he wrote on his bedside notepad. His pain medication offered some relief, but two nights later he was awakened again by "semi-acute pain just under the right shoulder blade towards the spine." In what was more wishful thinking than an accurate diagnosis, he scribbled in his notepad: "Am thinking it may be rheumatic or arthritic." On New Year's Day, he reported pain when taking a deep breath and speculated that it might be pleurisy. On January 2, he requested that the company plane come to Florida to take him north, for he had decided to be admitted to Roosevelt Hospital in New York.

Instead of arranging for the faster JetStar to come to Florida for him, he called Philip Hofmann, who was a houseguest of Henry McNeil on Eleuthera Island in the Bahamas, and asked if they would stop by and pick him up in the Convair, a slower prop plane, on their way north the following day. "He used the excuse of wanting to save on fuel, which was ridiculous," Hofmann said later. "I couldn't figure this out until I saw him at Fort Lauderdale Airport the next day. He was so weak we had to help him on the plane. He was scared, and he wanted someone with him on the flight."

"He went right to the sofa, and twice during the trip he went to sleep. When he was awake, I sat opposite him," Hofmann continued. "I remember him saying to me, 'Phil, I don't feel good at all.' When we got to Newark, his car was there to take him to Roosevelt, and he said to me: 'Well, kid, I'm going to the hospital and I don't know if I'm going to make it this time or not, but I'm sure going to try.'"

At the hospital, the doctors began a series of tests and put him on medication. After a few days he seemed to snap back, finding fault with the hard pillows, a malfunctioning light in the bathroom, and the inquisitive nature of the interns and residents making grand rounds. He sent Nurse Ferretti out to purchase new pillows—"We'll use them again"—he noted, to justify the purchase. He got the hospital to fix the bathroom light promptly, and he persuaded the doctors to skip him on grand rounds. Clearly, he was feeling more like his old self.

Redesigning the hospital bed also perked him up. Hospital beds were very uncomfortable and poorly designed, he complained, and his in particular. He spent hours sketching and providing the details of a new type of hospital bed that he believed would be far superior. Evie had come up from Florida to be with him, and on one of her visits he proudly showed her the sketches. This one was longer, and earlier he had maintained that all hospital beds should first be tested by the Green Bay Packers football team.

Having solved the hospital bed problem, he looked around for others.

After reading the newspapers one morning, he placed a call to New Jersey Governor Richard J. Hughes. The governor remembered it well: "He phoned me from the hospital to raise hell about something the Port of New York Authority had done, or did wrong, or failed to do—I forget exactly what, but it involved the interests of New Jersey, so Bob Johnson was involved." And at 4:30 one morning he wrote a memo to the chairman of The Robert Wood Johnson Foundation about a new plan he had for medical scholarships. Two days later, he outlined his views on the problems facing

the nation's hospitals: "I have been striving for some time to identify the problems facing hospitals, and I think I am getting close
to it." It was almost business as usual and, except for the medical
reports, there might have been room for optimism.

In mid-January, Dr. Hugh Murray received a letter from Johnson at his health clinic in Regina, Saskatchewan:

Dear Hugh:
Rumor may reach you that I am a patient in Roosevelt Hospital. That,
by the way, is true. I have been running into some difficulty of late
with what appears to be the liver area of my abdomen. I am here for
diagnostic analysis, and out of that will come some form of therapeutic treatment. As I see it now, nothing will interfere with our trip on
the *Golden Crest*. I will take off for Aruba as arranged. We are going
according to schedule.

Frank Farrell was confused. He too had received a message from
the General saying that the *Golden Crest* would sail as scheduled
on February 1. Yet he also heard reports that Johnson's health was
rapidly declining. "I wanted to visit him at Roosevelt," he said, "so
I called Dr. Winslow, who was also my doctor. He told me not to
visit him, and I asked him why not. He said that the General would
not want me to see him in his present condition and that he had
lost so much weight I would scarcely be able to recognize him. I
didn't go to the hospital."

Johnson's skin began turning yellowish. He was losing weight
rapidly and looked emaciated. It was painful for his nurses — all of
whom knew him well — to see him in this condition. Once again,
he began talking about Bobby, who was then a patient at Middlesex
Hospital in New Brunswick undergoing treatment for his recurring colon problem. This was the opportunity Nurse Ferretti had
been waiting for. After ten years of working for Johnson, she had
become a little more assertive. It was time to see Bobby, she told
him. She recalled later: "I wanted him to have a reconciliation with
Bobby because I was sure that's what he wanted, but he was, oh, so

stubborn. Every time I brought up the subject he would resist talking about it. He and Bobby had not seen or spoken to each other in over two years, and I was afraid they might not ever get the chance."

She continued: "I had not seen Bobby in a long time, so that weekend I decided to visit him at Middlesex Hospital. I reported on his father's condition, and he was concerned. We didn't talk about a reconciliation, but I told him I had been outspoken with his father, but I didn't say about what. He said not to let it bother me. Bobby was the only one who ever spoke back to the General.

"When I returned to Roosevelt on Monday, I saw the results of the General's most recent tests, which confirmed that he had cancer of the liver. We did not tell him. It was the one thing he feared most, the one thing he said he never wanted to have wrong with him."

Dorothy O'Neal, the missionary nurse, was also attending Johnson, and she picked up the story: "One night he asked me to call Bobby at the hospital to see how he was doing. I said, 'Why don't *you* talk to him?' and he replied, 'No, he won't speak to me. I've tried that.'

"The next day he said that while I had only been with him for three years he wanted to do something special for me. I told him: 'General Johnson, let me tell you something. I was a missionary for years and I went over there because I loved people. I do want something, but not that.' I didn't tell him then that what I really wanted was to have him call Bobby. I was trying to figure out a better way to approach it, so I let it lie there that night, and I prayed to God to let him live a little longer.

"The next day," Nurse O'Neal continued, "he asked me to read to him from the Bible. I said, 'All right, but I want to talk to you about something.' He told me to read from the Bible first, so I read him the Twenty-Third Psalm. He asked me why I read that one, and I said people like to hear that psalm when they are sick, and it makes you realize that, no matter how deep the valley is, you're going to know that God is with you. I told him that I read that psalm all the time, and we talked about it a little. He then asked me to read more, so I read a psalm praising the Lord—I think it was the 103rd, and he just loved that.

"Later that evening I said to him: 'You said you wanted to do something special for me. Well, this isn't an act, but what I really want is for you to make peace with your son. If you do that I'll be happy. I'll be walking on clouds.' 'Oh, God,' he said, and turned his head away. I told him there was nothing too difficult for God to work out. Then he said to me: 'First it's Miss Ferretti, then Miss Reilly, then Miss Feaster who's after me, and now it's you. Every day you're after me!' I said to him: 'We're all very much interested. Bobby loves you. He's concerned about you, and you're here worrying about him.'

"Then he took his hand out and started messing with the bed covers, and I put my hand on his and said, 'You would make us so happy.' For the rest of the evening he ignored me.

"The next morning he said, 'Miss O'Neal, will you dial Middlesex Hospital for me.' I did and got Bobby on the phone and told him that his father wanted to speak with him. He said, 'Okay.' Then I handed the phone to the General and left the room. I don't know what they said. When I came back into the room, the General said to me: 'Bobby is getting out of the hospital on Sunday and he is coming over to see me on Monday.'"

Monday came, with the General anxiously awaiting Bobby's visit. Looking wan and not very well himself, Bobby entered his father's room. The two greeted each other warmly, then father and son were left alone for more than thirty minutes. Only the two of them knew what was said.

"Before he left the hospital, Bobby thanked the nurses for helping to arrange the meeting," said Nurse O'Neal. "After that there was a noticeable difference in the General's spirits. He was a happy man."

Later, Bobby let it be known that although the meeting between the two had elated his father, it still had not erased all the bitter memories Bobby had of his departure from the company.

[597]

Seward came to the hospital to visit his brother. It was a tearful meeting and Seward left weeping like a child. Johnson wanted no other visitors, except Evie. In those final days, Evie and Johnson drew closer than they had ever been. "The only one he then wanted there was Mrs. Johnson," Nurse O'Neal said. "In the agony of his last days, he wanted her near him. She was understanding, and he leaned on her — and that said volumes to me."

•

Once again the General took his notepad and heavy black pencil and began making notations about his worsening condition. He dutifully jotted down the times he felt the pains — as though he was recording them in a ship's log — and as the seas became more turbulent the letters in each word became shakier. "Sunday 0430 sharp pain extreme right lung area — far beyond liver. very peculiar. Monday 0200 must move to control pain. took codeine. nose bleed left side. confusion but I am still thinking straight. sharp continuous pain lower right abdomen."

"He didn't want others to see him that way, but he wanted the nurses nearby," Nurse O'Neal said. "Especially Miss Ferretti. She was an excellent nurse and had been with him so many years. It was hard on her to see him like that.

"Then he realized we weren't telling him the truth, that he was dying. 'I want you to look right into my face and answer me,' he said. 'Do I have a liver abscess?' I said, 'What did the doctor tell you, General?' Of course, he knew all along he had cancer, but he never mentioned that word. Then he said, 'I have millions and I would give everything I have if someone could make me well.' I said to him, 'Well, General, at this stage I believe the only one you can rely on is God. I would strongly advise you to ask God to help you.' And I believe that he then reached some sort of experience in his prayers."

It was a few minutes before six on Tuesday evening, January 30, and Nurses O'Neal and Mary Feaster were on duty at the General's

[598]

bedside. Nurse O'Neal recounted what happened: "Mrs. Johnson had been there all day. She hadn't eaten and she was exhausted. She asked if I thought it would be all right if she went down to the cafeteria for a cup of tea. I said yes, because there was no significant difference in his breathing.

"She was gone only a few minutes when he sat straight up in bed, with his eyes wide open, as though he saw something. And he reached his arm out in front of him, and I took it to steady him. Mary took his other hand in hers. Then his head fell on my shoulder, and that was it. He died."

•

He died at 6:03 P.M., though the General would have recorded it as 1803. Philip Hofmann was patiently keeping vigil in the hospital waiting room and was the one to telephone New Brunswick with the news, and that call put in motion the plans that had been made earlier. Johnson's obituary, which this author had written weeks earlier, was released to the news media by the corporate public relations department.

It came as no great surprise to anyone who knew him that the General had left explicit instructions for his funeral and burial. They read as follows:

It is my wish that my funeral will be a simple procedure. In the days when we had one plant and I knew all the people it would have been appropriate to close down the units of Johnson & Johnson for a day as a tribute to my name. I do not consider this appropriate now. Therefore, I request that this should not be done.

I further request that my remains should not be on view in any funeral parlor nor at my home. As soon as possible the casket should be placed in the chapel of my church, Christ Church in New Brunswick. The pallbearers, honorary and otherwise, will be the Board of Directors of Johnson and Johnson.

Miscellaneous flowers should be avoided. The casket can be draped with one flower blanket. I do not wish an eulogy. A competent organist may be employed, but I do not wish any other form of music, such as a voice. The officiating minister is to use the classic service of the church. The ceremony at the mausoleum will be brief.

I will be deeply pleased if those who have worked with me for years are present in addition to the members of my family.

Robert Wood Johnson

Colleagues were troubled by Johnson's request that there be no eulogy, so the night he died this author was asked to write a tribute to the General and have it ready for review the next morning. Summarizing his life and accomplishments in a few hundred words seemed like a daunting assignment at the time. The following morning it was presented for review, and, as inadequate as it now seems, it was approved as written, with no changes. The decision was to call it a "tribute" as opposed to a "eulogy," to justify going counter to Johnson's wishes. No one believed that he would have been persuaded to change his mind, but they also knew that this time there would be no memo from him.

Johnson had neglected to note the type of casket he wanted — a major omission for him. Foster Whitlock told about the problems that caused: "Since I was familiar with New Brunswick, I was put in charge of funeral arrangements. The people at the Quackenboss Funeral Home told me the General's father had been buried in a very special bronze sarcophagus, and they had learned there was one just like it in New York City. Then I learned it weighed over eight hundred pounds and cost $25,000. I checked with Mrs. Johnson and she said okay. But we had to reinforce the entire floor of the old church to support the weight of the casket. Then I called the Steinway Piano Company in New York and asked for four burly piano movers. I bought them matching blue suits and they came out to New Brunswick to handle the coffin."

When Evie Johnson read the tribute to her husband, she asked whether a certain verse from the Bible could be added at the end: "I have fought the good fight, and have finished the course; I have run

[600]

the race and have kept the faith." When the Rev. Charles Newberry read the tribute, he questioned the lines she had added, perhaps because he had seen very little of Johnson in his church over the years. Said Whitlock: "We had put the General on a cloud and the minister wasn't sure he belonged there. At first he said he wouldn't do it, but after much persuasion he finally agreed to go along."

Fearing that his death might have an impact on the company stock because of his large personal holdings, Johnson had taken precautions to avoid that by writing an announcement to be distributed after his death. It read:

> To Whom It May Concern:
>
> In recent years a goal of General Johnson was the arrangement of his affairs in such a way that his death would not adversely affect Johnson & Johnson, its employees or its stockholders. To this end, he stressed within Johnson & Johnson the development of outstanding management. He arranged his personal financial affairs in such a way that a sale of Johnson & Johnson stock at the time of his death would not be necessary to pay expenses, bequests and taxes. We are advised by counsel that he succeeded in his endeavor and that the sale of Johnson & Johnson stock is neither necessary nor contemplated.

As one of the executors of Johnson's estate, Philip Hofmann was present when Johnson's safe deposit box was opened. "I lifted the first document out of the box and it was a U.S. Treasury bond for $1 million. It was meticulously planned. It wasn't necessary to sell a single share of Johnson & Johnson stock to pay the inheritance tax. All of his stock went to The Robert Wood Johnson Foundation, other than what was for his family and Evie and the trusts he had set up."

The funeral service was held on a rainy Friday morning, February 2. Christ Church was filled to capacity with family members, friends, public officials from afar, and a large representation from Johnson & Johnson, but many fewer than wanted to attend. The General got most of his final wishes. There were no flowers other than those draping the coffin. There was no vocalist. The twenty-three members of the Board of Directors — all of them his executives — were serving as honorary pallbearers. The service was brief and simple. Reverend Newberry rose to read the tribute, which Johnson certainly would have edited had he been given the chance.

Robert Wood Johnson was a very unusual man. Many of us will live an entire lifetime and never know another man quite like him.

He was born with opportunity, which sometimes has a tendency to spoil a man. Opportunity didn't spoil Robert Wood Johnson; instead, he used it to enrich his own life and the lives of an untold number of people who were fortunate enough to win his friendship or his admiration, or his concern.

He was born with a restless energy that was amazing to behold. It often left the people around him breathless and disbelieving, and perhaps capriciously, this stirred him to even greater effort.

Robert Wood Johnson possessed a tenacity of spirit that few men could match, and seldom was he without a challenger. But once he set his sights on a goal, there was very little doubt that he would achieve it. Even when he lost, he still managed to be philosophical.

Dignity was a characteristic that accompanied him all through his life. It was apparent in his bearing, in his appearance and in his manner. Yet he had a disarming wit that he loved to call into play at precisely the moment when it was least expected.

While other men were preoccupied by the past and the present, his thoughts always seemed to be probing the future — new ideas, new projects, an agile and adventurous mind that always seemed to function best when spurred by a sense of urgency. Great men have always been frugal with time, and Robert Johnson was no exception. For him, there always seemed to be so much to do, and never quite enough time in which to do it.

Of all the qualities that this unusual man possessed, none served the world better than the tender concern he had for those less privileged than he. The spirit of giving, not only of himself but of his worldly goods, has reached out and touched countless numbers of people in the far corners of the earth. It is impossible to comprehend all of the good that he did for his fellow men during his lifetime, and this is Robert Johnson's greatest legacy. His deeds are forever inscribed on the hearts of those to whom he was benefactor.

Perhaps his most inspired devotion was directed toward the men and women with whom he worked. He invested them with a sense of dignity. He provided in abundance the material needs for them and for their families. He constructed buildings that established standards years before their time, and he had the wisdom to make the working conditions as modern as the structures themselves.

He left his imprint on the business world, the field of medical care, the political arena, and as a public servant, statesman, patriot, soldier and humanitarian. The surprising thing is not that he did so many things, but that he did them so well.

So now we come to the parting of ways, we who were privileged to be close to him through the years. Life is fleeting at best, but think how much better ours has been because we were fortunate enough to cross paths with Robert Wood Johnson. Remember him in these ways, and we will have been worthy of his friendship.

There is a brief passage from the Scriptures that speaks for Robert Wood Johnson:

> *I have fought the good fight, and have finished the course,*
> *I have run the race and have kept the faith.*

When the service was over, the members of the Board of Directors left the church first and formed two lines. The bronze casket, which the General would have thought exorbitantly expensive, was wheeled between the two lines of directors to the hearse parked on Church Street. Standing four and five deep on the sidewalk across the street were scores of the old-timers from Johnson & Johnson, workers he had always considered friends. They had waited in the drizzling rain to bid him farewell.

The service at the family mausoleum was private and brief, just as Johnson had requested. One of his colleagues noted later: "After the funeral, we came right back to work."

That surely would have pleased him.

POSTLUDE

I

JOHNSON FAMILY
MEMBERS

Robert Wood Johnson Jr.   Bobby Johnson died at a Fort Lauderdale, Florida, hospital on December 22, 1970, less than two years after his father. He was fifty, and had never fully recovered from the illness he was battling in January 1968 when he went to Roosevelt Hospital in New York for a reconciliation with his father. His widow, Betty Johnson, gradually assumed the role of matriarch of that side of the family, as the aging Evie Johnson's health began to fail.

In Bobby's will the Robert Wood Johnson Jr. Charitable Trust was created. Betty Johnson and her three surviving children — Robert Wood IV, Elizabeth "Libbet," and Christopher — steered the philanthropy in the direction of providing support for a range of innovative cultural and art programs. Major funding was given to the Metropolitan Museum of Art for the Van Gogh in Aries and the Treasures of Tutankhamen exhibits, which toured the nation after making their debuts in New York. Other funding supported public television, including the "Live from Lincoln Center" series.

More recently, the Trust has developed a special interest in funding medical research projects on the autoimmune system. This came about when Robert Wood Johnson IV became a national leader of and fund-raiser for the Juvenile Diabetes Foundation International. The Trust also makes major contributions to environmental programs and wildlife conservation projects, areas in which Bobby Johnson had a personal interest during his lifetime.

J. Seward Johnson Sr. The General's brother, Seward, died on May 23, 1983, at the age of eighty-seven at his home at Fort Pierce, Florida, on the grounds of the Harbor Branch Foundation. The Foundation was an oceanographic research center he had set up with inventor Edwin Link. Seward had endured a long and difficult illness.

His six children — Mary Lea Richardson, Elaine Wold, J. Seward Jr., Diana Firestone, Jennifer Duke, and James — gathered in Florida for a private burial service at dawn, along with Basia, Seward's third wife. Later that morning a memorial service was held alongside the wharf at Harbor Branch for friends and other members of the family. It was an oppressively hot day, and the service ended with the plaintive notes of taps echoing from a bugle on the nearby hillside, followed by a response from two ship's horns, first from the research vessel *R/V Johnson* and finally from Seward's prized 61-foot ketch, the *Ocean Pearl*.

Then the family repaired to the quietude of the solarium at the house to exchange warm words about Seward. That moment in time should have lasted longer, but a bitter court battle over the distribution of his wealth ensued.

Evangeline Johnson Merrill Evangeline died on June 17, 1990, at the age of ninety-three. She had long outlived her two brothers, Robert and Seward. In 1975 she married her third husband, Charles Merrill, and they lived quietly at World's Edge Apple Organic Farm in Henderson, North Carolina, a long way from the glitter of Palm Beach social life where she had once reigned. Obituaries recalled her many contributions to the arts — she was a Fellow in Perpetuity of the Metropolitan Museum of Art in New York.

On a visit to Evangeline in Palm Beach several months before her death, we sat in her tree-shaded garden, and her vitality, when measured against her years, was amazing. She had lost none of her regalness. That day she was dressed in a flowing Thai-silk caftan of brilliant purplish red, and the sun danced on her shoulders as it filtered through the gently swaying trees. She was charming, witty, and, as always, amusingly saucy. We spoke mostly about the General—"Bob" to her. I said: "Did you know that the General once remarked, 'If Evangeline had been a man she would have been the one to run the company?'" It was a comment that had been repeated many times, and I was sure she had heard it before. But her answer surprised me: "I never knew Bob said that about me," she said, but the twinkle in her eye told me otherwise.

Evangeline had two loving and attentive daughters—Lyuba and Sadja—by conductor Leopold Stokowski, and she spoke proudly about them. All the while, a fluffy little dog circled frenetically beneath our chairs—the same dog that Evangeline would trip over some weeks later and take a fall that led to her death. Evangeline, however, did not believe that people actually died. She explained in a letter that arrived after her departure:

Dear Family and Friends:
Thank you for your friendship and love which has greatly enriched my long and happy life.

I am writing this letter to be sent to you after my so called death. I believe that there is no death, only eternal forms of Universal energies which are unending.

My wish for you is that you become ever more aware that you yourself are an expression of Universal energy and one with its beauty, harmony and rhythm.

Love always,
Evangeline

Evelyne Vernon Johnson   Evie outlived the General by twenty-eight years and spent much of that time keeping his memory alive.

She died on September 10, 1996, at Longleat, her estate home in Princeton, New Jersey, at the age of ninety-five. She was in fragile health the last ten years of her life.

For the first two years after her husband's death, Evie rarely ventured away from Longleat, except for attending Mass at Our Lady of Princeton Chapel and for occasional visits to the family mausoleum at Greenwood Cemetery in New Brunswick, where the General was entombed. Finally, during the third Christmas season after his death she was persuaded to go to New York City's Rockefeller Center to see the Yule tree and the Christmas displays in the windows of Saks on Fifth Avenue, which she had enjoyed so much in happier years. After that she began going out more.

The eulogy at Evie's funeral was given by this author, who recalled a comment made years earlier by Bishop Fulton Sheen: "Evie was a lady and the General was a gentleman." A past era was remembered, when the beautiful lady and the handsome gentleman danced in perfect harmony and were hailed by newspaper columnists as New York's most stunning couple. It was also recalled that Johnson had often commented on Evie's "great sense of style" and how proud he was of that quality in her. Following the service, Evie was interred next to the General at the family mausoleum.

Sheila Johnson Brutsch   The last surviving member of Robert Wood Johnson's immediate family, Sheila lives in Switzerland, with her husband, François. They also have a home in Palm Beach, Florida. Sheila's mother, Maggi Shea Johnson Eily, who was the General's second wife, died on February 26, 1997, at the Francis E. Parker Memorial Home in New Brunswick, at the age of ninety-four.

As an adopted child living in the musty expanses of the historic house called Morven, Sheila had quickly adapted to her new surroundings and to life as a Johnson. Though torn by the breakup of her parents some five years later, she remained close to both of them as she grew into womanhood with a notable sense of independence. Some thought it was an injustice that Johnson did not provide Sheila with substantial wealth, but instead set up a trust that could be described as modest when compared with the family's riches. He had always been wary of putting too much money in the hands of women, whom he felt could easily fall prey to male fortune-seekers. It was therefore lucky for Sheila that she was someone who preferred a comfortable lifestyle over a more opulent one. And it was not mere resignation on her part.

In the two years before her father's death, during the falling-out with Bobby, Sheila walked a tightrope in her relationship with her father and brother. The alienation was too complicated for her to mediate, so she followed the course of maintaining a loving relationship with both and not taking sides. She and Bobby had always been close, and during his final, lengthy illness Sheila visited him on many weekends and offered him comfort.

THE TYLENOL
TRAGEDIES

In the years following his death, Robert Wood Johnson's cherished Credo philosophy began losing some of the influence it once had within Johnson & Johnson. This was partly due to the continued expansion of the company into new global markets, and the difficulty of instilling corporate culture in the thinking of new managements and employees who had not experienced either the Credo's earlier impact on the company, or Johnson's personal crusade to keep it alive and relevant.

Philip B. Hofmann sensed this waning, and in the closing months of his chairmanship conducted a series of ten Credo dinner meetings attended by some 4,000 management employees. At these events, he spoke about preserving the values inherent in the Credo and making them a part of the decision-making process. The reaction of those present was supportive, but the Credo was still merely a nicely worded document that hung on the wall and had never been tested.

After Richard B. Sellars succeeded Hofmann as Chairman and Chief Executive Officer in 1973, he was confronted by an embarrassment to the Credo philosophy. The news media had publicly disclosed that Johnson & Johnson was one of a number of global companies that had been making illegal payments in certain overseas markets in exchange for favorable treatment that would enhance the business of those companies. Such activity was in direct violation of the Credo. The company had failed the test. Sellars met the issue head-on. He fired the offenders, apologized for the reprehensible actions of a few, and tightened management controls to ensure that it would not happen again.

His earlier association with Johnson had made Sellars a strong believer in the Credo philosophy. Another test of that came when the company began deliberating on where it would locate the new corporate headquarters it was planning to build. While New Brunswick had been the company's home since 1886, the city in the early 1970s was in rapid decline brought on by a combination of destructive economic factors. The downtown business district had an alarming number of vacant stores, small companies were moving out of the dispirited city, and morale among civic leaders was at a low.

Within Johnson & Johnson there was strong sentiment for joining the exodus from New Brunswick, a city that appeared to have lost its way. The company owned a score of possible building sites for the new headquarters, many of them on beautifully landscaped acreage in desirable suburban settings. The ultimate decision was up to Sellars, and he chose to have the company remain in New Brunswick.

"I looked at the Credo's commitment to the communities where we work and live," Sellars recalled, "and I reminded myself of General Johnson's deep sense of loyalty to New Brunswick, his birthplace. Those two factors influenced the decision to remain in New Brunswick, but I also knew that we would have to work to revitalize the city to make it worth staying here." Sellars had no way of knowing that bringing New Brunswick back to life would require his intense personal efforts for the next ten years.

Sellars began the arduous task by recruiting John J. Heldrich as project chief. Heldrich, a senior Johnson & Johnson executive, had strong personal ties to the area and a zealous determination

Giving a fiery
radio talk

On the town with
columnist Frank
Farrell

The new Chairman, Philip B. Hofmann, tours the baby products plant

RWJ in his office, with photo of Sheila in background

The *Pilgrim*

RWJ — the lure of the sea

Brother Seward

The *Golden Crest* in Australia, later Pilot Boat #2 in New York Harbor

The last voyage

The Board of Directors as honorary pallbearers

The people of New Brunswick bid farewell

The early Foundation building

Gus Lienhard

The Robert Wood Johnson Foundation in Princeton

Maker of Tylenol Discontinuing All Over-Counter Drug Capsules

Offers to Replace Them After Woman's Death From Poisoned Pills

By ROBERT D. McFADDEN

Johnson & Johnson yesterday discontinued the manufacture and sale of all its over-the-counter medications in capsule form to prevent the kind of tampering that recently killed a woman who took cyanide-laced capsules of Extra-Strength Tylenol.

The company also offered, at its expense, to replace about 15 million packages of its capsule products in stores and homes across the nation with caplets, which are oval-shaped tablets coated to make them easier to swallow. It said it hoped to rebuild the lost capsule market in less tamper-prone caplets and tablets.

The phamaceutical concern, which markets scores of products and had sales of $6.4 billion last year, estimated that its withdrawal from capsules would cost $100 million to $150 million, after taxes. This will include the expenses of replacing six kinds of capsules already on the market and of retooling its plants as well as other costs in trying to rebuild its market position

'Standards of Responsibilit

"We feel the company can guarantee the safety degree consistent ⸱tanda⸱

The New York Times / William E. Sauro

James E. Burke, chairman of Johnson & Johnson, at news conference with large model of oval-shaped tablet known as a caplet.

James E. Burke deals with the Tylenol crisis

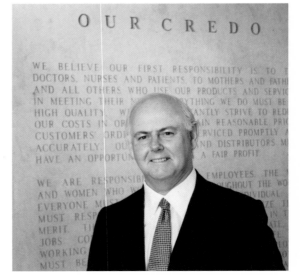

Chairman/CEO
Ralph S. Larsen
"The Credo lives on"

to save the city. He and Sellars began by recruiting and inspiring local leadership to share the same vision, and together they created the "New Brunswick Tomorrow" project. It took time, work, and money, but eventually they succeeded in turning the once-doomed city into a nationwide model of urban rebirth. The centerpiece for the revitalized downtown area was a handsome new Johnson & Johnson headquarters complex designed by associates of renowned architect I. M. Pei. Part of the credit for the turnaround went to the responsibilities outlined in Johnson's Credo.

Just before he succeeded Sellars as Chairman of the Board in 1976, James E. Burke had questioned the relevance of the Credo in terms that were challenging and upsetting to many in the Johnson & Johnson hierarchy—Sellars, and this author, among them. Reflecting later on the tensions he had generated, Burke explained—in an interview with the American Management Association—what happened next:

"I began to suspect that the Credo wasn't as meaningful to everyone in the company. While many had adopted it as our guideline for conducting the business, this wasn't universally true. The company had plants in some fifty or more countries, and the number of new employees had grown rapidly. I expressed these concerns to David Clare, our President and Chairman of the Executive Committee, and my closest associate in the company. He agreed, so we decided to do something about it.

"We began by bringing in about twenty-five of our managers and laying out for them what we called 'The Credo Challenge.' What we said, in effect, was this: If you do not believe in the Credo, and you aren't urging your employees to abide by it, then it is an act of pretension. In that case, you should take it off the wall of your office and throw it away.

"Then we began the debate—or the 'challenge'—as we called it. We went through every section of the Credo, challenging each one. The assignment was to come out of the meeting either recommending that we get rid of it, change it, or commit to it as it is. And if we were going to change it, I said, 'I want you to tell us how.' The debate continued for two days, and in the end the overwhelming majority voted to retain the Credo philosophy but urged some word changes that brought the document more in keeping with the times. In substance, however, the Credo received reaffirmation. It proved my point that everyone has a value system. But by giving them the opportunity through discussion and confrontation to buy into the Credo, it was now their philosophy as well, and not one foisted on them by a previous generation."

Many employees in the company, however, were distressed to find that the revised Credo omitted the reference to "God." The closing lines of the Credo had read: "We are determined with the help of God's grace to fulfill these obligations to the best of our ability." Those in charge of the Credo challenge process had bowed to the wishes of a few international managers from countries where God was not widely recognized. The decision generated an undercurrent of bitter disappointment within the company.

Burke continued: "The dynamics of that meeting became so important to us, in terms of management involvement in this critical philosophical issue, that over the next three years Dave Clare and I met with all the other managing directors. The same process ensued, and the results were the same as the first meeting. We then incorporated the recommended word changes into a revised Credo and reissued it in 1979 at one of our world meetings."

At the time, Burke had no way of knowing how important his decision to challenge the Credo would be when Johnson & Johnson was faced with the greatest crisis in the company's history in the fall of 1982. By encouraging the worldwide managers to discuss and debate the details of the document freely, Burke had paved the way for further institutionalizing the same set of beliefs throughout the company. Having been part of the evaluation process, the managers of all Johnson & Johnson companies now felt a new sense of ownership in the principles of the Credo, and many of their employees felt the same way. Belief in the Credo was once again palpable.

·

What began as Johnson & Johnson's darkest hour turned out to be its brightest in terms of corporate reputation. In late September 1982, one or more crazed criminals — still unknown to authorities — used Tylenol Extra Strength Capsules as a murder weapon by lacing them with cyanide poison and killing seven innocent people. The method used was diabolical beyond belief. The murderers purchased eight bottles of Tylenol from five food and drug stores within a twenty-mile radius of Chicago. About fifty of the red-and-white capsules were pried open, and the powdered medication was mixed with potassium cyanide, a powerful poison in crystalline form. The lethal mixture was then put back in the capsules, which were reassembled and put back in the original bottles and outer boxes. Each repackaged bottle was then secretly placed back on the shelf in the same store where it had been purchased, to ensure that there would be no questions raised at the checkout counters when unsuspecting victims repurchased them later.

The first word of the horror came on the morning of September 30, when a reporter for the *Chicago Sun-Times* telephoned Johnson & Johnson's Corporate Public Relations Department and informed veteran staff member James A. Murray of a suspected link between Tylenol and the death of a Chicago-area woman from cyanide poisoning. The news was quickly passed along to the company's senior management, and they were stunned and disbelieving. About the same time, the Cook County medical examiner was giving the same shocking report to the medical director of the McNeil Consumer Products Company at Fort Washington, Pennsylvania, the makers of Tylenol products. McNeil is one of Johnson & Johnson's Family of Companies.

This ignited what came to be known as the "Tylenol Tragedy." It was later likened to throwing a lighted match into a vast, dry forest where an evil wind kept it burning fiercely for months. It was the greatest crisis of its kind ever to strike an American corporation.

The stunned disbelief in New Brunswick and Fort Washington rapidly turned to shocking reality. Within twenty-four hours, five women and two men from the Chicago area—all under thirty-six years of age—died painfully after ingesting the poisoned capsules in the belief that they were taking a pain remedy. Three of the dead were from the same family. After one brother had collapsed and died, his grief-stricken younger brother and his wife came to the dead man's apartment. Shaken and distraught, they sat down at the kitchen table and took capsules from the same poisoned bottle. They died too. And a twelve-year-old girl who had stayed home from school with a sore throat took one of the tainted capsules and died almost instantly.

The nation's news media converged on the story with frenzied intensity, putting it on the front pages of newspapers and at the top of television and radio newscasts—where it would remain for seemingly endless weeks. There was good cause for the alarm. For the first time ever, terrorism with lethal consequences had invaded the sanctity of the home, making everyone vulnerable. In *Life* magazine, Loudon Wainwright Jr. wrote: "The killer, in effect, had appeared in everyone's home—every medicine cabinet had become a potential hiding place for some life-threatening horror."

A cold chill swept over the executives of Johnson & Johnson and McNeil as they realized that the poisoning might have occurred in the plant during manufacturing. Tylenol was the nation's most popular brand of pain remedy, with more than one hundred million users. There were thirty-one million bottles of Tylenol capsules out there—in homes, schools, hospitals, and work places, and on the shelves of tens of thousands of retail outlets across the nation. How widespread was this murderous act? How many other lives were threatened?

In Chicago there was pandemonium. Police and fire vehicles moved through the streets blaring warnings about using the product, as police and company representatives moved from store to store in the area of the murders, removing Tylenol capsules from the shelves so they could be tested to determine whether they had been poisoned. And agents of the Food and Drug Administration descended on the McNeil plant in Pennsylvania, where the tainted capsules had been produced, searching for clues. There was desperate uncertainty about how the poisoning took place and how far the wicked plot might reach. Then it was learned that some of the tainted capsules had been produced at a McNeil plant in Round Rock, Texas. The likelihood of an in-plant tampering at two widely separated plants seemed slight. With this information in hand, authorities intensified the search for the killers in the Chicago area.

The alarm spread quickly to other countries. At Heathrow Airport outside London, and at Orly and Charles de Gaulle airports in France, loudspeakers warned passengers from the United States of the possible danger and instructed them to bring any Tylenol they had to a customs desk for inspection. In Italy, the warning was broadcast over state television. In markets as far apart as Poland, Guatemala, the Philippines, and Singapore, authorities issued warnings and removed Tylenol from store shelves. The problem was worldwide. Tylenol products were on the market in twenty-three countries.

The senior management of Johnson & Johnson took two early steps to protect the public. From the very first call, the company was completely open and forthright with the news media and began a phased voluntary withdrawal of Tylenol Capsules that would later become both nationwide and worldwide. Cooperation with the news media was seen as the most effective way to warn all consumers about the potential danger, even though there was no evidence that the plot had reached beyond Chicago. The fright and mounting anxiety had gripped the nation, and this alone was seen as reason enough to get the capsules off the market. Johnson & Johnson's reputation and credibility were at stake, as was the compelling need to protect the public.

The Federal Bureau of Investigation quickly entered the case, giving it the highest priority. Working with authorities in Pennsylvania, agents of the Food and Drug Administration, after careful investigation, declared that the poisoning had not taken place at the McNeil plant. It was virtually impossible to gain access to the product during the automated production process, and even if that had been possible, it would have taken nearly a ton of cyanide in the mixing vat to contaminate the product in the concentration found in the capsules in Chicago. There was prayerful thanks at the company, where the worst fears were that the poisoning had taken place in the plant.

While there was no tangible evidence that the poisoning plot extended beyond Chicago, there was no certainty of that. Speculation was rampant, and often fed by the latest headline or newscast, even when hard facts were missing. Poison-control centers were flooded with calls from frantic people who claimed they were feeling ill and suspected they had been poisoned. Sometimes there was a link to Tylenol, but not always. Six hysterical residents of the Pittsburgh area went to local hospitals after viewing a graphic television program that described the symptoms of cyanide poisoning. They were sure they had been poisoned. The emotional scene was replayed in towns and cities all across the nation. Pathologists were quick to point out that everyone's blood has traces of cyanide and that heavy smokers test four times higher, thereby complicating the procedure and prolonging the final results.

The cases of mistaken illness were troublesome to deal with, but not nearly as alarming as news of sudden deaths of some 250 people all across the nation linked in some way, no matter how tenuously, to the use of Tylenol. One example was the death of a trucker who died in the cab of his vehicle along a Tennessee highway. Police found a bottle of Tylenol capsules on the seat beside him. He was a heavy smoker and tested positive for cyanide, but doctors found that he had actually died of a heart attack. In time, all the other sudden deaths thought to be part of the Tylenol plot were attributed to other causes, mostly heart attacks and stroke, but they contributed to the growing volume of press coverage. While medical tests were being performed on the deceased, reporters kept the story alive, often calling the company and announcing: "We think we have another one here."

Both the FBI and the FDA initially opposed the company's decision to withdraw all capsules nationwide (four other capsule products were included in the recall), because that would be capitulating to the terrorist and would threaten the nation's system of marketing food and proprietary drug products. "Sick minds would be encouraged to repeat these acts," another said in arguing against the nationwide withdrawal. FBI Director William Webster was concerned that because Halloween was coming it might trigger a wave of copycat crimes. But a bizarre coincidence in California—where strychnine was put in Tylenol capsules in an unsuccessful poisoning plot—convinced them that Johnson & Johnson's decision was the right one.

"Someone was using our brand as a vehicle for murder, and we had to remove the vehicle," Burke said. The prompt action saved lives. Two of the eight bottles of Tylenol capsules containing cyanide were recovered in the Chicago area before they could claim more victims. One bottle was removed from a store shelf, another was returned by a very lucky woman who had purchased it but had yet to take any of the contaminated capsules. Given that an estimated fifty capsules had been poisoned, it was a miracle that the fiendish crime had claimed just seven victims.

Consumers who had purchased Tylenol capsules were urged to return them to a testing center or throw them away, and McNeil promised to replace the capsules with the tablet product, which was above suspicion. To be absolutely certain the solid tablet product was safe, a group of company scientists were later asked to see whether they could find a way to contaminate tablets. They did discover a way, but it involved the use of a hyperbaric chamber and a process only a scientist could carry out. Even disposing of the capsules posed a problem for some officials. In San Francisco, there were warnings about contaminating the city's sewer system.

Investigators in Chicago were working around-the-clock but making little headway. What few leads they had took them down one blind alley after another. There were conflicts among local, state, and federal authorities over jurisdiction, adding to the turmoil. The Illinois attorney general took charge of the investigation — and as if that wasn't enough pressure, he also had an election coming up. He appointed a Tylenol Task Force to cooperate in the investigation, and this group would grow to an unwieldy 170 members. The media claimed they got in each other's way. The headquarters for the investigation was a converted garage in Des Plaines, and there a band of edgy reporters impatiently sought new information on the case. They came from as far away as London.

Quiet grieving for the seven victims and their families was taking place within the company. Despite the frenzy of work generated by the crisis, expressions of deep sorrow for the misfortune of "those poor people" were heard everywhere. They came from those who had manufactured the product with pride, from those who had sold it with confidence, and from top-echelon executives who were still disbelieving. Letters of condolence were written to the families, but numerous suggestions to show the company's deep sense of regret in more tangible ways fell victim to the legal ramifications of such actions. It was not a popular course, but one that had to be adhered to. The fact that the company had been held blameless — and was itself a victim — would later nullify the legal actions that eventually came.

Despite the absence of leads, the combined weight of the Tylenol news coverage throughout the nation was staggering. From the outset, senior executives at both Johnson & Johnson and McNeil were available to the press for interviews and television appearances, even though they could shed no light on the mystery. Making the executives available served to strengthen the belief that the company was blameless and not resorting to the run-and-hide tactic that infuriates the news media. This approach strengthened the relationship with the press, which continued to show surprising sympathy for the company's plight.

The enterprising reporters who were pursuing new angles to the story kept it in each day's news and often on the front pages. The combined network news coverage was now averaging an hour of air time a day. The story had taken on a life of its own. It was later determined that the case had commanded more print space than any news story since the assassination of President John F. Kennedy in Dallas in 1963, and more television coverage since the reporting of the Vietnam War. Both the Associated Press and United Press International ranked Tylenol as the second impact story of the year — the first being the ongoing coverage of the American economy.

A seemingly endless flood of press calls came day and night to Johnson & Johnson's corporate public relations staff — all of whom were former journalists, familiar with news coverage and the ways of wily reporters. Over time, the number of calls from the news media exceeded 2,500. Beginning with the first call, a log was kept recording the name and phone number of every reporter who phoned. When information wasn't immediately available, the reporter received a return call. The same practice was followed at McNeil. No public relations agency people participated in this phase of the crisis. The record of reporters who were covering the story would prove invaluable later.

Numerous false leads were pursued, and even those with no validity came back to haunt the company and prompted Burke to describe the situation as "an unremitting nightmare." Many of the suspicions that Tylenol capsules were involved in illness or death beyond the Chicago murders were totally unfounded. Scientists working on the investigation tried to emphasize that because cyanide absorbs water readily the gelatin that comprises the shell of a capsule contains water that would be quickly absorbed by the poison. Thus, a capsule containing cyanide would decompose and turn dark in a few weeks, making it easily recognizable as a contaminated capsule. Perhaps understandably, the scientific explanation was not very reassuring to most people.

One of the legitimate suspects that emerged in Chicago was a darkly brooding man with satanic symbols tattooed on his body and a predisposition to violence. When the police got a tip, they raided his apartment and found a horrifying collection of poisons and a guidebook on how to commit mass murder with them. It turned out, however, that the suspect had not been in Chicago at the time the Tylenol capsules were poisoned and placed on the store shelves. Enraged that a former co-worker had tipped off the police about him, the suspect killed the man he believed to be the informant — but he killed the wrong person. The newspapers in Chicago portrayed the bizarre mistake as an extension of the Tylenol tragedy, and now there were eight dead.

Suddenly there was an outbreak of brazen attempts at extortion, with Johnson & Johnson as the target. Conniving individuals thought they had found a way to make easy money by threatening to do more harm to the company by contaminating others of its products. In an attempt to catch one extortionist, an FBI agent, posing as a company executive, went to downtown Newark and boarded a bus. Following instructions in the extortion letter, he carried a briefcase supposedly containing a large amount of money, and as the bus passed a designated spot — a small park — the FBI agent threw the briefcase out the window, as the letter had instructed. Other FBI agents were nearby, disguised as workers. Several people descended on the briefcase lying on the ground in the park, but none of them was the extortionist. The trap had failed to catch its prey.

The only arrest ever made in the Tylenol case was a would-be extortionist. James W. Lewis, an unemployed accountant from Chicago, was apprehended in the New York Public Library after a stakeout by the FBI. It was yet another strange twist in an already bizarre investigation. Lewis had earlier been questioned about a murder in Kansas City before he moved to Chicago. After the Tylenol murders, he sent an extortion letter to Johnson & Johnson demanding $1 million to "stop the killing." The letter had been sent from New York, and investigators turned their attention to Manhattan in search of Lewis, who had also written letters to the *Chicago Tribune.*

When it became apparent that Lewis was reading the *Chicago Tribune* in New York City, the FBI began a surveillance of out-of-town newsstands and the New York Public Library. At the library, the FBI's patience paid off and Lewis was arrested. It turned out that Lewis had also written a letter to the White House, threatening to "bomb" it with plastic explosives dropped from a radio-controlled model airplane that Lewis said would be launched from a nearby park. It was a wild scheme, but it alarmed both the FBI and the Secret Service.

A few executives at Johnson & Johnson, working closely with the FBI, knew about the threatening letter to the White House but had been sworn to secrecy. Early one morning, James Litke, the Associated Press bureau chief in Chicago and one of the most tenacious reporters covering the murders, phoned Johnson & Johnson's vice president of public relations (the author) at home and asked bluntly: "What the hell is the Secret Service doing at the Tylenol Task Force?" (referring to the investigation meeting in Chicago). After a slight pause came the reply: "I don't know." It was the only time during the Tylenol episode that the press got an evasive response.

Lewis was convicted of extortion and served more than twelve years in prison. Investigators tried to implicate him in the Tylenol murders but could not make a case against him. Lewis stoutly defended his innocence in the murders, once telling Cable News Network: "It's just as impossible for me to be the Tylenol killer as it would be for me to be the killer of Julius Caesar." Lewis had been slated for parole earlier, but his letter in 1982, threatening the life of President Ronald Reagan, came back to haunt him, and the parole board decided he should serve his time.

The press had been inadvertently misled for several days early in the story when they asked the crucial question: Was cyanide used in the manufacturing process? After checking with production people, the reply was a flat "No." Investigators had asked the same question and were told the same thing. Several days later, the head of quality control at McNeil disclosed that a tiny amount of cyanide was indeed present in the testing lab, which was located in a building apart from the manufacturing plant. It was inconceivable that this small amount of cyanide could have been used in the murders — besides, none of it was missing. The issue was credibility, and Johnson & Johnson spokesmen had given their word. Almost immediately the Associated Press, the *New York Times*, and the *Newark Star-Ledger* learned of the error. In a display of journalistic fairness and responsibility, they noted the discrepancy well into the next day's stories, and discounted the importance of the presence of a small amount of cyanide in the testing lab.

Day in and day out the story dealt in tragedy, but every now and then a faint trace of humor merged. A ten-year-old New Jersey boy wrote a carefully worded extortion letter to Johnson & Johnson, demanding payment of $1 million. He then put his home address on the envelope, and because he didn't have a stamp he gave it to his father to mail, which he dutifully did without suspecting the contents. The father was left to judge what punishment, if any, should be meted out.

•

In addition to demonstrated marketing skills, Johnson & Johnson was known for having capable and competitive management. Once it was determined that the poisoning had not taken place in the plant, the marketing people began to discuss how to bring the Tylenol brand back. They turned to the marketer's stock-in-trade: consumer polling. The polls showed that while an astounding 99 percent of Americans were aware of the murders in Chicago, an encouraging 90 percent did not fault the company for what happened. This left the door open for the comeback that many of the marketing and advertising "experts" had already decided was impossible. They declared that the Tylenol brand was dead. In doing so, many even wrote off the tablet form, which posed no threats. Consumers had shown a strong preference for capsules over tablets because they saw them as being more like prescription medicine, which Tylenol was when first introduced by McNeil two decades earlier.

On the eighth day of the crisis, the decision was made to ignore the doomsayers and bring Tylenol capsules back, this time in tamper-resistant packaging that would ensure the product's safety. The groundwork had been laid to resurrect the $450 million business that had collapsed virtually overnight. Television advertising had been halted at the first word of the murders, so consumers would not be exposed to messages about pain relief when they were hearing newscasts linking the product to murder. The company promptly sent 450,000 telex messages to physicians, hospitals, and distributors, explaining the problem and seeking their confidence and support. Toll-free telephone lines were quickly set up by McNeil, and there were 136,000 calls from consumers seeking information about the poisonings, and thousands who offered moral support.

Everyone at the company knew that there were challenging days ahead. Burke put it clearly in a message to employees: "It will take time, it will take money, and it will be very difficult," he warned, "but we consider it a moral imperative, as well as good business, to restore Tylenol to its preeminent position." He went to the McNeil plant in Pennsylvania, where employees crowded into the cafeteria to hear him deliver an emotion-charged speech that set the fighting tone for the recovery effort. Burke was especially adept at rallying people to perform beyond even their own expectations. That day, he was brilliant at it.

The employees of McNeil and Johnson & Johnson—even those not directly involved—got caught up in the recovery effort and volunteered their services. The entire families who showed up on weekends to help out were assigned to answer the banks of toll-free phones and speak to customers who called in to accept the offer of a free exchange of Tylenol tablets for capsules they had purchased. Many callers, and others as well, expressed their sympathy for the company. When a group of McNeil employees formed a morale-boosting committee, they came up with the slogan "We're Coming Back" and placed an order for lapel buttons with a California supplier. Two days later, enough "We're Coming Back" buttons for the entire work force arrived. "No charge," a note with the shipment said.

Cooperation and goodwill came to Johnson & Johnson and McNeil from many sources. Even usually fierce competitors were reluctant to fill the empty store shelves with their pain-relief products—space only recently occupied by Tylenol capsules before they were swept away.

The technical problems associated with the design, manufacture, and installation of tamper-resistant packaging machinery were daunting. Early estimates were that it would take six months. Responding to McNeil's desperate need to get back on the market before memory of the product faded, outside suppliers of machinery and other production needs performed minor miracles in record time that no one thought was possible.

For generations, Johnson & Johnson had enjoyed a unique relationship with its millions of customers, a relationship that had a certain mystique. It went beyond a commitment to fulfill the responsibilities outlined in Robert Wood Johnson's Credo. There were other companies that performed admirably in these areas. And still, consumers consistently indicated in various studies that they had developed a special warm spot for the company that had been making Johnson's baby products for the better part of a century. It was not a marketing pipe dream, for the edge given Johnson

& Johnson showed up time after time in consumer surveys. As best the company could determine, it was the role that the use of baby products played in strengthening the bond between generations of infants and their parents — mothers in particular.

Studies conducted by psychologists and pediatricians, and independent of the company's interests, had long ago determined the importance of "touch" in the development of an infant. Touch conveyed love and a sense of security. In applying powder, lotion, and other baby products to the infant, touch played an important role and helped to strengthen the bond between mother and infant. Other studies showed that the distinctive floral fragrance of Johnson's Baby Powder was one of the most familiar of all scents and that it always brought back pleasant memories of the warm relationship between a child and its mother. This, the believers said, was powerful reason to have trust in a company whose products could stimulate such a deeply personal response. Though not fully understanding the mystique, Johnson & Johnson welcomed the advantage it offered them in its relationship with the public. It was a bitter irony that the gentle, loving relationship between mother and child should somehow be a factor in the comeback phase of a crime of evil-minded brutality.

If the public had trust and confidence in the company, as many believed, now was the time to draw on it. The first television advertising in the comeback was a brief campaign with one basic theme — "Trust Us" — and featured the medical director of McNeil, Dr. Thomas N. Gates, who had a calming, authoritative voice and could easily have passed for the family physician. From a professional office setting, Dr. Gates looked squarely at the camera and asked his audience to trust the company while it prepared to bring Tylenol back in tamper-resistant packaging.

The nation's news media immediately picked up on the "Trust Us" theme, and the commercials got wide attention in the news columns. To counsel him and help make key decisions, both in managing the crisis and planning to bring Tylenol back, Burke formed a seven-member strategy committee, which he chaired.* The committee met twice a day in Burke's office — early in the morning and again at the end of the day — for eight weeks. The meetings were lengthy and often marked by heated discussion and open debate, a hallmark of Burke's style of management. He not only encouraged debate on key strategy issues, he often precipitated it in order to arrive at the right decisions. Rank held no privilege in Burke's debates. When the smoke of battle cleared and he had heard all sides, he then made the final decision.

Communications within the management of Johnson & Johnson had always been good, despite its decentralized structure. That proved to be a great asset in managing the Tylenol crisis, noted David E. Collins, Chairman of McNeil and a member of the strategy committee. "It is not possible to refine poor communications at the heights of a crisis. A crisis only magnifies imperfections," he said.

Over the next several months, hundreds of people within Johnson & Johnson and McNeil changed their normal work schedules and worked day and night toward a common goal: to save the company's reputation and bring the product back to market as a way of demonstrating the company's innocence in the crime. Reflecting on the tenor of the strategy committee meetings and the pressures, David Clare, company president, later told author Martin Mayer: "We watched the news together, we lived together, we thought together, and we fought together, week after week. My memory of those months is one of unending stresses — and we still had to keep running the company in its other markets."

Many of the strategy committee's discussions revolved around issues that Johnson had addressed in his Credo. Copies of the

---

* In addition to Chairman James E. Burke, the members of the strategy committee were David R. Clare, President; David E. Collins, Chairman of McNeil; Lawrence G. Foster, Corporate Vice President of Public Relations; George S. Frazza, General Counsel; Wayne K. Nelson, Company Group Chairman; and Arthur M. Quilty, a member of the Executive Committee.

document were kept on the table in the meetingroom and referred to frequently. Often the answers were there, as Burke said later: "We had to make some of the most critical decisions in the company's history, and most of what we needed by way of direction was right there in the document. Had we not made these decisions according to the Credo, we would have broken faith with our people."

One of the company's traditional strengths was its close ties to its employees, which now totaled 79,000 worldwide. In the early days, the General began calling it a "Family of Companies," and now there were 160 affiliate companies in the family, with separate managements and different missions in health care but still closely tied to the parent, Johnson & Johnson. As Burke had noted, keeping faith with employees and gaining their support during the current crisis was essential. Seven years earlier, a Worldwide Video Network had been established to improve internal communications and was now being used to keep employees informed about the latest developments with Tylenol. Video monitors, converted so they could replay cassette tapes made in the United States, were in place at two hundred plant and office locations around the world. Global delivery services were used to get the tapes there quickly. Twelve hours of tapes on developments in the Tylenol story were made in the New Brunswick studio, keeping employees informed and giving them a sense of involvement.

In the final analysis, it was the public that would render the final decision on how responsible the company was and on whether Tylenol capsules would be restored to its once lofty position among pain-relief medications. To keep informed about what the public was thinking, photographers with video cameras were sent out every day, in various cities, to conduct informal, on-the-street interviews. They asked consumers their opinions about the Tylenol situation, how they thought the company was responding, and whether they would be likely to purchase the product again later.

At the end of each day, the photographers would send the tape cassettes to New Brunswick by the fastest means so the strategy committee and others in management could screen them carefully. Many nights, Burke would take the tapes home and review them again, looking for guidance from the public's reaction.

The outbreak of product-tampering in the nation was now accelerating at an alarming rate, with various other companies and their customers becoming the targets of the attacks. Hydrochloric acid turned up in eyedrops, and a strong irritant was found in a bottle of mouthwash. Shoppers had become wary and were now examining packaging for signs of tampering. When they became suspicious, they complained to store clerks. A tension had been added to shopping. In Washington, the FDA and Congress were working feverishly to come up with emergency legislation that would soon revolutionize consumer packaging with regulations on tamper-resistant packaging. There was no way to fully protect consumers from product contamination, but the new requirements for tamper-resistant packaging would at least provide some safeguards. It was clear that what began as one company's problem had now become society's problem.

As the relaunch of Tylenol capsules moved forward, consumer surveys were encouraging. Some 79 percent of those polled now said they would buy Tylenol again, in tamper-resistant packaging. "We are sensing a tremendous reservoir of goodwill and trust toward Johnson & Johnson and the brand," Burke told the *Wall Street Journal* with a note of optimism.

The marketing strategy for the relaunch was rapidly taking shape, and the new packaging equipment had been purchased and was being installed on production lines faster than anyone had thought possible, because people were working day and night. Several years earlier, the public-relations agency Burson-Marsteller had been retained by McNeil to publicize the Tylenol brand. The agency suggested that the capsules be reintroduced at a televised press conference that would be beamed via satellite to press conferences held simultaneously across the nation in dozens of other cities, thereby ensuring wider coverage by the news media. Management bought the idea, and the elaborate planning began.

In early November not even six weeks after the crisis began, the new Tylenol packaging was introduced to the McNeil sales force. The bottles included three tamper-resistant seals: an outer box with all the flaps glued shut, a red plastic band sealing the cap to the neck of the bottle, and a strong innerfoil seal over the mouth of the bottle. The design of the triple safety-sealed packaging went beyond the new requirements being drawn up in Washington, which would take effect in a few months. A race developed within the drug industry to see who would be on the market first. McNeil President Joseph R. Chiesa announced that the cost of the new packaging—two cents a bottle—would not be passed along to consumers but would be absorbed by the company.

The marketing effort moved into high gear, drawing on all the company's strengths. A huge task force of 2,250 sales people recruited from domestic Johnson & Johnson companies that marketed professional products was briefed on the Tylenol relaunch. They were assigned to help the McNeil sales force make presentations to physicians and other health-care professionals, with the target being one million visits. Thirty McNeil sales managers were given television training, and after the introduction they made appearances on more than one hundred local talk shows to promote Tylenol capsules in the new safety packaging.

The carefully planned relaunch took place on November 11 at the Sheraton Center in New York, where a hundred news media people had gathered for a closed-circuit television press conference that was also relayed by satellite to thirty other cities. In those locations, another five hundred news people had gathered, making the turnout one of the largest press conferences ever held. The number was high because personal invitations had been sent to every reporter who had worked on the Tylenol story. Their names and addresses were drawn from the log that the public relations staff had been keeping since the first press call.

At the press conference, the new tamper-resistant package was unveiled with great fanfare. The other news was that consumers would receive a free bottle of Tylenol capsules in the new tamper-resistant package. This clever marketing scheme would be backed by a massive advertising campaign, aptly named "Thank you, America," and include distribution of 80 million coupons worth $2.50 each when redeemed for the capsules. The rest would be up to the public, Burke said. "We are confident that consumers will make an eminently fair decision about the future of Tylenol," he told the press, which relayed the message in thousands of news stories about the comeback.

The public responded favorably, and sales of Tylenol capsules began to soar. In less than a year, the product had regained its preeminent position among pain-relief medications. Johnson & Johnson's reputation was intact, and the news media gave the company high marks for its performance during the crisis. The *Washington Post* said: "Johnson & Johnson has effectively demonstrated how a major business ought to handle a disaster." At Johnson & Johnson, much of the credit was being given to Robert Wood Johnson's philosophy of managing a business.

·

Three years and three months later, the unthinkable happened. On February 8, 1986, a young woman from Westchester County, New York, died of cyanide poisoning after ingesting a Tylenol capsule. Other capsules in the bottle had also been contaminated with potassium cyanide, but in this case the chemical profile was slightly different from the cyanide used in the Chicago murders. Tylenol capsules were promptly removed from store shelves in the immediate area. It was February 10 before the medical tests were completed and the press was on the story. The search for the killer focused on Westchester County because the improbability that the poisoning occurred during manufacturing had been established in 1982. The story was once again on the front pages, reviving all the horrors of the unsolved mystery in Chicago. Old television footage showed bottles of Tylenol being swept off store shelves in Illinois. The nightmare had begun again for the people at Johnson & Johnson and McNeil. They were devastated.

On Tuesday, February 11, the company called a press conference at corporate headquarters in New Brunswick for that afternoon. There was a wicked snowstorm that day. At the company's request, AT&T and New Jersey Bell worked feverishly to set up telephone lines to enable the news media from all over the nation to listen in on the news conference. Seventy members of the press came to New Brunswick. Seven hundred other news media people were on the telephone hookup. There was little news to offer, but the company wanted to show that it was cooperating with the press, as it had in 1982. No immediate recall was planned, Burke told the reporters. There were questions about the tamper-resistant packaging and how it had apparently failed. The contaminated bottle sold in Westchester had been manufactured in Fort Washington eight months earlier.

On Thursday there was a baffling development. A second bottle of contaminated Tylenol capsules was found on a store shelf in Westchester County. The bottle had never been opened — its safety seals were still in place. But the contaminated, discolored capsules could be seen through the bottom of the bottle, which had been produced in Puerto Rico seven months earlier. Investigators examined the bottle and found no visible signs of tampering, but it was sent to the FBI labs in Washington for closer testing.

On Thursday, Johnson & Johnson held another press conference in New Brunswick, where questions were asked about how the bottle could have been invaded and contaminated with the safety seals still in place. No one had an answer for that. Burke made it clear that Johnson & Johnson was itself a victim, again, and that the company was reluctant to give in to a terrorist. The investigation in Westchester had made no progress, but authorities believed there was no link between the crime there and the murders in Chicago three years before.

The public relations issues were many, and none were without risk. To get an outside viewpoint, Harold Burson, Chairman of Burson-Marsteller and widely respected for his experience and judgment, was invited to New Brunswick for a consultation. Meanwhile, there were other rapid developments, all of them discouraging.

In desperation, fourteen states banned the sale of Tylenol capsules. All across the nation there were reports of suspicious deaths and attempts to link them with Tylenol. Even where the evidence was sparse, overzealous reporters made it a big story, and the national frenzy was regenerated. A report came from Washington that the FBI had discovered how the terrorist had invaded the bottle taken from the store shelf in Westchester, but the technique was wisely withheld. The news was reassuring to the company, though no one believed the contamination could have taken place at the plant. It was a terrorist act, and in the three years since the Chicago murders the feeling that it could happen again had not diminished.

The strategy committee, reconvened by Burke, met later the same day to resolve a crucial question: Should Tylenol capsules be removed from the market? There was no easy answer. Sales of the product had soared to $550 million a year, with profits exceeding $90 million, making it a major contributor to the company's overall financial performance. Then there was the important consideration of employee morale. Hundreds of people had worked tirelessly over a long period to restore the product to its leading position in the analgesic market—and many had said it couldn't be done. Would it be fair to them to summarily wipe out their hard-earned achievement by abandoning Tylenol capsules? Those at the meeting who had worked hardest on the comeback stoutly defended keeping the product on the market and resolving the present difficulties, just as had been done before.

In time, the discussion turned to the Credo. Everyone in the room knew that it would. A copy of the Credo lay on the table around which the group was seated. Its presence there was disquieting. Someone raised a difficult question: If a terrorist had demonstrated that it was possible to invade the safety-sealed bottle without it being detected, how could customers ever be protected from danger? No one had the answer. Then came another question: If the first responsibility under the Credo was to the customer, wasn't there only one decision to be made? Burke set up a press conference for the next morning.

Standing before the crowd of news media representatives the following day, Burke announced that Johnson & Johnson would discontinue manufacturing all over-the-counter capsule products worldwide. "We feel that the company can no longer guarantee the safety of capsules," he said. Then he held up a large model of a Tylenol Caplet — a white, oval tablet that was virtually tamper proof. The company, he said, would replace all the capsules now in the hands of retailers and consumers with the new caplets. As he spoke, cameras pressed closer for a photo of Burke holding the model caplet with the red Tylenol logo emblazoned on the side. He paused, and for a minute only the sound of clicking cameras could be heard. The next day, the photo of Burke holding the enlarged caplet ran on front pages all across the nation, including the *New York Times*.

It appeared to be a carefully orchestrated marketing presentation, but it wasn't. Hours earlier, when the strategy committee concluded that the Credo had spoken, they pondered "What now?" They turned their attention to Tylenol Caplets. McNeil had developed the caplet product in the aftermath of the 1982 crisis, and it had modest success. As luck would have it, however, a huge quantity of caplets had just recently been produced for a special sales promotion and were sitting in a warehouse waiting to be distributed. The caplet model that Burke held up at the press conference was actually an old paperweight given away as a promotion at the time caplets were introduced. A secretary in public relations remembered seeing one on a desk in the building and borrowed it for the photo. It was perfect.

Four days later, at the National Press Club in Washington, President Ronald Reagan was addressing a group of business leaders and the press. He departed from his prepared remarks to praise Burke, who was in the audience, and Johnson & Johnson for the actions that had been taken in the public interest. As it turned out, consumers all over the nation shared these sentiments, and Tylenol Caplets became an overnight success.

Somewhere, Robert Wood Johnson must have been smiling. His Credo had helped to write the end of the story.

III

THE CREDO
LIVES ON

In the decade since becoming Chairman and CEO of Johnson & Johnson in 1989, Ralph S. Larsen has skillfully blended the Credo principles into the mainstream of several management programs aimed at strengthening the company. As a result, he has brought a new dimension of importance and utilitarian value to the Credo, lifting it beyond its traditional role of being a statement of responsible decision-making and making it a management tool. The process that the Credo has gone through in making these further contributions to the company's success is a tribute both to Robert Wood Johnson's foresight and to advancements that have been made in the art of management.

The 1982 Tylenol crisis thrust the Credo into the limelight, and the news media began referring to the document as the most widely known statement on corporate responsibility in American business. The passage of time did nothing to detract from the document's visibility. Some sixteen years later, in his 1998 book, *Eighty Exemplary Ethics Statements*, Professor Patrick E. Murphy, Chair of the Department of Marketing at the University of Notre Dame, wrote: "The Johnson & Johnson Credo is probably the best known ethics statement in the world, at least partially due to the central role it played in the tragic Tylenol poisonings."

The higher the pedestal, the more likely it is to be shaken when

Our Credo

We believe our first responsibility is to the doctors, nurses and patients,
to mothers and fathers and all others who use our products and services.
In meeting their needs everything we do must be of high quality.
We must constantly strive to reduce our costs
in order to maintain reasonable prices.
Customers' orders must be serviced promptly and accurately.
Our suppliers and distributors must have an opportunity
to make a fair profit.

We are responsible to our employees,
the men and women who work with us throughout the world.
Everyone must be considered as an individual.
We must respect their dignity and recognize their merit.
They must have a sense of security in their jobs.
Compensation must be fair and adequate,
and working conditions clean, orderly and safe.
We must be mindful of ways to help our employees fulfill
their family responsibilities.
Employees must feel free to make suggestions and complaints.
There must be equal opportunity for employment, development
and advancement for those qualified.
We must provide competent management,
and their actions must be just and ethical.

We are responsible to the communities in which we live and work
and to the world community as well.
We must be good citizens — support good works and charities
and bear our fair share of taxes.
We must encourage civic improvements and better health and education.
We must maintain in good order
the property we are privileged to use,
protecting the environment and natural resources.

Our final responsibility is to our stockholders.
Business must make a sound profit.
We must experiment with new ideas.
Research must be carried on, innovative programs developed
and mistakes paid for.
New equipment must be purchased, new facilities provided
and new products launched.
Reserves must be created to provide for adverse times.
When we operate according to these principles,
the stockholders should realize a fair return.

something goes wrong. The rocking of the pedestal came in 1983 when Zomax, McNeil's popular new prescription drug for intense pain, was linked to more than a dozen deaths caused by the severe allergic reaction known as anaphylaxis, which can lead to seizures and respiratory failure. While nearly 15 million patients were using Zomax without untoward incident, the recurrence of anaphylactic reaction sounded an alarm and prompted critics to ask: "Where was the Johnson & Johnson Credo in this scenario?"

McNeil's response was that the risks of taking Zomax—an oral drug as effective as injected morphine, but one that did not cloud the consciousness or cause addiction—were stressed in instructions to physicians. Unfortunately, the warnings were not always heeded. Despite the merits of the drug, Johnson & Johnson decided to voluntarily withdraw the product from the market when reports of anaphylactic reactions continued. The Food and Drug Administration was not happy with that decision because of the unique need Zomax filled for patients with intractable pain. The drug's supporters said the company had acted precipitously, but its critics said action was not swift enough. The merits of both arguments were debated in ensuing litigation.

This watershed event moved the Credo to a new level of importance within Johnson & Johnson and its Family of Companies. In the Tylenol episode, the company had been seen as a victim. With Zomax, the circumstances were different, and while the Credo had precipitated the decision to withdraw the product from the market, there was the question of timing. It was now abundantly clear that all future decisions of major importance made by the company would be measured against the yardstick that the Credo had become. Previously, Johnson & Johnson had been judging itself by these standards. Now the outside world was doing so as well. The Credo's new visibility brought added responsibility and made the company more vulnerable to criticism.

Sensing the Credo's new importance, Chief Executive Officer James E. Burke and his colleagues launched in 1985 a new program to make the document as relevant to employees as it had become to management. Known as the Credo Survey Process, it would become the foundation on which the next Chairman, Ralph S. Larsen, and his management would build.

The process began with a carefully thought-out questionnaire that would allow the company's employees to evaluate how management was performing in the four areas of responsibility covered in the Credo: consumers, employees, communities, and the stockholders. To encourage frankness, employees were assured that all responses would be held confidential. A special staff was assigned to handle the survey and the evaluation. After a test run at one of the affiliate companies, the Credo Survey Process was expanded to cover all of Johnson & Johnson's 77,000 employees worldwide. The complex survey took months to complete.

Asking employees what they thought of management's performance in carrying out the goals of the Credo was not without risk—but it was deemed a risk worth taking. The responses were tabulated and analyzed, and the results were given to managers, who then held feedback meetings with their people. At these sessions, deficiencies in the workplace and in other areas where the company was not performing to employee expectations were discussed. Managers were then required to present action plans to correct problems the survey had revealed.

At the end of the lengthy process, even skeptical employees seemed to have a new respect for what the Credo could accomplish in making Johnson & Johnson a better company.

Cultural differences, and the way overseas managers viewed the American concept of corporate responsibility, made the Credo more difficult to comprehend, and follow, for certain Johnson & Johnson international affiliates. Senior managers devoted a great deal of time to this learning process.

When a Japanese business delegation interested in promoting their nation's economic development came to the United States, one of their stops was to visit Johnson & Johnson's corporate headquarters in New Brunswick, New Jersey. Surprisingly, they focused on the Credo and came armed with penetrating questions about its effectiveness. While meeting with four members of the company's Executive Committee, they asked: "Can you give us an example of an important decision that was rescinded because it was in conflict with your Credo values?"

This was the reply: "One of our affiliate companies had recommended we close a textile operation because it was no longer profitable. In doing so the company would have been forced to close a plant in the South in an area already hard-hit economically. Many of our long-service employees, some with twenty to twenty-five years, would have been put out of work. When this decision came to the Executive Committee, the discussion centered on our Credo responsibilities. As a result, the plan was substantially altered. We asked one of our companies looking to expand to move into the plant to be vacated. They did, and we were able to utilize some two hundred people that otherwise would have been displaced. We also altered the severance and relocation programs for the remaining employees. Basically, this was about our Credo responsibilities."

When Ralph Larsen became Chairman, he began finding new ways to use the Credo as a management tool. An executive in Human Resources cited some of the objectives: "Our ultimate objective," he said, "is to have employees and their managements work together to enhance our culture and strengthen the business. Increasingly, employee feedback has been playing a key role in the startup of task forces and action plans aimed at improving the workplace. The survey process is no longer just a report card. It serves as an instrument with enormous potential to increase employee involvement, productivity, and the communication of values and business objectives. It is also a means of getting employee input into forming strategic plans."

The Credo Survey Process was now put on a bi-annual schedule and demonstrating that it was capable of identifying and resolving gaps between its guiding principles and the company's daily action.

The Credo's reputation in business was growing. In 1991, *Business Ethics* magazine cited it as a legendary document "and perhaps the nation's longest lasting and most effective statement of corporate ethical standards."

Expanding rapidly, Johnson & Johnson now had more than 150 affiliate companies around the world, and this complicated the task of applying the Credo principles to such a wide range of cultures and business practices. In preparation for the Worldwide Management Conference in 1995, an "Executive Survey of Credo Values" was sent to 246 senior managers. They responded with a list of significant components they felt would be required if Chairman Larsen were to achieve his goal of creating what he described as a "Credo-based leadership."

The managers decided that Credo leadership would require daily management behavior that supported the values outlined in the document, that communications about Credo values had to be purposeful and consistent, and that the company's reward system had to include recognition of management adherence to Credo principles. By wisely allowing managers to set the ground rules, Larsen was ensuring support for the program. From this, one of the conference's major themes evolved and was titled "What Does It Mean to Be a Credo Leader . . . *Specifically.*"

At this major conference of company management, Larsen made it clear that Credo leadership *at all levels* was needed to sustain the integrity of Credo values in a highly competitive global marketplace. The next step in the evolution of the Credo was a major new program titled "Standards of Leadership." In describing what was expected of management leaders, Larsen said: "Credo values represent the foundation stone upon which leadership is built. Certainly within Johnson & Johnson you cannot be a good leader if you don't believe in and try to live up to the Credo."

The "Standards of Leadership" as defined by Ralph Larsen and his colleagues embodied the following: renewed focus on the customer and the marketplace, innovation, interdependent partnering, organizational and people development, and mastering complexity. These goals, they said, defined the fundamental requirements for maintaining leadership in the global marketplace. To serve this purpose, the "Standards" became the driving force behind a series of human resources programs, and the focal point of discussion and review of the Succession Planning Process. In short, that determined who moved up in the organization and who didn't.

Of all his business skills, Robert Wood Johnson's talent for selecting and training a highly competent management paid the biggest dividends. For decades the company had been widely recognized for developing outstanding management—*Forbes* magazine referred to Johnson & Johnson as "one of the world's best managed companies." As with other successes in business, the last best performance becomes the launching pad for higher achievement if the upward momentum is to continue.

Chairman Larsen saw a problem on the horizon. Early in 1998, he wrote his senior management around the world: "It is increasingly evident that the competitive nature of the marketplace goes far beyond the issues of market share, product technology, and shareholder return. We are seeing increased competition for talent as well. A shortage of management talent can be a key restraint in achieving growth and performance objectives. Competition for top talent will become increasingly fierce. . . . It will be only your continued emphasis on leadership development that will enable Johnson & Johnson to retain our talented people for future growth opportunities."

In the highly competitive global game of attracting and keeping talented management, Johnson & Johnson's trump card has been the Credo. The principles expressed in the document are appealing to the type of person the company wants to attract. Some other companies subscribe to similarly high standards of conduct, but few are as overtly committed to a written set of guidelines as Johnson & Johnson.

At the important succession planning meetings, when upward

mobility in the company is discussed with managers, "Credo Values" is first on the agenda. "Business Results" is next in line. The behaviors associated with Credo values are noted: "Behaving with honesty and integrity. Treating others with dignity and respect. Applying Credo values. Using Credo survey results to improve the business. Balancing the interests of all constituents. Managing for the long term."

Like his predecessors, Ralph Larsen has had to deal with violations of Credo policy and has done so swiftly, clearly outlining the consequences of such infractions. One incident involved infiltration of a competitor's sales meeting. Larsen wrote his management: "Our behavior should deeply embarrass everyone associated with Johnson & Johnson. Our investigation revealed that certain employees had engaged in improper activities that violated our policies. These actions were wrong and we took steps, immediately, to discipline those involved and guard against a recurrence of this kind of activity."

It is better for global managements to assimilate the philosophy contained in the Credo than to have it force-fed to them. All five Johnson & Johnson Chief Executive Officers, beginning with Johnson, and then Hofmann, Sellars, Burke, and now Larsen, have been acutely aware of that. Managers have never been ordered to display the Credo, but they do with remarkable frequency. When professor and author Patrick Murphy visited the Janssen-Cilag pharmaceutical affiliate in Cork, Ireland, he noted: "An enlarged Credo hung both in the reception area and outside the managing director's office." Had he been in Malaysia, he would have seen what is referred to as the "Credo Wall" — the document translated into twenty-four languages.

To make a point regarding the universality of the Credo within the company, Chairman Larsen in 1997 collected sixty-five copies of the Credo in various languages and had them printed in a single volume. In his foreword to that book, he wrote: "We share a heritage so strong that it transcends cultural and language differences.

The bond that ties us all together is Our Credo, a simple yet profound document that clearly defines our responsibilities. . . . As you will see in the following pages, Our Credo looks different from country to country. But no matter what the language, its enduring principles remind us of the values that make up the character of Johnson & Johnson."

There has always been a pocket of criticism in business that dismisses such high-sounding philosophy as merely a form of self-delusion—that business success is more about numbers than it is about integrity and putting the customer first. That argument would be a tough sell with Ralph Larsen, who dealt with his numbers at the 1998 Shareholder Meeting in this way: "We are pleased to report another year of record sales and earnings for Johnson & Johnson. Importantly, net income passed the $3 billion mark for the first time to $3.3 billion, an increase of 14.4 percent." And then he added:

"We now have more than 90,000 people and 180 operating companies doing business in almost every country in the world. That makes the Credo and our value system more important than ever.

"In a sense, the Credo remains our North Star, and we are doing everything we can to make sure that its importance is more widely and deeply understood than at any other time in our history."

Robert Wood Johnson's Credo, now nearly sixty years old, continues to thrive.

IV

THE ROBERT WOOD
JOHNSON FOUNDATION

The year was 1936, and America was struggling to survive the Great Depression. Poverty and despair gripped the nation. Everywhere, people were in need. Hoping to ease some of the pain in his hometown of New Brunswick, New Jersey, Robert Wood Johnson used some of his personal funds to form a foundation to help those in need. The focus was on improving health care, but he also provided food and heat for families that were in great need.

Modest grants to the local hospitals were made to improve patient care, and young people who wanted to become physicians but could not afford the cost of a medical education were given financial support. These were the seeds that grew to become The Robert Wood Johnson Foundation, which today is the nation's largest private philanthropy devoted exclusively to improving health and health care in America. Since becoming a national philanthropic organization in 1972, the Johnson Foundation has made more than 10,000 grants totaling in excess of $3 billion. It has become a fountainhead of health-related philanthropy in the United States.

Johnson left virtually his entire estate, in the form of Johnson & Johnson stock, to the Foundation, having provided for his family earlier with a series of trust funds. Robert J. Dixson, a longtime colleague, explained Johnson's rationale: "The General was a very generous man, and I think he felt that the American people had made

[649]

Johnson & Johnson a very successful company and that he was discharging his responsibility by turning his money back to the people who gave it to him. I believe that is what he thought. But I also think he was motivated by another very pragmatic thought. He felt that if a substantial part of his stockholdings could remain in the Foundation, future managements of Johnson & Johnson would be more likely to conform to his philosophy of management. And his old colleagues serving on the Foundation Board would see to that."

It was not Johnson's nature to leave things to chance. He planned with meticulous care, yet he made no attempt to chart the course of his Foundation after his death, other than to stipulate that the money be used to improve health care in America. That came as no surprise to Philip Hofmann, Johnson's successor as Chairman of the company and his closest business associate, who explained Johnson's thoughts. "The General knew he could not run the Foundation from the grave," Hofmann said, "so he decided to leave the decisions to his associates, whom he knew and trusted."

At the time of his death, Johnson's holdings in Johnson & Johnson stock were valued at about $300 million, and all of it was designated to go to the Foundation once the estate was probated—a process that took some three years. His plan for continuing the strong ties between the Foundation and Johnson & Johnson made sense at the time, but he had no way of anticipating the drastic changes that would be made in the federal tax laws in 1969, the year after his death. Robert Dixson summed up the changes as they applied to foundations. "The new tax laws declared that business had better keep its nose out of foundations, and foundations had better keep their noses out of business."

While the changes in the tax laws had thwarted one of Johnson's goals—to preserve a link between his philanthropy and the company—his colleagues were free to carry out his management philosophy, as well as his values, in the way the Foundation was organized and run. After Johnson's death, Gustav O. Lienhard, Johnson & Johnson's low-key president who was approaching retirement, became the Foundation's chairman. It was a choice that Johnson himself would have applauded. Lienhard, financially conservative and a product of the green-eyeshade generation of accountants, had long ago won Johnson's approval. Johnson would refer to him as "the penurious Mr. Lienhard" — and Lienhard took it as a high compliment.

Following his retirement, Lienhard moved his office to the modest frame house that was then the Foundation's home, on Livingston Avenue in New Brunswick. Joining him as his assistant was Olga Ferretti, Johnson's loyal and competent nurse/secretary. Lienhard knew nothing about managing a foundation, but this was a plus for the learning process that followed. "In the year before we got the money," Lienhard later explained, "I visited most of the large foundations in the country and talked with their chairmen and presidents to get a better understanding of what their problems were. I learned what kind of staffing was needed. I laid the groundwork and organized ourselves in anticipation of what I knew would be coming when the money from the estate was released. I also began a search for a president to run the Foundation."

The first life of the Foundation that Johnson had formed thirty-six years earlier was about to end. During that period from 1936 to 1972, grants were awarded totaling $7.8 million. Now a new era was about to begin. The vastly increased resources worried Lienhard, who later said that the responsibility reminded him of the words of the Greek philosopher Aristotle: "To give away money is an easy matter and in any man's power. But to decide to whom to give it and how much and when, and for what purpose and how, is neither in every man's power nor an easy matter."

As Lienhard continued to educate himself on foundations, he began looking for a site for a new headquarters building. He finally settled on seventy attractively landscaped acres at a campus-like setting near Princeton, a short distance from the university. Again Johnson's influence came into play. "We didn't need seventy acres," Lienhard said later, "but this was the General's way of doing things.

When we were looking for plant sites, we would recommend buying ten acres, and he would say 'No, buy twenty, buy fifty so you have room to expand.' He was right. He had the vision that a lot of us didn't. Now, you might say that was dictatorial and autocratic, but he had darn good judgment. So we bought the seventy acres and built his type of building [precast concrete, and similar to many of the office buildings Johnson had helped to design]."

Lienhard's lack of traditional thinking about the way in which a foundation should be organized and managed may have been his greatest asset. "I fostered the philosophy that philanthropy should be productive," he said, "and that when we spend large sums of money it should be on programs that will allow grantees to carry on after we end our support. Productive philanthropy must be beneficial to society, and spent on programs that can be replicated by others. The Board was in full agreement on this."

Lienhard was keeping an eye on the dramatic growth in the value of Johnson & Johnson shares in the years just after Johnson's death, realizing that as the share price soared so did the size of the Foundation and the magnitude of his problems. A front-page *New York Times* story announced on December 6, 1971, that the Robert Wood Johnson Foundation would soon receive $1.2 billion in Johnson & Johnson stock, making it the nation's second largest philanthropy, next to the Ford Foundation. Since Johnson's death, the value of the stock had increased four-fold.

The day after the story appeared, this author visited Lienhard at the Foundation office on Livingston Avenue with a draft of the annual report on grants made that year. As he approached the rear entrance off the parking lot, two workmen were rehanging the door, which had been ripped from its hinges. Lienhard was agitated. "Some crazy jerks read in yesterday's paper that the Foundation was receiving $1.2 billion," he said, "and last night they broke in here trying to find it." With a glimmer of satisfaction, he added: "The only thing of value here was a roll of stamps."

After a careful search, the Board chose Dr. David E. Rogers, the innovative dean of the prestigious medical school at Johns Hopkins University in Baltimore, to be the first president of the Robert Wood Johnson Foundation. Rogers had gained wide acclaim as a physician and teacher and was an important contributor to the national debate on health policy. This would be his first venture into philanthropy. Rogers and Lienhard made a strange pair: the visionary physician with bold new ideas, as president, and the staid chairman holding on to the purse strings and demanding "productive philanthropy."

The two men spent many hours discussing program direction, and, according to both, the chemistry between them was good. The reputation and personal magnetism of Dr. Rogers attracted to the staff several of the most innovative thinkers in health care, among them Robert Blendon, Margaret Mahoney, and the venerable Walsh McDermott, who had helped form the National Academy of Medicine to advise the government on health issues. As a team, they wrote the script for the creative role the Foundation would play in changing the face of health-care philanthropy in the nation.

Surveys conducted by the Foundation indicated that many Americans were deeply concerned about their inability to get prompt medical help when they needed it. Using that information to help set the course, the Foundation decided to make one of its major goals improving patient access to out-of-hospital primary medical care. "We decided to listen to the public," Dr. Rogers explained, "and Americans were saying that they were concerned about getting help when they were sick."

Once the direction was set, creative programs were developed in several areas. One provided a grant for revamping the emergency medical response system, and this led to adoption of the "911" method now in use nationwide. Another program vastly improved child care in rural areas and brought about a sharp reduction in infant mortality rates. Health-care programs were developed for the homeless, and dental care for the handicapped. Attention was focused on helping youths who were at high risk for drug addic-

[653]

tion, alcoholism, and unwanted pregnancies. Other grants went to programs that dealt with health problems of the elderly and the chronically ill. As demonstration projects proved workable, they were replicated elsewhere in the nation, and soon the young Foundation's capacity for bringing about change began to grow. "We wanted to be outcome-oriented," Dr. Rogers said in assessing the early programs.

At the time some $50 million a year was being given in grants. Yet, when pitted against the many problems facing the nation's health-care system, that amount seemed inadequate. For every new solution, two new problems seemed to surface. The challenge was to use the money wisely and not duplicate the efforts of other philanthropies or government health programs. Through the influence of Lienhard and the Board, grantees were informed that "accountability" would be part of every grant agreement and that they must be prepared to give a detailed account of how the funds were spent. Lienhard referred to that as "keeping book," an expression carried over from his accounting days. Every grant had an evaluation component, so that results could be tracked and success or failure would not be left to speculation. Failure was tolerated, however, and Dr. Rogers said that the 10 percent failure rate they encountered was quite acceptable given the kinds of new ventures being funded.

The Foundation's program staff dealt with the grantees, and Lienhard remained in the background—a role he had always preferred in business too. Still, he and his fellow board members carefully reviewed every grant. "I told our grantees that we supply the money but that you fellows are the doers," he recalled. "Nobody in the foundation field knew me. They knew Dave Rogers. That was his job."

The success of the programs being funded gradually added to the Foundation's national reputation as the leading philanthropy in health care. Its innovative ways began to have a catalytic effect on the federal government, stimulating it to become involved with new programs where the Johnson Foundation had blazed the trail. An article in the *New York Times Magazine* in 1984 noted: "Many in the world of philanthropy look upon this organization as a model for the big and not so big foundations — streamlined, focused, flexible, accountable and living within its means."

Moreover, all this was being accomplished with a staff of about twenty-five professionals, far fewer than other philanthropies of similar size. David Rogers preferred small staffs, which would have endeared him to Robert Wood Johnson and his management philosophy. Johnson feared bigness, which could easily become bureaucratic, and Rogers was of the same mind. "With a small staff, you don't develop enclaves," he said at the time. "You can sit around a table, hear differences of opinion, and then make a decision." *Medical World News*, commenting on this aspect, wrote: "The Foundation's small staff has won a pervasive influence on American medicine through carefully targeted grants."

Johnson was a strong believer in decentralization, and the Foundation used that approach effectively in many of the national programs it funded. National program directors with the expertise required for particular assignments were recruited and given responsibility for managing the programs from their own base of operations. Subsidies made it possible for them to use their staffs to oversee the programs. This enabled the Foundation to keep its own headquarters staff smaller, more flexible, and constantly searching for fresh ideas and new approaches to providing better health care.

The conflict that some thought might develop between the Foundation and Johnson & Johnson never materialized. Author Waldemar A. Nielsen in 1985 wrote a widely acclaimed book titled *The Golden Donors: A New Anatomy of the Great Foundations* and addressed that point: "This could have resulted in a hopeless entanglement of the Foundation with the company and its interests, but it did not. All of the trustees soon separated themselves [retired] from the company, and not a trace of conflict of interest can be detected in their performance in the years since. After the

[655]

General's death in 1968, they set seriously to work to make the Foundation not only a good one but an outstanding one. . . . It seems evident that some deeper and built-in standards of ethics and social responsibility deriving from the character of the donor were at work and he had chosen from among his executive colleagues men of character and quality to be his trustees."

The Foundation's policies and its direction have experienced seamless continuity for close to three decades, despite changes in leadership that resulted from retirements. New and creative programs are always being added, and the best of the older ones receive continued support. Rogers retired as president, and Lienhard as chairman, in 1986. Leighton E. Cluff, M.D., who was senior vice president, succeeded Rogers and served until he himself retired in 1990. Robert H. Myers, the attorney who handled Johnson's estate, was chairman until 1989, when he was succeeded by Sidney F. Wentz, a New Jersey business executive. Wentz was succeeded as Chairman of the Board in July 1999 by trustee Robert E. Campbell.

Steven A. Schroeder, M.D., became the Foundation's dynamic and visionary president in 1990, and in 1999 he was also named chief executive officer. An honors graduate of Stanford University and Harvard Medical School, he trained in internal medicine, in epidemiology, and in public health and held faculty positions at three academic health centers. He was at the University of California at San Francisco, where he founded the Division of Internal Medicine, when he decided to join the Foundation. Dr. Schroeder had not worked in philanthropy, and he brought fresh thinking to the task of determining how to invest in health and health care wisely and responsibly. On his desk he keeps a framed quotation that reads: "Nothing so gives the illusion of intelligence as personal association with large sums of money." (That wisdom came from economist John Kenneth Galbraith.) Dr. Schroeder combines intelligence with boundless energy and wide-eyed enthusiasm for his work. If he has a problem, it is the increasing amount of money available for grants.

The more money there is, the more difficult it becomes to find meaningful programs that target the Foundation's mission. There is the temptation to stray. Spurred by the growth of Johnson & Johnson stock, the Johnson Foundation's assets had reached the $8 billion range, and at this level it would be required to give $400 million a year in grants in order to conform to the 5 percent pay-out requirement. This would be nearly five times the amount given in grants during Dr. Schroeder's first year as president. Some of the earlier goals are still in the Foundation's mission statement, which reads:

> To assure that all Americans have access to basic health care at a rea-sonable cost; to improve the way services are organized and provided to people with chronic health conditions, and to promote health and reduce the personal, social and economic harm caused by substance abuse — tobacco, alcohol and illicit drugs.

The Foundation still has a relatively small staff — some 150 in all — many of them young, knowledgeable, and passionately com-mitted to the programs they help develop. They take pride in the prevailing collegial environment. More than at most other major philanthropies, the staff interacts closely with the trustees during the quarterly two-day board meetings, including the time spent at meals and receptions. The board now has a smaller number of Johnson's former colleagues and a broader representation of the various disciplines that are needed to comprehend and improve today's complex health-care system — trustees who have distin-guished themselves in such areas as medicine, science, education, finance, and government. The commitment of the trustees is ap-parent too, and reflected in their remarkable attendance record at board meetings, seminars, and site visits.

At board meetings, staff members make carefully rehearsed pre-sentations on the grant proposals they have been reviewing and nurturing to this point of decision-making. Then come questions, often probing, from the trustees. The lively discussions sometimes

reach the debate level when a program proposal is a little too innovative or off-target. Usually the staff gains board approval, but
they are shot down just often enough to emphasize the importance
of adhering to policy and funding only programs that build on
the Foundation's goals. The relationship between the staff and the
trustees is open, and there is ample evidence of mutual respect.

Dr. Schroeder seems to be in perpetual motion, mentally and
physically. He has provided excellent leadership, is a good commu-
nicator, and shows a flair for innovation. He enjoys a good rapport
with his young staff, though he tends to protect them in a paternalistic way when they get caught in cross-fire at a trustees meeting.
The business-oriented board members, used to engaging in robust
give-and-take, seem to test the sensitivities of those reared in academic settings. The real test for Dr. Schroeder, however, is living
up to one of Robert Wood Johnson's favorite aphorisms: that any
fool can spend money, but that spending it wisely is the challenge. That means funding programs that are matched to specific
goals, to which Dr. Schroeder alluded in an article he wrote for the
July/August 1998 issue of *Health Affairs*.

"Goals have to be translated into action through programs,"
Dr. Schroeder wrote. "Let me illustrate this through a few ex-
amples: Programs to improve access include expanding health insurance coverage for the uninsured, making it easier for those who
need care to receive it, and training health workers to meet the
needs of underserved populations. In the chronic care area we have
concentrated on helping persons with chronic diseases to function
in their own homes; improving care giving at the end of life; and
promoting integrated care systems for persons with certain medical conditions, such as dementia. In the substance abuse area we
have supported community coalitions to counter drug and alcohol
abuse; state coalitions to lower smoking rates; a national center to
reduce smoking among children and youth; and programs to reduce the amount of binge drinking among college students. Within

[658]

each of the goal areas we have supported a wide range of policy-relevant research."

Additional exploration of the Johnson Foundation's impact on health and health care in the United States reveals a series of programs that tend to follow various themes as part of the overall strategy. The Clinical Scholars Program, for instance, is about training. It improves health care by giving young physicians who have just completed a residency the opportunity to rise to leadership roles by enabling them to expand their knowledge in non-clinical disciplines. These areas include epidemiology, biostatistics, economics, law, social science, ethics, and health services research. Some thirty scholars are chosen annually and spend two rigorous years studying at one of seven leading academic medical centers. Today, many of the more than seven hundred men and women who were Clinical Scholars hold positions of leadership in academic medicine, the private health sector, and government health agencies. One became the U.S. Surgeon General, the nation's highest health officer. The program has been called "a national treasure."

Author Waldemar Nielsen wrote: "Johnson is the finest of the activist foundations. It is willing to hang out there in controversy and make something happen." One example is its readiness to allocate resources for such controversial health problems as AIDS. In the 1980s, at a time when AIDS was seen as more of a social stigma than a serious threat to public health, the Foundation supported educational programs that offered effective prevention strategies. The early criticism diminished when medical authorities began to emphasize that the disease was endangering world health.

Willingness to help others has been a trait of Americans dating back to the days of the pioneers. The Foundation has invested heavily in programs that encourage volunteerism in communities all across the nation. Beginning in 1983 with the Interfaith Volunteer Caregivers Program, grants were made to local coalitions to mobilize volunteers in many religious congregations and in the community at large to provide informal support to the home-bound—primarily elderly people with chronic health problems. Ten years later the concept took a bold step forward with a $25 million program, Faith in Action, to provide eighteen-month seed grants of $25,000 to launch more than 1,000 caregiver projects throughout the United States. Its success has been phenomenal, and millions more dollars are being directed to replication and expansion of the program. Another of the many volunteerism efforts has encouraged the physician community to expand primary-care services to include people who lack health insurance and the ability to pay for medical care. "Reach Out: Physicians' Initiative to Expand Care to Underserved Americans" is a $12 million program with some forty sites both in rural areas and in inner cities.

As people grew increasingly conscious of health issues, they began relying more and more on the news media and other information sources to keep abreast of rapid developments. Information had become an important weapon in the battle against disease and addiction, and the Foundation, quick to recognize this trend, began building a communication component into many of its programs. Vast resources were targeted at communicating the danger of drug addiction, particularly among youths.

It was grants from the Johnson Foundation that helped move the hazards of smoking into the forefront of national concern. This resulted in a major shift in the way Americans view smoking—from that of being an annoying behavioral issue to its present recognition as a deadly addiction and the number-one preventable cause of death in the United States. Again, many of the programs are focused on getting youths to avoid the dangers of smoking. Today it is a national health issue, but when the Foundation first became involved there were far fewer people concerned.

The pervasive and seemingly overwhelming problems of poorer urban areas attracted the Foundation's attention and concern years ago. Under the Urban Health Initiative, major cities received four-year grants to build regional collaborations to improve the lives of their children and youths. Drawing on the forces already at work in these cities — health professionals, clergy, government, schools, and parents — the programs teach young people both the nature of these problems and the solutions to them. One goal is to inspire a new generation that will be more caring and responsive to the needs of their communities.

A similar approach was taken in the Foundation's efforts to help solve the problem of homelessness, which is often linked to health-related causes, including mental illness, physical abuse, and drug or alcohol addiction. The staff recognized that social change that considers the whole of the person and the whole of the environment would require long-range solutions.

The delicate subject of death and dying has been brought out into the open in recent years by the Foundation's program known by the acronym SUPPORT. As the population aged, the nursing-home residents became older and more feeble and end-of-life care became a major medical and social issue. Johnson's philanthropy stepped up to address it. Patients were encouraged to express their preferences for treatment, pain control, and resuscitation, and physicians were drawn into the dialogue in ways they had never been before.

To raise awareness about the need to improve care at the end of life, the Foundation's Last Acts campaign has engaged all of society — patients, families, health-care professionals, medical educators, the clergy, and others. The educational process, which now extends to reaching medical students during their formative years, has resulted in a reshaping of the nation's attitudes about end-of-life care. Access to palliative-care services is being institutionalized in a variety of clinical settings, and because of the Foundation's efforts the subject of death and dying has broken through the barrier that once existed in the news media. Television programs devoted to the subject, once largely considered taboo, have become routine.

As the nation became more ethnically diverse, it was clear that large segments of this population had limited access to health care. Part of the problem was that blacks, Hispanics, and Native Americans are underrepresented among the nation's health-care professionals. In an effort to correct this imbalance, the Foundation has made a substantial investment in the Minority Medical Education Program, which has benefited thousands of minority medical students. In addition, the Minority Medical Faculty Program has supported more than eighty fellows, many of whom serve as role models for minority medical students.

Substantial grants have been made to improve health policy in a constantly changing environment. The Foundation's "State Initiatives in Health-Care Reform" program recognizes the need for change at the state level, and more than $43 million has been directed to twenty states for financial and technical assistance to pursue interventions to expand insurance coverage, improve market function, and control costs. State and federal policymakers have been given the opportunity to weigh the results of the Foundation's demonstration projects and apply what was learned, and some of this experience has influenced new legislation. In support of good policy development, the Foundation has funded "Health Tracking," a major data-collection effort that attempts to provide the reliable and uniform data needed to make good policy decisions. As viewed by the Foundation, policymaking is a major forum through which health-care reforms can be initiated and which results in better health care for all Americans.

In deference to Johnson's longtime loyalty to the New Brunswick area and to New Jersey, the Foundation allocates a modest amount of its resources to carry on that tradition. It is known as "New Jersey Health Initiatives," and most of the grants fall within the overall mission. There are, however, a few sentimental exceptions, one being the old family homestead in Highland Park, New Jersey, that Johnson donated to the Cenacle nuns for use as a religious retreat. He used to make frequent visits there to personally inspect the home for needed repairs—a faulty furnace or a leaky roof—and then pay for them himself. Now the Foundation keeps an eye on what the nuns need to keep the home in good repair.

Those familiar with health care in America give the Johnson Foundation high marks for its performance and for the impact it is having. In the view of Jordan J. Cohen, M.D., president of the Association of American Medical Colleges: "The Robert Wood Johnson Foundation has been a powerful force for promoting change within the health-care system. The Foundation's strength has been its ability to identify systemic problems in American health care and to direct its resources to exploring multiple approaches to alleviate these problems."

"The hallmark of the Robert Wood Johnson Foundation has been creativity," said Kenneth I. Shine, M.D., president of the Institute of Medicine of the National Academy of Sciences. "It has been willing to take risks, adopt new approaches, try new strategies, implement new organizations, and develop new concepts. It has confronted some of the most difficult problems in improving health in America, when the issues have not been particularly popular."

"The Foundation has served a critical role as convener to bring together diverse voices in the search for solutions to various health issues," added Dorothy S. Ridings, president of the Council on Foundations. "It has communicated effectively, and many other foundations have taken a page from the Robert Wood Johnson book in telling the story of what they do, and what they have learned for the benefit of society, so clearly and compellingly."

And, from George D. Lundberg, M.D., former editor of the *Journal of the American Medical Association*: "I consider the Robert Wood Johnson Foundation, as it is currently constituted and functioning, to be one of a very few United States organizations with a stellar impact on the nation's public health and health education. Picking its spots carefully, RWJF spends substantial sums to ob-

[663]

tain the multiplier effect from carefully chosen people and places for now and for the future. Impeccably managed, RWJF is a joy to work with and a pleasure to laud."

.

A large portrait of Robert Wood Johnson hangs in the Foundation's spacious lobby facing the wide glass entrance doors of the building that bears his name. Directly in front of the portrait, suspended over a large reflective pool, is a broad, open stairway that leads to the main offices on the second floor. For someone who always wanted to keep an eye on things, the portrait is perfectly positioned.

Every now and then Johnson's curiosity gets the best of him and he steps down from the portrait and wanders around the building on one of his legendary inspection tours. Old habits die hard. These days, however, he moves quietly and unobtrusively, for now he can only observe—see but not be seen.

On this day he eases himself down and saunters over to the entrance. He looks for smudges on the glass doors. They are spotless. Good! He glances out the doors, past the circular driveway, and sees acres of neatly trimmed lawn and a line of trees shielding the building from the highway in the distance. Good planning. He turns and goes up the stairway, pausing on the landing to look down at the water in the reflective pool. It is crystal clear. He smiles.

It is the fall of 1998 and the Board of Trustees is in session. The General slips quietly into the boardroom and finds a seat at the rear. Looking around, he spots that old bronze bust of him setting on a pedestal against the rear wall—the same bust that he banished to a storage closet years ago. He grimaces. Oh, well, he thinks, they have to look at it, I don't. The room is filled with staff members seated around three walls of the room. The trustees sit around the long, polished wood table in the center, listening intently as the staff makes its presentations. He is impressed by the youthfulness of the staff, and their grasp of complex health matters. It pains him that he can't participate in the dialogue between staff and the trustees. He'd like to make a few points himself.

[664]

All the chairs around the board table are filled. Perfect attendance. That's good, he notes, smiling. They certainly couldn't have known I was going to be here. Among the trustees are many unfamiliar faces, but the name placards on the table help him identify those he does not know: Edward C. Andrews Jr., M.D., the Honorable Nancy Kassebaum Baker, Rheba de Tornyay, Ed.D., Linda Griego, the Honorable Thomas H. Kean, James R. Gavin III, M.D., Ph.D., Edward E. Matthews, Jack W. Owen, John H. Steele, Sc.D., Gail L. Warden, Dr. Schroeder, Sidney F. Wentz, and J. Warren Wood III, the general counsel and secretary, and five trustees whom he does know, all former colleagues at Johnson & Johnson: James E. Burke, David R. Clare, Robert E. Campbell, John J. Heldrich, and Lawrence G. Foster.

He leans forward as Dr. Schroeder begins talking about plans for reorganizing the Foundation to better manage future growth. The grant-making will be decentralized and two separate staff groups created: one for programs related to medical care, the other to concentrate on improving the overall health of Americans. Starting in the year 2000 each unit will compete for funds based on the quality of its past and current projects. The goal will be to have staff members develop fresh ideas for programs. "We hope to instill a little healthy competition," Dr. Schroeder explains. To Johnson the plan has a familiar ring: decentralization, competition, creativity. He nods in approval. Forming the Foundation, he reminds himself, was the right thing to do.

The Board meeting is almost over, and he slips quietly out of the room. Passing the Law Library, he pauses and instinctively steps inside. On one shelf he notices a copy of Nielsen's "The Golden Donors" and starts browsing through it. A comment on page 132 catches his eye:

"The Johnson Foundation, judged by the standards of performance normally applicable to foundations, is virtually in a class by itself. In the clarity and ambitiousness of its purpose, in the intellectual power that has governed its strategy and grant-making, in the social sensitivity and political skill by which its programs have been shaped, in the able and creative way in which its programs have been managed, and in the general qualities of integrity and independence that have

characterized all that it has done, the Robert Wood Johnson Foundation is the best of the big foundations today."

Leaving the library, he makes his way down the stairway to return to his place in the lobby, mulling over those words of high praise. In one respect they please him, but in another they make him uneasy. We are never as good as we think we are, he says to himself, and health-care philanthropy today is infinitely more complex. Time will tell.

He reaches the portrait, carefully steps back into it, and turns and settles himself so he is in just the right position to continue to keep an eye on things.

UMDNJ — Robert Wood Johnson Medical School

Robert Wood Johnson University Hospital

Nearly eighty years ago, a young and caring Robert Wood Johnson "adopted" the small and struggling Middlesex Hospital in New Brunswick, and for the next five decades he devoted his time, skills, and resources to improving patient care. Today this large, modern facility is the Robert Wood Johnson University Hospital, New Jersey's premier academic health center.

Coinciding with the hospital's name change in 1986, Johnson was accorded the additional honor of having the University of Medicine and Dentistry of New Jersey renamed UMDNJ — Robert Wood Johnson Medical School.

The quality of medicine taught and practiced at these two institutions has rapidly propelled them to the forefront of national recognition in the areas of medicine in which they specialize. Had he lived to see this remarkable progress over a relatively short span of time, Robert Wood Johnson would have been impressed, as others are.

As the state university of the health sciences, the UMDNJ — Robert Wood Johnson Medical School maintains programs at the undergraduate, graduate, and postgraduate levels and conducts continuing education courses for health professionals as well as community education programs. The 2,500 full-time and volunteer faculty members train approximately 1,500 students in medicine, public health, and graduate programs, and the school ranks in the top one-third of the country in the percentage of students who practice in the primary-care specialties after completing residency training. The graduate program in public health is the largest medical-school–based program in the United States.

The Medical School has twenty-one basic science and clinical departments and ranks also in the top third in the nation in terms of grant support per faculty member. In addition to its departments, the school hosts eighty-five institutes and centers. Among the largest are the Center for Advanced Biotechnology and Medicine, a center for molecular medicine, and the Environmental and Occupational Health Sciences Institute, the largest such institute in the world. Other facilities include the Clinical Research Center, the Child Health Institute of New Jersey, the Cardiovascular Institute, the Laurie Neurodevelopmental Institute, the Gerontological Institute, the Center for Disease Management and Clinical Outcomes, and the Coriell Institute in Camden.

The school integrates diverse clinical programs conducted at thirty-seven hospital affiliates and numerous ambulatory care sites in the region. The clinical faculty participates in more than 170 specialized health care programs through a multispecialty group practice of the medical school. With more than four hundred physician members, it is the largest multispecialty group practice in New Jersey. Affiliates throughout the state include a branch in Hamilton, Bayshore Community Hospital in Holmdel, CentraState Healthcare System in Freehold, Rahway Hospital, Raritan Bay Medical Centers in Perth Amboy and Old Bridge, Warren Hospital in Phillipsburg, Eric B. Chandler Health Center in New Brunswick, the Henry J. Austin Health Center in Trenton, the Plainfield Health Center, and the VNA Community Health Center in Red Bank.

In pursuit of a diverse student body, UMDNJ—Robert Wood Johnson Medical School makes special efforts to recruit and support students and other trainees from underrepresented minority groups and women. Furthermore, the graduation of medical students who are likely to pursue careers in primary-care medicine is a special concern.

·

The main focus of the Robert Wood Johnson University Hospital has been on critical-care patients and trauma victims, but it has gained renown for setting the standard of care in every measure of service to the community. The hospital gained Accreditation with Commendation from the Joint Commission on Accreditation of Healthcare Organizations, receiving an excellent score of 97 out of a possible 100. Only 15 percent of U.S. hospitals surveyed had attained this level of commendation.

Among the hospital's special strengths are the Heart Center of New Jersey, a "hospital within a hospital," and the Vascular Center of New Jersey, conducted by a multidisciplinary medical team. The hospital is also approved to do transplants.

The newer centers of excellence are Children's Hospital, with 70 beds devoted to children's services in forty-five medical specialties, and the Cancer Hospital of New Jersey. This new seven-story facility adds another 100 beds, bringing the hospital's overall total to 548. The Cancer Hospital works in partnership with the Cancer Institute of New Jersey.

An example of the medical center's vision is the new Health Science & Technology High School, which the New Brunswick Public School System is building within the hospital complex, and where young health care professionals of the future will be trained in a medical setting.

In combination, the Robert Wood Johnson University Hospital and the UMDNJ—Robert Wood Johnson Medical School provide New Jersey with innovative state-of-the-art medical care and education in every aspect of health care.

Acknowledgments

During the years that this work was in progress, more than one hundred of Robert Wood Johnson's colleagues and friends, including some of his critics, spoke with me about their recollections of him. Those who were interviewed at length are noted in the bibliography. Many of them, regrettably, are no longer here to receive my thanks. In addition to those who are listed, dozens of others provided me with important bits of information and impressions that contributed to the larger picture of the man. Each has my thanks and gratitude.

Following the General's death, Evie Johnson offered me strong encouragement to write this book about her husband and provided me with important information in a refreshingly candid way. She was familiar with his flaws. Evie was also generous in making available for the book many family photos. Sadly, she did not live to see the book completed.

Johnson's daughter, Sheila, had a special relationship with her father and in our interviews happily recalled the years they spent together. She was most generous with her time, and support, and also provided photos that appear in the book, including those of her mother, Maggi. Betty Johnson allowed me to review the Johnson Family Bible, which contained a rich trove of historical information. Her son, Robert Wood Johnson IV, recalled for me memories of his grandfather. They have my gratitude, along with the other members of the Johnson family and the staff at Longleat, who, each in their own way, contributed to the book.

For the last ten years of Robert Wood Johnson's life, Olga Ferretti spent large amounts of time with him, as his nurse-secretary, travel companion, and friend. She was most generous in sharing her recollections, as well as photos and newspaper clippings from their worldwide adventures aboard the *Pilgrim* and the *Golden Crest*. I also thank Dr. Hugh Murray for kindly sharing with me copies of the letters he sent to his parents in Scotland, in which he gave vivid accounts of his experiences aboard General Johnson's ships.

James A. Murray, a colleague of many years, called on his skills as an author, editor, and student of history and made invaluable contributions to this work, as he did with my earlier book on the history of Johnson & Johnson. Thanks, Jim.

Sam Vaughan, an admired friend of many years, has a place of special distinction in the publishing field as one of its most eminent editors. Ever since this book was in its embryonic stage, Sam has given me inspiration and direction, and I am truly grateful to him.

The research for this biography began many years ago, and I wish to express my appreciation to those who worked with me back then — Valerie Burkhart Tamis, Elaine Jaskol, Margaret Van Gluck Gurowitz, and Eunice McMurtry. In preparing the early manuscript drafts I had a great deal of help from Marion Lloyd, Terry McShane, Carol Dobrovolski and Tina Gordon, for which I thank them. Andy Baglivo, a fellow staff member on the *Newark News*, and an expert on New Jersey politics, was kind enough to provide insight into the tumultuous years when Johnson was active politically.

Elisabeth King, a skilled librarian and former colleague, helped me find elusive facts during the final writing of the manuscript, and I am grateful for her help. My thanks and appreciation also go to Gary Gorran, for financial details from the past, and to Peter Dinella, for sharing his knowledge of current Credo activities. At the Robert Wood Johnson Foundation, Frank Karel and Warren Wood were extremely helpful in providing background on that fine institution.

In my search for an editor for this book I asked Daniel W. Pfaff, a now-retired Penn State journalism professor, if he could recommend someone. He suggested Peggy Hoover, who, he said, had done excellent work editing his biography of Joseph Pulitzer II. Peggy graciously agreed to edit this book. She is a superb editor, and I greatly appreciate her contributions to this work, as well as her timely words of encouragement. My thanks also to Dan Pfaff for an inspired recommendation.

Preparation of the final manuscript was in the capable hands of Karen Kier, another of my former colleagues, who agreed to team up with me again. She is always a pleasure to work with. I also thank Kit Tacie for her earlier work on the manuscript.

When I was seeking a top-flight designer for the book, Janet Dietz, Production Manager and Associate Director at Penn State Press, informed me that Omega Clay was one of the best. Omega agreed to take the assignment, and her talents are evident here. She was an excellent choice, made possible by Janet's recommendation.

This book is dedicated to Ellen Miller Foster, my loving wife and patient friend. In addition to the usual sentimental reasons, this particular dedication also reflects my deep appreciation for her perceptive observations during her many readings of the manuscript. She has a sharp eye, and, importantly, a "feel" for what reads well. During our many happy years together she has been my compass—always keeping me pointed in the right direction.

About Lillian Press

Amid the often turbulent waters of trade book publishing, the Small Press is an island of refuge and hope for aspiring American authors. Creating one's own Small Press imprint, and staying the course throughout the arduous details of design and production, is a daunting experience. The reward is the opportunity to produce a book that meets the author's expectations, not someone else's. The risk is that a book produced by a fledgling addition to the ranks of Small Press publishers has to struggle to gain recognition among those who judge literary effort. Hopefully, this book will rise or fall on its overall merits, and not on how, or by whom, it was published.

The name Lillian was chosen to bring some small honor to a person who spent her entire life helping others — my mother.

LGF

Bibliography

Interviews by the Author

- John E. Avery Jr., Mexico City, Mexico
- Leonard P. Bailey, Edinburgh, Scotland
- George Bahash, New Brunswick, New Jersey
- William Baumer, New Brunswick, New Jersey
- Sheila Johnson Brutsch, New Brunswick, New Jersey
- James E. Burke, New Brunswick, New Jersey
- Harold Burnham, New Brunswick, New Jersey
- Mrs. Peg Campbell, Highland Park, New Jersey
- David R. Clare, en route to São Paulo, Brazil
- Mrs. Frank Cosgrove, Fort Lauderdale, Florida
- Rev. John Cronin, New Brunswick, New Jersey
- Thomas Deegan, Rye, New York
- Robert J. Dixson, New Brunswick and Bay Head, New Jersey
- Alan Donawa, New York City
- Brig. General Henry Dries, Salvation Army, New Brunswick, New Jersey
- Dr. René DuBos, New Brunswick, New Jersey

- Frank Farrell, New York City
- Olga Ferretti, Princeton and Sea Girt, New Jersey
- Captain Charles Hanna, New Brunswick, New Jersey
- Brig. General Donald J. Hittle, Washington, D.C.
- John Hoagland, New Brunswick, New Jersey
- Philip B. Hofmann, New Brunswick, New Jersey; Indian Creek Island, Florida; and aboard the *QE2* en route to Southampton, England
- Governor Richard J. Hughes, New Brunswick, New Jersey
- William J. Hughes, New York City
- Dr. Paul Janssen, New Brunswick, New Jersey, and Beerse, Belgium
- Betty Wold Johnson, Princeton, New Jersey
- D. Mead Johnson, Palm Beach, Florida
- Evelyne Vernon Johnson, Princeton, New Jersey
- Maggi Shea Johnson (Eily), Palm Beach, Florida
- Robert Wood Johnson IV, New York City
- John Kelly, Princeton, New Jersey
- Dr. Joseph H. Kler, New Brunswick, New Jersey
- Gustav O. Lienhard, Metuchen, New Jersey
- Doris Little, State College, Pennsylvania
- Eric Marsh, New Brunswick, New Jersey
- Sister Mary McGarry, Highland Park, New Jersey
- Sister Virginia McGarry, Highland Park, New Jersey
- Evangeline Johnson Merrill, Palm Beach, Florida
- Walter Metz, New Brunswick, New Jersey
- Helen Stevenson Meyner, New York City
- Governor Robert B. Meyner, Captiva Island, Florida
- Richard V. Mulligan, Fort Lauderdale, Florida

- Dr. Hugh Murray, Edinburgh, Scotland
- Robert R. Nathan, Key West, Florida
- Michael Norris, São Paulo, Brazil
- William Northam, Bay Head, New Jersey
- Dorothy O'Neal, New Brunswick, New Jersey
- Dr. D. Stanley ("Pat") Pattison, New Brunswick, New Jersey
- Dr. David Rogers, Princeton, New Jersey
- Andrew and Peggy Rohlfing, São Paulo, Brazil
- Richard B. Sellars, New Brunswick, New Jersey
- Bishop Fulton J. Sheen, New York City
- George F. Smith, Edison, New Jersey
- Paul Sprague, New Brunswick, New Jersey
- Alfred Tennyson, New Brunswick, New Jersey
- Kenneth Unger, New Brunswick, New Jersey
- Edward Van Nordheim, Mexico City, Mexico
- Edward and Shirley Walker, São Paulo, Brazil
- Patrick Whaley, New Brunswick, New Jersey
- Dr. Paul Dudley White, Newark, New Jersey
- Foster B. Whitlock, New Brunswick, New Jersey, and New York City
- Dr. Francis C. Wood, Philadelphia, Pennsylvania

Books and Articles by
Robert Wood Johnson

Books

1944   "*But, General Johnson,*" Princeton University Press.

1947   *Or Forfeit Freedom: People Must Live and Work Together,* Doubleday & Company.

1949   *Robert Johnson Talks It Over,* privately published.

1950   *Human Relations in Modern Business* (co-authored with fifty business leaders).

Articles

1944   "What Business Needs," *Saturday Evening Post*, July 15.
1945   "Christian Engineering," *America*, July 21.
        "The No. 1 Problem of All Businessmen," *American Druggist*, November.
1946   "Break It Up," *Saturday Evening Post*, January 5.
        "Women in Politics," 1946 *Yearbook of The Garden Club of New Jersey*.
        "Buyers in Khaki," *Ordnance*, May-June.
        "Executive Myopia," *Journal of Business* (University of Chicago), April.
        "Free Man and Watch Him Go," *Motive*, December.
1947   "Dig, Son, Dig," *Ordnance*, January-February.
        "Sugar, Spice and Everything Nice," *Vogue*, April 1.
        "Labor Contracts Must Include Good Will," *Saturday Evening Post*, September 6.
1948   "Business Faces the Future," *Canadian Business*, April.
        "You Profit, Too," *Canadian Business*, May.
        "An Employer Looks at Labor-Management Relations," *Industrial and Labor Relations Review* (Cornell University), April.
        "The Maginot Line of America," *Harper's*, August.
        "Defense Is Men," *Ordnance*, November-December.
1949   "What Doth It Profit?" *Motive*, January.
        "On the Human Side," *The Modern Hospital*, February.
        "Military Executive Competence," *Ordnance*, March-April.
        "Human Relations in Modern Business," *Harvard Business Review*, September.
1952   "Military Socialism," *Ordnance*, July-August.
        "Are We Giving Our GIs Inferior Weapons?" *American Legion Magazine*, August.

"How to Light a Candle," *Dun's Review*, November.

1953   "Tapping Latent Talent," *Dun's Review*, June.

Documents and
Archival Sources

The Kilmer Museum at Johnson & Johnson's corporate headquarters in New Brunswick was the source of an estimated 250,000 memos, letters, and other documents that helped shed light on the life of Robert Wood Johnson. This rich trove was carefully reviewed for this work, as it was for the author's book on the company history, published in 1986. Following General Johnson's death in 1968, Mrs. Johnson made available to the author, for his consideration, a number of her husband's personal papers and photographs, as did other members of the Johnson family. Numerous other archival sources were consulted, and the information gleaned from them has been woven into this story of his life.

Transcripts of various speeches that made reference to Johnson's career provided source material, as did numerous videotapes, including a ten-part series by the Harvard Business School.

Additional Sources

Books

Armour, Richard. *Drug Store Days*. McGraw-Hill Book Co., 1959.

Bill, Alfred Hoyt. *A House Called Morven: Its Role in American History*. In collaboration with Walker E. Edge, Princeton University Press, 1954, revised 1978.

Branyan, Robert L., and Lawrence E. Larsen. *The Eisenhower Administration, 1953–1961*. Random House, 1971.

Chandler, Lester V. *America's Greatest Depression, 1929–1941*. Harper & Row, 1971.

Coben, Stanley, ed. *Reform, War, and Reaction, 1912–1932*. University of South Carolina Press, 1973.

Cudd, John Michael. *The Chicopee Manufacturing Company, 1823–1912*. Scholarly Resources, 1974.

Duffy, John. *The Healers: A History of American Medicine*. University of Illinois Press, 1976.

Dulles, Foster Rhea. *Twentieth Century America*. Riverside Press, 1945.

Ellis, Edward Robb. *The Epic of New York City*. Coward-McCann, 1966.

Engel, Leonard. *Medicine Makers of Kalamazoo*. McGraw-Hill Book Co., 1961.

Fisher, Richard B. *Joseph Lister, 1827–1912*. McDonald and Jane's, 1977.

Freidel, Frank. *American in the Twentieth Century*. Alfred A. Knopf, 1960.

Friedson, Eliot, ed. *The Hospital in Modern Society*. The Free Press, 1963.

Godlee, Sir Rickman John. *Lord Lister*. The Clarenden Press, 1924.

Hays, Samuel P. *The Response to Industrialism*. University of Chicago Press, 1957.

Hoehling, A. A. *Disaster: Major American Catastrophes*. Hawthorne Books, 1973.

Hofstadter, Richard. *The Age of Reform: From Bryan to F.D.R.* Alfred A. Knopf, 1955.

Holliday, Robert Cortes. *Joyce Kilmer: Memoir and Poems*. George H. Doran Co., 1918.

Johnson, Hugh S. *The Blue Eagle from Egg to Earth*. Doubleday, Doran & Co., 1935.

Josephson, Matthew. *Edison*. McGraw-Hill Book Co., 1959.

Link, Arthur S. *American Epoch: A History of the United States Since the 1890s*. Vol. 1: 1897–1920, Vol. 2: 1921–1941. Alfred A. Knopf, 1955.

Marks, Geoffrey, and William K. Beatty. *Epidemics*. Charles Scribner's Sons, 1976.

Mayer, Martin. *Making News*. Doubleday & Co., 1987.

McCormick, Richard P. *Rutgers: A Bicentennial History*. Rutgers University Press, 1966.

McKean, Dayton David. *The Boss: The Hague Machine in Action*. Russell & Russell, 1940.

Mitchell, Edward P. *Memoirs of an Editor: Fifty Years of American Journalism*. Charles Scribner's Sons, 1924.

Mohr, Lillian Holman. *Frances Perkins: That Woman in FDR's Cabinet!* North River Press, 1979.

Morgan, H. Wayne. *William McKinley and His America*. Syracuse University Press, 1963.

Morris, Lloyd. *Incredible New York*. Random House, 1951.

Rauch, Basil. *The History of the New Deal, 1933–1938*. Creative Age Press, 1944.

Risley, Mary. *House of Healing: The Story of the Hospital*. R. Hale, 1961.

Rothstein, William G. *American Physicians in the Nineteenth Century*. Johns Hopkins University Press, 1972.

Slosson, Preston William. *The Great Crusade and After, 1914–1928*. Macmillan Co., 1930.

Stage, Sarah. *Female Complaints: Lydia Pinkham and the Business of Women's Medicine*. W. W. Norton & Co., 1979.

Stevens, Rosemary. *American Medicine and the Public Interest*. Yale University Press, 1971.

Stover, John F. *The Life and Decline of the American Railroad*. Oxford University Press, 1970.

Unger, Irwin, and Debi Unger. *The Vulnerable Years: The United States, 1896–1917*. New York University Press, 1978.

Vanderbilt, Byron M. *Thomas Edison, Chemist*. American Chemical Society, 1971.

Villalon, Luis J. A., ed. *Management Men and Their Methods*. Funk & Wagnalls Co., 1949.

Wallace, Paul A. W. *Pennsylvania: Seed of a Nation*. Harper & Row, 1962.

Whitney, David C. *The Graphic Story of the American Presidents.*
T. J. Ferguson Publishing Co., 1968.

Wrench, G. T. *Lord Lister: His Life and His Work.* T. Fisher Unwin,
1913.

Other

The American Red Cross: A Century of Service, by Louise Levathes.
National Geographic, 1981.

American Red Cross and Johnson & Johnson, Agreement of 1895,
signed by Clara Barton and R. W. Johnson.

Belladonna Illustrated, by Fred B. Kilmer. Johnson & Johnson, 1894.

Biographical Record of Northeastern Pennsylvania. J. H. Beers &
Co., 1900.

Biography of George J. Seabury, in *Dictionary of American Biography.* Charles Scribner's Sons, 1927.

"Blue Bahama Seas: The Cruise of the Zodiac," by Robert Wood
Johnson. 1922.

Centennial History of Susquehanna County, R. T. Peck & Co., 1887.

The Chronicle of Coca-Cola Since 1886. The Coca-Cola Company.

Collected Papers of Joseph Lister. Royal College of Surgeons of
England Library, 1909.

The Cyclopedia of American Biography. Press Association Compilers, 1932.

Diary of F. L. Gilbert, Field End, Corbridge, Northumberland,
England.

Dictionary of American Biography, vol. 4, Charles Scribner's Sons,
1943.

"E. Mead Johnson's Million: Feeding Babies" in *Medical Times* (*The
Journal of General Practice*), 1958.

The Epic of Medicine, by Felix Marti-Ibanez. Clarkson N. Potter,
1959.

"A Family Memoir," by Charles Heber Clark. Unpublished.

"Frederick B. Kilmer: A Notable New Jersey Pharmacist," by Roy A.

Bowers, Dean Emeritus, Rutgers University, in *Journal of the Medical Society of New Jersey*, 1984.

"Hadley Field, 1924–1968," an anniversary brochure.

Highland Park (N.J.) Borough Council organization meeting minutes, January 1, 1920.

History of Lackawanna County, at Carbondale (Pa.) Public Library.

History of Middlesex County, New Jersey, 1664–1920, by John P. Wall and Harold P. Pickersgill. Lewis Historical Publishing Co., n.d.

"History of Plasters," by Robert Wood Johnson, in *The Pharmaceutical Era*, April 1890.

Johnson Family Bible.

Johnson's First Aid Manual. 1901.

"Land Marks, 1886–1924," by Fred B. Kilmer. Unpublished.

"Living the American Dream in New Brunswick, New Jersey: Johnson & Johnson and Hungarian Pioneers and Immigrants." A paper by August J. Molnar, American Hungarian Foundation, 1976.

Middlesex Hospital, 1931 Annual Report.

Minutes, Seabury & Johnson trustee meetings, 1884–85. Kilmer Museum.

The Montgomery County (Pa.) Story, by Gordon Alderfer. Published by the Commissioners of Montgomery County, 1959.

The National Cyclopedia of American Biography, vols. 3 and 42. James T. White & Co., 1958.

Poughkeepsie (N.Y.) City Directory of 1864.

Prudens Futuri: The U.S. Army War College, 1901–67, by Colonel George S. Pappas, Wadsworth Publishing Co., 1968.

"Red Cross Notes," edited by Fred B. Kilmer. New Brunswick, N.J., 1906.

"The Slender Thread," by George A. Kellogg. Unpublished.

Transcription of Joseph Lister talk, International Medical Congress, Philadelphia, 1876.

200 Years: A Bicentennial Illustrated History of the United States. Vols. 1 and 2. A U.S. News & World Report Book, 1973.

Wyoming Seminary, 1844–1944, by Leroy E. Bugbee. Privately published.

Journals, Magazines, and Newspapers

America · *American Druggist* · *Associated Press* · *Athens (Georgia) Herald* · *Atlanta Constitution* · *Atlanta Journal* · *Barron's* · *British Medical Journal* · *Buffalo (New York) Courier Express* · *Burlington (Vermont) Free Press* · *Business Week* · *Camden (New Jersey) Courier* · *Catholic Men* · *Central Jersey Monthly* · *Central Pharmaceutical Journal* · *Chicago Sun-Times* · *Chicago Tribune* · *Collier's* · *Coronet* · *Corpus Christi Times* · *Cosmopolitan* · *Dallas Morning News* · *Denton (Texas) Record-Chronicle* · *Detroit News* · *Detroit Times* · *Drug Trade News* · *Dun's Review* · *Evening Post (New Zealand)* · *Factory Magazine* · *Forbes* · *Fortune* · *Harper's* · *Harvard Business Review* · *Holley (New York) Standard* · *Illinois Times* · *Johnson & Johnson Bulletin* · *Journal of General Practice* · *Journal of Labor, Dallas* · *Journal of the Medical Society of New Jersey* · *Labor Leader (New Jersey)* · *Lancet: The British Medical Journal* · *Life* · *Look* · *Marquette Alumnus* · *The Medical Standard* · *Medical Times: The Journal of General Practice* · *Modern Hospital* · *Modern Industry* · *New Brunswick (New Jersey) Daily Homes News* · *New Brunswick (New Jersey) Sunday Times* · *New Brunswick (New Jersey) Times* · *New Jersey Compass* · *New York American* · *New York Daily News* · *New York Herald Tribune* · *New York Journal* · *New York Journal-American* · *New York Mirror* · *New York Sun* · *New York Times* · *New York Times Magazine* · *New York World-Telegram* · *Newark News* · *Newark Star Ledger* · *Newsweek* · *Philadelphia Inquirer* · *Philadelphia North American* · *Philadelphia Record* · *Pittsfield (Massachusetts) Eagle* · *PM New York* · *Poughkeepsie (New York) Observer* · *Protestant World* · *Publisher's Weekly* · *Reader's Digest* · *Red Cross Messenger* · *Red Cross Notes* · *Rochester Courier-Journal* · *The Saturday Evening Post* · *Saturday Review* · *Slough*

(England) Observer · *St. Louis (Missouri) Globe-Democrat* · *Syracuse Post-Standard* · *Tennessee Press-Scimitar* · *Time* · *Trenton (New Jersey) Times* · *U.S. News & World Report* · *United Press International* · *United States News* · *Vogue* · *Wall Street Journal* · *Washington Daily News* · *Washington Post* · *Washington Star* · *Wenatchee (Washington) Daily Herald* · *Wichita (Texas) Beacon* · *Yachting*

Index

Cenacle retreat house, 371
Foundation support for, 662–663
Centennial Exhibition (Philadelphia), 26–28
Center for Advanced Biotechnology and Medicine, 668
Center for Disease Management and Clinical Outcomes, 668
central authority, 428
dangers of, 396
CentraState Healthcare System, 668
Cermak, Anton J., 201
Ceylon, 156, 158
"Challenge to the Business Man" (Bowles), 373
Chamber of Commerce of U.S., 213, 353
Chapman (Johnson fishing companion), 90
Charles de Gaulle airport, Tylenol warning, 619
Chase, Howard, 361–362, 380
Chase, Stuart, 297–298, 301
Chase National Bank, 229
Chattahoochee River, 170
Chicago Sun-Times, 617
Chicago Tribune, 255, 625
Chicopee Falls, textile mill, 204
Chicopee Manufacturing Company, 129
Chicopee Village, 170
sale, 582–583
Chiesa, Joseph R., 633

Child Health Institute of New Jersey, 668
Children's Hospital, 669
China, 156, 159
as cotton source, 158
Chinese, injury treatment, 12
chloris-soda ampules, 136
Christianity and business, 304, 307, 347–348
Christmas, 593
CIO Auto Workers Union, 289
CIO Electrical Workers Union, 290
civil defense, 444
"Civil Service Philosophy," 527
Civil War
Battle of Bull Run, 21
impact on New York City, 14–15
R. Nelson reaction to, 11
Wyoming Valley volunteers, 10–11
civilians, underground shelters, 360
Clapper, Raymond, 226
Clare, Archdale, 70
Clare, David, 615, 616, 630, 665
Clark, Charles Heber, 100–101
Clark, Vincent, 180
Clarke (butler), 275
Classen, Clara, 409
Clay, Omega, 673
Clean Government movement (1920s), 323, 324
cleanliness, xvi, 279, 317–318
Clee, Lester H., 231

Panama-Pacific International
Exposition gold medal, 127
Public Relations Department,
617
as publicly held company,
277–278, 284
"Railway Station & Factory
Supply Case," 61
reputation, 634
Robert's request for Seward's
involvement, 139–141
role in antiseptic and aseptic
surgery education, 58
sales force training, 63
security, 484
surgical dressings for Spanish-
American War, 78
wartime production, 134–135
welfare department, 433–434
Welfare Work Department, 97
workforce in Depression, 188
wound-healing product production in advance of WWII,
246
WWII production, 252
Johnson & Johnson Board of
Directors, 100
Burke as Chairman, 431
Executive Committee, 421
financial support for nurses'
training, 514
Hofmann as Executive Committee Chairman, 462
with Hofmann as head, 492
Johnson (II) as Chairman, 241,
462

Johnson (II) as Finance Com-
mittee chairman, 523
Johnson (II) at meeting 1943,
277
Johnson (II) continued mem-
bership, 491
Johnson (II) drunk at, 118
Johnson (II) election to, 119
Johnson (II) on Depression
business measures, 191
Johnson (II) recommendation
for expenditure constraint,
189
Johnson (II) selection of Hofmann as Chairman, 489–491
Johnson (II) views, 284–285
Johnson III as member, 420
position of President of J&J
Worldwide, 540
Sellars as Chairman, 453
Seward's attendance, 415
Johnson & Johnson Credo, xv, 278,
282–284, 367–370, 424–425, 567,
640
impact on decisions, 643
loss of influence, 613
as management tool, 639, 643
modified version, 336–338
origins, 589–590
revision in 1970s, 616
and Tylenol strategy decisions,
345, 630–631, 637
violations of policy, 646
"Johnson & Johnson Family of
Companies," 203

pacifism, 221

Pack, Arthur N., 196

packaging. *See* tamper-resistant packaging

Page, Barbara, 549

Page, Robert, 547

Pan-American Exposition (Buffalo, N.Y.), McKinley assassination, 79–80

Panama Canal, 534, 571

Panama-Pacific International Exposition gold medal, 127

Panic of 1907, 98

papaya fruit, experiments with, 74

Papeete, Tahiti, 570

Paris, 156, 157, 174

Paris Vogue, 186

Parker, Dorothy, 230

Parker, Henry G., 247

Parker Memorial Home, 515

parking lots, Johnson (II) attention to, 589

Parsons, Jim, 247

Pasteur, Louis, 60

patent medicine, 43–44, 73 articles exposing quack, 94

patents, Edison's generation of, 55

patient care, Johnson (II) concern for, 514

Patou, Jean, 175

patriotism of Johnson (II), xvii, 361, 398–399, 476

Patterson, Robert P., 272

Pattison, D. Stanley, 562, 563, 578

Pattison, Joyce, 564

Patton, George, 400

Paynter, Tom, 412–413

peacetime economy, 332 conversion to, 288

Pearl Harbor, Japanese attack, 251

Pearson, Drew, 255

Pei, I.M., 615

Peking, 156, 159

Pemberton, John Styth, 73

"The Pendulum of Hope" (Johnson; unpublished), 456

Penn, William, 4, 181

Pennsylvania Coal Company, 32

Pennsylvania, farming in, 4

Pennsylvania Military Academy, 266

pension, for James Johnson, 194

people factor, 293

Perkins, Frances, 204–205, 210

Permanent International Committee for Relief to Wounded Combatants, 71

Perri, John, 164

Pershing, John J., 131

Personal Products company, 238–239 Johnson III involvement in, 420

Perth Amboy, 137

Perth, Australia, 564

Pfaff, Charlie, 19

Pfaff, Daniel W., 673

Pfaff's, 19–20

pharmaceuticals, Johnson & Johnson expansion into, 437

pharmacy. *See* drugstores

9